# The NeXT Bible

Doug Clapp

**BRADY**

New York  London  Toronto  Sydney  Tokyo  Singapore

**BRADY**

Simon & Schuster, Inc.
15 Columbus Circle
New York, NY 10023

DISTRIBUTED BY PRENTICE HALL TRADE

Manufactured in the United States of America

10 9 8 7 6 5 4 3 2 1

**Library of Congress Cataloging–in–Publication Data**

Clapp, Doug, 1950–
    The neXT bible / Doug Clapp.
       p.   cm.
    1. NeXT (Computer)    I. Title.
QA76.8.N49C53    1990
004.165—dc20                               89–26317
    ISBN 0–13–620725–1                  CIP

# Limits of Liability and Disclaimer of Warranty

# Acknowledgments

To be honest, I don't have many people to acknowledge. Only three.

My wife took care of everything while I disappeared into the basement, night after night; weekend after weekend. Thanks, Patti.

David Durkee, my partner in business, carried me through NeXT's developer school, made sure I didn't botch the explanation of EPS files too badly, and contributed the illustration of the NeXT keyboard found in Appendix B. (He used Multi-Ad Creator to make the illustration; a great program that's deserving of a plug, if only because it pays the mortgage every month.) Thanks, David.

Finally, and most important, my son Hubert didn't bug me all those summer mornings (and many afternoons and evenings) while I labored on this book. He could have easily; he was upstairs most of the time. But he didn't. It was an awesome display of willpower, unmatched, I'm sure by any other eleven-year-old, before or since.

Thanks, Hubert. For you, there's a dedication. And next summer will be lowercase. Promise.

# Dedication

To Hubert. Again. I love you!

This book was written in WriteNow on a NeXT Computer. The files were converted to RTF and transferred to Word 4.0 for the Macintosh. The pages were designed and layed out in QuarkXPress on a Macintosh IIx. The screen images were captured on the NeXT, stored in EPS format and transferred to the Macintosh. Finished pages were produced on a Varityper 4300p.

Head font: Avenir
Text Font: Berkeley from Adobe Systems

Page design by Lee Busch, PageWorks, Cambridge, MA

Production Editors: Tom Dillon, Ozzievelt Owens
Editor: Mia McCroskey

# Contents

# Introduction

*There are two things which I am confident I can do very well:*
*one is an introduction to any literary work, stating what it*
*is to contain, and how it should be executed in the most perfect*
*manner; the other is a conclusion, shewing from various causes*
*why the execution has not been equal to what the author promised*
*to himself and to the public.*
p.292. 1755

> — SAMUEL JOHNSON 1709–1784

*Les livres ne se font pas comme les enfants, mais comme les pyramides...et*
*ça ne sert á rien! et ça reste dans le désert!...Les chacals pissent*
*au bas et les bourgeois montent dessus.*

*"Books are made not like children but like pyramids...and they're*
*just as useless! and they stay in the desert!...Jackals piss at*
*their foot and the bourgeois climb up on them."*
Letter to Ernest Feydeau (1821–73), Nov./Dec. 1857

> — GUSTAVE FLAUBERT 1821–1880

Ignore the second quote.

This is a book about The NeXT Computer.

It isn't exhaustive and it isn't definitive; it's too early for any book about The NeXT Computer to be either.

As I write this, the 1.0 NeXT software release is only a few weeks past. So the machine we'll talk about is an infant: a precocious infant, granted, but still an infant. Only a few third-party hardware and software packages have been announced as I type these words.

Thankfully (and craftily) the NeXT comes with a treasure chest of applications, developer tools, and reference material. If you own a NeXT, you'll never be without something to explore, even if you never buy another software package.

But this is, I hope, a modest introduction to this amazing machine. We'll look at the NeXT hardware, NeXT software, and explore not just the features, but the reasons behind the features.

In the process, we'll take a long look at UNIX and Mach. If you don't have at least a passing acquaintance with UNIX, you'll never really understand this machine.

I'll try and make it as painless as possible.

We'll also cover the extraordinary programming environment that's included with every NeXT computer. And here, let me disappoint you in advance: I won't do it justice. There's too much to say, and too few pages. We'll resign ourselves to only the main ideas behind object-oriented programming on the NeXT and a brief look at the marvelous tools to create applications. More specifics, in mind-boggling profusion, are found in the NeXT documentation.

We'll end with a further reading section, a few appendices, and you can be on your way. If your head starts spinning long before that, don't put all the blame on me. This machine's like that: amazing.

And about the title of this book: I don't like it. The title is pure and simple hubris. Thanks to this wonderful machine, I can be explicit:


**hu•bris** \ˈhyü-brəs\n

[Gk *hybris* – more at OUT]

(1884)

:exaggerated pride or self-confidence often resulting in retribution

– **hu•bris•tic** \hyü-ˈbris-tik\adj


A great dictionary is always close by when your computer is a NeXT.

Finally, here in the intimacy of an introduction, allow me a personal comment.

I haven't written a book for a long, long time. I'm delighted to be here.

Enough about me.

Here's your part:

Use this computer to make things better.

Just that.

Yes, I know: It's the best business computer ever. Hell, it's the best computer ever made!

But the real purpose of this tool is for

you

to make the world

a better place.

Go to it.

And God bless you.

*Doug Clapp*
*December, 1989*

# Section I

---

# Software

# Chapter 1

# In the Beginning: UNIX

*I must create a System, or be enslav'd by another Man's,*
*I will not Reason and Compare: my business is to Create.*
Jerusalem, pl.10, I.20
— **WILLIAM BLAKE** 1757–1827

*Art must be parochial in the beginning*
*to become cosmopolitan in the end.*
Hail and Farewell! (1911–14), 1925 edn., vol.i, p.5
— **GEORGE MOORE** 1852–1933

The history of UNIX begins twenty years ago, in the Computer Research Group at Bell Labs, with Ken Thompson and a project called MULTICS. The name was an acronym for MULTiplexed Information and Computing System.

MULTICS was a sophisticated multiuser, interactive computing environment. These were big ideas at the time, when computers were finally growing past the "batch" stage, where users approached computers holding stacks of cards that contained their programs.

But MULTICS was a large project, and it didn't perform as well as hoped. It was big, and it was slow. It required immense (at the time) computing resources. Although a few working versions were completed and installed, the project was a failure.

The alternatives for Ken Thompson, Dennis Ritchie, and other researchers at Bell weren't good. They were programmers; they wanted a system for programmers. What was needed was a fast, easy-to-use system that would allow interactive time-sharing. What they had was a clumsy GE 645.

Ken Thompson had an idea for an operating system. And he decided on the right computer to implement his ideas: the DEC-10. Thompson requested a DEC-10. He was refused. Management had been burned by the MULTICS project; they didn't want to get burned again. Management guessed that Thompson would reinvent MULTICS—the last thing they wanted.

Thompson kept requesting.

Management kept refusing.

## Space Travel

It might have ended there. UNIX might have never been. Except for a game: Space Travel.

Ken Thompson enjoyed Space Travel. A lot. The program let you land a spaceship on different planets in the solar system. Thompson finally got the program to run on the GE computer, but with poor results. Response time was terrible. And it was expensive to run on the timesharing system; Dennis Ritchie later said "$75 a game!"

Stymied, Thompson stumbled on a now-legendary "little-used PDP-7 sitting in a corner." Soon, Thompson and Ritchie had Space Travel running on the PDP-7.

Of course, a computer needs an operating system. Files need to be read and written and displayed. Directories of files are needed. Printers need to be supported. A way to enter commands is needed. And multiple users are a necessity.

Soon, the PDP-7 had a operating system—one that looked much like today's UNIX. It allowed multiprocessing: the ability to run more than one program at once. The file system was much like today's UNIX. Best of all, it was multiuser: two users could share the PDP-7!

The operating system was named UNICS, a play on MULTICS, then became UNIX. The researchers finagled a larger computer, a PDP-11/20, and ported UNIX to it.

How did they finagle the larger, more sophisticated PDP-11/20? Not by mentioning "operating systems research." The request was for *text processing* research. Management approved; the PDP-11/20 arrived.

True to their word, the Bell scientists produced a flurry of text processing tools. And UNIX has been a writer's playground ever since.

You may never use ms, nroff, troff, ditroff, or other typesetting-related UNIX programs. But other text manipulation tools are there, in abundance. If you enjoy mucking with words, UNIX is toyland.

The Bell Labs patent office was the first official UNIX site. They did, indeed, use UNIX for text processing: creating text, editing text, formatting text for typesetters, creating tables and indexes—all the normal, tedious text tasks. And they chose UNIX over commercial systems from other vendors—proof that something beyond Space Travel was in the wind.

## The Rise of UNIX

In 1971, Version 1 of UNIX was made official. The Second Edition appeared in 1972. (UNIX "Versions" are also called "Editions.") In 1974, the Fifth Edition was released and made available to universities for a pittance. In effect, UNIX was unleashed upon the world.

Universities loved it. In particular, The University of California, Berkeley, took UNIX to heart. The Computer Science Department at Berkeley embraced UNIX with a vengeance, adding a Pascal interpreter, a new editor, a new shell, and a variety of drivers, utilities, and bug fixes. The result was an operating system that was almost, but not quite, "Standard UNIX," if ever such a thing existed in a system designed to be altered so easily by users.

The Berkeley release was titled "1BSD," for "Berkeley Software Distribution." Since then, the Berkeley and AT&T flavors of UNIX have evolved in separate, but similar, paths. AT&T released Version 6, then System III, then System IV, then System V. The current AT&T offering is System V, Release 4.

Berkeley, meanwhile, unleashed 2BSD, 3BSD, 4.0BSD, and so on, up to the current 4.3BSD.

That's not all. Microsoft has XENIX, another version of UNIX. Other vendors have other "same but different" UNIX offshoots for a variety of computers.

Even the variants have variants! There's a UM BSD UNIX (courtesy of the University of Maryland), a JHU/BRL BSD UNIX (from Johns Hopkins University/

Ballistic Research Laboratory), and, of course, Carnegie-Mellon's silk purse transformation of BSD: Mach.

The AT&T and BSD versions are maddeningly similar. Both have much in common. If you know one, you'll feel at home in the other, but you'll wonder why some of the doorknobs have been moved and your socks are in the wrong drawer. BSD has a few commands missing in System V. System V has a few features not found in BSD.

What's the best version of UNIX? The question has religious overtones for "UNIX wizards," but both versions are excellent renditions of UNIX.

NeXT chose 4.3BSD, then went one step further and chose Mach as an operating system. We'll get to Mach in a bit. First, let's look at UNIX itself.

# Chapter 2

# The Design of UNIX

*An elephant is a mouse with an operating system.*

**— DON KNUTH**

Why is UNIX like it is? To answer that question, we need to go back once more, to the beginning: back to the men who designed UNIX, and the machines they designed it to run on.

Ken Thompson, Dennis Ritchie, and other UNIX designers were programmers, first and foremost. UNIX was designed by programmers for programmers. UNIX wasn't designed by market research or middle management. It wasn't designed to be easy to use by novices or casual users. The creators of UNIX were programmers, who wanted the best environment possible to write programs.

They wanted an operating system that was small, fast, and easy to program. The first UNIX *had* to be small, because it ran on a small computer. The PDP-11 had 64K of memory—half that of a 128K Macintosh; just that of a Commodore 64. And it had a disk for storage: 0.5 megabytes! What's more, the screen displayed characters at a snail's pace.

To make the most of all this, UNIX was designed as a small core—called a kernel—surrounded by small programs that performed useful tasks. Each small program did one thing, and did it well.

This is a no frills approach to computing. Many UNIX programs are razor-sharp utilities that do only one thing, but do it extremely well. The utilities don't have "interface"—no menus or buttons, just the name of the utility. Type in the name and the action is performed, fast. No fuss, no muss.

The burden is on the user to know his tools.

Simplicity has always been a hallmark of UNIX. That sentence may be hard to swallow by those baffled and confounded by UNIX over the years, but it's true: UNIX is a simple and beautiful design.

Simplicity, to the UNIX designers, was squeezing the most function possible from a handful of fundamental ideas. A few of those ideas were

- A hierarchical file system.
- An elegant method of creating asynchronous processes—the ability to run many programs at once.
- Choosing text files as the most common file type.
- The decision to make the Shell a separate program, which allowed it to be easily modified or replaced.
- Consistency of commands (though thousands of UNIX users-cum-programmers have muddled this grand idea).
- Generalizing the notion of standard input and standard output to apply to commands, files, and devices. And,
- Interprocess communications.

If this doesn't make immediate sense, don't worry. We'll get to each soon, or in subsequent chapters.

UNIX became a phenomenon for several reasons. First, it worked. It worked well; it was small, fast, and efficient. It had few built-in hardware requirements, so it could be ported to other computers with a minimum of agony.

Best of all, it was easy to modify and extend. There are no secrets in UNIX. The Bell researchers wanted an operating system they could get their hands into—anywhere, anytime. When UNIX was first offered to universities for "educational purposes," it came with full source code. The rule with UNIX has always been

"If you don't like the way it works, change it!"

And people have been changing it ever since. Hence the profusion of UNIX dialects and offshoots. Although NeXT may take the prize for the most sweeping

UNIX changes, underneath the glitz and convenience of the NeXT interface is the same old UNIX that users have loved and hated for years.

Actually, under the glitz and convenience is Mach, yet another UNIX variation! We'll get to Mach, but first let's delve into the UNIX basics.

## C

The first version of UNIX was written in assembly language, which made for quickness, but also made it difficult to port UNIX to other computers, which relied on other, incompatible assemblers. Later versions were written in C, a language created by the creators of UNIX. In a sense, C was developed to develop UNIX. The relationship has been incestuous ever since. Although C is a general-purpose language, its roots are in "operating systems programming"—UNIX.

The rise of C paralleled the rise of UNIX. Like UNIX, C is small, fast, and sharp. If you know what you're doing, you can do virtually anything, with little effort and little code. If you *don't* know what you're doing, watch out!

Although most UNIX systems include other languages (Pascal, LISP, and FORTRAN are common), C's sweet smell—or stench, depending on your preference—pervades UNIX.

## The Kernel

The kernel is elemental UNIX. It's the heart of UNIX: the lowest level. The kernel mediates between software and hardware: opening, reading, writing, and closing files, and printing— to printers, the screen display, or across networks. The kernel also handles process scheduling—it's the traffic cop that keeps programs from running into each other while running.

The kernel is made up of several hundred small, fast "system calls" which do the low-level dirty work. The design of system calls is what makes UNIX consistent in regard to devices, and what allows for UNIX features such as output redirection. The system call to open a file, for example, is also used to open a printer for printing. "Open" simply opens a device. The user determines what device to open.

Other programs call kernel routines, which enforces the UNIX philosophy of "loosely coupled architecture" and keeps programs small and straightforward.

## The Shell

Many UNIX users think that "the shell" is UNIX.

It's not.

Keeping the UNIX kernel and the UNIX shell separate was a fundamental design decision. The shell is similar to the Macintosh Finder, Microsoft Windows, or the MS-DOS prompt. In those other systems, though, the portion of the operating system that processes commands is an integral part of the operating system. In UNIX, it's been cleanly separate from the beginning, so Bell scientists could easily debug, change, modify, and enhance both the kernel and the shell.

The shell is a program you use to give commands to UNIX. Two NeXT applications, Shell and Terminal, let you access the traditional UNIX shell. Type in a command, and the shell does its best to execute it, or calls on another program to execute the command.

More than that, the shell is a complete language. It accepts commands (like "ls" to list files), but it can also execute complete shell programs. Shell programs, not surprisingly, are similar to C programs: C made easy, if such a thing is possible.

There are a variety of shells. Two of the most popular are the "Bourne Shell" (named after its creator, Stephen R. Bourne) and the "C Shell."

Both shells are available on the NeXT; "sh" and "csh" in /bin are the Bourne and C Shells, respectively.

On the NeXT, the Shell application calls on the C Shell. Most users consider the C Shell more powerful than the Bourne Shell, and C Shell scripts more closely resemble the C language. (The hidden file ".cshrc" in your root directory is the startup file for "Shell.") As we wind our way through this book, you'll see many examples of interaction with the Shell, and you'll be encouraged to use the shell. Although "The shell isn't UNIX," if you know the shell, you're well on your way to UNIX mastery.

The NeXT Workspace Manager is just another shell. Although you can't write Workspace Manager scripts, the NeXT shell gives you a large handful of traditional shell commands, in a pleasant guise. For those willing to lift the hood, Shell is always available.

## Utilities

If you come to NeXT from personal computers, you'll be amazed at the vast number of utilities that come with UNIX. More than 200 separate programs are here: utilities, languages, you name it. If you're new to computers, it's overwhelming.

Why hundreds of programs? Why hundreds of commands (many with many options) to learn?

Again, it's UNIX philosophy. Programs should be single-purpose. They should take in something, and output something else.

To add functionality, you don't add features to existing programs. Instead, you connect programs together. The output of one program becomes the input to a second program. The second program may send (or "pipe") its output to a third program, and so on. This philosophy is expressed in a famous UNIX aphorism:

"Use tools, not panaceas."

In other words, if you've got a hammer, don't add features until the hammer works "sorta like" a screwdriver. Let the hammer be a hammer. And fashion a screwdriver whose sole mission is driving screws.

This work paradigm makes only a few simple demands on utility programs. First, they shouldn't be fussy about their input, which may come from a user, a file, or another program. And program output should be bare-bones: no headers, footers, or other extra material. Since output from one program may be input to another program, it's necessary to keep to a "Just the facts, Ma'am," output. If a sort utility sorts lines in a file (which it does), it must also presume that its input—the file—contains lines of text, and lines of text only. No funny stuff.

These considerations resulted in a raft of small, specialized programs. Programs that can accept input from most anywhere, and which deliver bare-bones output. If one program won't do what you want, then maybe two, or more, connected together can.

That's the idea, anyway. Not all UNIX utilities, however, live up to those lofty ideals. You can't blindly connect anything to anything. Creeping features have crept into many utilities, resulting in a welter of options to remember, and utilities that behave more like full-blown applications.

## Multitasking

From the beginning, UNIX supported multitasking: the ability to run many programs at the same time. Each program is a task, or "process." Multitasking and multiprocessing refer to the same idea.

One of the beauties of UNIX is the way that it handles multiple processes. To the kernel, a process consists of one or more files and a chunk of memory. Processes can be applications like WriteNow or Digital Librarian. Other processes are invisible, doing their work in the background. The mail daemon, for example, is an invisible background process. You can't see it, you don't know it's there. But when you're notified that mail has arrived, the mail daemon is the cause—it's been watching for mail.

The kernel also takes care of scheduling—allocating CPU time to the various processes that are active. Processes have several characteristics, including:

- runnable;
- stopped;
- sleeping; and
- idle.

Processes run either in the foreground or background. On NeXT, the foreground process is usually an application with a key window—a black title bar. All other running applications are background processes. The foreground concept is important to both UNIX and the Workspace Manager for the same reason: only one process can be eligible to accept commands. Think of the confusion otherwise!

Let's take a closer look at processes (which we'll soon call "tasks," the correct Mach term). In the Shell, type:

```
localhost# ps cu
```

and you'll see:

```
USER    PID %CPU %MEM  VSIZE  RSIZE  TT STAT TIME  COMMAND
root    190  3.7  1.7   824K   280K  p3  S   0:00  csh
root    181  0.5  6.9  1.71M  1.10M  p2  S   0:03  DeskPad
root    180  0.0  6.7  1.68M  1.07M  p1  S   0:02  QuickShell
root    195  0.0  0.9   728K   144K  p3  R   0:00  ps
```

Ps means "process." The ps utility has many options. Here, we used "c" to display the command name (shown in the rightmost column) and "u" to create what's called a "user oriented display."

This is what NeXT is multitasking away at, this moment:

- the C Shell (csh);
- an application: DeskPad;
- another application: QuickShell; and
- The ps command itself.

But that's not all. Those are only *the most visible tasks*. There's more. We could ask to see absolutely everything:

```
localhost#  ps caugx
USER     PID   %CPU %MEM VSIZE RSIZE TT  STAT   TIME COMMAND
root     112   8.6 21.1 5.20M 3.38M ?   R      4:18 WindowServer
root     189   5.3  6.8 2.16M 1.09M ?   S      0:07 Shell
root       0   0.9 10.8 14.3M 1.73M ?   R <   36:38 kernel-task
root     190   0.7  1.7  824K  280K p3  S      0:00 csh
root     181   0.6  6.9 1.72M 1.11M p2  S      0:19 DeskPad
root      49   0.3  1.7 5.87M  280K ?   S      0:01 nmserver
root      45   0.0  0.1  584K   16K ?   S      0:00 biod
root      43   0.0  2.8 1.12M  456K ?   S      0:08 netinfod
root      41   0.0  1.4  960K  232K ?   S      0:00 nibindd
root      38   0.0  1.6  968K  256K ?   S      0:00 portmap
root      32   0.0  0.8  720K  136K ?   S      0:00 syslogd
root      46   0.0  0.1  584K   16K ?   S      0:00 biod
root      47   0.0  0.1  584K   16K ?   S      0:00 biod
root       2   0.0  0.2  592K   32K ?   SW     0:00 mach_init
root       1   0.0  0.5  616K   80K ?   SW     0:00 init
root      48   0.0  0.1  584K   16K ?   S      0:00 biod
root      71   0.0  1.6  984K  264K ?   SW     0:00 lpd
root      60   0.0  0.6  744K   96K ?   SW     0:00 inetd
root     179   0.0  6.3 2.09M 1.02M ?   S      0:01 Terminal
root     178   0.0  6.3 2.09M 1.02M ?   SW     0:01 Terminal
root     180   0.0  6.7 1.68M 1.07M p1  SW     0:02 QuickShell
root     186   0.0  8.0 2.38M 1.28M ?   S      0:51 Edit
root     119   0.0  7.3 1.84M 1.17M ?   S      0:04 Preferences
```

```
root      66   0.0   1.0   840K   160K ?  SW     0:00 sendmail
root     108   0.0   0.7   704K   112K ?  S      0:00 cron
root     117   0.0   8.1  2.43M  1.30M ?  SW     0:06 Workspace
root     105   0.0   0.1   584K    24K ?  S      0:00 update
root      82   0.0   0.0     0K     0K ?  SW     0:00 np_buddy
root      81   0.0   1.7  1.51M   272K ?  SW     0:00 npd
root     113   0.0   5.1  1.56M   840K ?  SW     0:05 loginwindow
root      76   0.0   1.4   960K   224K ?  S      0:00 pbs
root      78   0.0   0.3   680K    56K ?  SWN    0:00
  autodiskmount
root     209   0.0   0.9   728K   144K p3 R      0:00 ps
```

This is closer to "what's really happening." What's really happening is multitasking—in a big way! (The above listing is sorted by percent of CPU time used by each task. It's an instructive demonstration not only of UNIX's ability to multitask, but of Mach's efficient use of processor time, shown in the %CPU column.)

Not only can multiple tasks run at (what appears to be) the same time, but tasks can "spawn" new tasks. The new, or "child," task is a copy of its parent task. Children can produce other children. When you create new Shell windows, for example, you're actually "spawning" new shells, which then run in unison with the first Shell.

## Multiusers

The design of UNIX makes handling multiple users easy. UNIX has always been multiuser—although the most ancient UNIX could only handle two users! We'll cover multiuser issues more thoroughly in the networking chapters.

## Virtual Memory

A feature that's only now appearing on personal computers, virtual memory, has been a UNIX fixture since around 1978—about the time that consumers were buying Apple II's and Radio Shack TRS-80 Model I's.

Virtual memory allows programs to treat disk space as RAM memory. (You'll also hear RAM anachronistically called "core" by UNIX buffs.) Since disks are big and memory always limited (and expensive), virtual memory, in effect, gives programs all the space they need, and more.

Virtual memory came to UNIX from Berkeley. The researchers at Bell Labs had ported a version of UNIX to a DEC VAX—an impressive computer that allowed virtual memory. But Bell ignored the virtual memory capability.

Berkeley didn't. They quickly added virtual memory to UNIX. Virtual memory is a big feature; it assured the success of "the Berkeley Extensions," and paved the way for BSD to become a major UNIX variant.

We'll have more to say about virtual memory when we look at Mach in the next chapter.

## Device Independence

Computers are input/output machines. Something goes in, something comes out. The UNIX designers made that notion as general as possible. As a result, UNIX isn't fussy about where its input comes from, or where its output goes.

To UNIX, most everything looks like a file. Even devices such as printers or terminals look, to UNIX, like files. UNIX can happily read from a file or write to a file. It can write information to the screen as easily as writing the same information to a disk file, or a printer, or a modem.

That's device independence. Because UNIX isn't choosy, users (or programs) can redirect program output—send the output of a program most anywhere that makes sense—even to the input of another program.

## Interprocess Communication

Device independence makes interprocess communication possible. Commands can be chained to other commands. Two of the basic methods are called "pipes" and "filters." A pipe directs the output of one program to the input of a second program. A filter processes input data, changes it in some way, and outputs it—often through a pipe to another program.

For example, let's say we've got a file named "somewords." We could use the UNIX "cat" command to display the file:

```
localhost# cat somewords
now
is
```

```
the
time
for
all
good
men
to
go
ape
```

Or we could pipe the output of cat to the sort command (the "|" is the pipe symbol), like this:

```
localhost# cat | sort somewords
all
ape
for
go
good
is
men
now
the
time
to
```

A sorted list, quickly done, thanks to interprocess communication.

We'll see more UNIX (possibly more UNIX than you'd like!) soon. First, let's look more closely at Mach. And look at some of these ideas again; this time at a lower level.

# Chapter 3

# Mach

*Not choice*
*But habit rules the unreflecting herd.*
Grant that by this (1822)
　　　— **WILLIAM WORDSWORTH**  1770–1850

*L'embarras des richesses.*
*"The more alternatives, the more difficult the choice."*
Title of comedy, 1726
　　　　— **ABBE D'ALLAINVAL**  1700–1753

Making a computer means making choices. What microprocessor to use? How much memory? Disks: what kind and how much storage? And on and on.

The most important choice, though, may be the selection of an operating system. Here, NeXT made two crucial decisions. The first was the decision to adopt UNIX, and all that UNIX entails.

The second decision was better: choosing Mach.

If NeXT succeeds, the single most important reason may be Mach. Not the read/write optical disk, the beauty of the display, or the marvelous programming environment. Mach.

Mach, the "UNIX for the nineties," was developed at Carnegie-Mellon University. Mach is a complete rewrite of UNIX; it's UNIX dismantled, examined, and rebuilt. (Despite the rewrite, though, Mach is compatible with programs created under 4.3BSD. All that's necessary is a recompilation of the program under Mach, which uses a slightly different object file format.)

The time was right. UNIX began as a simple and elegant operating system. Early versions of the UNIX kernel fit in 40K of memory. Over time, features were added and the kernel grew, and grew, then bloated. Some versions topped out at over a megabyte as features that were once separate were "rolled into" the kernel.

What once was simple became complex and inconsistent. Difficult to understand, hard to change.

With Mach, UNIX returns to its "small is beautiful; simpler is better" roots. Carnegie-Mellon slashed away a morass of features, reducing UNIX to its most elemental state: the kernel. Then they rewrote the kernel, and modernized and extended the kernel's basic functions. The result, on NeXT, is a kernel of only about 420K—small, as UNIX kernels go.

The work paid off, not only in size and elegance, but in speed. On most computers, Mach is 15 to 25 percent faster than Berkeley UNIX. And some Mach operations are *five to seven times faster* than BSD UNIX.

Many features that were once part of the kernel are now separate programs. This increased modularity keeps the kernel small and fast; and the split-off programs are easier to maintain and debug.

The Mach kernel has only three primary duties:

- management of virtual memory;
- scheduling of processor time; and
- IPC—Interprocess Communication.

## Virtual Memory

Applications under Mach are allotted a four gigabyte address space to romp in.

Four gigabytes? Mach really is designed for the future!

The vast address space means that running applications (tasks) are constrained only by available disk space. Virtual memory allows only a portion of an application to reside in RAM memory. Applications are divided into "pages" of memory, each 8K in size. Some pages remain in RAM memory. Idle portions are written to a "swap file" on disk. When an application attempts to access a part of itself not in RAM, a "page fault" occurs, and the needed portion is loaded into RAM. If RAM is full, the least recently used page in memory gets sent to disk. (The disk file used, by the way, is /private/vm/swapfile.)

It works better than you'd think. Mach is extremely clever about RAM. And Mach's design is memory efficient to begin with, so Mach applications require less RAM than similar programs on other UNIX systems.

Mach shines in memory management. A major improvement over other UNIX variants is Mach's "copy-on-write" feature. To understand copy-on-write, consider traditional UNIX processes. When a process "spawns" a new process (when you create a second Shell, for example), UNIX makes a copy of the entire address space. Everything—all the data—is copied. That takes time.

Mach designers reasoned that since most "child" tasks only read data—not actually change it—why make a copy? Until changes are made in the child task, the "parent" is only referred to, not copied. Make a change, however, and the data is copied—fast. The scheme not only saves time, but greatly reduces memory needs.

Mach excels at fast, clever, low-level memory operations. The low-level prowess of Mach makes it easy to perform operations unthinkable on other computers. The NeXT Pasteboard, for example, allows you to copy two or ten megabytes of data as quickly as a single sentence. Thanks to Mach.

## Who Owns Mach?

UNIX was created at AT&T.

Mach was created at Carnegie-Mellon university, with taxpayer's money.

So Mach should be free, right?

Yes, no, and sort of.

Many companies offer custom versions of UNIX, created outside AT&T, yet still pay royalties to AT&T. Why? Because to avoid paying royalties to AT&T, it's necessary to rewrite every line in UNIX. Only then, can other UNIX suppliers legally avoid paying AT&T their due.

UNIX consists of hundreds of thousands of lines of program code. Tricky, complex code. "Rewriting from scratch" is enormously difficult. Although Carnegie-Mellon *has* completely re-written the UNIX kernel, the UNIX commands (grep ls, and hundreds of others) also need to be re-written from scratch, and they comprise over 500,000 lines of code.

Still, that's what Carnegie-Mellon set out to do: completely rewrite UNIX, and make it better, faster, and more modern in the process.

When they're finished, Mach—in theory, anyway—may be free, with the complete source code available to anyone with curiousity, and lots of available disk space.

But some AT&T program code still exists in Mach, so it's not free yet, if indeed it ever will be.

But maybe.

## IPC—Interprocess Communication

The Mach kernel is object-oriented; the idea of "message passing" is at the lowest level of Mach. The support for precise, low-level message passing makes communication between applications easy to implement at a higher level. Application Kit objects rely on this low-level support to provide features like "Send Selection" in NeXT applications.

In the last chapter, we mentioned how UNIX commands can be chained together using pipes and filters. Mach implements this idea on an even lower level. With Mach, commands can communicate with *themselves*. Read on.

## Tasks and Threads

Multitasking—the ability to run many programs at once—has always been a UNIX feature. Programs become "processes" that run concurrently, while the kernel handles scheduling.

Mach takes the idea of a process and splits it into two new concepts:

• tasks; and
• threads.

A task is similar to a UNIX process: one or more files and a chunk of memory. But a Mach task isn't a running application; instead, it's an environment where threads execute and a collection of "ports" which allow tasks to communicate with one another. Tasks are smaller, faster, and require less memory than UNIX processes.

What we think of as a "running program" actually takes place in threads. A task may have one thread or many threads, all sharing the task's address space. In hardware terms, a thread is similar to a microprocessor; a task is similar to memory chips and input/output channels.

The increased "granularity" of tasks and threads has important consequences.

UNIX users take multiprocessing for granted; UNIX has always been able to run multiple programs. But with Mach, the programs themselves can multiprocess! An application may consist of separate modules, in separate threads, each merrily churning along, while other modules perform other duties. The NeXT manuals use a word processor as an example: one thread devoted to handling keyboard input, another thread checking spelling, and so on.

Of course, this is an illusion, just as on other UNIX systems. There's only one processor, and only one instruction can be executed at a time. It's the fineness of kernel scheduling—a time slice here, a time slice there—that makes the illusion real. All done with mirrors.

This is making the best of a bad situation. The bad situation is the "Von Neumann bottleneck." Von Neumann laid the conceptual groundwork for today's microprocessors. The beauty of "Von Neumann machines" is that instructions and data can be stored together. The bottleneck is that only one instruction can execute at a time.

Mach threads break the bottleneck. Not only can applications written for Mach consist of separate threads, but each thread can run on a separate processor: true parallel computing. Threads can even execute on other networked computers, for completely transparent "distributed processing"—another Mach feature.

The current version of Mach only presents the illusion of true multiprocessing, as do other UNIX versions. The reason is that Mach is still under development at Carnegie-Mellon and at NeXT (where Avadis Tevanian, one of Mach's chief architects, is now NeXT's Chief Operating System Scientist).

Expect future versions of the NeXT/Mach operating system to offer full multiprocessor multiprocessing. If anything, this is NeXT's ace in the hole: parallel computing, supported at the lowest level.

With Mach multiprocessing, NeXT can take absolute advantage of newer, faster processors. Mach has a built-in, unbounded appetite for power and speed. The more you give Mach, the better it gets. Expect to see NeXT add-on boards stuffed with RISC processors, ready to blaze through jobs that would choke a Macintosh IIcx or the fastest IBM 80486 computer.

## Mach's Future

NeXT has no lock on Mach. Versions of Mach are also available for the DEC VAX (where Mach was first developed), the Sun 3, the IBM RT PC, and other computers.

And Mach's shine may fade as newer versions of UNIX arrive. Many of Mach's best features are promised for the next generation UNIX from AT&T. Still, talk is cheap and promises easy. NeXT couldn't ship promises. Mach is here, it's good, and it works. Future NeXTs may use Mach, or they may not. "We're not religious," NeXT officials say.

But right now, today, Mach is the best choice.

## Does the Version Matter?

BSD4.3, System V, Mach—versions of UNIX abound. Which version is better, and why, is a constant topic of discussion. At a lunch with NeXT developers, Steve Jobs took the high road, saying, "Once you've chosen UNIX, you're 90% of the way there. It doesn't really matter which version you choose, and people who argue about this kind of thing are people who don't have anything better to do."

So there.

# Chapter 4

## Files and Directories

*Brevis esse laboro,*
*Obscurus fio.*
"I strive to be brief, and I become obscure."
                          **— HORACE** 65–8 B.C.

Here's the most important fact about files: file names are case sensitive.

The file "myfile" isn't the same as the file "MyFile".

And the file "myFile" is yet a third file!

Once more. The file

usr/include/appkit/form.h

isn't the same as

usr/include/appkit/Form.h

See the difference? One capital letter. It makes all the difference. Nowhere in the bowels of the cube does "Form.h" exist. A file called "form.h" exists, but no file "Form.h."

This can create utter despair when dealing with UNIX. "Why isn't this working?" you think. "I did EVERYTHING RIGHT!"

If you ever get that feeling, remember: file names (and directory names) are case sensitive. Type an untoward capital letter and the cube is utterly blind to your request.

The NeXT keyboard makes an oblique nod to case's importance. Most computer keyboards have a Caps Lock key. NeXT, instead, requires Command-Shift to engage "Alphalock," or Caps Lock. This may be a gentle reminder of case sensitivity.

The moral? When creating new files, opt for all lowercase or uppercase file names, if possible. Then you'll never need to think "Was that 'MyFile,' or 'Myfile'?"

Now for less important information.

## File Names

The NeXT Workspace Manager relaxes some—but not all—of the UNIX file naming rules. UNIX doesn't allow file names containing spaces. "my file" wouldn't be allowed. The Workspace Manager permits spaces, which makes for much easier reading.

Some UNIX variants limit file names to fourteen characters. "thisisafilename" would be one character too long. 4.3BSD (and subsequently, Mach) removes this limitation. As a result, The Workspace Manager permits filenames longer than you're likely to use.

At the expense of some convenience, it's a good idea to follow UNIX conventions, particularly if you intend to work in the shell—and it's likely you'll find yourself drawn to the shell as your NeXT experience grows.

The other filename caveat concerns special characters. Don't use these characters in a filename:

"|, -, >, >>, <, /, \ , @, #, !, ?, *"

In general, it's best to use only characters and digits when naming files.

## File Types

UNIX files are either:

- binary files;
- text files; or
- directories.

Binary files are often compiled programs; "executable files," in UNIX terms.

Most other files are straight text, with no special structure imposed. Most of the files that UNIX uses to conduct its business are text files. The advantage is that programs and data are kept separate. Data needed by programs isn't hidden in compiled code; instead, it's open to view and easy to change. Change the text file and UNIX obligingly changes its behavior. Even the definition of text itself is in a text file! It's found in the (text) file "ascii" in the /usr/pub directory. Here's a sample from the file:

```
|000 nul|001 soh|002 stx|003 etx|004 eot|005 enq|006 ack|007 bel|
|010 bs |011 ht |012 nl |013 vt |014 np |015 cr |016 so |017 si |
|020 dle|021 dc1|022 dc2|023 dc3|024 dc4|025 nak|026 syn|027 etb|
|030 can|031 em |032 sub|033 esc|034 fs |035 gs |036 rs |037 us |
|040 sp |041  ! |042  " |043  # |044  $ |045  % |046  & |047  ` |
|050  ( |051  ) |052  * |053  + |054  , |055  - |056  . |057  / |
|060  0 |061  1 |062  2 |063  3 |064  4 |065  5 |066  6 |067  7 |
|070  8 |071  9 |072  : |073  ; |074  < |075  = |076  > |077  ? |
|100  @ |101  A |102  B |103  C |104  D |105  E |106  F |107  G |
|110  H |111  I |112  J |113  K |114  L |115  M |116  N |117  O |
|120  P |121  Q |122  R |123  S |124  T |125  U |126  V |127  W |
|130  X |131  Y |132  Z |133  [ |134  \ |135  ] |136  ^ |137  _ |
|140  ` |141  a |142  b |143  c |144  d |145  e |146  f |147  g |
|150  h |151  i |152  j |153  k |154  l |155  m |156  n |157  o |
|160  p |161  q |162  r |163  s |164  t |165  u |166  v |167  w |
|170  x |171  y |172  z |173  {|174  | |175  }|176  ~ |177 del|
```

Much of UNIX's malleability comes from the notion of keeping system information in text files. On NeXT, the "UNIX Expert" option in the Preferences application shows you most files. The Workspace Manager goes a step further: checking "All" in the "Filter..." panel shows all files—even files preceded by a period, which are initially hidden from view.

The hidden files, again, are text files. Even the file ".hidden" itself, which lists hidden directories, is a text file. (Filenames that begin with a period are hidden by default.) Since it's a text file, perusing .hidden is as easy as double-clicking the mouse to launch Shell and typing:

```
localhost# cat /.hidden
bin
clients
```

```
dev
etc
lib
lost+found
mach
odmach
private
sdmach
tmp
usr
vmunix
```

Remember, the first UNIX users were the UNIX designers. They wanted every aspect of UNIX to be easily changed or modified. Keeping data in text files made that easy, and now makes it easy for UNIX gurus (like yourself, one day) to quickly change the face and function of UNIX at will or whim.

## Directories

Directories are also text files. Directories contain the names of files and the names of other directories. Directories can be read like any other text file. They can't, however, be changed by users and "written" back to UNIX. Only UNIX commands can change the contents of directories—which is as it should be!

The UNIX directory structure is powerful but straightforward. Here's how it works:

- every file is in a directory;
- directories may contain other directories.

A directory might contain ten files. Five might be program or data files. The other five files might be directories which, in turn, contain other files and other directories, and so on.

To keep this nesting of directories in directories from becoming total confusion, UNIX imposes a tree-like hierarchy. The root of the tree is a single directory called (oddly) "root."

This is the root directory:

/

That's it, in typical UNIX terseness. Every file and directory is either in the / directory, or a subdirectory contained within the root (/) directory. No exceptions.

Since every directory and every file is, at root, in the root directory, it's possible to describe a path—beginning at root—to reach any file. The idea of paths and pathnames is central to the file system.

For example, the Shakespeare poem "The Rape of Lucrece" is in the directory "Various_Poems." The Various_Poems directory is nestled in the "Shakespeare" directory, and so on up the line, until we get to the root directory /.

The proper UNIX pathname always starts at root and works on down. In this instance, the path is:

```
/NextLibrary/Literature/Shakespeare/Various_Poems/The Rape of
    Lucrece
```

That's the proper way to describe the path. (Don't be confused by the two uses of /. It's both the name of the root directory and a pathname separator.)

Although NeXT's Workspace Manager looks for certain types of files in particular directories automatically, if you specify the full pathname of a file, you can be assured of getting where you want to go.

In fact, the Workspace Manager also uses paths to find files. When you launch an application the Workspace Manager uses this path

```
/Apps:/LocalApps:/NextApps:/NextAdmin:/NextDeveloper/Demos
```

to locate the file. The search is from left to right, until the file is found. First, the /Apps directory is searched (if it exists). Then /LocalApps is rummaged through. Next, /NextApps is searched. Finally, /NextDeveloper/Demos is perused for the file in question.

Now let's list the contents of the root directory, using the shell command ls. We'll add the -a option to show all files:

```
localhost# ls -a
/          .places        NextDeveloper/ lib/          sdmach*
/          .profile       NextLibrary/   lost+found/   tmp/
NeXT/      LocalLibrary/  bin/           mach@         usr/
cshrc      Net/           clients/       me/           vmunix@
hidden     NextAdmin/     dev/           odmach*
login      NextApps/      etc/           private/
```

The first two directory entries, ./ and ../, are hidden files found in every directory, and placed automatically in every new directory. The first entry, ./, is the current directory—the directory you're "in." The second entry is the current directory's "parent" directory. Again, the only directory with no parent directory is the root directory.

In everyday use, the periods are a fast shorthand.

.

means "this directory" and

..

means "the directory one back" (or "one up the tree" or "the directory of which this directory is a subdirectory")—you get the idea.

Once more: a forward slash (/) means "the root directory" and two periods (..) mean "the parent directory of this directory." Re-read the previous sentence thirty times. Why are we harping on this? You'll see.

The next few directory entries are hidden files, preceded by periods:

```
.NeXT/
.cshrc
.hidden
.login
.places
.profile
```

The / symbol means that the directory entry is another directory. So .NeXT/ is a directory. Listing the .NeXT/ directory yields this:

```
localhost# ls -a /.NeXT
/                    .NeXTdefaults.D  .dock
/                    .NeXTdefaults.L  .places
```

Again, the . and .. files appear, followed by files and directories used by the Workspace Manager. The .NeXTdefaults file, for example, holds system settings. ".dock" is a text file containing the names of applications in the NeXT dock.

Let's move back to the root directory:

```
localhost# ls -a
```

| / | .places | NextDeveloper/ | lib/ | sdmach* |
| / | .profile | NextLibrary/ | lost+found/ | tmp/ |
| NeXT/ | LocalLibrary/ | bin/ | mach@ | usr/ |
| cshrc | Net/ | clients/ | me/ | vmunix@ |
| hidden | NextAdmin/ | dev/ | odmach* | |
| login | NextApps/ | etc/ | private/ | |

It's now easy to see which files are directories; any filename ending with / is a directory.

Filenames ending with * are binary files; either executable programs, or binary files used by other programs, or binary files needed by UNIX. "odmach*" stands for "Optical Disk Mach." "sdmach" for "SCSI Disk Mach." These files are used by Mach, not by users. They're in the root directory, we can assume, to make them quickly available.

## Links

Finally, filenames ending with @ are "symbolic links" to other directories. Symbolic links are a Berkeley innovation. So far, we've been talking about files in directories. Of course, the physical files don't actually reside in tidy clumps inside the computer called directories. The actual files may be scattered all over your disk.

To UNIX, a directory is a list of pointers. Each pointer holds the address of the actual file. So the path

```
/NextLibrary/Literature/Shakespeare/Various_Poems/The Rape of
    Lucrece
```

is really a list of pointers to other pointers, finally ending with the file in question. The pointers are called links. In this case, hard links. Whenever you create a file, UNIX creates a link that holds the location of the file. Remove a file and UNIX removes the link.

A symbolic link is a soft link. It's a pseudonym for the actual pathname. Although a file can have only one "true" hard-linked pathname, it can have multiple symbolic links.

Symbolic links are a clever alternative to copying files from one directory to another. Say, for example, that you'd like Shakespeare's poems right up there with NeXTApps in the root directory. Fire up the shell and type in:

```
ln -s /NextLibrary/Literature/Shakespeare/Various_Poems /
```

The Various_Poems directory now appears in your root directory:

```
localhost# ls
NeXT/       LocalLibrary/    Various_Poems/   lost+found/    tmp/
cshrc       Net/             bin/             mach@          usr/
hidden      NextAdmin/       clients/         me/            vmunix@
login       NextApps/        dev/             odmach*
places      NextDeveloper/   etc/             private/
profile     NextLibrary/     lib/             sdmach*
```

And the original pathname still exists. So you now have two ways to get to Various_Poems.

Okay: a little more explanation of that command. "ln" is another of those verbose UNIX commands. It stands for "make links." The default is to make a hard link. The "-s" option makes a soft link. One way to invoke the command is

```
ln [ -s ] sourcename [ targetname ]
```

In this case, the sourcename is the pathname

```
/NextLibrary/Literature/Shakespeare/Various_Poems
```

And the targetname is the home directory, or

```
/
```

All that's required between the sourcename and the targetname is a space, which we cheerfully included. Type it in, hit Return, and the shell makes the link. In the best UNIX fashion, that's it. No words of praise, no confidence-building remarks like "Link successfully created" from the Shell. Zip. That's the way it is; real programmers don't want needless blather from their computers. But when you next look in your root directory, there's the new directory.

## Absolute and Relative Pathnames

Pathnames such as

```
/NextLibrary/Literature/Shakespeare/Various_Poems/The Rape
```

```
of Lucrece
```

seem to go against the UNIX tradition of terse typing. The pathname above is called an "absolute pathname." It begins at the root directory (/) and *absolutely* specifies the complete path to a file or directory.

The alternative, to save keystrokes, is using a relative pathname. A relative pathname takes advantage of the fact that the shell always knows the present working directory.

For example, the poems in the Various_Poems directory can be specified as

```
/NextLibrary/Literature/Shakespeare/Various_Poems/A_Song
/NextLibrary/Literature/Shakespeare/Various_Poems/Epitaphs
/NextLibrary/Literature/Shakespeare/Various_Poems/Gloves
```

and so on. But if you first change the current directory (abbreviated as "cd") to Various_Poems with this shell command

```
localhost# cd /NextLibrary/Literature/Shakespeare/
  Various_Poems
```

you can then use relative pathnames:

```
A_Song
Epitaphs
Gloves
```

For example, to read a file from the Shell, you could

```
localhost# cat gloves
gloves: No such file or directory
```

Notice my slip: I used the wrong case. Don't let this happen to you! Once again...

```
localhost# cat Gloves
{\ rtf0\ mac{\ fonttbl{\ f0\ froman Times Roman;}}{\ f1\ fmod-
  ern Courier;}}
{\ pard\ f0\ fs28{\ fs48\ b
Various Poems\
_____}\
\
        `Upon a pair of gloves that master sent to his mis-
```

```
    tress'\
                            The gift is small,\
                            The will is all:\
                            Alexander Aspinall\

    }}
```

Although only "glove" was entered as the filename, UNIX happily expanded it to

    Present Working Directory + filename,

or

    /NextLibrary/Literature/Shakespeare/Various_Poems/Gloves

(If the listing looks odd, it's because the file is in RTF format; Digital Librarian or WriteNow "interpret" the file to restore the formatting.)

Relative pathnames save time and typing. If you intend to work with more than one file in a directory, use cd to change the directory, then use relative pathnames. And remember that .. means "the parent directory of this directory." Typing "cd .." is a fast way to move "one back" in the shell. The parent directory is now the present working directory. Later, we'll see how this directory shorthand is useful in The Workspace Manager.

## Relative Linking

Now let's combine our knowledge of relative pathnames and linking. We're going to link a directory to the NextDeveloper directory.

First, let's find out what directory we're in.

```
localhost#  pwd
/
```

We're in the root directory. Now we'll make /NextDeveloper the current directory with cd (Change Directory).

```
localhost# cd /NextDeveloper
```

Did it work?

```
localhost# pwd
/NextDeveloper
```

Good. Now for a link. The /usr/include directory contains files that are useful and interesting to developers. The trick, of course, is remembering that /usr/include is where to go to find the files. Linking the directory to the /NextDeveloper file would help.

```
localhost# ln -s /usr/include
```

Done. Since the working directory is currently /NextDeveloper, we didn't need to specify the "targetname" for the command.

/NextDeveloper was used by default. All that was needed was:

```
Command        -option      filename
```

We used a directory name instead of a filename, which works just as well. And we used the -s option to make a soft link.

Another advantage of soft links is that they can span file systems. You can link a file or directory that exists on another networked cube, and have it appear to reside in your own directories.

## Permissions

Because UNIX was multiuser from the beginning, the idea of file permissions was addressed at the start.

We've seen how easy it is to go in and muck around with UNIX itself. On a multiuser system, it's just as easy to go in and muck around with someone else's files on another computer! Obviously, this can't be allowed indiscriminately. A system as complex as UNIX (did I say it was simple earlier?) needs someone doomed to act as a System Administrator. This "Superuser" might need full access to everything everywhere. Mere users, however, shouldn't have the power to change (or remove!) files on other users' systems, without express permission.

The security issue led to file permissions. The permissions are in three groups:

- owner (usually the person who created the file);
- group; and
- others.

For each group, permissions can be set to allow files to be read, written, or executed. Directories have an additional permission: search. In UNIXSpeak:

```
r w x
```

for Read, Write, and eXecute.

The read and write permissions apply to nonbinary files. Execute means "run" or "launch." A dash in the place of an r, w, or x means that permission isn't granted, as in:

```
-rw-r-r-  1 root            77 Apr  4 22:36 .hidden
```

The .hidden file contains the names of hidden files. Since it's not a binary file, it can't be executed, hence the dashes instead of x's. The file also can't be written to except by the owner (although UNIX takes care of this for you).

Because there are three categories, there are three sets of "rwe" for every file.

If you type

```
ls -l
```

in the shell, you'll see something like this:

```
localhost# ls -l
total 1146
drwxr-xr-x  2 root          1024 Sep 24 04:17 .NeXT/
rw-r-r-  1 root             457 Jun 26 12:00 .cshrc
rw-r-r-  1 root              77 Apr  4 12:47 .hidden
rw-r-r-  1 root             187 Mar 20  1989 .login
rw-rw-rw-  1 root           741 Sep 26 08:54 .places
rw-r-r-  1 root             259 Jun 26 12:00 .profile
drwxr-xr-x  3 root          1024 Sep 25 21:17 LocalLibrary/
lrwxrwxrwx  1 root            11 Sep 24 04:21 Net@ ->
    private/Net/
drwxr-xr-x  2 root          1024 Sep  8 00:05 NextAdmin/
drwxr-xr-x  6 root          1024 Sep 10 17:44 NextApps/
drwxr-xr-x  5 root          1024 Sep  8 00:05 NextDeveloper/
drwxr-xr-x 10 root          1024 Sep  6 19:08 NextLibrary/
```

The first clump of initials are the permissions for each file or directory. The preceding "d" means directory. (But you know that anyway, because directory names end with a slash.) On the line

```
lrwxrwxrwx  1 root           11 May 31 18:05 Net@ ->
   private/Net/
```

the preceding "l" means link—but you know that, because of the @ suffix.

To examine individual file permissions, select a file in the Workspace Manager, choose More Info, and examine the panel that appears.

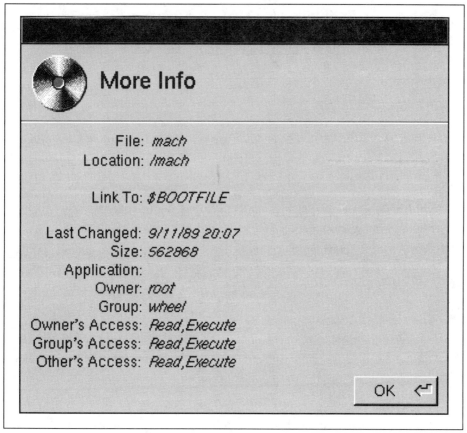

*Figure 4.1*

Permissions for newly created files are determined by settings in the Preferences applications

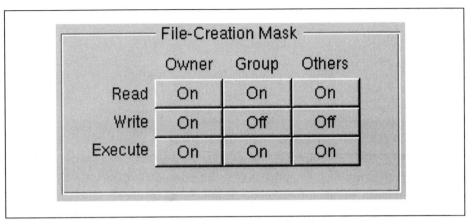

Figure 4.2

## Files on Disk

With that short glance at files and directories, we're ready to look at something truly interesting: how the NeXT operating system builds an optical disk.

UNIX commands may come from you, sitting before the MegaPixel display, or from across the network, or from UNIX itself. In the case of BuildDisk, you click a button in the BuildDisk application, and UNIX does the gritty work of initializing the disk, building the directory structure, and copying over the requisite files.

As often happens, the commands used by BuildDisk reside, mostly, in a text file. The file, in this case, is private/etc/BLD.od. (An interesting file to read, but don't change it, please!)

Here's the complete transcript from BuildDisk as it builds an optical disk. The NeXT comments, preceded by #, should give you a good idea of the process.

```
localhost# cat /private/etc/BLD.od
# NeXT File System build procedure
# Build Optical disk from booted file system
# Release 1.0
#
# Build the read-write partition (a)
# First fill in the root directory
```

```
symlink a $BOOTFILE                      /mach
copy    a /.places                       /.places
chmod   a 666                            /.places
copy    a /.hidden                       /.hidden
copy    a /.login                        /.login
copy    a /.cshrc                        /.cshrc
copy    a /.profile                      /.profile
load    a /.NeXT                         /.NeXT
# Build the "private" symlinks
symlink a private/etc                    /etc
symlink a private/dev                    /dev
symlink a private/tmp                    /tmp
symlink a private/Net                    /Net
# Lay down the files we need most at boot
load    a /usr/template                  /usr/template
load    a /usr/etc                       /usr/etc
load    a /bin                           /bin
exec    a /usr/etc                       ./newclient -p od
   /mnta/usr/template/client /mnta/private
# Now lay down what we want close together after boot
load    a /usr/shlib                     /usr/shlib
load    a /usr/lib/NextStep              /usr/lib/NextStep
load    a /NextApps                      /NextApps
load    a /lib                           /lib
load    a /usr                           /usr
load    a /NextDeveloper                 /NextDeveloper
load    a /NextAdmin                     /NextAdmin
load    a /NextLibrary                   /NextLibrary
# Put kernels on the disk
copy    a /odmach                        /odmach
chmod   a 555                            /odmach
link    a /odmach                        /sdmach
symlink a mach                           /vmUNIX
# Build the home directory
load    a /usr/template/user             /me
rchown  a me                             /me
chmod   a 777                            /me
```

That's it: the optical disk is loaded with UNIX and NeXT files; ready to go.

## NeXT Files

We've seen how UNIX files are typically either text files or binary-executable files. The files often have filename extensions to clue users to the file's purpose. For software development, some common extensions are:

.c      for C source code;

.h      for C header files; and

.o      for binary object code.

On NeXT, you'll also see:

.m      for Objective-C source code;

.s      for MC68030 assembly source code;

.asm    for DSP56001 source code;

.lnk    for relocatable DSP56001 object code; and

.nib    for archive files created by Interface Builder.

Another NeXT file suffix is ".app," which we'll get to in a bit.

## Proprietary Formats, Standard Formats

Most applications have a proprietary file format. Files saved in Mathematica format, for instance, can't be read by other applications. That's unfortunate, but necessary. Applications often need to save specific information in files. That application-specific, binary information would be meaningless to other programs—even if the programs could read the file format.

Still, as applications proliferate, application-specific file formats also proliferate. Standard formats that can be read by many applications make life simpler for users, and simpler for developers, who then only need to support a few standards, not every application-specific format that comes along.

## ASCII

As in UNIX, ASCII has a place on The NeXT Computer. ASCII is the lowest common denominator for text files. Almost any computer can create text files, and almost any computer can read text files. Need to get an IBM PC file into your

NeXT? Save it as ASCII text. Most word processors can optionally save as ASCII. Edit, and other programming editors save ASCII text by default, because compilers prefer ASCII (compilation's difficult enough without requiring compilers to determine exactly why you boldfaced the word loadNibSection!).

When you telecommunicate, you'll also typically send and receive text files.

ASCII files are also the basis for other file types: files with the virtue of being "plain vanilla ASCII," yet still capable of containing formatting (often complex formatting) information. One example is...

## EPS

EPS files have become a standard graphic file type on many computers. The abbreviation stands for "Encapsulated PostScript." You'll also see "EPSF," for "Encapsulated PostScript File," which means the same thing. NeXT EPS files don't typically have an ".eps" extension. Just the filename itself.

EPS files *are* PostScript. And they're particularly elegant. In general, an EPS file has three sections: header information, PostScript code, and graphic information.

Here are the first few lines of an EPS file generated by Scene:

```
%!PS-Adobe-2.0 EPSF-1.2
%%Creator:Scene
%%Title:IB2.dump.eps
%%Origin:0 720
%%BoundingBox: 0.000 0.000 1120.000 832.000
%%EndComments
/picstr 280 string def
gsave
0.000 0.000 translate
1.000 1.000 scale
1120 832 scale
1120 832 2
[1120 0 0 832 neg 0 832]
{currentfile picstr readhexstring pop}
image
FFFFFFFFFFFFFFFFFFFFFFFFFFFFFFFFFFFFFFFFFFFFFFFFFFFFFFFFFFFFFFFFF
FFFFFFFFFFFFFFFFFFFFFFFFFFFFFFFFFFFFFFFFFFFFFFFFFFFFFFFFFFFFFFFFF
```

The file begins with comments, which continue until the line

```
%%EndComments
```

Then comes actual PostScript code. If you know PostScript, it's straightforward (and PostScript isn't a difficult language to learn; it's different, but not difficult).

Notice the Image command. After this command, what follows is hexadecimal data representing a "bit-image" of the graphic itself. Lines and lines and lines of

```
AAAAAAAAAAAAAAAAAAAAAAAAAAAAAAA10AAAAAAAAAAAAAAAAAAAAAAAAAAAAAAAA10
AAAAAAAAAAAAAAAAAAAAAAAAAAAAAAA10AAAAAAAAAAAAAAAAAAAAAAAAAAAAAAAA10
AAAAAAAAAAAAAAAAAAAAAAAAAAAAAAA10ABFFFFFFFFFFFFFFFFFFFFFFFFFCAA10
ABAAAAAAAAAAAAAAAAAAAAAAAAAA4AA10ABAAAAAAAAAAAAAAAAAAAAAAAAAAAA4AA10
ABAA80001AAAAAAA0A0AAAA82AA4AA10ABAA800006AAAAAA0A0AAAA82AA4AA10
ABAA82AA42AAAAAAAA0AAAA82AA4AA10ABAA82AA82AAAAAAAA0AAAA82AA4AA10
ABAA82AA82A0AA0A0A0AA0082AA4AA10ABAA82AA0AA0AA0A0A0A80002AA4AA10
```

After this, nothing. End of file.

In EPS files created by other applications, PostScript drawing commands—of which "Image" may be one—may replace or supplement the hex data. In fact, any valid PostScript command can appear in an EPS file.

The beauty of EPS files is this: EPS files can be sent anywhere text files can be sent. And read by any program or device (or human) that can read ASCII.

One drawback is that EPS files must be interpreted before display (or before printing). Some programs, like WriteNow, automatically convert EPS files into graphic images. Other applications, like Edit, merely treat EPS files as the ASCII files that they are, and load them in, and display them as shown here. Another drawback is size. An EPS "dump" of the NeXT screen is almost half a megabyte!

EPS files, like PostScript itself, have become a standard for another reason: device independence. An EPS file can display at 92 dpi on the NeXT screen, print at 400 dpi on the NeXT Laser Printer, or print at 2,400 dpi on a photo typesetter.

NeXT developers will also use files with these extensions:

.ps       for files of PostScript code;

.psw      for files of pswrap declarations; and

.pswm     for files of pswrap declarations and Objective-C "Methods."

## TIFF

TIFF—for Tagged Image File Format—is another standard graphic format. Originally devised by Aldus Corporation, TIFF files are now standard fare on Macintosh, NeXT, and other graphic computers. On NeXT, TIFF files are used to represent icons, bitmaps, and cursors. All Webster pictures are also TIFF files.

TIFF was created because a standard was needed for representing grayscale images. Unlike EPS files, TIFF files are binary concoctions. There's no ASCII in a TIFF file.

Four TIFF class are defined:

- Class B for 1-bit (black and white) images;
- Class G for grayscale images, (8-bit image maximum; double the NeXT display);
- Class P for palette color images; and
- Class R for full-color RGB images.

For an overwhelming look at NeXT TIFF files, launch the shell and type:

```
localhost# find . -name '*tiff' -print
```

You'll be presented with a listing of all available TIFF files.

To wander through the many TIFF images used in NextStep, launch the Scene application and check out NextApps/Librarian.app/images and NextApps/ Librarian.app/targets. Ever wondered where those images of folders in The Workspace Manager come from? Try NextApps/Librarian.app/Images/OpenFolder.tiff. There's lots more. Have fun.

## RTF

This one's interesting.

RTF stands for "Rich Text Format." The RTF file format was created by Microsoft Corporation. (Microsoft also calls it "Interchange format.") The goal was this: a format that allowed word processing files to retain formatting information across different computer platforms. Between IBM and Macintosh, to put it simply.

Microsoft, somewhat altruistically, knows that what's good for the computer industry in general, is good for Microsoft in particular. So they made the RTF specifications available to developers, and urged its adoption as a means for various word processors to communicate.

As you can see, there are file formats and there are file formats. Some are well-conceived and well-implemented. Some aren't. Some are clear, some are murky. Some are easy for developers to support. Others, with variation upon variation to support (TIFF comes to mind) are support nightmares.

Microsoft, like Adobe with EPS, did it right. RTF is a joy. Like EPS files, RTF files are ASCII-based. To display the formatting in RTF files, it's necessary first to interpret the files.

For developers, interpreting RTF files isn't child's play, but it's not too difficult. The RTF format is clear and logical. Microsoft did a first-class job with RTF.

Here's a snippet from Hamlet. Like all NeXT Shakespeare files, it's in RTF. First, the interpreted, formatted version.

# Hamlet

3.1

*Enter King Claudius, Queen Gertrude, Polonius,*

*Ophelia, Rosencrantz, Guildenstern, and lords*

KING CLAUDIUS  *(to Rosencrantz and Guildenstern)*

And can you by no drift of circumstance

Get from him why he puts on this confusion,

Grating so harshly all his days of quiet

With turbulent and dangerous lunacy?

And here's the uninterpreted version:

```
{\rtf0\mac{\fonttbl{\f0\froman Times Roman;}{\f1\fmodern
  Courier;}}
{\pard\f0\fs28{\fs48 Hamlet
}\
\
{\b\fs36 3.1}
\
{\i              Enter King Claudius, Queen Gertrude,
  Polonius,\
                Ophelia, Rosencrantz, Guildenstern, and
  lords\
}{\b \fs24 KING CLAUDIUS}{\i   (to Rosencrantz and
  Guildenstern)\
}        And can you by no drift of circumstance\
        Get from him why he puts on this confusion,\
        Grating so harshly all his days of quiet\
        With turbulent and dangerous lunacy?\
```

Without getting too involved, notice how backslashes signal possible format changes, and curly braces group formatted characters.

On NeXT, WriteNow and Edit support RTF. And RTF is becoming increasingly popular on other computers. Let's hope that Microsoft is successful in making RTF a uniform standard; it would make life simpler for everyone.

## WriteNow

While developers prefer to support only a few standard formats, there's an even more preferable way to conduct business: have everyone else support *your* format! Create your own application-specific format, then publish it for other developers. Let them do the dirty work of supporting. If your format becomes a standard, so much the better. Your reputation is enhanced; other programs now "come to you," not vice-versa.

This is the tack taken by WriteNow. On Macintosh, it's been moderately successful. The WriteNow format is easier to support than, say, MacWrite. The WriteNow file format specification is clear and well-documented. Developers can support WriteNow formatted files without too much effort. Rummage around almost any expansive bulletin board and you'll find T/Maker's WriteNow file format spec.

WriteNow obviously has the edge on NeXT, where it's the "free with every cube" word processor. WriteNow was used to create NeXT documentation, and many NeXT documentation files on disk are WriteNow formatted.

Thankfully, WriteNow also supports RTF formatting, a more widely used standard. As other word processors appear for NeXT, they may also support WriteNow's format.

## Sound and Music Files

The most elemental NeXT sound files are suffixed with ".snd". The sound files can be included in applications (most easily with Interface Builder), or heard by using the SoundPlayer application. Files ending with ".midi" contain binary MIDI-standard data.

## Mailbox Files

The extension ".mbox" is automatically added by NeXT to mail messages. The .mbox files are located, logically, in the Mailboxes directory.

## .app Files

The .app file suffix doesn't denote a file type. Instead, ".app" signals that what appears to be a single application is, in fact, a collection of files.

It's like this. As applications became more sophisticated, separate support files became commonplace. Word processors, for example, come with dictionaries, thesauruses (not needed on NeXT, of course), settings files, you name it.

Applications need to know where their files are. On other computers, this means keeping all the files in one directory (common on IBM's), or in the System folder (on Macintosh).

The files are a bother to users. They clutter up the screen, they clutter directories.

NeXT solves this with the notion of .app files. The files appear as single filenames or single icons, but may contain many files in addition to the main application file. Digital Librarian, for example, has the filename Librarian.app. It appears as a single icon—in The Workspace Manager's Icon view—or a single filename otherwise. A quick trip to the Shell, however, shows that it's really a directory:

```
localhost# ls /NextApps
.places              Librarian.app/      Preview*
  Terminal*
BuildDisk*           Mail.app/           PrintManager*
  Webster*
Edit*                Mathematica.app/    Quotations*
  WriteNow.app/
InterfaceBuilder*  Preferences*          Shell*
localhost# ls /NextApps/Librarian.app
.places       Librarian*  aux/       images/       targets/
```

Listing the Librarian.app/ directory yields:

```
localhost# ls /NextApps/Librarian.app
.places       Librarian*  aux/       images/       targets/
```

Here we find the application itself (the * means that it's an executable file), and three directories. The directories contain, respectively, help files, and TIFF and EPS images used by Digital Librarian. In all, files you don't need to see. And won't see, at least in The Workspace Manager.

## Skirting Doom

Hit the power key, wait for the cube to wind up, there's the Login window, type "Root," hit Return twice.

And there's the Login window again. What?! Try it again: Root, Return, Return. And, the Login window reappears.

I'm stuck! Trapped. I can't get into the cube!

I type passwords, I type other login names, I type old-world curses. Doesn't work. In months of working with the cube, this has never happened.Okay, I'll go into the Monitor, set my parameters, and boot from there. That doesn't work, either.

So I grab the phone and call NeXT Technical Support—something I've never done.

Here's what happens: I'm transfered to a support person immediately. No waiting, no being placed on hold and listening to Muzak. That's good.

The support guy is great. He guides me through a sequence of UNIX commands—you can weasel into UNIX even if you can't get NextStep "up." He tells me what to type, I type.

In five minutes, we've found the problem. My fault. I did it. User error strikes again.

Here's what happened: I foolishly renamed the NeXT directory containing the Window Server. When the cube tried to boot, it couldn't find the Window Server file, and "returned me to the gate." Once I renamed the directory, everything worked fine.

The moral?

*Don't rename NeXT files or directories. (And don't move NeXT files into other directories.)*

Other files—including start-up commands—need to find files where they're supposed to be. Consider the NeXT directories sacrosanct. Muck with your own directories all you want, but don't muck with NeXT directories. In my case, I renamed the NextApps directory; a big no-no. (In System 1.0, things are a bit different, but it's still a no-no.)

But I'm glad I had the chance to try out NeXT's technical support. In this case, at least, it was great.

Nice to know.

# Chapter 5

# Hands-on UNIX

*A sympathetic Scot summed it all up very neatly in the remark,
'You should make a point of trying every experience once, excepting
incest and folk-dancing'.*
Sir Arnold Bax (1883–1953), Farewell My Youth (1943), 'Cecil Sharp'
**— ANONYMOUS, ENGLISH**

One way to learn UNIX is to fearlessly enter the shell and wildly type characters. Anything could happen.

A better way is start with a handful of useful commands. As your experience grows, you'll add other commands. Eventually, you'll be piping, redirecting, and greping with the best of them.

Let's fire up the shell. If it's not on your dock, open The Workspace Manager, click on the NextApps directory, then double-click "Shell" in the browser listing.

If the window that appears is empty, hit Return. Hit Return a few times anyway.

```
localhost#
localhost#
localhost#
localhost#
localhost#
localhost#
```

No harm done. To clear the window of all those prompts, hit Command-K. To abort a long listing, or if you see a line such as

```
—More—(16%)
```

at the bottom of the shell window, but don't want any more, type Control-c or Control-z, which gently tells the shell to STOP and returns you to the

```
localhost#
```

prompt.

## Who and where am I?

Now let's ask the Big Question.

```
localhost# who
root        ttyp1    Aug 15 16:22    (localhost)
localhost#
```

UNIX obligingly reports that I'm root. My terminal name is "ttyp1," and it's August 15. The next field, 16:22, isn't the current time; instead, it's the length of time that I've been logged on. Must've left the NeXT on last night.

The who command gets its information from the file /usr/adm/wtmp. Does it really? Let's see.

```
localhost# cat /etc/utmp
ttyp1   root   localhost    $ :Dlocalhost#
```

The command cat printed the contents of the file /etc/utmp. The /etc/utmp file does indeed include much of the information the who command uses. The last field "$ :Dlocalhost#" gives itself away with $. The dollar sign marks shell variables. In this case, the variable is for the shell prompt: localhost.

We could also ask the existential question

```
localhost# whoami
root
```

and receive a concise answer: root. Logging in as root gives you Superuser status—the ability to do anything anywhere in the system (provided, of course, you know how). Single-user NeXTs grant their masters Superuser status automatically. On networked NeXTs, you'll need the proper password to elevate yourself to Superuser status. The "#" character after the prompt assures you of Superuser status.

After whoami is where am I?

```
localhost# pwd
/
```

With UNIX, "where" means "what directory am I in?" The pwd command is a pithy way to say "Present Working Directory." Here, we've been informed that we're in the root directory: /.

Pwd is a command you'll use often. It's a must learn. pwd. pwd. It should ripple off your fingers. As is often the case, you can get the same result with a different command:

```
localhost# dirs
/
```

The dirs command is for use with the csh, or "C Shell." Since the C Shell is the default shell on the NeXT, either command works.

We're in the root directory, so let's see what files are here.

```
localhost# ls
.NeXT/              NextDeveloper/      me/
.cshrc              NextLibrary/        odmach*
.hidden             TheBook/            phonelist
.list               bin/                poems@
.login              clients/            private/
.places             dev/                sdmach*
.profile            etc/                tmp/
Life With NeXT.edit lib/                usr/
Net/                lost+found/         vmUNIX@
NextApps/           mach@
```

ls is another command you'll use often. Sure, you can do much the same thing in the Workspace Manager, but using ls is faster, and gives you a slew of options for listing files. Here's the beginning of the manual entry for ls:

```
NAME
    ls - list contents of directory
SYNOPSIS
    ls [ -acdfgilqrstu1ACLFR ] name ...
```

Optional arguments to commands begin with "-". Some commands (like whoami) require no arguments. Other commands must have arguments. If you omit a needed argument, the shell will prompt you.

Some of the most useful ls options are:

-l for a long listing, and

-t for lists ordered by time; most recent files first.

Again, notice that UNIX is case sensitive. ls -a is different from ls -A.

So far, we've glanced at six UNIX commands. Here's a handy command that shows what we've done so far.

```
localhost# history
    1  who
    2  cat /etc/utmp
    3  whoami
    4  pwd
    5  dirs
    6  ls
    7  history
localhost#
```

The history command shows previously executed commands. How many commands to remember is set in the hidden file .cshrc. The default is to remember 100 commands.

Hate to type those long command names? Entering !! reexecutes the previous command. And a single exclamation mark before any event number executes that command. So

```
    !4
```

reexecutes the command pwd.

As you're learning UNIX, history is a good command to rely on. Despite the effortless attitude that UNIX books (and the UNIX documentation) convey, in truth it's tough to remember the UNIX commands and tougher to learn the many UNIX options. History can jog your memory a bit.

## Using man

The most important UNIX command is man. Short for "manual," the command displays the proper UNIX manual "page" in your shell window that explains the command in question.

Let's try man on itself.

```
localhost# man man
MAN(1)          UNIX Programmer's Manual          MAN(1)
NAME
    man - find manual information by keywords; print out the
    manual
SYNOPSIS
    man [ - ] [ -M path ] [ section ] title ...
    man -t title ...
    man -k keyword ...
    man -f file ...
DESCRIPTION
    Man is a program which gives information from the program-
    mers manual. It can be asked for one line descriptions of
    commands specified by name, or for all commands whose
    description contains any of a set of keywords. It can also
    provide on-line access to the sections of the printed
    manual.
    When given the option -t and the title of a manual page,
  man
—More—(16%)
```

There's more, not shown. Now let's try man on "who."

```
localhost# man who
WHO(1)          UNIX Programmer's Manual          WHO(1)
NAME
    who - who is on the system
SYNOPSIS
    who [ who-file ] [ am I ]
```

```
DESCRIPTION
     Who, without an argument, lists the login name, terminal
     name, and login time for each current UNIX user.
     Without an argument,...
```

it continues. Also useful is the -k option, which shows all occurrences of the word.

```
localhost# man -k who
from (1)        - who is my mail from?
getname (3)     - returns the string login id of the entry in
   the password file whose numerical user id matches .I userid.
getpwwho (3)    - get password file entry using liberal name
   matching.
rusers (1C)     - who's logged in on local machines (RPC ver-
   sion)
rwho (1C)       - who's logged in on local machines
rwhod (8C)      - system status server
users (1)       - compact list of users who are on the system
w (1)           - who is on and what they are doing
who (1)         - who is on the system
whoami (1)      - print effective current user id
whois (1)       - DARPA Internet user name directory service
```

From there, you can "man" your way among the entries. As you're learning UNIX, you'll rely constantly on man.

Many of the manual entries are quite long. If so, only a few lines (by default, 22) will appear in the Shell window. On the last line, you'll see something similar to this:

```
—More—(7%)
```

to alert you that there's more to read. The percent is the amount of the entry already displayed. To see the next 22 lines of the entry, hit Return or space. Or type "h" for a surprise:

```
Most commands optionally preceded by integer argument k.
   Defaults in brackets.
Star (*) indicates argument becomes new default.
```

```
<space>        Display next k lines of text [current screen
   size]
z              Display next k lines of text [current screen
   size]*
<return>        Display next k lines of text [1]*
d or ctrl-D       Scroll k lines [current scroll size, ini-
   tially 11]*
q or Q or <interrupt>  Exit from more
s              Skip forward k lines of text [1]
f              Skip forward k screenfuls of text [1]
b or ctrl-B       Skip backwards k screenfuls of text [1]
'              Go to place where previous search started
=              Display current line number
/<regular expression>  Search for kth occurrence of regular
   expression [1]
n              Search for kth occurrence of last r.e [1]
!<cmd> or :!<cmd>    Execute <cmd> in a subshell
v              Start up /usr/ucb/vi at current line
ctrl-L          Redraw screen
:n             Go to kth next file [1]
:p             Go to kth previous file [1]
:f             Display current file name and line number
.              Repeat previous command
```

"More" is, itself, a command! With a full set of viewing features. Like other aspects of the shell, it's worth exploring.

Why use the shell for this? Why not Digital Librarian? Because, as elsewhere with NeXT, using the shell usually gives you more options, more speed, and more flexibility. The "more" options are a case in point.

## Into the Shell

The shell isn't UNIX. It's just the shell—a separate program that delivers commands to other programs, or to the UNIX kernel.

To be precise, the shell is an interpreter. Like many versions of the BASIC language, the shell is a language that interprets your commands and acts on them. Also like BASIC, you can write programs and have the shell execute them.

We mentioned the .cshrc file earlier. .cshrc contains a shell program—a "shell script" that's executed automatically on startup:

```
if ( ${?prompt} ) then
  set host=`hostname`
  set prompt="${host}# "
  # number of commands to remember
  set history=100
  # some default aliases
  alias ls ls -F
  alias mail /usr/ucb/Mail
endif
```

If you've programmed in any language, that shouldn't look too forbidding. The shell programming language is an extremely stripped down version of C. (As you wander among the many UNIX special purpose command/languages, you'll notice that most pay stripped-down homage to C—the father of all things UNIX-like.)

The shell script above first checks to see if the shell prompt is set. If not, the prompt is set. (Lines beginning with # are comments.) Next, history gets a 100-command memory. Finally, aliases are set. An alias is a stand-in for another command. In the shell script above, the line

```
alias ls ls -F
```

substitutes ls -F for ls. Whenever ls is entered in the shell, ls -F is the command actually performed. (The -F option to ls is a benign option; it merely prints directory names with a trailing /, to alert you that name is, in fact, a directory.)

The second alias

```
alias mail /usr/ucb/Mail
```

spares you from typing usr/ucb/Mail to execute mail from the shell.

If you often use a particular option ( ls -l, for example, for general file listings), you might want to add more alias lines to the script.

Shell scripts can become marvelously detailed and ridiculously powerful. The shell can execute a lengthy script or a single command. As UNIX evolved, some of the most useful shell scripts were compiled into standalone programs. The compiled programs were smaller than the text scripts, and ran faster without the overhead of shell interpretation.

## Creating a Command

Shell scripts let you create custom commands. Let's do it.

Most UNIX commands are in the /bin directory. When you enter a command, the shell first checks to see if it's a built-in command. If not, it checks /bin.

Since our file should reside in /bin, just like other commands, let's change the working directory with cd, for "Change Directory." Easily done:

```
localhost# cd /bin
localhost#
```

Now, notice that

```
localhost# hello
localhost#
```

does nothing. Amazing. There's no UNIX command for hello! But we can fix that. We'll use the echo command, which works like this:

```
localhost# echo "this is some text"
this is some text
localhost# echo echo
echo
```

So far, not very exciting. Echo merely echos text to the terminal.

Now to make a file.

```
localhost# echo echo "I love you, won\'t you tell me your
    name?" > hello
```

Here's what happened. Everything after the first "echo" up to > was echoed. The > is the redirection symbol. Instead of being echoed to the display, the text was redirected to a new file: hello. The > operator creates a new file if no file is found that matches the filename. (But be careful: > will overwrite the contents of an existing file!)

The \ in "won\t" means "treat the next character as a character, not as a grouping symbol."

To view the contents of the new file, we cat:

```
localhost# cat hello
echo I love you, won\'t you tell me your name?
```

The one line file contains the UNIX command "echo," and a drab of text. Not much, but enough. UNIX commands, after all, should be tightly coded.

Now let's make it an executable file.

```
localhost# chmod +x hello
localhost# file hello
help:  commands text
```

Chmod is used to CHange the MODe of a file. We made the file "executable" by setting "+x" to add "eXecute" permission. (Execute means the same as "run" or "launch.")

One way to determine if chmod was successful is with the "file" command, which reads the first part of file, in an effort to determine the file type. In this case:

```
localhost# file hello
hello: commands text
```

We've now created our first command. From now on:

```
localhost# hello
I love you, won't you tell me your name?
localhost#
```

Okay, it's a trivial example. But how about this:

```
localhost# help
Type man man or type cat whatis
```

This short help message could be created as we created the more whimsical message.

## Altering Unix files

Learning UNIX is a lifetime endeavor. And, as you learn, you'll want to alter UNIX: a little change here, a tuck there.

Go for it. Unix was designed to be diddled with.

But before you change any UNIX files, make a back-up. Don't ever think "Well, this is such a little change."

There are *no* little changes. That last little change may completely scrog your cube (as in "the oil spill scrogged 300 miles of virgin coastline").

"Back up!" is advice often given, but seldom taken.

Take it.

Make a directory somewhere; call it "backups." Then, before even the slightest diddle, make a back-up in the Workspace Manager. Select the file, hit Command-d, then drag the file into your backup folder. Simpler yet: hold down the Command key and drag the file into the backup folder. This makes and moves a copy in one motion.

Now diddle.

## Printing from the Shell

So far, our examples have been either displayed on-screen, or directed to a file.

What about printing from the shell?

Easy.

Another UNIX daemon is "lpr," for Line PRinter. The name is an anachronism in these days of laser printers, but the daemon has kept pace with the times. If you type "ps -x" into the shell, you'll see all current processes. One process will look like this:

```
71 ? S   0:00 /usr/lib/lpd
```

That's the NeXT "Line Printer Daemon." Its duty is to lurk until a print request comes along. When it does, it calls the lpr program to print the request.

Printing from the shell is ridiculously easy. To print a file, just enter

```
lpr <filename>
```

and hit Return. That's it.

NeXT applications print by constructing PostScript "bit-images" of pages. Those pages of bits are blasted to the laser printer. The Shell—and UNIX itself—doesn't know bit images. Here, we're character-based. Characters can go to the screen, to files, or to printers. There's no tricky "make a bit image of the page" processing happening. Instead, the stream of characters is sent to the printer—right now.

Needless to say, printing from the shell is fast. What to print? In general, anything that can be shown (cat'ed) on the display. Just "lpr <filename>."

Or really enjoy yourself and use a pipe. This assemblage

```
localhost# ls | lpr
```

takes the output of ls (the familiar LiSt files command) and uses it as the input to lpr. A few seconds later, a printed file listing glides from the laser printer.

Once you realize how easy (and fast) it is to use lpr from the shell, you may find yourself printing from the shell often.

That's barely a taste of the UNIX ocean. If you're not busy for the next few years, consider learning UNIX inside and out.

## Do I really need to learn Unix?

NeXT corporate is schizophrenic about UNIX. On one hand, NeXT points to the selection of the Unix/Mach operating system as "the absolute right choice." On the other hand, they downplay UNIX. "We don't like to talk about UNIX," I was told by more than one public relations type. The idea, probably, is that NeXT offers the power of UNIX without the pain of UNIX. A "have your cake and eat it" scenario. The Workspace Manager and NextStep free you from needing to know UNIX.

UNIX, after all, is complicated, and NeXT doesn't want to be perceived as offering a "UNIX box." Everybody offers UNIX boxes. And NeXT wants the general business/consumer market. NeXT believes that excutives and middle-managers won't want to grep, awk, or even ls.

It's a problem. How to trumpet UNIX while ignoring UNIX?

Public relations machinations aside, is NeXT correct? Do you really need to learn UNIX to use The NeXT Computer?

No. And yes.

The real answer—and it's wishy-washy—is that "It depends."

It depends on

• what you use the NeXT computer for,

• how hard you use it, and

• how much you want to know.

Those considerations are intertwined, of course. If you only use the NeXT occasionally, and only use a few applications, you can probably find happiness without UNIX. But if you use NeXT hard and often, you won't find joy without at least a smidgen of UNIX understanding.

If you want to truly understand The NeXT Computer—and tap all the power of the cube, you must know the basics of UNIX.

Mach—the NeXT UNIX of choice—is the bone and sinew underlying this computer. And Mach is merely UNIX done better. It's still UNIX.

Understand UNIX, even a little UNIX, and suddenly much of NextStep and The NeXT Computer and networking and much of Computing In General begins to make sense.

That's my belief, anyway. The organization of this book, as you've discovered, is based on that belief. Even a little UNIX goes a long way. But don't worry. You can still hate UNIX if you want. I do, about 80% of the time.

But that 20%…

# Chapter 6

# NextStep Fundamentals

*You can't step twice into the same river.*

— **HERACLITUS**  fl 513 B.C.

Not long ago, the acronym GUI wasn't needed; there was only one graphic user interface for mass-market computers: Apple's Macintosh interface. Now GUIs are everywhere: from lowly Commodore 64s to the highest high-end workstation and everything in between.

In one sense, NextStep is just another GUI. But on closer look, NextStep is exceptionally well-thought-out; a rich, consistent graphic interface firmly based on AppKit programming objects. While fundamental user actions are similar to Macintosh, Microsoft Windows, GEM, and IBM's Presentation Manager, NextStep adds to and enhances many basic interface operations.

Users of other GUIs will quickly feel at home, and soon find that NextStep does more than other graphic interfaces.

## Mouse Actions

NextStep is staunchly mouse-based. Although some keyboard equivalents exist for mouse actions, you *will* use the mouse or you won't use NextStep.

Mouse actions, for the most part, are familiar: click to activate a window or bring a window forward; click on buttons, other controls, or menus; drag to select a range, and so on. We won't cover these in detail; the NeXT owner's manual does a fine job of introducing basic mouse skills.

61

NextStep does make some additions to the mouse-movement pantheon. The first is mousescaling. Rapid mouse movements result in greater cursor movement. Slow hand movements make for short cursor moves. It takes some getting used to, but it's handy. In time, you'll find yourself making fast cursor throws to quickly traverse the NeXT display.

The idea is this: if you're moving the mouse slowly, you're probably doing detailed mouse work. Or you're a novice who wants to see precisely where you're going (stalking the wily Hide button, maybe).

Mousescaling is set in the Preferences application.

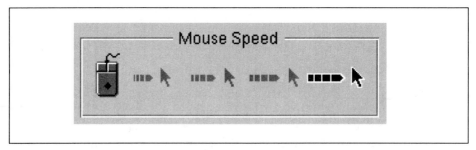

Figure 6-1

The rightmost button, shown selected, sets mouse speed and scaling to the speediest settings (experienced mousers may wish for a still faster setting, however).

As on Macintosh, holding down the Shift key while clicking extends a selection. NeXT also adds the Alternate key for alternative click behavior: The Alternate key is pressed during mouse clicking, pressing, or dragging.

Alternate scroll arrow click, for example, scrolls a screenful—not a line—at a time (this one also works in The Workspace Manager Browser window; it's a fast way to move through long lists of files).

Alternate key clicks aren't as firmly defined as Shift key use. Third-party software may use Alternate key/mouse actions for other purposes (or add Control key/mouse actions).

Another wrinkle is discontiguous selection. Commonly, click-Shift key makes the range of a selection larger or smaller. On NeXT, applications may also let you make multiple, discrete selections. The first and third paragraphs of text may be selected, for example, but the second paragraph can remain unselected. In a spreadsheet, you may select a column here, and also a block of cells somewhere else. A very useful feature.

Discontiguous selection is performed by Shift-dragging. Let's hope that all NeXT applications embrace the idea.

## Windows

Which to begin with? Windows or controls?

Windows.

Here's a NeXT application window, courtesy of the Edit application:

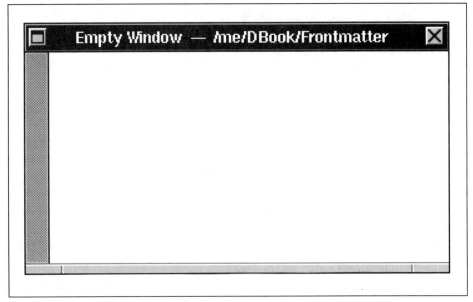

*Figure 6-2*

Windows consists of a content area surrounded by controls. This is a sparse window: at the top, a title bar contains two controls. If the content area contained more information than could be shown, a scroller would also be present.

All NeXT document windows have title bars. Application windows typically contain the name of the file associated with the window. The filename is usually the complete pathname. For example, the WriteNow window I'm currently typing in has this title bar:

*Figure 6-3*

The filename, followed by the complete pathname, from root on down. (Now you're glad you suffered through those UNIX chapters, right?)

NeXT applications sometimes use the title bar to display transient messages. Edit shows Loading and Saving messages in the title bar. Mathematica puts "Running..." in the title bar during computations.

Dragging the title bar moves the window.

The area below the title bar is the content area, where applications draw and users use. The content area is surrounded, for the most part, by controls.

The Miniaturize button,

*Figure 6-4*

on the title bar's left, corresponds to the Miniaturize item on the main menu. A click in the Miniaturize button reduces the window to a mere fraction of its former self:

*Figure 6-5*

The Miniaturized window is deposited at the bottom of the display, where it awaits a double-click to spring to fullness again. Miniaturizing *doesn't stop* an application, it merely puts it in a mini-window. If the application was performing some action when you shrunk it, it'll probably keep right on keeping on (though this choice is up to developers).

On the title bar's right, the close button

*Figure 6-6*

stands in for the main menu's Close command. The action is identical to choosing Close; if the window hasn't been saved, you'll be asked to save changes before closing. Otherwise, it's gone.

NeXT adds a nice touch here. If a document window has been changed—but not yet saved—the close button appears as a partial x:

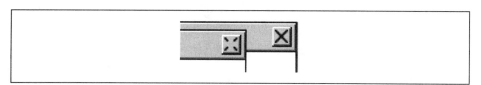

*Figure 6-7*

The window at left has been changed; you can still click the close button, but you'll be presented with the Save changes? panel. The window at right is clean—it hasn't been changed.

This is a good feature. You don't want to close a window that hasn't been saved, right? But has it been saved? It's often hard to remember. Changing the close button informs you at a glance, without having to suffer through a Save changes? panel.

Window resizing is accomplished with the Resize bar at the bottom of the window:

*Figure 6-8*

Yes, it's small. If you'd like a few more pixels to grab, write to NeXT and tell 'em. (An earlier, awkward method of resizing is now history thanks to many cards and letters.)

Size aside, the Resize bar is a convenient way to resize. Notice the two bezels? Dragging from the rightmost area resizes from the bottom right corner. Dragging on the left resizes from the bottom left corner. Dragging anywhere in the center limits resizing to vertical changes. (As a final flip, if your first mouse movements are mostly horizontal when dragging from the corners, window resizing is constrained to horizontal changes.)

The final often-seen window control is the Scroller.

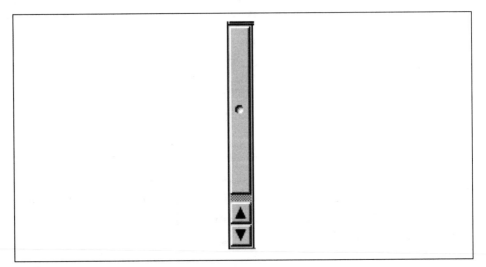

*Figure 6-9*

You'll also see horizontal scrollers, as shown in Figure 6-10.

Scrollers are well-thought-out gadgets. Scroller arrows are arranged, together, at the window's bottom left. (See Figure 6-11.)

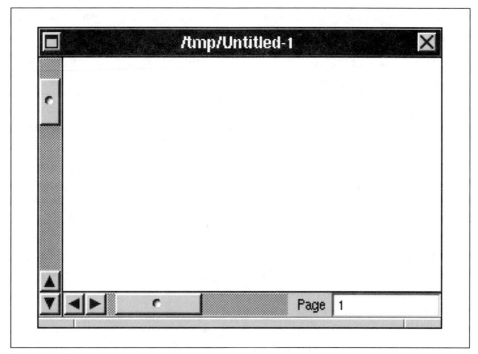

*Figure 6-10*

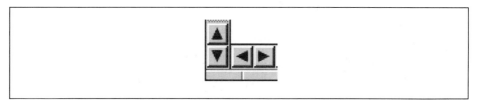

*Figure 6-11*

This minimizes the mouse throw needed to scroll on one axis, then the other axis. A single click produces a small scroll increment. Pressing an arrow produces a smooth scroll. In most applications, holding down the Alternate key while clicking a scroller arrow moves a screenful.

The knob and bar are more interesting. First, scrollers are continuous by default. In other words, when you drag the knob, the window's image moves *while you drag*. On Macintosh, nothing happens until you mouse-up; only then is the image redrawn. This is great if you get lucky and drag to the area you wanted to see. This happens less frequently, of course, as documents become large.

NeXT's method is better. But it's possible only because of the 68030's speed: continuous, smooth redrawing takes processing muscle (and in this case, also puts the lie to any contention of Display PostScript being slow).

The knob also gives you an indication of the file's length. The longer the document, the smaller the knob. As files become longer, the knob becomes smaller. And vice-versa: if the file becomes shorter in length, the knob lengthens. If the entire image is contained in the window, the knob vanishes altogether. If the file is enlarged, the knob reappears.

There's more. You can also click on the bar—the area surrounding the knob. A click brings the knob under the cursor, and moves the image appropriately. If you keep the mouse button down, the knob is immediately in your control, for finer viewing adjustments. Click in the bar, then drag to adjust.

This is a feature you should use, and one you'll miss when using other GUI's.

In large documents, dragging the knob results in a blisteringly fast sequence of images. To slow things down, hold down the Alternate key while dragging the knob. This changes the mouse *movement/scroll speed ratio* and performs a smooth, slower scroll.

To summarize, scrolling on NeXT is well-thought-out: the knob gives you information about the length of your document. Alternate-click and Alternate-dragthe-knob are useful additions to traditional scrolling behavior. Now, if you could only scroll from the keyboard...

We'll come back to windows. But let's continue with controls.

## Controls

NextStep defines six standard controls. Other custom controls may be created by developers. The standards are:

* Buttons;
* Scrollers;
* Sliders;

- TextField;
- Matrix; and
- Form.

NextStep buttons may appear and act like Macintosh or Microsoft Windows buttons. But, as with scrollers, NeXT extends and enhances the everyday button. NeXT buttons, when clicked or pressed, may:

- highlight only during a click:

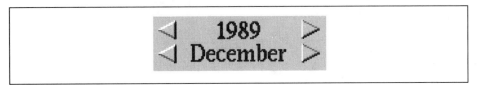

*Figure 6-12*

- highlight and remain highlighted:

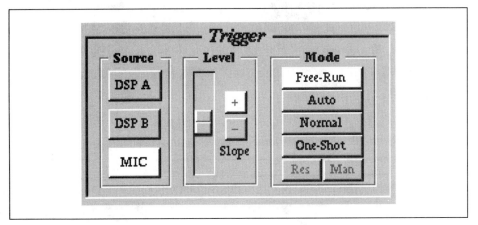

*Figure 6-13*

- show a pushed-in appearance:

*Figure 6-14*

- highlight *and* show a pushed-in appearance:

*Figures 6-15, 6-16 & 6-17*

- change the image associated with the button:

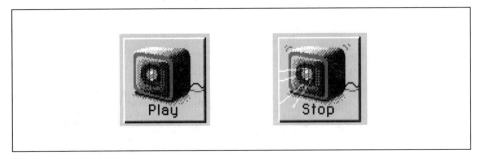

*Figures 6-18 & 6-19*

- or change the bitmap, highlight, *and* appear pressed:

*Figures 6-20 & 6-21*

The paradigm at work here is *always give the user feedback to a mouse click or mouse press.* On NeXT, that feedback often goes far beyond a mere highlight-when-pressed approach, as you can see.

NeXT buttons, while often more sophisticated than buttons in other GUI's, can sometimes be confusing at first use. The reason has to do with state. Those two buttons in Figures 6-20 and 6-21 (from Digital Librarian) are actually one button. When you click to begin a search, the button changes to the STOP image. To stop a search, click the button. It's a terse and graphic way to say: *Search in progress. Press Stop to terminate search before completion.*

Another example. Here's a button:

*Figure 6-22*

Does the button mean *This is now on. Click to turn off*?

Or does it mean *This is now off. Click to turn on*?

The first answer is correct, in this case. A click does *turn off,* after which the button changes to

*Figure 6-23*

And your next click is then an on click.

In other words, sometimes NeXT buttons display the state of an action, and other times they inform you what the state will be *after* you click the button. These two buttons from Quotations show the *current* state:

*Figures 6-24 & 6-25*

This isn't bad interface on NeXT's part. Instead, it's just an indication of a flexible, powerful interface with many options for developers. It's up to designers to make application controls clear, simple, and obvious to users.

Switches are more straightforward. As in real life, switches are either on or off. One, many, or all switches in a collection may be on or off. Here, they're all off:

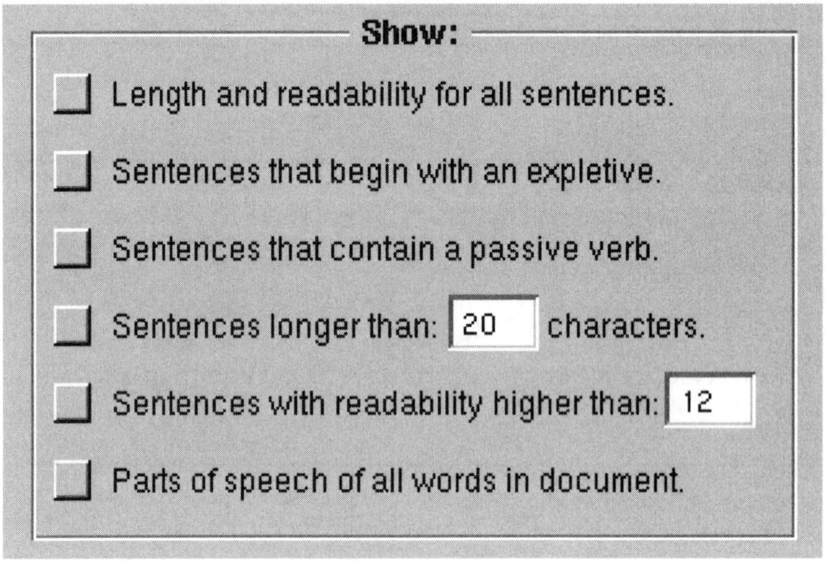

**Show:**

☐ Length and readability for all sentences.

☐ Sentences that begin with an expletive.

☐ Sentences that contain a passive verb.

☐ Sentences longer than: 20  characters.

☐ Sentences with readability higher than: 12

☐ Parts of speech of all words in document.

*Figure 6-26*

NeXT switches aren't limited to *switch on the left; text on the right.* A variety of text positions are possible:

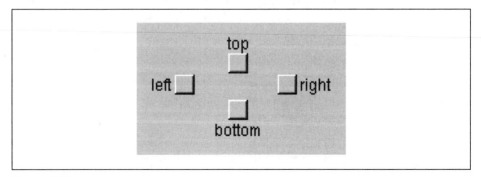

*Figure 6-27*

Switches may also be bordered or disabled:

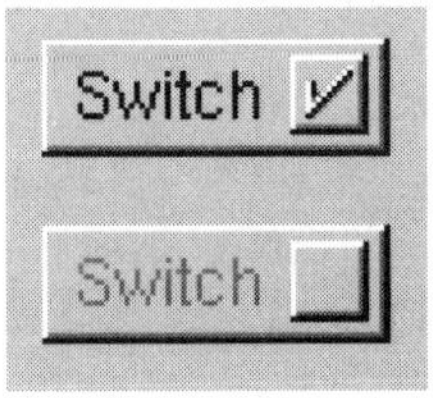

*Figure 6-28*

Radio buttons (NeXT breezily calls them *radios*) behave differently. As with push-button car radios, only one button in a group may be *on:*

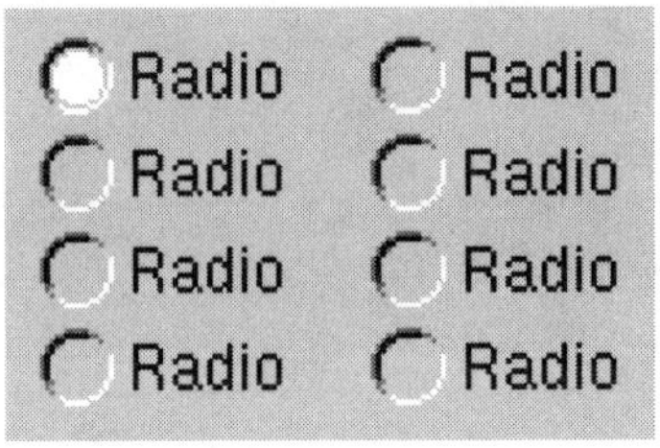

*Figure 6-29*

Here's a better example:

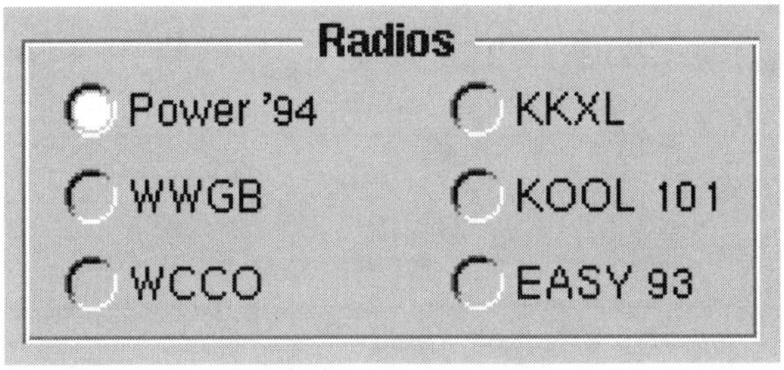

*Figure 6-30*

(The bezeled boxes and titles are created in Interface Builder, where numerous box and title options are found.)

Although it needn't concern you unless you're a developer, the grouping of radios above is called a *matrix*. NeXT makes it easy for developers to group controls into matrixes, then deal with them en masse.

Beyond buttons, switches, radios, and sliders are custom controls, which may look like just about anything! Here, from the Preferences application, is a custom button, at the top, to enable or disable the *menu button* option:

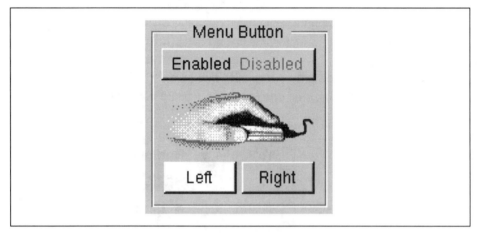

*Figure 6-31*

Where to click? On the light gray *Disabled,* or on Enabled?

The answer? Either. The button is a toggle. Clicking anywhere in the button toggles the feature, and reverses the name dimming. You'll see this type of button now and again on NeXT.

Another custom control is the pop-up list. Unpopped, it looks like this:

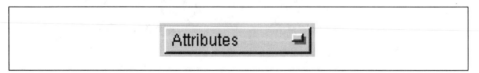

*Figure 6-32*

Mousedown on the control and a list appears:

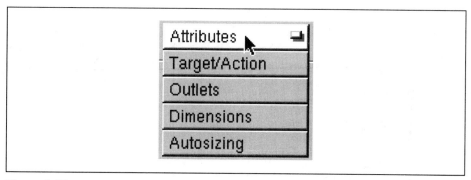

*Figure 6-33*

Keep the button down and drag to your choice. Let go. The button's title changes to your choice and, hopefully, something useful occurs.

Sometimes clicking isn't enough. To enter numbers or characters, text fields are used.

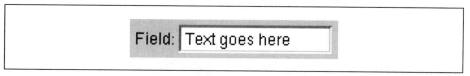

*Figure 6-34*

Click inside the box and type. You can use traditional Cut, Copy, and Paste actions, though typing and backspacing will get you by. In many applications, you can type out of the field and your characters are preserved, although you won't see them (this is misery for bad typists). Press Return when you're done, or merely click somewhere else.

Forms are a matrix of text fields. Forms are important to developers, who can easily deal with groups of text fields. To users, it means that some text field conveniences are built in: the ability to Tab or Return to the next field, or Shift-Tab backwards through fields. Figure 6-35 shows a well-done arrangement of text fields (from the Statlab demo).

Finally, there's a scrolling list control. These are typically used to display, not enter information. In a sense, these are just like word processor views: a content area and a scroller.

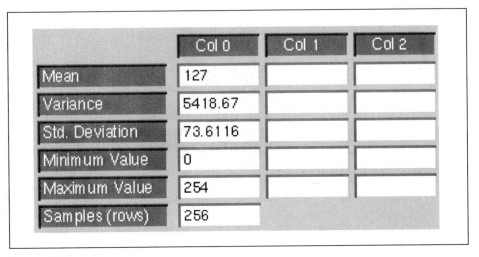

*Figure 6-35*

Now let's put all these controls together: fields, sliders, switches, radios, buttons, and scrolling lists. Here's a tasty example:

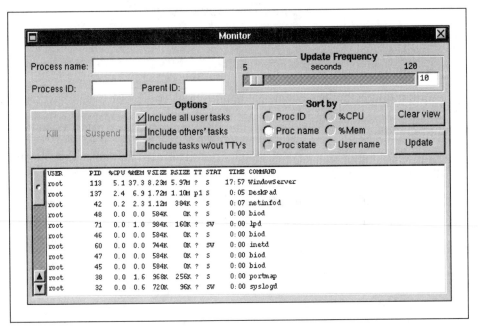

*Figure 6-36*

# Needed in NextStep

NextStep. Great. Love it.

One small addition, one additional convention would make a world of difference.

It's this: keyboard key <something> to Cancel.

In most panels, Return stands in for a click on an OK (or an OK-like) button. Click the button or hit Return. That's wonderful. Just as it should be. Saying "Yes, do it." is a ubiquitous command; it obviously should have a standard keyboard equivalent.

But what about Cancel? Certainly "No!" and "Never mind" and "Just looking, thanks," are equally common. The always seen "OK / Cancel" combination is almost mandatory in panels. Users need both a way to confirm, and a "way out" of panels.

So why isn't there a keyboard shortcut for Cancel? No reason, probably, except that NeXT hasn't implemented one, and hasn't pressed for a standard "Cancel" keyboard shortcut.

Well, let's do it. It'd be enormously convenient. The Command-Period combination is already an unspoken convention for "Stop!"; let it stand for Cancel. Better yet, use (and trumpet) "Esc" as a substitute for clicking Cancel. It makes sense: When you Cancel, you're "Escaping" from a mode, or a behavior, or a panel.

Oh, to Command-O to Open, then hit Escape to Cancel. And to Cancel whenever, with nary a click. Fingers would stay on keyboards more often. Work would fly. U.S. productivity would soar. Users would be much less cranky. I'd have one less sidebar.

## Key Windows

Back to windows. We've glanced at document windows: application windows where you carry out your work of typing, drawing, fudging numbers, or whatever.

A second type of window is like that in Figure 6-36 above: a panel. Panels contain information or controls.

Let's look at The Workspace Manager's Info panel. When you choose *Info...* from the main menu to bring up the panel, the title bars of other workspace windows dim. Like this:

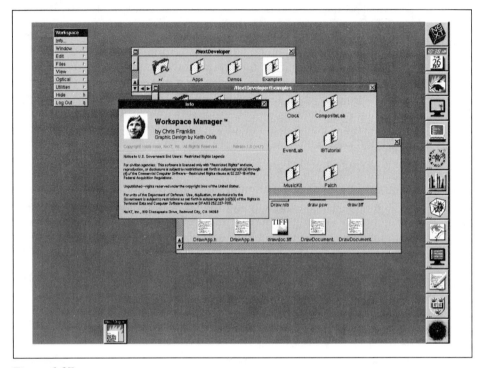

*Figure 6-37*

The reason is that the Info panel is a *key window,* an important concept on NeXT that applies not only to panels, but to all NeXT windows and all NeXT applications.

Let's pause for a moment and consider the NeXT interface.

When using your NeXT, you may have many applications running. Each application may have many windows: some document windows, some attention-getting panels.

So here's the question. Who's on top? Who gets the clicks and the keystrokes?

Obviously, it's a question that needs to be answered. But the answer isn't simple.

The first notion is that key windows have black title bars. Above, the Info panel has a black title bar; it's the key window. Hit Return and the Info panel gets the keystroke *event* and goes away.

But notice that The Workspace Manager menus *also* have black title bars (yes, menus are windows, too). So menus are always *key windows* in applications.

Finally, notice the Miniature window in the lower left. That's a shrunken Write-Now window. Although Miniature, it has a black title bar. So it's also available to receive events—either a mouse drag to move it, or a double-click to open it, which would also bring WriteNow to the fore, hide The Workspace Manager menus, and show WriteNow's menus. Which would, of course, now have black title bars...

Also notice that the window directly behind the Info panel has a dark gray title bar. NeXT adds this addition to window ranking: a main document window. If the main window isn't the key window (as in this example), its title bar is dark gray.

Is there always a key window?

No.

Imagine this. You're running an application. The Workspace Manager, for example. Now you launch a second application—Digital Webster, maybe—which comes up, frontmost, sporting a key window.

Meanwhile, The Workspace Manager's windows have dimmed, as they should; it's no longer the active, frontmost application. It looks like Figure 6-38.

Now you quit Webster. The display (less the Dock, not shown here) looks like Figure 6-39.

Where's the key window? There isn't one! And no menus.

It makes sense. After all, *you* determine the active application. Here, you've quit from one application, but not yet activated another application. Hit a keyboard key now and you'll be rewarded with only a beep—a signal from NextStep that there's nothing to receive the keyboard event. Click outside the windows and you'll also be beeped; the display's background isn't part of any application; it's only the background.

Click *in* one of the windows, however, and The Workspace Manager (in this example) becomes the active application, and the window you clicked becomes the key window, and The Workspace Manager menus appear, and you can go on with your life.

The key window concept has to do with layers: applications under other applications, and so on. On a multiwindow, multitasking computer like NeXT, layers

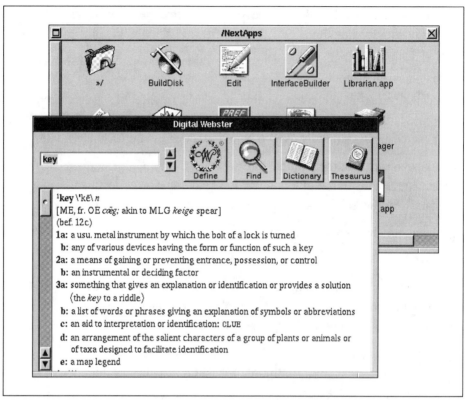

*Figure 6-38*

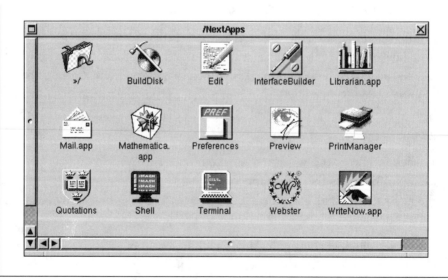

*Figure 6-39*

are a fact of life. NextStep imposes a strict hierarchy of layers, for obvious reasons! We'll list all the layers in a bit.

## Responding

Before we get to panels, there's one more important point. We just mentioned that key windows receive mouse or keyboard events. Technically, the key window is called a *first responder.* Responder because it can respond to events. And *first,* because it's *first in line* for events. But that doesn't mean that the key window is the *only* object that can receive events—only that it's got first crack at them.

Here's an example. We have three overlapping windows. Let's focus on the top left of the windows:

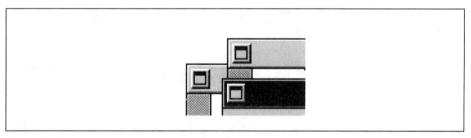

*Figure 6-40*

The key window is frontmost (as it should be). The other two windows are behind, with dimmed title bars. Now, obviously, we can click the Miniaturize button on the frontmost window. Zip, it's shrunk.

But we can *also* miniaturize the other two windows, even though they're not the key window!

Let's say we click the Miniaturize button on the backmost window. In the bowels of NeXT, something like this happens:

1. Mouse click. Is the click in the first responder?

2. No.

3. Hmm. Is the click in the next window back?

4. No.

5. Hmm. Is the click in the window one more back?

6. Yes! (Joy in NeXTVille.)

7. Where's the click?

8. In the Miniaturize button.

9. Do it.

So key windows aren't the only objects which can receive events; they're only first up to get the event.

## Panels

Panels always appear on top of application windows. Panels are either:

* modal; or

* modeless.

Modeless panels can be used in conjunction with working in an application. When a panel is chosen (usually by choosing a menu item), it appears as the key window. A click in the application window makes the application window the key window once more, and dims the title bar of the modeless panel. Find panels are typical modeless panels. (See Figure 6-41.)

A click in the Find/Replace panel blackens the title bar and makes it active.

WriteNow takes modeless panels a step further. This panel, when visible, is always dimmed. The title bar never blackens; it's dimmed for life. (See Figure 6-42.)

This is an extremely modeless panel. What's the design philosophy here? Well, consider this: The Find Next button finds the next likely misspelling and selects it. Since the application window containing the selected word is the active window, you can immediately begin typing to correct the word—without first needing to click the window and make it active. Because the application window and panel don't trade active status, you save a mouse click. In practice, it's easier to use than to explain, and works well.

## Canceling Panels

NextStep panels differ from Macintosh dialogs in one respect: There's often no Cancel button. And there's often no OK button either! The Preferences panel in Quotations makes the point. (See Figure 6-43.)

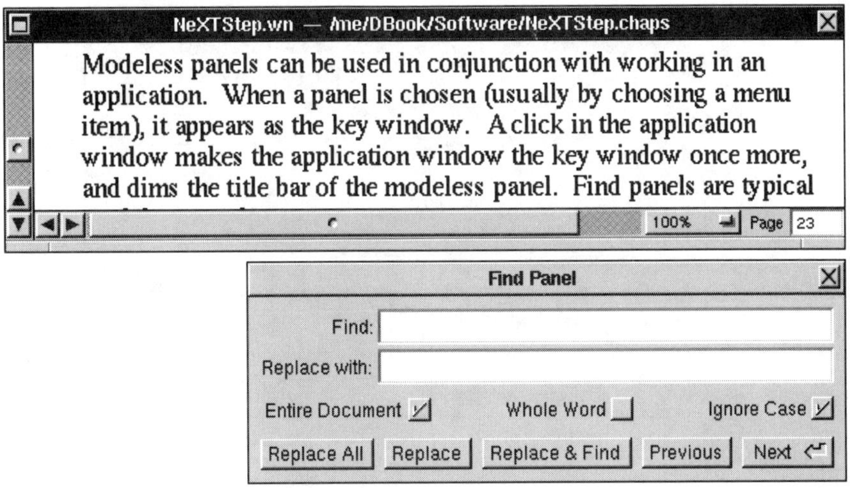
NeXTStep.wn — /me/DBook/Software/NeXTStep.chaps
Modeless panels can be used in conjunction with working in an application. When a panel is chosen (usually by choosing a menu item), it appears as the key window. A click in the application window makes the application window the key window once more, and dims the title bar of the modeless panel. Find panels are typical
100%
Page
23
Find Panel
Find:
Replace with:
Entire Document
Whole Word
Ignore Case
Replace All
Replace
Replace & Find
Previous
Next

*Figure 6-41*

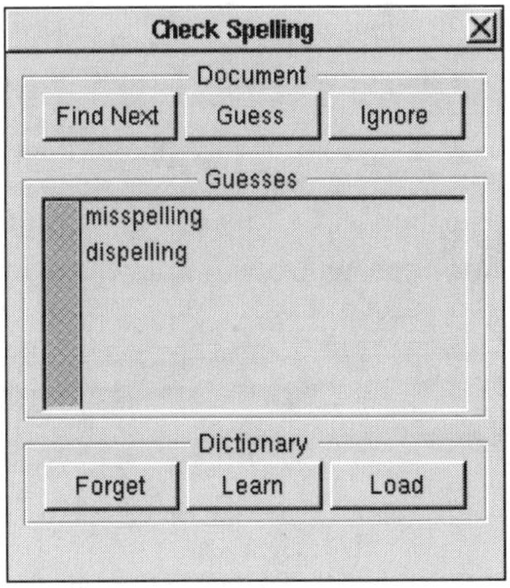
Check Spelling
Document
Find Next
Guess
Ignore
Guesses
misspelling
dispelling
Dictionary
Forget
Learn
Load

*Figure 6-42*

The close button stands in for both actions. This isn't universal, but it's common. Developers can, of course, add OK and Cancel buttons if they wish.

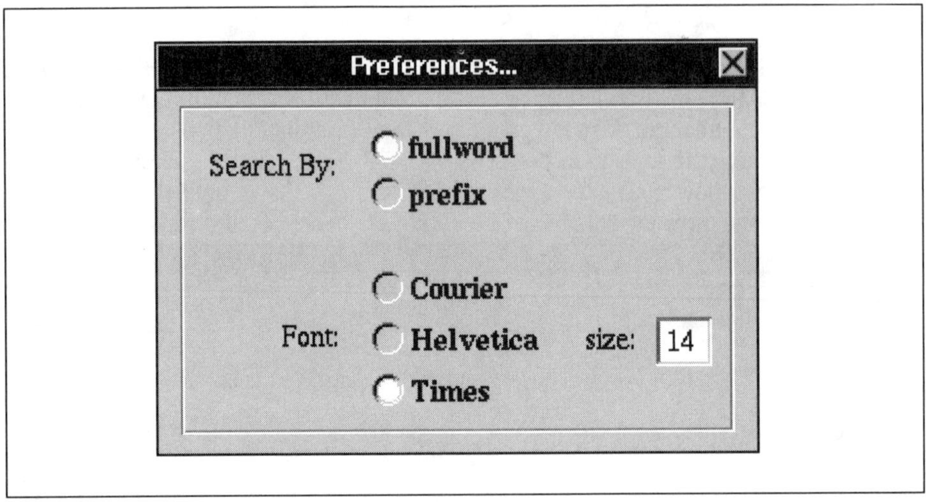

*Figure 6-43*

Ditching the buttons has the advantage of freeing up room on panels. Panels can be smaller and filled with more panel-specific options. There's a subtle consideration here, though, that developers need to address. It's this: Sometimes Cancel means *Cancel anything I've done in this panel and close it.* Other times, Cancel means *I'm done now. Keep the settings I've made and close the panel.*

And OK means *I'm done. Put my changes into action.*

So which is it? For panels closed by the close button, it seems the latter: OK. Clicking the close button means Done, rather than Cancel. If that's the case, however, the only means to Cancel is to backtrack: to undo your changes one by one and *then* hit the close button.

## Modal Panels

Modal panels, on the other hand, aren't as easygoing. Modal panels can't be *left up* while you go on with your work.

Modal panels require an action, even if it's only Cancel, before continuing. NextStep defines a number of modal panels that developers can use to provide users with consistent *looks* across applications. We'll provide examples when we discuss menus.

A more extreme form of modal panels are attention panels. Attention panels, by convention, appear centered on the screen. They demand attention; they can't be dismissed by clicking on a back window in the application. Until they're dealt with—on their own terms—they're in front: fixed.

Here's a fanciful example:

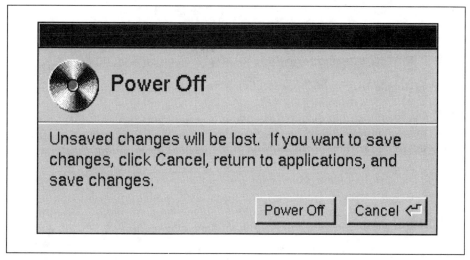

Figure 6-44

Until one of those two buttons is pushed, the attention panel stays right where it is. (This is a wishful thinking panel. Expect a much better 2nd edition of this book if this feature is implemented in a NeXT word processor.)

A modal panel you will see is this:

Figure 6-45

This is a classic modal panel: No close button, no title. And, thoughtfully, the default button produces the least destructive choice.

The most modal panel of all is an alert. Alerts look like the panel above and often contain the word "Alert" to make the point even more clearly.

Alerts apprise you of conditions that must be dealt with, one way or another. Read the buttons carefully before making a choice.

## Standard Panels

NeXT provides a default alert panel, which applications add text to, as in Figure 6-46, and five standard panels, shown in Figures 6-47 through 6-51:

- Print;
- Page Layout;
- Font;
- Open; and
- Save.

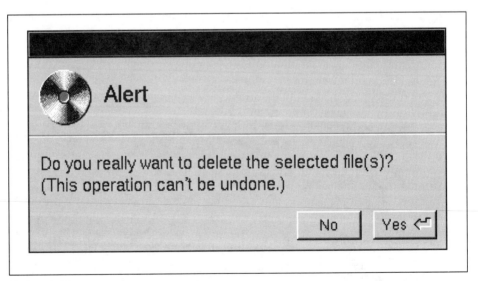

*Figure 6-46*

Notice that the Open and Save panels include resize bars. (Some applications may also include resize bars on the Font panel.)

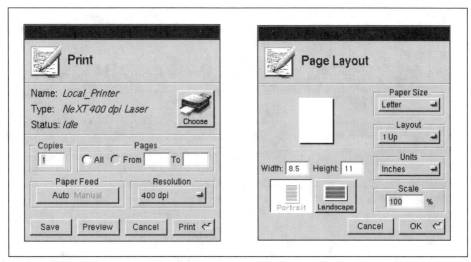

*Figures 6-47 & 6-48*

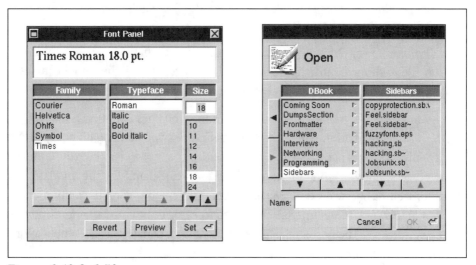

*Figures 6-49 & 6-50*

Panel resizing is a welcome addition in the 1.0 software release. Now, when opening or saving, you can widen the view, a great convenience when working with nested subdirectories (Figure 6-52).

A last panel note. Panels, whether modeless or modal, are local to applications. Even when an attention panel is frontmost, you can always switch to another application. You may be locked in a mode in one application, but you're *not* locked

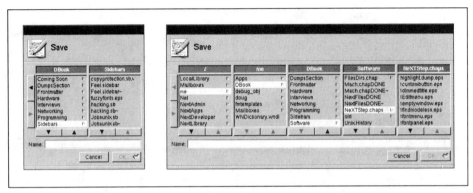

*Figures 6-51 & 6-52*

out of other applications. Click on a docked application, for example, and work somewhere else for a while; or click on the window of another application, bringing it to the front and making it the active application. When you return to your original application, however, that pesky attention panel will also return, right where it was when you left.

For the Power Off panel further back, that's just what happened: I hit the Power key, then slipped into the Scene application, captured the panel's image, then clicked on the Power Off panel to make it active, and Canceled.

Modal panels, modeless panels. It's a murky business. It's not as clear cut as the NeXT documentation would have you believe. As you can see, it's possible to make a really modeless panel. So it's a matter of degrees, not a clear-cut division between modeless, modal, and attention panels. As an example, the modal/modeless approach has been used on Macintosh computers for years, but only recently has Apple tried to address interface issues concerning "sorta modal" and "kind of modeless", dialogs. The best advice is experiment with panels in NeXT applications and test the limits of modality.

## Menus

We'll take a look at standard NeXT menus here, then answer "Who's on top?"—a necessary question that window-based interfaces need to answer. We'll end with a look at some of NextStep's unique features.

Menus are a standard fixture of graphic interfaces. NeXT menus are both different from, and similar to, Macintosh menus and Microsoft Windows menus.

First, basic concepts. Menus are merely another type of window. As such, they have title bars. The title bar contains the menu's name.

Menus, when shown, are always active. Applications could, in theory, dim the title bar of a menu (to show that an entire menu is inactive, for example), but that hasn't shown up (or dimmed out) in NeXT applications.

More specifically, menus are windows full of buttons. One of the beauties of NextStep is this creation of interface elements from simple, elemental pieces: windows, buttons... For developers, it makes programming (relatively) easy: a menu is just a type of window; a menu item is just a type of button.

So menu items are buttons like other buttons: click them to perform an action. Or press them; if a submenu is attached, the press displays the submenu.

If an action associated with a menu item can't be performed, the item is shown dimmed.

In Figure 6-53, text hasn't been selected, so Cut, Copy, and Delete are unavailable. Since Paste *isn't* dimmed, the Pasteboard must not be empty. (Just *what* the Pasteboard contains is another matter. NeXT doesn't request that developers include a "Show Pasteboard" command.)

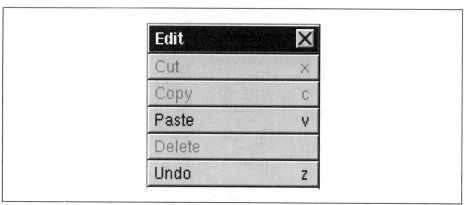

Figure 6-53

Often, the situations that determine the availability of a command are complex. An interesting exercise is to pull off all the submenus in your favorite application, then use the application—keeping an eye on menu dimming. It's a good way to get insight into the many "states" and "modes" that applications pass through.

## Where's the Menu?

By convention, every NeXT application has a main menu. When an application is launched, the main menu appears at the upper left of the display. From there, the main menu can be dragged to any convenient location. If you choose the "Enable Menu Button" option in Preferences, pressing the "mouse menu button" brings the main menu up under your cursor.

## Canonical Menus

NeXT doesn't want developers to create menus willy-nilly. To prevent that, NeXT has defined "canonical menus." The first canonical menu is the main menu. NeXT prefers that all main menus, in all applications, use this as a starting point. (See Figure 6-54.)

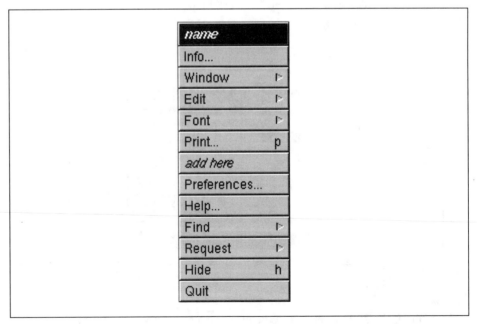

*Figure 6-54*

The triangles point to submenus. Keyboard equivalents, accessed by Command-letter, are at the right of some items. Case counts here; Command-s isn't the same as Command-S, and both may be used. (Some equivalents are predefined by NeXT; they're listed in Appendix A.)

Much thought, we can assume, has gone into this menu. Let's examine it in detail.

First, every application should have an Info panel—just as every Macintosh application should have an "About box." The Info panel contains the application's name, the company that created/markets the application, the version number, copyright information, maybe a winning icon, an OK button, whatever.

We'll come back to submenus after we get to the bottom of the main menu. The next non-submenu is Print, which brings up a standard Print panel.

Then comes the *"add here"* item, a placeholder for application-specific items.

NeXT wants all applications to include a Preferences item and a Help item. Preferences would bring up an application-specific panel for setting application-specific settings. The Preferences are saved with the application. (System-wide preferences are saved in the file /.NeXT/NeXTdefaults.L.)

NeXT also wants Help in every application, and gives the Help item prime real estate on the Main menu. This is a considerate move. Applications are becoming ever more complex. Help is more welcome now than ever. The default Help item is both a nudge to developers and a welcome consistency (if the nudge works) to users.

Find, except in applications where it makes no sense, is also a mandatory item. So is Hide. In a multiwindow interface such as NextStep, it's vital that users can "clear the view" by temporarily hiding applications. Without some Hide-like mechanism, the NeXT display could quickly become a morass of overlapped windows. To forestall that, there's Hide. And NeXT doesn't want the "Hide" item hidden in a submenu.

After Find comes Request. In the 0.9 version of NextStep, this item was absent from the main menu. 0.9 called the command "Send Selection," and relegated it to the Edit menu. In 1.0, it becomes "Request," and gets a more prominent position.

The Request menu item is used for communication between applications—one of the most useful features of the NeXT system.

Finally, Quit. Only The Workspace Manager is exempt from this required item.

Now the submenus. This is the default Windows submenu:

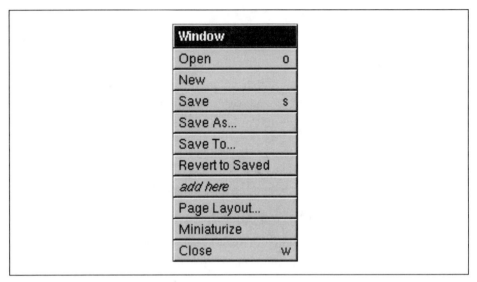

*Figure 6-55*

Most items are self-explanatory. If not, check your NeXT manual. A few items are noteworthy, however. Save To..., for example, may not be seen in all applications. Its purpose is to allow you to Save As without overwriting your original file. If you're working on file "foo," you can Save To "foobar" without disturbing "foo." Save As, in contrast, lets you rename the file, then replaces the previous file with your newly named foobar.

Revert to Saved replaces your on-screen file with the latest saved version of the file. Some applications, WriteNow for one, also add "Revert to Backup," which uses a particular named backup file on disk to replace the on-screen file.

Both Revert to Saved and Revert to Backup are useful. The problem with both, though, is that you typically won't remember when you last saved, and what changes you've made since. If that's the case, Save To can come to the rescue: Use Save To to save under a new name, then open the Save To'd file, and compare it to your original. Keep the version you wish by using Save As—you don't need to rename the file if you don't want to.

The Miniaturize command collapses the current active window into a mini-window, which is placed at the bottom of the screen. When you double-click the mini-window, the window springs back, just as you'd left it. The action is identical to clicking the Miniaturize button on a window's title bar.

Hiding is similar to Miniaturizing, but affects the entire application: menus, all open windows, everything. The files you're working with remain open. NextStep, in effect, takes a "snapshot" of the application when you choose Hide. If the application you hide is Docked, no mini-window is created. If the application *isn't* on the dock, a mini-window is made, just as if you chose Miniaturize.

The Edit submenu gives Apple ground for suit. With only a few exceptions, it's identical to the Macintosh Edit menu. Cut, Copy, Paste, Delete (Clear on Macintosh), Undo, and Select All work identically to the Macintosh versions, and use the same keyboard equivalents. (See Figure 6-56.)

Basic editing commands—Cut, Copy, and Paste—employ a global, unseen object called the "Pasteboard." The Pasteboard is a Mach server that's initialized on start-up (which means that Pasteboard contents vanish when you logout). If you root around in the Shell (use the "ps -aux" command), you'll see it as "pbs," for Pasteboard server.

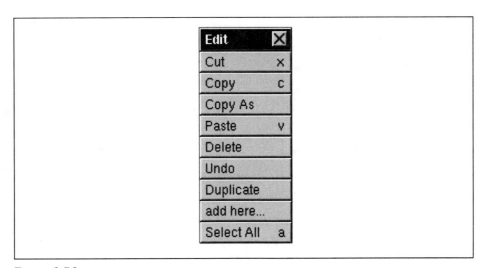

*Figure 6-56*

The Pasteboard contains data Cut or Copied from applications. The data formats supported by the Pasteboard are:

- plain ASCII text;
- Encapsulated PostScript (EPS) version 1.2;
- Rich Text Format (RTF) version 1.0;
- Tag Image File Format (TIFF) version 5.0;
- sound objects; and
- archived objects.

This Pasteboard flexibility is reflected in another new addition to NeXT's 1.0 software, the Copy As menu:

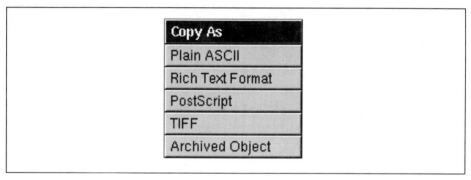

*Figure 6-57*

The global file formats were discussed earlier (in the "Files & Directories" chapter, if you're browsing). Applications may also use application-specific formats that can't be read by other applications.

The Pasteboard object is The Right Thing, done in The Right Way. NeXT applications can easily trade text, formatted text, PostScript images, and grayscale TIFF images. And because the Pasteboard is a Mach process, it's fast, powerful, and efficient. Don't be bashful about Copying or Cutting gouts of data to the Pasteboard.

Applications have some leeway in how they employ Undo. In general, Undo undoes your last action. Typing may also be undone in some applications. Just how *much* typing is up to the application. Try it and see.

A final Edit menu thought. NeXT wants all applications to contain an Edit menu. Fine. Except for this: in many applications, it makes no sense to offer an Edit menu! But there it is, anyway. Cut, Copy, and Paste, endlessly waiting in applications where there's nothing to Cut, nothing to Copy, and nothing to Paste. A triumph of convention over common sense.

NeXT also has specific ideas on how font handling should be presented to users. The Font menu recommended for all applications is this:

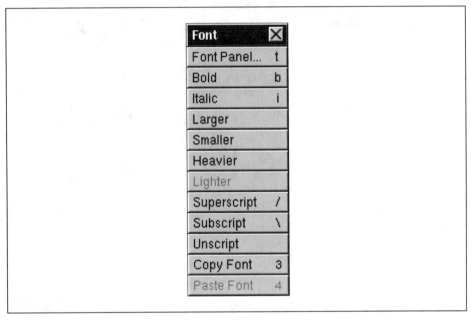

*Figure 6-58*

The first item produces a standard font panel. (See Figure 6-59.)

The Resize bar is new in the 1.0 release. WriteNow and most other applications allow vertical Resizing (to see more font sizes), but don't allow horizontal Resizing. As you add fonts to your system, you'll appreciate the Resize bar.

The remaining menu commands, Bold through Lighter, change the attributes of the selected text.

One thing to notice is this: fonts are made up of families and typefaces. Times Roman, for example, is a complete font—a complete set of designed characters.

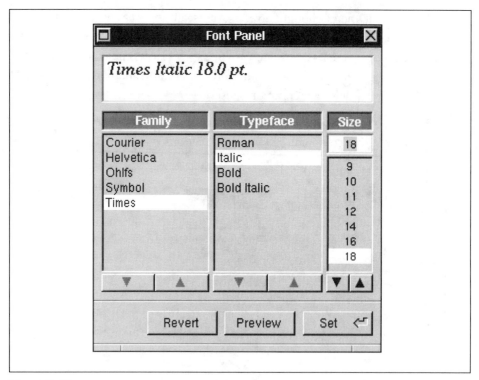

*Figure 6-59*

Times Bold is another complete set of characters. When you choose Times Bold, you're actually changing the typeface used.

But not all fonts have Bold typefaces. If not, the Bold command will still be available, but "Boldness" will be computer-generated, not substituted for the previous typeface.

This helps explain the "Heavier" and "Lighter" typefaces. Some font families have heavy and light typefaces. If so, they'll be used when asked for. (Some fonts may have more than one "heavy" or "light" typeface.) If fonts *don't* have typefaces for heavy and light, choosing those menu items will merely bold and unbold. A glance at the Font panel will give you an idea of what to expect from each font.

The recommended Heavy and Light items may seem needless now (they are), but NeXT is looking ahead here. More fonts will arrive soon, with a variety of typefaces and degrees of boldness and lightness. The standard menu will be here when they arrive.

Expect applications to add to the default Font menu. Here's the WriteNow Font menu:

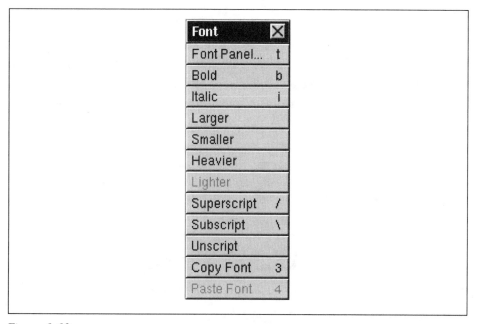

*Figure 6-60*

which adds Superscript, Subscript, Unscript (to remove super or subscripting), and allows you to Copy and Paste fonts.

The default Find submenu will be found in text-oriented applications:

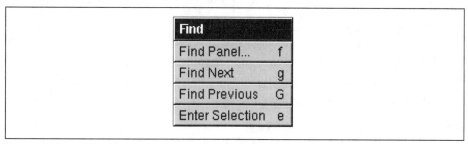

*Figure 6-61*

This one, we can guess, is NeXT's attempt to head off developers before they create hundreds of applications with hundreds of different Find looks and options.

As in other menus, a standard panel heads the list. "Standard" here, though, is more loosely defined. Different applications need to find different things, in different ways.

Let's hope the remaining Find items are implemented consistently by applications. In practice, then, you'll be able to Command-e to enter the selection, and Command-g to find the next occurrence—fast. And to use that same combination in many applications. That, after all, is the reason behind NeXT's menu standards: so users can bring already acquired knowledge and skills to new applications.

## The Request Submenu

Except for those applications where it's clearly needless, NeXT mandates a Request menu. Here's a robust example:

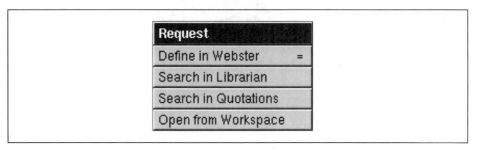

*Figure 6-62*

One of NeXT's great advantages is message-passing between applications. At a low level, it's Mach interprocess communication. At an application level, it's seen as Request. Make a selection, get the Request submenu up, and Request away. If the application you're sending to hasn't yet been launched, it launches automatically, comes to the front, and processes the request. Webster, for example, will launch and define the selected word. If you're a programmer, an "Open from Workspace" item will launch a selected filename—handy for fast access to source-code files.

As NeXT matures, it should be fascinating to watch Request be used by applications. This is landmark stuff, after all. Applications, for the first time, can say "Wake up and do this!" to other applications. Today's Request examples may well look timid, soon.

## The Order of Things

Menus, windows, panels, cursors, the dock—what's on top? What isn't?

From front to back, top to bottom, it goes like this: the cursor is *always* topmost and can't be obscured by anything. You may have to look for it (it's a big screen!), but it's always present on the display. And the screen background is always on the bottom. (The background defaults to dark gray, though you can change it via the Scene application.)

Now it becomes more interesting. First, modal attention panels are topmost: in front of application windows, menu, even the dock. It wouldn't do to obscure attention panels with other windows.

Next come menus. The Main Menu is always on top of submenus. And submenus are on top of windows. Within the "menu layer," submenus act like windows. If two submenus overlap, clicking one will bring it to the front. Clicking the submenu that's now behind brings it to the front.

Next in line is the dock—a menu of applications, if you will.

Only now do application windows come into play. The windows are ordered like sheets of paper. Click on the title bar of a backmost window to bring it to the front.

Mini-windows behave as application windows: they can overlap, or be clicked to the front of other application windows. (Which means that you can also misplace them by positioning them behind many other application windows. That's probably why the mini-windows are placed by The Workspace Manager at the bottom of the display.)

Mini-windows differ from application windows in this: when brought to the front with a single click, they don't also bring up their associated application.

Figure 6-63 is an artless "screen dump" that shows the layering:

From the top: modal panel, main menu, submenu, dock, and finally, application window.

If another application were now launched, what would happen? This: The WriteNow menus would disappear, but the WriteNow application window and the modal panel would still be visible, though dimmed. A subsequent click on any

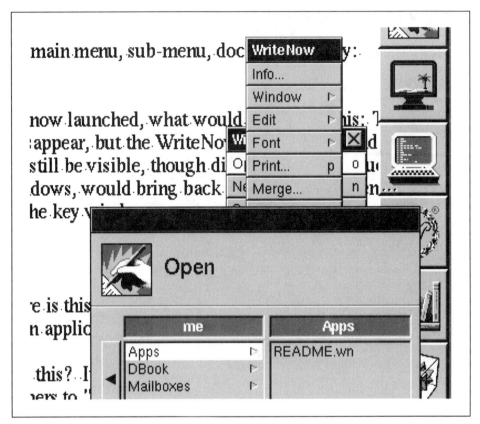

*Figure 6-63*

WriteNow windows would bring back the WriteNow menus and make the modal panel the key window.

## Sliding Icons

One unique NextStep feature is this: the ability to drag an icon from The Workspace Manager onto an application window!

What happens when you do this? It depends. The NeXT programming environment allows developers to "register" their application windows with the NeXT Window Server—the low-level system software that manages the NeXT display. If the application has registered a window, it's notified with one of its icons dragged onto an application window. The application, once notified, can do whatever it pleases. Usually, this means loading the file into the application window; but it's up to the programmer.

## Running Multiple Copies of an Application

Most applications allow this, though you'll seldom need the feature. Just launch the application twice. If this doesn't work, duplicate the application, then launch the duplicate.

## Archiving

It would be a poor world if applications couldn't save files.

Not to worry. NeXT applications that allow you to open and change files also allow you to save them. But NeXT adds an enhancement to saving files: archiving.

With archiving, the entire "state" of an application is saved. Think of taking a snapshot of a running application: where the menus are, what panels, if any, are open, even where the insertion bar is located. Archiving lets you stop work in an application, then pick up later *exactly* where you left off.

Archiving is another option available to developers. It's up to them to implement the feature, and make it clear to users.

## Crafting an Interface

Creating a good graphic interface isn't easy. It *looks* easy, especially in relation to "writing programs," which appears difficult (and often is!). But in truth, creating a consistent, easy-to-use interface is very difficult. There's much going on. Priorities need to be set. Events need to be dealt with. User actions require feedback. Applications need to present a consistent interface to users, while performing radically varying duties.

It's hard to have an opinion on window server event processing (to take just one low-level example), but it's easy to say "Ah...shouldn't that Resize bar be larger?"

To their credit, the NeXT software designers have crafted the most elegant and most useful graphic interface ever to grace a computer.

That said, let's note that interface design is a process. NeXT is committed to serving its customers. If a better way is found, NeXT will implement it. As NeXT was developed, NextStep changed. It changed for the better, often as the result of customer requests and comments.

As you explore NextStep, remember that NeXT is actively seeking your suggestions for future improvements. Personally, I've never seen a computer company as receptive to suggestions as NeXT.

Join the process.

Now let's examine NextStep in application action.

# The Feel of the Computer

How does it feel to use The NeXT Computer? Really?

Awkward. And graceful. And…

Here are my feelings. My feelings only.

First, background. I'm an excellent touch-typist. Typing has been my life since about 1972. A ways back. I've used personal computers, full-bore, since 1978; first a Radio Shack Model I, then the IBM PC, then the short-lived Apple III, then the IBM PC again, then a Macintosh for five long bleary years. My opinions were formed on those machines. Now, the NeXT.

What do I like about The NeXT Computer? Basically, every single thing that isn't in this sidebar. Every "amazing" and "marvelous" elsewhere in this book is heartfelt. No computer has ever been this good. Period.

My personal dislikes? Enough to fill a sidebar, but only that.

Let's start with the keyboard. It's far better than the Macintosh keyboard. It's not quite as good as the IBM PC keyboards—and we're not talking about "IBM clone" keyboards, which are usually cheap and mushy.

The IBM PC keyboards have a marvelous "snap" that's totally lacking on Macintosh. NeXT lies somewhere between; it's a nice feel, but it's not typing nirvana. Not enough snap; my opinion only.

Keyboard access to commands is still lacking on NeXT. Is this a religious issue at NeXT? Why don't cursor keys lead you up and down browser lists?

Most applications implement cursor keys for this task, but the NextStep interface balks.

The idea should be—but isn't—this: anything you can do with a mouse, you can do from the keyboard. *Anything*.

Granted, it's a goal that won't be reached, but it should be strived for. NeXT isn't striving very hard. (But hey! He said apologetically. They've been busy. Maybe they'll get to it. Let's hope.)

The two-button mouse? After years on one-buttoning, it was a transition. Now I prefer it. The ability to bring up a main menu anywhere is worth the extra button. The mouse itself, to me, fits the hand better than a Macintosh mouse.

Then there's mousescaling: a fine idea. The faster you move the mouse, the quicker it moves. Almost a necessity on a large display.

But I wish I could fine-tune the scaling a bit more. I'd like the cursor to move faster when my movements are slow. Petty? You bet. But use a computer (use anything!) eight or more hours a day and petty annoyances become constant aggravation.

The seamless multitasking of NeXT is a great joy. What would make it better? A keyboard way to "cycle" through open applications. Command-Anything would do. On the subject of cycling, a keyboard method to cycle through windows in a single application would also be welcome. That feature, though, can easily be implemented by developers. Maybe NeXT could lead the way here?

Now for fonts. The curse of PostScript. First, let's say this: NeXT did the absolute right thing by embracing PostScript and PostScript fonts.

Unfortunately, what looks great printed looks jaggy on the display. Not really jaggy, but...jaggy.

In Real Life, you watch the screen often, and print seldom. Screen fonts should be impeccable. You earn your living, after all, while looking at the screen.

The jagginess is understandable. PostScript fonts are designed for 300 dpi or greater printers. The NeXT screen is 94 dpi, and font readability suffers. NeXT/PostScript fonts are designed for maximum printed readability, not maximum on-screen readability. As a result, what's beautiful printed isn't beautiful on-screen.

The solution is automatic on-screen font smoothing. That's a tricky, low-level business, but readability is important. I hope NeXT implements it.

More gripes. Twelve Dock slots aren't enough. Granted, the cry of the wild User is always "More!" "More!" But...how about the option of two vertical Dock columns?

But that's a trivial complaint. My biggest complaint has to do with vision. And age.

Here's a truism: Computer interfaces are designed by young people for use by old people.

The cube I'm using to write this book cost $15,500—developer's price! A ton of money.

Designers usually love what they design. They're intent upon the object of their creation. Not so the user, for whom the product is just...well...another product, however good or bad.

What's this leading up to? Size. The screen's big, but the letters are puny. The menu items are itsy-witsy (the technical term). Worse, they're on a gray background, which makes them even harder to read. Ditto for most panel text: tiny.

The optimum distance from a computer display is about the length of your arm. At that distance, menu text and browser text and most panel text is too small. And it's on a gray background, for chrissakes!

Other than that, I love it. How's the bumper sticker slogan go? Something about prying it from my cold, dead fingers?

# Chapter 7

# The Workspace Manager

*Invention breeds invention.*
Works and Days
             — **RALPH WALDO EMERSON** 1803–1882

The Workspace Manager is UNIX with a new face. That truth, however, takes nothing away from the marvelous NextStep interface.

Traditionally, command-line interfaces are easy to program but hard to use. And graphic interfaces are easy to use, but hard to program. Hence the few good graphic interfaces around.

What's more, command-line interfaces reward expert users (and expert typists) while frustrating novices who just want to "make the damn thing work!" Conversely, graphic interfaces reward novices—who can "see what they're doing"—while frustrating expert users who know what they want, and want it *now*.

The Workspace Manager tries to serve both groups. Mousers and novices will be immediately at home. Good typists aren't forgotten. Truly expert users still have the Shell, where anything goes.

## First Thoughts

Daemons aside, The Workspace Manager is the only NeXT application (sure it's an application) which is always available. It may be hidden, but it's always there. If unseen, a double-click on the NeXT icon brings The Workspace Manager's main menu to the front. And the NeXT icon is permanently fixed at the top of the dock. When using The NeXT Computer, you may lose your mind or your patience, but you'll never lose The Workspace Manager.

You'll also never Quit The Workspace Manager. Where other applications have Quit on the menu, The Workspace Manager has "Log Out." To leave The Workspace Manager, you must leave the entire system.

(Okay. Absolute power UNIX users can avoid The Workspace Manager, NextStep, and the Window Server entirely if they wish. The file to manipulate is /private/etc/ttys. The first few lines are:

```
#
# name  getty                type      status        comments
#
# If you do not want to start the window server by default, you can
# uncomment the first entry and comment out the second.
#
# console    "/usr/etc/getty std.9600" NeXT          on secure
console /usr/lib/NextStep/loginwindow   NeXT          on secure
window=/usr/lib/NextStep/WindowServer onoption="/usr/etc/getty std.9600"
ttya    "/usr/etc/getty std.9600"       unknown       off secure
ttyb    "/usr/etc/getty std.9600"       unknown       off secure
ttyda   "/usr/etc/getty D9600"          unknown       off
ttydb   "/usr/etc/getty D9600"          unknown       off
```

Although it's not detailed above, the login window passes control to the Window Server, which starts up The Workspace Manager as a matter of course. The Dark Ages of terminal-based computing are still available for NeXT Luddites and masochists. Now back to our program.)

The Workspace Manager, in general, handles the duties of most graphic shells:

* launching applications;
* moving, copying, renaming, and deleting files; and
* working with disks: mounting, initializing, naming, and so on.

Still, it's UNIX underneath. Many Workspace Manager commands call UNIX commands. In many cases, you can get the same results from the Shell, if you know what you're doing.

## Workspace Views

Working with computers means working with files. As we saw earlier, the shell offers many (probably too many) options for viewing files. The Workspace Manager takes a handful of those options and wraps them in NextStep.

In general, The Workspace Manager consists of:

* menus;

* windows displaying files; and

* the application dock.

The default file displays are shown in "directory browser" windows. Here's the most modest browser possible, shown alongside The Workspace Manager main menu:

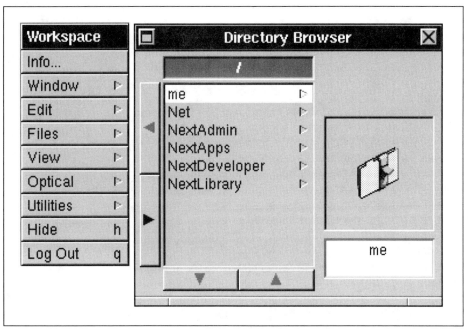

*Figure 7-1*

At left, the main menu should look familiar: a column of items, with submenus marked by triangles. At right, the browser is an elegant face on the UNIX ls command that we looked at earlier. At the top of the browser column is the parent directory. Here, we're seeing the root directory, so the parent directory is /, for root.

Browser view is the graphic equivalent of the Shell's ls command:

```
localhost# ls
.NeXT/          LocalLibrary/   Various_Poems/  lost+found/  tmp/
.cshrc          Net/            bin/            mach@        usr/
.hidden         NextAdmin/      clients/        me/          vmUNIX@
.login          NextApps/       dev/            odmach*
.places         NextDeveloper/  etc/            private/
.profile        NextLibrary/    lib/            sdmach*
```

except that the Shell typically shows *all* files and directories. The browser above shows only the simplified "non-UNIX-expert" view of files. Where the Shell marks directories with trailing /s, the browser marks directories with trailing triangles, to remain consistent with menu's "more to the right" triangles. In The Workspace Manager, "folder" is synonymous with "directory." *Folders are directories.* From now on, we'll use both terms to keep you off guard.

The buttons that surround the browser's file listing are used to scroll. Here, we're in the root directory, so the left scroll arrow is dimmed. Because the entire file list is shown, the up and down arrows are also dimmed.

When the browser window is resized, more directories can be viewed. Remember the pathname example given earlier?

```
/NextLibrary/Literature/Shakespeare/Various_Poems/The Rape of
    Lucrece
```

With The Workspace Manager, wending your way to The Rape of Lucrece is a matter of clicking on the NextLibrary directory to display its contents, then clicking on the Literature directory to display *its* contents, and so on, until you have something like Figure 7-2.

The full pathname can be seen two ways: by reading the column titles ending with the filename shown in the icon well at right, or by reading the highlighted directories in the browser. Remember, the column titles are the parent directory of the listing below—the "one back" directory.

If we'd left the browser view in a meager one-column display, the columns would have scrolled to the left as you clicked in successive directories.

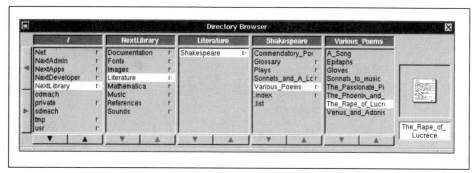

Figure 7-2

The icon well contains the selected file or directory:

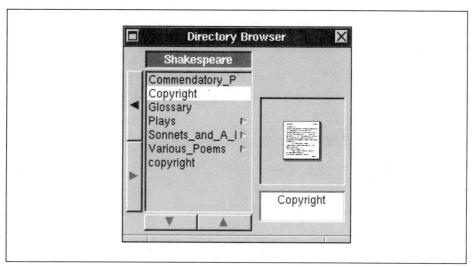

Figure 7-3

The text field below shows the file or folder's name. To rename a file or folder, use the edit field: select the name with the mouse and type a new name. If, as shown above, you've selected a file, a double-click on the icon opens the file, and its associated application (Edit, in this case).

You can also launch (open) a file by double-clicking its name in the browser listing.

If you've selected a directory folder, not a file, it's also shown in the icon well:

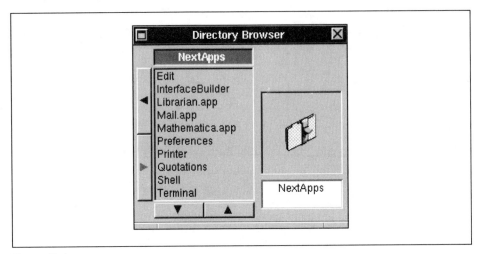

*Figure 7-4*

Double-clicking on the directory folder opens it, and displays the directory contents in a new window:

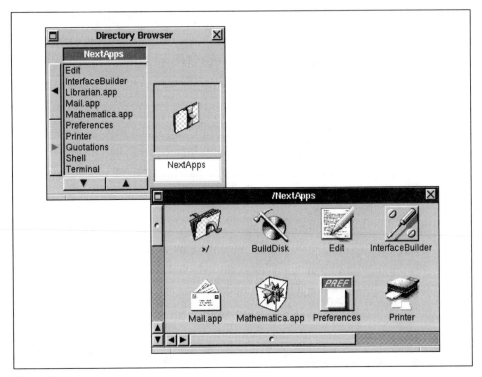

*Figure 7-5*

(Double-clicking folder names in browser listings *doesn't* open a new window; you must double-click the folder image in the icon well.)

By default, the new window displays files as icons. If you change the view, however, The Workspace Manager remembers your view preference the next time you open the directory.

The window's title bar contains the directory name. The parent directory, as in all nonbrowser views, is shown as an open folder. In icon views, the open "parent directory folder" is always at the top left corner of the window.

If the icon window contains additional directories, they can be opened by double-clicking (or clicking to select, then choosing Open from The Workspace Manager's Window menu. Or clicking to select, then a fast Command-O). The result might look like this, a typical Workspace Manager display:

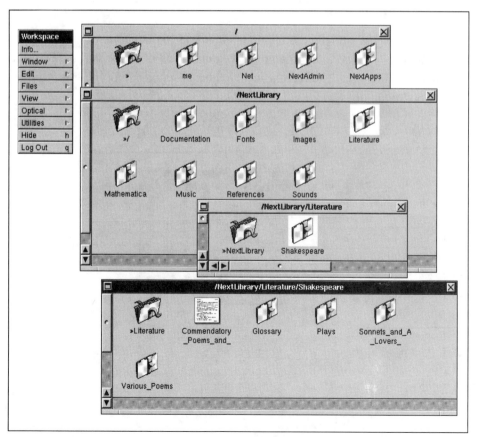

*Figure 7-6*

Notice that the chain of pathnames is similar to that in browser windows, only here it's given in the window's title bars. This clicking began at the top, in the root directory, then wandered down through NextLibrary, into Literature, and so forth. And each window contains a folder at the top left representing the parent directory. A double-click on the parent directory folder brings the parent directory window to the front and makes it the key window. If the window isn't open, a double-click opens it, then displays it.

Workspace Manager windows behave like other NextStep windows. A click in the Close box removes them from the screen. The Hide button miniaturizes the window and places it at the bottom of the display. Opening, then Hiding directory windows is a good way to keep the display uncluttered, yet have the directories instantly available.

## The Files Menu

We'll come back to directory views. First, let's look at The Workspace Manager commands. With one important exception—filename expansion—all commands are found in menus. Submenus, for the most part (except for the Info..., Hide, and Logout commands).

The Files submenu contains commands that act on files or directories.

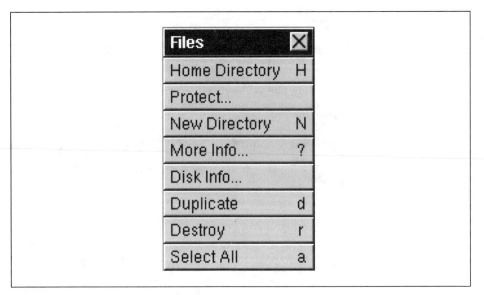

Figure 7-7

Home Directory means "root directory." The command displays the root directory window, bringing it to the front if open, opening then bringing it to the front otherwise. The key equivalent is *capital* H. Command (lowercase) h is reserved, as elsewhere, for Hiding the entire application and all its windows.

Protect brings up this panel:

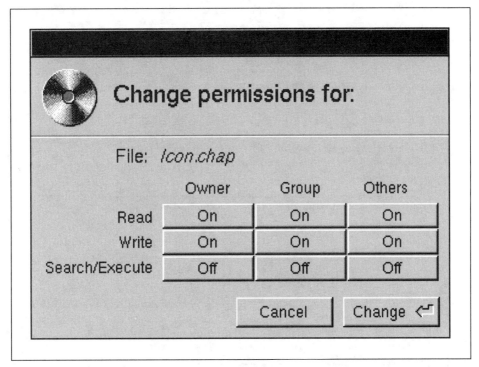

*Figure 7-8*

The panel is a NextStep version of the UNIX file permissions we saw earlier; here in button format. Each "permission button" cycles between "On," "Off," and "No Change." In the case of "Icon.chap" above, Search/Execute is Off because the file is text—not executable.

The Protect panel can also be used to protect directories. If you don't want prying network eyes to view your "Personal" directory, for example, set the "You" permissions to On, and all others to Off.

New Directory creates a new, empty subdirectory. In all views except browser view, the directory becomes a subdirectory of the key window's directory. In browser view, the new directory is deposited in the rightmost directory. Here's a shot before the New Directory command:

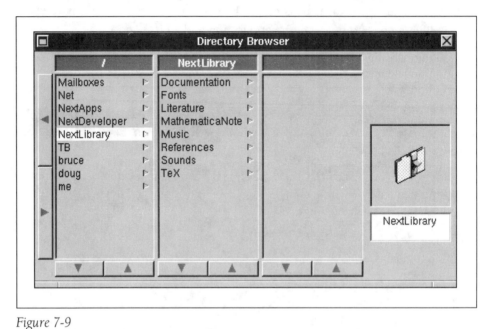

*Figure 7-9*

and the result after the New Directory command:

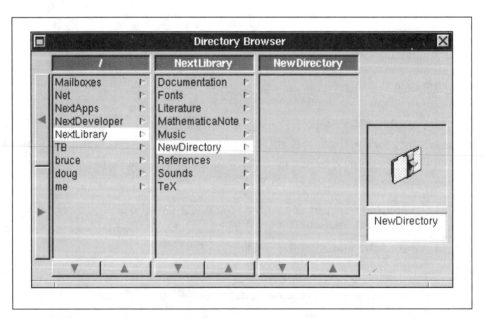

*Figure 7-10*

The Workspace Manager creates the directory and titles the rightmost column with the directory's name. You could now click under the folder icon to rename the directory.

After a file or directory is first selected (by clicking on it), the More Info command gives additional information:

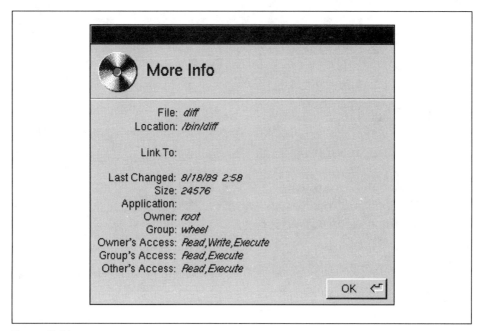

*Figure 7-11*

With the exception of the "Link To" field, this information is also shown in various Workspace Manager views, as we'll see.

Disk Info is a new command in the 1.0 software release. (See Figure 7-12.) Previously, this information could only be had in the Shell, through various UNIX commands. The Shell is still a good stop, though. Compare the panel above to the UNIX df (for "disk free") command:

```
localhost# df
Filesystem          kbytes    used   avail capacity Mounted on
/dev/sd0a           446719  279048  122999    69%   /
/dev/sd0b           216311       9  194670     0%   /clients
```

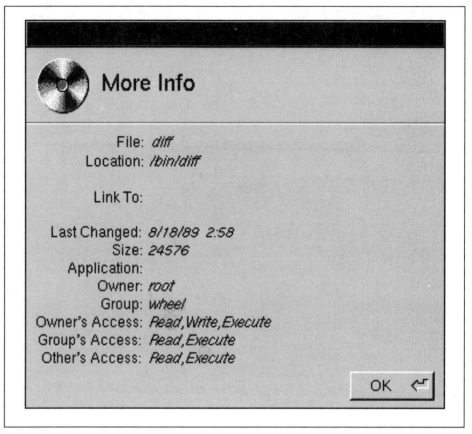

*Figure 7-12*

The Duplicate command copies a file within its directory, with the prefix "Copy of." The file "Thisfile" would be duplicated and named "Copy of Thisfile." (NeXT's 0.9 software put underscores between words. The 1.0 software seems to assume that you'll work with files in The Workspace Manager—where filenames may contain spaces—not in the Shell.)

Destroy does just that: destroys a file. It's essentially a shortcut to dragging a file to the Black Hole, then choosing Destroy Deleted Files. A panel appears before the actual file deletion, giving you one last chance to change your mind.

Select All selects all the files in the current directory. In icon view, selected files are highlighted. In browser view, they're also highlighted, and the icon well shows a "handful" of files:

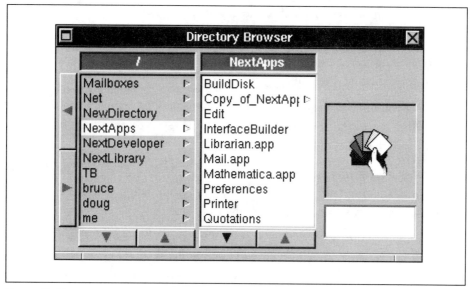

*Figure 7-13*

Since you can't rename many files at once, the text field is blank.

## Moving, Copying and Linking Files

What good is a handful of files? This: files shown in the browser's icon well (one file or many files) can be dragged into other directory windows. There are three possibilities:

- moving a file;
- copying a file; or
- linking a file.

All are easy. To copy a file or directory, just drag it from one window to another window. In Browser view, you'll need to drag the image in the icon well. In other views, just drag the icon into another window. Since windows represent directories, dragging the icon to another window copies it to that directory. After the copy, the file or folder exists in two directories.

The same actions are used to move or link files. To move a file, hold down the Command key while dragging (the letter to remember is "C": Command to Copy). Move, unlike Copy, doesn't leave a copy behind.

Linking works as explained previously: you aren't physically moving the file, just making it appear in two directories.

Again, the basic action is the same: drag it. To link, however, you hold down the Control key while dragging.

After you mouseup to start the move, copy, or linking action, a panel may appear to inform you of the file handling progress. After everything's safely moved, copied, or linked, the panel disappears.

When you're first starting out with The Workspace Manager, this business of moving, copying, and linking files may be intimidating. There's a tendency to think, "Jeez, I hope I don't accidentally ruin something here!"

To build confidence, try this: copy a folder, then create a new directory. Spend a few hours moving, copying, and linking the files in the copied directory and the new directory. You won't hurt anything—you're only working with copies of existing files—and you'll get the hang of it quickly. When you've dragged yourself out, make a few final drags. Placed the copied files (one last drag) into the Black Hole for eventual disposal.

## The View Menu

Back to views.

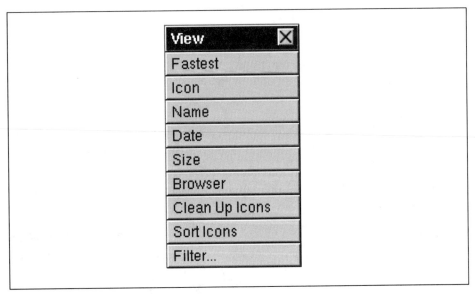

*Figure 7-14*

The View menu offers these choices for file-gazing:

* Fastest;

* Icon;

* Name;

* Date;

* Size; and

* Browser.

You'll probably use the Browser and Icon views most frequently. The other views are useful with directories filled with many files, because the displays are smaller.

The least obtrusive of the non-Browser views is Fastest, which merely lists the files alphabetically, with no other information:

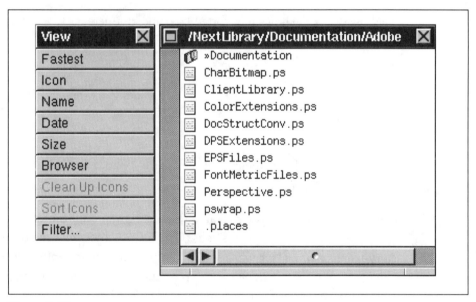

*Figure 7-15*

It is, indeed, a fast way to display files, but all views are fast. Fastest view is really "simplest" view. As in Icon view, you can double-click to open directories and perform all relevant dragging feats in this view, or any other non-Browser view.

The remaining three views, Name, Date, and Size, all give the same information. All that's different is the file order. Here's Name view:

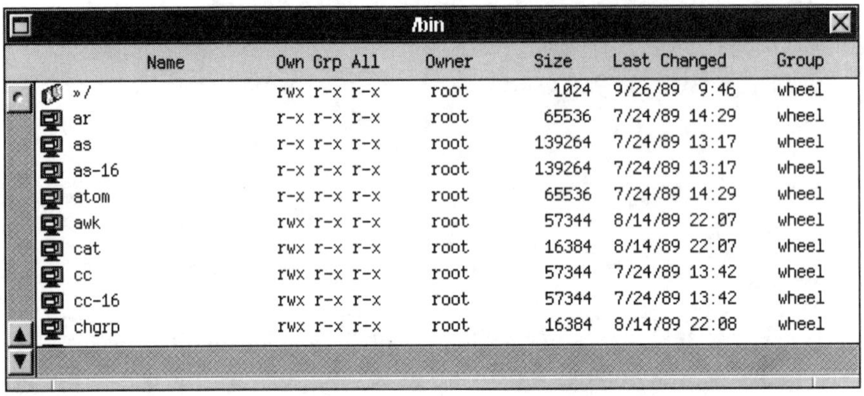

| Name | Own Grp All | Owner | Size | Last Changed | Group |
|------|-------------|-------|------|--------------|-------|
| »/ | rwx r-x r-x | root | 1024 | 9/26/89  9:46 | wheel |
| ar | r-x r-x r-x | root | 65536 | 7/24/89 14:29 | wheel |
| as | r-x r-x r-x | root | 139264 | 7/24/89 13:17 | wheel |
| as-16 | r-x r-x r-x | root | 139264 | 7/24/89 13:17 | wheel |
| atom | r-x r-x r-x | root | 65536 | 7/24/89 14:29 | wheel |
| awk | rwx r-x r-x | root | 57344 | 8/14/89 22:07 | wheel |
| cat | rwx r-x r-x | root | 16384 | 8/14/89 22:07 | wheel |
| cc | rwx r-x r-x | root | 57344 | 7/24/89 13:42 | wheel |
| cc-16 | rwx r-x r-x | root | 57344 | 7/24/89 13:42 | wheel |
| chgrp | rwx r-x r-x | root | 16384 | 8/14/89 22:08 | wheel |

*Figure 7-16*

Name view, like Fastest, shows files sorted by name. But here, as with Date and Size view, more information is shown. From the left are:

- the file name;
- permissions for the file;
- the file's owner;
- the file's size in bytes;
- the date and time of the last change to the file (in 24 hour format); and
- what group the file belongs to.

If your cube isn't networked, you're granted "wheel" group status automatically. Groups are another hierarchy of permissions. (The name comes from the mists of UNIX history, when only the "big wheels" had this rarified network status.) If your cube *is* networked, you'll be assigned a group by the system administrator (who probably *will* belong to either the wheel group or the "staff" group).

The View menu also holds commands to Sort Icons and Clean Up Icons. Sort Icons attempts to put similar files near each other. Clean Up Icons "snaps" the icons' positions to an invisible grid. Though not seen, grid spacing can be determined from the Utilities menu, where the Icon Grid item brings up this panel:

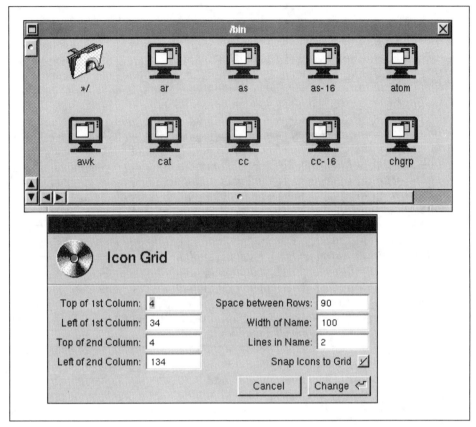

*Figure 7-17*

The "Snap Icons to Grid" checkbox gives you the freedom to create a truly unruly icon display.

The final item on the View menu is Filter. (See Figure 7-18.)

The icons are clicked to select. Usually, you'll want to display all file types. Filter is most useful with crowded directories, when you're looking for one or more particular file types—possibly in preparation for a move or copy. The "Special Files" checkbox is used to show hidden files. By default, it's unchecked, to reduce visual clutter.

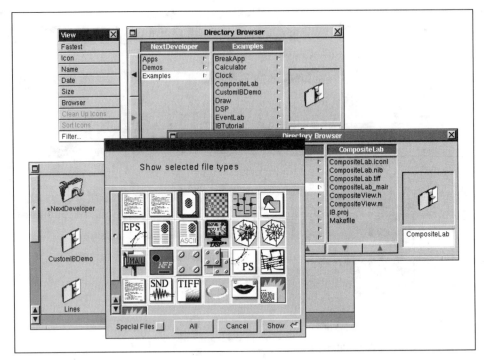

Figure 7-18

## The Optical Menu

The Optical menu concerns itself with optical disks:

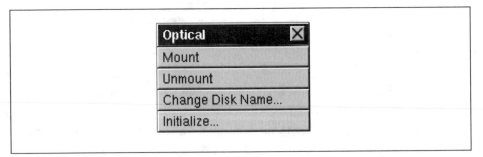

Figure 7-19

One of the cube's invisible servers is "autodiskmount." It endlessly paces in the background, waiting for an optical disk to be inserted. When you slide in an optical, you're actually "mounting" a new directory onto your present directory structure. With NeXT, that's all it takes; a big improvement over traditional UNIX, where mounting directories takes the appropriate Shell incantations.

The Mount command is only necessary on optical-only cubes. Imagine: You've only got one optical drive. There's a disk in the drive. You want to mount a different disk. What to do? Choose Mount.

The Mount command ejects the optical and prompts you to insert a disk. Swapping then commences. Eventually, things settle down, and the new disk remains in the drive.

(The Mount panel is one of the few rough edges in NeXT's 1.0 software release: it's modal and hard-edged; one of the few panels that didn't get attention prior to the release of 1.0.)

The Unmount command does just that and, as a by-product, ejects the optical disk. Earlier versions of the software also had an "Eject" item. Unmount now serves that function.

The Change Disk Name is *only* used for optical disks. Hard disks, because of the UNIX conventions, don't have names. Instead, they have root directories. There can be only one root directory, no matter how many hard disks are attached, so naming hard disks doesn't make sense.

The Initialize command, again, is used for opticals only. (Now you can see why the menu was named "Optical.") Unlike building an optical disk, which can take three hours or so, initializing is a fairly speedy process.

## Utilities

The Utilities menu contains some useful, if seldom used, commands:

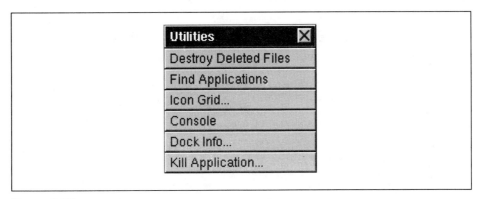

*Figure 7-20*

The Destroy Deleted Files command erases files in the Black Hole. Notice that NeXT makes you explicitly erase deleted files. Merely logging out, or shutting down the cube *doesn't* erase files in the Black Hole. In truth, the Black Hole is merely a directory. When you choose Destroy Deleted Files (or "Destroy" from the File menu), the directory contents are erased.

If you're fortunate enough to have a 660 megabyte hard disk, you may let files molder in the Black Hole for weeks before destroying them. If you've got room, why not?

The Find Applications command updates The Window Manager. Use it after you've moved a new application into any of these directories:

- ~/Apps;
- /LocalApps;
- /NextApps;
- /NextDeveloperApps;
- NextAdmin; or
- NextDeveloper/Demos

We mentioned the icon grid above. Moving along, the Console command brings up the console window, a relic of the cube's prerelease days:

*Figure 7-21*

The console is a read-only window. It displays the pathname of the home directory and the standard application directories.

Its real purpose, though, is displaying error messages. If you crash while running a NeXT application, or some other malfunction occurs, it's likely that a message will be written to the console window. If you leave your cube on for days at a time, the console window may contain a slew of messages. They're interesting, but instructive only to NeXT developers.

The dock is a convenience. It spares you from wading through directories searching for an application to launch. The Dock Info panel is used only to auto-start docked applications. To place an application on the dock, you merely drag it to the dock area. To remove an application, you drag it off the dock:

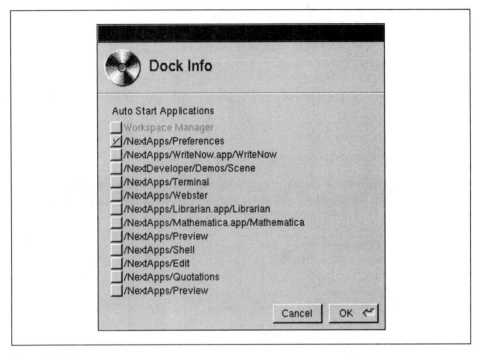

*Figure 7-22*

You can put an extra application on the dock by moving the Black Hole. That brings the total docked applications to twelve plus the omnipresent NeXT Workspace Manager icon: thirteen in all.

## Filename Expansion

The Workspace Manager gives typists their due with one important feature: filename expansion.

Filename expansion lets you select any file, or deselect files. All from the keyboard. Once a file is selected, hit Return. Then:

- If you've selected a directory, it opens.
- If you've selected an application, it launches.
- If you've selected a file, it opens and launches the application needed to display it.

And there's more. If you're a good typist, it's a godsend.

## Going Down

Here we are in The Workspace Manager. One humble Browser window is onscreen. Nothing is selected. The mouse is drowsing by the keyboard, untouched:

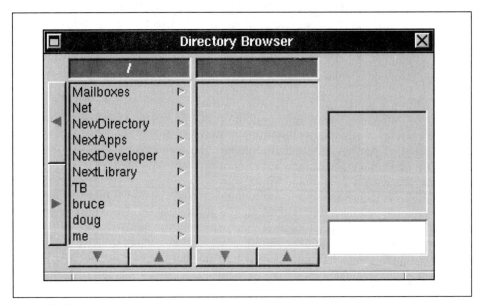

*Figure 7-23*

Now type a quick "N:"

The Name Expansion window opens. It displays the N that was typed. And the first directory name that matches is selected. If you now hit Esc, the name would expand to "Net."

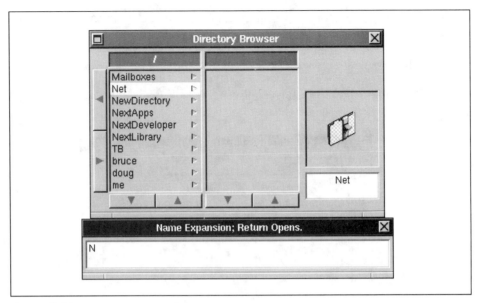

*Figure 7-24*

But we don't want to select the "Net" directory. We want the "NextApps" directory. Keep typing. An "e," then a "x," and we're rewarded with:

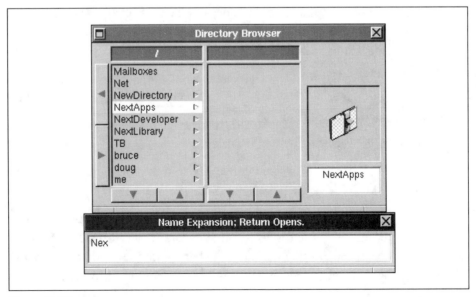

*Figure 7-25*

*That's* the right directory. If we hit Esc *now*, the characters in the name expansion window would expand to "NextApps". But let's not.

Hit Return.

The Name Expansion window vanishes and the NextApps directory opens:

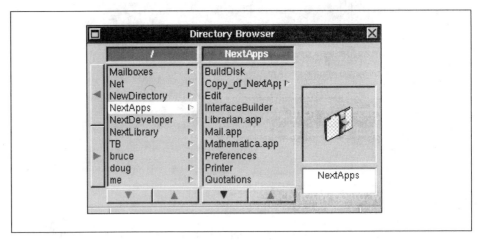

*Figure 7-26*

The process can be repeated until the desired file is selected. As subdirectories are selected and Return is hit, the subdirectories open. If a file is selected, Return opens the file. Hit Esc at any time to expand the characters in the name expansion window.

As you start out with filename expansion, you might want to enlarge the Browser view somewhat. (See Figure 7-27.)

That's one strategy.

Filename expansion isn't just a convenience in the Browser; it's available in all Workspace Manager views. (See Figure 7-28.)

Above, it's necessary to type "Mat" to match "Mathematica.app." Merely typing "M" or "Ma" matches—and selects—the Mail.app icon. If that's what you want, you can stop. Typing a "t" deselected Mail.app and selects Mathematica.app. As soon as you've typed enough letters to uniquely identify a file or folder, hit Return.

There's more to filename expansion than finding and opening files. Remember the earlier discussion of the UNIX "cd" (Change Directory) command? And the

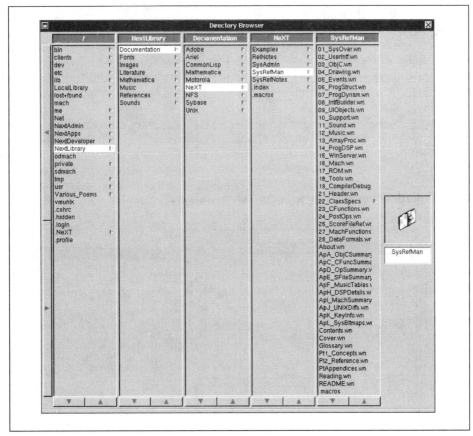

Figure 7-27

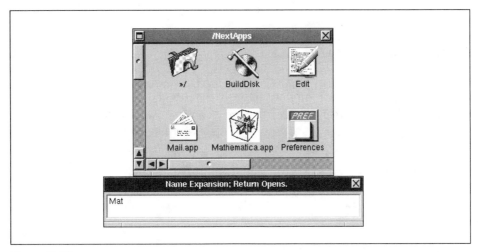

Figure 7-28

fuss we made about "/" for the root directory, and ".." for "the parent directory of the current directory"?

This is where it pays off. As you work with The Workspace Manager, you'll often end up with many open windows. Things may become confusing. Where's that root directory window? How about the directory "above" this directory?

As an example, say you're rummaging in /NextLibrary/Literature/Plays/Macbeth and decide you'd like to return to the root directory. All it takes is one keystroke:

/

followed by Return. Here's before Return, and after Return:

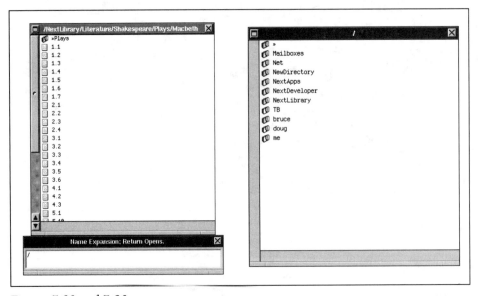

*Figures 7-29 and 7-30*

Back to root in one swoop. And notice that the same window is used. Changing directories in this manner doesn't open new windows; it only changes what's displayed in the current, key window. This means it's possible to have a directory displayed in more than one window. Two windows containing views of the root directory, for instance:

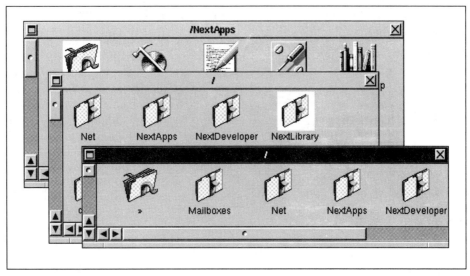

*Figure 7-31*

With name expansion, you can also quickly change to the "UNIX-expert" file view. Just type the name of a UNIX directory. On Return, the view is instantly changed to UNIX-expert view.

Filename expansion can also be used in all NeXT Open and Save panels. Use the same techniques as in The Workspace Manager.

Filename expansion isn't a NeXT invention. It's been a UNIX feature for years—and a feature you should use in the Shell. NeXT merely carried the feature into their graphic interface.

The only problem with filename expansion is this: You might forget that it's available. After all, until you hit a key the file expansion window isn't shown (and it's never shown when you're using Open and Save panels). When you're mousing around in Icon view, it doesn't seem that the keyboard is available. There's no visual hint that, yes!, you really *can* use the keyboard. But you can, and should, if only to hit / and .., which are tremendous timesavers.

Advice: Use this feature. Go into The Workspace Manager and practice, practice, practice. In time, Browser windows will be your Steinway. There's an East

European saying that goes, "Tell me a hundred times. Show me once." It's hard to show anything well in the strictured confines of paper and ink. Here, as elsewhere, you'll need to try it for yourself. When you do, give yourself some time to "know your tools."

## In Conclusion

The Workspace Manager is one application that you'll use constantly. Use it hard; learn how it works, and use the available shortcuts, Command key menu equivalents, and filename expansion.

# Section II

## Hardware

# Chapter 8

# The NeXT Display, Keyboard, and Mouse

*Not only is there but one way of doing things rightly, but there is only one way of seeing them, and that is, seeing the whole of them.*

— JOHN RUSKIN  1819–1900

The NeXT MegaPixel Display is hardware; what you see displayed is the result of both hardware and software. This chapter, then, is in the "Hardware" section by default only; we'll touch here on both aspects of the display. We'll also cover the NeXT keyboard and mouse.

The NeXT MegaPixel Display is manufactured by Sony, not by NeXT. The display never sets...ah...tractor rollers in NeXT's manufacturing plant. MegaPixel Displays are shipped directly from Sony to dealers. The computer, in one box, comes from NeXT. The display, in another box, comes from Sony.

NeXT efficiency at work.

## The Physical Display

The 17-inch grayscale monitor is a compromise between big screen size and manageability. It's imposing, but not overwhelming.

The 17-inch display raises, once again, computing's common denominator. NeXT (for now, anyway) has one display, and it's big. Every NeXT owner will have 17 inches of display, guaranteed. Software developers don't have to worry about supporting various screen sizes, or alphabet soups of display software standards. With NeXT, everybody gets the big one.

135

The display itself rests on a moveable, cast metal base. Two tractor rollers allow you to easily move the display forward and back; moving side-to-side requires picking up the display; and it's heavy. Although not immediately apparent, the display screen also tilts forward and back (though not left and right), giving you about a 30-degree range of play to find your angle of choice.

## The Display

The NeXT display has roots in what the academic community once called the "3-M" computer: a dreamed-of ideal university computer. The 3M computer would have:

- 1 megabyte of memory;
- 1 million instructions per second of processor speed; and
- 1 million screen pixels.

Some variants allotted one "M" to a $1,000 price for the computer.

NeXT delivered a computer to academia that far exceeded the paltry 3-M specifications. In every respect, that is, except one: the display.

The MegaPixel display actually offers not 1 million pixels, but 931,840 individual picture elements: a 1,120 by 832 display.

"Nearly MegaPixel Display" doesn't have the same ring.

Still, 931,840 pixels is a bunch: a big, rich graphic canvas; far greater than found on most workstations. (Higher-resolution displays, while available, are hideously expensive. They should be: they're difficult and expensive to manufacture. And conforming to FCC emission standards becomes a murderous task. A higher-resolution monitor would have knocked the price of the cube thousands of dollars higher.)

If you want to get picky, there actually are a million pixels. To see why, compare a monitor like the NeXT display to a common television screen. A problem on both displays is resolution "drop-off" at the edges of the screen. Television sets solve this with "overscan," which means that TV images extend beyond the screen. If you could see the entire image—which you can't—you'd notice that it gets fuzzy on the edges.

On computer displays, though, every pixel tells a story. You can't just chop the edges of the picture. So the NeXT/Sony monitor takes a different approach: a margin of pixels surrounding the display are blacked out and declared off-limits for drawing. The edges contain perfectly good pixels, but if the display reached to the very edge, the images displayed might drop off: get fuzzy.

The margins are 39 pixels on both the left and right of the display, and 16 pixels at the top and bottom of the display. Here's how it's expressed in the NeXT software source code, where NPPB means "Number of Pixels Per Byte" and MW means "Maximum Width."

```
#define NPPB    4        /* # pixels per byte */
#define VIDEO_W         1120
#define VIDEO_MW        1152
#define VIDEO_H         832
#define VIDEO_MH        910
```

Blacking out a margin isn't a new idea; other computers use the same technique. Even with margin blacking, other computer monitors can't match the edge-to-edge sharpness of the NeXT monitor. Spend a minute and look at the clarity of image in the extreme corners of the NeXT display. And when you next happen into a computer store, look at a few monitors as experts do: check the edges and the corners. The NeXT display is better. Detail counts.

The pixel density is 92 dots per inch (dpi). In contrast, the Macintosh display is 72 dpi. The 92-dpi resolution, combined with a 68-Hz refresh rate, and a 100-MHz bandwidth, produces a completely flicker-free, rock-steady image. This, at a time when computers from other manufacturers still leave visible "ghosts" when images are scrolled on screen.

NeXT and Sony have crafted an impeccable, beautiful display.

The 92-dpi screen has some interesting consequences. The high pixel density means that NeXT documents on screen can more closely approximate their printed forms. But laser printers are 300-400 dpi. In practice, the result is that what you see on the NeXT display is 78 percent of the printed size. It's What You See Is What You Get, Only Smaller (or WYSIWYGOS). Until we see 300 dpi or 400 dpi screens (don't hold your breath), it's the most we can expect.

Still, for accurate proofing of documents, NeXT offers a way out. The standard NeXT Page Layout panel offers "Scale" as an option, which should delight Desktop Publishers:

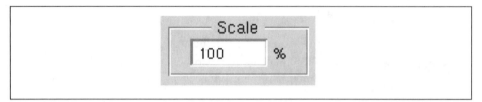

*Figure 8-1*

By changing the value of scaling, screen images can match the size of printed images.

The display offers two-bit grayscaling. Each individual pixel can contain one of four values: 00, 01, 10, and 11. The four values correspond to four shades: black, white, light gray, and dark gray.

Admittedly, black and white aren't spectacular shades. In practice, however, the effects are impressive. Let's look at the NeXT Login panel, shown as the TIFF file that it really is:

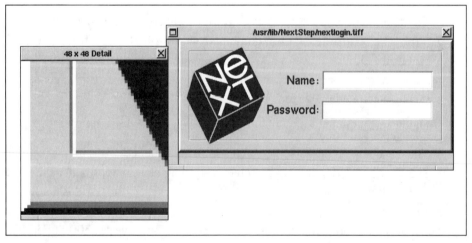

*Figure 8-2*

The "Detail" window at left is courtesy of the Icon application. Here, it details the lower left 48 x 48 pixels of the login image.

Notice how the two gray shades add to the image's depth. See the fineness of detail at the bezel's corner? At the bottom of the detail, see how light gray gives way to dark gray, then black—creating the illusion of three dimensions? And look at the one pixel line of dark gray pixels along the cube's edge.

Or consider this image of a custom control:

Figure 8-3

Again, all four shades are used to create the image. But here, a pattern is also used: to create a shadow behind the switch's handle:

Figure 8-4

Or consider these TIFF images, shown actual size and enlarged:

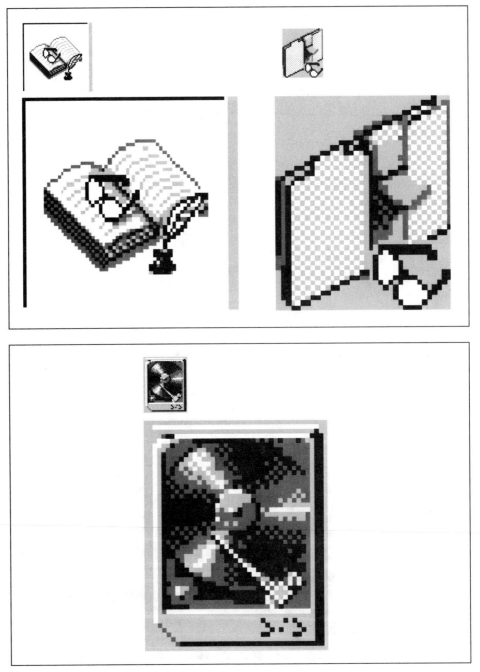

*Figures 8-5 and 8-6*

"Two-bit grayscale" sounds low-rent. But, as you can see, two bits—and untold pattern combinations—provide a wide field for artistry.

The pattern combinations can be generated automatically by NeXT software. Developers can specify four "pure" shades: black, white, light gray, or dark gray; all given as predefined values. Ask for a gray value that's not predefined, and NeXT software automatically "dithers" to create the desired shade, by alternating pixels of different shades.

While users are never satisfied (and shouldn't be, and should be), this should be said: It's taken years to exploit the deadly monotonous black-and-white-only Macintosh display. Breathtaking images have been composed on Macintosh, using only black pixels and white pixels.

NeXT will eventually deliver color and (as a good guess) 256-shade grayscale (or higher) monochrome displays. That's fine. But what NeXT offers, today—as standard equipment—is an order of magnitude greater than what's routinely offered on other computers.

## Jacks and Plugs

The rear of the MegaPixel Display contains connectors for (from left):

- stereo headphones,
- left and right channel stereo output,
- the main power cord, and
- a microphone.

The microphone and headphone jacks are standard mini-jack plugs, like those for "Walkman" headphones. When shopping for microphones, make sure you select a "high impedance" model; again, with a mini-jack end.

The stereo output jacks are RCA standard. They're also gold-plated, which supposedly results in a better signal (gold is an excellent electrical conductor).

The main cable is an engineering and esthetic feat. It contains all the signals that come from—and go to—the cube: power, sound (both ways), video, keyboard and mouse data. The backs of most computers look like the back of your TV/stereo/VCR—and you know what a mess that is! With NeXT, everything is in one cable. These people know how to build computers.

Despite its complexity, the cord is reasonably supple. It's also 3 meters—almost 10 feet—long, so the cube can be tucked away under a desk or on a shelf. If, that is, you have a hard disk, or seldom need to swap disks.

Inside the display are two circuit boards. One is an analog board containing a "step-up" transformer, which generates the high voltages needed to drive the display. (Again, it's easy to forget that large monitors are engineering feats. It's difficult to create the high frequencies and high voltages needed by big monitors, yet still keep radio frequency emissions at the level required by the FCC. Sony did a good job.)

The second, digital board handles input and output for sound, the keyboard, and the mouse. A high-performance, 3-inch speaker delivers the sonic goods.

## The Keyboard

The NeXT keyboard doubles as a control center. The keyboard isn't merely for typing. It's also where you control the computer. The cube proper has no On/Off switch; the display has no controls for brightness or speaker volume. Those controls are all on the keyboard.

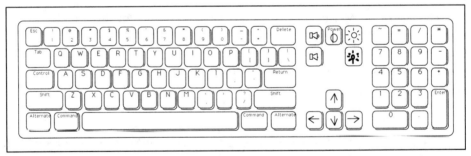

*Figure 8-7*

With one caveat, this makes sense. The keyboard, after all, is where your hands are; why not put the system controls there?

The keyboard is divided into four groups:

- the keyboard proper;
- system controls;
- cursor keys; and
- a numeric keypad.

All keytops are labeled, which takes the fun out of touch-typing. Some keys also have green labels on their keyfronts. The green labels represent Command key combinations. The Command key is held down while one of the green-labeled keys is pressed to perform some standard action. Thus:

| **Key** | **With Command key** |
| --- | --- |
| Shift | AlphaLock (caps lock) |
| z | Undo |
| x | Cut |
| c | Copy |
| v | Paste |
| Return | Enter (the Enter key on the numeric keypad can also be used in most cases) |
| Volume down | Mute speaker |

These are only the absolutely standard Command key combinations. An appendix lists other common Command key equivalents. And applications usually define yet another tier of Command key combinations.

And notice that Command key combinations are case-sensitive. Cut is Command-x, not Command-X.

The system control keys, arranged in an upside-down "U," are:

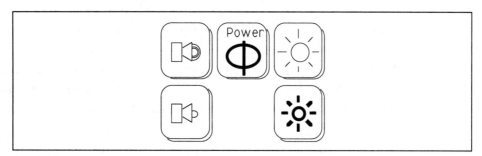

*Figure 8-8*

It's a convenient location for the volume and brightness keys. And a terrible location for the power key. If you change volume or brightness frequently, you're sure to hit the power key accidentally once in a while. Fortunately, a panel appears that lets you cancel the inadvertent power off.

The main keyboard contains all the familiar letters, and a few computer-specific and NeXT-specific keys. Forgoing the letters, we have these keys to consider:

## Return

Return sets a carriage return (paragraph marker) in text. It's also the all-purpose "Do it!" key, often associated with the default "OK" button in panels. Also used, when telecommunicating, to say "Hello? I'm here!" In general, when in doubt, hit Return. If the application is well-behaved, you'll be rewarded with the default action (if there is one).

## Command

In The Workspace Manager, holding down the Command key while dragging a file icon to another window makes a copy of the file. Otherwise used in combination with other keys to perform specific actions. Many applications use Command keys for their own devious purposes.

## Alternate

Alternate has two main uses. The first use is to access special keyboard characters. Alternate-<alphabet key> produces an alternate character.

The problem with Command key equivalents is that developers quickly run through all the memorable combinations. The alphabet quickly becomes suffocatingly small when trying to assign tens (or hundreds) of commands to keyboard combinations. The Alternate key, like the Macintosh Option key, brings some aid, at the cost of requiring users to memorize yet another set of combinations.

Alternate has many predefined NextStep uses, most often Alternate-mouse actions: Alternate-scroll arrow click to scroll a page at a time, for example.

## Shift

Primarily used to capitalize letters. Some applications use the Shift key as yet a *third* Command key, usually to add a "superset" action to an existing action. In WriteNow, the Shift-cursor key both moves the cursor and selects the area passed over as the cursor moves—a superset of cursor key movement. Mathematica, as another example, uses Shift-Return to signal that an equation should be processed.

## Tab

A holdover from typewriter days, Tab moves the insertion point to the next "tab stop" in word-processing applications. In the NextStep interface, Tab is used most often to move forward between text fields. Considerate applications often add Shift-Tab to move backward through text fields.

## Esc

The Esc (for "Escape") key is often used in UNIX applications, most notably in the EMAC's word processor, where Esc stands in for the Command key.

## Delete

The Delete key is a "destructive backspace." In text, it moves the insertion point backwards, erasing anything in its path. In other applications, it mimics the Clear menu command. The Delete key autorepeats, as do the alphabetic keys. How fast it autorepeats, and how soon the autorepeating begins, is set in Preferences.

## The Mouse

The NeXT mouse is optomechanical. You move the mouse, which rolls the mouse ball, which moves the cursor on-screen. Two Teflon pads on the mouse's bottom ensure smooth rolling. And a black rubber band around the mouse puts an end to those noisy mouse-keyboard collisions. (The keyboard is also swathed with a thin rubber strip, thank goodness. God is in the details, as they say.)

One mouse button is dedicated to bringing up the main menu (unless you uncheck "Enable menu button" in Preferences), and the other button is used for traditional NextStep duties: clicking, dragging, and so on.

Other manufacturers offer one-button mice (Apple), two-button mice (Microsoft and others), and three-button mice (DEC and others.) As always, it's a trade-off: more buttons allow for more functionality, at the expense of confusing users with too many functions.

NeXT's choice was sound. If you don't care for the "bring up the Main Menu under the cursor" feature, both buttons act identically, giving you a two-buttoned "one-button" mouse.

Developers may use both buttons for their own purposes. Though we haven't yet seen it, some applications may implement "press both buttons" to access a feature.

# Chapter 9

## Inside the Cube

**Hardware** *n.* The easy part of the system.
  — STAN KELLY-BOOTLE in *The Devil's Dictionary*

*We want to own the term "workstation"*
  — STEVE JOBS

This is where the real computer is. The heart of the NeXT. Inside the cube. The motherboard, the power supply, disk drives, and the system bus.

Let's back up and out for a minute. Before you design a computer—before you design anything—you need to make some basic decisions. The most important is this: what, exactly, do you want to make?

That decision was made by NeXT, and The NeXT Computer is the result. But what is it? Is it an academic computer? A workstation? A high-end personal computer? (There's a title that's fallen out of favor. Most households don't have an extra $10,000 lying around to pop for a computer.) Or is it a scientific computer? Or a business computer?

## Designing Computers

The answer, of course, determines the design.

So what is it? These days, NeXT is calling it "a general-purpose business computer."

That makes sense. Business, after all, is the largest market for computers. To sell a lot of computers, call it a business computer.

But to call The NeXT Computer a "business computer" is to give it far less than its due. (Or to give other computers more credit than they deserve!) My hunch is that NeXT's design strategy is simpler and more encompassing. NeXT set out, pure and simple, to make the best computer in the world.

Period.

How's that done? By combining high speed, and vast storage, and CD-quality sound and music, and wonderful graphics, and built-in networking. And slots for extensibility. And an unparalleled development environment. And more.

Making the best computer in the world takes great software and great hardware.

Making great software is simple. It requires only great people, much money, and time.

Making great hardware? Now it becomes interesting. With the exception of the read/write optical disk, NeXT hardware features are found on other computers—though they're seldom all found in one computer.

It's not hard. You just take a bunch of chips and string 'em together. Naturally, to include all the features above, you'll need a lot of chips. They won't all fit on one circuit board, so you'll need a number of circuit boards.

That's how it's traditionally done. The chips cost money, the boards cost money, the "card cage" to hold everything costs money, and a huge power supply to keep all those boards cool costs money.

And that's why high-end, powerful computers are expensive. They're expensive to make. Software investments (in a simplified view) are one-time investments. Hardware costs, in contrast, dog each machine.

Great hardware design means "doing the most with the least." Using only a minimum of chips. And squeezing maximum function from each chip. Great hardware designers say things like "I can do that with...two chips." (When IBM announced the IBM Personal Computer, a hardware engineer at Apple took one look at the IBM motherboard and said, "Too many chips. It looks like it was designed by a kid in high school.")

Fewer chips mean lower manufacturing costs, and greater reliability—since there're fewer parts to fail. And fewer chips require less power, so money's also saved on the power supply.

It's not hard to make a powerful computer. It's hard to make a powerful *affordable* computer. Until now, the Macintosh was acknowledged to be the most artful hardware design: a wealth of function from very few chips.

That crown now belongs to NeXT. The NeXT motherboard is an engineering marvel. All the cube's hardware functions (with the exception of a small digital board in the display) are contained in 45 chips.

It's difficult to overstate the importance of this engineering feat. (I'm trying my best, though.)

NeXT didn't stop there, however. They also designed for maximum "throughput."

Computers are complex webs of devices. Some devices are fast, and some are slow. It's misleading to judge overall system speed based on only one component.

It's misleading, but it's done all the time. Other companies have been quick to make comparisons with NeXT based on MIPS: how many Millions of Instructions Per Second can be squeezed from the machine.

It's getting to be a MIPS world. Intel and Motorola are escalating the MIPS wars, announcing faster and faster chips. 20 MIPS here, 50 there, this new chip that pumps 100 MIPS on the way. Journalists join the fray; when there's nothing new to talk about (always a problem with IBM PCs), they talk about MIPS and faster clock speeds.

So how fast is the NeXT? 5 to 7 MIPS, give or take. But NeXT doesn't like talking about MIPS. They'd rather talk about "total system throughput."

Which makes sense. If you've got the fastest microprocessor in the world, and a slow hard disk, will the computer seem fast?

No.

What if the screen is slow on the draw? If your RAM chips are slow and your processor is fast, guess what happens. How about bus speed?

NeXT is right on this one. It's a mistake to look merely at processor speed.

The NeXT attitude is reminiscent of Rolls-Royce. You'll never see a "top speed" given for a Rolls-Royce. Ask a Rolls-Royce salesman how fast the car goes and you'll be told "As fast as you require, sir."

Computers haven't gotten to that stage, yet. For now, boosting overall speed means maximizing throughput: find the slow components, the devices that bog down system performance, and concentrate design efforts there. Eliminate the weak links, or at least improve their performance as much as possible.

As we look at the individual components, remember the goals: few chips, maximum function, maximum throughput.

## The Motherboard

The NeXT motherboard contains 45 chips. The major components are:

- three microprocessors:
  a Motorola MC68030 microprocessor,
  a Motorola MC68882 floating-point math coprocessor, and
  a Motorola DSP56001 digital signal processor;
- two custom VLSI (Very Large Scale Integration) chips designed by NeXT:
  an ICP (Integrated Channel Processor) to handle input/output, and
  an OSP (Optical Storage Processor) to control the Canon optical disk drive;
- 4 to 16 megabytes of RAM memory;
- a NuBus-like system bus,
- interfaces to networks, hard disk drives, serial devices, printers, and the MegaPixel Display, and
- other, support, components.

## The MC68030

The MC68030 microprocessor is NeXT's central processing unit. The 68030 is a successor to the 68000 processor first widely used in the original Macintosh computer. Motorola followed the 68000 with the 68010, then the 68020, and 68030. Each processor built on the strengths of the 68000: many address and data registers and a clean "orthogonal" instruction set. What that means is that the low-level microprocessor instruction set presents a consistent face to programmers. Motorola also made sure each new processor was "backward compatible" with programs written for earlier processors. If programmers didn't do anything tricky, they could be assured that software written for 68000s would run fine on new, faster, snazzier 68020s and 68030s.

This doesn't mean that Macintosh software will run on NeXTs (though NeXT marketing types may dream of such things often). But it does mean that NeXT software should continue to work fine if NeXT moves up to the newest Motorola offering: the 68040.

As the 68000 evolved, the quest has always been for more speed. Since backward compatibility has always been a must for Motorola, the need for speed limited improvements to certain areas. You can't reinvent the wheel and still achieve compatibility with existing software. So the evolution of the 68000 focused on a few particular areas.

The first was faster clock speed. Like car engines, microprocessors can run at different speeds. The microprocessor speed is determined by its "clock rate," given in megahertz. The faster the better. The 68000 was first offered at 8 MHz, followed by a 10 MHz version. (As the chip-manufacturing process improves, higher rates are possible.)

The 68020 was offered in a range of speeds: 12.5, 16, 20, 25, and 33 MHz. The 16 MHz version of the 68020 was used by Apple in the Macintosh II.

The 68030, used by NeXT, is available in speeds from 16 to 33 MHz (the 12.5-MHz version isn't offered, presumably because no manufacturer would want such a slow processor). NeXT uses the 25-MHz version.

Why not go all the way up to 33 MHz? Two reasons. First, the higher the clock speed, the more expensive the processor. Production "yields" on high-speed processors are small, so chip makers are forced to charge more (much more) per chip. The smaller yields also mean that manufacturers often can't be guaranteed desired quantities. Had Apple, for example, used a 33-MHz 68020 in the Macintosh II, demand may have outstripped Motorola's production. Users would have been crabby and Apple's revenues would have suffered.

In general, mass-market computer makers shy away from the fastest chip offerings. They're expensive, less reliable, and available in reduced quantities. Only when production improves, and prices fall, do the faster chips become standard issue.

Early versions of The NeXT Computer used a slower, 20-MHz version of the 68030. The 25-MHz chip was then substituted. As Motorola ramps up production, NeXT may eye the 33-MHz version for future machines. Still, a faster processor isn't a panacea. Overall system speed is still the watchterm at NeXT. Clock speed is only one factor.

Another way to improve microprocessor speed is through tricky design. Here the 68030 shines. One trick is doing two things at once. While one portion of the 68030 is processing an instruction, another processing area is off getting (and decoding) the next instruction. It's called instruction pipelining. It means that the 68030 uses its speed to the best advantage: when an instruction can be processed, it's right on the doorstep.

Another trick is the use of caches. Computer programs consist of instructions and data. The instruction might be ADD and the data might be two numbers. The microprocessor needs to "fetch" both instructions and data from memory; either from RAM memory or from disk. This takes time.

To minimize all this shuffling and fetching of memory, the 68030 has two on-chip caches, one for instructions and one for data. Each cache contains 16 entries of the most recently used instructions and data, and their addresses in memory. When the 68030 needs something, it first checks its own on-chip cache. If the instruction or data is there, it's used—bam. The performance speed-up is dramatic.

Internally, the 68030 is a 32-bit processor. With microprocessors, the more bits the better. The original Apple II used an 8-bit processor, the 6502. Mainframe computers often use 64-bit processors (though 32 bits was considered "main-frame" not long ago.) More bits mean longer computer "words"; more information can be processed in a single clock cycle.

While the 68xxx line has always had an internal 32-bit architecture, earlier mod-els—like the 68000—talked to the rest of the computer through a "bus" of 16-bit address lines. In contrast, the 68030 has full 32-bit address and data lines. Where the 68000 had 64 or 68 "pins" (depending on the model) to connect to memory, the 68030 is festooned with 128 pins. Better still, the 68030, unlike earlier proces-sors, doesn't use one set of lines for both addresses and data. Address and data lines for the 68030 are separate, which makes for a less complex design and more speed.

The greater the number of address lines, the more total system memory can be "reached" by the microprocessor. That's why early personal computers, which typically used 8-bit processors, could only access 64K of RAM memory.

What do 32 bits translate to?

Four gigabytes.

In theory, The NeXT Computer can handle 4,096 megabytes of RAM memory! 4,096 megabytes of RAM! Or, to put it another way: 4,096 megabytes of RAM!

Expect to see add-on memory boards, for those times when 16 megabytes of RAM (the maximum you can stuff on the motherboard) isn't enough. We'll have more to say about RAM soon.

## The PMMU

Making microprocessors faster requires figuring out ways to both make them do more, and make them do less. Do more, by making sure that the central processing unit is seldom idle. Do less, by off-loading computations whenever possible.

We covered virtual memory earlier. We said then that virtual memory, in a sense, "tricked" applications into thinking they were living in a world of unlimited RAM memory.

That's not actually true (sorry about that). What *really* gets tricked is the central processing unit in the 68030.

Hardware designers think in terms of physical memory and logical memory. Physical memory is where something really is. Logical memory is where some component thinks it is. My apologies for speaking of these guys in human terms.

To the central processing unit in the 68030, it's simpler to perform computations on logical addresses. And simpler is faster. That means, however, that additional computations need to be done somewhere else, to translate between the logical and physical addresses.

That task, traditionally, was done by specialized processors called "paged memory management units." The PMMUs handled the translation of addresses, and all other computations involved with virtual memory. The central processing unit, unhindered by these memory-management computations (which aren't trivial), blazed about its business, logically churning through computations of logical addresses.

Time passes. Microprocessor technology improves. (It's easy to forget how awesomely hard it is to create these small wonders. The 68030 contains the equivalent of 600,000 transistors in a single component smaller than a breadbox.) Soon after the development of the 68020, it became possible to put all the functions of a PMMU chip on the main processor chip—in this case, the 68030.

As with on-chip caching, placing memory management functions on-chip resulted in dramatic speed-ups. It also saved on motherboard "real estate," lowered overall power consumption, and cut component prices by about 20%; it's cheaper to buy one somewhat more expensive CPU than it is to buy both a CPU *and* another chip for memory management.

As processors like the 68030 add more on-chip functions, it becomes more and more erroneous to speak of microprocessors as chips that merely process instruction after instruction. The 68030, more than any other current chip, has a large degree of "parallelism." Many things are happening at once. At the lowest levels in the computer, parallel processing is in effect. At higher levels, Mach is multitasking away. At still higher levels, NextStep is letting you run many applications at once. At the very highest level, you're trying to remember just which applications you've set in motion.

Before we leave the 68030, let's note that computer journalists are usually "microprocessor skirt-chasers." While the 68030 is a marvelous processor, there's always a "better, faster, neater" processor just up ahead, just going into production.

The design of The NeXT Computer began over three years ago. At that time, the 68030 *was* that better, faster, neater chip. Today, the 68030 is still fast, and still neat. To add a faster, newer processor wouldn't necessarily make the cube any faster. A faster, whizzier processor might only drag its heels waiting for slower system components (memory chips, for example) to do their job.

## The 68882

Floating-point numbers are the bane of microprocessors. Integers are the microprocessor's diet of choice. Integers can be easily expressed as binary numbers, then manipulated extremely quickly.

Floating-point numbers, however, are a pain. Imagine: $1.00045678 \times 34.567^{532}$. Those numbers first need to be converted to binary before the computation can be performed. This takes time. Microprocessors grind out floating-point calculations at a (relative) snail's pace.

Specialized floating-point microprocessors are the answer. These "coprocessors" are microprocessors in their own right; they have data registers, instruction sets, and other microprocessor features. But they're specialized for floating-point calculations. Math coprocessors don't do address calculations, for example.

The 68030 has built-in instructions for common math operations. If a math coprocessor is present, however, the coprocessor handles the math—and every cube has a math coprocessor: Motorola's MC68882 Floating Point Math Coprocessor.

In addition to the common math operations, the 68882 adds instructions for floating-point, trigonometric, and transcendental math. (Transcendental numbers are those like pi, which has been computed to millions of decimal places. You can imagine how much fun it is to express transcendental numbers in the limited "bits" available in a microprocessor!) A few of the built-in instructions of the 68882 are:

| Instruction | Function |
| --- | --- |
| FABS | Absolute Value |
| FACOS | Arc Cosine |
| FASIN | Arc Sine |
| FATAN | Arc Tangent |
| FATANH | Hyperbolic Arc Tangent |
| FCOS | Cosine |

and many more, including FSINCOS (Simultaneous Sine and Cosine). These instructions are microcoded, on-chip instructions. In all, forty-six instructions, including thirty-five arithmetic instructions. A carefully chosen instruction set—and they really rip. Also "hard-coded" on-chip in ROM (read-only memory) are twenty-two constants, including e, pi, and powers of ten.

The 68030 and the 68882 FPU (for "Floating Point Unit") are closely mated. When a floating-point number comes along, it's automatically off-loaded to the 68882 for processing. Programmers need do nothing special to access the 68882;

if floating-point math is required, the 68882 kicks in. (Fanatical speed freaks can directly access the 68882 using assembly language.)

Once in the FPU, the number is converted to an 80-bit extended-precision real data format: a 64-bit mantissa plus a sign bit, and a 15-bit signed exponent. The FPU has eight general-purpose data registers to hold these incredibly precise numerical representations.

Although numbers are converted internally to an 80-bit format, the FPU accepts these data types from the 68030:

- bytes;
- word (two-byte) integers;
- long word (four-byte) integers;
- single-precision real numbers;
- double-precision real numbers;
- extended-precision real numbers; and
- packed binary coded decimal string real numbers.

The 68882 is particularly well-suited to Display PostScript, which is staunchly floating-point-based. When a programmer sets a line's width using a Display PostScript command, for example, it's done like this:

```
PSsetlinewidth (2.0);
```

Integers are never, never sent when using Display PostScript. That way lies death for programs.

The 68882 is a successor to Motorola's 68881 coprocessor, which is an option on the Macintosh II. Overall, the 68882 is 1.5 times faster than the 68881.

The features of the MC68882 go on and on. It's an amazing chip and worth a closer look if you're interested in mathematics or computer hardware.

## The DSP56001

Math coprocessors, however marvelous, are now common fare in many high-end computers. Sometimes they're included in every computer—as they are in the cube—and sometimes they're optional.

One chip you won't often see is Motorola's DSP56001. To include the DSP56001 as standard equipment in every NeXT computer was a bold, visionary move by NeXT. The DSP56001 is a sophisticated, expensive chip. It's usually only available (if it is available at all) on add-on boards costing thousands of dollars. By including a DSP56001 in every cube, NeXT raised the "lowest common denominator" of computing in a single stroke.

The DSP prefix stands for "Digital Signal Processor." The 56001, like the 68882, is a specialized processor. The DSP's specialty is extremely fast processing of, well...sound. And more.

When it comes to the DSP, NeXT doesn't shy away from touting MIPS. Clocked at 25 MHz, the DSP processes an instruction every two clock cycles, which translates into a 10 MIPS rating. That's enough speed to process sounds in "real-time," with no lag—an amazing feat considering the massive computations needed to manipulate sound.

As an aside, here's a personal experience. I was fortunate to be involved in the design of a Macintosh program called SoundWave, which allowed users to record and manipulate sound. (The software came with an audio digitizer which converted sounds into streams of data for use by the SoundWave software.) One of SoundWave's features was an on-screen "graphic equalizer." To boost the high frequencies, for example, you moved (moused, actually) a slider, just like in "real life."

The problem was that, unlike in real life, you didn't immediately hear the difference. The program had to first apply a "fast Fourier transform" to the digital sound data before you could hear the result. And it was slow. Painfully slow. Really, really slow. Not because of programming; we had a great programmer who did the best possible job. The fast Fourier routine was even written in assembly language for maximum speed. But it was still slow: move the slider, go out for lunch. That kind of thing.

It was slow, simply, because the fast Fourier transform, like most routines that manipulate digital sound, requires hundreds—thousands—of complex calculations. The fact that the DSP can process sound in real time is a remarkable hardware achievement.

The DSP's speed, like that of the 68030, comes, in part, from parallelism. The DSP has three on-chip processing units: an arithmetic logic unit, an address generation unit, and a program control unit, all of which can operate at once. The chip also has 8K of fast (zero wait state) static RAM to ensure that data is quickly available for processing, or output to other components.

The DSP's instruction set is a remarkably tightly-coded set of 62 mnemonics tailored for processing sound, and "matrixes" of x and y data. Every instruction can execute in just two clock cycles.

Computers digitize sound by "slicing" it into chunks of data called "samples." The sound quality that results depends on two things:

- how frequently the sound is sampled; and

- how many bits are used to contain the sample.

Higher-quality sound contains more digital information than low quality sound—just as a detailed screen image contains more pixels than a lower resolution image. The more bits used, the more information is contained.

The DSP uses two 16-bit channels for sound sampling—two-channel stereo. The sampling speed is typically either 22.05 kHz or 44.1 kHz. The lower sampling rate, 22.05 kHz or 22,050 samples *per second,* digitizes into average sound quality; about what you'd hear over a good phone line. The higher sampling rate of 44.1 kHz (44,100 samples a second) produces CD-quality sound; breathtakingly pure with a dynamic range encompassing all of human hearing. Words can't do justice to the sound quality. (Nor can the cube, in fact. An external amplifier and speakers—just use the display's line-out jacks—are what's needed.)

The DSP can be used in many ways. One of the most basic is playing sounds. Sound playing puts only the slightest burden on the 68030. In effect, the DSP handles all the sound playing while other applications run, at the same time, unbothered.

Applications use the DSP to record sounds. Mail and SoundPlayer, both shipped with the cube, use only the lower sampling rate, and only hint at the recording possibilities of the DSP. Software from other vendors, some shipping and some to come, will make more complete use of this remarkable chip for recording and altering sound.

Let's pause at the words "altering sound" for a moment. We've only mentioned the most mundane DSP capabilities so far. The DSP is also a synthesizer-on-a-chip. Any sound you can imagine (and many you can't) can be synthesized by the DSP. The possibilities for musicians and music academicians are immense. Record one note from a Stradivarius, for example, then create a string ensemble of Stradivaria. (There are some legal issues here that you should examine, however, before "using" sounds created by others—particularly if you'll use the synthesized sounds for commercial purposes.)

Support for the DSP is contained in the MusicKit, which consists of 29 predefined classes for working with sound and music. Here's a glance:

```
localhost# ls
NoteSender.wn        ScorePerformer.wn
Conductor.wn         Orchestra.wn         ScoreRecorder.wn
Envelope.wn          Part.wn              ScorefilePerformer.wn
FilePerformer.wn     PartPerformer.wn     ScorefileWriter.wn
FileWriter.wn        PartRecorder.wn      SynthData.wn
Instrument.wn        Partials.wn          SynthInstrument.wn
Midi.wn              PatchTemplate.wn     SynthPatch.wn
Note.wn              Performer.wn         TuningSystem.wn
NoteFilter.wn        Samples.wn           UnitGenerator.wn
NoteReceiver.wn      Score.wn             WaveTable.wn
```

For most uses, that complete set of classes should be enough. For more control over the DSP, programmers can create "DSPWraps," which "wrap" a C language interface around a small chunk of DSP assembly language code. For ultimate access to the DSP, NeXT provides Motorola's DSP assembler. If you already know some variant of assembly language, you'll find DSP assembly language programming...challenging, at the least.

The DSP isn't limited, however, to digitizing, playing, and synthesizing sound. The DSP56001 is a full-fledged microprocessor, ideally suited to manipulating any data that can be expressed in lists, tables, or x-y pairs of data. So it's perfect for matrix math calculations, sophisticated image processing, or two-dimensional graphics generation. Other uses? Voice recognition. Face recognition. Speech synthesis. Real-time data filtering. Data compression and decompression.

Or how about a "modem on a chip?" The DSP contains most everything needed to make a modem. NeXT lore has it that the DSP was originally planned as the heart of a built-in 9600-baud modem. But adding all the features necessary would have entailed a smoosh more hardware and (more important at the time) a complete motherboard redesign. It didn't happen, but adding a NeXT-specific, DSP-based modem still requires only very little additional hardware. And given the power of the DSP, a "NeXTFax" would also require little additional hardware.

## RAM and ROM

The NeXT motherboard has 16 SIMM (for Surface-mount In-line Memory Modules) sockets for RAM. Currently, NeXT ships 1-megabit SIMMs. The RAM chips have a rated speed of 100 nanoseconds. That's quicker (and more expensive) than most RAM chips, but necessary to keep up with the rest of the system.

Eight megabytes is the default memory configuration. Adding more RAM boards ups the count in 4-megabyte increments to 12, then 16 megabytes of RAM: the maximum possible without using additional cube slots or higher-megabit RAM chips.

But what if you do use higher-megabit RAM chips? It can be done. It's now possible to buy 4-megabit RAMs. In that case, each RAM board would contain *16 megabytes* of RAM. The total RAM—on the motherboard only, remember—would then be a staggering *64 megabytes* of RAM.

It's certainly possible, but the cost would stagger your pocketbook. As this book was written, 4-megabit SIMMs cost about $1,000 per four-megabyte module, so 64 megabytes of RAM would set you back...$16,000.

The good news is that industry analysts say 4-megabit RAM prices will fall. By late 1990, that same 64 megabytes of RAM may cost only $9,500 or so.

Wishful thinking aside, what's the "right amount" of system RAM?

Sixteen megabytes.

Which is an unfair statement. Certainly, the more RAM the better. That's always the way. But for most users, and most uses, 8 megabytes will get you by just fine. You won't be able to run as many applications as *smoothly* as if you had 12 or 16 megabytes, but you won't be unduly cramped. In practice, very few users actually need to run concurrently processing applications. You might have *launched* more than one application, but in most cases, you're only working in the frontmost application. The other applications aren't really doing anything, they're just hanging around, waiting for a double-click to bring them to life.

The motherboard also has other, strategically used, chunks of memory. The largest is 256K of dual-ported RAM devoted to the video display. The screen image never uses main system RAM; it's all contained here, which keeps memory design simple and screen updating fast.

There's also 32K of fast 45-nanosecond static RAM divided between the DSP (24K) and the Optical Storage Processor (8K, used for memory buffers to speed optical disk reads and writes).

That's the RAM. What about ROM? Other computers typically use Read-Only Memory to hold start-up procedures, system information, routines used by graphic interfaces, fonts...many things. Macintosh, for instance, has 256K ROMs that contain Quickdraw software routines and other software that makes Macintosh uniquely Macintosh.

NeXT took a different approach. NextStep isn't in ROM. The Appkit routines used to create NeXT applications aren't in ROM. Instead, system software is on disk: optical disk. When NeXT upgrades to 2.0 and 3.0 and beyond, users won't have to purchase "ROM upgrades," but merely slide a disk in a slot.

Still, the motherboard has two small chunks of ROM. The first is 128K of ROM containing system diagnostic code and a small set of instructions to "bootstrap" the operating system into memory. Basically, only enough code to make a few system checks, then load the complete operating system from disk. Another chip holds 65K of EPROM (for Erasable Programmable Read-Only Memory) full of system settings. These settings, unlike the contents of RAM, are preserved when the cube is off.

## The ICP

Mainframe computers handle immense amounts of input and output. Terminals, disks, printers, plotters—the demands on the CPU are immense. Memory is read, and written to, constantly. To speed operation, mainframes often use specialized "Input/Output processors" to handle memory transfers. The I/O processors are memory "go-fers," if you will. Personal computers usually let the microprocessor handle all these chores.

The demands on NeXT's 68030 are also immense. To maximize system through-put, NeXT took a page from mainframe computer design, then did it one better. First, they dedicated 12 I/O channels with direct memory access (DMA) to system RAM. In conventional mainframe design, each channel would have an I/O processor chip, and possibly additional hardware.

What NeXT did next was startling and smart. They wrapped all twelve channels into a single, NeXT-designed custom chip. The VLSI (for Very Large Scale Integration) chip is a paragon of bit-blasting. Each channel has the equivalent of microprocessor registers to hold data and a 128K buffer to make sure that registers seldom need to wait for data. The chunks of data are blasted in chunks directly to and from memory. The increased system speed is remarkable, particularly in the frequent cases where repetitive data needs to be written to memory (white space on a page being prepared for printing, for example).

NeXT calls it an "Integrated Channel Processor," or ICP. The ICP is probably one reason that NeXT considered calling the cube a "personal mainframe."

Here's what's on the chip:

- two disk channels: one for the optical disk drive, the other for the SCSI hard disk drive;
- two sound channels: one for sound input, one for sound ouput;
- a channel to handle both serial ports;
- a channel for the DSP chip;
- a channel to send bit-images to the Laser Printer;
- a video channel, which writes data to the 256K video memory;
- two 32-bit Ethernet channels, one for input, one for output;
- a memory to DMA register channel; and
- a DMA register to memory channel.

The last two channels speed moving data between locations in main memory. The chip designer probably thought, "Well, as long as I'm here..."

The result of all this is speed. Sophisticated processors don't need to wait for data from main memory, or incoming data from various ports. And output devices, whether the display, speaker, printer, or network, get their data quickly. And, of course, all channels can be active at once, processing away at I/O. How fast? Well, up to 32 megabytes *a second,* in some cases. To users, the proof comes in those moments when you realize how many things are happening at once, or when you perform an action (saving a file is a good example) then notice that "Jeez that was fast!"

NeXT uses a second custom-designed VLSI chip: an Optical Storage Processor (or OSP) chip to handle the Canon optical disk. We'll cover it when we look at disk drives.

## I/O Ports

For the most part, the ICP channels work with the various input and output ports. The cube is loaded with ports, both conventional (serial and SCSI ports), and unconventional.

The every-cube-has-one Ethernet port marks NeXT's commitment to the idea that "networking is a given." It's powered by an AM7996 Ethernet transceiver chip with a maximum speed of ten megabits per second.

The monitor port sends +12 volts and -12 volts of DC power to run the display and carries the wealth of data that passes to and from the display: sound, video, mouse actions, and keyboard events. A number of ICP channels lend assistance with this.

The DB-25 SCSI port is Mac-compatible. It uses the lastest NCR SCSI interface chip (the 53C90) and has a maximum "burst" transfer rate of 4.8 megabytes per second. In theory, any Macintosh-compatible SCSI hard disk can be plugged in and used.

The DB-9 serial printer port has a maximum transfer rate of 5 megabits per second. When printing at 300 dpi, bits leave the cube at 1.8 megabits per second. 400-dpi printing ups the speed to 3.2 megabits per second.

Two RS-422 serial ports are provided. Both use 8-pin "mini-DIN" connectors—the same connectors used by Macintosh serial ports (so a Macintosh modem cable should work fine with the cube). A Z8530 chip is charged with both ports. Speed? When moving data in one direction only—synchronously—speed is 230.4 kilobits per second; the same as Apple's LocalTalk network. Asynchronous (two-way) transfers move at 38.4 kilobits per second.

The two serial ports *aren't* identical, though they have identical pin arrangements. In a thoughtful move, NeXT provides +5 volts of power on pin 7 (top middle) of serial port B. Consider this: early Macintosh models also offered five volts on a serial port. Hardware designers took advantage of this easy way to power devices. Digitizers, scanners, and other peripherals could be powered by simply plugging them into the serial port. No bulky "AC/DC adapters" to plug into the wall.

Unfortunately, these powered peripherals tended to overload the Macintosh power supply. Blown power supplies were common. Much finger-pointing ensued between hardware developers and Apple. We won't try and place the hardware design blame here. But Apple pulled the plug on the Macintosh Plus and subsequent models. No more powered serial ports. AC adaptors were needed to power devices.

So the five volts of power is a thoughtful move. Unlike Apple, NeXT needn't worry about power-supply overloading. The NeXT power supply, which we'll get to soon, has power to spare and more.

The final port is for exclusive use of the DSP56001. The connector is a DB-15, and provides both synchronous and asynchronous serial communication. You may also hear it referred to as a "MIDI port." It is that—this is where you'd plug in a musical keyboard. But it can also accept input from, and pass output to, a variety of devices. Time will tell just what those devices are.

## The Almost NuBus

The system bus is the backbone of the computer: the wires that carry signals and the "bus slots" to hold additional cards. The NeXT motherboard occupies one slot. Three more remain to fire—for now—the imagination of users and designers.

The importance of system buses was reflected in the "old days" when classes of computers were known by their buses. "S-100" computers used buses of 100 pins, which often lured you into believing that S-100 cards from one computer could be used in other S-100 computers.

Buses need to be fast, since they carry data, and they need enough wires to carry all the necessary signals. Beyond that, more esoteric considerations come into play. Hardware mavens will endlessly debate over which bus architecture is best.

But there's broad agreement that a bus developed by Texas Instruments, NuBus, is superb. Apple first brought NuBus to mass prominence by using a NuBus variation in the Macintosh II. NeXT added its own variations to NuBus and named the result "NextBus."

NextBus has a "NuBus-compatible backplane," according to NeXT. That doesn't mean that Macintosh cards will work; Apple doesn't match the IEEE 1196 NuBus specification for electrical bus signals.

One of the NeXT bus enhancements is speed. (You're probably getting the impression that these folks like speed. Speed is survival, these days.) NextBus runs at a clock speed of 25 MHz, to match processor speed. In contrast, the NuBus spec calls for a paltry 10 MHz bus speed. NeXT also uses a CMOS-level signal, instead of bipolar "TTL" logic. Here's a more detailed comparison, based on NeXT's "Next-Bus Preliminary Specification [993.AA]."

|  | NextBus | NuBus |
| --- | --- | --- |
| Clock speed | 25 MHz | 10 MHz |
| Duty cycle | 50%/50% | 75%/25% |
| System clock signals | 3 | 1 |
| Burst speed | double | regular |
| Bursts (in words) | 4/8/16/32 | 2/4/8/16 |
| Flow control | master/slave | slave only |
| Drivers | CMOS | TTL |
| Termination | none needed | required |
| Store and forward | yes | no |
| Parity bits | 4 | 1 |

Even if your degree isn't in electrical engineering, NeXT's bus looks better, doesn't it? (Request a copy of the entire bus specification from NeXT, if you want the whole story.)

An advantage shared by NextBus and NuBus is "form factor"—the allowable hardware board size. It's 10.840 inches by 10.637 inches, about 11" by 11". This is big. And it's the reason that the cube is a one-foot square: to make room for cards.

Although we can't expect third party card makers to duplicate the wizardry and compaction of the NeXT motherboard, an 11" by 11" card size, again, is *big*. With that much real estate to design on, expect tremendously powerful hardware add-on boards. The room is there, the chips can be had, and the power supply is generous. Remember, NeXT easily found room for sixteen megabytes of RAM on less than a quarter of the total motherboard area.

Hardware designers wishing to design for NextBus should contact NeXT to purchase a "bus interface chip." The price is nominal; about $25.

## The Power Supply

Power supplies and power supply designers get little respect. These are mere analog devices, after all. No digital magic here. Just analog conversion of alternating current into direct current to feed computer circuitry.

The design of computer power supplies is often a "do as little as possible" affair. Power supply components add greatly to a computer's cost. The more power you make available, the more money you'll spend on each power supply. And the larger the power supply becomes. And the heavier the computer becomes. So shipping costs rise! Everything is touched, it seems. As a result, firms stint on power and power supply design.

NeXT didn't stint. The NeXT power supply is a beautiful—and canny—engineering work.

Put yourself in the place of the power supply designer. On one hand, you've presumably got 60 Hz, alternating current coming in. Voltage should be 115 volts, but it could just as well be 110, 112, or 120 volts. It varies, somewhat, from place to place. A close look at the quality of electricity that spews from the everyday wall plug isn't for the faint-hearted. It ain't pretty. Very few homes or businesses receive the electrical equivalent of filtered spring water.

On the other hand, you have a myriad of devices to power, all of which expect pure, filtered, pristine direct current. The disk drives, display, fan, and motherboard slot all need power. The three remaining slots also need power—and hardware designers want all they can get. There's also that nasty "power-up pull" when everything wants power at once.

Oh—those are only *U.S.* voltages given above. Other parts of the world have 220 volt outlets (which could, of course, really be 213 or 237...).

Here's what NeXT did. They crafted a big, rugged power supply. 300 watts of power, allocated thus: 50 watts for the display (where a step-up transformer ups the voltage to needed levels), a hefty 25 watts for each slot (100 watts total), and most of the rest going to the optical and SCSI disk drives. With 300 watts to start with, there's a healthy spare cushion of power. (The design here is similar to stereo amplifiers, which are rated in watts per channel. More wattage does mean the stereo has more volume, but it also means that the sound is purer, because input variations don't momentarily overtax the amplifier.)

The NeXT power supply—and this is really clever—is "auto adjusting." It can handle input frequencies of 47 to 63 hertz. It can handle input voltages of 90 to 270 volts: a remarkable range. Not only can the cube take ragged U.S. electricity in stride, it can also be plugged in virtually anywhere in the world. And run just fine. No add-ons, no adjustments needed.

Anyone who thinks that NeXT intends to be a small U.S. computer company should look at the power supply.

## The Fan

Yes, there's a fan. With the potential of four 11" by 11" boards drawing 100 watts and spewing heat, along with an optical and SCSI drive, a fan is a must. The cube's fan is mounted above the power supply. It's quiet though noticeable, unless the optical disk is being accessed, which usually causes the neighbors to complain.

Pre-1.0 versions of the cube drew air in from the bottom—an invitation to collecting dust—and blew it out the back. Today's cube reverses that arrangement, which probably makes for a cleaner cube inside.

## Leave it on? Turn it off?

Your NeXT computer: should you leave it on or turn it off?

Programmers and assorted UNIX wizards tend to leave their computers on, always. Most users, though, turn off their computers when they're finished—at least at day's end.

Which is better?

The NeXT manuals come down hard on neither side of the issue, saying merely that the cube consumes roughly 100 watts of electricity. And that it's okay to turn it off or leave it constantly on.

So which is better?

On the face of it, the "leave it on" school has logic on their side. Constant on/off's, they say, are hard on hard drives, and deliver jolts and shocks to the computer circuitry. It's better to just leave the thing on, always.

I say this: bosh. Turn if off when you're done.

Here's why. If a single cube consumes 100 watts, then 10,000 cubes burn 1,000,000 watts. Let's say that NeXT sells 40,000 cubes in 1990. That's...ah...4,000,000 watts worth of cubes. Once NeXT hits 1 million in sales (and they will), it'll be 100,000,000 potential watts of power being drawn from...where? Smoke-stack spewing power plants? Nuclear reactors?

It's simple ecology. Power down your cube, save a planet. Everything helps. If everyone extinguished just one little candle...

While you're at it, fire up the Shell and "npppower off" if you're not using the Laser Writer. Why should it be on, even if when "on standby" it only consumes a dribble of electricity?

# Chapter 10

## Disks and Drives

*Cras ingens iterabimus æquor*
*"Tomorrow we'll be back on the vast ocean."*
             — **HORACE** 65–8 B.C.

No puny 20, 40, 80 or 100 megabyte drives here. NeXT offers massive mass storage options:

- a 330 megabyte internal hard disk;
- a 660 megabyte hard disk; and
- a 256 megabyte removeable read/write optical disk.

A minimum system has only the 256 megabyte optical disk. A loaded cube has the optical and a 660 megabyte hard disk. NeXT computer book writers, by default, have loaded cubes. Those hungry for still more storage can add an external SCSI hard disk.

Before we get into disk details, let's consider the rationale behind this massive disk capacity, and see which configurations make the most sense for various groups of users.

Although the puniest cube has only the optical disk, it's also possible to use the cube as a "diskless workstation."

A computer with no mass storage, not even a floppy disk, seems odd if you're accustomed to Apples, IBMs and other run-of-the-mill business computers. But workstations are usually networked, and workstation networks are often collections of powerful computers, standalone file servers, and terminals. Think of terminals as lobotomized computers: a display, keyboard, and not much else. The terminals use disk and processor resources on the network.

The cube is much more than a mere computer terminal. Take away the disk and you've still got immense computing power. You just don't have mass storage. The sharing of disk resources by these diskless computers is, for the most part, transparent to users. Files shown in directories reside on a server, not within your computer. For businesses, this is an economical way to go.

NeXT, not wanting to overlook this market, offers "Ethernet" as a startup option. When the cube is powered-up, it then looks not to a disk, but to the network for the necessary start-up files.

One step up is the "optical-disk only" cube. Despite the immensity of 256 megabytes on line, this isn't a recommended system for most users. The NeXT 1.0 software release comes close to filling a 256 megabyte optical! Although many files can be removed from the disk (Shakespeare can easily live on a back-up in a drawer), you may still find yourself swapping files between two optical disks. This isn't too painful for small or few files, but it's not recommended for copying large amounts of data.

Still, can you find happiness with only an optical drive? If it's a question of an optical-only or no cube, the answer is yes. A better solution for those on a budget is buying the minimum cube, then adding a third-party SCSI hard disk (any Macintosh-compatible SCSI hard disk should do). An additional $500 or so should buy enough capacity to take the load off the optical. If you want, you can "daisy chain" many SCSI hard disks together. Two, three, even four hard disks can be connected to the cube.

A two-optical, no-hard-disk arrangement is also possible. I'm not sure what the audience for this is. Maybe "naked cubes" for university students? The students could "bring their worlds with them" and system administrators wouldn't need to worry about tampering with the contents of a fixed disk. That's just a guess, and probably not a good guess.

A standard configuration is an optical with an internal 330 megabyte hard disk. Most users will be comfortable with this combination.

Only *comfortable*? Uh-huh. On most computers, this would be an awesome amount of disk storage. But most computers don't use UNIX, or offer the applications and reference material standard on The NeXT Computer. Roughly speaking, UNIX and NeXT system files, and bundled NeXT applications, take up about 80 megabytes of disk storage. UNIX manuals, NeXT documentation, dictionaries, and other reference material consume an additional 120 megabytes. In all, that is about 200 megabytes of programs, data, and references that are free with every cube. Not something to complain about.

The maximum configuration, an optical and 660 megabyte disk, is recommended for software developers, or those needing 100 or more free megabytes. (I've already heard of users putting years of New York Stock Exchange data on disk.) The larger hard disk is also the choice for cubes to be used as network file servers.

Considering their capacity, NeXT's prices are reasonable. The optical is $1,495; the 330 megabyte hard disk is $1,995; the 660 megabyte hard disk is $3,995.

## Hard Disks

Both the 330 and 660 megabyte hard disks are manufactured for NeXT by Maxtor. They're quiet and quick hard drives. Both drives have a maximum raw transfer rate of 4.8 megabytes per second, in "burst mode." Sustained transfer rates are 1.4 megabytes per second. Average seek times are 14.5 milliseconds for the 330 megabyte drive, and 16.5 milliseconds for the 660—both good times for hard drives. If you're accustomed to using a SCSI disk on another computer, you won't be disappointed. They really zip.

Benchmarks? The saying "Lies, damn lies, and benchmarks" comes to mind. It doesn't really matter how fast a hard disk is in theory. What matters is actual, everyday use. By that criterion, these are fast disks. I just rummaged around for a large file and came up with a 195K, 32,000 word, formatted WriteNow file. It opened in less than two seconds—and much of that time was probably due to WriteNow.

## The Optical Disk

Remarkably, the NeXT read/write optical disk is controversial. It's slow, say the technoids. It's expensive, say the pundits. And where's the floppy disk?

Floppy disks are right where they belong: on less powerful, less capable computers.

Floppy disks contain from 360K to about 1.5 megabytes, depending on type of floppy and formatting. In contrast, the NeXT optical disk has 235,600K or about 235 megabytes of available storage. (80 megabytes are reserved for error-correction code and Mach uses a small chunk for system information.)

How much is 235 megabytes? Enough for about 39 million (English) words.

At the introduction of The NeXT Computer, the optical disk was touted as "your world on a disk." It is that. For students, a single optical disk can easily hold four years of academic coursework. Most writers' life output will never fill a single optical disk.

What about storing images? As an example, let's assume the images are NeXT "screen dumps." To capture the four-bit-per-pixel NeXT screen image requires about 473,500 bytes: about half a megabyte per image. So an optical disk can hold 235,600,000/473,500 or about 500 of these large, detailed images.

Sound? A single optical can hold about 30 minutes of CD-quality, stereo sound. Or about an hour of good-quality, single-channel sound. Or hours of "telephone quality" sounds. Or lengthy multi-media productions combining text, sounds, and images.

But these are worst-case examples. Images and sounds can be, and usually are, compressed mightily. Text is also often compressed. The UNIX "compress" utility squeezes text files down to about 40% of their original size. So instead of 39 million words, a single optical disk could hold...well, it's humbling.

A single optical still isn't recommended as the sole storage device. But that's only because of the immense amount of data shipped on disk and used by the NeXT system. Empty opticals are capacious.

Here, as elsewhere, NeXT did "the right thing the right way." Computers were once calculation machines and fancy typewriters. With puny disks and limited RAM, that's about all they could be. With immense, removable, storage, computers can become what they should be: information machines.

## Anatomy of an Optical

To be precise, the cube uses a magneto-optical drive. The disks and drive mechanism are manufactured by Canon, which owns 16% of NeXT. The technology needed to make it work— contained, for the most part, in a single VLSI chip—was invented by NeXT.

More than any other system component, the read/write optical defines the cube. It's bold technology; NeXT says it "bet the company" on the creation of this technology. That may be hyperbole, but it may not be. Although other read/write opticals can be had, their cost is often that of a complete NeXT system, or more.

The optical disks are as wide as 5.25-inch floppy disks, and about 1/2" longer. And something over 1/4" deep. They won't fit in your shirt pocket, but a knapsack or briefcase (or hand) will do.

Unlike CD-ROM disks, the NeXT opticals are enclosed in a smoked-plastic case. The disk itself is made of three layers. The top layer is clear polycarbonate—the same plastic material used by CD-ROMs. It protects the disk. The bottom layer is reflective aluminum.

The middle layer is the key. It's an alloy: a rare-earth concoction that has characteristics of both crystals and metals. Like crystals, the alloy has a precise structural alignment. Like metals, the alloy can "change state." It can melt, then solidify.

Creating this alloy was a stunning achievement. It's good to see chemistry get its due in technology.

The fabrication of this alloy made the magneto-optical disk possible. Reading and writing to the disk is a "good cop, bad cop" combination of magnetics and laser beams.

Writing data to the disk uses both methods in three passes. The first pass across the disk is made by a high-powered laser beam. The beam heats the alloy to the "Curie point," a temperature which causes the crystal structure to "forget" its previous alignment. At the Curie point, the molecular alignment is up for grabs. Now, a magnetic field snaps the malleable matter to an alignment representing zero. The heat and magnetic field have, in effect, written a string of 0's to the disk.

The next pass writes data—1's—to disk. Again, the laser and a magnetic field are used in combination. At locations where a "1" is to be written, the laser again heats the alloy, and the magnetic field yanks the crystalline structure to the proper position.

The final pass uses only the laser, which scans the disk to verify the accuracy of the write operation.

Reading data uses only the laser beam. A low-power laser beam is used, to prevent melting—writing—on the disk. The beam passes through the alloy, then is reflected upwards by the aluminum backing. The reflected beam passes through a filter and into a photodetector. The beam's intensity when it reaches the detector has been polarized by the alloy's alignment. The polarization results in two beam intensities which correspond to the 1's and 0's previously written to disk.

Amazing technology.

In many ways, the optical drive is more rugged and more reliable than hard "Winchester" drives and floppy disk drives. A speck of dust on a hard disk can cause a "head crash" akin to a Ferrari hitting the side of a mountain at 200 miles per hour. Opticals don't have heads flying directly over the disk's surface.

Floppies and hard disks can be accidentally erased by stray magnetic fields; optical disks can't: only a strong, precise, close magnetic field can affect opticals. Finally, floppy disk "media" are relatively unprotected. Optical disks, like CD-ROM disks, are shielded in plastic. To sum it up, hard disks and floppy disks crash. Opticals don't.

It's one thing to invent a new technology and another to make it practical and affordable. To bring this technology out of the laboratory and into BusinessLand required devotion to speed, and data integrity.

Those two areas are the rest of the story.

## The OSP

The brains behind the optical drive are in another NeXT-designed VLSI motherboard chip: the OSP, for Optical Storage Processor. The OSP implements all disk controller hardware for the optical drive, and also controls internal and external SCSI drives, if present.

As elsewhere, parallelism is used to increase speed. The OSP has two buffers, each 128 bytes, to hold data that's simultaneously read from the optical disk and written out (through a DMA channel) to the 68030. During this double-buffered read/write operation, the data is also corrected if necessary, using a Reed-Solomon algorithm, which is microcoded on chip. The goal of the OSP is to process data as fast as it's received—from both the optical and 68030—while providing error detection and correction "on the fly."

## Optical Speed

Now for speed. The optical is slower than most hard disk drives, and much slower than the NeXT internal hard disk. From the explanation above, it's clear that writing data—which takes additional passes over the disk—is slower than reading data. Compared directly to the NeXT SCSI hard disk, it looks like this:

|  | **Optical** | **SCSI** |
|---|---|---|
| Average seek time: | 92 ms | 14.5 ms (330 MB disk) |
|  |  | 16.5 ms (660 MB disk) |
| Raw transfer rate, burst: | 1.14 MB/second | 4.8 MB/second |
| Raw transfer rate, sustained: | .83 MB/second | 1.4 MB/second |

"Seek time" is the time needed for the drive mechanism to travel to the desired location on disk, in preparation for reading and writing. That's where one of the big "performance hits" occurs, so seek time is widely quoted as one indication of overall disk speed.

It's clear that the NeXT hard disk is much faster here. For comparison, it's common to find IBM AT computers with hard-disk seek times of about 30 ms. Macintosh internal hard disks also have seek times of about 30 ms. Both those groups of hard disks would be slower than the NeXT SCSI disk (about twice as slow), but three times faster than the NeXT optical—judged only on seek times.

It's important to note that these are "average" seek times. How long it really takes a drive to get ready depends on a few factors. The farther the drive head has to move, for example, the longer it takes. "Close seeks" are much faster. The NeXT optical, when looking within five megabytes of its current position, performs a seek quickly, in about 20 ms. Part of the operating system's job is reducing the fragmentation of hard-disk files, so the drive head can sweep smoothly and quickly across the surface of the disk. The fewer far seeks, the faster.

Although the NeXT SCSI disk is noticeably faster in burst transfer mode (so-called because it can't be sustained for long periods), during sustained transfers of data, the optical comes out pretty well: 0.83 megabytes per second to the SCSI drive's 1.14 MB/second.

What does all this mean? First, that disk speed is iffy. And that disk speed, in large part, can be optimized by system software, just as NeXT has already optimized the disk hardware. For now, the optical is slower than the SCSI drive, though constant fine-tuning should improve the optical's overall times.

In real life, it feels like this. The optical is acceptably fast when reading data (most easily perceived when you're launching an application or loading a file). It's not gangbusters, but it's fine. Faster than a floppy disk. As fast as many hard disks found in IBM XTs. About what you'd expect, or faster than you'd expect—if you've been exposed to yabbering about the "slow optical."

When writing data—saving or copying files to the optical, for example—it's "thunk..thunkthunkthunk" instead of the SCSI's "..z..ziip." (Stop me if I'm getting too technical.)

## Using a Third-Party Hard Disk

Installing a SCSI hard disk—a non-NeXT hard disk, that is—isn't too difficult. It's not for the timid, but you probably won't need a "disk guru."

Here's how it's done.

First, connect the drive. If it's an external hard disk, just plug it in. If it's an internal drive, connect the drive to the power cable and SCSI "ribbon" cable.

If your drive is supported by NeXT, you can now build the disk and be done. In addition to the Maxtor drives, these hard disks are supported:

- the Hewlett-Packard 9754XS 324-megabyte drive;
- the Hewlett-Packard 8754BS 648-megabyte drive;
- the CONNER CP3040 40-megabyte drive;
- the CONNER CP3200 200-megabyte drive;
- the Sony SRD2040Z;
- the Quantum P40S 40-megabyte drive; and
- the Quantum Q250 40-megabyte drive.

By far the simplest course is to buy one of the hard disks, plug it in, format it, and go on with your life.

If your disk isn't in the list above, you've got some work to do.

Launch Shell. Enter:

```
localhost# /usr/etc/scsimodes /dev/rsd0a
```

You'll see a listing *similar* to this:

```
SCSI information for /dev/rsd0a
Drive type: MAXTOR XT-8760S
1024 bytes per sector
28 sectors per track
15 tracks per cylinder
1632 cylinder per volume (including spare cylinders)
4 spare sectors per cylinder
45 alternate tracks per volume
676415 usable sectors on volume
```

This listing details the NeXT internal 660-megabyte drive. Your drive may be different. Those differences must be communicated to the NeXT system.

Now you need to change a UNIX file: disktab. Its location is /etc/disktab. You should become familiar with disktab; you're about to change it. So open the file using Edit and learn the structure of disktab.

Basically, disktab contains information about the physical characteristics of hard disks (and the NeXT optical). The BuildDisk application relies on disktab's information.

Before making any alterations, make a backup of the disktab file. Using Duplicate in The Workspace Manager is the simplest method.

Okay, back to the original disktab file. You'll now change disktab to contain the information you gleaned from the "scsimodes" command.

You can do this in two ways. Either add a new entry, or change an existing entry. The less fearsome approach is to change an existing entry. You might choose the first entry to alter. Here it is:

```
XT-8760S-512|MAXTOR XT-8760S-512|Maxtor 760MB w/512 byte sectors:\
        :ty=fixed_rw_scsi:nc#1626:nt#15:ns#26:ss#1024:rm#3600:\
        :fp#160:bp#0:ng#0:gs#0:ga#0:ao#0:\
        :os=sdmach:z0#32:z1#96:ro=a:\
```

```
:pa#0:sa#413980:ba#8192:fa#1024:ca#32:da#4096:ra#10:\
       :oa=time:ia:ta=4.3BSD:\
:pb#413980:sb#220000:bb#8192:fb#1024:cb#32:db#8192:\
       :rb#10:ob=time:ib:tb=4.3BSD:
```

Some notes about the entry. First, the backslashes are only to make the listing readable. A backslash means "this line continued on the next line," and is ignored when the file is read. So what we've got here, really, is one very long line.

Now go in and change whatever's necessary to make the entry conform to the information detailed by scsimodes. The disktab file explains what each variable means. You should be able to match everything up with no trouble. If you *do* run into trouble, you may need detailed specifications from your hard disk's manufacturer. A good technical person should be able to guide you through any necessary changes over the phone.

Once the file is changed, save it. Now run BuildDisk as you would to build any disk. And keep your fingers crossed.

## Distribution

NeXT took care not to reinvent the entire computer industry. One area it hasn't yet tampered with is third-party software distribution.

Software distribution, at least as this book is being written, is a thorny issue. The thorn is the price of optical disks. The blank disks cost developers $50 each, with no quantity discounts, and can be purchased only from NeXT.

In comparison, blank floppy disks are about $1 each, in quantity. After commercial disk duplicators copy applications on floppies, the cost is still reasonable: about $1.50 a disk or less.

For consumers, that means higher application costs. The price of the optical disks must either be shouldered by developers (don't count on it) or passed on to purchasers.

That's the bad news. The good news is that optical disk prices will fall as production increases. To...maybe...$25, even $13 a disk. And remember, this is for a *256-megabyte* disk. Even at $50 a disk, the price per megabyte is good.

The other side of the "higher application prices" coin is this: NeXT applications aren't constrained by disk space. Today, some IBM applications come on ten or more floppy disks. You could hide the contents of ten measly disks on an optical disk and they'd never be found. NeXT optical disks allow developers to think big. To create applications bursting with and accompanied by data, sample data, templates, sound, music, speech, illustrations, maps, help files, tutorials, animations, simulations, catalogs, entire manuals, entire supplementary manuals, and really nifty Info panels.

NeXT has done their part here to "raise the common denominator" of computing. It's up to developers to follow through.

# Chapter 11

# The NeXT Laser Printer

*Vim et virtutem et consequentias rerum inventarum notare juvat;
quæ non in aliis manifestius occurrunt, quæ in illis tribus
quæ antiquis incognitæ, et quarum primordia, licet recentia,
obscura et ingloria sunt: Artis nimirum Imprimendi, Pulveris
Tormentarii, et Acus Nauticæ.*

*"It is well to observe the force and virtue and consequence of
discoveries, and these are to be seen nowhere more conspicuously
than in those three which were unknown to the ancients, and of
which the origin, though recent, is obscure and inglorious; namely,
printing, gunpowder, and the magnet [i.e. Mariner's Needle].
For these three have changed the whole face and state of things
throughout the world."*

— **FRANCIS BACON**  1561–1626

*"Desktop publishing"*

— **PAUL BRAINERD**  Aldus founder.

Printers don't get much attention. They're not glamorous.

That's as it should be. Printers should be "low attention" devices; as dependable as refrigerators.

The NeXT Laser Printer fits the bill. Its dependability comes, in large part, from what *isn't* in the printer.

The printer costs $2,596. (Student price is $1,995.) Laser printers typically cost $3,000 to $8,000. The main reason for the low price is that the NeXT printer doesn't contain a PostScript processing board. The Apple LaserWriter, Hewlett-Packard's LaserJet, and other popular laser printers are essentially self-contained

PostScript computers, with microprocessors (usually in the 68xxx line) and ROM software containing PostScript imaging software. Hook a dumb terminal up to these laser printers and you've got both a computer and a language (PostScript) to program it with.

NeXT crafted a brainless laser printer, hence the $1,995 price. This makes perfect sense. Why duplicate the PostScript interpreter in the cube?

## The Printing Process

Other computers send PostScript as a stream of ASCII text to laser writers for processing and imaging. On NeXT, the imaging is done in the cube. Applications create PostScript files. The PostScript files are converted by The Window Server into bitmaps. The bitmaps are then sent to the Laser Printer.

This is a burdensome process, even for the cube. Imaging is memory- and processor-intensive. Under the 0.9 operating system, the percentage of total CPU time used by The Window Server during imaging rose to as much as 99%—which caused other applications to momentarily "freeze." NeXT employees are spending much time (let's hope and assume) making sure that imaging doesn't slow down other current processes.

The image itself, when created, is big. Big enough that NeXT dedicated a Direct-Memory-Access (DMA) port to blasting the bloated bit images to the Laser Printer. The maximum transfer rate is 5 million bits per second—fast.

If your printing needs are great—if you'll be printing large, complex graphics—more memory helps. Sixteen megabytes isn't too much if you plan on printing while running other memory-intensive programs (like Mathematica, for one).

Inside the printer is a custom engine designed by Canon, now a shareholder in NeXT, Inc. The engine pumps out an *average* of eight pages a minute. Actual performance varies greatly depending on the complexity of the image. Complex graphics are slow, as you'd guess. Straight text flies. Top speed is possible (though for text only) directly from the shell, where the lpr command prints in a flash. Just type "lpr filename" in the shell for remarkably fast printing of text files.

The laser printer uses EP-S toner cartridges, as do Apple LaserWriters.

Let's take a paragraph for some "soft information."

The NeXT Laser Printer is a good product. NeXT designers did the printer right. It's powered by the cube, so you never have to fumble for a hidden "on" switch. The lever to open the top is *on top,* in plain view; a radical idea. Trays are easy to attach. If you wish, you can detach the output tray and have the printed sheets fall gracefully (onto a desk, in my case). For foreign operation, a switch to set voltage is in plain view under the cover. The input paper tray has the best, and easiest-to-use, paper-holding design I've seen. Feeding single sheets is particularly easy and—unlike with Apple LaserWriters—the single sheets don't sometimes print "kinda crooked," because you fed them "kinda sideways." In all, it's a very well-crafted machine.

It's also quiet, thanks in part to dual operation modes. When not printing, the Laser Printer goes into a quiet "standby mode," and sips a mere 110 watts—about the same as the cube. During printing, the power consumption leaps to 640 watts. Even during printing, though, the printer isn't objectionally loud. There's a "whine-up" and a hum, which ends soon after printing.

## 400 dpi

In a field where 300 printed dots-per-inch is the norm, the NeXT Laser Printer offers both 300 and 400 dpi. Nobody's ever figured out a reason for 300 dpi (other than saving printer toner, maybe), but it's an option.

Is 400 dpi a gimmick? No. It's noticeably sharper than 300 dpi. It's not a huge difference, but it's a difference. For an empirical rule of thumb, answer this question: What's the smallest type size, at 300 dpi, that you'd be willing to read in a book?

This is an iffy question. It depends on the font, and how it's set. Fuzzy laser printer print (compared to 1200 dpi and higher resolutions) needs to be "set" with additional leading—the space between lines—to be clear and easy to read. Books have been typeset on dot-matrix printers (even typewriters!) so it's not a question of what's possible, only what's "good." What isn't displeasing to read?

To me, 300-dpi printers produce good-looking type at 13 points or higher with most serifed fonts. Below that, it gets fuzzy fast. I'd prefer not to read a book set in 12-point Times Roman, for example, and printed on a 300-dpi LaserWriter.

At 400 dpi, the lower limit seems to be 12-point type. 12-point type looks good at 400 dpi: acceptably sharp and crisp. Anything larger only gets better.

When dpi is put into "square inch" perspective, the difference is clear. Three hundred dpi means 90,000 dots per square inch. Four hundred dpi is *160,000* dots per square inch—almost double the resolution.

## The Print Panel

NeXT offers developers a standard Print panel for use in applications.

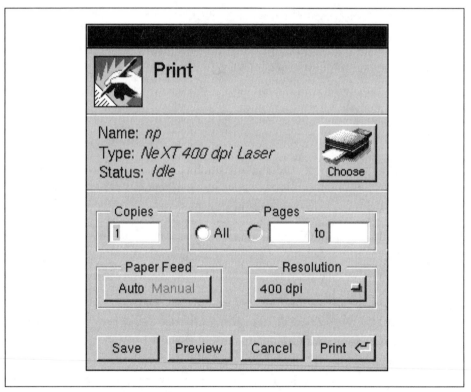

*Figure 11-1*

At the top left are the printer's name, type (the cube can support non-NeXT printers), and printer status information.

The print options are:

- the number of copies to print;
- whether to print all, or only a range of pages;
- auto or manual (fed by hand) paper feed;
- printer resolution (300 and 400 dpi are standard); and
- Save, a "print to disk" feature that creates a PostScript file which can be printed from another application, or transferred to another computer for printing.

The Preview button redirects printing. Instead of printing to the Laser Printer, the Preview application is launched, and Preview "Prints to Screen," for final proofing. Preview lets you page forward and backward through multiple-page documents, and zoom in and out of the document for closeup (and far-away) views of the document.

If it looks good, you can print the document from Preview. Take a look at Preview's options:

*Figure 11-2*

Back to the standard Print panel. The Choose button brings up another panel where you can choose a particular printer:

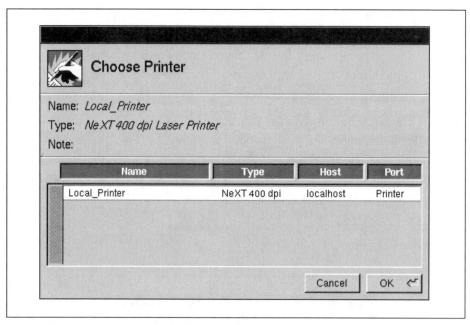

*Figure 11-3*

Other printers, if available, would be shown under "np" (for NeXT Printer). To choose a printer, click on a line and hit OK. The printers needn't be NeXT printers. Linotronic or other high-end typesetters may also be on the network and available for high-quality printing.

## Printer Definition Files

Of course, printers don't just magically appear in the Choose Printer dialog. For a printer to be supported, a Printer Definition File must be present. The "pdf" file resides on your boot disk (or on a network server, if you boot off the network).

The cube comes with three printer definition files that define:

- the NeXT Laser Printer;
- the Apple LaserWriter; and
- the Linotronic 100—a high-end, 1,270-dpi typesetter.

For an additional printer to appear in the Choose Printer panel, a new pdf must be created. This isn't particularly hard, but it takes good knowledge of both the printer in question, and PostScript.

Here's the first few lines in the "L100-380.pdf" file, which describes the Linotronic 100:

```
*% Adobe Printer Description File
*% For "Linotype" version 38.0
*% Produced by "GETapd.ps" version 2.0 edit 47
*% Date: <12/21/1987>
*FormatVersion: "2.0"
*LanguageVersion: English

*Product: "(Linotype)"
*PSVersion: "(38.0) 0"
*NickName: "Linotronic 100 v38.0"

*% General Information and Defaults ================
*ColorDevice: False
*FileSystem: True
*?FileSystem: "/initializedisk where{pop(True)}{(False)} ifelse = flush"
*% Edit *Throughput and remove this comment:
*%Throughput: "8"
*Password: "0"
*ExitServer: "serverdict begin exitserver"
*FreeVM: "182356"
*Reset: "
systemdict /quit get exec
(WARNING : Printer Reset Failed.) = flush
"
*End
*VariablePaperSize: True

*DefaultResolution: 1270dpi
*?Resolution: "
save
  initgraphics
```

```
0 0 moveto currentpoint matrix defaultmatrix transform
0 72 lineto currentpoint matrix defaultmatrix transform
3 -1 roll sub dup mul
3 1 roll exch sub dup mul
add sqrt round cvi
(            ) cvs print (dpi) = flush
restore
"
*End

*% Halftone Information ================
*ScreenFreq: "90.0"
*ScreenAngle: "45.0"
*DefaultScreenProc: Dot
*ScreenProc Dot: "
{abs exch abs 2 copy add 1 gt {1 sub dup mul exch 1 sub dup mul add 1
sub }{dup mul exch dup mul add 1 exch sub }ifelse }
```

## The Printer Application

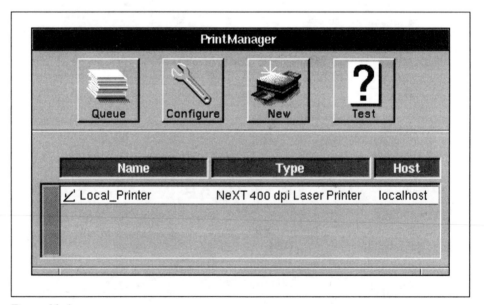

*Figure 11-4*

NeXT also offers a Printer application:

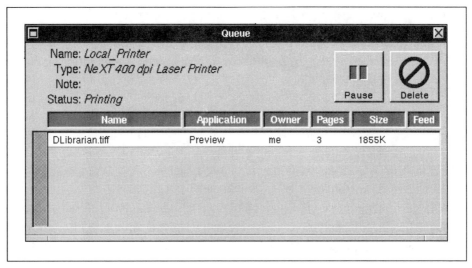

*Figure 11-5*

The Queue button brings up this panel:

where you can pause printing, or delete print "jobs" from the printing queue. The

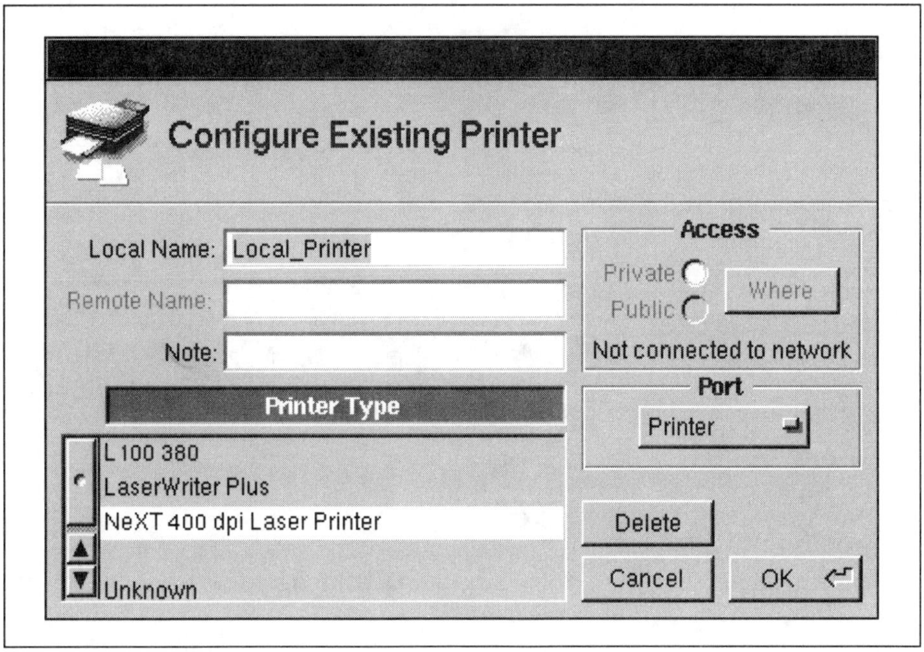

*Figure 11-6*

Configure and New buttons bring up essentially the same panel:

The Configure panel has a Delete button, not needed when putting a new printer on the network. The Port pop-up lets you attach the printer to the printer port, or the serial A or serial B port.

The Test button prints a lovely test sheet.

## Printer Problems

Your most common problem—as with all laser printers—will be paper jams. Thanks to a short (two feet), straight paper path in the Laser Printer, paper jams are infrequent. Unjamming is easy, though annoying. Just pop the printer open, and gently pull the jammed sheet out. A smooth pull is the way to do it; you don't want to rip the paper.

Jams and other errors are reported by panel or by voice: your choice, determined by a Preference setting.

Running out of toner is also a problem. To coax a few more pages from a toner cartridge, remove it and shake it, in a horizontal back-and-forth motion. This toner redistribution will get you a few more pages. You can also turn the contrast knob to darker printing. (Remember to turn it back when you replace the toner cartridge.)

## Choosing Paper

Paper that's too thick jams in the printer, and paper that's too thin comes out two sheets at a time. The double sheets are a minor inconvenience; you can always run the blank bottom sheets through again. Paper jams, though, are a hassle.

The way to prevent paper jams is proper paper selection. I've found that ordinary 20 lb. paper works fine. You can try heavier, thicker paper, but you'll jam eventually.

Buy paper in reams; either a ream at a time or a box of reams at a crack. Look for something that says (I'm reading a label on a ream right now...) "for laser printers, xerographic copiers, and offset duplicators." Copier paper, in other words.

And don't pay too much. For ordinary printing needs, you should currently be able to get a ream of good paper for $4-7. Paper's cheap; get a lot. Laser printers eat reams of paper, almost unbeckoned.

## Buying Toner

The best advice here is: Don't pay $100 for a toner cartridge.

Laser printing is big business these days. Making and refilling toner cartridges is also big business. You should be able to purchase EP-S toner cartridges for less than $70. Maybe as little as $60, if you shop around.

Many companies will take your old toner cartridge, refill it, and send it back—at a great savings over buying new toner cartridges. One company I'll recommend is Black Lightning, Inc. They'll sell you new toner cartridges, refill your old cartridges, offer you a variety of toner types, and do it all fast, at good prices. A great company. For prices, or a brochure of their services, call (800)252-2599. (436-3257 in Vermont). Or write them at RR1-87, Depot Road, Hartland, VT 05048.

A last toner note. Don't be cowed if your sales rep maintains that using third-party cartridges voids your NeXT warranty. It's a violation of U.S. antitrust laws to require exclusive use of manufacturer's parts. You can use any spark plug you want in your car; you can use any toner cartridge you want in your Laser Printer—without voiding your warranty.

# Intermission

## Images

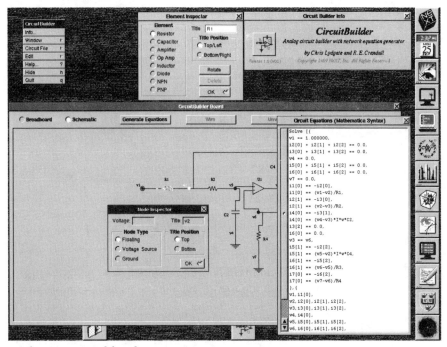

The CircuitBuilder demo

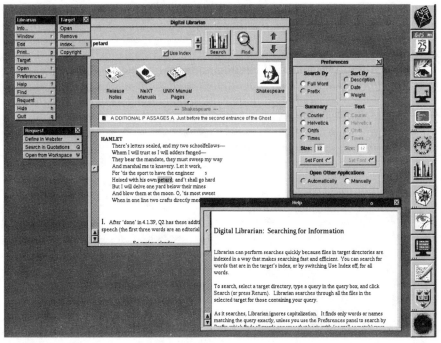

Digital Librarian

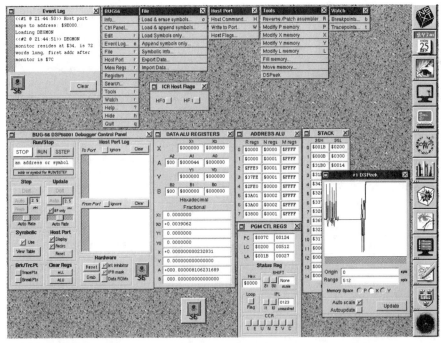

The DSP Debugger

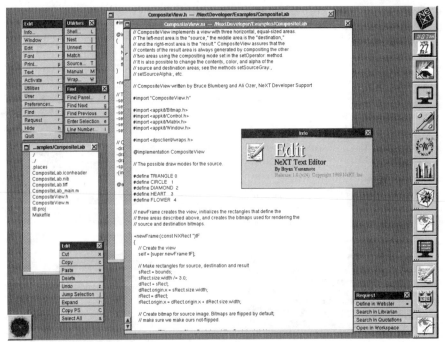

The Edit application

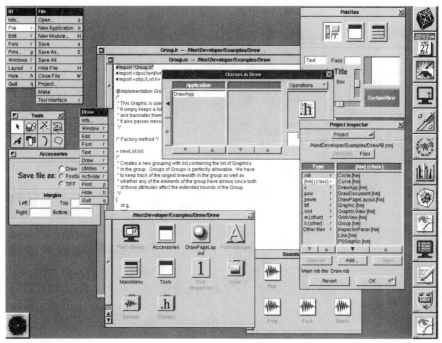

Interface Builder

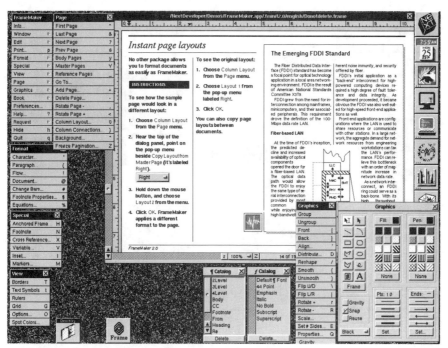

The Framemaker demo

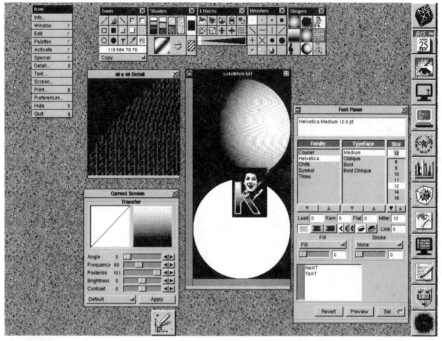

The Icon application

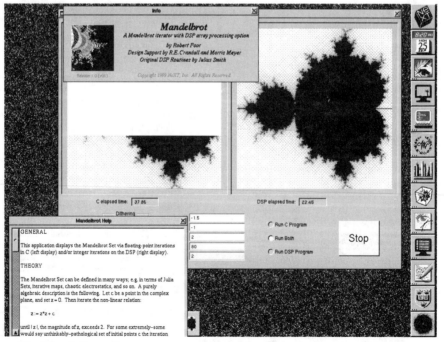

The Mandelbrot demo

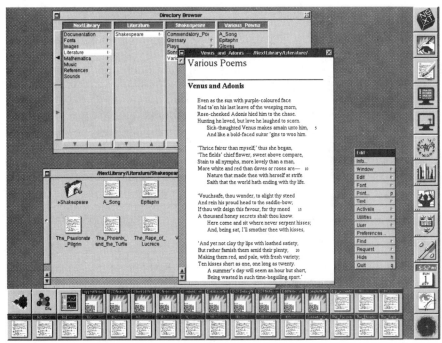

The Edit application and the Workspace Manager

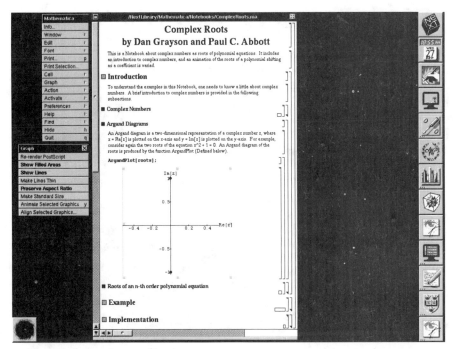

The Mathematica application

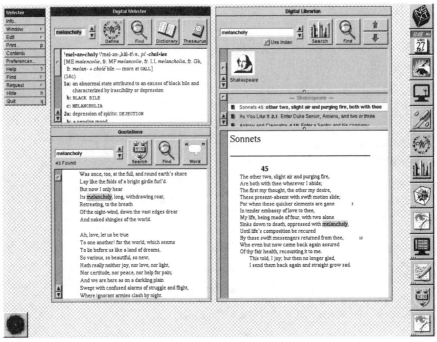

Digital Webster, Quotations, and Digital Librarian

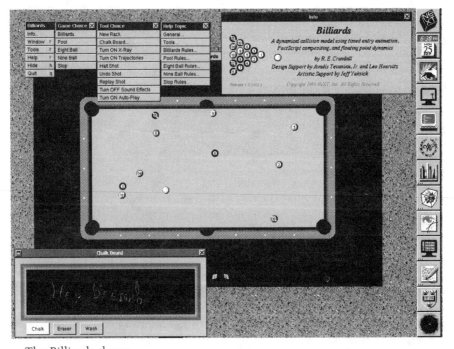

The Billiards demo

Ray—a ray tracing demo

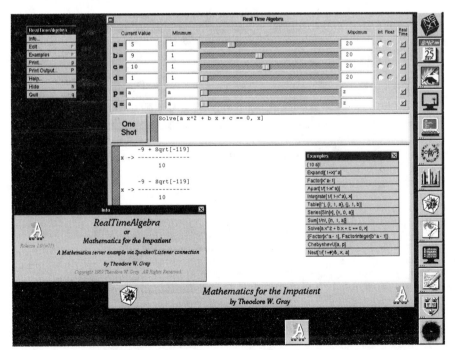

The RealTimeAlgebra demo

The Saturn Demo

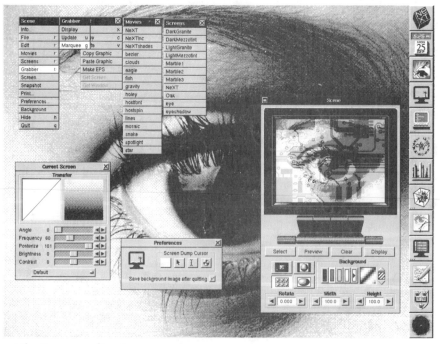

The Scene application

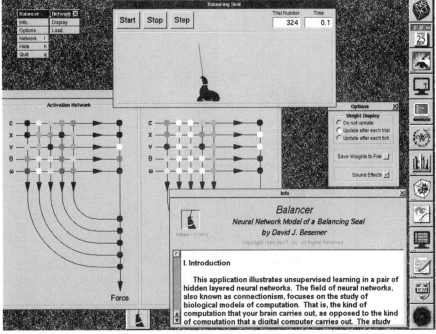

Balancer—a neural network simulation

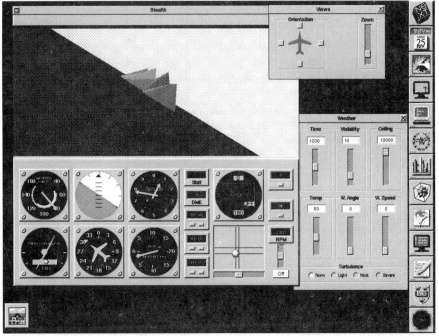

The Stealth flight simulator demo

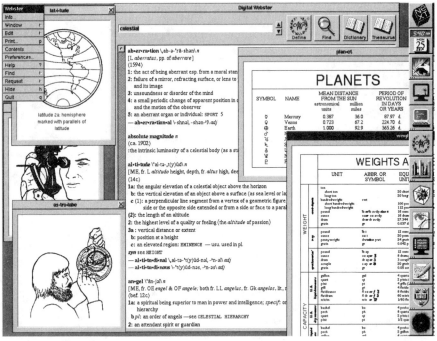

Digital Webster

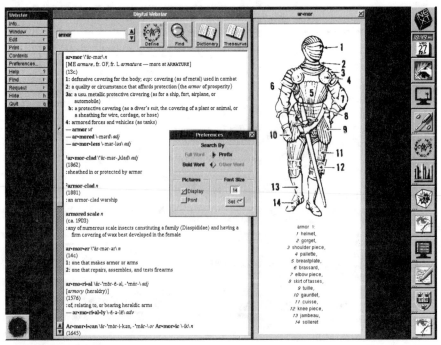

Digital Webster

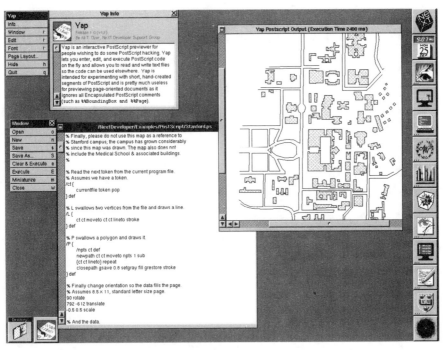

YAP—an interactive PostScript previewer

The Chess application

# Section III

## Networking and Communications

# Chapter 12

# A Networking Primer

**network** n. & v.trans. [From *net* "reduced slightly from gross" + *work.*]
1. *n.* The antisynergetic interconnection of noncompatible nodal systems
divided by a common protocol. 2. *v. trans.* To reduce [net] the work rate
(of a computing resource) by adding it to a network.

> — **STAN KELLY-BOOTLE** in *The Devil's DP Dictionary*

*I only ask for information. [Miss Rosa Dartle.]*
David Copperfield, ch.20

> — **CHARLES DICKENS** 1812–1870

Welcome to NFS, TCP/IP, FTP, SMTP, RPC, and, of course, finger.

It's networking time. Networking is a book-length topic. Even on NeXT, where
it's remarkably easy, it's a book-length topic. Here, it gets a chapter.

We'll begin with generalities and history. Gory details will be gradually folded in.

## The NeXT Goal

During the design of The NeXT Computer, this was a goal:

> *Networking is built-in from the start. A given on every NeXT computer.*
> *It's not an add-on or an afterthought.*

The goal was met with dizzying thoroughness. If workstations are known by
their ability to provide sophisticated networking, then the cube is a workstation to
the bone. Every cube comes ready to network: stuffed with networking hardware
and software; graced with an Ethernet connector. Plug and play.

Unfortunately for users (but happily for computer book writers), it's not that
simple. But revolutions are never simple, and networking is indeed a revolution.

Today, we take telephones for granted. Soon, we'll take networking for granted. And not merely networks of a few computers cabled together. The networking revolution means this: Your computer has near-instant access to other computers—other information—around the world. It's the difference between a single book and a library; between a friend and a fellowship.

Now, we think of computers as boxes: Some built-in software and the hardware to make it work. Self-contained. To do something else, to use another program, slide a disk into a slot. Once we get the software "in there," the computer does (hopefully) what we want.

Networks dissolve that definition. There's a world of data out there. And a world of software. And interconnected communities of scientists, engineers, philosophers, guys who like to fix up cars, and people who'd just like to meet someone new—you.

That's only part of it. The other part is called "distributed computing." With distributed computing, what you see on the display may not come from computations in your cube.

Mathematica is a good example. It consists of two parts: an interface you interact with, and a computational engine called a "kernel" which does the actual processing. The default is that both interface and kernel reside on a single computer. But the kernel can just as happily reside on another cube—or a VAX in Michigan, or a Cray supercomputer in Massachusetts.

You're "using Mathematica," but the real computing action is taking place somewhere else; possibly thousands of miles away. The boundaries have dissolved. It doesn't matter "where" the processing takes place, it doesn't matter "where" the data is. *It only matters that you get what you want.* (It's easy to forget that, after all, you're the reason for all this. Be flattered.)

A program may run on your computer, or it may run on a cube down the hall—or some other cube with time on its hands. It "seems" as if it's running on your cube, but it may not be. And *it doesn't matter.* Networking and distributed computing have dissolved the boundaries.

But that, too, is only part of it. The network revolution is also a "bandwidth" revolution. As you read this, the nation is being strung with optical-fiber cables: hundreds of thousands of miles of optical-fiber cables—and more added daily. Fiber optics is being used in over 20 countries, replacing existing lower capacity telephone cables. Soon, the United States and Europe will be connected by undersea fiber-optic cables, with a U.S.-to-Asia connection to follow. Those cables may make communications satellites obsolete.

Why? Bandwidth. Capacity. A single fiber-optic cable can carry a staggering amount of information. The reason is frequency: higher frequencies require less bandwidth to carry information. That's why FM radio offers more sound quality than AM while occupying less of the radio spectrum. It's why microwaves are used to ferry telephone conversations: the frequency is much higher; more information in less bandwidth.

Fiber-optic cables use light to carry information. The frequency? One hundred thousand times that of microwaves! Capacity? Fiber optics can carry untold numbers of telephone conversations. Or transmit 80 million television channels at once. Your TV Guide for Tuesday will soon come in a large truck.

This immense information capacity means more than video telephones (though that's surely one result). It means that television, telephones, and computers will soon melt and meld together. Today, we use computers to transfer simple files—an often tedious, error-prone process. Soon, fiber optics will bring us text, graphics, high-definition video, and CD-quality sound—all at once: right now. As a trivial example, expect a NeXT-TV card sometime in 1990. Read Shakespeare while keeping an eye on the Vikings bashing the Bears.

The fiber-optic grid will one day connect every home, every business, every computer in the world. Visionaries call the idea ISDN: the Integrated Services Digital Network. The first tentative moves toward ISDN protocols are already being made.

And protocols, as we'll soon see, are what communication is all about.

## Clients, Servers, and Daemons

Let's start unraveling this magic. One of the basic networking ideas is the "client-server" relationship. It works like this. Clients make requests. Servers fulfill requests.

Servers provide services. You'll see the words "server" and "services" frequently, in many contexts.

So a server is anything that offers a service. The NeXT Laser Printer is a server, for example. The service it provides is printing files. A cube that contains files accessed by other users is a file server.

Clients make requests. At a high level, any individual NeXT computer can be a client. If you're "logged on" to another computer, then you're the client. The computer that's processing your requests is the server. At a lower level, individual applications can be clients or servers. When WriteNow asks for a file to be printed, it's a client of the Laser Printer server.

Servers aren't only hardware devices. The NeXT Pasteboard, which contains material Cut or Copied from applications, is also a server. The service it provides is the managing the Pasteboard and handling Cut, Copy, and Paste requests from client applications.

Below the NeXT Workspace Manager is the Window Server, which handles requests to move windows, display images, and the like.

That's only the tip of the iceberg. Remember the discussion earlier of Mach processes? When your NeXT is booted to life, Mach creates (spawns) unseen background processes called "daemons." The daemons hang around, unseen, periodically checking for requests. The requests may come from applications, from other daemons, or from across the network. When a request is made, the appropriate daemon starts up the appropriate server. Or, the daemon may itself be a server. On NeXT, autodiskmount is a server daemon. The service? Automatically mounting optical disks.

So a server can be hardware, an application, or an invisible process. And a client is anything that requests a server to do something. One additional thought: servers are passive. They perform, but don't initiate actions. Clients, the "entities" that make requests, are active.

The cube is a hive of clients and servers. Some, like the Window Server, run constantly. Others awake if called. To glimpse a few servers, run the Shell and type:

```
localhost# man -k server
```

to see manual entries that mention servers. Here's a portion of the response:

```
\ (3)               - get receive rights to a standard server port
NSWSd (8C)          - NextStep(tm) Window Server front-end daemon
bootparamd (8)      - boot parameter server
```

```
comsat (8C)            - biff server
fingerd (8C)           - remote user information server
ftpd (8C)              - DARPA Internet File Transfer Protocol server
inetd (8)              - internet "super\ server"
kern_loader (8)        - kernel server loader daemon
kl_util (8)            - kernel server loader utility program
mountd (8C)            - NFS mount request server
named (8)              - Internet domain name server
nmcontrol (1)          - control the operation of the Mach network server
nmserver (8)           - Mach network server
nmtest (1)             - Generic test program for the Mach network server.
nmtime (1)             - Timing program for the Mach network server.
nmxlog (1)             - translate a Mach network server debugging log
pft (1)                - communicate with PostScript Window Server
rexd (8C)              - RPC-based remote execution server
rexecd (8C)            - remote execution server
rlogind (8C)           - remote login server
rshd (8C)              - remote shell server
rstatd (8C)            - kernel statistics server
rusersd (8C)           - network username server
rwalld (8C)            - network rwall server
rwhod (8C)             - system status server
sprayd (8C)            - spray server
talkd (8C)             - remote user communication server
telnetd (8C)           - DARPA TELNET protocol server
tftpd (8C)             - DARPA Trivial File Transfer Protocol server
timed (8)              - time server daemon
tnamed (8C)            - DARPA Trivial name server
yppasswdd (8C)         - server for modifying yellow pages password file
yppoll (8)             - what version of a YP map is at a YP server host
ypserv, ypbind (8)     - yellow pages server and binder processes
ypset (8)              - point ypbind at a particular server
ypwhich (1)            - which host is the YP server or map master?
ypwhich (8)            - what machine is the YP server?
ypxfr, ypxfr_1perday, ypxfr_1p
```

If most of that is meaningless, good. To understand it, let's see where it all came from.

## Networking History

We'll skip over the invention of the alphabet, Gutenberg, Marconi, Bell, and James Joyce. The story begins in 1957, when the Sputnik satellite shocked and humiliated the United States. Suddenly the U.S. was in second place.

President Eisenhower responded by creating ARPA: the Advanced Research Projects Agency. ARPA was a unique Pentagon agency. It had little bureaucracy. It had no real charter, except to foster technology. It had a ton of money. And it was run by scientists, not bureaucrats. (NASA, in fact, is an ARPA spin-off agency.)

These were days, remember, when scientists were respected; the stuff of wonder and movie serials (look here for Commander Cody and the genesis of Indiana Jones).

Wondrously unhampered, ARPA funded basic computer research for decades. Most of the money went to MIT, Carnegie-Mellon, Stanford, USC, and the University of California, Berkeley. The United States took the lead in computers and technology—a grasp that's grown increasingly feeble under recent Republican administrations.

It's only a small understatement to say that computer science sprang from ARPA's deep pockets.

Let's pause in 1959, about a year after ARPA's inception. Where...

At MIT, John McCarthy was frustrated with "batch" computing. Computers were large and expensive. Computer programs were punched into cards, which were fed into computers—after users first waited in line to approach the "computer operator" who did the actual card feeding. Then there was the wait for the program's results: hours, even days later, depending on how many card-carrying supplicants were ahead of you in line.

McCarthy wrote a memo to his MIT colleagues outlining a new idea: time sharing. The idea was simple: a number of terminals would be connected to a single computer and "share" the computer's CPU time.

In 1961, thanks to ARPA funding, it finally happened. A team of programmers wrote software that allowed multiple terminals to share an IBM 370 computer. The IBM 370, graciously, was the "host" for the terminals.

ARPA took to the idea and funded Project MAC. The acronym meant both "Multi-Access Computer" and "Machine-Aided Cognition." (McCarthy is also the founder of MIT's Artificial Intelligence Laboratory and the inventor of the AI language LISP, so a bit of McCarthyism may have snuck in there.)

After being developed at universities (Dartmouth, in particular, made large contributions), time sharing became a commercial success in the 1960s. By 1968, GE had 31 time-sharing centers and 50,000 time-sharing customers, to cite just one example.

Still, the idea was this: one host computer, many dumb terminals. Time sharing. It worked fine as long as the host computer was fast and powerful, and few terminals were attached. As more and more terminals clamored for the host computer's CPU (a finite resource), things bogged down. Programmers would work at night (many still do), when "activity was low" and they could compute at something greater than a snail's pace.

That wasn't good enough for ARPA. Powerful computers now existed at universities and defense installations around the country. What was needed was a way to tie these many disparate "hosts" into a single, resource-sharing network.

The ambitious project was coined "ARPANET." Its chief architect was the legendary Lawrence Roberts, who came to ARPA from (not surprisingly) MIT.

To implement ARPANET, Roberts chose a new idea, then fought for it—often against disdain and ridicule.

The idea was called packet switching.

To understand packet-switched communications, consider the opposite approach: circuit switching. Telephone calls use circuit switching. The path between yourself and the person you call is a circuit. A direct circuit that remains in place until the call ends. You're billed for the time that the circuit exists—it doesn't matter whether either person talks! Silence costs as much as wisdom, because you're paying not for the information, but for the time that the circuit is open.

Packet switching, instead, slices information into packets: bullets of information. Each packet contains a small segment of the entire message. Like letters, packets contain addresses of the recipient.

Many different messages may be sent simultaneously as packets. A stream of bullets: messages interspersed with other messages. The packets, after being appropriately routed, are reassembled by the receiving computers.

It was a Big Idea. So big that the word "network" now actually means "packet-switched network." A larger, more accurate phrase is "connectionless packet delivery service." With packet switching, unlike circuit switching, once a packet was sent, the sender could pull the plug and go home; the message was on its own, on the way.

In practice, it worked like this. Large host computers were tied together via smaller computers, called IMPs (for Interface Message Processors). The IMPs took care of monitoring the network and routing packets. When the packets arrived at their destination, the IMP reassembled them into a single file and delivered the file to the host. (IMPs were the forerunner of the UNIX TIP software—the Terminal Interface Processor, which allows you login to a remote "host.")

All well and good. The low-level details, however, are gritty. Back to the story.

In 1970, ARPA became DARPA—*Defense* Advanced Research Projects Agency. Funding for basic research was cut dramatically by Congress. From now on, direct military applicability was a requirement for funding. (Historians may someday finger the event as a turning point in the United States' technological rise.)

Still, work on "DARPANET" continued throughout the 1970s. In communications, "work" often means creating protocols. Creating an inclusive set of communications conventions—a protocol—is tough. Packet-switched networks are inherently complicated. Host computers may be fast or slow, big or small, running a variety of operating systems from a variety of vendors. Networking wouldn't work unless each computer agreed on everything, from the smallest packet detail on up.

But by 1979, most of the protocols had been decided upon. Those protocols formed the basis of DARPA Internet. Once protocols were agreed on, Internet flowered, and commercial packet-switching networks like Telenet and Tymnet blossomed. The commercial networks, called VANs (for Value Added Networks), allowed anyone with a modem to dial up a host computer, provided they knew the proper authorizations and incantations. The VANs used (and still use) the packet-switching protocols laid down by ARPA and used on Internet. If you subscribe to MCI Mail or CompuServe or BIX or GEnie, you're a beneficiary of this research.

It's important to note that Internet isn't a program or collection of hardware. It's not a noun—though Internet is referred to as a "thing" both in this book and in the real world.

Instead, Internet is set of protocols, a language for network communications, much like computer languages are protocols for language compilers. The "thingness" of Internet is really the networking software that uses Internet protocols to connect groups of national, regional, and local networks together. (Today, Internet connects over 500 networks, each consisting of a few, to hundreds of computers. In all, over 60,000 computers have Internet access.)

Once the protocols were in place—and only then—could applications be written. To network users, the most familiar applications are:

- file transfer programs, including electronic mail; and
- terminal software, such as UNIX's TIP and CU, that allows "remote login" on other host systems.

The Internet protocols are the foundation of UNIX networking. Protocols, of course, aren't useful unless many people use them. To ensure adoption of the Internet procotols, DARPA—like AT&T before them—offered the goods to universities at "low cost."

Sound familiar?

The University of California, Berkeley, had earlier jumped hard on UNIX. Now they leaped on the Internet protocols. Soon, Internet protocols were part of Berkeley's BSD UNIX. As before, Berkeley added a raft of utilities; this time networking utilities. Suddenly, in addition to cp (CoPy files), there was rcp, Remote Copy. The new commands were similar to other UNIX commands. The melding of UNIX and Internet had begun.

Berkeley's biggest contribution to networking was the idea of "sockets." From the beginning, UNIX has been gracious about input and output. Either could be easily directed or redirected; input could be from the keyboard or from a file, for example. Output could be to the screen, a file, a printer, or some other device.

Sockets make the idea of "generalized I/O" even more general, by adding options for network and Internet access. Like other Berkeley innovations, sockets were controversial (it often seems that Berkeley innovates and others criticize). But the sockets stuck.

To get an idea of what sockets are all about, let's peruse the manual:

```
localhost# man -k socket
```

```
accept (2)         - accept a connection on a socket
bind (2)           - bind a name to a socket
bindresvport (3N) - bind a socket to a privileged IP port
connect (2)        - initiate a connection on a socket
getsockname (2)   - get socket name
getsockopt, setsockopt (2)  - get and set options on sockets
listen (2)         - listen for connections on a socket
recv, recvfrom, recvmsg (2)  - receive a message from a socket
send, sendto, sendmsg (2)  - send a message from a socket
socket (2)         - create an endpoint for communication
socketpair (2)     - create a pair of connected sockets
```

Now let's rummage for Internet-related topics:

```
localhost# man -k internet
ftpd (8C)          - DARPA Internet File Transfer Protocol server
icmp (4P)          - Internet Control Message Protocol
inet (4F)          - Internet protocol family
inet_addr, inet_network, inet_ntoa, inet_makeaddr, inet_lnaof,
   inet_netof (3N)
                   - Internet address manipulation routines
inetd (8)          - Internet ``super\ server''
ip (4P)            - Internet Protocol
named (8)          - Internet domain name server
sendmail (8)       - send mail over the internet
tcp (4P)           - Internet Transmission Control Protocol
udp (4P)           - Internet User Datagram Protocol
whois (1)          - DARPA Internet user name directory service
```

Obviously, you won't get more than a networking glimpse in this book. The Further Reading appendix, however, lists some excellent books on networking: both high-level and low-level. (Though be warned: "low-level" networking is low, indeed!)

Back to glimpsing.

## TCP/IP

Communication protocols are onions of layers, each layer built upon a lower, more primitive protocol. At the top are Network Level Protocols. One step below are

Host Level Protocols. Today, most computers with the smallest smidgen of intelligence (even an Apple II will do) are "hosts," as your shell prompt reminds you.

Next come Application Level Protocols. And down and down, lower and lower. In all, a flurry of all-caps acronyms. At the Application level, you might stumble across:

| Protocol | Meaning |
|----------|---------|
| FTP | File Transfer Protocol; specifies how files are moved between Internet hosts. |
| TFTP | Trivial File Transfer Protocol. |
| SFTP | Simple File Transfer Protocol. This one's more sophisticated than TFTP, but less complex than FTP. |
| SMTP | Simple Mail Transfer Protocol. |
| FINGER | Provides information on a user's current activities. |

And on. And on. An onion of protocols.

At the bottom, the notion of packet switching. While packet switching is the right idea, the lowest level protocols don't guarantee that packets will actually even arrive, let alone arrive intact!

To remedy that failing, a new Host Level Protocol, TCP, came into use on Internet in 1980. In January 1983, DARPA mandated that all computers using Internet also use TCP/IP protocols. The initials stand for "Transmission Control Protocol/Internet Protocol."

Here's a snippet from the UNIX manual pages:

```
NAME
    tcp - Internet Transmission Control Protocol
DESCRIPTION
    The TCP protocol provides reliable, flow-controlled, two-way
    transmission of data. It is a byte-stream protocol used to
    support the SOCK_STREAM abstraction. TCP uses the standard
    Internet address format and, in addition, provides a per-
    host collection of "port addresses." Thus, each address is
    composed of an Internet address specifying the host and net-
    work, with a specific TCP port on the host identifying the
    peer entity.
```

The key advantage of TCP/IP is the word "reliable." TCP/IP is a protocol (not a program, remember, just a set of conventions) that ensures reliable transmission of data across networks.

And notice the phrase "standard Internet address format." One of the great networking complications is addressing. Packets require addresses. Gateways that route packets between networks require addresses. And Internet now consists of hundreds of individual, interconnected networks, each requiring a unique address.

## Names and Addresses

DARPA never envisioned this many networks, this many computers on Internet. (Notice how "Internet" becomes a noun unbidden!) Originally, all network names and addresses were kept in a single file. The file was updated periodically and mailed to each site. As Internet grew, this became impractical.

Today, all network addresses are assigned by the Network Information Center, a part of SRI International (a quasi-commercial spinoff from Stanford University. CHECK). Computer manufacturers, such as NeXT, go to SRI and purchase a block of Internet addresses.

There are three classes of Internet addresses: Class A, Class B, and Class C. Each address has two main parts:

- a network ID; and
- a host ID.

Class A addresses devote more bits to the host portion of the address, allowing up to 65,536 hosts! DARPANET has Class A numbers. Let's see...that means an additional 65,000-odd networks (not individual computers, but networks) can still join DARPANET!

Class B addresses can handle from 256 to 65,536 hosts.

At Class C we get to NeXT addresses. Class C addresses can specify up to 255 hosts. Since each NeXT is a host, and NeXT/Ethernet networks are typically composed of less than 30 computers (the recommended maximum), Class C more than suffices. Each computer on a NeXT network can have a unique address.

The 32-bit binary addresses look like this:

```
10000000 00001010 00000010 00011110
```

but are usually shown in "decimal dot notion," which looks like this:

```
128.10.2.30
```

Now to find some NeXT addresses.

```
localhost# cat /etc/networks
#
# NeXT customer networks
# NOTE: This file is never consulted if NetInfo or Yellow
  Pages is running
#
loopback        127            loopback-net software-loopback-net
next-default    192.42.172     NeXTether ethernet localnet
#
# Internet networks
#
arpanet         10             arpa
ucb-ether       46             ucbether
```

Notice that the NeXT default address is 192.42.172. (We're working our way toward NetInfo and Yellow Pages.)

And here's part of the file /usr/template/client/etc/hosts:

```
localhost# cat /usr/template/client/etc/hosts
#
#   NOTE: This file is never consulted if NetInfo or Yellow Pages is running.
#
#
#   To do anything on the network, you need to assign an address to your
#   machine. This default host table will get you started. "myhost"
#   can be used for the first machine on the network, and client[1-8]
#   can be used for subsequent machines. You must make sure that no two
#   machines have the same address. If you need to add more machines
#   just keep adding entries. Each digit in the four digit number must
#   be between 1 and 254 inclusive.
```

```
#
192.42.172.1    myhost
192.42.172.2    client1
192.42.172.3    client2
192.42.172.4    client3
192.42.172.5    client4
192.42.172.6    client5
192.42.172.7    client6
192.42.172.8    client7
192.42.172.9    client8
```

Although only nine host addresses are shown above, the sequence would continue, after more entries...

```
192.42.172.198    client198
192.42.172.199    client199
192.42.172.200    client200
192.42.172.201    client201
```

Why must the final numbers be between 1 and 254? Because these are Class C Internet addresses. The first digits (192.42.172) contain the network address. The last digit(s) contains the host number. Only 255 individual host computers can be specified. Still, more than enough for a NeXT network. The last allowable computer on this local network (and would be a very slow network!) would be 192.42.172.254.

One of the beauties of the Internet address scheme is this: Messages on Internet don't need to know the complete address of the recipient—only the address of the local (or regional) network. Once packets arrive at a local network, Internet calls it a day and the local network takes care of final routing. As you can imagine, this simplifies things considerably!

So it's important that each computer on a local network have the same network number: the same leftmost digits. The NeXT default network address, again, is 192.42.172. If your network *isn't* connected to Internet, 192.42.172.xxx is a fine address. On the other hand, if your local network will be connected to Internet, you need to be assigned a unique Internet address, so you're not confused with another 192.42.172 somewhere else.

## Domains

But enough about numbers. Nobody likes numbers. From the beginning, Internet users wanted names, not numbers, for their networks. DARPA, obligingly, kept track of the network names associated with each Internet address.

This scheme, of course, also fell, as tens, then hundreds of networks came on board. With only 26 letters in the alphabet, it's hard to keep coming up with unique, meaningful names.

To solve the problem, an enforced "hierarchical namespace" was created. The namespace is a tree, just like UNIX directories are trees. At the top are a handful of fixed names—called "domains." Below are subdomains. And sub-subdomains, and so on. The namespaces look like this:

```
local.site
```

The names go from smaller to larger, with periods used to separate portions of the name. The rightmost word is the topmost domain.

Central to this idea—just as with Internet 32-bit ID's—is enforcement. Anyone wishing Internet access must request a domain name, just as they'd request an Internet ID. The top Internet domain names are:

| Domain | Given To |
|---|---|
| COM | commercial companies |
| EDU | educational institutions |
| GOV | the Federal Government |
| MIL | the military |
| NET | network support centers |
| ARPA | temporary ARPANET domains |
| ORG | unclassifiable organizations |
| country-codes | domains in countries other than the United States |

As an example, take NeXT. They apply for a domain name and get "COM," naturally. NeXT also receives permission to use:

```
next.com
```

as their local.site appellation.

From there on, it's out of Internet administration's hands. NeXT can merrily add local networks. Subdomains and sub-subdomains. The lower-level domains identify departments, machines, or individual users. The arrangement and policing of the hierarchy is up to NeXT.

One convention often used in domain names is @ to represent "at." As an example, Avadis Tevanian, Jr., bearer of the imposing title: "Manager, System Software Group / Chief Operating System Scientist, NeXT, Inc.," has the domain name:

```
avie@next.com
```

The names can become frightfully long as the domain name tree spreads its branches. As NeXT prospers and grows, we may see domain names such as:

```
frank.processgroup.mach.osgroup.software.68xxx.dev.next.com.
```

But let's hope not.

So networks and individual machines are represented both by names and by numbers. But what matches the names to the numbers? A "name server." Just another of the many clients and servers within NeXT computers and NeXT networks.

## UUCP

This Internet stuff is all well and good, but how do you actually *do things* on Internet?

The answer is: just as you'd do them on your own computer. Almost.

One of the most common UNIX commands is cp, to copy a file. Like this:

```
cp [options] file1 file2
```

File1 gets copied to file2. If file2 already exists, it's history. (Using a –i option:

```
cp -i file1 file2
```

produces a prompt, and a way out, if a file will be overwritten.)

A necessary command, cp.

Early on in the history of UNIX, in 1978, a variation of cp appeared: uucp, for UNIX-to-UNIX CoPy. Where cp copied a file within a single computer, uucp copied a file to or from *another* computer. It was now possible to transfer files between connected computers. And with Internet, the connected computers can be separated by miles or oceans.

The syntax for uucp is similar to cp:

```
uucp [options] source destination
```

Using uucp, it's possible to:

* transfer files between remote UNIX systems;
* send mail to remote systems; and
* access resources—even run programs—on remote computer systems.

Heady stuff.

Let's look at the uucp syntax again:

```
uucp [options] source destination
```

"Source" is usually a file you wish to send. (Though it could also be a quick note you type into the Shell, thanks to UNIX redirection.) "Destination" needs to be specified like this:

```
systemname![username | pathname]
```

Systemname must be a system that your computer "knows about." Another UNIX command, uuname, lists remote systems you can access (or ask your System Administrator for the names of remote systems).

Username and pathname are handy, often-used options. The "|" stands for "or." In most cases, you'll be sending to a particular someone, and you may also want to deposit the goods in a particular file or directory.

A further note about systemname. The C Shell used on NeXT wants to run the history command when it sees "!". To prevent this, you need to place a backslash before !, to cause the Shell to treat ! as a character, not a command. So the actual uucp syntax becomes:

```
systemname\ ![username][pathname]
```

Systemnames can be strung together. Remember that all this is done at the lowest level, by connectionless packet delivery. So you usually just specify the address, not the actual route. The actual route...well, who knows? It depends. A message from San Francisco to Sacramento might be routed through Little Rock. To have more control, it's possible to string systemnames together to "forward" your message through various sites.

Maybe you'd like to drop a note to the Australian UNIX Users Group? The systemname is:

```
uunet!munnari!auug
```

When sending to remote systems, the feeling is often akin to placing a note in a bottle, then dropping the bottle off the dock. (Uucp does have options, though, to alert you when a message has been received, and other options to alert the *recipient* when a message arrives, and...well, uucp has *lots* of options.)

Needless to say, there's much behind-the-scenes magic going on during uucp. Daemons begin running, modems are automatically dialed, packets are routed, and more. This glimpse at uucp is much like a Woody Allen joke, which goes like this:

"I just read *War and Peace*."

"I've always wanted to read *War and Peace*! What's it about?"

"Russia."

For more information about using uucp, breeze through the UNIX manual entry (man uucp) or pick up "Using UUCP and Usenet," a wonderful, clearly written handbook. It's listed in the Further Reading appendix.

A final uucp note. Although uucp is on the System 1.0 disk, uucp *isn't supported* by NeXT.

What's that mean? I'm not sure. Probably that NeXT isn't willing to say, "Oh sure it works." It also means you can't call NeXT with uucp problems.

## Ethernet

We've gotten this far and never mentioned LANs once. That's okay. LANs—local area networks—weren't the forerunners of the national networks. First came uucp, then ARPANET, then the VANs, and finally the LANs.

The spine of NeXT networks is Ethernet. And, like UNIX and DARPANET, Ethernet is an oldtimer.

Along with windows, icons, and mice, Ethernet comes from Xerox PARC; the child of Robert Metcalfe, who in 1973, at the ripe age of 27, invented Ethernet.

Like most good ideas, LANs are obvious in hindsight. Hard disks and printers are expensive. Many computers should share those resources. Users should be able to access common databases. Or share files. Or send messages across the room—not just across the country!

Metcalfe got the idea for Ethernet from Alohanet, which used radio waves to link terminals on the Hawaiian islands to a central computer. Metcalfe whimsically dubbed his creation Ethernet, playing off the 19th-century idea of...well, let's use Webster:

**ether** \ 'e-ther\ *n*
[ME, fr. L *æther,* fr. Gk *aithe<sup>a</sup>r,* fr. *aithein* to ignite, blaze; akin to Gk *aithos* fire,
    OE ad pyre — more at EDIFY]
(14c)
1a:  the rarefied element formerly believed to fill the upper regions of space
  b:  the upper regions of space: HEAVENS
2a:  a medium that in the undulatory theory of light permeates all space and
      transmits transverse waves

Ethernet became a success because it was fast, simple, and cheap. (And, let's hope, because it had a great name.)

It works like this. Each computer (or other device) connects, by a short cable, to a transceiver. The transceivers can transmit and receive data packets. The transceivers are connected to a longer cable that ties everything together. Ethernet isn't a circular cable; the end doesn't attach to the beginning. It's more like a hose. Computers and servers tap into the cable. The end of the cable is plugged.

In networking, "routing" is always a concern. For access to and across Internet, routing tables are used by routing daemons to make sure everything gets where it should. Look:

```
localhost# man routed
ROUTED(8C)            UNIX Programmer's Manual            ROUTED(8C)

NAME
   routed - network routing daemon0

SYNOPSIS
   /etc/routed [ -d ] [ -g ] [ -s ] [ -q ] [ -t ] [ logfile ]

DESCRIPTION
   Routed is invoked at boot time to manage the network routing
   tables. The routing daemon uses a variant of the Xerox NS
```

```
Routing Information Protocol in maintaining up to date ker-
nel routing table entries. It used a generalized protocol
capable of use with multiple address types, but is currently
used only for Internet routing within a cluster of networks.
```

Ethernet takes a different approach from the Internet routing scheme—one that gives it 3-megabits-per-second speed across local networks. On Ethernet, packets are "broadcast," not routed. Every computer on the network gets every message. Each station grabs the messages addressed to it, and ignores all other messages. The idea is simple, fast, and takes only a minimum of hardware to implement.

In the grand tradition of Making a Protocol a Standard, Xerox quickly began licensing Ethernet (the Ethernet protocols, actually) to other companies. The price was the traditional "nominal fee."

It worked. Other companies, including 3Com, responded, installing hundreds of Ethernet networks and making millions of dollars. In 1983, the IEEE (the Institute of Electrical and Electronics Engineers) dubbed Ethernet the standard LAN protocol. Others would come, but Ethernet was the first.

And the protocol onion had another layer. And another set of addresses: Ethernet addresses. And the appropriate software to translate from Internet addresses to local Ethernet addresses.

Fortunately, NeXT makes setting up Ethernet networks and Internet connections relatively painless. We'll look at NeXT applications to manage networks after one more stop.

## NFS

This is the end of the Networking Today road. So far, we've seen Internet, uucp, and Ethernet. But we're not done. Ethernet provides a means to network computers, but it *doesn't* provide an easy way for users to actually share files on a network. Unless, of course, users spend all day doing remote logins to other computers, or uucp'ing each time they want to transfer a file.

What's needed is distributed computing, the idea that began this chapter. What you want is "transparency." You want system resources—files, applications, directories—to look like, and act like, they're "local"—on your screen, as if they're in your cube. You want to *use* things, not worry about where they "really" are.

Networks that offer this transparency, called "distributed computing networks," have been around for quite a while. Intially, they only existed for networks of compatible computers. All-IBM networks, for example.

Designing this type of distributed network is relatively easy. Designers can make sweeping assumptions about hardware, because they know that computers and servers will exist on the network. It's easy to make a "tight fit" between hardware and networking software.

But that's not what's needed. What's needed are networks of various computers: mainframes, minis, and micros. DECs, IBMs, Apples, and, of course, cubes. Nobody wants to be locked in to one manufacturer. Everybody wants to purchase hardware (maybe a bargain hard disk, to use for a file server) from whomever they please.

Again, it's not easy. These connected computers don't just vary in hardware, they also have entirely different operating systems! A Finder here, an MS-DOS command line there, a UNIX terminal somewhere else.

Still, networking software for "distributed networking in heterogenous environments" arrived. Once again, in the form of a protocol.

It's called NFS, for Network Filesystem. It was created by Sun Microsystems, a brash upstart in the "workstation wars" of the early '80's.

Here's what happened. Stanford University designed a single-board, 68000-based computer, tailored to run UNIX. The university licensed the board (known as the Stanford University Network board, or SUN) to computer makers. The result was a rash of UNIX clones: the first affordable UNIX workstations. Suddenly, for as little as $10,000, you could buy a multiprocessing UNIX workstation. Universities, institutions, and businesses gobbled them up. Suddenly, workstations were a big market.

Sun Microsystems, which still bears the name of that first board, survived the frenzy and became the dominant player in the UNIX workstation market.

Sun's success, in part, stemmed from the philosophy that "the network is the computer," and Sun's willingness to adhere to existing UNIX standards. Sun also treated the concept of "proprietary" as anathema. After Sun devised NFS, it freely made the protocol available to other vendors. By adhering to existing standards, and creating new standards, Sun itself become "the standard" for UNIX workstations and networking software.

Back to NFS.

The NFS software lets users access files in remote directories, then treat them as local files. The directory that appears in your Browser window may exist on another cube, somewhere else on the network.

Distributed networks are either "stateless" or "stateful." On a stateful network, you're tied, in a sense, to the servers containing your mounted directories. There are advantages to these stateful networks; they're fast, for one thing, because once a user opens a file on a server, it stays open until the user finishes their work.

But there's a dark side to stateful schemes. If the server crashes, you crash.

NFS, instead, is stateless. This means that files are opened and quickly closed for each network "transaction." NFS uses caching to reduce the inefficiencies inherent in all this opening and closing of files (which takes time). The good news is this: if a server crashes, you don't. To you, the server only appears slow. Assuming that someone reboots the server, eventually.

The NFS protocol is a piece of work. It's:

- machine independent;
- operating system independent;
- network architecture independent; and
- transport protocol independent.

This doesn't mean that it's child's play to cobble IBMs, cubes, and Lord-knows-what-else together on a network. But NFS makes the process fairly straightforward.

## Yellow Pages

To keep track of "who's who" on networks, NFS uses a read-only database called Yellow Pages. Great name. Yellow pages are text files of fields filled with information about machines and addresses. A number of Yellow Pages commands (ypinit, yppoll, yppush, and others) are used to query and change the Yellow Pages database.

## NetInfo

And that's enough about Yellow Pages. Though it's a well-known fixture of UNIX networks, NeXT has its own ideas about network administration. By default, Yellow Pages aren't used on NeXT networks. Instead, NeXT offers NetInfo, an application and associated utilities for managing networks. NetInfo is similar, however, to Yellow Pages—it's a database of network information. The databases are grouped into *domains*. As we saw above, every machine must belong to at least one domain.

The domain actually is a group of directories. The directories contain lists of properties. Those properties determine the configuration of the domain.

In traditional UNIX distributed networks, the task of system administration means, in large part, going in and editing files containing network information: setting passwords, entering new users on the network, changing addresses. Mucking around in various files that configure the network.

System administration on *other* computers requires far more knowledge than we've given here. But system administration on the cube is much less painful.

Way back, we mentioned that a NeXT goal was to make networking a "given." They had another goal: to make it easy.

Did they? Well, as you've seen, networking is a complicated affair. That said, NeXT has made network configuration and administration easier. Easier than setting up and maintaining other UNIX networks, which is saying a lot.

*Now* we'll get into specifics.

## UserManager

Under NeXT's 0.9 operating system, system administration was straightforward, if somewhat daunting. The 1.0 software release makes system administration even simpler—proof of NeXT's commitment to making networking easy.

One of the most basic networking tasks is adding new users. The NeXT UserManager application handles that duty.

The two UserManager views correspond to two levels of network detail. In the short view, all that's needed to add a new user is typing a full name, account name, and password:

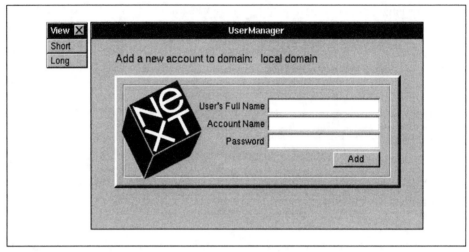

Figure 12-1

Retype the password to verify it (the password isn't shown as you type it), and an alert allows you to confirm your actions:

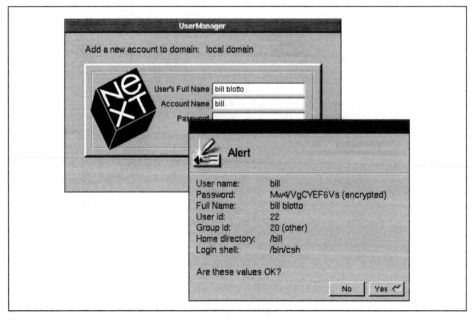

Figure 12-2

Notice that many of the values have been automatically filled in by User Manager. Click "Yes" and the application writes the necessary files and creates a login directory for the new user:

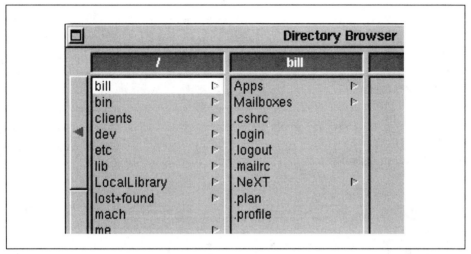

*Figure 12-3*

Bill, the newest NeXT user, now has his own login directory, his own subdirectory of applications (empty for the moment), his own mailboxes, and startup and preferences files.

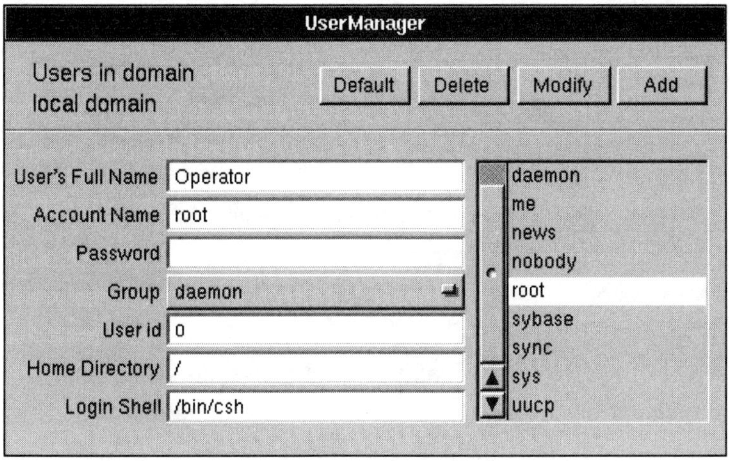

*Figure 12-4*

For those wishing more control over the business of adding and changing accounts, UserManager has a long view (see Figure 12-4), where users can be defined with many more options, including group ownership, login shell, and user ID.

The NeXT manuals give adequate detail on "long view." For most purposes, you'll only need long view when deleting user accounts.

## NetManager

One of NeXT's biggest network advances is this: A NeXT network configures itself automatically. You may never need to venture past the default values in the NetManager application:

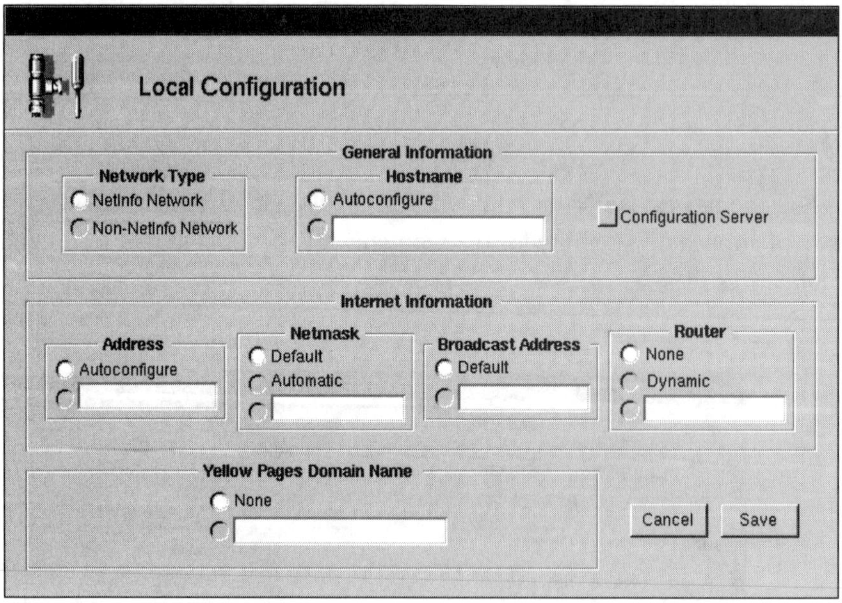

*Figure 12-5*

If you do choose to go beyond autoconfiguration, however, NetManager still tries to help out by suggesting values (which should look familiar from our earlier discussion):

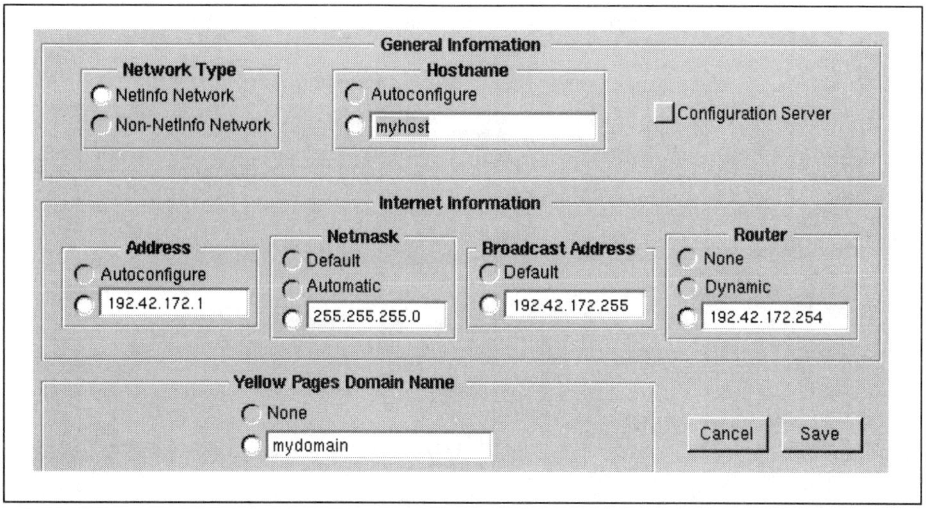

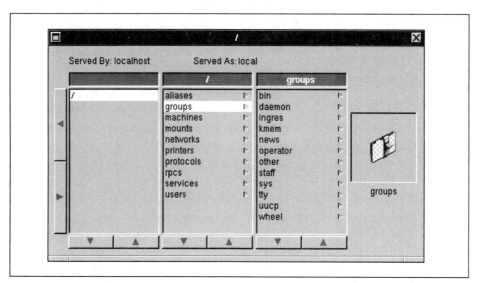

*Figure 12-6*

To go beyond autoconfiguration requires expertise you won't find here. A thorough reading of NeXT manuals and a very good grounding in UNIX networking are required.

## NetInfoManager

For truly exquisite control over domain properties, there's NetInfoManager:

*Figure 12-7*

Here, you can edit properties in the many directories that make up the NetInfo database.

NetInfo properties have two parts: a name and a value. To edit NetInfo properties, you click on a rightmost directory, which opens a Property Editor panel:

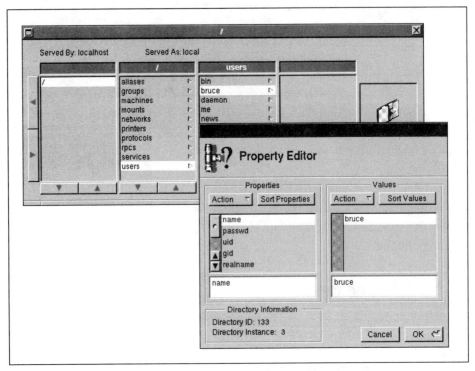

*Figure 12-8*

Names are on the left; values on the right. The property being edited above is the name of user "Bruce."

NetInfo contains a wealth of system information, as you can see. Despite the NextStep ease-of-use, the best advice is to leave this low-level system maintenance and configuration to someone trained in NeXT system administration.

# Usenet

Usenet (for USEr's NETwork) is, among other things, the world's greatest bulletin board.

First, some history: From early days, UNIX systems could be connected either directly, or through "dialup"—telephone lines. The origins of Usenet were at Duke University and the University of North Carolina, where a simple dialup network was based on uucp (the Unix to Unix CoPy utility).

It worked, it was fun, it was useful. Modems became affordable and more UNIX sites wanted in. Public domain software started to appear. More sites wanted in. Usenet was a good place to find bug fixes or a guru to help with UNIX problems.

It was free. More sites wanted in.

Today, Usenet serves tens of thousands of Unix users. (You may also hear it called "The Net," "NetNews," or simply "News.") The network spans four continents and thirty countries. Usenet is still about Unix, but it also includes forums about everything from fantasy games to food to hunting to dating. In fact, the discussion group 'soc.singles' in the most popular Unix 'newsgroup.' In all, the complete "feed" for one day of Usenet news may be four or more megabytes!

There's no central Usenet administration, and no single group controls Usenet. Instead, Usenet is a loose collection of sites connected to other sites. Most sites are universities.

How to get on? If you attend a university, there's a good chance that your school is already a Usenet site—or can access a nearby site.

If you're a mere individual, it's still possible to experience (and that is the correct word) Usenet. Many commercial telecommunications services provide a "gateway" to Usenet. It's not free (the commercial companies obviously can't provide the largesse of universities—which even foot the bill for international calls!), but it's not prohibitive.

To research this book, I subscribed to Portal, a communications service based in California. Portal is accessed through Telenet, which means that only a local call is needed in over 600 cities served by Telenet. The price? A startup fee of $15, a flat fee of $10 a month, reasonable surcharges for dowloading, and a couple bucks an hour (off-peak) for Telenet. Not bad.

Another possiblity for Usenet access is The Well (for Whole Earth eLectronic Link). The Well is a famous—and fun—BBS. It offers numerous enticements besides Usenet. Cost: $8 a month, $3 an hour. Add $20 an hour for prime-time Telenet, or $4 an hour of Telenet off-peak charges.

NeXT has its own Usenet newsgroup: /comp/sys/next. It's the place to go for rumormongering, NeXT help, programming problems and tips, and rabid speculation (often of the "If I ran NeXT" variety). Best of all, NeXT employes check in frequently to answer questions and calm the waters.

# Section IV

---

# Programming
the Cube

# Chapter 13

# Programming The NeXT Computer

*And there began a lang digression*
*About the lords of the creation.*
1 I.45

— **ROBERT BURNS** 1759–1796

## Objective Programming

Object-oriented programming has progressed from a curiosity, to a good idea, to The Right Way to Program. The message for developers is this: Learn object programming, or prepare to become a programming relic.

Why? Why not program traditionally? Pick a language, write a program. A traditional program: algorithms, data, functions, procedures. Like it's always been.

For better or worse, that's no longer good enough. After programming in an object-oriented language, going back to non-object programming is like mowing your lawn with scissors. You could do it, but you wouldn't want to.

Object-oriented programming gives you many advantages. Programs are written more quickly. Object programs are easier to debug, easier to maintain, and easier to enhance.

Again: why? Because object-oriented programs are easier to understand! If programmers can't understand what they've written—can't clearly see the consequences of their code—then programming becomes harder and harder, slower and slower.

In small programs, it's possible to "keep everything in your head"—or at least to have some certainty about what does what. As programs become large, or many programmers collaborate, that certainty collapses. Large programs, unless created with extreme care, become nightmares of complexity. And complexity means bugs, missed ship dates, terror, agony, fear, and—worst of all—decreased income.

## Encapsulation

One Big Idea in object programming is encapsulation. Functions, procedures and data are rolled together into objects. Applications are made up of interacting objects. Each object has a specific functionality.

Objects may have instance variables, which contain data. The instance variables are private data. The procedures and functions used by objects are called methods. The methods are also specific to a particular object.

Objects are black boxes. Once you've created an object, defined what it is, and what variables and methods it needs, you can use it without worrying about "what's happening inside" the object. You only need to remember what the object does and what methods are used by it. All the functionality of the object—data, procedures, and functions—is safely tucked away; encapsulated within.

It's programming without the mess.

Object programming—once you get the hang of it—is a joy. As it should be: Object-oriented languages are "higher-level" languages than traditional languages like Pascal or C. You can accomplish the same results with fewer lines of code. The biggest stumbling block to learning objective programming, in fact, may be that it's easier than you think! It takes a while to get used to how little code is needed to get the results you want. Remember: The purpose of object-oriented programming is to make programming easier for you, the programmer.

## Objects and Classes

Encapsulation keeps algorithms and data private to objects. The "black box" approach keeps programs simple.

But there's another problem with traditional programming: bulk. Thousands and thousands and thousands of lines of code. Hundreds of procedures and functions. Large programs that are confusing, hard to maintain, and hard to debug.

If you've programmed on a large project, you know the feeling. You want to do something: center a window, say. You know that somewhere in that pile of code is a procedure you've written that centers a window.

Okay. Just find the procedure, see what needs to be passed as arguments, and call it.

But no. It turns out that the procedure only centers a particular window type—not the type you're working with.

Now you've got a choice. You can rewrite the procedure to deal with your particular window (which may require other changes in other procedures—God knows how many or where they are!). Or you can take the easy way out: Write a new procedure to deal with this particular case. The two procedures will be similar, but different.

Repeat this process 700 times. Your program is now 1,200K when compiled. Code bulk has struck. And it's a mess.

Objective programming reduces code bulk dramatically. It does it by grouping objects into classes. The classes are arranged in a hierarchy. Every class is a subclass of another class.

And every class—except one—has a superclass that's one step higher in the hierarchy. Each class shares the "instance variables" of its superclass—which eliminates much duplication of program code.

Everything begins with the Object class: The Father of All. Other classes are always defined relative to the Object class.

Object is the only class without a superclass. *Every object exists in a subclass of Object.*

Let's work from the bottom up and arrive at Object.

Let's say we want to program a button. On the NeXT, it's easy: There's a Button object. It has methods to create buttons, set the button type, display the button, modify the button—you name it. It's unlikely that you'll need to add or change anything. Just look up the method you want and use it.

But first, you need to make an "instance" of Button, by making a new button object. It's done like this:

```
id myButton;
myButton = [Button new];
```

To set the title of a button, you can now write:

```
[myButton setTitle:"Click me!"];
```

The Button class has a slew of methods. What's interesting, though, is what isn't defined for buttons! For example, there's no method to set the font of a button.

## Inheritance

Why is that? Because *the Button class only contains methods particular to buttons.* The business of setting fonts is found in the Control class, the superclass of Button. The Button class *inherits* methods (and variables) from its superclasses—including a method to set the font of a button.

In this case, the method to set the font of a button is found in the Control class. Control itself is a subclass of View. And View is a subclass of Responder, which brings us to the top: Object.

Each subclass defines a more specific set of behavior, by defining additional instance variables and methods.

In this case it looks like this:

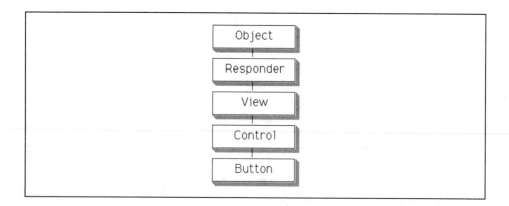

Here's the beauty of the scheme: Each subclass automatically "inherits" the instance variables and the methods of its superclass, and that class's superclass, and so on, all the way up the line to Object.

Again, from Object to Button, each subclass defines additional methods and variables that are used to create more specific behavior. For instance variables, think of C structures or Pascal records that become larger and larger as more functionality is added. And remember that methods also are inherited. (If you come from a C background, think of methods as functions.)

So setFont doesn't need to be defined in Button. It's in Control, one step higher. Besides Button, the Control class has other predefined subclasses:

* Matrix;

* TextField;

* Slider; and

* Scroller.

Or think of it as:

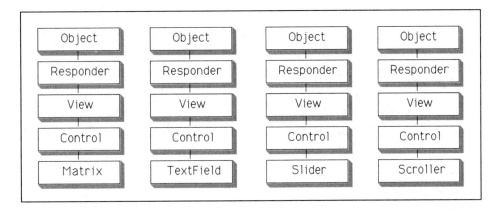

Or, more succinctly:

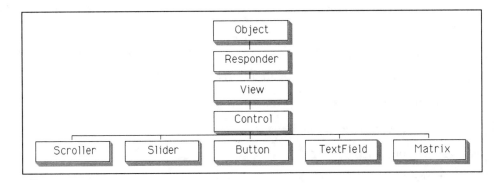

Each is a subclass of Control, each a particular type of control. The method for setting control fonts is found in the Control class—it isn't duplicated in Button, Matrix, and TextField.

In practice, it works like this: You write:

```
[myButton setFont: [Font: newFont: "Times-Roman": size: 12.0]]
```

When your application is run, the runtime system comes upon setFont. It knows that myButton is a Button object, so it looks in the Button class. No setFont there. So it looks one level higher: to the Control class.

There it is. Button inherits setFont from Control. Your application knows where to look. If setFont wasn't found in Control, the Responder class would be the next likely place, and so on up the line.

(In practice, the look-up process is smarter and faster than this explanation; but that's how it works conceptually.)

Let's look at another example of inheritance. This time, menus. Starting from the bottom:

The Menu class is a subclass of Panel.

That makes sense; menus are always contained in panels. The Panel class, though small, contains keyDown and commandKey methods, which are used by menus. By making the Menu class a subclass of Panel, there's no duplication of code.

Panel itself is a subclass of Window, which also makes sense. Panels are nothing more than specialized windows. Why reinvent the wheel to offer panel functionality found in the Window class?

Inheritance is a tremendous advantage. If the classes are properly thought out and written, there's very little duplication of code.

In most cases, the classes and objects in NeXT's Application Kit can be used "as is." Just make a new instance of an object and have at it.

If you want new behavior, you can:

• add new instance variables;

• add new methods; or

• override existing methods.

The idea is to create new features and new behavior with a minimum of code. And a minimum of complexity.

As you program on the NeXT, you'll seldom need to override the default behavior of many objects—especially "interface" objects, such as Button. The NeXT Application Kit is marvelously complete and flexible. If there's something you need, chances are that it's there, and it works just as you'd like.

You will, though, usually create subclasses in creating your application. The classes you'll subclass most often are View and Object.

## Messages

Objects communicate with other objects by sending messages. Think of messages as procedures or function calls supported by classes. Message statements contain:

- the object's name;
- the method to use; and
- method arguments; if any.

Messages are enclosed in square brackets. The syntax is:

```
[nameOfObject methodname]
```

If the method has arguments, the syntax is:

```
[nameOfObject methodname: argument]
```

The colon is necessary. It means "and the argument is :"

Object syntax has a "declarative" feel to it—a martinet, demanding ring. Like C or Pascal functions, messages can return values. Or be nested within functions, macros, or other messages:

```
[[myPanel contentView] addSubview:panelText];
```

Or be used where a C statement or function would be used:

```
if (viewIsDirty) [view dirty];
if([myText charWrap] == YES)
        [myText setCharWrap:NO];
```

## Objective-C

Objective-C is a superset of the ANSI C language. All the traditional features of C are provided. In fact, the Objective-C compiler assumes ANSI C programs—which meet the de facto definition of "what C programs are."

To achieve the richness of an object environment, very little was added to the C language: one new type, one new expression, and not much else. As you create programs for the NeXT, you can mix and match traditional C and Objective-C, though you'll find that the object style is seductive—and that the NeXT Way of Life is Objectified from top to bottom.

But those few additions make a world of difference. While traditional C programs can be obscure and confusing, Objective-C programs are usually crystal clear.

The Brad Cox interview, elsewhere in this book, delves into Objective-C at more length.

# Programming Advice

What's the best way to learn to program the NeXT?

It depends on your desires and your programming prowess. Let's start at the top of the programming heap and work down to more casual programmers. Advice:

## If you're a professional programmer who's new to NeXT.

First and most important: Attend the week-long NeXT Developer Camp. Call NeXT at 415-366-0900 for information.

It's not cheap, but it shouldn't be. It's a mandatory investment for serious programmers.

You'll learn NeXT programming with 30–40 other programmers. The course covers the fundamentals of NeXT programming. Lectures are relaxed, but thorough; hands-on labs are frequent. A good grounding in C is advised. Some time spent with a cube prior to "Camp" also helps. If you're acquainted with PostScript, so much the better.

You'll learn a lot, have fun, and possibly make some enduring friendships. And eat wondrous "Continental breakfasts" provided by NeXT. And probably get a T-shirt.

When you return home, you'll wish that camp had been a week longer. No matter. Dive into NeXT's documentation. Don't come up for air until you know the Responder classes like the back of your hex calculator.

## If you've programmed in C, but are new to object-oriented languages.

If you're not a professional programmer, skip developer camp. But order printed copies of NeXT's developer documentation (about $300 from NeXT) and read, read, read. The documentation is well-done, but rigorous. Prowl the bookstores for books on NeXT programming. They should appear shortly. Buy 'em.

Pore through the many example programs that come with the cube. Master Interface Builder, which requires a good understanding of "outlets," "target-action" paradigms and other objective notions.

Finally, program. Writing programs is the only way to learn programming. To get started, begin with an example program and add features. Add font-handling to "Little," for example.

Keep at it and don't get discouraged. It'll take time, but it'll come.

## If you're a casual programmer with experience in Pascal or another high-level language experience, but no C experience.

Here, there are two schools of thought. One is: Dive right into Objective-C and NeXT programming. The other is: Learn C first, *then* tackle Objective-C.

There are good arguments for both. I think, though, I'd suggest learning the basics of C first, if only because of the many good "introductory C" books available. Find the book that fits you best (look for one that isn't computer-specific), and write a few C programs using only Edit and the Shell. Once you understand the basic C ideas, apply your skills to Objective-C and Interface Builder. If you can afford it, buy the NeXT developer documentation; you'll be frequently stymied without it.

## If you're a hobbyist who's programmed only in Basic or HyperTalk.

Hmmm. The easiest advice is "forget it." But that would be wrong.

Well...you could try your hand at shell programming. It's not too tough, once you get the hang of it. Beyond that...

Let's hope that a language similar to HyperCard is developed for the cube. The NeXT Computer's object-oriented, graphic rich environment cries out for an easy-to-program language-cum-application. Professional programmers struggle 40-plus hours a week to create NeXT programs. That effort can't be expected from everyone.

But it's early. HyperCard-like programs will come.

## If you've never programmed, period. But you *really want to learn programming.*

Oh boy.

I've been hacking away at programming since 1978, and I'm still no good.

Let's face it. Programming—despite anything you've been led to believe—is hard. It's not up there with neurosurgery, but it's a long road.

If you're sincere, though: if you're really sincere about learning to program "from scratch," I'd advise this:

Learn assembly language first. It's boring and brain-dead, but it's also the well-spring of all programming languages. If you can get around in assembler, you'll never be cowed by any high-level language. Know assembler and C "pointer arithmetic" makes perfect sense, and Objective-C "isa" pointers also make perfect sense.

Learning assembler is like running with ankle weights. You won't be fast, and it may not be fun, but you will know where your feet are. And when you finally take the weights off: ah...

# Chapter 14

# The Window Server and Display PostScript

*Accustom your children constantly to this; if a thing happened
at one window and they, when relating it, say that it happened
at another, do not let it pass, but instantly check them; you
do not know where deviation from truth will end.*
                                    **— SAMUEL JOHNSON** 1709–1784

Earlier, we mentioned that The Workspace Manager is always "launched" and available. At a lower level—immediately above the Mach operating system—is the cube's most fundamental process: the NeXT Window Server. Let's look in the shell:

```
localhost# ps -auxc
USER    PID   %CPU %MEM VSIZE RSIZE TT STAT   TIME COMMAND
root    161   26.1  5.8 2.46M  952K ?  R      0:09 Shell
root    129   14.0 17.9 8.40M 2.86M ?  S      5:25 WindowServer
root    162    1.2  1.6 1024K  256K p1 S      0:00 csh
root      0    1.0  7.9 14.3M 1.26M ?  R <   22:34 kernel-task
root    173    0.3 10.3 3.12M 1.64M ?  S      0:16 WriteNow
```

The Window Server process is shown first. It's been running for five-odd minutes. Since power-on, in this case.

At the moment, it's using 15.4% of the total CPU time and 24.6% of RAM. When this "snapshot" was taken, the Window Server was "sleeping," according to the S in the STAT field. A process that's idle for less than 20 seconds is sleeping. After sleeping 20 seconds, the process is termed "idle." Even though the Window Server is central to all screen activity, it shares time with other processes.

251

Considering all it contains, the Window Server is a modest 500K. It's located in usr/lib/NextStep, with other NextStep-related files.

The Window Server manages the NeXT display. It creates, draws, and manages all windows (and everything on the NeXT display is shown in a window). It's responsible, in fact, for all drawing on the NeXT display. NeXT's vaunted Display PostScript imaging software is embedded in the Window Server.

The Window Server also processes all events—mouse actions, keystrokes, and other events. If the event can be performed by the Window Server (dragging a window, for example), it's done. If the event can't be serviced by the Window Server, it's posted to the appropriate application for processing. This low-level event processing takes the burden off NeXT applications. Many typical window actions—moving windows, hiding windows, and many more—are handled by the Window Server.

More precisely, the Window Server communicates with applications by putting events on the application's event queue. The application object, in turn, relays the event to the proper object in the application.

Essentially, the Window Server takes care of all window updating. If you're a Macintosh programmer, you'll appreciate this: On the NeXT, all window updating is done automatically—you don't need to write a line of code to redraw windows that have been covered, then uncovered, by other windows.

Communication between applications and the Window Server is a critical factor in the cube's overall speed. As you learn more about programming the cube, you'll notice that many additions and enhancements are designed specifically to speed up the application/Window Server "connection."

The Window Server communicates with applications using interprocess communication. Because of this, the Window Server and applications can even reside on different machines, and everything still works fine.

## Packages

There's a programming concept called "granularity." It has to do with how discrete, how self-contained, various program portions are. In general, the more granular the better: Everything is well separated and easy to modify, debug, or enhance. A case in point: Microsoft recently decided to rewrite all their applications, to separate interface code from algorithmic program code. The result of this increased granularity will be applications that can be ported relatively quickly to new machines and new interfaces. ("Over here, Bill!")

The NeXT software is granular indeed. The closer you look, the more impressive it is. The NeXT system software seems to have been designed first, then programmed. NeXT scientists took their time, and it shows.

One example is NeXT's use of "packages": low-level code collections that live in the Window Server. Packages handle those portions of the NextStep interface governed by the Window Server: window movement, window activation, and other actions.

Because packages are self-contained collections of PostScript code, NeXT (or other enlightened programmers) can alter the fundamental behavior of NextStep. For a look at one package, spend some time nosying through usr/lib/NextStep/windowPackage1.0.ps. You'll learn much about the foundation of NextStep, even if you don't know PostScript. Look, that is, but don't change—or you'll likely be in a world of trouble.

## Display PostScript

NeXT uses Adobe System's PostScript imaging model for both screen display and generating images for the NeXT Laser Printer. Using PostScript as a display imaging model was a much-heralded move by NeXT, and justly so. For programmers, there's only one model to learn for both screen drawing and "drawing" to the printer. For users, Display PostScript presents screen images of exceptionally close correspondence to printed images. Because of the lower screen resolution, displayed images are smaller and fuzzier than printed images. Other than that, they're exactly the same. It's a great aid to desktop publishing—a market that NeXT wants.

PostScript has other advantages. It's both device independent and resolution independent. PostScript files can be sent to the NeXT Laser Printer or to higher-resolution printers. The screen illustrations in this book, for instance, were created on NeXT (natch), proofed on the NeXT Laser Printer, then printed on a higher-resolution imagesetter for inclusion in this book. PostScript automatically took advantage of the higher resolution. The same holds for the screen display: If NeXT releases a higher-resolution screen—or a color display—developers won't need to rewrite one line of code.

The PostScript language and PostScript-based printers have been around now for years. Display PostScript is a new thing. When NeXT announced its choice of Display PostScript, and Adobe began to show "beta" versions of Display PostScript, the attitude in the computer industry was: We'll believe it when we see it.

After all, it's one thing to print. Nobody minds waiting a few seconds, even a few minutes, for a beautiful page to slide out of a printer. But could PostScript ever be fast enough to manage a graphic screen display?

The answer is "yes," it's fast.

The PostScript language, like Basic or HyperTalk, is an interpreted language. The PostScript interpreter reads in ASCII files, interprets the instructions, and performs them. That's how traditional PostScript printers work: The computer sends ASCII commands to the printer; the PostScript interpreter (in printer ROM) deciphers the commands, then builds the image, then prints the image.

This takes time. If this approach were used to draw to a screen, well...forget it. It would require a supercomputer to provide the necessary response time.

At a hardware level, as we've seen, throughput is maximized by caching, numerous DMA channels, video display RAM, and other cleverness.

Other speed increases are accomplished in software. Adobe took the interpreted PostScript language and, in effect, turned it into an encoded interpreted language: Display PostScript. The encoded tokens are interpreted much more quickly than ASCII characters. Adobe also added extensions to make Display PostScript work in a multiprocess environment.

As we wind along, you'll notice "PS" for PostScript and "DPS" for Display PostScript—not to be confused with "DSP" for the Digital Signal Processor, another prefix you'll run into.

The Display PostScript routines were then given a C interface, to present a consistent face to developers. Here are a few:

```
void    PScurrentlinecap(int *plinecap)
void    PScurrentlinejoin(int *plinejoin)
void    PScurrentlinewidth(float *pwidth)
```

NeXT provides a gaggle of these predefined functions. As you create programs for the cube, you'll spend much time poring over lists of PostScript operators and predefined PostScript functions.

But, of course, you won't always find what you need. In that case, you'll need to write your own PostScript routines. Are you then back to a slow, interpreted way of life?

Nope.

The mechanism is called "PSWraps." It works like this: You create PostScript routines that begin with "defineps" and end with "endps." The routines contain PostScript code but are set up as C functions. They're in a C "wrapper," hence the name. PSWraps, like all routines, can be simple or fiendishly complicated.

Source code files containing PSWraps are suffixed with a ".psw." CustomDrawing.psw, maybe. When you make your application, the compiler converts the PostScript code to fast, binary routines, like the predefined PostScript routines. In your program, the PSWrap functions are called just as you'd call any other C function.

If that's not enough, you can send PostScript directly to the PostScript interpreter embedded in the Window Server. This isn't advised, though, because it's slow, as you can imagine, and also defeats the purpose of the Application Kit.

In all, the development environment helps you out as much as possible but doesn't tie your hands. If you really want to do something "the hard way," you can.

## Compositing

Two notable additions to Display PostScript are compositing and instance drawing.

Compositing is a marvel devised by the scientists at Pixar, the LucasFilms graphics company owned in part by Steve Jobs. To speak of compositing, we need to look at pixels.

The shade of each pixel in a NeXT window is determined by its data: one of four predefined values resulting in "pure" colors, or some other data value, which produces a dithered image. That's called the "data channel."

NeXT also provides another channel, an "alpha channel." Here you can set the transparency of pixels, just as you'd determine the "grayness" of ink.

The alpha channel contains a value that represents the transparency of a pixel. Zero (0.0, in the correct floating-point notation) makes the pixel completely transparent—invisible. A value of 1.0 makes the pixel opaque. Values between 0 and 1 result in degrees of transparency. By default, pixels are opaque.

Here's an image from Molecule, a 3-D-like demo:

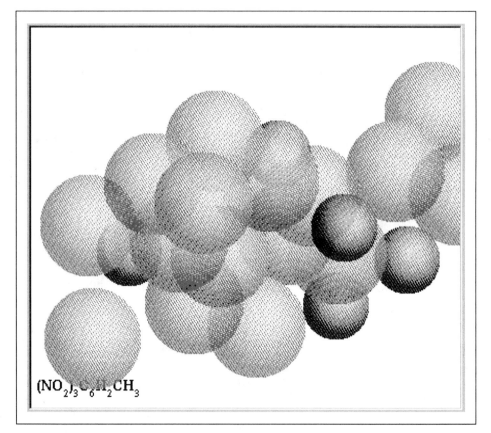

$(NO_2)_3C_6H_2CH_3$

*Figure 14-1*

Yes, it's Trinitrotoluene. TNT. And the atoms have varying degrees of transparency, due to compositing. (This one's more fun on the cube, where the molecules spin in 3-D space.)

Compositing is a method of combining images with differing alpha values. The images are overlaid (usually off screen), then copied to the display. All image copying on the NeXT is done with compositing.

The compositing modes are: Copy, Sover, Dover, Sin, Din, Sout, Dout, Satop, Datop, Xor, Plus, PlusD, and Clear. At first glance, the names are gobbledygook. The designers aren't really trying to needle you, though. The compositing operators assume a "source" image and a "destination" image. So Sover means "Source Over" and Dout means "Destination Out," and so on.

Satop? That one means that the portion of Source that's "on top" is shown (the union of Source and Destination), and the portion of the Destination not covered by Source is shown.

Learning these powerful compositing operators is a requisite to programming the cube. The operators are fast and easy to use, once you get them all straight. "Compositing is your friend," developers are told. NeXT Developer Camp devotes a lab exercise to compositing. For those who can't attend, or those who didn't finish the lab, here's the "solution":

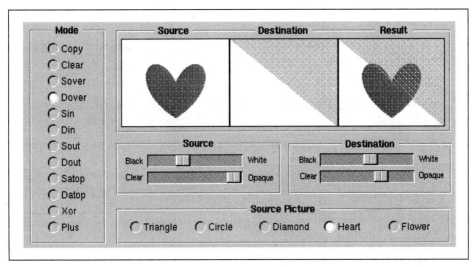

*Figure 14-2*

Shown is Dover, or "Destination Over." The destination "paint" is partially transparent, which results in the underlying source image being visible though overlaid by the destination.

If you're a programmer, you're probably familiar with operations such as AND, OR, and NOT. The compositing operations may seem magical. In fact, they're highly optimized bit-level operations. All selection highlighting, for example, is done by compositing. It's very fast.

This amazing low-level bitwork is only the first surprise to come from Pixar. If your math background is up to it, the July 1984 issue of Computer Graphics contains an article, "Compositing Digital Images," where the authors of compositing explain more than you probably want to know.

## Instance Drawing

Instance drawing is a NeXT addition to Display PostScript. Its purpose is to provide a convenient way for temporary drawing.

Display PostScript, as we've seen, involves some overhead despite many design speed-ups. Also, most drawing to the display is first done off screen. Images are composed in off-screen buffers, then copied to the screen.

In contrast, instance drawing is low-overhead drawing that's done directly to the screen. Instance drawing is usually in response to a user action; the drawing is also usually a transitory image—it's drawn, then gone. For example, when you drag a rectangle in The Workspace Manager to select a group of icons, you're using instance drawing. The blinking insertion point in text is also low-overhead instance drawing.

# Chapter 15

# Interface Builder

*In* Architecture *as in all other* Operative *Arts, the* end *must* direct *the* Operation. *The end is to build well. Well building hath three Conditions.* Commodity, Firmness, *and* Delight. Elements of Architecture (1624), pt.I.

**— SIR HENRY WOTTON** 1568–1639

Interface Builder is one of the few applications in computer history with an overly modest title. Interface Builder does indeed let you build interfaces, but it also lets you create much of an application—sometimes an entire application—graphically.

Creating an application in Interface Builder is a process of:

- Designing the basic "looks" of your application: windows, buttons, scrollers, views, icons, sounds...

- Diddling with the interface until it looks and acts as you wish. Because the graphic objects are truly objects—not mere images—what you're actually doing is setting instance variables. When you resize a button, Interface Builder changes the frame variable accordingly, for example.

- Creating new subclasses, of View and Object, to hold the algorithmic portions of your application. (You'll have to write this code yourself, an obvious oversight by Jean Marie Hullot, builder of Interface Builder.)

- And connecting the objects together. Connections are of two types: target/action connections and outlets. In the first case, a button might send a predetermined message to a target object when pressed. By setting an outlet, an object contains the address of another object to which it can then send messages.

## Nibs and Projects

Interface Builder maintains a "project" that contains:

- a project file (IB.proj) that tracks changes and holds information about the project;
- one or more ".nib" files (for NeXT Interface Builder); and
- other files that make up your application.

The .nib file contains the complete interface specification: objects used, their sizes and locations, the messages they send, and connections between objects.

If you're familiar with Macintosh or Windows programming, it's tempting to think of the .nib file as the application's "resources." But .nib files don't contain resources in the Macintosh sense of the word, and you can only view the contents of a .nib file (in a meaningful way, at least) or alter a .nib file in Interface Builder. What's more, the .nib file format is considered by NeXT to be proprietary, which discourages "hacking" the .nib files of existing applications. (In most cases, the .nib files are "rolled in" to applications and are not amenable to change or discovery.)

Project files are shown in an "Inspector Window." (See Figure 15-2.)

All the file types shown under "Type" above can be included in Interface Builder projects. Notice that traditional C files, as well as Objective-C ".m" (for method) files, may be included. Projects (and applications) may contain multiple .nib files, which reduces complexity, memory requirements, and results in faster launching (at the expense of a small pause to load additional segments).

Interface Builder uses the information in the project file to create two files needed to compile the application: a makefile and a main file. The makefile contains instructions needed by the compiler; the main file, as in traditional C programs, is the entry point for the application.

The Inspector window is a busy place. In Figure 15-2, a click on:

*Figure 15-1*

changes the display to the project's attributes. (See Figure 15-3.)

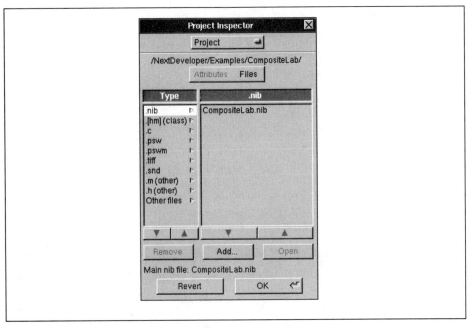

Figure 15-2

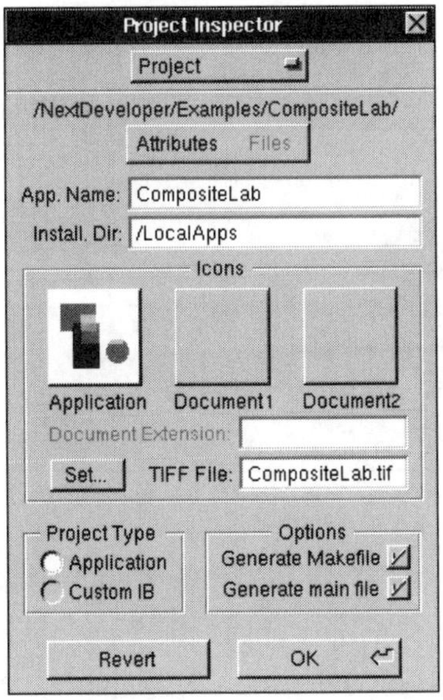

Figure 15-3

Here, much of the busy work involved with creating applications is grouped together. By default, you'll create applications, not custom Interface Builders. It is possible to customize Interface Builder somewhat, but full customization won't be possible until subsequent versions of Interface Builder.

We'll come back, soon, to the Inspector Window.

## Free Interface

The basis of a new application is a gift from Interface Builder. Choosing "New Application" presents you with this:

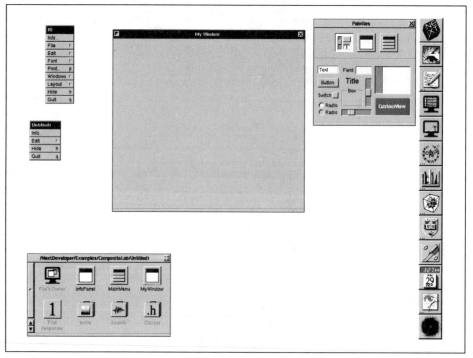

*Figure 15-4*

At the bottom left is the File window, which contains the project's high-level objects and resources. At top right is the Palette window, which holds interface objects. The interface objects—buttons, switches, panels, windows, menus—are dragged off the palette.

Interface Builder automatically creates a main window, an Info window, and a main menu containing Info, Hide, and Quit items. A First Responder object is also created to handle certain events.

Again, these aren't mere images or templates. They have built-in, default functionality. If you wish, you could save the project and compile it now. The resulting application would have:

- an empty, draggable window with a Close box, a Hide box, and controls at the bottom for resizing;
- a menu with Info, Hide, and Quit items, all functional;
- and an Info panel containing three textfields and a button (as an icon place holder).

As you can see, what's created is a real application. It just doesn't do anything of consequence yet.

## Creating an Interface

To add to this sparse interface, objects are dragged from the Palette window. The Palette window has three views: View, Window, and Menu. The View view (for want of a better term) contains the NeXT canonical views and controls: button, field, form, radio matrix, title, box, slider, scrolling list, and custom view. Just drag them into a window and they become part of the interface.

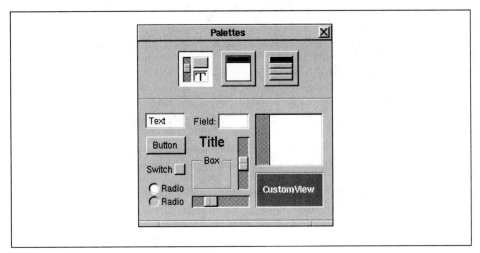

*Figure 15-5*

Clicking on the Window button changes the view:

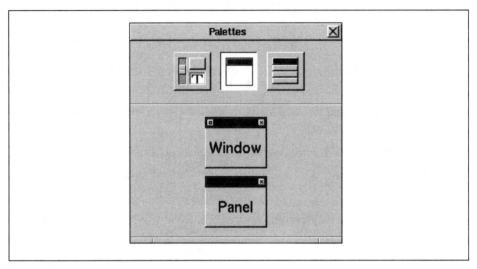

*Figure 15-6*

To add a window or panel to your application, drag it off the Palette window. Drag off as many windows and panels as you need. Each is added to the project and shown in the Files window.

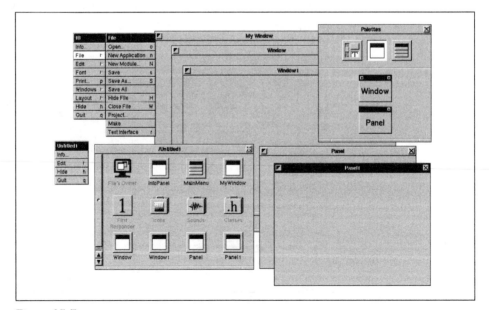

*Figure 15-7*

The final Palette window view is Menu.

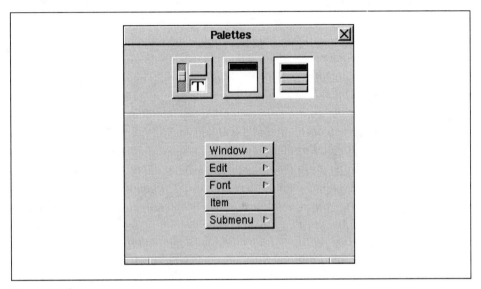

*Figure 15-8*

Your main menu has already been created by Interface Builder. Additional items and submenus are dragged onto the main menu. Once there, they can be dragged to be repositioned on the menu, or double-clicked to be named.

## Inspectors

After much dragging—but no coding—most of your interface will be in rough order. To fine-tune the interface, Interface Builder offers Inspectors. While controls can be changed, repositioned and resized by hand, some specifications need to be typed in—or at least clicked in.

Each object type has its own Inspector. Here are a few. (See Figures 15-9–15-15.)

As you can see, the Inspectors let you fine-tune the appearance and behavior of objects. We won't cover all the attribute options (that'd take a while!), but you can glean much from studying the illustrations.

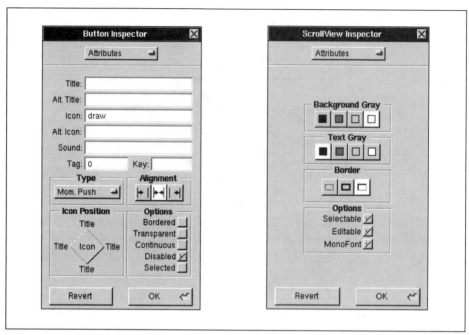

*Figures 15-9 and 15-10*

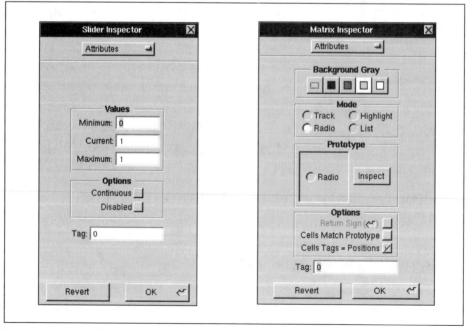

*Figures 15-11 and 15-12*

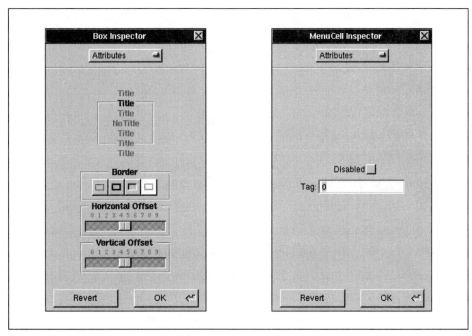

*Figures 15-13 and 15-14*

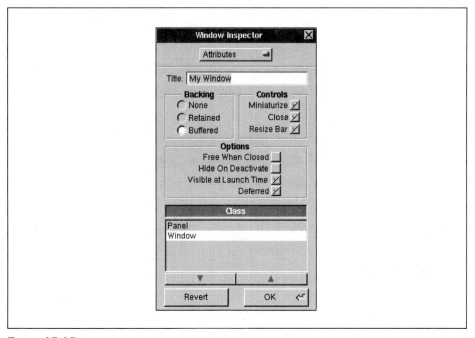

*Figure 15-15*

At the top of each Inspector window is a pop-up menu. Choosing an item changes the contents of the Inspector window to display either:

- the object's attributes;
- connections between objects;
- autosizing settings;
- miscellaneous values such as size; or
- class information for the object.

Let's take Miscellaneous and Autosizing first. Miscellaneous is used to set the size of the control or object. Entering numbers is more precise than dragging to resize.

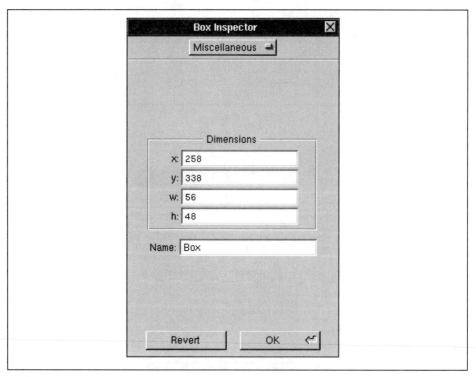

*Figure 15-16*

Autosizing lets you answer the question: "If my window contains controls, and the window is resized, do the controls move or not?"

The choice is yours. You can have the controls move proportionally to the new window size, or resize proportionally, or both, or neither. Effecting these choices is a matter of clicking on a few lines. ("Doodads," I think, is the technical term). At left, no autosizing whatsoever. At right, the works (for the particular selected object):

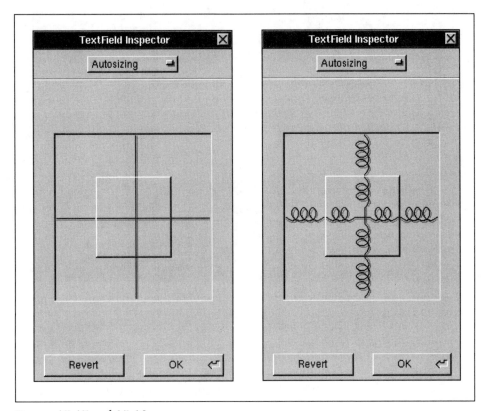

*Figures 15-17 and 15-18*

This is pretty neat: another NextStep innovation. While it's nice that controls can move when a window resizes, the truly clever aspect is that the controls may also resize when the window resizes. Same functionality, new size. Very clever.

When you've finished dragging and clicking your way to a beautiful interface, the result will look exactly like Figure 15-19.

The application window is at the top center. Below it is the Classes window, here widened to show many of the Application Kit classes. The pop-up menu at the top right of the Classes window contains commands to parse, unparse, subclass, and instantiate classes.

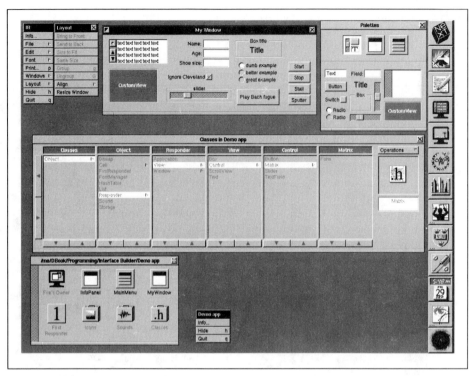

*Figure 15-19*

As always with the cube, there's more.

At any time, after setting any attribute, or adding or changing any object, you can test your interface by choosing Test Interface from the File menu.

Interface Builder steps aside and your application now "works," at least to the extent of bringing up windows, pressing buttons, moving sliders, and the like.

The only visible indication of Interface Builder is the Build/Toggle switch, which replaces Interface Builder's dock icon. (Or appears on screen if you haven't docked Interface Builder.)

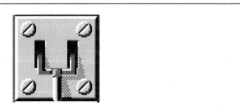

*Figure 15-20*

Use the interface until you're satisfied or dismayed with your work, then hit the switch to leave the "test" mode.

You can also return to Interface Builder by choosing your application's Quit menu item.

## Connections

Well, enough diddling. We now come to conceptual matters having to do with Objective-C.

As you know, Objective-C programs are collections of interacting objects. The objects contain instance variables of private data, analogous to Pascal records or C structs. The objects also have methods, analogous to procedures or functions. The methods are used to send messages to other objects, which may invoke subsequent methods, and so on. Old hat.

Using Interface Builder, then, is a matter of:

* creating objects;
* setting the instance variables of those objects; and
* specifying what messages to send to other objects.

Talk is cheap, right? Fortunately, the Application Kit defines a ton of useful classes all stuffed with pre-written methods. And Interface Builder lets you define— subclass—new objects and allows you to make the connections between objects.

One of the Big Concepts behind this is "target/action." Objects may be the targets of other objects. A click on a button, for example, may send a certain message to a predefined "target" object. The target receives the message and takes action.

Many target/action connections are pre-defined in Interface Builder. The standard "bare-bones" menu provided by Interface Builder provides a good example.

The standard menu has commands for Info, Edit, Hide, and Quit. And the menu commands are predefined by Interface Builder.

Consider: Clicking the Info item should display the Info Panel.

How's that done? With a method. A method that brings a window to the front and makes it the key window.

Obviously, the method needs a window or panel to serve as the target of the message.

Enough preamble. Click on the default menu. The Inspector window changes to the MenuCell Inspector display. Now set the pop-up to Connections. A number of methods appear.

Click makeKeyAndOrderFront under "Actions of Destination."

And this happens:

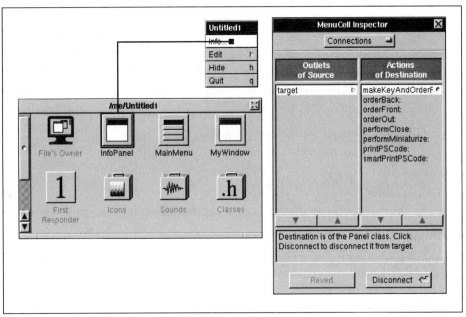

*Figure 15-21*

You're shown the connection that already exists! The target is the InfoPanel, the action is makeKeyAndOrderFront, and the connection has been pre-made by Interface Builder. (The dot to the right of the method name in the Inspector window means a connection exists.)

Many methods and connections are provided. You can also make your own connections. Let's say we have a slider and a text field. We want to connect them and have the text field display the value of the slider.

Click on the slider and watch the inspector window:

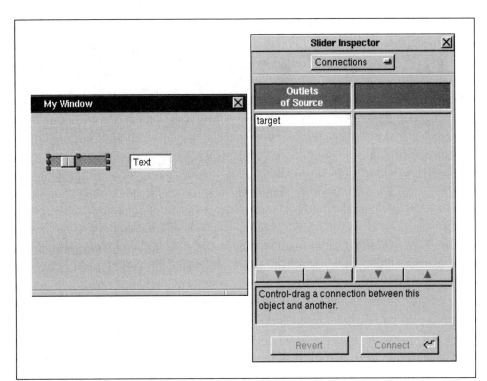

*Figure 15-22*

Instructions are given in the Inspector window. We Control-drag to make the connection and are shown the result. (See Figure 15-23.)

We can now select a predefined method from the Inspector window (takeFloat-ValueFrom:, maybe) and click Connect to make the connection.

This doesn't mean you don't need to write code. Sure, you need to write code. In practice, it's a back-and-forth process between Edit and Interface Builder. You can create source files, then have Interface Builder "parse" them. Once they're parsed, you can add and modify in Interface Builder.

Or you can go the other way: Define your classes in Interface Builder, then "unparse" the classes to create source code files. The files created by Interface Builder will be bare-boned method skeletons, which you can then flesh in with handcrafted code.

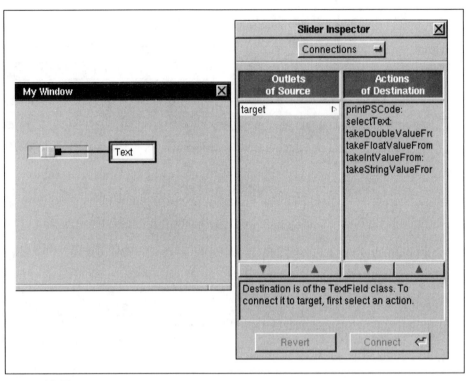

*Figure 15-23*

# Chapter 16

## The NeXT Application Kit, Part I: Non-Responsive Classes

*The bearings of this observation lays in the application of it. [Bunsby]*
Dombey and Son, ch.23
— **CHARLES DICKENS** 1812–1870

Many computers keep their built-in software in ROM. Often, the ROM routines are grouped into "managers." A Window Manager here, a Dialog Manager there. Programmers are given the high-level data structures and the interface to the ROM routines—a collection of pre-written functions and procedures.

With NeXT, the software is on disk, not in ROM, but the process is the same. To create programs, you first learn the "interface routines," then use them well—because interface is a primary part of the program. The interface is the program in many respects. When all's said and done, and the program is happily compiled, interface code will probably be the largest contributor to code size.

Interface is "where the program happens." Programs with graphic interfaces—most commercial programs, these days—must be interactive. Users don't want to click a button, then wait, and wait. Action must be snappy. The user does something, the program does something: now.

When graphic interfaces first came along, programmers thought of them as a shell around "the real program." There's the shell: buttons, menus, windows, and such. But the real program is underneath.

That philosophy is still around. And it's not without merit. It makes porting applications easier, for example.

But more and more, the move is away from that programming style. Because interface is "where the program happens," and because graphic applications need to be quick, basic program functionality has moved up and up—into the interface itself.

Apple's HyperCard is a good example. "Open" a button and you'll often see a script of program code. The functionality is in the button. The button is the function. Interface and algorithm are married, intertwined, one. Om.

That's the way it is on NeXT. Don't think of the Application Kit as the "graphic face" on your application. The interface is the application. Application Kit objects aren't mere images; they're self-contained, marvelously functional classes of object "templates." They already know how to do many things, and do them fast and well.

When you create programs using the Application Kit (and the SoundKit and MusicKit), you'll use this predefined functionality. For the most part, you'll employ pre-written routines. You'll create instances of existing Application Kit objects. Or you'll subclass Application Kit objects to create your own objects. You'll write your own methods, and you'll take advantage of the hundreds of pre-written methods available.

That said, here's the Application Kit, on the facing page.

Notice that most of the Application Kit is devoted to interface. One easy division, in fact, is dividing the Application Kit into two parts: interface classes and non-interface classes, or "algorithmic classes," for want of a better term.

Stripping away the interface classes leaves these common classes:

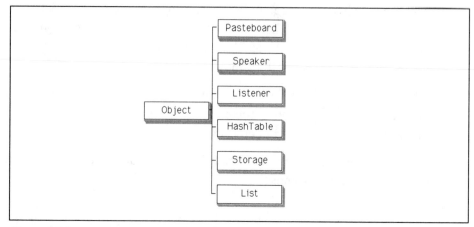

*Figure 16-1*

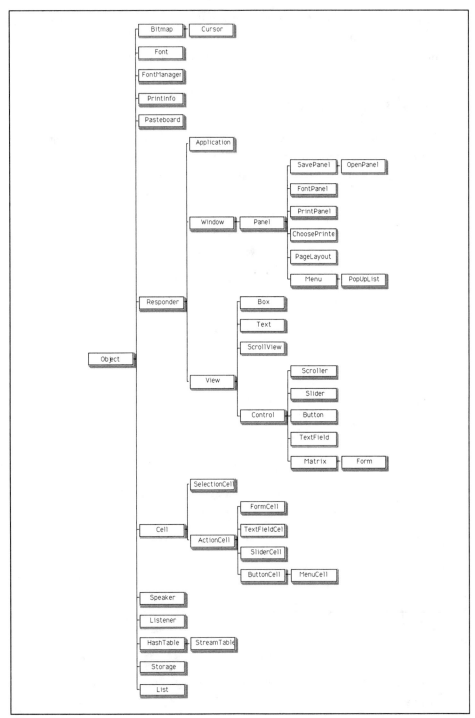

*Figure 16-2*

Not many classes there, but a wealth of functionality. If you're a dedicated programmer, you might want to add other classes here. Maybe a "BinaryTree" class (by subclassing "List") or a "NeuralNetwork" class (you tell me).

## Into the Application Kit

Now let's briefly cover each Application Kit class, beginning with Object. To keep everything moderately grouped, these "foundation classes" will provide the framework. Collapsing the Application Kit into top-level classes yields:

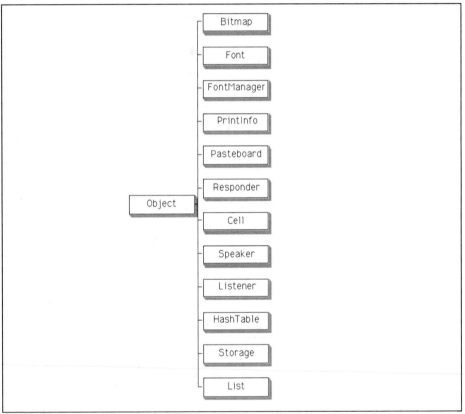

*Figure 16-3*

A much more manageable list.

As we proceed, we'll consider subclasses together with their respective superclasses.

The Application Kit requires a book, not this brief glance. Sorry. So, imagine that you're standing on a hill. Down below, in a pleasant valley, there's a party going on. You can see swirls of color and hear faint laughter...

A final apology: This isn't hard information. It's early for NeXT and early for the Application Kit. This information covers NeXT's 1.0 software release. The exact structure and content of the Application Kit may have changed slightly from what's given here.

## Object

The Object class is the top of the Application Kit tree. Object is the only class with no superclass. Every class in the Application Kit inherits from Object. As always, both the instance variables and the methods of Object are inherited by its subclasses. In this case, by all other classes, since all classes are subclasses of Object.

Other classes call on Object methods to:

- initialize classes;
- create, free, and copy instances;
- identify classes and instances;
- test inheritance relationships or class functionality;
- send run-time messages;
- get method handles;
- handle errors; and
- archive objects.

This, the seminal class, has many methods but only one instance variable: the "isa" pointer.

This pointer—inherited by all classes—is the key to Objective-C messaging. The isa pointer provides a path for the low-level msg() call to follow. The msg() function uses the isa pointer to find the class structure. Once there, it checks the dispatch table to find the requested method. If it's there, fine; the method is performed.

If the method being sought isn't found, the isa pointer is employed again, this time to find the class's superclass. Once again, the method dispatch table is checked. If the method isn't found, the process is repeated, hand over hand, using the isa pointer.

The Object class is the end of the road—the top of the isa pointer chain. If all subclasses have been checked unsuccessfully, the Object class is checked for the method. If the method is found, it's performed. If it's not found, the message request falls out of the cube (through the fan grill), rolls under the table, and no harm's done. (Though applications that send messages to nonexistent methods shouldn't be trusted.)

In practice, this laborious searching of dispatch tables isn't done. Instead, a 2,000 entry cache is used to hold the most frequently called methods. If the method sought is in the cache, it's called—fast. If it's not in the cache, the process described above takes place: isa to isa to isa, all the way up to Object.

After applications have run for a while, according to NeXT, 98% or more of the messages will find their methods in the cache. This means that applications become faster as you use them! Amazing. Frequently used commands are faster than infrequently used commands. That's pretty neat.

Perusing Object's methods will give you a good idea of the basic housekeeping methods available to Application Kit classes. Remember: Every class inherits these methods. They can be called by any instance of any object, anywhere. Some—like copy—are straightforward and easy to use. Others will rarely be used but are great conveniences for times when you really need something like:

- `shouldNotImplement:(SEL)aSelector;`

One of the most interesting methods in Object is the factory method:

+ `poseAs: aFactoryId;`

which allows you to change the fundamental behavior of objects. If you're familiar with the concept of "patching ROM routines" to alter basic behavior, you'll appreciate this means to bend the Application Kit to your will, at a very low level.

## Bitmap

The Bitmap class helps out in drawing—particularly in drawing icons. On NeXT, icons are TIFF images. The class includes methods for:

- setting the size of a bitmap (usually an icon);
- getting information about the bitmap; and
- compositing bitmaps.

The Bitmap class has a single subclass: Cursor. The Cursor class adds, as instance variables:

- a "hotSpot," declared as a NXPoint; and
- a C structure containing two flags: onMouseEntered and onMouseExited.

In other words, the Application Kit provides built-in means to determine if the cursor has entered an area on screen. Another construct, called a "tracking rectangle," is used with this feature.

## Font

The Font class encapsulates our friends, the fonts, into objects. Some of the instance variables used to describe fonts are expected:

- name;
- size;
- style; and
- PostScript font number.

Other instance variables include flags to denote whether a particular font is stored in the Window Server, stored in the printer, is a screen font, or has an associated screen font.

Factory methods are provided to create or free font objects. Other methods query font objects for point size, style, and other attributes.

A "set" method makes a font the current font. Finally, methods are provided to read and write fonts to and from archived files.

## FontManager

If you've used Interface Builder to add a Font menu to an application, you've noticed that the Font menu brings with it a wealth of no-coding-necessary features: all the features on the standard Font menu, plus the Font panel. This class—FontManager—is where that functionality comes from.

Three of the instance variables defined in the FontManager class are objects:

* panel: used for the Font panel;
* menu: for the Font menu; and
* selFont, which holds the id of the selected font.

A "whatToDo" variable holds the "what" to be done on receiving a convertFont message. Another variable, traitToChange, contains the trait to change (bold, for example) if the "what" in whatToDo is NX_CHANGETRAIT. Finally, a multiple-Font flag is provided. It's true if the selection contains multiple fonts.

## PrintInfo

The PrintInfo class contains information about the current print job and lets you determine some aspects of printing. Another class, PrintPanel, handles the familiar Print panel. Since printing is really drawing to another device, making the actual print images is handled by the View class.

In general, PrintInfo methods let you query or set various print parameters:

* all four margins;
* the scaling factor;
* image orientation (vertical or horizontal "landscape");
* centering: either vertical or horizontal centering of the printed image;
* spooling;
* manual feed;
* the page order of printing;
* printer name;
* printer type;
* printer host;
* print resolution.

These are helpful methods. There's even a method to set the number of "pages per sheet" to print.

Two additional methods will make you appreciate the Application Kit, if you don't already. SetVertPagination and setHorizPagination are methods to paginate printer output. Unless your needs are picky, you'll never need to write your own pagination routine.

SetVertPagination and setHorizPagination each take a single argument: a mode to specify the type of pagination you want. The modes are:

- NX_AUTOPAGINATION, which leaves pagination up to the Application Kit (usually with good results—it's a sophisticated algorithm);
- NX_FITPAGINATION, which scales the image to fit on the page, while retaining the aspect ratio; or
- NX_CLIPPAGINATION, which clips the printed image.

## Pasteboard

The Pasteboard is similar in function to the Macintosh Clipboard, but more powerful. The NeXT Pasteboard is actually a Mach server: pbs, for PasteBoard Server. The pbs server is initialized on startup and hangs around waiting for data.

Using the Pasteboard is a breeze. The NeXT Pasteboard doesn't contain data. It contains only a pointer to the actual data and a Count that represents the data's length in bytes. The use of pointers means that it's fast and easy to transfer huge amounts of data. The data isn't first copied to the Pasteboard, only a pointer.

Only one factory method is provided: New, which is used by the NeXT system, never by programmers. A mere seven other methods take care of reading and writing the Pasteboard and freeing the Pasteboard's contents.

## Cell

Cell is a major Application Kit class. The Cell class and its subclasses are:

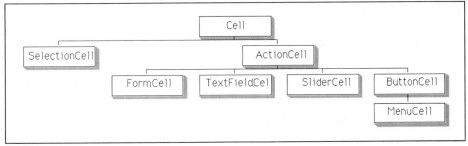

Figure 16-4

You could do everything that Cell (and its subclasses) provides using only the View class, but it'd be very painful. Using Cell and Cell subclasses also relieves you of the overhead of the massive View class.

Consider a humble text field. The field itself is a View, right? Since there's text inside, you'll need the Text class, right?

No. These low-level functions, in part, are built into Cell. (Other TextField functions are in the TextField class.)

Also in Cell are a variety of methods to set the appearance of cell-based interface items. And there's an additional convenience: the Cell class comes with predefined cell data types. So your fields can be preset to contain integers, floats, even a "date-type."

Cell has many methods. But they're not tricky, tough-to-learn methods. You won't have any conceptual difficulties here. The Cell methods allow you to:

- create or free cells;
- set the size, type, and state of cells;
- enable or disable cells;
- set the content of cells;
- set parameters for cell contents ("pinning" input to a range, in other words);
- modify graphic or text attributes, or images in cells; and
- edit cell text.

There's more. Cell methods are provided to validate the contents of text cells (more functions you won't need to write yourself!). And other Cell methods are used to interact with other cells:

-takeDoubleValueFrom:

- takeFloatValueFrom:

- takeIntValueFrom:

- takeStringValueFrom:

And there's a handful of target/action methods:

- action

- getPeriodicDelay:andInterval:

- isContinuous

- sendActionOn:

- setAction:

- setContinuous:

- setTarget:

- target

And a keyEquivalent method for attaching a keyboard equivalent to a cell. And...

• a few methods to display cell contents; and

• four methods for tracking the mouse; and

• a method to change the cursor appearance while in a cell; and

• archiving methods for use with cells.

And more.

Granted, it's a lot. But keep in mind that the methods in Cell aren't complicated. They're a complete set of handy routines. If they weren't here, you'd probably end up writing them yourself. For example: Is a cell highlighted? Just call:

isHighlighted

to find out:

if [myCell isHighlighted] <additional code>

The methods in the Cell class will quickly become second nature. Many of these methods are put into place as you click and drag your way through Interface Builder; and Interface Builder Inspector windows let you set most Cell instance variables.

## Object > Cell > SelectionCell

Let's move down the class tree to one of Cell's two subclasses: SelectionCell.

SelectionCell has no subclasses. It's a small class, and we won't spend much time on it. Why? Because you won't often use SelectionCell. For most programmers, SelectionCell will be a curiosity, not a frequently used class.

SelectionCell's purpose in life is making it easy to create and use NeXT-style hier- archical menus. Since you'll probably never make menus "by hand," you won't need to use SelectionCell directly. Interface Builder provides menu-making means.

Innovative programmers, though, may use the functionality in SelectionCell to display data in innovative ways.

## Object > Cell > ActionCell

In contrast to SelectionCell, ActionCell is a large class. It's subclassed by NeXT to provide definitive NextStep cell-based objects:

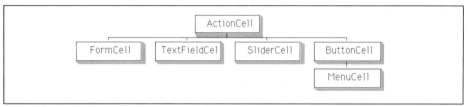

*Figure 16-5*

Let's pause before we get into these various cells and take a look again at the NeXT Application Kit. (See opposite page.)

To look at this elegant structure is to believe. Or, at least, to want to believe that, yes!, everything is precisely grouped, and subclassed, and sub-subclassed in perfect symmetry. Life is good.

But the illustration is misleading. Not monumentally misleading, just slightly misleading. In truth, the Application Kit isn't quite as elegant as the illustration.

A few classes sort of...slop over into other classes. In particular, consider our present position: ActionCell and its subclasses.

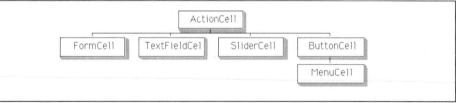

*Figure 16-6*

Now consider these classes:

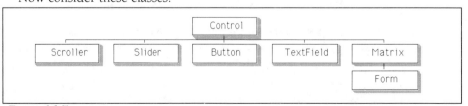

*Figure 16-7*

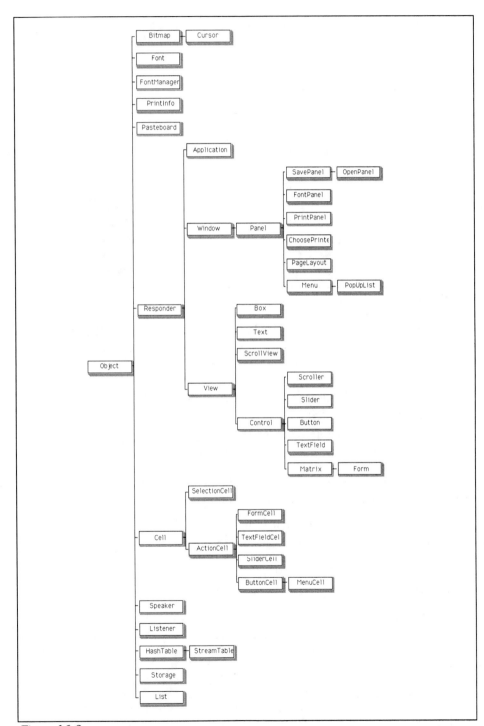

*Figure 16-8*

Similar but different, right? The Cell subclasses have more to do with "looks," and the Responder subclasses are more "responsive" to user actions, right?

Yes, to a degree. But there's overlap between the two groups of subclasses. Let's home in on ButtonCell and Button. Or:

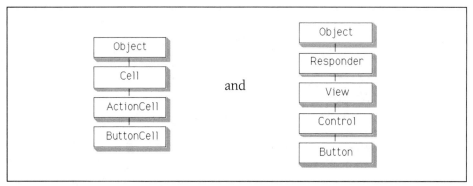

Figure 16-9

The two classes, ButtonCell and Button, are similar but different. They each have methods unique to their respective classes, but they also have methods in common.

On one hand, this is a convenience, because it increases the likelihood you'll find the method you want, if you're looking for one of the methods common to more than one class. On the other hand, the fuzziness between classes may make it difficult to find what you want. Is it in the Cell classes or in the Control classes?

When NeXT, or some third-party company, delivers an honest-to-goodness "method browser," finding the right method will be easier.

For now, just remember that Cell classes deal more with "looks" and Control classes deal more with actions and events.

Now back to ActionCell, FormCell, TextFieldCell, SliderCell, ButtonCell, and MenuCell.

ActionCell is the superclass of more specific Cell classes:

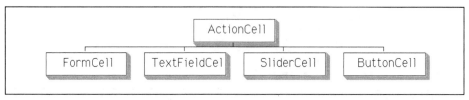

Figure 16-10

As such, it adds only a few variables and methods for use by all the ActionCell subclasses. ActionCell doesn't define much, but what is defined is important.

ActionCell methods are also high-level, geared for use by NeXT cells or cell objects that you create by subclassing.

One method not in ActionCell is a "new" factory method. That method is found in ActionCell's superclass: Cell.

ActionCell does offer a copy method, which copies an ActionCell. Other methods handle:

- setting stringValue's of ActionCells;
- displaying ActionCells;
- targets and actions;
- assigning tags to ActionCells; and
- archiving ActionCells.

## Object > Cell > ActionCell > TextFieldCell

All subclasses of ActionCell use ActionCell methods and instance variables. That should be obvious. In this part of the tree, however, superclass methods and variables are indeed used often.

The TextFieldCell class adds only two instance variables:

- textGray; and
- backgroundGray.

No other variables are needed.

Two factory methods create new text fields. A couple of specialized draw methods cater to drawing text. One draw method takes textGray and backgroundGray into account, for example. Other methods deal with the "looks" of text fields, and reading and writing text fields with typed streams.

## Object > Cell > ActionCell > FormCell

FormCells are matrices of TextFieldCells. As such, the FormCell class doesn't offer much in the way of awesome new functionality; only a handful of methods, mostly dealing with the appearance of the FormCell array of TextFieldCells.

## Object > Cell > ActionCell > ButtonCell

ButtonCell, however, is a different story. NeXT went wild with buttons. As a result, buttons can be virtually anything you want them to be. Buttons may contain:

- text; and/or
- icons; and/or
- sounds.

If you want, buttons can even be transparent. Sure, there's a use for transparent buttons, isn't there?

For basic button behavior, NeXT defines these button types:

NX_MOMENTARYPUSH

NX_MOMENTARYCHANGE

NX_PUSHONPUSHOFF

NX_TOGGLE

NX_SWITCH

NX_RADIOBUTTON

You'll most often choose a button type in Interface Builder, but you can also "code in" your choice.

The many button instance variables are put to use by the methods of ButtonCell. Nothing tricky here, just creating buttons, modifying buttons, drawing buttons, setting icons, sounds, and alternate images.

The built-in methods for key equivalents are a nice touch. You should include them in your applications. Good typists will appreciate your thoughtfulness.

Also noteworthy are methods that allow you to set or "get" the "state" of a button as a value. They allow you to query a button's state. Is the button on or off?

Some Application Kit classes are powerful and sometimes difficult to understand. ButtonCell and its kin offer powerful methods, but they're not complex classes. They're fun.

## Object > Cell > ActionCell > SliderCell

SliderCell is a particularly elegant class.

The NeXT SliderCell improves on Macintosh-like "scroll bars." NeXT sliders can be continuous. If you choose to make your SliderCell continuous, a mousedown begins a modal loop that sends message after message to a specified target. Whatever is updated by the slider can then be updated continuously, not just once, on mouseup.

Using SliderCells is a matter of:

• setting minimum and maximum values for the slider to produce; and
• deciding whether to make the slider continuous.

Once those decisions are made, SliderCell methods let you determine the look of sliders and track the mouse. If you prefer a custom look for your slider, you can easily override the SliderCell methods.

## Object > Cell > ActionCell > ButtonCell > MenuCell

Cell's lowest subclass is MenuCell.

MenuCells are a specific type of button used in menus. The characteristics of MenuCells are:

• text is drawn left-justified;
• a keyboard equivalent may be shown at right; and
• an arrow may be drawn to indicate a submenu.

MenuCell inherits the wealth of ButtonCell functionality and adds menu-specific methods and a single instance variable: updateAction.

Updating may highlight or dim a menu item, or it may change the string associated with a menu item. Updating-related methods are also found in the Menu class (another example of class overlap).

There are only a few other MenuCell methods: a "hasMenu" boolean method, read and write methods for use with archiving, and not much else.

## Speaker and Listener Classes

The Speaker class and Listener class put easy to use, high-level programming interfaces on Mach's low-level message-passing abilities.

Speakers and Listeners aren't optional niceties. They're a necessary part of every major NeXT application.

The Application Kit creates the objects for you. Using Speakers and Listeners is easy, and they provide immense functionality to your program, at little cost. Creating a Speaker object is as easy as creating a button:

```
mySpeaker = [Speaker new]
```

Beyond that, using Speakers and Listeners requires only:

- setting a port (when you're speaking); or
- checking in (if you're listening).

Your Listener object then receives remote events automatically along with other events. Do with them what you will.

When speaking—sending information to other applications—you can send data or send data and methods: a powerful option.

Spend some time with the Speaker and Listener classes. NeXT has made them easy to use. Use `em.

## HashTable

The HashTable class implements everything you need to create and use hash tables. It also implements a data structure of matching keys and values for fast look-up of information.

Three instance variables are defined: a count and two pointers—one for the key description, the other for the value description. And four factory methods handle creation of hash tables.

Here's a good spot to note something you'll see often in the Application Kit: a variety of "new" factory methods with varying degrees of detail. You may use whichever method you prefer. But when your program is run, the factory method with the greatest detail is eventually called. The detailed factory methods let you determine the initial state of the object's instance variables. If you don't wish to do that—and simply use "new"—Objective-C's runtime system plugs in default values for you.

In general, it's better to specify as much as possible when creating a new object. It's somewhat faster and gives you control over the initial state of an object.

## Storage

The Storage class is a pre-built "array handler." Using it allows you to create, manipulate and access arrays without having to subclass them yourself. If you prefer, you can also use a Storage object as a stack.

You don't need to explicitly set the capacity of arrays. The Storage object grows as needed (as does the List object).

A single factory method creates an array of Count elements of elementSize size, and type description.

## List

It's hard to program without making lists. The List class is a great convenience. It's a small, peaceful class for managing collections of elements. You can create and use:

* fixed-length lists;
* variable-length lists;
* sets; or
* ordered collections.

Only three instance variables are needed:

* a pointer to the list object's data;
* numElements; and
* maxElements.

Two factory methods let you create a new list and, optionally, set the list's initial number of elements.

Methods, similar to those in the storage class, let you add, insert, remove, or find the index of list elements.

# Chapter 17

# The NeXT Application Kit, Part II: Responder and Its Subclasses

*Ambo florentes ætatibus, Arcades ambo,*
*Et cantare pares et respondere parati.*
"Both in the flower of their youth, Arcadians both, and matched
and ready alike to start a song and to respond."

— **VIRGIL** 70–19 B.C.

*This method is, to define as the number of a class the class*
*of all classes similar to the given class.*
Principles of Mathematics, pt.II, ch.11, sect.iii (1903)

— **BERTRAND RUSSELL** 1872–1970

When you program the cube, this is where you'll spend most of your time: in Responder and its subclasses.

These classes form the heart of NeXT applications. In particular, the View class is important.

View is a bear, though: It's a complex class. The power of NeXT applications, in great measure, comes from the View class. Learn the View class, and learn it well, and no other Application Kit class will trouble you unduly. Well, that's enough for one day. Take a break, go to the beach.

Now let's back up to Responder.

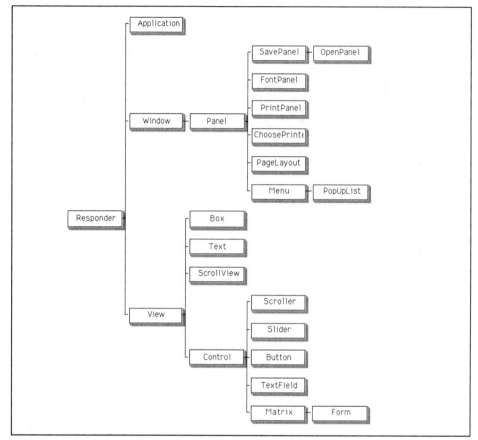

*Figure 17-1*

## Responder

Responder is termed an "abstract class" by NeXT. In other words, it's a conceptual class. You won't find a Responder object in an Interface Builder palette.

Responder isn't a large class, but it's fundamental. It deals with one key concept: responsiveness.

On NeXT, entities that can receive and act on events are "responders."

Earlier, we mentioned "key windows." At a programming level, the key window usually contains the "first responder." It's the object that gets first crack at handling— responding to—the current event.

The Responder class, then, encapsulates responsiveness to events. And that's about all it does. Exactly how the events are handled is determined by Responder subclasses.

The Responder class defines only one instance variable, which contains the object (id) fingered as the nextResponder.

At first glance, the notion of responders may seem overly complicated. But consider: Windows may contain many objects. Not merely visible, discrete objects like buttons and sliders, but also views where information is displayed. And views, or other objects, may overlap.

So it's not enough to merely "hit-test" to find mouse click locations, then pass the event to the object "under" the mouse click; there may be many objects under the mouse click.

What's needed is a definitive way to say: "Hey, you! You're the first responder. If you can't handle the event, give it to nextResponder. See if it can handle the event."

And that's the way it works. FirstResponder gets the events. If FirstResponder doesn't have a method to deal with the event, the event is passed to the nextResponder.

It follows, then, that Responder methods deal primarily with "who's the responder" and with key and mouse events.

FirstResponders are usually View objects. After all, users do their work in windows. Window objects are primarily the window frame and associated controls. Inside windows are Views, and Views are usually responders.

## Object > Responder > Application

Every NeXT application has one—and only one—Application object. The Application object has some important duties:

* It manages a "windowlist" of all application windows. Since Views are contained in windows, all Views are linked in the windowlist.

* It serves as a connection between the application and the Window Server and Display PostScript.

* It receives events from the Window Server and dispatches events it can't handle (most events, in other words) to other objects in the application.

The application object is assigned a global variable—one of the few "globals" you'll see in the AppKit: NXApp.

Application has many methods. In general, the methods:

- monitor or change the application's state;
- deal with events;
- or deal with application windows.

Other methods are used with the Pasteboard, speakers and listeners, archive files, and .nib files. (Large applications often consist of multiple .nib files.)

## Delegates

It's time to introduce delegates.

Many Application Kit objects have delegates: objects that "stand in" for the primary object. The purpose behind delegation is simplicity. You can get the same result by subclassing objects, but using a delegate is simpler and doesn't carry the burden of superclass overhead. Delegates are "Let George do it" objects.

The methods used by delegates are usually "did" and "will" methods. When "something will happen," or "something did happen," a delegate—if there is one—gets a crack at doing something, if it wants to.

If an application delegate is present, certain messages are sent. If there's no application delegate, the messages aren't sent. The delegate can do something on receipt of the message or ignore the message. Often, the messages are ignored. But if you want to act on a message, you can easily do so. Maybe you'd like to code in a trumpet flourish when you receive an appDidUnhide message? Or, on a more practical level, send some clean-up messages after appDidResignActive.

## Object > Responder > Window

Window is another large class: many defines, about 30 instance variables, and about 130 methods. Again, it's a class you need to know well.

Window instance variables and methods are geared to making and managing windows: moving, resizing, displaying, ordering, even printing window contents.

## Object > Responder > Window > Panel

Window has a single subclass: Panel.

Panel, itself, however, has many subclasses: SavePanel, FontPanel, PrintPanel, ChoosePrinter, PageLayout, and Menu. As a result, the Panel subclass holds only those variables and methods common to its subclasses.

This class, like all Application Kit classes, is well-documented in the header file. A welcome addition in the NeXT 1.0 release was careful and thorough documentation of all Application Kit classes, objects, and methods. Other companies should take note.

The Panel class encapsulates variables and data common to its subclasses. All panel subclasses can avail themselves of Command-key equivalents defined here, in Panel, for example.

The subclasses of Panel include the standard NeXT panels:

- SavePanel;
- FontPanel;
- PrintPanel;
- ChoosePrinter; and
- PageLayout.

The remaining standard Panel class is OpenPanel, which is a subclass of SavePanel. A glance at the header files reveals why: SavePanel is the more functional of the two panels. Making OpenPanel a subclass of SavePanel is a concise move.

Before you begin subclassing Panel for your own distinctive panels, spend some time with the NeXT standard panels. You'll pick up Panelizing in a hurry.

## Object > Responder > Window > Panel > Menu

The Menu class inherits the ability to understand Command-key equivalents from Panel. Beyond that, Menu adds only a few features. Prominent menu methods are used to:

- change menu items or menu titles;
- add menu items; and
- update menus.

You won't need the Menu class often, unless your application is fond of changing menu items' appearance in response to user actions: toggling between "Hide Graphics" and "Show Graphics," for instance.

You might subclass Menu to create your own Menu-related objects.

## Object > Responder > View

This is it: the View class. Know View and prosper. Someday, NeXT magazines will be filled with NeXT Programmer Wanted ads. When that day comes, you'll be ready, If you're a ViewMaster.

Views are where drawing happens. You don't draw in Windows; you draw in Views.

View is always subclassed, which isn't hard. Typically, you'll make one or more View subclasses in Interface Builder, like Figure 17-2.

Views can have many subviews, and many views can be contained in a window. (See Figure 17-3.)

View objects are used to display information. They're also used to handle mouse and keyboard events. All controls are subclasses of View. All displayed text, whether full-blown text objects or mere TextFields, are subclasses of View.

Remember that View is a subclass of Responder. All Responder subclasses can respond to events. Once you get down to the View class, objects not only can respond but also can draw to the screen.

All graphic objects are subclasses of View.

All windows have a minimum of two views. One view displays the window's title bar and border. That view is created and maintained by the Window Server. Programmers shouldn't muck with it.

The second view that all windows have is the contentView. Other views that you create in windows are subclasses of contentView. One thing you can't do is make contentView a subview of another views.

All window views exist in a hierarchy. Views may have subviews. Those subviews may have other subviews. The hierarchy of views makes drawing easier and allows subviews to take information easily from superviews. Subviews also allow

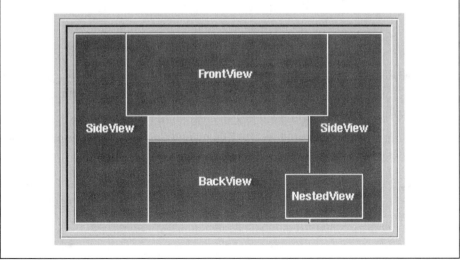

*Figures 17-2 and 17-3*

you to use different coordinate systems for different views. For example, a subview that displayed the contents of a superview, but added 12 degrees of rotation, would be easily accomplished.

Two instance variables contain a view's location. Both are NXrects. The first, frame, is the view's rectangle expressed in the coordinate system of the view's superview. The other variable, bounds, is the rectangle expressed in the coordinate of the view itself. Much of the View class is devoted to coordinate system manipulations.

Other View methods:

- manage the hierarchy of views in a window;
- inform other views of changes;
- prepare to display views;
- display views (through numerous methods);
- move, flip, and rotate, or adjust images;
- scroll views;
- archive views;
- handle "hit-testing" (to find where the user clicked); and
- print views.

View is loaded with methods you'll need to learn well to master NeXT programming.

But remember: The methods add functionality you don't need to create "from scratch." On other computers, for example, rotating text involves low-level wizardry. Most free-rotation routines, even when crafted in assembler, are slow. On NeXT, rotating text—or anything else—is child's play, thanks to the sophistication of Display PostScript, and the many methods of View.

Another bonus comes when it's time to print, because the printing of views is built-in. *Views know how to print themselves.*

As all programmers know, printing is a pain. On NeXT, thanks to the "single image" model, it's remarkably easy. You can even avail yourself of automatic pagination, if you wish.

## Object > Responder > View > Box

Box is a small class that allows you to make and change boxes, and add views and subviews to boxes. Here's a nice set of nested boxes, filled with controls:

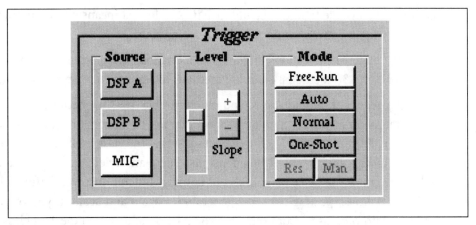

*Figure 17-4*

Most often, you'll work with boxes in Interface Builder. However, effects like the italicized "trigger" label above are done with Box class methods; Interface Builder offers only some of the available box attributes.

## Object > Responder > View > Text

Text is the largest Application Kit class. (View and Window vie for second place in size.)

It's a big class because NeXT text objects are extremely functional. Want to write a word processor? You'll find many of the necessary features in an off-the-shelf text object.

Text is a subclass of View. Like views, text objects are displayed in frames, or "bounds rectangles." The Text class adds an additional frame: body rectangle, which is nested inside the bounds rectangle. The text itself is displayed in the body rectangle. The area surrounding the body rectangle—out to the bounds rectangle on all four sides—contains the text margins.

Text objects can be left aligned, right aligned, centered, or fully justified; or contain mixtures of fonts, faces, and sizes. Foreground and background colors (whites, blacks, and grays for now) may be set. Underline is available, as are superscripting and subscripting. Even "paragraph styles," something usually found only in "power" word processors, are included in the Text class.

Two text formats are supported: ASCII and RTF, for Rich Text Format. Built-in support for RTF is a great blessing; RTF is widely used on Macintosh and IBM computers. Being able to interpret and save in RTF format means it's easy to transfer formatted text between various makes of computers.

This, the largest Application Kit class, has a boatload of instance variables, followed by about 130 methods, counting methods allotted for text object delegates.

Still, the Text class shouldn't give you much trouble, possibly because text handling is more...immediately familiar to most people. It has something to do with Western Civilization, probably. Or maybe it's just that the class itself, though large, doesn't introduce any brain-twisting concepts. There are style "runs," a few tables used to determine the behavior of text, but nothing difficult. Just wonderfully useful. At the risk of repeating the same general idea again and again: If you've ever written a word processor "from scratch," you'll be delighted with the Text class. If you haven't ever written a word processor, count yourself lucky.

## Object > Responder > View > ScrollView

The ScrollView class adds methods to relieve some of the scrolling burden from programmers. In general, ScrollView methods implement traditional scrolling at the Application Kit level. They also provide methods for "autoscrolling"—scrolling initiated, for example, when a user drags an object to the window's edge.

## Object > Responder > View > Control

Like Responder, Control is an abstract class. It contains only the common elements of its subclasses:

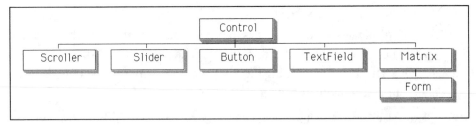

*Figure 17-5*

Control's instance variables are few. There's a integer "tag" for each control, because it's useful to identify a given control by number. And there's the cell object associated with the control, defined as an "id," naturally. (Not all controls will have companion cells, however.) Finally, a set of flags denote whether a control is enabled, is capable of being edited, and more. There's even a flag saying whether the control's editing has been validated.

Control methods are used to:

* create controls;
* resize controls;
* manage the "field editor," which handles editing in text controls;
* enable or disable controls;
* set the value of a control;
* assign control tags; and
* manage the cursor.

The Control class also implements target/action methods and includes methods to interact with other controls.

## Object > Responder > View > Control > Matrix

First, the conception. A matrix is any group of controls. The control cells may be the same, or differing, types.

One control, radio, is always expressed as a matrix. A single radio button would be...silly. Interface Builder knows this and won't allow creation of a single radio; only matrices of radios are allowed.

Other controls, however, also may be matrices. In addition to radios, here's what can be matricized:

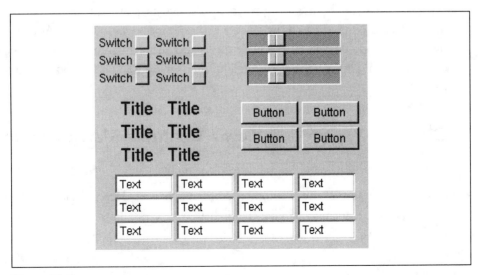

*Figure 17-6*

This is interesting. Even titles can be a matrix.

Notice, though, what can't be expressed as matrices: scrollViews, boxes, and custom views. Also, "form" textfields can't be made into matrices. Those objects become entry forms and are handled by the Form class, a subclass of Matrix.

Notice one final restriction: The cells must be the same size.

Now it gets fun.

Four modes are defined for matrices. Your choice. These are pretty neat modes, as modes go.

- NX_TRACKMODE is the basic mode. Here, the mouse location is "tracked" as it moves over the matrix. Tracking doesn't require a mousedown; just moving the cursor over the matrix begins tracking. You might use this mode to let users move sliders without having to mousedown on the slider knob.
- NX_HIGHLIGHTMODE adds a feature to TRACKMODE. Here, the control is highlighted as it's being tracked.
- NX_RADIOMODE allows only one matrix cell to be selected.
- NX_LISTMODE allows multiple cells to be selected and highlighted. No tracking is done.

These modes are where the real utility of matrices is found. With thoughtful use, you can create some sophisticated matrix-based interfaces.

Methods, as you'd guess, are provided to select, display, edit, resize, and modify matrices. Additional methods let you set and send messages to targets. As a final flip, predefined methods watch for double-clicks and allow different messages to be sent depending on whether the user single-clicked or double-clicked on a matrix element.

## Object > Responder > View > Control > Matrix > Form

Form, the only subclass of Matrix, is a "convenience class."

Since "entry forms" are a common computer fixture, NeXT decided to take the basic features of forms and give them their own class: Form. Here we have two forms, side by side:

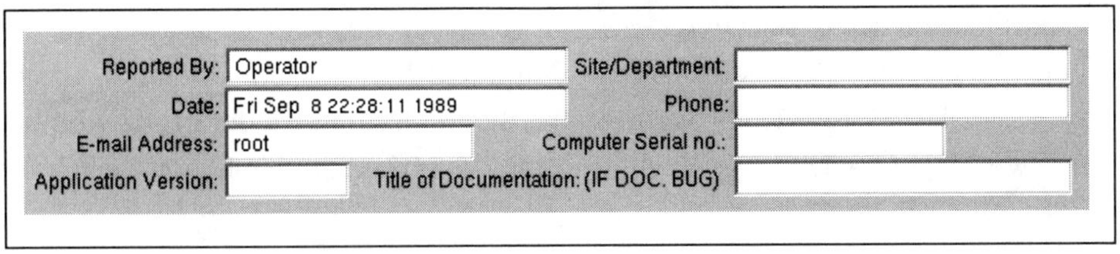

| Reported By: | Operator | Site/Department: | |
| Date: | Fri Sep 8 22:28:11 1989 | Phone: | |
| E-mail Address: | root | Computer Serial no.: | |
| Application Version: | | Title of Documentation: (IF DOC. BUG) | |

*Figure 17-7*

Essentially, forms are titled and indexed matrices. These basic features are provided:

- A click in a form cell readies it for editing;
- A Tab selects the next entry for editing.

When editing of an entry is complete—when the user hits Return or clicks outside the entry—the contents of the entry are sent to the entry's target, if there is one, or to the target of the entire form.

The Form class adds not a single instance variable.

Form methods are used to create forms, lay out forms, resize forms, set form values, return and set indexes, edit text, and modify form attributes.

Also, two methods let you determine targets and actions. These two methods are identical to methods in the Matrix class, with one addition: index. It's a good example of how to subclass: Take from a superclass, then add more functionality. And keep it clean and simple.

Before you try your hand at subclassing, spend some time investigating how NeXT went about subclassing. With few exceptions, the Application Kit demonstrates elegant subclassing.

## Object > Responder > View > Control > TextField

This is a modest class. TextField allows for displaying, selecting, and editing text. Use TextField when you don't need the power and overhead of full-blown text objects—which are indeed full-blown.

Since TextFields are controls, they send messages, like all controls. With TextFields, the messages are sent when the user hits Return. You can also set a nextText instance variable to another object. Then, when the user hits Tab, the nextText object is selected, if it's a text object. So, in a sense, you can make TextFields act somewhat like forms, although if that's your intention, the Form class makes it easier. (Still, as elsewhere, the Application Kit doesn't tie your hands. If you've got something particular in mind, you can probably achieve it without too much effort.)

## Object > Responder > View > Control > Button

Button is another straightforward class. Buttons are controls that send messages on mousedown events. No instance variables are defined in Button.

If you want to venture beyond ordinary button behavior, this class won't disappoint you. NeXT wants you to have exactly the button you desire.

Notable among other methods are "PeriodicDelay" methods, which let you create buttons that send messages continuously during mousedowns. You can even set the interval for message sending.

## Object > Responder > View > Control > Slider

Slider is a surprisingly small class. It adds no instance variables to Control and has only a few methods.

Methods unique to Slider involve setting maximum and minimum values to be sent by sliders. NeXT sliders are continuous by default (a great feature), although you can disable "continuousness" if you're old-fashioned.

## Object > Responder > View > Control > Scroller

Scroller is a specialized control class used with scrollViews. The familiar scrollers on most NeXT windows are scrollers. Note the difference here:

- Sliders are controls, usually found in panels, that set values.
- Scrollers are used to "scroll" images or text, and work with scrollViews.

Like this:

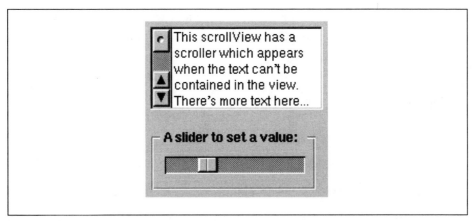

*Figure 17-8*

As this book was written, summer was turning to fall...no, that's not what I meant to say. As this book was written, the Scroller class was becoming more "private." We won't go into scroller details here, because you're better served dealing directly with the ScrollView class, which handles scrollers as a matter of course.

The Scroller class will remain, however, for adventurous souls who wish to subclass Scroller for devious, tricky purposes. If that's your wish, you'll find methods in Scroller:

- to determine whether clicks occurred in the knob, bar, or arrows; and
- to send messages based on the events received.

You can also create custom scrollers with the methods provided. A custom knob, maybe.

## To Come

Because the Application Kit is on disk—not in ROM—NeXT can easily change and extend it. And they probably will. Classes may be augmented with additional methods, or existing methods may be "rolled in" to fewer, more powerful methods. New classes may be offered.

If Brad Cox has his way, Stepstone Corporation will offer additional "Software-IC" modules to augment the Application Kit. If you're a professional programmer, you may also craft new classes, then market them to other programmers.

NeXT has provided the framework. Deep and wide as it is, it may look bare-boned in a few years as NeXT and other companies build on today's Application Kit.

## Dreaming

But wait.

Don't become stressed-out by the immensity of this functionality.

Take your time. Write some programs. Some simple programs.

Remember that Interface Builder helps out—a lot. Make your objects, and set your outlets, and define your classes in Interface Builder. You'll still need to write some code. But hopefully, you enjoy writing code. Writing code, after all, is fun. With this much to work with, it's really fun.

And take some time to sit back and dream. Go through the Application Kit header files. Think of all the things you can do. Dream. And dream some more.

Then make us great NeXT applications.

# Chapter 18

# Sound and Music

*All art constantly aspires towards the condition of music.*
The School of Giorgione
> — **WALTER PATER** 1839–1894

There has never been sound like this before. The NeXT Computer combines impressive, finely tuned hardware and a raft of NeXT-designed sound routines, grouped into a Sound Kit and Music Kit.

No mass-market computer has ever approached this level of aural sophistication. NeXT didn't simply add sound processing hardware and leave the rest to technically minded users. The aural features can be used by everyone who uses the cube:

- Casual users can create and listen to voice mail with less effort than dialing a telephone.

- Programmers can incorporate sound in applications merely, literally, by dragging an icon over an image. Or perform complex signal analysis with pre-built "plug and use" algorithms.

- Hardware engineers can use the cube as a real-time oscilloscope—a feat traditional mass-market computers can't attempt.

The oscilloscope is bundled with every cube. As you can see, it's not a toy. It has all the features found in commercial midline oscilloscopes. It's a software marvel, made possible by the DSP chip.

- For audio engineers, there's real-time spectrum analysis. Like the oscilloscope, the Spectrum Analyzer is bundled with the cube.

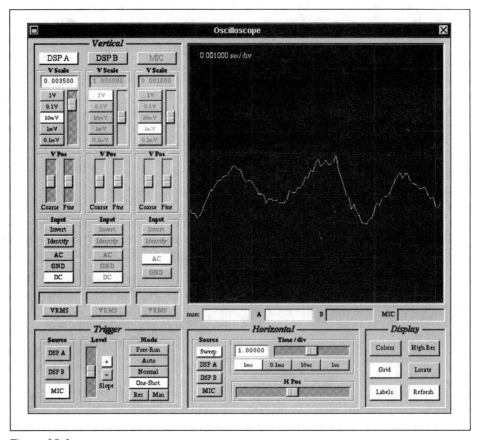

*Figure 18-1*

The oscilloscope and spectrum analyzer, alone, will sell many cubes. They should: They're amazing applications, yet only the forerunners of DSP-related applications.

- Musicians can turn the cube into a synthesizer, as powerful and easy to use as those in the highest-tech music shops.
- Composers can create single notes never heard before, or compositions of dazzling beauty and complexity.

It's hard to stop listing potential applications. Music education. Sound presentations. Medical applications in hearing analysis. Voice recognition. Speech synthesis. Things undreamed of, to come.

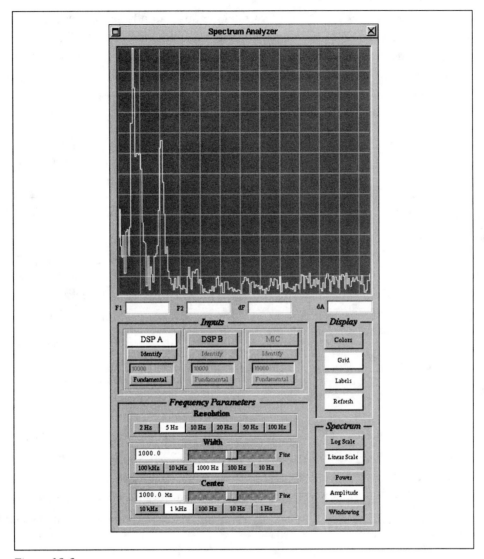

*Figure 18-2*

## Digital Sound

We glanced at the process of digitizing sound in the hardware chapter, during the discussion of the DSP. To recap, the cube offers two predefined sampling rates: 22,050 samples a second (22.05 KHz) and 44,100 samples a second (44.1 KHz). The lower rate produces average-quality sound. The higher sampling rate captures more information, resulting in higher-quality sound: CD-quality sound.

Why even offer a low sampling rate? Because sound files are hideously large. Even a few seconds of sound contain much detailed information. The more detail is captured, the more bytes are produced, and the larger the sound file. (There's no need to sample more often than 44,100 times a second; humans couldn't discern the additional detail.)

Consider these numbers:

| Recording time | Average quality 22.05 mono (approx.) | Average quality 22.05 stereo (approx.) | High quality 44.1 stereo (88.2 mono) (approx.) |
| --- | --- | --- | --- |
| 1 sec | 44 K | 88 K | 176 K |
| 5 sec | 220 K | 441 K | 882 K |
| 30 sec | 1.3 megabytes | 2.6 megabytes | 5 megabytes |
| 1 min | 2.6 megabytes | 5 megabytes | 10.6 megabytes |
| 5 min | 13 megabytes | 26 megabytes | 53 megabytes |
| 10 min | 26 megabytes | 53 megabytes | 106 megabytes |
| 30 min | 79 megabytes | 159 megabytes | 315 megabytes |
| 1 hour | 159 megabytes | 317 megabytes | 635 megabytes |

One minute of CD-quality stereo sound requires over ten megabytes of disk space! This is one reason—maybe the major reason—why NeXT offers massive storage as standard equipment.

Getting sound into the cube requires an analog-to-digital (A/D) converter. Sound output requires a digital-to-analog (D/A) converter. The cube has both, located in the MegaPixel Display.

First, output. Digital sound is sent from the motherboard to the display, where a 16-bit, two-channel D/A converter transforms the stream of bits into sound. The two channels can be used as left and right stereo channels (although you'll need to connect external speakers to hear stereo effects). The D/A converter accepts data sampled at the higher 44.1 KHz rate, so it's capable of producing the highest-quality, CD-like sound.

The sound is wonderful, even through the less-than-amphitheater-size speaker in the display. It's also just fine through a Walkman-type headphone, which can be plugged into the rear of the display.

For sound input, the display uses an 8 KHz "CODEC" chip to perform analog-to-digital conversion. The word CODEC comes from "COder/DECoder." The CODEC chip uses encoding/decoding algorithms based on a standard logarithmic scale called mu-law scale. The purpose of the CODEC technology is to compress the dynamic range of sound, while retaining as much dynamic information as possible. That it does. Although the A/D chip only has 8-bit accuracy (compared to the 16-bit, CD output of the D/A converter), it still manages to capture a 12- to 16-bit dynamic range, thanks to CODEC cleverness.

Still, built-in sound input isn't as good as built-in sound output. You can hear CD-quality sound, but you can only input "telephone quality" sound using standard equipment.

But it's fine. Offering CD-quality input would have required additional hardware. More important, it would have resulted in huge files. Even at the lower sound sampling rate, your five-minute voice mail message will be more than 26 megabytes. This monstrous file would not only have to be stored, but also sent across a network to some unwary recipient. Do you really want CD-quality voice mail, at a cost of twice the file size?

Nah. NeXT made the right decision here.

## Sound Hardware

Playing sound requires no additional hardware. Just click on some button in some application, lean back, and listen.

To record sound, you'll need to purchase a microphone. For best results, get a high-impedance microphone. If voice mail is your only need, buy something inexpensive at Radio Shack. You shouldn't need to spend more than $10 or $15. Better quality microphones can be had for $30 and up. The microphone should have a male "mini-jack," although you can buy an adapter for a few bucks that accepts a larger microphone jack. (I've been using a microphone that came with one of my kids' toys. Something you'd see for 50 cents at a garage sale. It works fine.)

It's possible (and easy) to record CD-quality 44.1 KHz sound, but you'll need additional hardware: a high-resolution A/D converter to stand in for the display's A/D converter.

One unit that's now available is "Digital Ears" from Metaresearch. It's a small hardware unit that connects directly to the cube's DSP port. It has two input plugs and gain controls for each. It can be used as:

- a two-channel, 44.1 KHz, 16-bit A/D converter; or
- a single-channel 88.2 KHz converter (for amazingly precise monophonic input).

It accepts either AC or DC input. Digital Ears is a breeze to use: Plug it in and go. The product also comes with remarkable software to record, play, and analyze sound. Highly recommended.

Most users will access the cube's vast sound capabilities through applications: everything from software oscilloscopes to music composition programs. Those programs aren't here yet (with the exception of the software oscilloscope, the spectrum analyzer, Mail, and a few others), but they're coming.

They're coming because of NeXT's Sound Kit and Music Kit: two object libraries that make creating these applications easier than it's ever been.

## The Sound Kit

Internally, NeXT sounds are lightweight Mach threads that run concurrently with other application threads. Thanks to the DSP chip, and Mach itself, sound can accompany any NeXT application without noticeably slowing other applications.

But you'll seldom need to be aware of low-level sound handling. Instead, you'll use the predefined objects and methods in the Sound Kit.

Considering the complexity of digital sound, the Sound Kit is surprisingly straightforward. The Sound Kit contains only three classes: Sound, SoundView, and SoundMeter.

The lynchpin of the Sound Kit is the sound object, a subclass of Object—so it's a high-level object. What can the sound object do? It can:

- represent all the data that comprises a sound;
- read soundfiles;
- play sounds or soundfiles;
- write data to soundfiles;

- record sampled sound,
- convert between sampling formats; and
- provide ways to edit and name sounds.

And it's easy.

Remember how we made a button?

```
id myButton = [Button new];
```

Making a new sound object is just as easy:

```
id mySound = [Sound new];
```

Once created, all it takes to play, record, or stop sounds is:

```
[Sound play];
[Sound record];
[Sound stop];
```

Or you might want to name your sound with:

```
[mySound setName:"heavyMetalSound"];
```

It's that easy.

## SoundView

The second object in the Sound Kit is SoundView, a subclass of the Application Kit View object.

The SoundView object lets you display and edit sounds as easily as text objects. Portions of a sound can be shown, selected, cut or copied, or pasted or deleted. Messaging methods are also provided, so that SoundView objects can easily communicate with other program objects—maybe when a part of the sound is selected or changed.

## SoundMeter

The SoundMeter class is a new addition to the Sound Kit 1.0 release. SoundMeter objects are attached to sampled sounds. Once hooked up, SoundMeter objects display the average output level and peak hold of the sampled sound in a bar graph display.

The SoundMeter class is a good example of the kinds of classes you can write to augment the Sound Kit's capabilities.

## Using Sound in Applications

It's never been this easy for developers to add and use sound in applications. But will they?

That's an unknown. Many developers may forego sound entirely, believing that the Sound Kit, despite being easy to use, is designed only for "sound applications," not all applications.

If so, it will be a shame, a waste, and a mistake. Applications that incorporate sound are not only more pleasant to use, but potentially more useful than mute applications.

The problem with visual communication is this: People can see only one thing at a time. As applications add features, they also add visual interface to access features. Visual clutter results. On a screen as large as NeXT's, visual clutter is almost encouraged: The screen's there—use it!

Sound is a way out. Sound conveys information without bespotting a single pixel. Users can keep their eyes on visual tasks while being informed by the application. Suddenly, the person/machine bandwidth is expansive. All things being equal, a mute application can't match the functionality of a sound-enhanced application, because sound can help users accomplish more in less time.

For now, though, it's a one-way street. Applications can speak to users, but users have only tactile means of response.

That will change soon. Speech recognition is coming. Then the street will be two-way. The cube's ready, now, to bear the traffic.

## Music

Sound is easy. Music is something else.

The Sound Kit is spare and functional. The Music Kit is large and amazingly full-featured. Wandering into the Music Kit is like visiting Elf Hill. You'll have a great time, but when you stumble out, years will have passed.

There's nothing halfhearted about the Music Kit. While it's possible to categorize Application Kit features as "similar, but better" than other computer software, that comparison can't be made with the Music Kit. Nothing comparable to the Music Kit has ever been offered on any computer before. The Commodore Amiga is the only other general-purpose computer to offer more than rudimentary musical features. Compared to the cube, the Amiga is...tissue paper on a comb.

NeXT hired the top people in the computer music field, then turned them loose. The result is the Music Kit. Like the Application Kit, it has high-level objects and subclasses. There's less subclassing here than in the Application Kit, though; the Music Kit defines many foundation classes and not too many subclasses.

It's hard to find anything that can't be done with the Music Kit.

* If your interest is creating new synthesized sounds, SynthPatch and UnitGenerator subclasses do everything you once did with knobs and patch cords. And more.
* If you want to compose, there's a fully defined ScoreFile language.
* If you're not always even-tempered, there's a tuningSystem class to tailor.
* Performance? There's a Performer class that works with lower-level musical entities to bring your work to life.

On the surface, there's not much to making music. You can:

* use the Music Kit to create music; or
* use the high-level ScoreFile language; or
* use MIDI input to create sound files.

In days to come, you'll create music using applications created by the Music Kit. The applications may be graphic "click to make a note" programs, similar to "music construction sets" on other computers. With other applications, you'll plug in your keyboard and play. And watch the score be written, in real time, on the NeXT display.

If that's your desire, be patient. Those applications are being written now, and should be available in 1990.

The DSP chip makes all this possible. It's extraordinarily fast, and it puts no restrictions on signal processing. The DSP's speed, combined with its generality, makes it an ideal musical synthesizer. You could directly program the DSP in assembler, if you wished, but it's difficult. The Music Kit builds on the DSP capabilities.

## Music Kit Classes

Here's a quick look at the Music Kit classes.

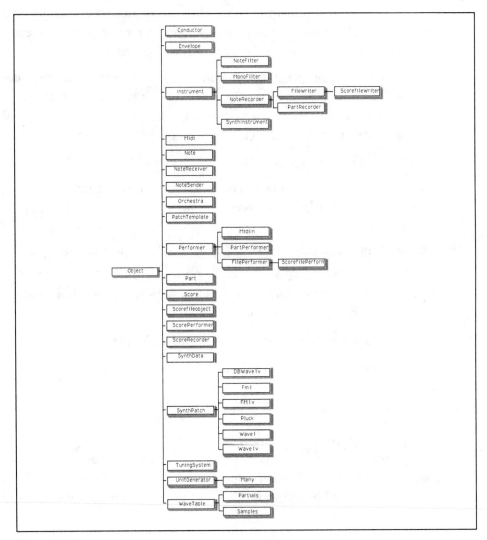

*Figure 18-3*

It goes on, doesn't it?

If this class holds interest for you, here's a consolation: It's likely you'll concentrate on only one or two general areas in the Music Kit. To use the Application Kit, you need a good understanding of almost all the classes. With the Music Kit, it's possible to take a narrower approach. Thank goodness.

The Music Kit works from a few general notions:

- Notes are fundamental objects that contain all parameters needed to define musical notes: frequency, amplitude, brightness, velocity, and more. If you're astute in matters of note, you'll also welcome parameters for stereo panning and for portamento: the transition time between notes. (Webster defines portamento as "...a nonsignificant sound..."). All MIDI parameters are also represented as optional note parameters.
- Performer objects take the notes, sequentially, and send them to
- Instrument objects, which "play" the notes.

That's not too complicated.

There's another important object: a conductor. Every performance requires a conductor object. As in life, conductor objects are responsible for timing: tempo (beats per second), and the length of beats themselves. The Music Kit provides default conductors for performances.

The Music Kit provides ways to group the tens, hundreds, or thousands of small sonic events we call music:

- Notes are gathered into Part objects.
- Parts combine to form scores.
- Scores are saved in scorefiles.

Because each note must be defined, even short musical passages become lengthy scorefiles.

The ScoreFile language is a true language. Scores consist of header statements and body statements, as do computational language source files. The language allows for constants, variable declarations, and assignments. Predefined constants are integer YES and NO, and these MIDI constants:

| | | |
|---|---|---|
| resetControllers | monoMode | sysActiveSensing |
| localControlModeOn | polyMode | sysReset |
| localControlModeOff | sysClock | sysUndefined0xf9 |
| allNotesOff | sysStart | sysUndefined0xfd |
| omniModeOff | sysContinue | |
| omniModeOn | sysStop | |

The language includes a subset of C operators and adds a few operators of its own:

| Operator | Operation |
|----------|-----------|
| ( ) | Grouping |
| - | Unary minus |
| dB | Decibel computation |
| ^, ~ | Exponentiation, pitch transposition |
| *, /, % | Multiplication, division, modulus |
| +, - | Addition, subtraction |
| @ | Envelope lookup |
| & | String concatenation |
| = | Assignment |
| , | Sequence separator |

The ScoreFile language is not the same as "scorefile files." The language is just that: a language to create music. Scorefile is a file format, and only that. The file format is much simpler than the ScoreFile language. The format is what's written to disk; the language is what's read. In a sense, the process is akin to RTF files, which are interpreted by the host application. On disk, RTF files are mere sequences of ASCII characters.

## Synthesized Sounds

To create synthesized sounds, you'll use these classes:

- SynthInstrument ( a subclass of Instrument);
- SynthPatch; and
- UnitGenerator.

The lowest level is UnitGenerator. Each subclass of UnitGenerator describes a single, elemental DSP function. Working down here, you're close to the bone: UnitGenerators are just a smoosh higher than assembly language.

Subclasses of SynthPatch manage UnitGenerator objects. Synthesized sounds are created when SynthPatch connects various UnitGenerators—much like "patch cords" connect various oscillators in old-school synthesized music.

The music isn't actually heard (or "realized") until SynthInstrument comes into play. Each SynthInstrument object oversees one or more SynthPatches, and each SynthPatch corresponds to a single type of note.

SynthInstrument is the software equivalent of a one-channel MIDI synthesizer. Note that one-channel doesn't mean "one voice." SynthInstrument can easily be polyphonic: Each SynthPatch corresponds to a single voice. Three-part harmony entails three SynthPatch subclasses.

NeXT offers many pre-made SynthPatches: Pluck (which simulates a "plucked string" instrument), Wave1 (for wave table synthesis), and many more. Eventually, other vendors may offer libraries of synthetic instruments for immediate use, or for further customization.

Let's note something beyond words. The cube's synthesizer capabilities go far, far beyond making sounds that "sound like synthesizers." Electronic music isn't just cold, spacey, futuristic whines and screeches. Here, you can craft violins that will break your heart. Oboes as dark and sweet as Guinness, and trumpets fit for Gideon. The musical palette is as wide as your imagination.

## What's Needed

That said, know this: The Music Kit is daunting. Bring all your programming skills; you'll need them.

What's needed? First, a great book (or five) that explains the Music Kit. (Remember my bias here. I also think the solution to world hunger is a good book.)

Second: applications. And maybe not just high-level applications. The Music Kit is complex; a few "mid-level" applications to create higher-level, custom applications would also be welcome. The world is filled with music educators and researchers who'd welcome tools that don't require Music Kit programming skills. It's a market with deep musical knowledge, but little or no programming skills. NeXT itself may address that market. Until now, they've been busy, as you've seen. Now that the foundation is laid, the musical NextStep can be made.

# Section V

## A Software Treasure Chest

# Chapter 19

## WriteNow

*True ease in writing comes from art, not chance.*
**— ALEXANDER POPE** 1688–1744

WriteNow is the mid-level word processor bundled with the cube. Some would call it "entry-level."

WriteNow's history is worth mention. It begins when Macintosh was in development. MacPaint and MacWrite were to be bundled with Macintosh, and were also in development. MacPaint, authored by programmer extraordinaire Bill Atkinson, was coming along fine. From the beginning, it was solid: fast, neat, with few bugs.

MacWrite, however, was a difficult birth. Granted, it's not easy to create a new type of word processor, especially when the computer you're developing for is also being created. The MacWrite authors had a difficult task, compounded by the fact that Mac was a "moving target."

The situation was ideal for finger-pointing.

Still, Apple needed a word processor for Macintosh, and some thought that MacWrite might not be completed on time.

Legend has it that Steve Jobs commissioned a second group of programmers to create another word processor. Macintosh was important enough to hedge a bet.

Whatever the truth of that, we know this: WriteNow is owned, in whole or in part, by Steve Jobs. The version of WriteNow bundled with the cube is copyrighted by NeXT, Inc.

MacWrite *was* completed in time to make the release of Macintosh. It became the standard Mac word processor in the early years.

WriteNow also, eventually, was finished. (Nothing's as easy as it looks.) It was marketed by T/Maker, and became the "alternative of choice" for many MacWrite users. Power wordsmiths chose Microsoft Word; MacWrite and WriteNow battled for the low to mid-range market.

## Here and Now

WriteNow/NeXT carries the WriteNow philosophy into the NextStep interface. It serves as a standard for other NeXT applications, but it also feels much like WriteNow/Macintosh: easy-to-use, moderately-powered, carefully graphic, and predominately mouse-based.

On graphic computers, most word processors have you create documents in "galley view," with headers, footers, footnotes, and page breaks hidden, for the most part. The other approach is often called "page view," where *everything* is shown, just as it would be when printed.

WriteNow is a page-view word processor.

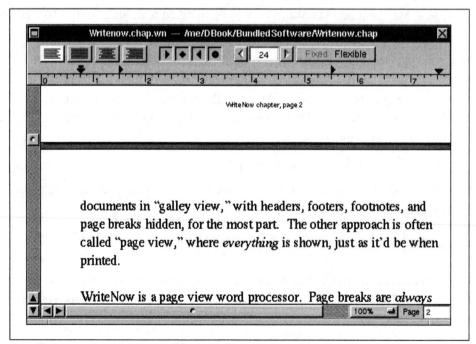

*Figure 19-1*

Page breaks are *always* shown, as are headers, footers, and footnotes. In Figure 19-1, you can also see the visual page break. With WriteNow, you'll never be surprised by what slides from the printer. What you see is what you get, like it or not.

Most people like it. To counter the popularity of WriteNow's exactness, other Macintosh word processors now offer page view as an option. In Microsoft Word, for example, you can compose in either page view, or the less cluttered galley view.

WriteNow seems designed as a "correspondence" word processor. It's a fast tool for creating letters, reports, and small- to medium-sized documents. Much of this book was written with WriteNow, and it was just fine. Chapters were 2,000 to 6,000 words with limited formatting, and no tricky typography. (That may come later, as this book is formatted for printing using Microsoft Word on Macintosh—which may tell you something...if only that few publishers have cubes yet.)

WriteNow has a handful of useful features, but doesn't try for do-it-all fame. The basics are here, and done well:

* excellent spell-checking;
* the ability to import EPS graphics, then easily resize them;
* a sturdy mail merge feature, modeled on Microsoft Word;
* extensive options for headers, footers, and footnotes;
* superscripted and subscripted text;
* optional alternating binding margins;
* hide or show formatting markers, or graphics, or spaces in text;
* character, word, and paragraph counts (greatly appreciated by professional writers); and
* line spacing in one-point increments.

Like all good NeXT applications, WriteNow also features a "Send Selection" menu item, with options to "Define in Webster" and "Search in Librarian." Digital Webster also provides a superb thesaurus for WriteNow to call on (though it's easy to forget the feature is available!).

WriteNow also edges toward desktop publishing with options for one, two, three, or four column format options. Multicolumn output, however, is all or nothing: If you choose a two column format, the *entire* document will be in two columns. FrameMaker has nothing to fear from WriteNow.

## File Formats

As NeXT's one and only word processor, WriteNow needs to be generous in file support. In addition to WriteNow format, you can save files as:

- ASCII text without line breaks;
- ASCII text with line breaks; and
- RTF.

The line break option is useful when preparing files to telecommunicate—WriteNow sees a paragraph as a single line, and long lines often muddle file transfers. The best option is RTF, which makes it possible to transfer WriteNow-created documents to other word processors (Word, primarily), while preserving text formatting. WriteNow also loads RTF and ASCII files.

## Other Word Processors

If NeXT is a success, which it will be, WriteNow is destined for competition. Consider the features absent in WriteNow:

- hyphenation;
- macros;
- style sheets—a necessity for complex documents;
- high-end typographic controls for kerning, scaling, fractional leading, and more;
- mixed column formats;
- tab leaders; and
- other high-end features.

The fact that WriteNow is "free" in every cube might dissuade other developers, but probably won't. Word processing is too big a market to ignore, even when your competitor is free. And, although WriteNow is now bundled with the cube, it may someday be cut loose to freely compete with other word processors.

NeXT bundled a word processor to make the cube immediately useful. In the long run, though, the success of NeXT will require a wealth of software, in all categories. Just as Apple eventually "unbundled" MacWrite and MacPaint, so might NeXT cast off WriteNow, to encourage the development of other word processors.

Until then, you'll find WriteNow a competent word processor. If you outgrow WriteNow, look to FrameMaker, which can satisfy the most demanding word-smith. If, however, you don't want or need all the desktop publishing clutter of FrameMaker, you'll have to wait for a "power word processor" to appear.

It will.

# Chapter 20

# Edit

*Tenet insanabile multos*
*Scribendi cacœthes et ægro in corde senescit.*

*"Many suffer from the incurable disease of writing, and it becomes*
*chronic in their sick minds."*
vii.51

                            —JUVENAL A.D. C.60–C.130

Text editors are classic UNIX applications.

The UNIX creators, programmers all, needed text editors to write programs. So UNIX text editors appeared early.

The first official UNIX site was Bell Labs' patent department: a hotbed of document creation. More text editors appeared: some simple, some complex. Text manipulation tools came along: programs to create indexes, programs to create bibliographies, programs to create tables in text, and more.

When UNIX escaped into the world, more text editors appeared, including emacs, a legendary text editor/word processor crafted by the legendary Richard Stallman. If you loved WordStar, or pine for feature-riddled word processors like Word Perfect, emacs will make you swoon.

The UNIX editors in every cube include:

- ed, a bare-bones editor used most often in Terminal;
- vi, a screen editor (the "vi"stands for "visual") which enhances the features of ed;
- sed, a "stream editor" which applies scripts of editing commands to text files. Think of sed as a batch-processing text editor;

- And, of course, emacs, the power text processor of choice on character-based UNIX systems.

The UNIX text editors are fascinating and useful. The UNIX man pages can get you started with them.

But those are side roads. On NeXT, WriteNow and Edit are the tools to use.

Edit joins the grand tradition of UNIX text editors. It's fast and capable. Although designed to create and edit source code files, Edit is also a serviceable word processor. It doesn't have advanced formatting commands—no headers, no footers, no pagination commands, not even page numbers! But Edit does have the basics: multiple fonts and sizes, bold and italic, and paragraph justification. About half of this book was written using Edit (and the remainder cobbled together in WriteNow).

Where Edit shines, though, is in creating source code, working with files, accessing the Shell, and more. Edit isn't just a "graphic text editor." It's a labor of love, full of programmer-oriented features. Here, we'll highlight just a few.

## The Main Menu and Window Menu

The Edit main menu belies the wealth of options and features you'll find in Edit submenus. (See Figure 20-1.)

The features start with the Window menu. (See Figure 20-2.)

Edit's most obvious NextStep addition are the directories which can be opened with the Open Directory command. (See Figure 20-3.)

The directory windows are a shortcut. You can use the familiar Open panel to select files, or double-click a directory window:

- If you double-click a directory, a new directory window opens; and
- If you double-click a file, it opens.

Another way to open a new directory window is the Open Directory command in the Window menu. This brings up a panel. Type in the directory name, hit OK, and the directory window appears.

The Manager menu item is used to close groups of windows in one swoop; either all "ancestors" or all "descendants" of the current window can be closed.

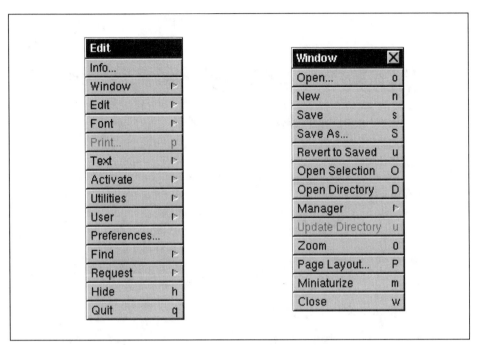

*Figures 20-1 and 20-2*

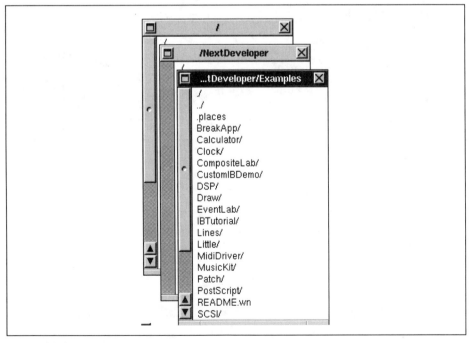

*Figure 20-3*

Edit's Preferences panel is a model for other applications:

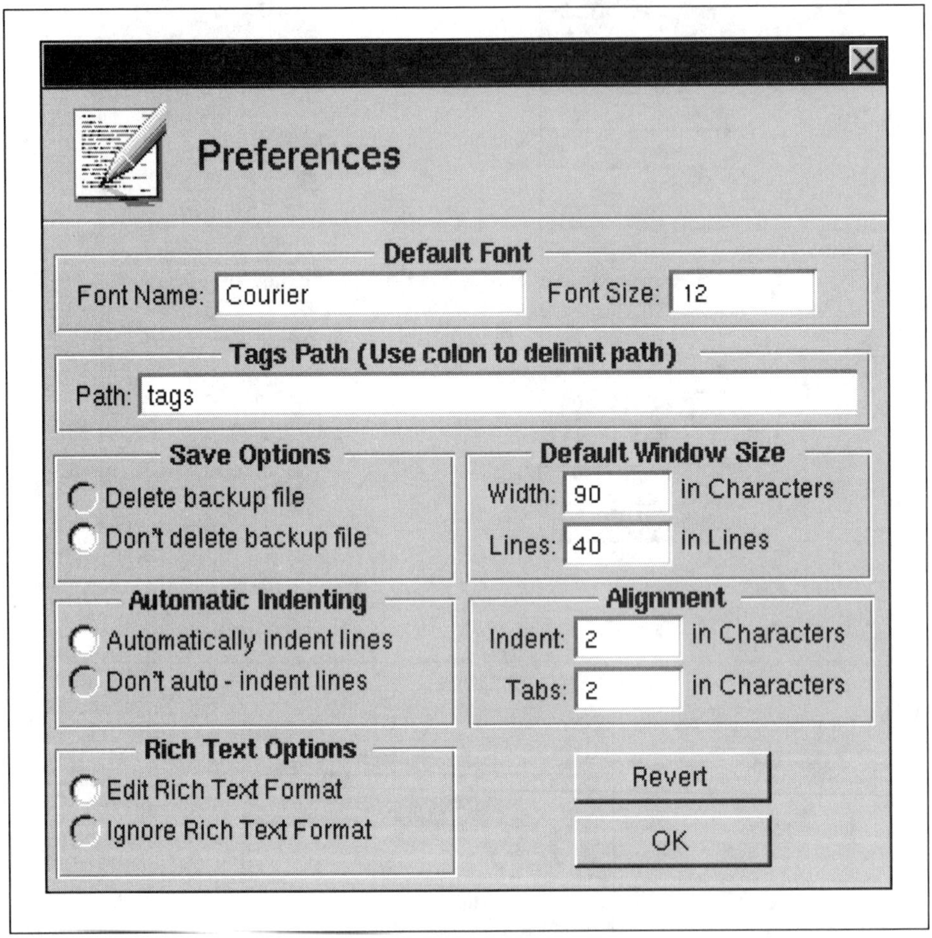

Figure 20-4

Automatic indenting is included for source code editing, where indented lines are often followed by subsequent indented lines. One mystifying item is "Tags Path," which we'll cover in the Utilities menus.

## Zooming

This one's fun and useful. The Zoom command lets you "zoom out" of an edit document. Here's an unzoomed Edit view:

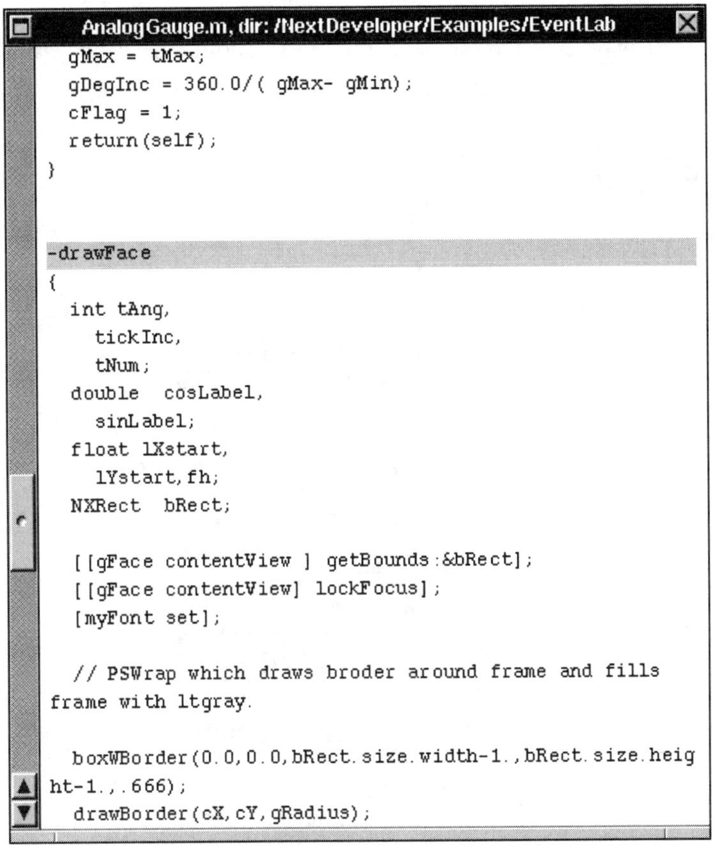

```
┌────────────────────────────────────────────────────────────┐
│ ■    AnalogGauge.m, dir: /NextDeveloper/Examples/EventLab  ☒ │
├────────────────────────────────────────────────────────────┤
│   gMax = tMax;                                               │
│   gDegInc = 360.0/( gMax- gMin);                             │
│   cFlag = 1;                                                 │
│   return(self);                                              │
│ }                                                            │
│                                                              │
│                                                              │
│ -drawFace                                                    │
│ {                                                            │
│   int tAng,                                                  │
│     tickInc,                                                 │
│     tNum;                                                    │
│   double  cosLabel,                                          │
│     sinLabel;                                                │
│   float lXstart,                                             │
│     lYstart,fh;                                              │
│   NXRect  bRect;                                             │
│                                                              │
│   [[gFace contentView ] getBounds:&bRect];                   │
│   [[gFace contentView] lockFocus];                           │
│   [myFont set];                                              │
│                                                              │
│   // PSWrap which draws broder around frame and fills        │
│ frame with ltgray.                                           │
│                                                              │
│   boxWBorder(0.0,0.0,bRect.size.width-1.,bRect.size.heig     │
│ ht-1.,.666);                                                 │
│   drawBorder(cX,cY,gRadius);                                 │
└────────────────────────────────────────────────────────────┘
```

*Figure 20-5*

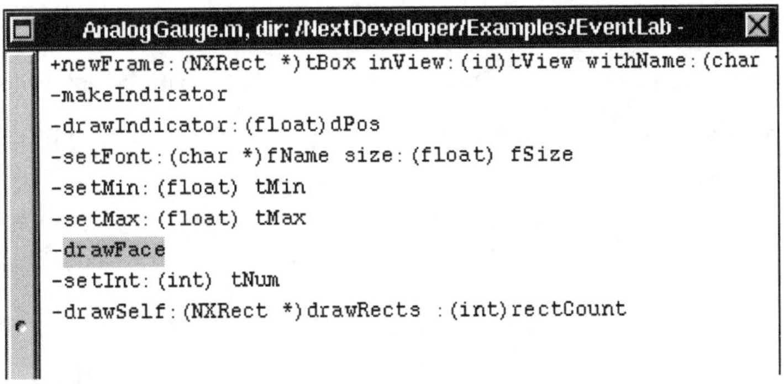

```
┌────────────────────────────────────────────────────────────┐
│ ■    AnalogGauge.m, dir: /NextDeveloper/Examples/EventLab - ☒│
├────────────────────────────────────────────────────────────┤
│ +newFrame:(NXRect *)tBox inView:(id)tView withName:(char     │
│ -makeIndicator                                               │
│ -drawIndicator:(float)dPos                                   │
│ -setFont:(char *)fName size:(float) fSize                    │
│ -setMin:(float) tMin                                         │
│ -setMax:(float) tMax                                         │
│ -drawFace                                                    │
│ -setInt:(int) tNum                                           │
│ -drawSelf:(NXRect *)drawRects :(int)rectCount                │
└────────────────────────────────────────────────────────────┘
```

*Figure 20-6*

Choosing Zoom shows only method headers. (See Figure 20-6.)

It's a fast way to move between methods. Zoom, select a method, then Zoom again: The full view is centered on the method you selected.

## The Edit Menu

You'll notice some enhancement in Edit's Edit menu.

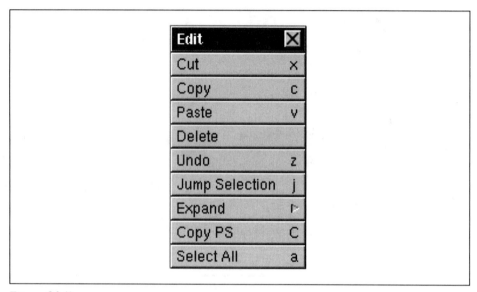

Figure 20-7

Beyond the ordinary:

• Jump Selection scrolls the window, bringing the selection into view; and

• Expand leads to a submenu which leads to this panel. (See Figure 20-8.)

Here, you can enter abbreviations which are expanded by typing the abbreviation, followed by Esc. If you're tired of seeing "The NeXT Computer" over and over again in these pages, it's because

```
t <Esc>
```

is all that's needed to insert the phrase.

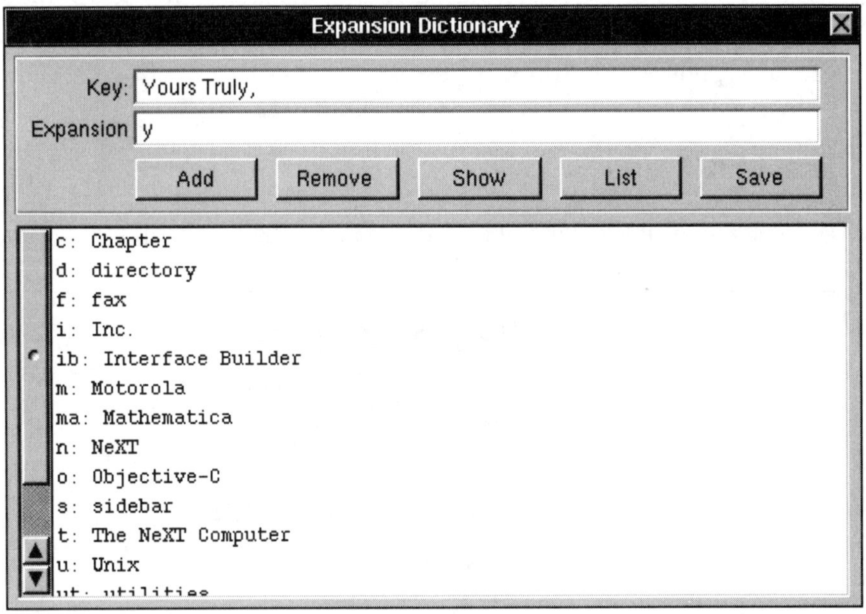

*Figure 20-8*

## The Font Menu

The expected choices are here: less than you'd find in a full-bore word processor, more than usually found in text editors. You may recognize this menu as the "standard" NextStep font menu:

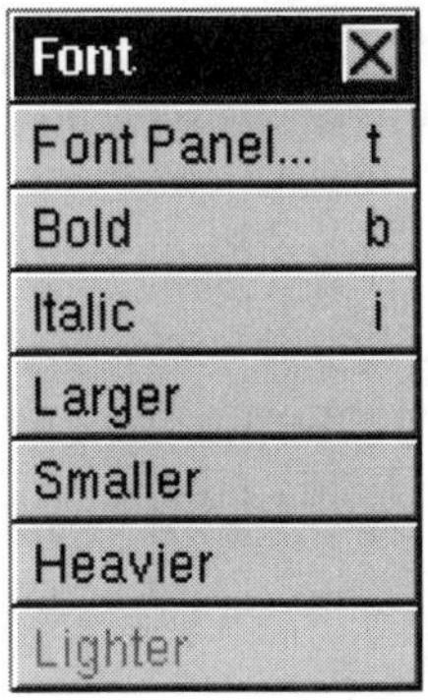

*Figure 20-9*

Later versions of NeXT software may include "Underline" as an option. The attribute is defined in low-level NeXT software, but hasn't yet been added as a standard option.

## The Text Menu

The Text menu allows Edit to be used as a better-than-makeshift word processor.

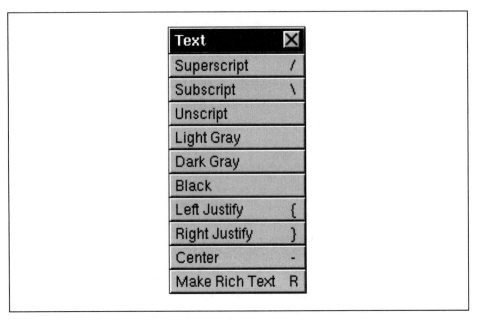

*Figure 20-10*

The top six commands are odd additions to a text editor. *Gray scale text in a text editor?* Edit's author probably had time on his hands.

The last four items are more useful. In particular, Make Rich Text brings Edit up to word processor status.

Unless Rich Text is chosen, only one font and size is allowed. Choose Make Rich Text, however, and you can bold, italicize, and use various fonts and sizes.

There's a catch, though. Converting a document to Rich Text Format (RTF) precludes using many of the programming features. If your interest is text—not program—editing, you won't mind.

## The Find Menu

Find provides the Command-e and Command-g shortcuts, which let you quickly select text, then find the text's next occurrence.

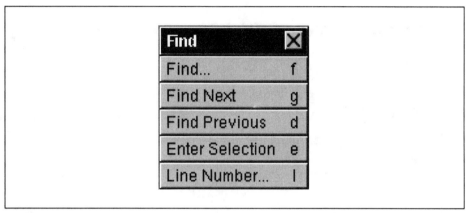

*Figure 20-11*

The Find panel does WriteNow one better by allowing for UNIX regular expressions to be used.

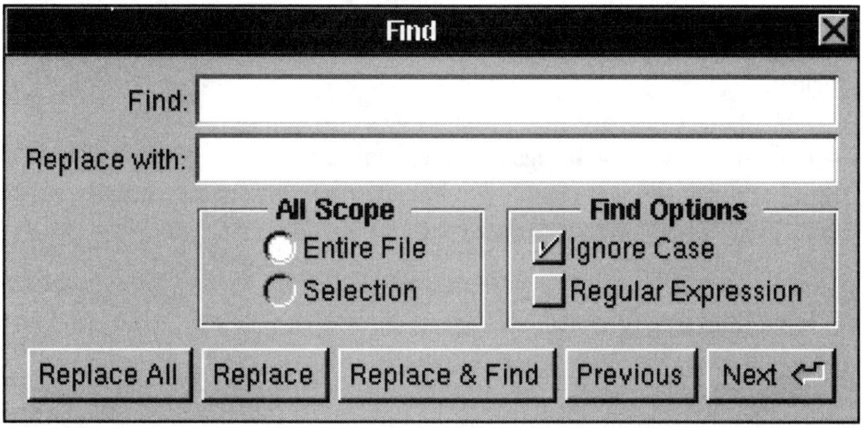

*Figure 20-12*

Grouping, single or multicharacter wildcards—any "grep-like" expression can be used. If you're more than a casual editor, regular expressions are worth learning.

## The Activate Menu

The Activate menu helps manage a morass of Edit windows and directory windows. All open windows are listed in the Activate menu.

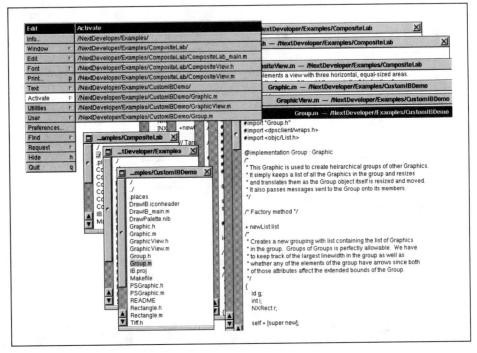

*Figure 20-13*

Choosing a window brings it to the front. If you choose a directory window, it's brought to the front. If you work with many windows, you'll find it worthwhile to tear off Activate, and keep it close at hand.

## The Utilities Menu

Here's where Edit really comes into its own. (See Figure 20-14.)

The Shell command lets you access a predefined UNIX pipe. UNIX commands consist of:

- the command itself;
- "standard input" to the command; and
- "standard output"—where the results of the command are sent.

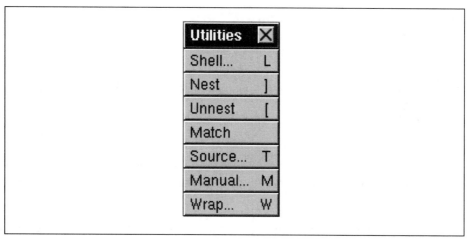

Figure 20-14

You can use the Shell command in two ways. The simplest is this: Choose Shell. This panel appears:

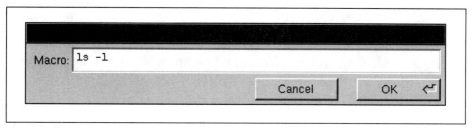

Figure 20-15

Type in any valid Shell command. It's performed, and the command's ouput is placed in your Edit document at the insertion point.

The more advanced use is this: Select text to be used as an argument to a Shell command. Now choose Select, and enter a command in the panel. The command uses the selected text as the command's argument, performs the command, and replaces the selection with the command's output.

The Nest and Unnest items are used to quickly format source code.

Match is another source code shortcut. Select a delimiter, choose Match, and all code up to and including the next delimiter is selected. Delimiters can be:

- { };
- [ ]; or
- ( ).

(A shorter shortcut is double-clicking a delimiter, which does the same thing.)

The Source item is the way to access tags. It requires some explanation.

As everyone knows, hypertext existed in UNIX, as a programmer utility, long before the term "hypertext" was coined. (Someday, when a faster-than-light drive is invented, UNIX programmers will say, "They're using it for spaceships?! We always used it as a UNIX utility.")

The command is ctags. The ctags command races through source code files, collecting object declarations, typedef locations, cross references, and more. The information is indexed and made available to text editors.

In Edit, it works like this: First you process the source with ctags. Open the Shell and type:

```
ctags <filename>
```

Ctags does its work (fast!) and creates a new "tags" file. Then, from Edit, you make a selection and choose Source from the menu. If, for example, your selection is a typedef, you're presented with a file window containing the definition. If there isn't a selection, a panel appears where you can type in a tag entry.

Creating the tags files can be a bother, but it's worth it for lengthy source code files.

The Manual command give you Edit access to the UNIX manual pages. Type "ctags," select it, hit Command-Shift-m, and a new window appears, containing:

```
CTAGS(1)        UNIX Programmer's Manual     CTAGS(1)
NAME
    ctags - create a tags file
SYNOPSIS
    ctags [ -abdgmrstuvwx ][ -f infile ][ -o output ][ -n max-
    refs ] files ...
DESCRIPTION
    Ctags creates a file called tags from the specified C,
    Objective-C, Yacc, Lex, Pascal, Fortran or Lisp source
```

```
files. The tags file is a sorted index giving the
locations of object declarations in files, as well as
type information.
```

and more. The ctags command deserves a book of its own.

The Wrap panel lets you choose between:

- word wrap;
- character wrap; or
- no line wrapping.

"Word" or "none" are the common choices. No one's yet found a use for character wrapping—where words are split, if necessary, at line's end. We're not talking about hyphenation here; that isn't an option in Edit.

## The User Menu

New Edit users who haven't read the manual will be perplexed by the User menu: It's empty. Just a submenu title. Nothing underneath. Perplexing.

That's because the User menu is your menu. You: the user. The commands on the User menu are custom commands: You make them.

My User menu currently sports Word Count, Style, Spell, and Diction:

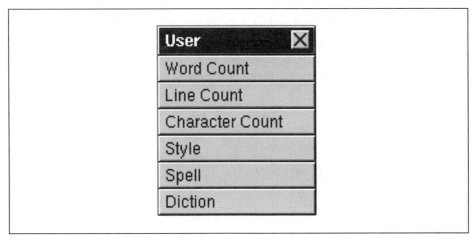

*Figure 20-16*

To make a custom User menu, first create a new file in Edit. Name it .userdict (the period makes the file hidden) and save it into your "me" directory. Then add Shell commands in the form:

```
Menu name        shell command
```

My .userdict file includes:

```
Word Count    wc -w |
Style         style |
Spell         spell |
Diction       diction |
```

The vertical bar sends output to a new window. To use the custom menu, save the finished product, quit Edit and launch Edit again. Edit reads in the .userdict file and makes the custom user menu. You're ready to go. Just make sure to Select All before choosing a command.

## Keyboard Commands

Quick typists will appreciate Edit's additional keyboard commands. The commands are a subset of the never-ending emacs keyboard commands.

```
Keyboard Command          Action
Control-A                 Move to beginning of line
Control-B                 Move back one character
Control-D                 Delete current character
Control-E                 Move to end of line
Control-F                 Move forward one character
Control-K                 Kill forward to end of line
Control-N                 Move down one line
Control-P                 Move up one line
Control-W                 Kill region
Control-Y                 Restore previous kill from buffer
Delete or Control-H       Delete previous character

Esc <                     Move to beginning of text
Esc >                     Move to end of text
Esc b                     Move back one word
Esc d                     Delete current word
Esc f                     Move forward one word
```

```
Esc h                    Delete previous word
Esc-N                    Move down one page
Esc-P                    Move up one page
```

"Previous kill from buffer" means "whatever you last deleted."

The keyboard moves are worth learning, if you're a heavy Edit user.

## Credit Due

Edit was written by NeXT's Bryan Yamamoto, who also wrote Mail, another feature-rich, solid NeXT application. Even in early versions, Edit was fast, rugged, reliable, and (for me, anyway) bug-free.

This is good software.

# Chapter 21

# Mail

*I knew one that when he wrote a letter he would put that which was most material in the postscript, as if it had been a bymatter.*

*It is generally better to deal by speech than by letter.*
47. Of Negotiating

— **FRANCIS BACON** 1561–1626

Mail is a strategic NeXT application. It's needed to fufill the promise of networking. Just as every cube has networking hardware built-in, so every cube has a sophisticated, easy-to-use electronic mail application.

Mail's inclusion also reveals NeXT's marketing goal: capture of the Fortune 500 market. In large companies, networking is vital, and electronic mail is more than a convenience: It can make workgroups exponentially more productive. Of all the bundled NeXT applications, Mail is potentially the most useful—at least in settings with many networked cubes. It's also the application that most fully exploits the many advantages of the cube:

- easy networking;
- multi-media communication of text, sound, and data; and
- the power and simplicity of NextStep.

This is an important application to NeXT, and it shows. Mail was written by Bryan Yamamoto, who also wrote Edit. Like Edit, Mail is finely crafted. And it's obviously been lavished with attention; both in features and interface:

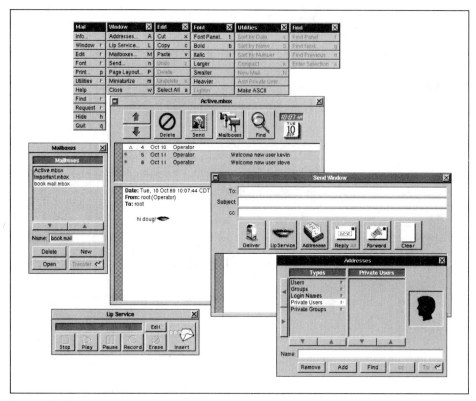

*Figure 21-1*

It may look intimidating at first, but it's not a complicated application. The many mail windows, in fact, simplify operating the program. You'll spend most of your time in Mail with two windows: a window where you read mail, and a "Send window," where you compose mail, or otherwise prepare to send most anything. (See Figure 21-2.)

The Send window is shown at the bottom. Type in the message and hit the "Deliver" button. Or click "Addresses" for a panel containing an "address browser," where you can add addresses, or select a name to be inserted in the Send window's "To:" or "CC:" fields.

The window at the top is the mailbox window. When you begin using Mail, you'll likely have only a single mailbox, but you can easily add more with the Mailboxes panel. (See Figure 21-3.)

Here, three additional mailboxes have been added: Important, Personal mail, and book mail. If you wish, all mailboxes may be open at once. (See Figure 21-4.)

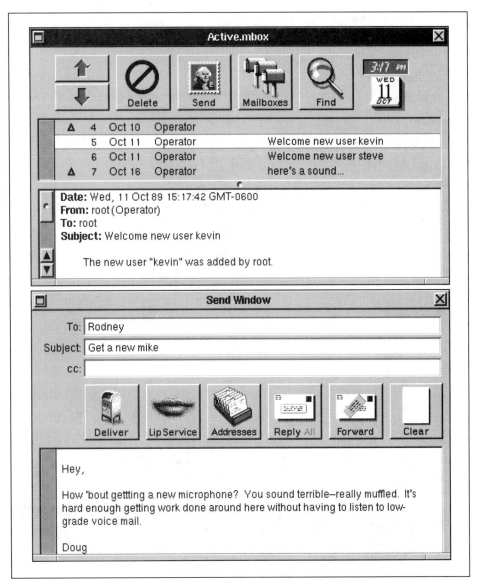

*Figure 21-2*

Notice the times shown at the upper right in the mailbox windows. In the front-most window, a message is selected, and the time and date shown represent when the selected message was sent. That's just one of the many nice touches of Mail.

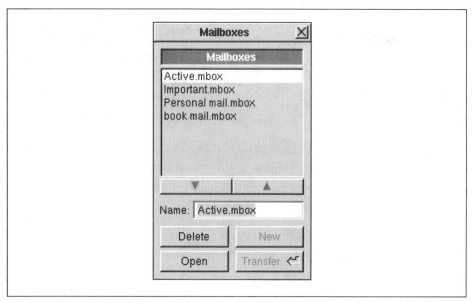

*Figure 21-3*

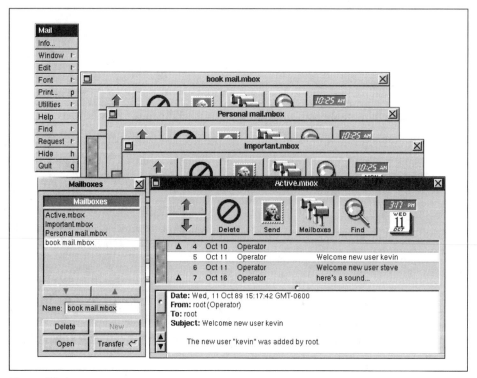

*Figure 21-4*

# File Transfer

One of Mail's most remarkable abilities is file transfer. It's not remarkable that it can be done—Mail would be puny if it couldn't transfer files—but it's remarkable how easy NextStep makes the process.

To transfer a file, simply drag it from a Workspace Manager window into the Send window.

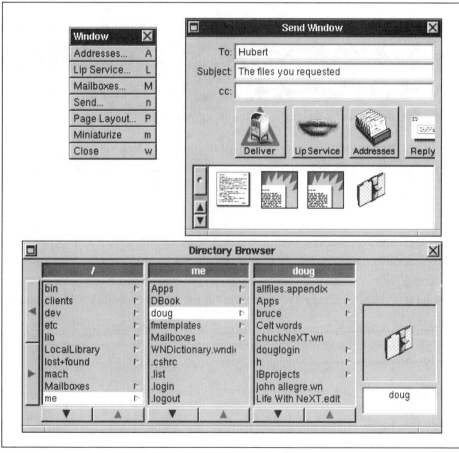

*Figure 21-5*

Above, three files (two WriteNow files and an Edit file) and a directory folder have been dragged into the Send window. Yes, you can also transfer entire directories (though you'll slow down the network if you send many, many megabytes of files).

Because files are about to be sent, the "Deliver" button now contains a triangle—a visible reminder that NeXT files can't be sent to non-NeXT computers. Text mail can be sent to any computer on the network.

## Voice Mail

Plug a microphone into the NeXT monitor, and you're ready to create voice mail. Just click the "Lip Service" button in the Send window to bring up this panel:

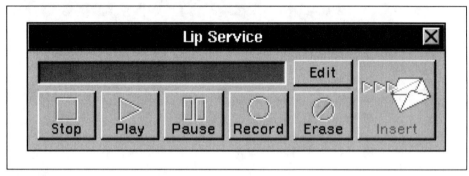

*Figure 21-6*

Click "Record," and say your piece. If you can run a cassette recorder, you can create voice mail. The Edit button brings up yet another panel, where you can Cut, Copy, Paste, or Delete portions of the sound you've recorded. The Insert button places the sound file into your message at the location of the insertion point.

For best results, buy a good-quality directional microphone, then tape it to the top of the cube, pointing squarely at your face.

## Help

Mail's elegant help system may soon be mimicked by other NeXT applications. When you choose Help, Mail makes The Workspace Manager the active application, and requests a new browser containing the Mail help files (which are hidden in the Mail.app folder).(See Figure 21-7.)

The help files themselves are Edit files. Click on a topic and Edit is launched and the help file displayed. It's a sensible arrangement, and one that shows off messaging between applications.

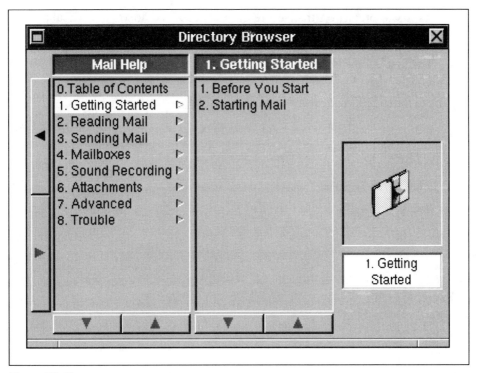

*Figure 21-7*

## Using Mail

You won't have problems using Mail. Although a wealth of options are available, nothing is difficult to master. The best Mail advice is:

Use it.

E-Mail really does make you more productive. Use it to write notes and memos. Use it to transfer files. And use voice mail. It's fun, it's easy, and it's fast—particularly if you're not an expert typist.

## Face Mail

What's next?

Face mail.

It's a safe prediction that future cubes will offer "video mail" capabilities. The technology is here now. But two problems must be overcome.

The first is expense. Microphones are cheaper than video cameras—even small, low-resolution, black-and-white video cameras. The second is file size. Images make for large files. *Real-time* images make for even larger files.

But neither will delay face mail for long. Solid-state-hardware video cameras are dropping in price. And the DSP chip excels at file-compression tasks.

# Chapter 22

# Mathematica

*Mathematics, rightly viewed, possesses not only truth, but supreme beauty—a beauty cold and austere, like that of sculpture.*
Mysticism and Logic (1918), ch.4

> — **BERTRAND RUSSELL** 1872–1970

*Science is nothing but trained and organized common sense, differing from the latter only as a veteran may differ from a raw recruit: and its methods differ from those of common sense only as far as the guardsman's cut and thrust differ from the manner in which a savage wields his club.*
Collected Essays, iv. The Method of Zadig

> — **T.H. HUXLEY** 1825–1895

*Angling may be said to be so like the mathematics, that it can never be fully learnt.*
The Compleat Angler (1653), Epistle to the Reader

> — **IZAAK WALTON** 1593–1683

Mathematica, "A System for Doing Mathematics by Computer," is an application, a language, a milestone in computer science, and a core NeXT application.

Mathematica can be:

- the best "quick and dirty" calculator you've ever had;
- a sophisticated number-crunching machine;
- an intelligent mathematics assistant; or
- a mathematics word processor.

Mathematica is easy to use, yet rich in features, powerful, and deep. Sounds like NeXT itself, doesn't it?

For all that, Mathematica isn't the first symbolic math program. Programs similar to Mathematica have been offered for mainframes, minicomputers, even microcomputers. One excellent program that never garnered much attention was MuMath, marketed in the early 1980s by Microsoft. MuMath was written in LISP, which excels in symbolic computations.

But MuMath moldered, and subsequent symbolic math programs were either ignored, or relegated to the curious realm of arcane scientific applications.

Suddenly, Mathematica arrived, full-blown, with versions for Macintosh, NeXT, 80386-based IBMs and IBM compatibles, Suns, and other computers. Unlike its forerunners, Mathematica was hailed.

Why? Again, because Mathematica was approachable, feature-rich, powerful, and deep.

A good analogy might be Lotus 1-2-3's ruin of VisiCalc.

VisiCalc was the first spreadsheet program and a fine piece of work. In its heyday, VisiCalc was the single most important application for the Apple II. It *made* the Apple II: VisiCalc "sold hardware." Many people bought Apples for one reason, one use only: VisiCalc.

When the IBM PC was released, VisiCalc was among the first programs offered. No fool, IBM.

Then 1-2-3 appeared and blew VisiCalc away. 1-2-3 wasn't simply VisiCalc done better, it was VisiCalc raised to a new power. 1-2-3 wasn't just a spreadsheet, it was a *huge* spreadsheet. And 1-2-3 did graphs, and 1-2-3 had not-so-rudimentary database features. And 1-2-3 had macros. And 1-2-3 was, for the time, incredibly fast.

VisiCalc couldn't touch it.

Mathematica is like that. On the surface, it's another symbolic math program. But look closer, and it's a universe: an expanse of features. A marvel of a program, created with care and lavished with programmer attention.

It may be the best application ever written for a computer. And "NeXT Mathematica" is its finest incarnation.

## Using Mathematica

Mathematica consists of a "front-end" and a kernel. The front-end is the Mathematica interface. The actual computation is done by the Mathematica kernel—a 1.4-megabyte engine which varies little, if at all, between various computer platforms.

By default, you'll use the Mathematica kernel in your cube. After launch (which takes a while), you're presented with a spare window:

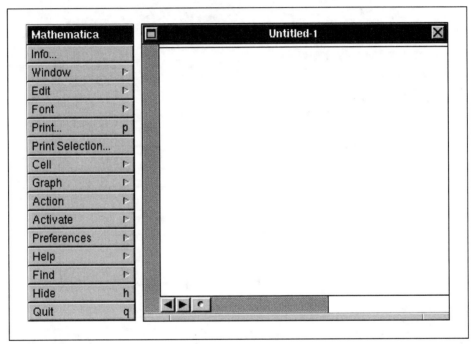

*Figure 22-1*

At the window's bottom right is a status indicator. It has various uses, including display of timing information.

But much of Mathematica is hidden in menus and submenus:

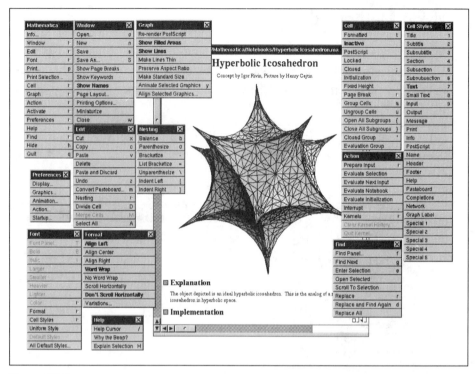

*Figure 22-2*

As you can see, the functionality is vast. And the options continue in Mathematica panels.

Starting out, however, is easy. Type in an expression, then hit:

- Shift-Return;
- Command-Return; or
- Enter.

Mathematica evaluates the expression, and displays the result:

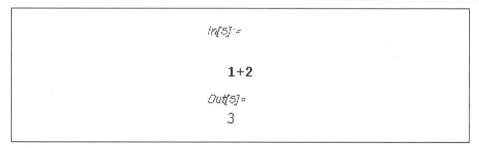

*Figure 22-3*

If you wish, you can leave it at that. Mathematica is a superb calculator, capable of ferociously fast calculations. The factorial of 200? It takes about two seconds.

Or you can avail yourself of Mathematica's built-in functions: numerical functions, pseudorandom-number functions, integer and number-theoretical functions (including MoebiusMu[n] and LatticeReduce[{v1, v2, ...},]), combinatorial functions, transcendental functions, gamma functions, zeta functions, exponential integral functions, Bessel functions, Legendre functions...

and many more. Anyone for confluent hypergeometric functions? They're here, too. In all, hundreds of predefined functions. Or you can define your own functions, then use them in subsequent calculations or Mathematica programs. Numerical precision is virtually unlimited, although Mathematica "follows your lead" in precision, unless told otherwise.

## Symbolic Math

But Mathematica isn't just a sophisticated calculation machine. It's better defined as a "rule-based expert system." Mathematica's fundamental principle, according to its creators, is:

> Take any expression, and apply transformation rules until the result no longer changes.

The expression may be numerical or symbolic. Whichever, the process is the same: Mathematica churns away, applying transformation "rules," until the result no longer changes, or until Mathematica runs out of rules. If the expression can't be transformed, it's returned unchanged.

Mathematica's rules encompass the traditional algebraic rules to expand, factor, and simplify expressions. A simplify[] function can be applied explicitly to complicated expressions.

You can ease into Mathematica programming by assigning expressions. If you enter:

```
y = Sin (x)
```

y will expand to Sin (x) in subsequent calculations. (Unless you'd rather make the assignment only in a specific instance, that is. Although Mathematica's default behavior is what you'd expect, most anything can be changed. The variations and options are mind-reeling—not just in numerical or symbolic behavior, but in every aspect of Mathematica. You can even choose "Mac-like" scrollers, or choose to have a "tm" displayed after Mathematica, and Mathematica may be displayed in italic, if you wish. Jeesh.)

There's little that can't be symbolically swallowed. Power series, integration, and partial and total differentiation—all are fair game. Results can be returned as exact symbolic expressions or numerical approximations.

## Lists

Lists are easily created and manipulated.

```
{2, 3, 6, 7, 12, 34}
```

is a list of numbers. You can also generate tables of values, or multidimensional tables by iterating over expression lists.

As a simple example, this input:

```
Table[ n!, {n, 1, 20} ]
```

creates a list of the first twenty factorials.

Functions can be applied to lists. Typically, the function is applied to each list element. Variations are possible.

If you're familiar with LISP, you'll appreciate the many ways that numerical or symbolic lists can be massaged, including Permutation, which returns all possible permutations of a list, Flatten, and other LISP-like list functions:

- Length;
- MemberQ;
- Count;
- First;
- Last;
- Drop;

and many others.

Lists may be used to represent sets, or grouped or partitioned, or nested in other lists. There's beauty and elegance in these list manipulations. If you've previously used LISP for symbolic pursuits, you may find Mathematica has everything you need, except all those parentheses.

APL fans will also find a home in Mathematica, where vectors are lists, and matrices are simply lists of lists. Vector and matrix computations are straight-forward and fast. The speed comes from both the Mathematica kernel and the DSP's array-processing abilities.

## Graphics

Graphics are Mathematica's "drop-dead" component. They may be as simple as this plot:

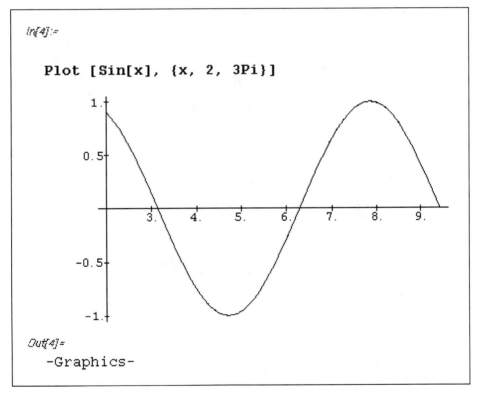

Figure 22-4

Or as stunning as this three-dimensional plot:

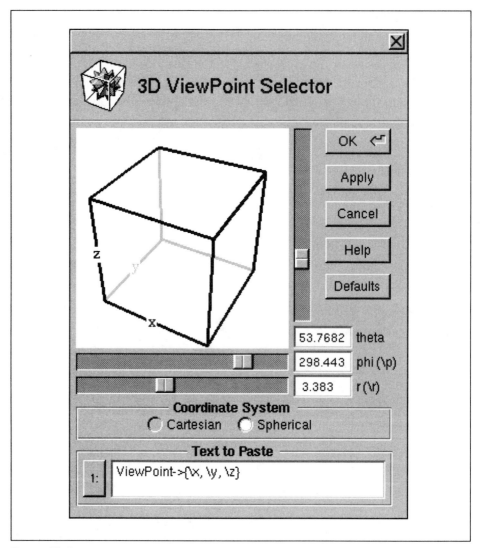

*Figure 22-5*

Once the graphic is created, you can:

- convert it to PostScript, TIFF format, or Bitmap format;
- show lines for a "wire-frame" look, hide lines, or show only filled areas. Here, lines are hidden, but filled areas are shown. (See Figure 22-6.)
- And, of course, you can change the viewing angle. (See Figure 22-7.)

*Figure 22-6*

Or set the number of points to plot, and the "lighting" of the plot. (See Figure 22-8.)

It doesn't stop there. You can also animate your creations. Take my word for it.

## Notebooks

Most applications create documents. In Mathematica, you create *Notebooks*. The Notebooks may contain text, expressions, graphics, or Mathematica programs. Notebooks are similar to outlines: You can expand or collapse the entire Notebook, or sections or subsections.

The Notebook feature lifts Mathematica even higher: from the greatest symbolic math program ever, to an *information provider*.

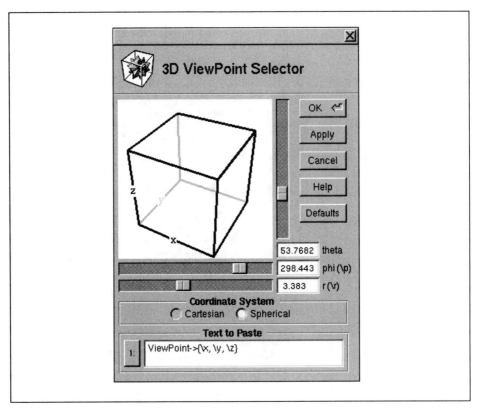

*Figure 22-7*

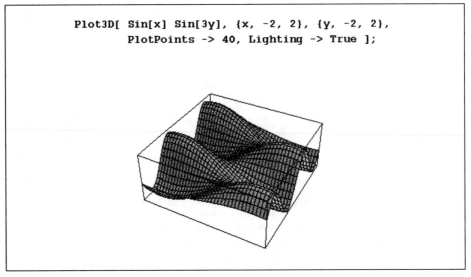

*Figure 22-8*

Each cube comes with these notebooks:

* ComplexRoots;

* PointPlots;

* HyperbolicIcosahedron;

* Animation;

* ComplexRoots;

* MinimalSurface; and

* TourOfMathematica.

Let's look at the Tour of Mathematica. At first blush, the Tour window shows only major headings:

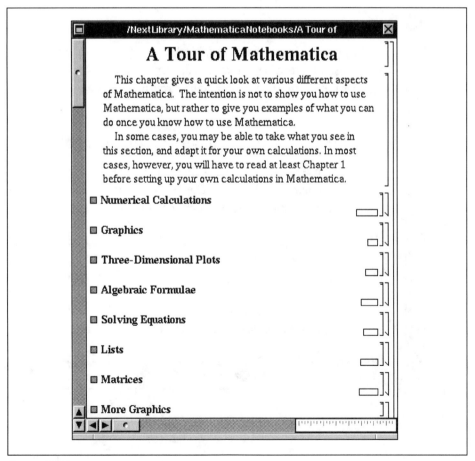

*Figure 22-9*

The brackets and rectangles at right are used to expand or collapse sections and subsections. Clicking the innermost bracket to the right of "Numerical Calculations" expands the sections:

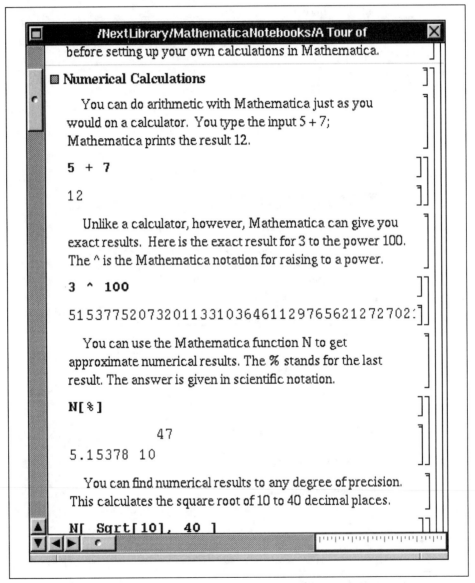

*Figure 22-10*

The sections are called "cells." Besides containing most anything, cells can be formatted to your exact requirements.

The authors of Mathematica envision many more "live" Notebooks of explanatory text and Mathematica commands to demonstrate the topics. Those live Notebooks may soon be a staple of university math courses. For now, the Notebooks included with the cube will keep you busy and fascinated.

## Programming Mathematica

Another blind man approached Mathematica and, after a detailed examination, determined that it was a mathematical programming language.

He was right. Mathematica *is* a programming language. It's geared to math, but remarkably general. If you're proficient in any high-level language, you'll be up to speed quickly in Mathematica programming.

Like C, Mathematica programs are function-based. The syntax is a mixture of C, Pascal, and Mathematica. Here's a sample program from the "Tour of Mathematica." It builds continued fraction expansions, as any fool can see:

```
CF[x_Real, n_Integer?Positive] :=
      Block[ {
              xi,
              xp = x,
              r = {}
              },
              Do[
                            xi = Floor[xp] ;
                            AppendTo[r, xi] ;
                            xp = 1 / (xp - xi) ,
              {n} ] ;
              Return [ r ]
      ]
```

It doesn't look much tougher than Basic or Shell programming, and isn't. The learning curve also isn't steep. After defining a few functions, you can ease into writing programs without any trouble.

## Packages

It goes on.

Mathematica has vast built-in capabilities. If those aren't enough, you can define your own functions. If that's not enough, you can write Mathematica programs. And if *that's* not enough, you can load "packages" of additional functions, definitions, or Mathematica programs. The packages are "plug-in" modules of math smarts.

Here's the "ReadMe" file which introduces the packages included with NeXT Mathematica.

```
This directory contains various subdirectories of
Mathematica packages.

With the standard setting for $Path in Mathematica, you can
read a file into Mathematica using for example
<<Graphics/Polyhedra.m. Note that on some systems you will
have to use a character other than a slash to separate the
directory name from the file name.

Note that the packages in this directory are in most cases
more intended as examples than as complete applications.
They have not been tested as thoroughly as the internal
code of Mathematica.
```

Here's a close look at the files in the Packages directory:

```
Algebra:
CountRoots.m            GosperSum.m      ReIm.m        Trigonometry.m
Calculus:
InverseLaplace.m        ODE.m
DefiniteIntegrate.m     Laplace.m        VectorAnalysis.m
DataAnalysis:
DescriptiveFunctions.m
ConfidenceIntervals.m                    DescriptiveStatistics.m
ContinuousDistributions.m                DiscreteDistributions.m
DataManipulation.m
DiscreteMath:
CombinatorialSimplification.m
```

```
ClebschGordan.m              Permutations.m
CombinatorialFunctions.m     Tree.m
Examples:
EllipticCurves.m      Mortgages.m
CellularAutomata.m    Factor.m               RingTheory.m
CollatzProblem.m      FunctionalProgramming.m RungeKutta.m
CrystalStructure.m    ModularArithmetic.m
Geometry:
Polytopes.m Rotations.m
Graphics:
Graphics.m            Polyhedra.m            ThreeScript.m
Colors.m              ParametricPlot3D.m     Shapes.m
LinearAlgebra:
Cross.m               Vectors.m
Miscellaneous:
PhysicalConstants.m   Units.m
NumberTheory:
IntegerRoots.m
ContinuedFractions.m Recognize.m
NumericalMath:
ListIntegrate.m
Approximations.m      RungeKutta.m
InverseStatisticalFunctions.m
Utilities:
Record.m              ShowTime.m
```

If you're not a math sissy, you may now drool. My personal favorite is Units.m, which defines every unit of measure—both common and scientific—that I've ever heard of, and many I've never heard of, including:

```
Ounce::symbol = "oz";
  Ounce -> 28.350 Gram,
  AvoirdupoisOunce -> Ounce,
  TroyOunce -> 31.103 Gram,
  Pennyweight -> 1.555 Gram,
  Slug -> 14.5939 Kilogram,
  Geepound -> Slug,
  Stone -> 14 Pound,
  Shekel -> 14.1 Gram,
```

```
Obolos -> 715.38*10^-3 Gram,
Drachma -> 4.2923 Gram,
Mina -> 0.9463 Pound,
Talent -> 60 Mina,
Libra -> 325.971 Gram,
Pondus -> 0.71864 Pound,
```

Take a look at this package. It rolls on and on, a testament to the thoroughness you'll see everywhere in Mathematica.

One of the smaller packages is IntegerRoots. This is the entire package:

```
(* Copyright 1988 Wolfram Research Inc. *)
BeginPackage["NumberTheory`IntegerRoots`"]
BreakRoots::usage =
    "BreakRoots[expr] extracts the integer parts of rational roots of
    integers in expr."
Begin["`private`"]
BreakRoots[expr_] := expr /. (n_Integer)^(p_Rational) :>
                FactorRoot[n, Numerator[p], Denominator[p]]

FactorRoot[n_Integer, p_Integer, q_Integer] :=
    Block[ { nf = FactorInteger[n], ip = 1, rp = 1, t } ,
        Do[
            t = nf[[i]] ;
            ip = ip * t[[1]]^Quotient[p t[[2]], q] ;
            rp = rp * t[[1]]^Mod[p t[[2]], q] ,
        {i, Length[nf]}
        ] ;

    ip rp^(1/q)
    ]
End[ ]
EndPackage[ ];
```

Packages make Mathematica still more open-ended. To make the program smarter, add another package. Already, many additional Mathematica packages are available. Many are available on Usenet. And note that Mathematica packages are text files. Because Mathematica kernels vary little between computers, a package created on a Sun or a Mac or a Cray can be used by NeXT Mathematica. And vice versa.

# Help

If you're not yet overwhelmed by Mathematica, it's my fault: you should be.

So it's deep. So it's amazingly powerful. So: How do I learn it?

Many ways. And you'll enjoy it.

First, there's a mandatory purchase: *Mathematica: A System for Doing Mathematics by Computer.*

The book is written by Stephen Wolfram, the creator of Mathematica. It is beautifully written: lucid and clear. Not stuffy. Such a book this is. Wolfram is widely acclaimed as a genius. If so, genius makes for exceptional clarity. Where was this guy when I struggled through algebra?

Don't even think of using Mathematica before reading—or at least skimming through—this book.

Now I want you to believe this truism: Great applications have great help.

Remember WordStar? That early word processor had tremendous help. Aldus PageMaker? Great help. 1-2-3? Great help. HyperCard? Great help.

Mathematica? Extraordinary help.

It comes in levels and flavors. The creators of Mathematica expended more effort on help than most programmers use for entire applications.

First, there's the somewhat traditional Help panel. (See Figure 22-11.)

Here, you can page and scroll through menus and menu items.

There's also a "help cursor." Choose the "Help Cursor" menu item and the cursor becomes a question mark. Click on what you don't understand. Up comes help. The panel even has a "Verbose" switch, for those wanting still more explanation.

Most panels also have Help buttons for context-sensitive help.

Since working in Mathematica means throwing expressions at the kernel, some of your tosses will miss the mark. If so, Mathematica beeps. Why the beep? Choose the "Why the beep?" menu item to find out.

You can also make a selection, then choose "Explain selection" from the Help menu.

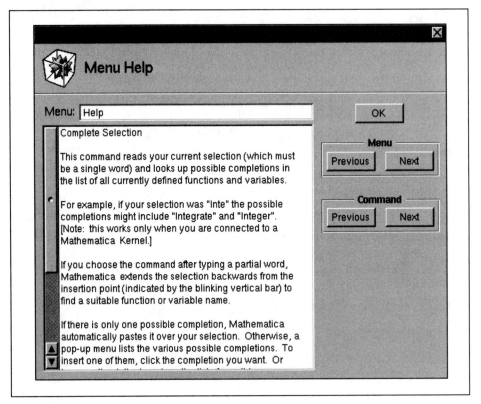

*Figure 22-11*

To get help on a particular subject, type:

? <name>

in a Mathematica window.

?ListPlot

produces:

```
ListPlot[{y1, y2, ...}] plots a list of values. The x
  coordinates for each point are taken to be 1, 2, ....
  ListPlot[{{x1, y1}, {x2, y2}, ...}] plots a list of
  values with specified x and y coordinates.
```

Preceding your request with *two* question marks yields verbose help:

??ListPlot

```
ListPlot[{y1, y2, ...}] plots a list of values. The x
 coordinates for each point are taken to be 1, 2, ....
 ListPlot[{{x1, y1}, {x2, y2}, ...}] plots a list of
 values with specified x and y coordinates.
Attributes[ListPlot] = {Protected}
ListPlot/:

  Options[ListPlot] =
   {PlotJoined -> False,
    PlotRange -> Automatic,
    PlotStyle -> Automatic,
    DisplayFunction :> $DisplayFunction, 1
    AspectRatio -> ———-,
                      GoldenRatio
  PlotColor -> Automatic, Axes -> Automatic,
    PlotLabel -> None, AxesLabel -> None,
    Ticks -> Automatic, Framed -> False}
```

If that's not enough help (and there's never enough help), Mathematica has a stash of about 380 error messages. Do something incorrectly, and you'll be told why. To Mathematica, the error messages have this format—you'll only see what's to the right, with placeholders replaced with meaningful descriptors.

```
Pattern::nonsymb = "First element in pattern `1` is not a symbol."
Pattern::noblanks = "No blanks found in second element of pattern `1`."
Pattern::multi = "Name `1` used for both fixed and variable length patterns."
General::optform = "Optional object `1` is not a single blank."
Optional::blanks = "Default value for optional argument `1` contains blanks."
```

And about 370 additional error messages. You'll never be alone.

Developers should take a cue from this avalanche of help. There's no such thing as "Too much help." Help shouldn't be an afterthought; it should be crafted in, throughout the application.

Mathematica excels here, again. This, truly, may be the best computer application ever.

## The Math Object

It goes on.

Mathematica is not just a world to itself, it's a body of knowledge to be accessed by any NeXT application.

Although it didn't make it into NeXT's 1.0 software release, future versions of the AppKit will include a Math Object. The Math Object will message the Mathematica kernel. Applications that use the Math Object can offload math calculations just as they'd send a word to Webster for definition, or to Librarian for look-up. The Math Object will allow Mathematica's talents to pervade the entire NeXT system.

# Chapter 23

# Digital Webster

*dic-tio-nary* \ *'dik-she-,ner-ē*\  *n,  pl* *-nar-ies*
*[ML dictionarium, fr. LL diction-, dictio word, fr. L, speaking]*
*(1526)*
*1: a reference book containing words usu. alphabetically arranged along with*
*information about their forms, pronunciations, functions, etymologies, meanings,*
*and syntactical and idiomatic uses*
*2: a reference book listing alphabetically terms or names important to a particular*
*subject or activity along with discussion of their meanings and applications*
*3: a reference book giving for words of one language equivalents in another*
*4: a list (as of phrases, synonyms, or hyphenation instructions) stored in machine-*
*readable form (as on a disk) for reference by an automatic system (as for*
*information retrieval or computerized typesetting)*

The Digital Webster application contains the complete "Webster's Ninth New Collegiate Dictionary," and the complete "Webster's Collegiate Thesaurus."

"Complete" is an understatement. Not only are all the words, pictures and tables included in the digital edition, but many cryptic abbreviations have been expanded. In creating the digital edition, thousands of new words were added, and other entries were expanded or enriched. Webster's digital edition isn't merely an electronic copy; it's better.

And, of course, there are viewing and searching options undreamed of in mere paper dictionaries.

Michael Hawley, in his preface to the "digital edition" of Webster, says it best:

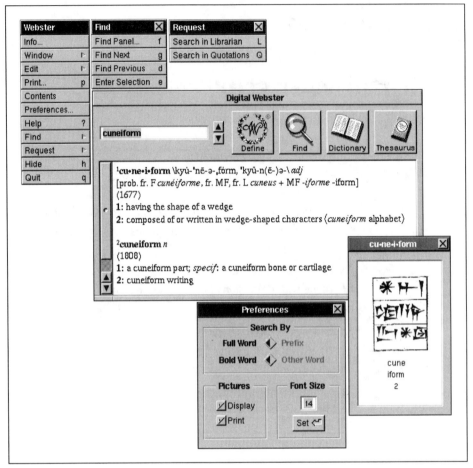

*Figure 23-1*

ENORMOUS KNOWLEDGE IS AVAILABLE IN A GREAT DICTIONARY, and this is the first time in history that such powerful access to this resource has really been placed at your fingertips: any word on the display, or in your imagination, can now be located in the dictionary in an instant. Cross-references can be followed by simply clicking a button.

And further on:

Finally, because the dictionary is packaged with the computer, every user and every application will have Webster at its fingertips—and that will be as valuable to a scholar as indoor plumbing is to a homeowner. Because of this, from now on and for all time, any computer that lacks a great dictionary will be considered barbaric.

This is one of the great sentences in the history of computing: "Because of this, from now on and for all time, any computer that lacks a great dictionary will be considered barbaric."

Yeah.

## How it Works

Webster's dictionary (ignoring the thesaurus for the moment) consists, primarily, of:

* the Webster application;
* the dictionary text; and
* illustrations and indexes

The Webster application is found in NextApps. The files used by Webster are in the NextLibrary/References/Webster-Dictionary directory:

```
localhost# ls -l /NextLibrary/References/Webster-Dictionary
total 36096
-rw-rw-rw- 1 root      217 Sep 8 00:04 .places
-rw-r-r- 1 root    15077052 Jul 8 16:04 full-index
-rw-r-r- 1 root     2677247 Jul 7 19:09 index
drwxr-xr-x 3 root      1024 Aug 23 15:16 info/
drwxr-xr-x 2 root     21504 Aug 23 15:00 pictures/
-rw-r-r- 1 root    19131602 Jul 7 19:08 source
drwxr-xr-x 2 root      1024 Aug 10 12:11 tiff/
```

The file "source" contains the actual dictionary text and all other indexed material—over 19 megabytes of material!

The Webster source is formatted by the Webster application. If you look at the first few lines of Webster "source" in the shell, you see only:

```
localhost# cat source
a 1an,pl a's or as \ z\ often cap, often attrial-1 mu-2
ed-51a the 1st letter of the English alphabet1b a graphic
representation of this letter1c a speech counterpart of
```

```
orthographic a2 the 6th tone of a C-major scale3 a graphic
device for reproducing the letter a4 one designated a esp.
as the 1st in order or class5a a grade rating a studen-
t's...
```

Webster uses two indexes to speed dictionary look-ups. The first-used index is "index," a scrawny 2.6-megabyte file. The file "full-index" is a more complete 15 megabytes of data—almost the size of the dictionary text itself. The full-index is only used when the smaller index doesn't contain the desired entry.

As ratios of "indexes to source" go, this is good. Indexes are often many times the size of the indexed material. Still, Webster (like other reference works) justifies the need for NeXT's immense storage capacity.

The illustrations for Webster are found in the directory NextLibrary/References/Webster-Dictionary/pictures. How many pictures?

```
localhost# cd /NextLibrary/References/Webster-Dictionary/pictures
localhost# ls | wc -l
   890
```

Actually, 889 illustrations; word count added in the ".places" file found in every directory.

Unfortunately, there's no way to browse through Webster's illustrations. The TIFF format used isn't compatible with formats used by the Scene or Icon applications.

The remaining files in NextLibrary/References/Webster-Dictionary contain supplementary material and explanatory text.

## Using Webster

Webster is a core NeXT application. It can be used as a standalone application, or called from other applications.

The AppKit makes it easy for other applications to access Webster. It takes only a few extra lines of code, a Request menu item, and a Request submenu. That done, Webster can be called by any application. If Webster hasn't been launched, the Request message does the launching automatically.

As NeXT applications proliferate, it's hoped that software developers include the ability to call Webster (and Digital Librarian) in their applications.

As a standalone application, Webster can be used to search the dictionary, thesaurus, or both. If both are chosen (by clicking buttons to "open" the file icons), the dictionary definition is shown first, followed by the thesaurus entry:

**won•drous** \ `wen-dres\ adj

[alter. of ME *wonders*, fr. gen. of 1*wonder*]

(15c)

:that is to be marveled at: EXTRAORDINARY

— **wondrous** *adv, archaic*

— **won•drous•ly** *adv*

— **won•drous•ness** *n*

° **Thesaurus:**

**wondrous** *adj*

   **syn**   MARVELOUS 1, amazing, astonishing, astounding, miraculous, spectacular, strange, stupendous, surprising, wonderful

Once a definition has been produced, Command-double-clicking on any word in the view area defines the clicked-on word. It's a fast way to learn: From the definition of "bone," you might travel to "calcareous," then to "carbonate," then to "carbon"...picking up more knowledge at each stop.

It's not hypertext, but it's neat, fun, and immensely useful.

You can search by whole word, or find all words matching a prefix. The prefix search is useful to find a word's spelling. If, for example, you can't remember how to spell the name for the outer layer of exine, a prefix search on "ex" turns up (among other entries):

**ekt•ex•ine** \ (`)ek-'tek-,se$^a$n, -,sı$^a$n\ n

[Gk *ekto-* ect- + E *exine*]

(1947)

:a structurally variable outer layer of the exine

Another option is a full-text search. Enter a word and you'll be shown every occurrence of the word throughout the dictionary or thesaurus or both. *Every* occurrence. This isn't recommended for use with common words.

Is this a useful option, or mere showing off?

It can be tremendously useful. Here's an example:

As a relief from delving into The NeXT Computer, I've been reading about Celts: the barbarian tribes of prehistoric Europe. Fascinating stuff.

While the Celts didn't have a written language, they did, of course, have a spoken language. That language has echoes in modern European languages, and in English.

So which words have Celtic origins? That's a hard question to answer. But with Digital Webster, it's easy: just set your preferences to "full-text index," enter the word "Celt," and click "Define."

Not too many seconds later, each definition containing the word "Celt" is delivered up. Amazing.

I now know that these words have Celtic origins: barnacle, basket, bat, battle, billet, biretta, bray, brier, brigand, brisance, British, Briton, brock, bruise, bushel, butcher, cant, car (!), carpenter, chance,...and more, down to vassal, Walloon, and Welsh. Just reading that list teaches you something about the Celts.

Amazing. Try doing that with paper.

## Finally

I've got one more comment that didn't seem to fit in anywhere. It's about the dictionary's supplementary material.

Most people go to dictionaries only for specific information. But all good dictionaries have much more to offer. In particular, the section titled "The English Language In the Dictionary" contains 10,608 fascinating words that do what good dictionaries should: Inform the reader.

# Chapter 24

# Quotations

*I hate quotations.*
May 1849

— **RALPH WALDO EMERSON** 1803–1882

Here's a really useless reference: The Oxford Book of Quotations. It occupies disk space better spent filled with C include files, shell scripts, or obsolete UNIX utilities.

It is, after all, the 1990's. The Oxford Book of Quotations (even the title is ponderous!) is a dinosaur. Good for nothing and nobody.

And, like, who are these people? They're all dead, or mostly all dead for one thing. John Brown? Thomas Brown? Somebody called T. E. Brown? I mean, really!

And, you know, the really good quotes are in *US* magazine. Or *Rolling Stone*. And the people who said them are like alive, you know? And they're, like, movie stars and rock stars. Or at least rich. Some of those quotes are really good.

The quotes in The Oxford Book of Quotations are just dumb. Put another way:

*Dumb as a drum vith a hole in it, sir. [Sam Weller.]*
PickwickPapers, ch.25

— CHARLES DICKENS 1812–1870

Pick up an *US* magazine. That's where the *really* good quotes are.

# Chapter 25

## Digital Librarian

*This, books can do—nor this alone: they give*
*New views to life, and teach us how to live;*
*They soothe the grieved, the stubborn they chastise;*
*Fools they admonish, and confirm the wise.*
*Their aid they yield to all: they never shun*
*The man of sorrow, nor the wretch undone;*
*Unlike the hard, the selfish, and the proud,*
*They fly not sullen from the suppliant crowd;*
*Nor tell to various people various things,*
*But show to subjects, what they show to kings.*
The Library, l.41

> — **GEORGE CRABBE** 1754–1832

*Come, and take choice of all my library,*
*And so beguile thy sorrow.*
Titus Andronicus IV.i.34

> — **WILLIAM SHAKESPEARE** 1564–1616

Digital Librarian is a means to cope with the ocean of information that comes with the cube. Not master, not learn: cope.

Digital Librarian isn't the innovation it seems at first glance, however. UNIX has had these capabilities for years, from a command called index. Digital Librarian is a new face on index. That's to the good, because index is a particularly forbidding UNIX command, as you can see from the UNIX manual page:

```
NAME
        index - build an index to a directory
```

```
SYNOPSIS
    index [ -i index ][ -lxfv ][ -m # ][ -P # ][
-pargString ][
    -c cmd ][ -s file ][ -[nNtT] str ] [files | directories]
```

Digital Librarian offers some of index's options in a more pleasant guise:

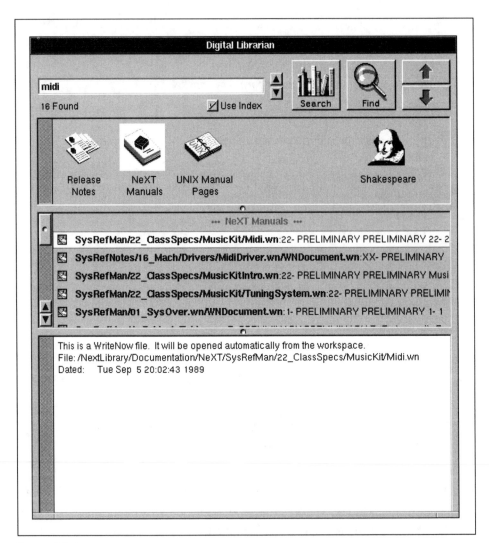

*Figure 25-1*

## How It Works

Digital Librarian lets you search for words in files. It's a super Find panel, in essence. The files or directories that Digital Librarian can search are shown in the topmost area. To add a file or folder to the collection, drag it in from The Workspace Manager.

To make room for additional target icons, drag down this custom control (which you'll see in other NeXT applications):

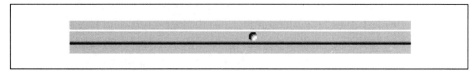

*Figure 25-2*

Once in the target area, the files or directories (we'll just say files from now on) can be searched.

If that's all there was to it, however, Digital Librarian would be slow, and not too useful. The key that makes Digital Librarian useful is indexing.

Consider a file of words. If it's a typical file, it contains many duplicated words. And it also contains many "noise words" like "it, a, the, and, or, if" and "so on." The noise words are generally articles, prepositions, and pronouns.

You'll seldom care about noise words, which carry little information, hence the name "noise." Noise words, essentially, are text static.

Once the noise words and duplicate words are stripped from a file, the file is smaller, and faster to search. But there's more that can be done. The indexing routine can guess which words are plurals of other words. If so, they're eliminated. Smart indexing routines are also wise to contractions and hyphenated words.

When the indexing process is complete, a manageable "key word" list results. Despite the list's reduced size, it still contains most of the information in the original text. With some difficulty, you could still read it, and know pretty much what it contained.

The indexing routine next takes the word list and creates a "hash table": a data structure that makes it easy for other routines to conduct extremely fast searches.

Except when indexing extremely long documents, you'll probably index 100% of the key words. Indexing fewer words results in smaller index files and somewhat faster searches, however—though search speed isn't a problem in Digital Librarian. More important, indexing only a small percent of the words usually ensures that the words you want to index *will* be indexed. Here's a bit of the NeXT documentation that makes the point:

> Word frequency information is efficiently encoded in a special data structure called a *word frequency* table. This data structure provides a compact, rapidly accessible cache; once the cache is primed, **frequency(word, domain)** can be computed with just a few instructions. On disk, the information is represented as a single file of modest size. For example, **DefaultEnglish.wf** occupies about 300 Kbytes. The information is loaded from disk with a single read operation to prime the cache.

> Using these facilities, **pword** needs about 30 seconds to compute a keyword index for *Alice in Wonderland,* which contains roughly 300 Kbytes of prose. In a test using a very stringent peculiarity threshold, **pword** selected 382 words from the text, including, in order from most significant to least significant, *alice, queen, thoughtfully, hedgehog, tart, treacle, hatter, herself, ... mimsy, borogroave, outgrabe, ... jabberwock ....* The list occupies less than 6 Kbytes, or approximately 2% of the space occupied by the original text, and includes the names of all of the principal characters, and many of Carroll's made-up words.

The indexing process begins automatically when you drag a file icon into the Librarian.

The Index panel appears first. Click Create Index and the Index Settings panel appears. The topmost checkbox, "Use stop list," is a custom noise word file. If present, and the option is checked, the indexing routine won't index any words found in the stop list file.

Building an index is a lengthy, computationally intensive task. In other words, it takes a long time and slows down all other applications. A good thing to do while indexing is lunch.

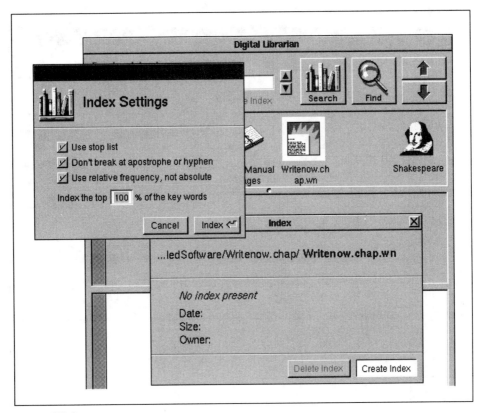

*Figure 25-3*

## Using Digital Librarian

Beginning a search means:

- Clicking one or more files to determine "where" to search;
- Entering a word to search for; and
- Hitting Return or clicking on the Search button to begin the search.

If an index has been created, the "Use indexes" radio button will be highlighted. If you'd rather perform a slower but more thorough search, click it off before beginning the search. A "no stone unturned" linear search will then be performed.

As matches are found, the files containing the match are shown below, in a scrolling list. To the left of the filenames are icons that represent the file type.

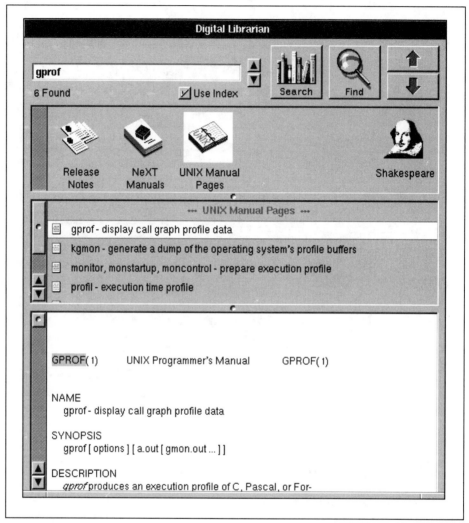

*Figure 25-4*

Below the file list, another view shows the actual text, if Digital Librarian can display the file. Files that can't be displayed by Digital Librarian—formatted Write-Now files, for example—aren't displayed. How those files are shown is determined by your preference settings (Figure 25-5.) You can choose to have Digital Librarian automatically open the file containing the first occurrence of a match, or you can open files manually, by double-clicking on the filename. Or make settings for searching, sorting, or fonts.

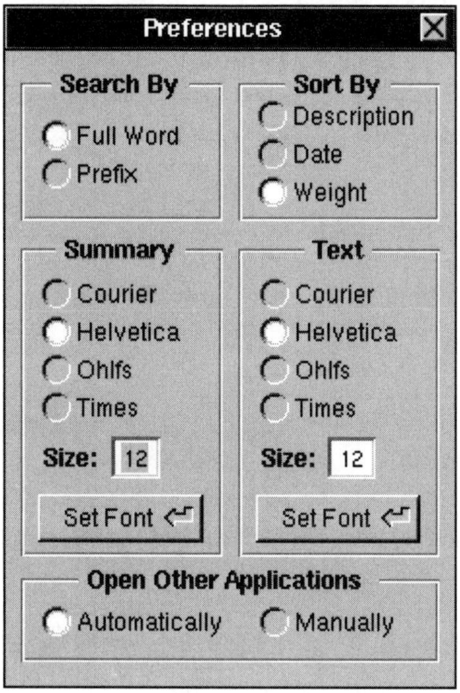

Figure 25-5

Back to controls:

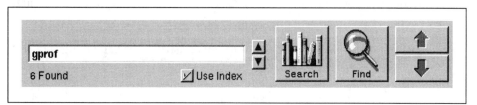

Figure 25-6

The Find button finds the next occurrence of the word in the highlighted file. The arrows at right move between files. And the small arrows at left let you move backward and forward through words you've typed in the search entry field. You should try each, to get the hang of moving within and among files.

## Cross-Referencing

There's a shortcut that allows immediate cross-referencing: Command-double-click on a word displayed in the text view. The word will be quickly found in the selected target files.

## Advanced Searching

This is useful, but limited. For more powerful searching, you can use the Boolean operators:

- and;
- or; and
- not

You can use these words in the entry field, or their algebraic stand-ins:

- "&" for "and,"
- "|" for "or," and
- "!" for "not."

Don't type the quotes.

*Now* you're getting into useful search constructions. Without Boolean operators, you'll often be overwhelmed by files which match your search string. Using the operators lets you narrow your search to, for example, all files that contain the word "pollution" *and* the word "industrial."

Another way to narrow a search is to use constructions containing "not." Maybe "rock ! Beatles."

To widen a search, use "or." Searching for "lymphoid | lymphocyte" makes sure you get all files containing either word. If you wish you can string many "and's" and "or's" together.

When you're comfortable with these operators, try more sophisticated constructions:

- rock and Stones ! Beatles;
- pollution & sludge | EPA & dump | toxic & waste;

- numinous & gnostic & logos; or
- voltage & spike | transient.

One note. Digital Librarian, like Quotations, "groups" words from left to right. In effect, they're automatically parenthesized. So the examples above would be converted internally to:

- (rock and Stones) ! Beatles;
- (pollution & sludge) | (EPA & dump) | (toxic & waste);
- (numinous & gnostic & logos); and
- (voltage & spike) | transient.

So the first example would only find files containing both the words "rock" and "Stones," but not containing the word "Beatles."

To override the gratuitous grouping, insert your own parenthesies.

## Sending Selections

If you want to branch out, you can send the selection in the lower view panel to Webster, to Quotations, or—if it's a filename—to The Workspace Manager for opening.

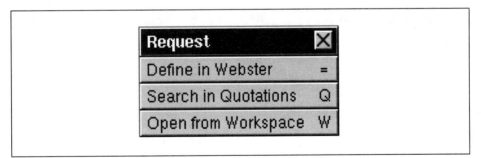

*Figure 25-7*

## Using Index

After using Digital Librarian, after learning how to create advanced Boolean search strings in your sleep, you might want to consider ditching Digital Librarian altogether and using UNIX's Index command instead. You'll have a few more options than allowed by Digital Librarian. You'll also have access to other UNIX commands—and there are many—that work with indexes; among them: dbadd, dbclean, dbfiles, dbkey, dbrm, and dbstat.

We won't go into that here. The UNIX manual pages have more information (start with the index entry). But it's a thought, if your indexing needs are extensive.

## If Only

Despite Digital Librarian's options and ease-of-use, the program is often an exercise in frustration. Two additions, one minor and one major, would be great improvements.

The first improvement is "soundex" searching. It's based on a soundex algorithm which "guesses" the correct spelling of a word. It's a remarkably accurate, well-known routine. Using it allows you to type in a word *the way you think* it's spelled, instead of being forced to use exact spellings. As it stands now, if you can't spell it, you can't find it. With the choice to use the soundex routine, you could enter "newmonia" and find "pneumonia," which is probably the word you wanted.

The second, major addition would be the ability to search on phrases, not mere words. This one would challenge NeXT programmers, but they could do it. They're good.

While using Boolean operators can often produce what you want, adding the ability to search for phrases would increase the usefulness of Digital Librarian by… a zillion times? A lot, anyway.

# Chapter 26

# Terminal and Shell

*Sweet Echo, sweetest nymph, that liv'st unseen*
  *Within thy airy shell*
*By slow Meander's margent green,*
  *And in the violet-embroidered vale.*
                    **— JOHN MILTON** 1608–1674

*I do not know what I may appear to the world, but to myself I*
*seem to have been only like a boy playing on the sea-shore, and*
*diverting myself in now and then finding a smoother pebble or*
*a prettier shell than ordinary, whilst the great ocean of truth*
*lay all undiscovered before me.*
L.T. More, Isaac Newton (1934), p.664
                    **— SIR ISAAC NEWTON** 1642–1727

Before either of us was born, computing was done with the aid of teletypes: large, heavy, clattering things. They were typewriters cum printers; known by the acronym "tty," for TeleTYpe. Eventually, they transformed into video terminals, which were quieter, but not much smarter. The terminals were called "glass tty's," which is somewhat like calling cars "horseless carriages."

Terminals, being easy to make, were made by most everyone in the 1970s and 1980s. Each manufacturer had their own terminal ideas. Making UNIX and other operating systems work with terminals of widely varying characteristics ("It sends what for backspace?") was, and still is, a pain.

For a first-hand look at a mind-boggling collection of terminals—all with their own characteristics—read the file private/etc/termcap. You won't understand it, but you should find the comments interesting, and often amusing.

The DEC VT100 was one of the most popular terminals, and became a loose standard for terminals. Telecommunication programs often have a "VT100 emulation mode" as a result.

Computer terminals are still around, but computers like the cube offer "virtual terminals." The NeXT terminals are Terminal, an application program, and Shell, another "tty window" application.

Terminal emulates, somewhat, a VT100 terminal. A discussion of just how closely it emulates a VT100 could span several pages. Let's just say that the Terminal window is smaller, lighter, and thinner than a VT100, and that programs designed to run in VT100s will usually consent to live in Terminal. A higher standard of VT100 emulation is offered by third-party software vendors.

Some users are perplexed over NeXT's decision to offer two terminal emulation programs: Terminal and Shell. The reason, we can guess, is that NeXT wanted to provide features which would have made terminal emulation incompatible with VT100 standards. So two terminal emulation programs are bundled: a robust, somewhat-mouse-based Shell application, and a stripped-down, but VT100-compatible, Terminal application.

Let's clear up some naming confusion here. UNIX includes programs, called "shells," for communicating with the UNIX operating system. The two most common are the "C Shell" and the "Bourne Shell." By default, NeXT uses the C Shell.

You communicate with the shell through terminal emulation programs: either Terminal or Shell. You can enter identical commands into either application, and they're passed onto the C Shell for processing.

But that's not all you can do. You can also run *other* programs within either the Terminal or Shell application—though usually you're restricted to using the Shell application, because programs which run in a terminal window prefer thinking they're doing their stuff in a DEC VT100 terminal.

On traditional, character-based UNIX systems, *everything* is done in the equivalent of a terminal window, except that there's no window. Your terminal is your view into UNIX. The terminal is hardware, and all your actions are accomplished using either the C Shell or the Bourne Shell.

## Terminal

Terminal emulates a VT100 terminal. VT100s are character-based terminals that display 24 on-screen lines of 80 characters each. Terminal approximates the VT100 display with a 12-point, monospaced Courier font and a "block" cursor. VT100 terminals have never heard of mice, and NeXT's Terminal application hasn't either. A resize bar is Terminal's only concession to NeXTness. You may resize the Terminal window, but you can't scroll with the mouse: there's no scroller. To move forward or back, you need to know keyboard scrolling commands—which may vary between applications you run in Terminal.

Terminal's main menu has a mere three items: Info, Hide, and Quit.

When you launch Terminal, it runs the C Shell by default. In a sense, then you're running two programs: Terminal and, inside Terminal, the C Shell.

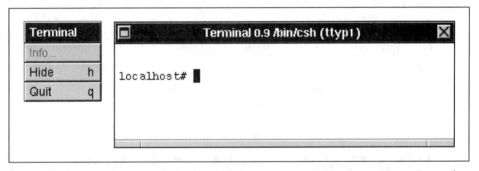

*Figure 26-1*

The pathname of the currently running program is displayed in the title bar. In this case, it's the C Shell (or csh), which is located in the /bin directory (so named because it's the home for executable "bin-ary" programs). You'll want a larger window than shown; this is resized to fit on paper.

The title bar also contains (ttyp1). Since NeXT and UNIX are multiprocessing, we can launch Terminal as many times as we want. (See Figure 26-2.)

Here, we've launched Terminal three times. The titles show (ttyp1), (ttyp2), and (ttyp3). Each is a full-fledged (which isn't saying much) Terminal window. All three are running /bin/csh. Commands can be entered, or programs run, in all three windows.

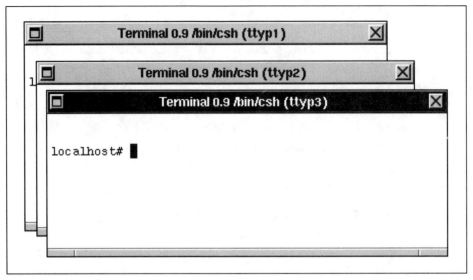

*Figure 26-2*

Although Terminal runs /bin/csh by default, Terminal can be launched and immediately run another program, or the program to be run can be specified from within Terminal. For instance, typing "emacs" (don't type the quotes) launches Emacs, a powerful, character-based, UNIX word processor:

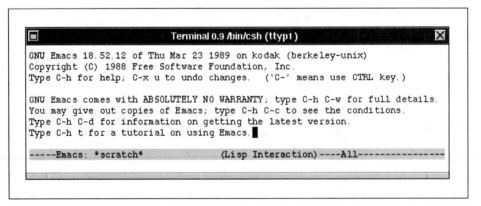

*Figure 26-3*

We'll leave Emacs here. It's worth investigating, though. Take some time and go through the extremely well-done Emacs tutorial for a taste of power UNIX word processing. In the window above, the line "(Lisp Interaction)" hints at Emacs' real purpose: creating and editing source code files. If you're a programmer, the goodies in Emacs (and there are tons) might just make you forego Edit and write your masterpiece in this anachronistically wonderful word processor.

The big question to answer about Terminal is this: When, and why, to use it? The answer, probably, is to use Terminal when you wish to run a UNIX program that balks at running in Terminal's more sophisticated sibling: Shell.

## Shell

Shell is Terminal all grown-up. It's NeXT's feature-laden version of a "standard text editor." Where Terminal gives only the slightest nod to windows and menus, Shell gives you this:

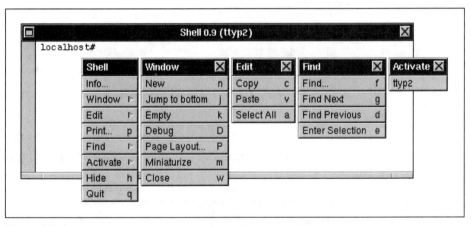

*Figure 26-4*

Although it's not shown above, Shell does offer a scroller, if the window's contents overflow the visible area (a frequent occurrence).

The Shell runs /bin/csh by default. Shell running in Shell, to be confusingly precise. All the UNIX examples that have peppered this book were performed in Shell.

In addition to standard NeXT menu options, Shell includes:

- commands to "Jump to bottom," which scrolls to the end of the window's text, and "Empty," which clears the window contents. Empty shouldn't be ignored; it's easy to have a few megabytes of text in a Shell window in short order;

- a Find/Change panel, and a full set of Find commands; and

- an Activate menu, which lists active Shell windows. Choose one to bring it to the front. (The inclusion of an Activate menu presumes that users will frequently open many new Shell windows, then yearn for an easy way to move between them.)

The most useful menu command, if you're a programmer, is Debug. Shell doesn't just run Shell, it can also run other programs. (When you're running the C Shell, in fact, *it's* usually running other programs!)

On NeXT, the default source-level debugger is "gdb," for GNU Debugger. Type "gdb" into the Shell window and you're off.

Gdb lets you debug a running application. But this presents a problem: how to enter debugging commands in the Shell window without making Shell the key window. Put another way, how do you enter debugging commands without activating and deactivating the application you're debugging?

Shell allows this with some nonstandard cleverness. When Debug is on, Shell is activated whenever the cursor enters the Shell window; no clicking necessary. And the previous key window (the application you're debugging, it's assumed) *remains* the key window.

This makes it easy to debug running programs. And presents the only display of two applications, both with key windows, that you'll see on NeXT.

Debug aside, you'll usually run the C Shell in the Shell window, and run other UNIX programs "from the C Shell." Learning and using UNIX is a never-ending process of typing into the Shell window, then being gratified or puzzled by what happens.

# Chapter 27

# And More...

*They are as sick that surfeit with too much, as they that starve
with nothing. It is no mean happiness, therefore, to be seated
in the mean: superfluity comes sooner by white hairs, but competency
lives longer.*
The Merchant of Venice
— **WILLIAM SHAKESPEARE** 1564–1616

*Damn the torpedoes! Full speed ahead.*
— **DAVID GLASGOW FARRAGUT** 1801–1870
At the battle of Mobile Bay, 5 Aug. 1864. "Torpedoes" were mines.

We've touched on the major applications bundled with The NeXT computer.
But there's more. Much more.

Beyond the applications in the NextApps directory, there's also:

+ a directory full of demo applications;

+ a directory of example applications, which include full source code; and

+ other languages, applications, and development environments lurking in
  other folders.

Let's start with a few of the applications in the Demos directory. We won't mention all the applications.

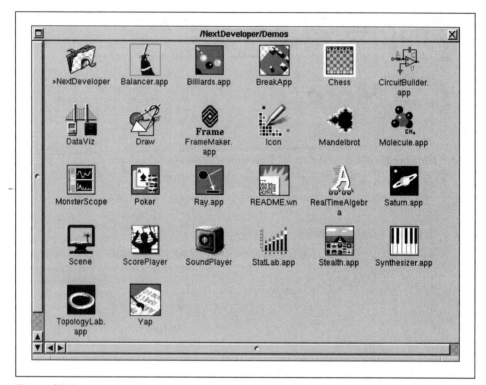

*Figure 27-1*

## Icon

With Macintosh, the tradition began: Every great computer has an artist on the design team.

For Macintosh, it was Susan Kare. For NeXT, it's Keith Ohlfs. This guy:

*Figure 27-2*

The whimsy, humor, and grace in NextStep are Ohlfs' fault. Ohlfs also created the Ohlfs font and, we presume, named it after a favorite relative. And he wrote the Scene application, which is used to set backgrounds and capture screen images (all the illustrations in this book were produced with Scene). His head really is that big, by the way.

Ohlfs is also responsible for the Icon application:

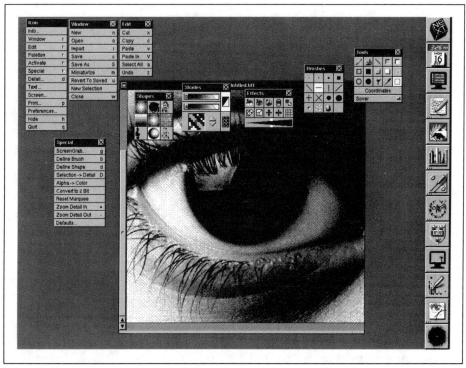

*Figure 27-3*

As the name suggests, Icon is the app to use to make icons. But it's more than that. Too much more, maybe—and we're not just talking about the mandatory "bullet hole" image on the Shades Palette.

There's a clever help system: In addition to Help in the Info panel, you can also Control-click-on items to get specific help. Despite that, Icon remains vastly underdocumented. That may be why it's in the Demos directory, and not in NextApps.

Look at the illustration of Icon. Is that Post-Modern, or what? I don't even know what Post-Modern means, but I've heard the term often used to describe Icon, so I'll use it too. Whatever it means, it feels right. Someday, when someone figures out Icon, maybe they'll explain it to "the rest of us"—sorry, wrong computer. Until then, Icon is the cube's MacPaint. Or maybe it isn't.

## Chess

One of the best things about UNIX has always been games. From the early days, Berkeley UNIX came with games—lots of games. Granted, they were all character-based; no graphics, obviously. But still: Adventure, Hunt the Wumpus, space games, number games...lots of games.

NeXT gives you everything included in Berkeley UNIX, *except* the games. NeXT Corporate probably looked disdainfully on these Terminal-based amusements. Or maybe they just didn't want to waste time recompiling them to run on NeXT. Or maybe they didn't want anyone to think that the cube is a "game computer" (fat chance). Anyway:

Boo.

NeXT's only redemption is the Chess application, included with other demos. It's based on UNIX GNU Chess, which has always played a ferocious game. It still plays a ferocious game, only now it does it in three dimensions. (See Figure 27-4.)

There's also a classic 2-D display. (See Figure 27-5.)

If you love chess, you'll love it. Even at the easy setting (60 moves in five minutes), it handily trounces an unnamed writer who once fancied himself a good chess player. For those who dare, you can play "one move an hour" chess. Don't say I didn't warn you.

## Allegro CL Common LISP

The cube also contains Allegro's version of Common LISP: the standard, complete implementation of the LISP language. If you like LISP, it's cause to rejoice.

LISP was created in the 1960s. It began as a small language that was fluid, easy to learn, and capable of wonderful feats of symbolic manipulation. In truth, LISP was the first "object-oriented" language.

Figure 27-4

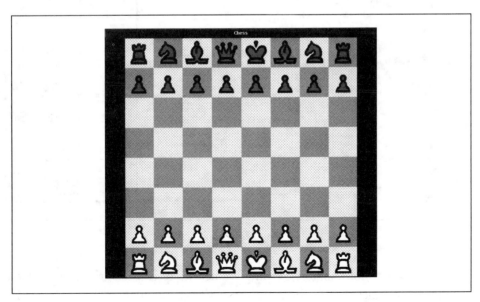

Figure 27-5

Today, LISP is big, rugged, and powerful. It's still capable of marvelous feats; it's ideal for natural-language or other string-processing tasks, and it's the language of choice for artificial-intelligence programs. LISP partisans, in fact, say LISP is ideal for most everything—and they may be right.

Today's LISP, however, isn't small and it isn't particularly easy to learn. The Common LISP standard is all-encompassing: Common LISP (not to be confused with lesser implementations of the language) adds almost every feature imaginable to LISP.

The good news is that Common LISP supports everything you're likely to want. The bad news is that Common LISP is a universe to explore, which takes time. Here's some of what you'll find in the cube:

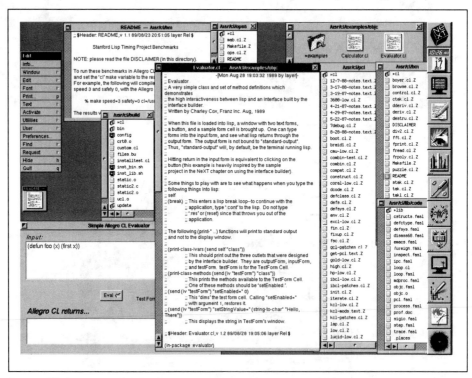

*Figure 27-6*

If you're a professional LISP programmer, it's reason enough to buy the cube. (There's so much in the cube that *everybody* has a reason to buy one—which is the whole idea, of course.)

One caveat: Common LISP isn't as tightly integrated into Interface Builder as Objective-C is. You'll need to run LISP from Shell or Terminal or—the preferred way—from within the Emacs word processor (which runs only in Terminal).

In fact, the version shipped with NeXT's 1.0 software is a *beta release*. (Version 3.1.beta.44, to be exact.)

Look for upcoming software releases to bring Common LISP out of beta and give it parity with Objective-C as a complete NextStep development environment.

## Sybase SQL Server

When the cube was announced, one of the big announcements was that an SQL database program was to be included, free.

This is it. How you feel about it will depend on your desires and programming skills.

First, it's not a database. If you think that "a database" comes with the cube, you're wrong.

Boy, are you wrong.

What you get is a complete—very complete—set of C-compatible SQL database routines, and all the Sybase accoutrements needed to craft "from scratch" databases, or include database capabilities into applications that you create.

It's not for the faint of heart. (See Figure 27-7.)

The Sybase directories, put another way, include:

| | |
|---|---|
| /usr/sybase | the Sybase home directory |
| Install | files needed to install Sybase |
| SPR | Software Performance Reports |
| bin | executable Sybase files |
| database | a directory for your database files |
| doc | manual pages to use with Digital Librarian |
| include | library header files |
| lib | host language libraries |
| sample | sample Sybase programs |
| dblibrary | DB-Library examples |
| scripts | Sybase scripts |

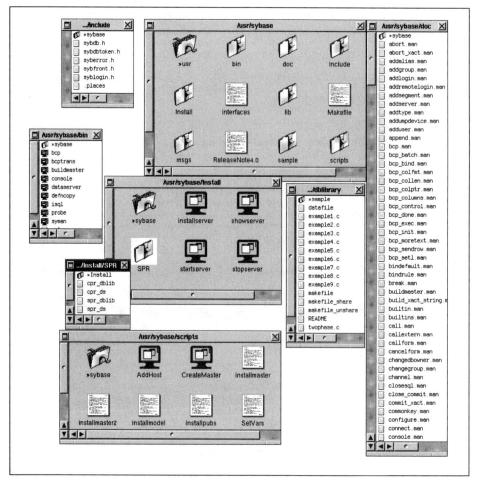

*Figure 27-7*

Here's the beginning of a sample Sybase script:

```
/* installpubs 44.1 4/23/89 */
set nocount on
if exists (select * from master.dbo.sysdatabases
        where name = "pubs")
begin
  drop database pubs
end
go
print 'Creating the "pubs" database'
```

```
create database pubs
go
use pubs
go
if exists (select * from master.dbo.sysdatabases
        where name = "pubs")
begin
  execute sp_addtype id, "varchar(11)", "not null"
  execute sp_addtype tid, "varchar(6)", "not null"
end
go
if exists (select * from master.dbo.sysdatabases
        where name = "pubs")
begin
  create table authors
  (au_id id,
  au_lname varchar(40) not null,
  au_fname varchar(20) not null,
  phone char(12),
  address varchar(40) null,
  city varchar(20) null,
  state char(2) null,
  zip char(5) null,
  contract bit)
end
go
grant select on authors to public
go
if exists (select * from master.dbo.sysdatabases
        where name = "pubs")
begin
  create table publishers
  (pub_id char(4) not null,
  pub_name varchar(40) null,
  city varchar(20) null,
  state char(2) null)
end
```

If you're a good programmer, and you know the ins and outs of SQL, it's a treasure chest, and a wonderful bonus to the already capacious NeXT programming environment. It's particularly appropriate for Fortune 500 firms who write their own database applications for internal use.

As with Common LISP, the Sybase environment has a "rough and ready" feel to it. (The Sybase software didn't even show up until NeXT's 1.0 release. Future versions, let's hope, will be more friendly and NextSteppy.)

## TeX

If you're an old hand at UNIX, TeX is probably old hat. If you're not:

TeX?

Here's the story. Don Knuth, the Obi-Wan of computing in our time, wanted to typeset some of his mathematical equations. But he found the available typesetting software deficient for his precise math typesetting needs.

So he decided to write a program to typeset equations. The first version of TeX appeared in 1977. Today's version can literally typeset anything. It's all done by inserting "codes" into text. You might prefer FrameMaker, trust me.

Before using TeX, you need to install it. Instructions can be found in the file:

```
/NextLibrary/Documentation/NeXT/RelNotes/TeXNotes.wn
```

Better yet, go into Digital Librarian, click on UNIX Manual Pages, then search for the word "TeX." What follows will get you started.

## DataViz

DataViz is an application to make it easy to transfer files between NeXTs and other computers. On the NeXT, it looks like Figure 27-8.

(Notice the icon: a cube and a Mac and a bridge. Cute, huh?)

But don't think that you're off the hook. You still need to buy software to manage the other end of the connection. The DataViz software costs $199 and comes with disks and cables for both Macintosh and IBM-compatible computers. (You can also get versions for other computers.)

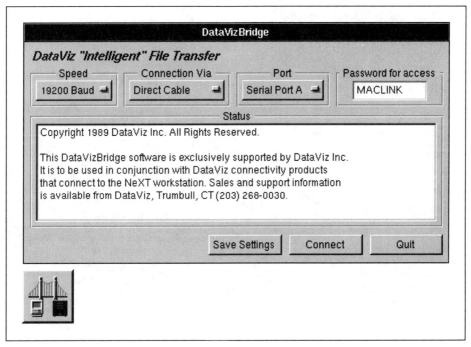

*Figure 27-8*

Most of the smarts are on the non-NeXT end. See the Other Products appendix for details. In brief, though: It works great.

## FrameMaker

The cube also comes with a demo version of FrameMaker. Don't scoff at the word "demo." The version does most everything except save files. And "most everything," with FrameMaker, is a boatload.

If you have even the slightest need for desktop publishing software, buy it. It's an extraordinary program. If you've used PageMaker or Quark Xpress or Ventura Publisher, you'll like FrameMaker much better. A terrific program.

More information can be found in the Other Products appendix, or turn to the "dumps" section to take a peek.

## Demos and Examples

The NextDeveloper directory contains a "demos" directory and an "example" directory. The difference? The examples are source code which you can compile into applications. The Calulator directory, for example, holds these files:

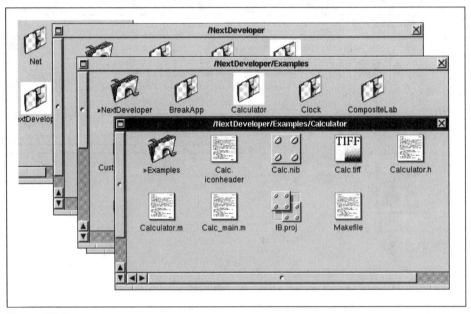

*Figure 27-9*

which you can "Make" into an application with a wave of your hand, either in Interface Builder, or through Shell.

The other program examples are shown in Figure 27-10.

Of all the examples, "Draw" is the most full-featured, and contains much code that you'll want to "lift" for your own first applications. (Sure, that's how it's done.) Most NeXT features are shown in code in the other examples. Start here if you know C and want to program the cube.

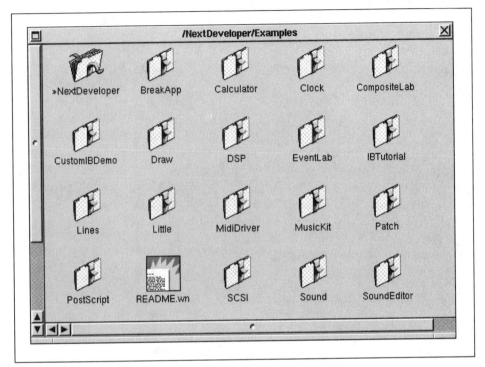

*Figure 27-10*

## What Else?

There's probably a thousand or so other applications lurking in the cube. I just haven't found them yet.

# Section VI

---

# The Present
# and Future

# Chapter 28

## Coming Soon...Maybe

*To complain of the age we live in, to murmur at the present possessors of power, to lament the past, to conceive extravagant hopes of the future, are the common dispositions of the greatest part of mankind.*
Thoughts on the Cause of the Present Discontents (1770)
— EDMUND BURKE 1729–1797

Enough facts. This chapter is raw speculation. Guesses, conjecture, and—in a few cases—hopes.

First, a caveat. I'm not a NeXT insider. I don't have a "deep cube" to tell me what's really going to happen. It's just me, the computer trade press, Usenet and other networks and bulletin boards, years of prognisticating experience (with mixed results), and an unbridled lust for more, more, more.

That said...

## Color

When NeXT was introduced, one of the few disappointments was the lack of color.

Why no color? First, because it's expensive. Color monitors cost more than monochrome monitors (and require more voltage, increasing the strain on the power supply).

Color requires additional memory. How much memory depends on the number of available colors. That, in turn, depends on the number of bytes associated with each pixel for color information. If three bytes are allotted to each pixel, twelve times the memory of the grayscale display would be required. Moving that additional memory to the display takes more "bandwidth" and makes greater demands on the NeXT bus. For an example, take a look at Macintosh "32-bit" color. It's beautiful, but it's slow.

Color also makes demands on the 68030, already burdened with a multiprocessing, multiuser operating system and 931,840 monochrome pixels to update (each with 4 levels of gray).

Display PostScript adds another problem. It only supports 8 bits of color information per RGB plane, and Steve Jobs has said he doesn't want "baby color" for the NeXT. (Though he didn't define what "adult color" was.)

And remember: NeXT is a small company, with limited resources. It's better to do only a few things, but do them well. Color is swell, but for most users it's not a necessity.

The bottom line, though, is cost. Fast "real" color is expensive. For now, foregoing color keeps costs down.

But color is coming, and it promises to be spectacular. Steve Jobs owns a chunk of Pixar, the renowned LucasFilms graphics company (responsible for the special effects in *Star Wars, Willow,* and the "Indiana Jones" epics). The Pixar color wizards are hard at work on NeXT color. When it appears, expect a separate (pricey) color board stuffed with video memory, a graphics coprocessor to handle the graphic load, and whizzy options.

At a NeXT developer conference last year, Jobs reminded color-hungry developers that NeXT has "three other slots and a lot of technology." Wait until next year, he said.

It should be worth the wait.

## Color Printers

Canon now owns 16% of NeXT. And Canon is a world leader in color printer technology. What good is color if you can't print it?

## True Multiprocessing

UNIX terms running applications processes. Mach processes are called tasks. The tasks are made up of threads. Each thread may be a portion of an application. A routine that determines page breaks in a word processor may be assigned a thread, for example. By clever scheduling of the 68030, tasks appear to run simultaneously, and threads within tasks also appear to run simultaneously.

Mach was designed to allow each task—even each thread—to have its own processor. That's true multiprocessing.

As this book was written, NeXT didn't allow true multiprocessing. But the choice of Mach is a sure signal of NeXT's intention to offer true multiprocessing. And, because NeXT system software is distributed on optical disk, not embedded on hard-to-replace ROM chips, upgrading to a new, improved version of Mach will be easy.

With multiple processors cranking away, The NeXT Computer will truly be a "personal mainframe." It's difficult to imagine the power and speed of, say, ten 68030s working in tandem? Twenty processors? More?

The mind reels.

Once Mach supports true multiprocessing, adding the necessary hardware will be straightforward. The hard part is taken care of in software, by Mach. NeXT, or third-party vendors, will most likely offer a board stuffed with additional processors, for use in any empty slot (the cube isn't fussy about which card goes in which slot). Needed on-board hardware, other than the additional processors, will be minimal.

Cost is anyone's guess. The best hope for users is that many third-party vendors offer coprocessor boards, and capitalism takes over: Prices fall, and NeXT users have near-supercomputer power for hand-calculator prices.

The best guess, though, is that early buyers, as always, will pay the most. Still, the MIPS (Millions of Instructions Per Second)-to-dollars ratio should be attractive, even for early buyers.

## Faster Processors

NeXT isn't wedded to the 68030 processor. When The NeXT Computer was first designed—now a few years back—the 68030 hadn't even begun shipping in volume quantities. Reduced-Instruction-Set Processors (RISC chips) were still a "coming thing," not a major contender for traditional Complex-Instruction-Set (CISC) processors like the 68030.

Times have changed. RISC chips are here, and they're fast. The computer industry is driven by speed; in part, because it's easier to substitute a faster chip than to design a new operating system—or an entire computer!

If the newer, faster processor is compatible with programs written for the current processor, it's a no-brainer: Users have always been willing to pay a higher cost for a faster processor.

For the IBM Personal Computer using Intel processors, the path has been from 8088 to 8086 to 80386 to 80486. Each chip retained essential compatibility with previous processors, but was faster and more powerful than its predecessor.

On the Motorola side, Apple's Macintosh has sported the 68000, 68020, and now the 68030 processor. Each faster and better.

The key for microprocessor manfacturers is compatibility. Both Intel and Motorola have taken pains to ensure that their latest offerings are both compatible and more advanced—not an easy task.

For NeXT, the choice of a next NeXT processor is between Motorola's 68040 and 88000. Of the two, the 68040 is fully compatible with the current 68030. When in volume production, the 68040 will be less expensive than the 68030 for computer manufacturers, primarily because hardware required by the 68030 is included on the 68040 chip. It also more fully supports multiple-processor architectures, which plays into Mach's (and NeXT's) expected plans for parallel processing.

To users, the big question is: How much faster is the 68040?

Roughly speaking, the 68040 is 20-40% faster. A noticeable but not remarkable speed increase.

Motorola's 88000, on the other hand, is a flat-out screamer. It's not "some percent" faster than the 68030, it's many times faster than the 68030.

Just how fast can't yet be accurately determined. As this book was written, the 88000 hadn't yet been shipped to manufacturers, although some computer makers had already announced machines to contain the new processor. Still, early tests show the 88000 capable of 14-20 MIPS, compared to 5-7 MIPS of the current NeXT—three to four times faster. In "best case" situations, the 88000 is capable of 50 MIPS!

Unfortunately, the 88000 isn't backwardly compatible with the 68xxx line. An enormous amount of software would need to be rewritten to support the 88000. But there's another alternative: a 68030 "main" processor, and 88000s used as co-processors; possibly graphics coprocessors to free the 68030 from screen display calculations. Oh, but that would be fast.

NeXT isn't wedded to the 68030, but it is committed to speed and power. After all, the NeXT isn't a "personal computer." It's a workstation, and the workstation arena rewards slowness with death in the marketplace.

Whichever chip NeXT chooses, expect NeXT to be in the forefront of the speed/power race. And expect a new motherboard, with a faster, more advanced processor in 1990, or a "drop dead" coprocessor board.

## Other System Enhancements

Time flies. One day the NeXT optical drive is radically new technology. A week later, it's "only single-sided."

One day, expect NeXT drives for double-sided optical disks. Sony already markets a standalone, double-sided, read/write optical drive. The disks hold 650 megabytes. The cost? $4,650. Count your blessings.

## NeXT TV

Oh, sure. It's already available for Macintosh: an add-on "TV tuner" board that puts a television screen on your computer screen. Give it the bottom left of your display; nothing much happens there anyway: Why not watch the soaps while you work?

Is this a good idea? Oh yes. The medias are melding. In our lifetime (knock on wood), we'll see computers, TV, telephones, newspapers, magazines, libraries, and more come together. If NeXT stays on track, the cube will be the best spot to meet.

## Peripherals to Come

Here, some guesses are easy to make. Expect third parties to offer:

- hard disk drives;
- printers;
- modems; and
- scanners.

Because most of the hardware needed by modems is already present in the cube, modem prices may (just may) be low. A reasonably-priced 9600-baud modem would be a sure seller.

More interesting are fax modems. Again, most of the hardware is already present. If the fax modem doubled as an inexpensive single-page copier, so much the better. Canon, which owns a good chunk of NeXT, is a prime candidate here for offerings.

For musicians, expect at least a few high-quality MIDI keyboards. Many existing keyboards can be plugged directly into NeXT. As NeXT sales increase, keyboard manufacturers may begin to directly pitch NeXT users, and create NeXT-specific products.

In general, the variety (and quality) of peripherals will hinge on the success of NeXT. If The NeXT Computer is a sales success, third-party hardware vendors will clamber aboard. If cube sales are less than stellar, peripherals may be few.

Another consideration is the role of NeXT as a peripherals manufacturer. Both IBM and Apple make a good percentage of their total revenues from the sale of peripherals: printers, modems, and the like. To date, NeXT has limited itself to one computer and one laser printer.

The best guess is that NeXT will stay out of the peripherals market, at least for now. NeXT doesn't yet have the staff needed to create and market peripherals.

More important, NeXT wants to attract other vendors to support the NeXT cause by offering additional hardware. Usurping a market isn't a good way to attract vendors.

## Books and Magazines

Many NeXT books are now being written. Expect some good books on programming the cube to appear. (Soon, please.) More than one company is also considering a NeXT magazine. Is the market large enough to support a NeXT magazine? Maybe. NeXT developers would love a NeXT-specific advertising venue.

## Cheaper Cubes

The NeXT Computer is a good value. It's not cheap, but it's a good value. The cost of NeXT's bundled software alone, purchased separately, would approach the price of the entire cube (although much of NeXT's software couldn't be had on other computers).

Still, few consumers will plunk down $10,000 on a NeXT computer. And small businesses with moderate computing needs won't purchase a NeXT for $14,000 (when all's said and done) when a Macintosh or IBM can be had for $4,000-6,000—or much less!—and perform adequately.

Before looking ahead, let's answer this: Is The NeXT Computer "worth the money?"

Yes. If.

Yes, if you require an unequalled software development machine. I've spoken with universities and government agencies who will buy NeXTs solely to design and explore user interfaces! Yes, if you want awesome sound and music capabilities; NeXT has no competitors—for now—when it comes to sound and music creation, analysis, and performance.

The biggest component of NeXT's value is the hardest to quantify: ease of use and productivity. How much more productive is a worker equipped with seamless networking, voice mail, and a host of on line applications?

That's a hard question. But here's an easy answer: Regardless of how "good" The NeXT Computer may be, the cheaper it is, the more will sell.

At a recent developer's camp, Steve Jobs said, "The NeXT Computer is affordable now. We want to make it affordable with a capital 'A.'"

In the computer industry, talk is traditionally cheap. In this case, though, the sentiment is crucial. NeXT doesn't want to be "another workstation vendor"; The NeXT Computer is a "general-purpose business computer," according to NeXT. They don't want only the workstation market. They don't want only the university market. They don't want only the high-end music market.

They want it all.

To have it all, price is paramount.

In general, the way to get prices down—and still make a profit—is to reduce production costs. From the start, NeXT has tailored both the cube, and NeXT itself, to keep costs low.

First, the NeXT motherboard contains a mere 45 chips. Much of the essential circuitry is contained in two proprietary Very Large Scale Integration (VLSI) custom chips. The design costs of those chips needs to be paid only once. In the long run, that creates a great savings over using (and buying!) many more chips to fill the same functions.

The NeXT has the most sophisticated interface and development environment ever offered. The AppKit, NextStep, and Interface Builder are marvels. But again: Those development costs need only be paid once. A manufacturer only pays for custom software once; after that, it is "free" in every computer—unlike hardware.

This is the Macintosh lesson. Apple has been able to extract healthy prices for Macintosh, primarily because of the software that makes Macintosh what it is (and because of the software built on the Macintosh ROM routines). Because that software foundation is, in general, already "paid for," Apple has large profit margins. And large margins mean price flexibility. When Apple wants to lower Macintosh prices, they can.

(As an aside, consider IBM. They took the other tack with the IBM Personal Computer: a large hardware investment and a small "proprietary software" investment. As a result, all that clone manufacturers had to do was offer the same hardware. They did, and were willing to take smaller margins for comparable equipment. Hence the "clone wars," and IBM's eroding share of the market it created.)

If anyone knows The Macintosh Lesson, it's Steve Jobs: creator of Macintosh. It's the NeXT software that makes the difference; both in the machine's capabilities and the machine's profit margins.

Manufacturing is another key. The NeXT manufacturing facilities are, without doubt, the most efficient in the world. So efficient that NeXT can purchase chips from Japan, build NeXT computers in California, and ship the finished computers back to Japan.

And still spend less than by building computers—for the Japanese market or any market—in Japan, in the first place.

This is startling. But then, Steve Jobs is a fiend on manufacturing. His original idea for a Macintosh manufacturing plant was this: a building open on two ends. In one end goes sand (silicon in the making). Out the other end come Macintosh computers. What could be simpler, or more efficient?

The Macintosh manufacturing facilities in Fremont, California, are testimony to Jobs' devotion to manufacturing technology. NeXT's production is, if anything, superior. In an age when computer makers fashion their wares overseas, to save on labor costs, NeXT saves labor costs by requiring fewer people—NeXT motherboards are untouched by human hands during production, as an example. (As a counterexample, Apple II computers are made in Southeast Asia. Labor costs, we can assume, are the reason.)

Finally, consider what may be the single most expensive NeXT component: the read/write optical disk. NeXT purchases the optical disks from Canon.

And Canon now owns 16% of NeXT. If your major supplier is also a business partner, it's likely that your costs will decrease (at the expense, it must be said, of sharing some of your profits).

Again, NeXT wants it all: a computer that's both "workstation powerful" and a mass-market product. Powerful has already been achieved. Consumer mass-market will come when the price falls.

But before "mass-market" comes "general-purpose business computer." NeXT will compete here with IBM and Apple in the intricate dance of price, performance, and features.

In the 1990s, NeXT will dance with the best of them. And prices will come down.

## Multimedia

This isn't something to come, really, but something that's already here—but largely unnoticed.

This book, like other NeXT books, spends much time discussing trees, and little time discussing forests. But consider: great text, great graphics, animation, sound, music, speech. It's all here. Multimedia. *The NeXT Computer is the finest multimedia computer ever made.* And it's got the voluminous storage needed for high-quality graphics and sounds.

It's not an accident. The cube was designed for multimedia creations. But will developers take advantage of what's offered? Will they think "big enough?" Will they stretch beyond spreadsheets, paint programs, drawing programs, and databases? Will they?

Oh sure. Soon, let's hope.

## Speech Recognition

Here's a fun one.

NeXT legend has it that speech recognition was an early goal during development of the cube. Imagine the unveiling: The NeXT Computer, in all its glory. You talk, it listens and responds. It would have brought down the house.

Unfortunately, the time hasn't yet come for useful speech recognition. Nor would reliable speech recognition be a fait accompli. Crafting an operating system that utilized speech input would be a momentous (though fascinating) task. It wouldn't be enough to use speech to merely give menu item commands. What about moving or resizing windows? Scrolling? Selecting text by voice?

It goes on. Wouldn't a dictionary of verbal synonyms be necessary? After all, the idea is to train the computer, not train the human. Then there's security: What better security than a computer that responded only to a particular voice? "His master's voice" meets the 1990's.

So besides being a thorny technical problem, speech recognition presents many design problems.

But speech recognition is coming. The NeXT DSP chip has all the power required—if not the software needed—to process speech. And software to recognize speech is now remarkably accurate: Researchers at AT&T have reported recognition rates upwards of 98%—near perfect.

If it's possible, will it happen? I think so. Don't expect NeXT to unveil speech recognition soon, though. It's still immature technology and NeXT has higher priorities. But if NeXT succeeds in the crowded mainstream computer market, the time may come for NeXT to commit corporate resources to make speech recognition a reality.

# Chapter 29

# Interview: Brad Cox

*Dr. Brad Cox is the Vice-President and cofounder of the Stepstone Corporation. Stepstone licenses its Objective-C compiler to NeXT, where Objective-C is the heart and soul of the NeXT programming environment on the NeXT Computer.*

*DSC: What's the history of Objective-C?*

Brad Cox: It begins in 1982. But there's some prehistory. I wrote an article in "SIGPlan Notices" about four years before about a little language called "OOP-C." A precompiler for C, was I think the acronym. And that was sort of the spiritual ancestor of Objective-C.

*DSC: Where were you working at the time?*

Brad Cox: ITT.

*DSC: And they let you just muck around, inventing languages?*

Brad Cox: Well, we were building what's come to be called "groupware." It was a research group that was trying to get at programmer productivity by affecting team productivity, instead of programmer productivity. So we were building groupware tools to try and do that.

   And I felt that the groupware tools ought to be on an object-oriented "substrate." And beneath that substrate, there ought to be C and UNIX. So I branched off to build OOP-C as the object-oriented substrate. And the team built coordination tools on top of that.

*DSC: Did you eventually throw all that away, and start over with what became Objective-C?*

Brad Cox: Yeah. I left ITT and went to Schlumberger.

DSC: *Who?*

Brad Cox: Schlumberger. It's a very large oil-field services company. But I felt that the day of object-oriented programming was soon arriving, and that we should focus on that and provide some tools for that. So we started a company. It was called "PPI" [Productivity Products International] in those days.

DSC: *Which became Stepstone?*

Brad Cox: Yes.

DSC: *When was that?*

Brad Cox: The spring of '82. That's when I left Schlumberger and went off into the proverbial garage for six months, and built Objective-C.

DSC: *All by yourself?*

Brad Cox: Yep.

DSC: *There must have been some thoughts of "Am I ever going to make any money off this?"*

Brad Cox: (Laughs) Well, yeah. That was the whole purpose. It was a company that we founded to build, to support, and then to train people in the use of an object-oriented extension to C.

In those days, it was just me and a partner, Tom Love.

DSC: *What computers did you use?*

Brad Cox: The first computer? We went down the road to ComputerLand and bought ourselves a Fortune. Cheap UNIX boxes weren't widely available then, so we got a Fortune computer and did all the development on that.

DSC: *What were the largest influences? Smalltalk...*

Brad Cox: Oh yes. Smalltalk. And the "Use tools, not panaceas" approach from UNIX was the other big influence. It was that influence that said that this should be viewed as an extension to C, rather than the "ultimate programming language."

DSC: *So from the beginning, the idea was: You can still do ANSI C if you want?*

Brad Cox: Yeah, yeah. In fact, in those days, it was before ANSI C. There wasn't any ANSI C.

*DSC: How long before you actually had it up and were writing programs in it?*

Brad Cox: A couple months.

*DSC: What was the hard part?*

Brad Cox: I can't really say that there were any. Technically, programming languages are no longer a very hard problem in the UNIX world, once you know all the tools. We no longer use those tools, because Objective-C has been hand-optimized, but in the original version, I used program-generation technology.

*DSC: YACC and things like that?*

Brad Cox: Yeah. I used both YACC and LEX in the original version. And that left only a reasonably small piece of the job undone. And that I did in Objective-C. It was a bootstrap process all along, so the first compiler was actually written in LEX, YACC, and Objective-C. It was written in itself.

*DSC: Is there a kernel, or...*

Brad Cox: There's a...well, the irreducible kernel of Objective-C is the central messaging routine, which is just a piece of C code that was originally just patched in assembly language to do some things you can't do in C.

*DSC: When did C++ come along? Had you started before C++ was in development?*

Brad Cox: Well, we'd been in touch with the C++ group—with Stroustrup— pretty much all along. I was down at Bell Labs...when was that? He invited me down...I don't remember if it was after we started the company, or back in ITT days. But we had various philosophical debates, like the relative importance of machine efficiency versus programmer efficiency. And the outcome, I believe, was that we agreed to disagree.

I felt that the problem that languages needed to focus on was programmer productivity, and he felt as strongly the opposite, so...we sort of diverged from that basic disagreement.

*DSC: How do you compare the two languages?*

Brad Cox: I have a chart, in which I use hardware terminology. The chart is a sequence of layers. The bottom layer is called "gate-level integration"; second one: "block-level." Above that, "chip-level," "card-level," and "system-level."

Five layers.

And I'd describe Bjarne's [Stroustrup] focus as being "improving C's support for gate-level and block-level integration tasks."

What that means is...gate-level is expressions and variable declarations and conditional statements...all the stuff you see inside the curly braces in C is gate-level integration.

And Bjarne's focus was improving C at that level.

He also focused at block level. Now block level is...it's the main reusability workhorse of the programming industry. You know: libraries and functions. X-windows is block-level integration—it's all composed of function calls. The Mac toolbox is a block-level integration approach.

And Bjarne also focused on improving the way C handled function calls by doing, for example, strong type-checking across function boundaries.

My focus, all along, has been to add a level that was never there, called "chip-level."

That's what Objective-C does.

*DSC: This is the "software IC" concept.*

Brad Cox: Exactly. Objective-C has 100% coverage at chip-level integration tasks.

*DSC: So Objective-C objects are more...discrete than C++ objects? They're more transportable between programs? They're higher-level entities?*

Brad Cox: Yes, and they're entities that a larger segment of the human race is prepared to deal with. The same way that more people know how to plug chips on a board than know how to build chips out of blocks.

*DSC: In the past, when speed wasn't an issue, the highest-level languages always "won."*

Brad Cox: Exactly. The higher-level language is a better tool for the job, when the problem you're solving is this: providing access to computing power for a larger segment of the human race.

That's what NeXT is all about.

*DSC: What's the biggest stumbling block to learning Objective-C? My problem was that I was trying too hard. It was hard to realize that, really, it's simple.*

Brad Cox: There's a tremendous amount of hype and misinformation out there about object-oriented programming, often of the form "You've got to go through this fundamental mind-set...you've got to train all your people...it's a hard, high threshold to get across..."

And all that is just nonsense. Because what object-oriented programming is all about is just making things simpler.

*DSC: Talk about being approached by NeXT.*

Brad Cox: I was involved in some of the early trips out there. Basically, they were looking for a technology to relieve the pain they felt when they were building the Mac ROMs. In other words, just the difficulty of getting up a user interface on a block-level integration scheme.

That was what was in their mind. Even when he was at Apple, Steve [Jobs] was interested in object-oriented technology. Of course, they were so hard up against the machine limitations [at Apple] that they couldn't afford to look at some of the productivity problems.

So I think part of his idea in NeXT was building a machine with enough power that you could afford to spend some of it on the programmer.

*DSC: How far along had they gotten when you became involved?*

Brad Cox: Oh, they were still moving into their building! This is a long time ago.

*DSC: So they were still drawing diagrams on blackboards?*

Brad Cox: Yep.

*DSC: So they did their initial work using Objective-C?*

Brad Cox: Yes, they've been using Objective-C all along. They do low-level stuff in C and microcode, I suppose, but the interface that users see is all Objective-C.

*DSC: What's the ongoing relationship? They bundle the language, you get royalties, they get the latest compilers and decide when to release them to the public?*

Brad Cox: Pretty much. There's also some discussion of building Objective-C inside C. That's something they'd probably do, because we have to keep Objective-C portable. And, of course, they're not motivated to do that.

*DSC: Getting rid of the Objective-C preprocessor was part of that.*

Brad Cox: Right. So it's sort of a cross-development effort. They have the sources and they're licensed to sell the product and pay royalties.

*DSC: What's interesting is that in your book* [Object-Oriented Programming, An Evolutionary Approach], *there are more classes than NeXT has implemented.*

Brad Cox: There're more!?

*DSC: Well, more algorithmic sorts of objects.*

Brad Cox: Oh, yeah.

*DSC: It seems like what they're presenting in Objective-C is sort of "How to program NextStep" objects. Once you get past those, I think there's...hash table, storage, stream, and I think one other one, and that's it.*

Brad Cox: Yes, and that's always been our focus. I only described, I think, five low-level things in the book, but our focus has always been to solve the low-level data-structure problems once and for all, and let our customers solve their high-level problems by just reusing our stuff.

When people buy Objective-C directly from us, they get a fairly rich library of data-structure things: stacks and queues and ordered collections and sets...

*DSC: Could I buy Objective-C from you, put it on my NeXT, and have a richer programming environment than I had when I bought my cube?*

Brad Cox: Yeah, that's the idea in principle. That combination hasn't been through Q/A yet, though, so there might be a "gotcha" lying around somewhere.

*DSC: What would you guess it'll be like in a year from now? Will NeXT be releasing the "full implementation" or will there always be a more robust version that you have, and a more "NextStepping" version that NeXT offers?*

Brad Cox: (laughing) My crystal ball's not that good! I'm a lot more comfortable speaking as a scientist, not as a businessman.

As a scientist, something that I hope to see in a year or so is that we take advantage of some of the potential of the NeXT machine that came from the Mach operating system. Have you heard the term "lightweight processes?"

*DSC: Oh yes. I've spent so much time on this stuff that my wife can't remember my first name!*

Brad Cox: I think that lightweight processes are more significant than most people think. Remember my chart?

*DSC: Yes.*

Brad Cox: Well, lightweight processes are "cards." So they're not just a technical "whiz-bang" that a bunch of gurus use. They're actually a level of integration that's higher than objects, as Objective-C defines them.

So my view of the future is that we integrate support for "card-level integration" right within an object-oriented language. So that we've got all the modularity options that a hardware engineer has.

*DSC: And the vision behind Mach is that you can have multiple processors running these threads.*

Brad Cox: Yes, exactly.

*DSC: Any regrets when you look back at the design of Objective-C?*

Brad Cox: No, not really. Certainly, the biggest insecurity we had at the beginning was whether the world would accept a hybrid approach. And I think the answer is now clear that at least part of the world will accept a hybrid approach. In other words, the NeXT world.

There's another segment of the world that resists hybrids at all costs, and they tend to go to C++.

*DSC: Did you expect that object-oriented programming would become as big, as fast as it has?*

Brad Cox: No, I thought we were going to lose our shirts! (Laughs.) So I've been pleasantly surprised to see that.

Right now the thing I'm most anxious to change is to...encourage people to take a broader definition of object-oriented programming than the one supported in Objective-C, or Smalltalk, or anywhere else. A broader definition that includes concurrent objects, and lightweight processes.

You know, so we can take a system like Metaphor or Fabrick or some of these dataflow languages, and feel free to talk about 'em as object-oriented languages that don't support inheritance.

*DSC: Am I going to have to learn new things, when concurrent processing really comes along?*

Brad Cox: That comes back to the training thing. I think: "No!" You've got to forget all this crap that we learned as programmers. You just have to learn to use the mental techniques that you use to cross the street in the morning!

*DSC: You have to convince yourself that it really is easy.*

Brad Cox: Yeah, right.

*DSC: So if someone came to you, cold, and said, "I want to learn to program. I want to learn C. I want to learn Objective-C," what would you say? Start with C, or start right off with Objective-C?*

Brad Cox: Oh, absolutely Objective-C. No doubt about it. And if we had one of these dataflow languages, start with that. Start at the highest level you can get away with! And leave all this "bit-twiddling" to...

*DSC: People who like it.*

Brad Cox: (Laughing) Yes.

*DSC: One of the things that always comes up is performance hits. On a computer like the NeXT—on a fast machine—can the user even notice any lesser performance?*

Brad Cox: No. I mean, if you want to see one of the fastest-looking systems in the world, run a NeXT and look at the user interface. That thing is fast!

As a programmer, one thing I can suggest is just write a tight loop. Call an empty function—you know: a C function. Call that a million times or so. And then send a message a million times. Use a stopwatch and compare 'em.

When I do that on my Sun, I get a number...in the range of about 2. In other words, I can call two functions in the time I can send one message.

But make your own measurements. Because it depends on how tightly someone optimized their version of the messaging routine for that particular machine.

If you did that measurement in C++, you're going to get a number of about 1.8.

*DSC: So they're about the same.*

Brad Cox: There's a marginal difference that has to do with some low-level efficiencies. If you look at the low-level code, you'll see that there's some register-saving optimizations that you can make in the C++ approach that we can't get to in Objective-C without endangering, you know, something else somewhere.

Our philosophy is to use a central messaging routine. Whereas C++'s approach is to not have a central routine, but to go directly from the calling site to the target site.

*DSC: What platforms do you support, other than NeXT?*

Brad Cox: Roughly speaking, anything that runs C.

*DSC: That's a lot!*

Brad Cox: Yeah. There're some exceptions. To my eternal frustration, we still don't have a product on the Macintosh. We have some ports that run on the Macintosh, but we [don't have a complete product]...and that has to do with market expectations. You know: documentation, and does it have the Mac interface, that kind of thing.

Objective-C runs on essentially all the UNIX systems. We've done ports to VMS; it runs on MS-DOS, OS/2, PS/2...

*DSC: Was OS/2 tough?*

Brad Cox: No more than most. I think that probably the toughest system was the old MS-DOS, and VMS. But the Objective-C system has always been designed with portability in mind. Since it generates C code, that solves most of the problems.

*DSC: What do you think of NeXT's Interface Builder?*

Brad Cox: I think it's absolutely strategic. I also think...I think it's important, very important. But the idea can be pushed much further than NeXT has taken it, to date. And I think it'll always be limited from its true potential by the absence of concurrent objects.

In other words, when we get these "card-level" objects into the toolkit, then Interface Builder's going to turn into something really important.

*DSC: I can't...it's hard to envision that...*

Brad Cox: I'll tell you a simple way to envision it. Imagine sitting down...and imagine what you do on a piece of paper, when you're doing the top-level design of some application. Let's say a little data-processing application.

You sit there and draw bubbles and arrows, right? Well, imagine drawing the bubbles and arrows on the screen, instead of the paper.

*DSC: Ah...*

Brad Cox: I mean, it's just the old CASE approach.

And when you're done, run it! That's all I'm saying.

*DSC: So it's truly visual programming.*

Brad Cox: Yes, exactly. Because now these card-level objects are higher-level objects than the objects in Smalltalk.

They're larger, more like cards...they have their own thread of control and their own user interface. And you program with them by drawing your problem onto the screen.

And the modules you're working with on screen are things you buy from the software store.

*DSC: That's the fundamental idea in your book: the very high-level "Software-IC." Do you think we'll see objects not just in stores, but in the public domain?*

Brad Cox: Yes, it'll be like any other marketplace. Public domain is a marketplace where charges are low to zero. The fundamental idea of the book is relying on a marketplace in cards and chips, instead of continually building them all from scratch.

*DSC: So the future for Stepstone is improving and porting the compiler, and providing collections of objects?*

Brad Cox: That's why we founded Stepstone in the beginning, to create an option, so people didn't have to continually build everything from scratch.

A lot of people think of Stepstone as "a language company," a place that sells Objective-C. But our main product is Software-ICs. In fact, most of our income is from Software-ICs, not from compilers. So the future...is today.

*DSC: Well, take out your crystal ball one more time. Where do you see yourself and Stepstone in five years?*

Brad Cox: The Intel of software.

*DSC: Will we see applications that are undreamed-of now, because it's so much easier to make them using object languages?*

Brad Cox: Absolutely. I was looking at Microsoft Word and Excel...there's a thing in Word where you bring up About Word, and you Command-click on the Microsoft icon, and it shows the names of the programmers who worked on Word.

What it tells you is the number of people who had to cooperate to get that product to market.

*DSC: Six or eight maybe?*

Brad Cox: In that range; about ten or so.

And Microsoft Word is about at the limit of complexity of what programmers can accomplish today, right?

*DSC: A lot of people think it's over the limit!*

Brad Cox: So a team of about ten people working for "n" years—I don't know how long they've been at it. And the result is about the limit of human [programmer] capability.

And I think that what this object-oriented stuff is all about would be to enable products that do what you were saying earlier: products that have a lot more "in them." That have richer things. So we can see products that are closer to our dream of "what computers are all about."

And nobody can use Word without criticizing it for what it lacks: grammar tools, regular expressions...programmable this and that...

It doesn't take much work to envision something way beyond anything we can do in C.

*DSC: Everybody wants everything.*

Brad Cox: Think of objects as a way of making that possible. Because you can imagine shipping products with a kernel—maybe somewhat like Microsoft Word—and then all of these other objects are available from second sources. So you can "drop in" your grammar tools, and "plug in" your regular expressions.

*DSC: It's like having a company, instead of being alone in your basement.*

Brad Cox: It's having a marketplace. You can go to Intel and buy accelerator chips, so you oughta be able to go to a marketplace in Software-ICs and buy tools that drop right in, and integrate themselves into something like Microsoft Word.

*DSC: Allen Kay said that "In the future, everyone will be a programmer."*

Brad Cox: That's exactly what this is about.

*DSC: But they won't think of it as "programming."*

Brad Cox: Think of the bubbles and arrows diagram on screen. That's something everybody can do!

*DSC: Show the computer what you want, and it figures out how to do it.*

Brad Cox: Ah...that's how the AI people would put it. I'd put a different slant on it.

A better model is the hardware store model. You don't show the hardware store what you want, and then it "figures out how to do it." A hardware store is where you go to buy the things you need, to do what you want.

And the hardware store's role is to make what you want available.

*DSC: This is getting very long! But I've gotta ask: Are you having fun?*

Brad Cox: Oh, absolutely. What we're all talking about here is a software revolution. It means fundamental changes in the way programs are built. And that's exciting stuff.

We don't see fundamental change...I mean everytime somebody announces a new modem, they describe it as a "revolution."

I'm not talking about that kind of revolution. I'm talking about something that's directly comparable to the Industrial Revolution. And that's happening right here, in our lifetime.

"Revolutionary" is a cultural change. And that doesn't depend just on faster hardware. It means changing the way we go about building software. And we've never done that before, ever.

*DSC: Thank you, Dr. Cox.*

# Appendix A

# Command-Key Combinations

These are the canonical NeXT Command-key equivalents (NeXT calls them "Alternates") for NeXT applications. NeXT hopes that third-party developers will embrace this standard to promote consistency across applications. Time will tell.

| Alternative | Menu command | Menu |
|---|---|---|
| Command-b | Bold | Font |
| Command-B | Unbold | Font |
| Command-c | Copy | Edit |
| Command-d | Find Previous | Find |
| Command-e | Enter Selection | Find |
| Command-f | Find | Find |
| Command-g | Find Next | Find |
| Command-h | Hide | Main |
| Command-i | Italic | Font |
| Command-I | Unitalic | Font |
| Command-o | Open | Window |
| Command-p | Print | Main |
| Command-s | Save | Window |
| Command-v | Paste | Edit |
| Command-w | Close | Main |
| Command-x | Cut | Edit |
| Command-z | Undo | Edit |

Notice that some commands have both unshifted and shifted alternatives. These usually are used with commands that toggle: between Bold and Unbold, for example. You may also see:

Command-S        Save As...              Window

and some applications implement:

Command-n        New                     Window

# Appendix B

# Keyboard Key Codes

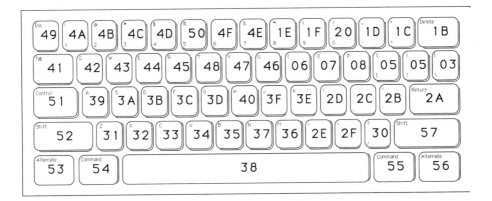

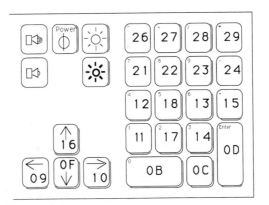

This illustration shows the key codes associated with keys on the NeXT keyboard. Also, shifted and unshifted characters are shown on the top and bottom of the keys, respectively.

# Appendix C

# Special Characters

These are some of the most common special characters you'll encounter when working with UNIX. For a more detailed listing of special characters, consult a detailed book on UNIX. See further reading for a list of some of the best.

\#

When the Shell prompt ends with #, you're in superuser mode and NeXT is your oyster—very little will be denied you.

The # is also used as a "comment" character. Lines beginning with # are ignored. Handy if a text file contains commands to be used by other programs. Here's the beginning of the .cshrc file:

```
#
# Default .cshrc file for root.
#
# set up the path
set path=(/etc /usr/etc /usr/ucb /bin /usr/bin /usr/local/bin
  /LocalApps /NeXTApps)
```

$

In Shell programming, $ denotes a variable ($1, for example). Mach uses strings beginning with $ as "metalinks" to hold kernel variables. $HOST is a metalink to the kernel variable "hostname."

&

When you enter a Shell command, it executes. When finished, the prompt is returned. Ending a command with & runs the process in the background. Use & with commands that take a long time to complete.

\*

In a search or substitution string, * matches zero to any number of any character. For example, to find the names of all files that begin with ".pl":

```
localhost# ls | grep .pl*
.places
```

.

Shell shorthand for the current directory.

..

Shell shorthand for the parent directory of the current directory. A fast way to move to a higher directory is:

```
localhost# cd ..
```

:-)

Smiley face. A symbol used on Usenet and other telecommunications services. Most frequently employed to convey the attitude "Just kidding."

<

A redirection operation. Used to take input from a file. Think of < as "from." To count the words in the file "words,"

```
localhost# wc -w < /usr/dict/words
  24259
```

>

Another redirection operator. This one means "to." Use it to redirect output.

```
localhost# echo "this is going to a new file" > newfile
localhost# cat newfile
this is going to a new file
```

>>

Similar to >, but appends information to the end of a file:

```
localhost# echo "This will be appended to newfile" >> newfile
localhost# cat newfile
this is going to a new file
This will be appended to newfile
```

[ ]

In searching or patterning matching, [ ] groups characters together. [a-z] means "match any lower-case character." [A-Z] means "match any upper-case letter." [0-9] matches any digit.

?

A wildcard character that means "any single character" in a search string. Thus "t?m" matches tom, tim, ten...

! !

In the Shell, repeats the previous command.

```
localhost# date
Wed Jun 28 10:50:49 PDT 1989

localhost# !!
date
Wed Jun 28 10:50:50 PDT 1989
```

|

The Shell pipe symbol, |, is used to connect the output of one command to the input of another command.

```
localhost# ls
.NeXT/        .profile       TheBook/       mach@          sdmach*
.cshrc        .userdict      bin/           mach man.edit  temp
.editdict     .userdict~     clients/       me/            tmp/
.editdict~    Mailboxes/     dev/           newfile        usr/
.hidden       Net/           doug/          odmach*        vmUNIX@
.list         NextApps/      etc/           personal/
.login        NextDeveloper/ lib/           phonelist
.places       NextLibrary/   lost+found/    private/
localhost# ls | wc -w
    38
```

The first command, ls, lists files in the current directory. The second command, ls | wc -w, pipes the output of ls into wc (Word Count), here given with the -w option, which limits wc to only counting words (without options, wc counts lines, words, and characters).

The result? The number of files in the directory.

Pipes allow you to, in effect, make new commands from existing commands. Just think "What commands can I connect to do what I want?"

# Appendix D

# NeXT/UNIX Files and Utilities

This appendix briefly describes some of the files and utilities included with The NeXT Computer. Not all: some.

Frequently, the results of typing the command into the Shell are shown. "Localhost#" is the Shell prompt.

Some commands are built into the Shell. The remaining utilities are found in various directories. The directory path searched by the Shell to find commands is listed in your .profile file. Here's the line in question:

```
PATH=/etc:/usr/etc:/usr/ucb:/bin:/usr/bin
```

Although these directories aren't displayed unless you've checked "UNIX Expert" in Preferences, the directories are always available from the Shell.

You might be interested in how I compiled this list.

From the PATH variable in .profile, I knew that some of the files I wanted were in /etc. So I fired up the Shell and entered:

```
localhost# ls /etc > TheBook/uwords
```

The ls command lists directory contents. Since directories are also text files, they can be easily redirected. The > operator redirected the output of ls /etc to the file uwords, in TheBook directory. Because there was no file named "uwords," UNIX obediently created it on the fly.

Next, the remaining directories were appended to uwords in the same fashion:

```
localhost# ls /usr/etc >> TheBook/uwords
localhost# ls /usr/ucb >> TheBook/uwords
localhost# ls /bin >> TheBook/uwords
localhost# ls /usr/bin >> TheBook/uwords
```

The >> operator both redirects and appends. Had I merely used >, each command would have clobbered the previous contents of the file.

The uwords file now contained a list of directory entries. The entries were then sorted, and a new file created to hold the sorted words.

```
localhost# sort -u TheBook/uwords > TheBook/sorteduwords
```

The -u option (for "Unique") removes redundant entries.

Now to check the file.

```
localhost# cat TheBook/sorteduwords
.list
.places
BLD.od
BLD.sd330
BLD.sd660
MAKEDEV*
MAKEDEV@
Mail*
Mail.rc
MakeTeXPK*
NETMSG_CONFIG
[*
ac*
accton*
addbib*
```

... and so on.

Ta da.

Granted, I still wasn't completely there. I had more fiddling to do. But I'll spare you the details.

The important point is this: It works! The commands listed below are powerful and marvelously flexible.

A "UNIX Wizard" would sneer at my clumsy attempts to use the Shell. With a bit more effort, I could have written a "Shell script" that would have done the above, and more, in one swoop.

So what? I'll get better. Life goes on.

For your part, don't be buffaloed by UNIX, the Shell, or any of the commands below. You may only use a few of these commands. You may never "program the Shell" or create intricate pipes and filters.

That's okay. Learning UNIX is a gradual process. It all stems from thinking "What do I want to do?" then determining if the needed tools are available. If the ideal tool isn't in the list below, think: "What if I connected this to that, then..."

That's the way to do it.

A final note. These are brief descriptions. Complete descriptions would have filled this entire book! If you'd like a more comprehensive list of "what's what," read the file whatis. More properly:

```
/NextLibrary/Documentation/UNIX/ManPages/whatis
```

The whatis file contains one-line descriptions of many of the files, commands, programs, languages, and utilities that litter your disk. Be warned that the descriptions are often delphic one-liners ("what version of a YP map is at a YP host" is my favorite), and that some of the files noted in whatis (games, in particular) aren't shipped with The NeXT Computer. Still, like this appendix, it's a good starting point.

For a more complete explanation of these commands, type:

```
man <entry name>
```

in the Shell. Although not all commands have manual entries, most do. The man command, in fact, may be the most useful command of all.

## ac

Gives the total connect time for users logged on to the system.

```
localhost# ac -p
        me        35.26
        root    6566.44
        doug       5.48
        total   6607.18
```

## addbib

Used with a database of entries to create a nicely formatted bibliography.

```
localhost# addbib
You must specify a bibliography file (database).
Usage:  addbib [-p promptfile] [-a] database
          -p: the promptfile defines alternate fields
          -a: don't include prompting for the abstract
```

The -p option gives individual totals.

# apply

A UNIX command with roots in LISP, apply uses this syntax:

```
apply [ -ac ] [ -n ] command args ...
```

to run the named command on each argument in turn.

# ar

An archiving utility, used primarily with C program files.

# arp

An acronym for "Address Resolution Protocol." The arp program displays and modifies the Internet-to-Ethernet address translation tables.

```
Usage: arp hostname
       arp -a [/vmUNIX] [/dev/kmem]
       arp -d hostname
       arp -s hostname ether_addr [temp] [pub] [trail]
       arp -f filename (file entries "name eaddr ...")
       arp -e filename (file entries "eaddr name ...")
localhost# arp -d localhost
localhost (127.0.0.1) -- no entry
```

# asm56000

The assembler used to create DSP programs. At present, using an assembler is the only way to directly program the DSP chip.

## at

To perform one or more commands "at" a later time. The usage is:

```
at [ -c ] [ -s ] [ -m ] time [ day ] [ file ]
```

which looks more daunting than it really is. The first two options, -c and -s, specify which Shell to use. Ignore these until you've used the command a few times.

The -m option automatically sends you mail after the commands have been performed; telling you that all is well, or that errors occurred. This is one of the few instances of UNIX graciously informing you about anything; be thankful.

The time and, optionally, the day specify when to perform the command(s), and [file] is the name of the file that contains the commands.

## atom

A programmer's utility that converts standard C a.out files to a format that Mach can stomach. The name? "A.out" TO "Mach": atom.

## atq

Prints the list of jobs waiting to be run. The jobs, we assume, we created by "at" described earlier. Stands for "AT Queue."

## atrm

"AT ReMove." Removes jobs from the at queue.

## autodiskmount

A NeXT utility to automatically mount an optical disk directory. You'll never call this directly; it's here for The Workspace Manager's use.

## awk

More than a command or utility program, awk is a full-blown language for scanning and processing text files. Awk programs can contain variables, operators, functions, even associative arrays. An amazing language. The manual entry for awk has enough detail to get you started.

Simply put, you give awk one or more files to process. Awk scans the files looking for patterns you specify. It then does what you tell it to after finding (or not finding) the pattern. An awk program consists of lines with this format:

```
pattern {action}
```

When awk finds the pattern, it performs the specified action, which might be as simple as writing the lines to the screen, or changing or formatting the lines containing the pattern.

Entire books have been written about awk. The best, *Awk — a Pattern Scanning and Processing Language,* is written by the authors of awk: Alfred V. Aho, Brian W. Kernighan, and Peter J. Weinberger.

## basename

A utility to strip filename affixes. You probably won't use this unless you begin writing Shell programs that manipulate filenames.

## bc

Another language. Bc is a language for doing arbitrary precision arithmetic—a "desk calculator" language. Having Mathematica at your mousetips obviates the need for bc, but if you're interested in computer languages or math you should at least give bc a glance. It's quite an effort.

## bison

UNIX spawned a raft of "compiler compilers." A compiler compiler, of course, is a compiler that produces a compiler. Actually, compiler compilers create "parsers," a vital part of any compiler.

It works like this: You specify the rules (or grammar) that your language will obey. The compiler compiler takes the rules and creates a parser. And you're on your way to creating your personal computer language!

The act of writing compiler compilers became so widespread in the UNIX community that the most famous compiler compiler of them all is named "YACC," for Yet Another Compiler Compiler.

Bison is similar to YACC, but even more powerful. Why the name bison?

Simple: A bison is a hairy YACC!

UNIX humor...

## buildafmdir

A file for use by the NeXT FontManager. It's installed automatically, and helps to quickly convert fonts.

## cal

Here's one you might like. Watch:

```
localhost# cal
usage: cal [month] year
localhost# cal 1989
                              1989
         Jan                  Feb                  Mar
 S  M Tu  W Th  F  S    S  M Tu  W Th  F  S    S  M Tu  W Th  F  S
 1  2  3  4  5  6  7             1  2  3  4             1  2  3  4
 8  9 10 11 12 13 14    5  6  7  8  9 10 11    5  6  7  8  9 10 11
15 16 17 18 19 20 21   12 13 14 15 16 17 18   12 13 14 15 16 17 18
22 23 24 25 26 27 28   19 20 21 22 23 24 25   19 20 21 22 23 24 25
29 30 31               26 27 28               26 27 28 29 30 31
         Apr                  May                  Jun
 S  M Tu  W Th  F  S    S  M Tu  W Th  F  S    S  M Tu  W Th  F  S
                   1       1  2  3  4  5  6                1  2  3
 2  3  4  5  6  7  8    7  8  9 10 11 12 13    4  5  6  7  8  9 10
 9 10 11 12 13 14 15   14 15 16 17 18 19 20   11 12 13 14 15 16 17
16 17 18 19 20 21 22   21 22 23 24 25 26 27   18 19 20 21 22 23 24
23 24 25 26 27 28 29   28 29 30 31            25 26 27 28 29 30
30
```

```
            Jul                     Aug                      Sep
 S  M Tu  W Th  F  S      S  M Tu  W Th  F  S      S  M Tu  W Th  F  S
                   1             1  2  3  4  5                      1  2
 2  3  4  5  6  7  8      6  7  8  9 10 11 12      3  4  5  6  7  8  9
 9 10 11 12 13 14 15     13 14 15 16 17 18 19     10 11 12 13 14 15 16
16 17 18 19 20 21 22     20 21 22 23 24 25 26     17 18 19 20 21 22 23
23 24 25 26 27 28 29     27 28 29 30 31           24 25 26 27 28 29 30
30 31
            Oct                     Nov                      Dec
 S  M Tu  W Th  F  S      S  M Tu  W Th  F  S      S  M Tu  W Th  F  S
 1  2  3  4  5  6  7            1  2  3  4                      1  2
 8  9 10 11 12 13 14      5  6  7  8  9 10 11      3  4  5  6  7  8  9
15 16 17 18 19 20 21     12 13 14 15 16 17 18     10 11 12 13 14 15 16
22 23 24 25 26 27 28     19 20 21 22 23 24 25     17 18 19 20 21 22 23
29 30 31                 26 27 28 29 30           24 25 26 27 28 29 30
                                                  31
```

Granted, the Preferences application also shows a calendar (though only one month at a time). But cal is good for any year, or any month of any year.

## calendar

Unlike cal, calendar is a reminder service. And another remarkably handy UNIX utility.

To use calendar, you must have a file named "calendar." The calendar command searches the file and displays any entries that contain today's or tomorrow's date. Any reasonable month/day combination is recognized.

Calendar is also a good example of a UNIX command that calls on other UNIX commands as subprocesses. In the course of its business, calendar calls on sed (a text "stream" editor), egrep (to search for patterns), and mail (to deliver you the goods).

One suspects that calendar began life as a Shell program, and it was so useful that it was compiled into a utility program.

## cat

Here's one you should know and use. Cat is short for "concatenate." The usage is:

```
cat [ -u ] [ -n ] [ -s ] [ -v ] file ...
```

The useful options are -n, which numbers lines, -s, which removes empty lines, and -v, which displays nonprinting characters.

At its most basic, cat reads and displays a file.

```
cat filename
```

shows you the contents of the file.

```
cat ThisFile ThatFile > AnotherFile
```

tacks ThisFile and ThatFile together and sends the resulting concatenation to the file AnotherFile.

## catman

A specialized form of cat used to create UNIX manuals. Investigate only if you're also willing to learn nroff, troff, and other old-time UNIX text-formatting commands.

## cb

For "C Beautifier." Converts jumbled looking C program listings into properly spaced and indented, hopefully readable listings.

## cc

The C compiler; the linchpin of program development on The NeXT Computer. It's in the /bin directory.

## checkeq

Used with eqn and neqn to typeset math. Mathematica is easier.

## chfn

A command used by system administrators to change passwords.

## chgrp

To "CHange the GRouP" file permission setting.

## chmod

Changes the file permissions of a file. Only the owner of a file—or a superuser—may change file permissions.

## chown

Changes the owner of a file. Only a superuser may use chown.

By now, you've probably figured out the algorithm used to name UNIX commands. It goes something like this:

1. Determine what the command does (CHange OWNer, in this case).
2. Join the words into one word (changeowner).
3. If the resulting word is longer than five or six characters, start throwing out letters; if so inclined, leave a vowel—but only one—to give a tantalizing clue as to what the command actually does.

The algorithm has only one fault. Given enough time, a random expansion of the command, by adding consonants and vowels, can result in a descriptive name. Fortunately, the possibilities, though not infinite, are great enough to discourage casual users.

## chsh

Changes or alters a password.

## clear

Clears the screen. This only works in the Terminal window.

## cmp

Compares two files for differences. The syntax is:

```
cmp filename1 filename2
```

Without options, nothing is reported if the files are identical—the Shell prompt merely reappears. If there are differences, the byte and line number where differences occur are given.

Given two files, Alinote and Copy_of_Alinote, and given that I've made a slight change to Copy_of_Alinote, then:

```
localhost# cmp Alinote Copy_of_Alinote
Alinote Copy_of_Alinote differ: char 760, line 15
```

The output of cmp (like the output of any command) could also be sent to a new file, created on the fly, like this:

```
localhost#  cmp Alinote Copy_of_Alinote > diffsfile
```

## col

Filters out reverse line feeds. Not often used on NeXT.

## comm

A more powerful cousin of cmp, used to select or reject lines common to two files. The files first must be sorted.

## compress

A very useful utility to compress files. Uses a Lempel-Ziv algorithm, which produces greatly scrunched files. You'll need to use the uncompress command to uncompress the files before use. Consider compressing before transmitting files; it saves time. Many options; see the manual entry.

## cp

For "Copy." One of the most fundamental UNIX commands. The syntax is:

```
cp file1 file2
```

Cp embodies much that is UNIX. It's terse, it's fast, and it works silently.

It can also be dangerous. If the file you're copying to doesn't exist, UNIX makes a new file and copies to it. If the file does exist, however, cp blithely copies over it without a quibble, as UNIX users have often found over the years, often to their dismay.

A necessary option to cp—unless you're very sure of yourself—is -i, which prompts you if a file will be overwritten.

If you plan to copy files from the Shell, consider adding the line:

```
alias cp cp -i
```

to your .chrsc file. The alias will ensure that you'll always be given notice before an existing file is overwritten by a cp.

## cron

A UNIX clock daemon, cron is useful and fascinating.

Like other UNIX daemons, cron runs invisibly, in the background. Every minute, cron comes to life and checks the file "crontab," which contains the names of commands, and the time when the commands should be run.

Cron also gives insight into UNIX background processes and UNIX itself. Cron, just another UNIX process, runs in the background, but gets marching orders from a text file. Although you can't change cron (and you wouldn't want to!), you can easily change cron's instructions, by changing the crontab text file.

## crontab

See cron, above.

## crypt

A utility to encrypt a password. The UNIX manual page (type "man crypt" in the Shell) gives a interesting look at the goals and methods of encryption. Not required reading, but very interesting.

## csh

For "C Shell," this is, essentially, the Shell application, found in NextApps/.

## cu

Used to telecommunicate, or to connect to another machine over phone lines, cu means "call UNIX." Cu is a vestigial command; it works, but tip (which does much the same thing) is preferred. See tip.

# date

Prints the date.

```
localhost# date
Mon Sep 11 06:51:52 PDT 1989
```

Day of the week, time (to the second), time zone, and year are bonuses.

# dc

A reverse Polish calculator, accessible from Terminal or Shell. A piece of work, but stick with Mathematica.

# dd

Dd is cp (CoPy file) with exquisite control over file conversion during copying. Many options for converting: change case, only copy some portions of a file, change from ASCII (standard text character mapping) to EBCDIC (IBM's preferred mapping), even swap every pair of bytes in the file while copying! (I'm sure there's a use...)

# deroff

To understand this one, know that nroff and troff are two utilities which format text files for printing. Deroff removes the commands and such that nroff and troff use to set formatting. Think of it as "un-nroff."

# df

Reports on disk space. Disk Free = df. On my system at the moment:

```
localhost# df
Filesystem        kbytes     used    avail capacity  Mounted on
/dev/sd0a         446719   197541   204506     49%   /
/dev/sd0b         216311       12   194667      0%   /clients
```

Sd0a and sd0b refer to the two partitions on the sd (for SCSI Drive). This is valuable information, not available from The Workspace Manager (though most NeXT users won't often run out of disk space). Also see du—the disk usage command.

# diction

Diction is a wonderful and humbling experience. Diction should be up there with other "NeXT bundled applications"—it's that useful.

Diction blisters through any text file, searching for poor diction, or suspect phrases. A humbling experience for a writer. Diction alerted me to my overuse of:

- "very";
- "fairly";
- "one of the";
- "quite";
- "in the course of";

and many other phrases and "nothing words" that should have been excised before they reached my fingertips.

Diction uses a default database (just another text file, of course) of suspect phrases and words. If you like, you can specify another file to be used in addition to the default file, or you can have diction ignore the default file entirely.

Another program, explain, does just that: It explains why words and phrases flagged by diction are undesirable. Watch:

```
localhost# explain
phrase?
in the course of
use "while, during" for "in the course of"
phrase?
in the amount of
use "for" for "in the amount of"
phrase?
retreat backward
phrase?
```

If explain doesn't have the phrase in its database, it merely prompts for another phrase.

# diff
# diff3

Two commands used to compare files or directories. Diff sorts the contents of two directories, then compares files for differences. Unlike cmp, diff can run through many files. Diff3 does a three-way file comparison.

# disktab

UNIX files ending in "tab" are text files of database-like information, usually presented in fields. Disktab contains detailed—very detailed—information about disks, both optical and SCSI drives. Though it's long, I can't resist adding at least the beginning of this file.

```
localhost# cat /etc/disktab
#
# Copyright (c) 1983,1986 Regents of the University of California.
# All rights reserved.  The Berkeley software License Agreement
# specifies the terms and conditions for redistribution.
#
#       @(#)disktab     4.11 (Berkeley) 5/31/86
#
# Disk geometry and partition layout tables.
# Key:
#       ty      type of disk
#       ns      #sectors/track - DEV_BSIZE sectors
#       nt      #tracks/cylinder
#       nc      #cylinders/disk
#       rm      rpm, 3600 default
#       ss      sector size -- MUST ALWAYS BE DEV_BSIZE (1024) FOR NOW
#       fp      # DEV_BSIZE blocks in front porch
#       bp      # DEV_BSIZE blocks in back porch
#       ng      #alternate groups
#       gs      #sectors per alt group
#       ga      #alt sectors per group
#       ao      sector offset to alternates in group
#       os      name of boot file
#       z[0-1]  location of "block 0" boot code in DEV_BSIZE blocks
#       hn      hostname
#       ro      read only root partition (e.g. 'a')
```

```
#       rw      read/write partition (e.g. 'b')
#       p[a-h]  partition base in DEV_BSIZE blocks
#       s[a-h]  partition sizes in DEV_BSIZE blocks
#       b[a-h]  partition block sizes in bytes
#       f[a-h]  partition fragment sizes in bytes
#       c[a-h]  partition cylinders-per-group
#       d[a-h]  partition density (bytes-per-inode)
#       r[a-h]  partition minfree
#       o[a-h]  partition optimization ("space" or "time")
#       i[a-h]  partition newfs during init
#       m[a-h]  partition mount point name
#       a[a-h]  partition auto-mount on insert
#       t[a-h]  partition file system type ("4.3BSD", "sound" etc.)
#
# Entries may also be used for other compatible drives
# with the same geometry.
#
# Internal drives
#
omd-1|OMD-1|Canon OMD-1:\

  :ty=removable_rw_optical:nc#1029:nt#15:ns#16:ss#1024:rm#3000:\
        :fp#256:bp#256:ng#153:gs#1600:ga#16:ao#784:\
        :os=odmach:z0#80:z1#168:ro=a:\
        :pa#0:sa#242352:ba#8192:fa#1024:ca#6:da#8192:ra#10:oa=time:\
        :ia:ta=4.3BSD:aa:
#
# SCSI drives
#
# NOTE: Drives that use "cylinder-oriented sparing" do not have
# simple values for sectors and tracks, since not all tracks have
# the same number of available sectors.  Therefore, the tracks and
# sectors in these entries don't match the physical device, but are
# chosen so that their product exactly matches the number of USABLE
# sectors per cylinder.  The slight lie about physical sectors/track
# is covered up by tuning the file system rotational latency parameter
# appropriately.
#
# MAXTOR XT-8760S with 1 spare sector/track and 512 byte sectors
#
```

```
# 'b' partition on XT-8760S is intended for NetBoot client private
  trees
# If not supporting NetBoot clients, it may be mounted as desired.
XT-8760S-512|MAXTOR XT-8760S-512|Maxtor 760MB w/512 byte sectors:\
        :ty=fixed_rw_scsi:nc#1626:nt#15:ns#26:ss#1024:rm#3600:\
        :fp#160:bp#0:ng#0:gs#0:ga#0:ao#0:\
        :os=sdmach:z0#32:z1#96:ro=a:\
        :pa#0:sa#413980:ba#8192:fa#1024:ca#32:da#4096:ra#10:oa=time:\
                :ia:ta=4.3BSD:\
   :pb#413980:sb#220000:bb#8192:fb#1024:cb#32:db#8192:rb#10:ob=time:\
                :ib:tb=4.3BSD:
```

## domainname

Shows or allows changing of the network domain name. See the networking
chapter for details on domains. The file is used with Yellow Pages; domainname
isn't typically used by NeXT.

## dread

Reads the text file containing user defaults, or preferences. On NeXT, these include
the settings made in the Preferences application, as well as preferences for specific
applications. The -l option gives a long listing.

Here's an example:

```
localhost> dread
Usage:  dread [owner] name
        dread -l
        dread -g [name]
        dread -o owner
        dread -n name
localhost> dread -l
FrameMaker AuthorizationNum 00-0000-000-0000
FrameMaker AutoBackupOnSave On
FrameMaker AutoSave On
FrameMaker AutoSaveTime 5
FrameMaker DefaultEditors "Icon PlaySound Preview"
FrameMaker DefaultTemplate
   /me/fmtemplates/StandardTemplate/Newsletters/Newsletter1.frame
FrameMaker GreekSize "7.0 pt"
```

```
FrameMaker NonDocWinLayer SubMenus
FrameMaker SerialNum 0-000
GLOBAL NXFont Times-Roman
GLOBAL NXFontSize 12.000000
GLOBAL NXMenuX "  80"
GLOBAL NXMenuY " 783"
Librarian AutoOpen YES
Librarian ContentFont Helvetica
Librarian ContentSize 12
Librarian Sort Weight
Librarian SummaryFont Helvetica
Librarian SummarySize 12
NeXT1 AutoDimTime 40800
NeXT1 ClickTime 30
NeXT1 MouseButtonsTied No
NeXT1 MouseClick 1
NeXT1 MouseHandedness Left
NeXT1 MouseScaling "5 2 2 3 6 4 10 5 15 6 22"
NeXT1 SystemBeep Bonk
NeXT1 TimeZone 4
NeXT1 TimeZoneLabel GMT-0600
Preferences LayoutOrder "0 1 2 3 4 5 6 7"
Quotations ByQuote TRUE
Quotations FontSize 12
Quotations SearchBy FullWord
Scene DeleteBackground 0
Terminal WinLocX 124.000000
Terminal WinLocY 124.000000
Webster DictionaryOpen YES
Webster ExactMatch YES
Webster FontSize 14
Webster FullWordIndex NO
Webster PrintPictures YES
Webster ShowPictures YES
Webster ThesaurusOpen NO
Workspace BrowserH 356
Workspace BrowserW 668
Workspace BrowserX 253
Workspace BrowserY 428
```

Your defaults file might be different. As NeXT evolves, more applications preferences may be found in this file.

Also see dwrite, which writes back defaults.

## dremove

Removes an entry from the defaults file (see above). Not recommended; use the Preferences application instead.

## dsp...

Files beginning with "dsp" are related to the Motorola DSP56000 Digital Signal Processor.

## dspasm
## dspasmr

Two files used to assemble a dsp source code file using Motorola's asm56000 assembler. A peek inside dspasm reveals:

```
localhost# cat /usr/bin/dspasm
echo asm56000 $2 $3 $4 $5 -a -b -l -I/usr/lib/dsp/smsrc/ $1
asm56000 $2 $3 $4 $5 -a -b -l -I/usr/lib/dsp/smsrc/ $1
```

The usage is "dspasm filename." Forget the filename and you'll be prompted:

```
localhost# dspasm
asm56000 -a -b -l -I/usr/lib/dsp/smsrc/
asm56000: Missing source filename
```

There are many DSP-related files. In lieu of explanations, read the manual pages:

```
/NextLibrary/Documentation/UNIX/ManPages/man1/dspabort.1
/NextLibrary/Documentation/UNIX/ManPages/man1/dspbeep.1
/NextLibrary/Documentation/UNIX/ManPages/man1/dspimg.1
/NextLibrary/Documentation/UNIX/ManPages/man1/dsploadwrap.1
/NextLibrary/Documentation/UNIX/ManPages/man1/dspmsg.1
/NextLibrary/Documentation/UNIX/ManPages/man1/dsptest.1
/NextLibrary/Documentation/UNIX/ManPages/man1/dspwrap.1
```

or go right to the source and read this file:

```
/NextLibrary/Documentation/Motorola/dsp_assembler_manual.txt
```

Then tackle these files:

```
localhost# find / -name 'dsp*' -print
/usr/lib/sound/dsprecord.snd
/usr/lib/dsp
/usr/lib/dsp/smsrc/dspmsgs.asm
/usr/lib/dsp/test/dspasm
/usr/lib/dsp/test/dspasml
/usr/include/dsp
/usr/include/dsp/dsp.h
/usr/include/dsp/dsp_errno.h
/usr/include/dsp/dsp_structs.h
/usr/include/dsp/dsp_messages.h
/usr/include/dsp/dsp_memory_map_mk.h
/usr/include/dsp/dsp_memory_map_ap.h
/usr/include/musickit/dspwrap.h
/usr/bin/dspimg
/usr/bin/dspmsg
/usr/bin/dsptest
/usr/bin/dspbeep
/usr/bin/dspabort
/usr/bin/dspwrap
/usr/bin/dsploadwrap
/private/dev/dsp
/NextDeveloper/Examples/DSP/SoundDSPDriver/dsp_example_1
/NextDeveloper/Examples/DSP/SoundDSPDriver/dsp_example_1/dsp_example_1.c
/NextDeveloper/Examples/DSP/SoundDSPDriver/dsp_example_1/dsp_example_1.asm
/NextDeveloper/Examples/DSP/SoundDSPDriver/dsp_example_2
/NextDeveloper/Examples/DSP/SoundDSPDriver/dsp_example_2/dsp_example_2.c
/NextDeveloper/Examples/DSP/SoundDSPDriver/dsp_example_2/dsp_example_2.asm
/NextDeveloper/Examples/DSP/SoundDSPDriver/dsp_example_3
/NextDeveloper/Examples/DSP/SoundDSPDriver/dsp_example_3/dsp_example_3.c
/NextDeveloper/Examples/DSP/SoundDSPDriver/dsp_example_3/dsp_example_3.asm
/NextDeveloper/Examples/DSP/SoundDSPDriver/dsp_example_4
/NextDeveloper/Examples/DSP/SoundDSPDriver/dsp_example_4/dsp_example_4.c
/NextDeveloper/Examples/DSP/SoundDSPDriver/dsp_example_4/dsp_example_4.asm
/NextDeveloper/Examples/DSP/SoundDSPDriver/dsp_example_4/dspstream.asm
localhost#
```

In most cases, you can save time (at the expense of not knowing what you're doing) and type the command into the Shell. Usually, you'll be prompted for necessary arguments, as in:

```
localhost# dspmusic

Usage:  dspmusic [-simulator] [-trace n] [-delay seconds] [-lowsrate] [-o
offsetTimeSamples] [-begin sample] [-pause] [-verbose] *.dsp *.img

See /LocalLibrary/Sounds/DSP for a list of files.
By convention, files with suffix '.img' require the -lowsrate (abbreviated -l).
```

If the command doesn't require an argument, it's done:

```
localhost# dsptest
Booting DSP with AP monitor
DSP is running system 1.0(14).
Unit internal X memory test [x:2#1]
  ... wins.
Internal X memory test [x:2#244]
  ... wins.
External X memory test [x:8192#6944]
  ... wins.
Internal Y memory test [y:2#244]
  ... wins.
External Y memory test [y:15136#0]
  ... wins.
Internal P memory test [p:128#384]
  ... wins.
External P memory test [p:8192#0]
  ... wins.
External X/Y partitioned memory test [x:40960#2848]
  [y:40960#4096]
  ... wins.
Fence-post buffer-size test [x:8192#513]
  ... wins.
Fence-post buffer-size test [x:8192#512]
  ... wins.
Fence-post buffer-size test [x:8192#1025]
  ... wins.
Fence-post buffer-size test [x:8192#1024]
  ... wins.
Fence-post buffer-size test [x:8192#1536]
  ... wins.
External X memory packed 16-bit mode test [x:8192#6944]
  ... wins.
External X memory packed 8-bit mode test [x:8192#6944]
```

```
... wins.
External X memory unpacked 24-bit transfer test [x:8192#6944]
 ... wins.
External X memory packed 24-bit transfer test [x:8192#6944]
 ... wins.
————————-
```

## du

For Disk Usage. Compare df and du:

```
localhost# df
Filesystem      kbytes  used    avail    capacity  Mounted on
/dev/sd0a       446719  198166  203881   49%       /
/dev/sd0b       216311  12      194667   0%        /clients
localhost# du
8        ./lost+found
1        ./.NeXT/.NeXTtrash/MyDisk
532      ./.NeXT/.NeXTtrash
22       ./.NeXT/targets
567      ./.NeXT
10       ./usr/template/user/Apps
2        ./usr/template/user/.NeXT
1        ./usr/template/user/Mailboxes
20       ./usr/template/user
7        ./usr/template/client/etc/nulib
7        ./usr/template/client/etc/zoneinfo/Australia
10       ./usr/template/client/etc/zoneinfo/US
9        ./usr/template/client/etc/zoneinfo/Canada
20       ./usr/template/client/etc/zoneinfo/SystemV
84       ./usr/template/client/etc/zoneinfo
33       ./usr/template/client/etc/sendmail
64       ./usr/template/client/etc/uucp/UUAIDS
82       ./usr/template/client/etc/uucp
18       ./usr/template/client/etc/yp
35       ./usr/template/client/etc/netinfo/local.nidb
36       ./usr/template/client/etc/netinfo
524      ./usr/template/client/etc
4        ./usr/template/client/adm
^Clocalhost#
```

The list was stopped with Control-C—it would have continued until it had listed all mounted files and directories. The left column shows sizes in K, or thousands of bytes. (A byte is equivalent to one character.)

# dvips

Converts TeX files to PostScript for printing.

# dwrite

Writes user preferences to the NeXTDefault.L file. See dread.

# echo

Displays the contents of a variable on the standard output, which is usually the display screen.

```
localhost# echo "hi"
hi
```

Echo is often used to print out the value of variables when debugging a Shell script to life.

# ed

A venerable and absolutely bare-bones text editor. Ed allows you to enter text from the Shell. Of little use on NeXT. If you'd like to experience a full-bore UNIX editor, explore Emacs instead.

# edquota

A command to allow superusers to edit user quotas. See quota entries for details.

# egrep

Egrep is the power-hitter of the grep pattern-matching family. The greps—grep, fgrep, egrep, and Job-Bob—search for patterns in text files. These commands have many options; they're almost one-word applications. If you're a beginning grep'er, check out fgrep, the simplest and quickest grep. Egrep is a "where eagles dare" grep: extraordinarily powerful, but likely to consume gouts of memory as it works; "exponential" memory space; hence the "e" in egrep.

## emacs

Emacs is a legendary text editor written by the legendary Richard Stallman. Stallman founded the Free Software Foundation and has committed his energies to fashioning a public-domain UNIX named GNU (for "Gnu's Not UNIX," naturally).

The Free Software Foundation provided much of NeXT's program development software. Besides Emacs, the NeXT C compiler and the gdb debugger (for Gnu DeBugger) are licensed from the Free Software Foundation. Philosophically, I'm in total disagreement with the aims of the Free Software Foundation. Regardless of that opinion, I urge you to support their efforts. For a copy of the latest "GNU's Bulletin," write to:

Free Software Foundation, Inc.
675 Massachusetts Avenue
Cambridge, MA 02139
Or call 617-876-3296.

The newsletter's free, but enclose some money anyway. You know: ten, twenty dollars. You're reading a book about The NeXT Computer—pricey hardware. You can spare ten bucks, can't you? It's a good cause. Doomed, and wrong, but good.

## enroll

A mail command, used to send "secret" encrypted messages, which can only be read by the recipient.

## enscript

Both a command and an environment variable, enscript allows you to convert text files to PostScript format, and print the files from the Terminal or Shell.

Worth investigating if you have special requirements for printing—enscript has a slew of options. From the UNIX manual pages:

```
NAME
      enscript - convert text files to POSTSCRIPT format for
```

```
    printing
```
SYNOPSIS
```
    enscript [ -12BcGghKklmoqRr ] [ -Llines ] [ -ffont ] [
    -Fhfont ] [ -bheader ] [ -pout ] [ spoolopts ] [ files ]
```

Some of the more useful (or interesting) options are:

2 —to print in two columns,

r —rotate 90 degrees; landscape mode,

l —line printer mode: 66 lines per page, skip headers,

ffont —sets the font for body copy. The default is Courier, which you
probably don't want, and

pout —send the PostScript file to a named file on disk, not to the printer.

# eqn

A preprocessor for troff, used to typeset equations. Like much in UNIX, fascinating stuff, but you're better served, in almost all cases, by Mathematica.

# expand

Converts tabs to spaces. Unexpand, its faithful companion, converts spaces to tabs.

# explain

Used with diction. See diction.

# expr

Maybe this appendix was a bad idea. It seemed so simple: Just briefly explain all those files cluttering the NeXT disk. No problem.

Okay: expr evaluates its arguments as expression. You won't need or use expr until you've reached the depths of Shell programming.

# false

False, like true, is predefined for your use in creating whizzy Shell scripts.

## fgrep

A member of the famous grep family, which also includes grep and egrep. All are used to find patterns in files. Fgrep is the baby of the family: It searches only for fixed strings. Fgrep is the one to use if you know exactly what you're looking for, and don't need the power of the other greps. (Still, like all greps, fgrep has many options.) Fgrep, though limited in power, is fast.

## file

A clever, simple, and useful command. File does its best to tell you the filetype of a file.

```
localhost# file .places
.places:        data
localhost# file grep
grep:   mach-O executable
localhost# file file
file:   mach-O executable
localhost# file /phonelist
/phonelist:     ascii text
```

## find

This is one you must learn. Find finds files. Given the vast amount of disk space on the NeXT, and the vast number of files, find is mandatory. It works like this:

```
find pathname options string -print
```

Pathname tells find where to start looking. Find starts where told and looks recursively—in other words, it searches a directory until it finds a nested directory, searches that directory, and any other directories within that directory, until it "bottoms out." Then it backs up one directory and repeats the process, which may involve delving into other directories, bottoming out, and so on. This goes on until everything "below" pathname has been examined, or you stop the process with Control-Return (or Control-c).

To look everywhere, use / for pathname. So far, the command would be:

```
find /
```

Find has many options. For everyday use, the -name option says "find the file with this name." Which makes the command:

```
find / -name
```

Now enter the file's name. Maybe:

```
find / -name Active.mbox
```

Now for the final, and strangest, option. Unless the command ends with -print, the results of find won't be displayed! It's easy to forget to end with "-print." Don't. The -print option displays the full pathname of the found file—where, exactly, the file is.

```
localhost# find / -name clouds.movie -print
/NextLibrary/Images/Scene_movies/clouds.movie
```

You may also use wildcards. NeXT sound files, for example, end in ".snd." Given that, we can find them all:

```
localhost#  find / -name '*snd' -print
/usr/lib/sound/booter.snd
/usr/lib/sound/codec.snd
/usr/lib/sound/mulawcodec.snd
/usr/lib/sound/mono.snd
/usr/lib/sound/monobyte.snd
/usr/lib/sound/dsprecord.snd
/usr/lib/sound/encodemulawsquelch.snd
/usr/lib/sound/mulawcodecsquelch.snd
/usr/lib/sound/decodemulawsquelch.snd
/usr/lib/NextPrinter/manualfeed.snd
/usr/lib/NextPrinter/nopaper.snd
/usr/lib/NextPrinter/paperjam.snd
/usr/lib/NextPrinter/printeropen.snd
/NextDeveloper/Demos/Stealth.app/farm.snd
/NextDeveloper/Demos/Stealth.app/crunch.snd
/NextDeveloper/Demos/Stealth.app/approach.snd
/NextDeveloper/Demos/Stealth.app/atis.snd
/NextDeveloper/Demos/Stealth.app/cDeparture.snd
/NextDeveloper/Demos/Stealth.app/ctower.snd
/NextDeveloper/Demos/Stealth.app/departure.snd
/NextDeveloper/Demos/Stealth.app/take-off.snd
/NextDeveloper/Demos/Balancer.app/Sound2.snd
/NextDeveloper/Demos/Balancer.app/oops.snd
/NextDeveloper/Demos/Balancer.app/sorry.snd
/NextDeveloper/Demos/Billiards.app/ball22.snd
```

```
/NextDeveloper/Demos/Billiards.app/cue22.snd
/NextDeveloper/Demos/Billiards.app/pocket22.snd
/NextDeveloper/Demos/Billiards.app/rail22.snd
/NextDeveloper/Demos/Billiards.app/gong22.snd
/NextDeveloper/Demos/FrameMaker.app/.fminit2.0/english/sndfiles/welcome.snd
/NextDeveloper/Demos/FrameMaker.app/.fminit2.0/english/sndfiles/titanic.snd
/NextDeveloper/Demos/FrameMaker.app/.fminit2.0/english/sndfiles/costs.snd
/NextDeveloper/Demos/FrameMaker.app/.fminit2.0/english/sndfiles/margin.snd
/NextDeveloper/Demos/FrameMaker.app/FrameDemo/greatjob.snd
/NextDeveloper/Examples/IBTutorial/Sounds/drum1.snd
/NextDeveloper/Examples/IBTutorial/Sounds/drum2.snd
/NextDeveloper/Examples/IBTutorial/Sounds/drum3.snd
/NextLibrary/Sounds/Bonk.snd
/NextLibrary/Sounds/Pop.snd
/NextLibrary/Sounds/Tink.snd
/NextLibrary/Sounds/Basso.snd
/NextLibrary/Sounds/Frog.snd
/NextLibrary/Sounds/Funk.snd
/NextLibrary/Sounds/SystemBeep.snd
/NextLibrary/Images/Scene_movies/holey.movie/guns.snd
/NextLibrary/Images/Scene_movies/gravity.movie/Bonk.snd
localhost#
```

Find has many, many options—a testament to its profound usefulness. If you only learn a handful of UNIX utilities, make sure find is one.

## fmt

For "ForMaTter." Fmt is the most brainless text formatter UNIX has.

But it's nifty. All it does is this: reads a text file and attempts to even out each line to 78 characters, without breaking words. The output shows up on screen; you'll probably want to pipe it somewhere.

What for? Preparing text files for modem transfer is one use. Fmt was created to massage mail files prior to sending. UNIX mail, not NeXT Mail, which doesn't require that files be massaged.

## fsck

A disk utility, fsck both checks the integrity of disks and repairs disks, when necessary. During boot, fsck gets its instructions from the file /etc/fstab. Here's the contents of fstab:

```
#
# NOTE: This file is never consulted if NetInfo is running.
  It is only
# used during bootstrap.
#
/dev/sd0a / 4.3 rw,noquota,noauto 0 1
/dev/sd0b /clients 4.3 rw,noquota 0 2
```

Let's decipher this. /dev/s0a and /dev/sd/0b are the two partitions of the SCSI drive, which is the current boot device. 4.3 is the number of the file system. "rw" means that the drive is opened for both reading (loading) and writing (saving and changing ) files. Noquota means that no usage limits are enforced (they may be on networked systems). The final numbers are used by fsck to prioritize checking of file systems during reboot. The fsck file is read by UNIX, but never changed. Only systems administrators, or other people with profound knowledge of UNIX, should mess with it.

## fsirand

A program to increase the security of systems with NFS (Network File Server) protocols.

fstab

fstab.client

fstab.od

fstab.sd330

fstab.sd660

These are files used by fsck. They contain settings for disk drives. See fsck.

## gdb

For Gnu DeBugger, the standard program debugger for use with Objective-C.

## gettytab

UNIX is a multiuser operating system—plug and play. Over time, users have cobbled a variety of terminals onto UNIX systems. A file called termcap attempts to describe the various terminals. Gettytab is a simplified version of termcap, which describes terminal line settings for classes of terminals.

## grep

Grep is a "find" command. It finds strings in text. It has many options. It has a less powerful sibling, fgrep, and a more powerful sibling, egrep. The syntax is:

```
grep [ option ] ...  expression [ file ] ...
```

"Expression" can become complex and powerful, but grep can also be used simply:

```
grep stringtofind filename
```

To look for the word "really" in the file UNIXdesign, we could:

```
localhost# grep really UNIXdesign
```

As expected, grep has many options. If you wish, grep can find all lines not containing the string in question. And remember: You can pipe grep output to other commands, or use other commands as input to grep. Also see fgrep and egrep.

## group

A text file containing information about groups, thus:

```
localhost# cat /etc/group
wheel:*:0:root,me
nogroup:*:-2:
daemon:*:1:daemon
sys:*:2:
bin:*:3:
uucp:*:4:
kmem:*:5:
news:*:6:
ingres:*:7:
tty:*:8:
operator:*:9:
staff:*:10:root,me
```

```
other:*:20:
localhost#
```

Each line contains the group name, password (shown encrypted), group id, and a list of all users allowed in the group. The example above is bare-bones. "Root" and "me" are obviously the big wheels in my one-person network.

## halt

This command stops UNIX—everything, dead in its tracks. It doesn't reboot the machine, it just shuts 'er down. Unless asked not to (with an -n option), halt calls sync before shutting down, to ensure the integrity of disk information.

## hostconfig

A well-documented text file that contains network settings.

```
localhost# cat /etc/hostconfig
#
# /etc/hostconfig
#
# This file sets up Shell variables used by the various rc scripts to
# configure the host.  Edit this file instead of rc.boot.
#
# Warning:  This is sourced by /bin/sh.  Make sure there are no spaces
#           on either side of the "=".
#
# There are some special keywords used by rc.boot and the programs it
# calls:
#
#       -AUTOMATIC-     Configure automatically
#       -YES-           Turn a feature on
#       -NO-            Leave a feature off or do not configure
#
HOSTNAME=-AUTOMATIC-
INETADDR=-AUTOMATIC-
ROUTER=-NO-
NETMASTER=-NO-
YPDOMAIN=-NO-
localhost#
```

## hostid

Displays, in hex, the identifier of the current host machine:

```
localhost# hostid
0x1002495
```

## hostinfo

Here's another command you don't need to learn. Just type:

```
localhost# hostinfo
Mach kernel version 1.0.
Kernel configured for a single processor only.
1 processor is physically available.
Primary memory available: 15.99 megabytes.
slot 0: MC68030 (NeXT) UP
localhost#
```

## hostname

Reports the current hostname. More properly: displays the contents of the hostname variable.

```
localhost# hostname
localhost
localhost#
```

## hosts

A text file containing default network numbers for NeXT computers. This file was discussed in the Networking chapter.

## hosts.equiv

A text file containing the names of "trusted" hosts. Trusted hosts aren't required to submit passwords, and have full Shell access.

## ifconfig

A low-level command used to configure network parameters.

# index

Digital Librarian in a UNIX guise.

# indxbib

A utility to index bibliographies.

# inetd

For "Internet Daemon." This is a high-level, low-level daemon, if that makes sense. Put another way (please), it's a network daemon that enlists other daemons to service network requests. Used with...

# inetd.conf

Which configures the daemon. This file also provides a fascinating look at network commands and daemons:

```
localhost# cat /etc/inetd.conf
# @(#)inetd.conf  1.1 87/08/12 3.2/4.3NFSSRC
#
# Internet server configuration database
#
ftp         stream  tcp   nowait   root    /usr/etc/ftpd      ftpd
telnet      stream  tcp   nowait   root    /usr/etc/telnetd   telnetd
Shell       stream  tcp   nowait   root    /usr/etc/rshd      rshd
login       stream  tcp   nowait   root    /usr/etc/rlogind   rlogind
exec        stream  tcp   nowait   root    /usr/etc/rexecd    rexecd
# Run as user "uucp" if you don't want uucpd's wtmp entries.
#uucp       stream  tcp   nowait   root    /usr/etc/uucpd     uucpd
finger      stream  tcp   nowait   nobody  /usr/etc/fingerd   fingerd
#tftp       dgram   udp   wait     nobody  /usr/etc/tftpd     tftpd
tftp        dgram   udp   wait     root    /usr/etc/tftpd     tftpd -s
/private/tftpboot
comsat      dgram   udp   wait     root    /usr/etc/comsat    comsat
talk        dgram   udp   wait     root    /usr/etc/talkd     talkd
ntalk       dgram   udp   wait     root    /usr/etc/ntalkd    ntalkd
echo        stream  tcp   nowait   root    internal
discard     stream  tcp   nowait   root    internal
```

```
chargen      stream  tcp    nowait    root    internal
daytime      stream  tcp    nowait    root    internal
time         stream  tcp    nowait    root    internal
echo         dgram   udp    wait      root    internal
discard      dgram   udp    wait      root    internal
chargen      dgram   udp    wait      root    internal
daytime      dgram   udp    wait      root    internal
time         dgram   udp    wait      root    internal
NSWS         stream  tcp    wait      root    /usr/lib/NextStep/NSWSd NSWSd
#
rexd/1       stream  rpc/tcp wait root /usr/etc/rpc.rexd       rpc.rexd
#ypupdated/1 stream  rpc/tcp wait root /usr/etc/rpc.ypupdated  rpc.ypupdated
rquotad/1    dgram   rpc/udp wait root /usr/etc/rpc.rquotad    rpc.rquotad
rstat_svc/1-3dgram   rpc/udp wait root /usr/etc/rpc.rstatd     rpc.rstatd
rusersd/1-2  dgram   rpc/udp wait root /usr/etc/rpc.rusersd    rpc.rusersd
sprayd/1     gram    rpc/udp wait root /usr/etc/rpc.sprayd     rpc.sprayd
walld/1      dgram   rpc/udp wait root /usr/etc/rpc.rwalld     rpc.rwalld
localhost#
```

## install

A command used to move binary files to new locations.

## installman

Install files into the UNIX on-line manual.

## iostat

Reports nitty-gritty statistics and input and output. Read the manual entry for details, but here's the command in action:

```
localhost#  iostat
      tty           od0         od1          SE0          SE0          cpu
   tin tout bps tps msps  bps tps msps  bps tps msps  bps tps msps  us ni sy id
     0    1   0   0 0.0    0   0 0.0    4   1 22.7    0   0 0.0    7  0  4 89
localhost#
```

I don't know much about this one. But..the SEO field, under "msps," reports the average seek time of the hard disk. Here (I'm only using a single 660-megabyte hard disk) it reports a 22.7-millisecond average seek time. That's slower than the NeXT specs, which state a 16.5-millisecond average seek time. Maybe I've got a slow hard disk—though it doesn't seem slow to me!

## join

Creates a relational "join" between two files.

## kill

To kill a current process. This is most often used with "hung" applications: programs which have crashed but are still around—frozen zombies with open windows, dead to mouse clicks. To kill a program, first run the ps command. Enter "ps -aux" into the Shell. You'll see a listing of all processes. The second column contains the process id, abbreviated "PID."

Now, PID in hand, enter "kill <the PID number>" in the Shell. Bam, it's gone.

## last

Yields information about who's logged in recently. Without options:

```
localhost# last
root      ttyp2 localhost   Mon Sep 18 04:47   still logged in
root      ttyp2 localhost   Mon Sep 18 03:00   - 04:47  (01:46)
root      ttyp1 localhost   Mon Sep 18 00:44   still logged in
reboot    ~                 Sun Sep 17 21:00
shutdown ~                  Sun Sep 17 21:00
shutdown ~                  Sun Sep 17 10:50
root      ttyp1 localhost   Sun Sep 17 05:08   - down   (05:41)
root      ttyp1 localhost   Sun Sep 17 03:53   - 05:08  (01:14)
root      ttyp1 localhost   Sun Sep 17 02:26   - 03:53  (01:27)
root      ttyp1 localhost   Sun Sep 17 02:01   - 02:26  (00:24)
```

And on and on and on.

## ld

Combines a number of Mach object files into a single file.

## less

Now I've seen everything. Read the entry for "more," then come back.

Back? Okay: Less is "more's" less. It lets you scroll backward (with more options than either of us want to know about) through Terminal displays.

Less only works in Terminal. Try less in Shell (where you should be, if you're using UNIX) and you'll see:

```
localhost# less
WARNING:terminal cannot "clear to end of line"
WARNING:terminal cannot "clear screen"
WARNING:terminal cannot "home cursor"
WARNING:terminal cannot "move cursor to lower left of screen"
WARNING:terminal cannot "scroll backwards"
   (press RETURN)Can't take input from a terminal  (press RETURN)
localhost#
```

## lex

A program to create text, or lexical, analysis programs. For input, lex requires input files which contain regular expressions and actions—written in C—to be performed when the regular expressions are found. Lex chews on this, then creates a program that performs the analysis on text files.

## lib56000

A utility to group separate DSP files into a single file.

## ln

To create links between files. The default is to make a hard link; the -s option makes a soft link. Links allow directories to appear in more than one location.

## lnk56000

A cross-linker for Motorola DSP56000 files. Linking is part of the compilation process.

# login
# login.std
# logout.std

Files containing commands to be performed during login and logout. Here's .login (located, as a hidden file, in your root directory):

```
localhost# cat .login
#
# Default .login file for root
#
# initialize the terminal parameters
set noglob; eval `tset -Q -s`; unset noglob
set term=$TERM
stty decctlq intr "^C" erase "^?" kill "^U"
stty -tabs
```

# look

Look is a poor person's grep. It finds lines in a file—which must be sorted—which match a string. The syntax is:

```
look [-df] string [file]
```

The -d option limits the comparison to dictionary order. The -f option "folds" upper-case letters into lowercase; it considers uppercase as lowercase for comparison purposes.

If a filename isn't given, look uses the default UNIX word list /usr/dict/words, which betrays the origin of the utility: It's a simple, fast way to look up words in a word list. Also handy if you're looking for the spelling of a word, and know the first few letters. As in:

```
localhost# look reb
reb
Rebecca
rebel
rebelled
rebelling
rebellion
rebellious
```

```
rebuke
rebut
rebuttal
rebutted
rebutting
```

## lookbib

Builds an index for a bibliography, or finds references in an existing bibliography. Lookbib is one of a handful of programs for creating and formatting bibliographies. The others are refer, addbib, sortbib, and roffbib.

## lpr

A no-hassle way to print a file listing, complete with headers and page numbers. Many options are available; multi-column output is one.

This is a fast way to get minimal formatting, without the rigors of troff, or other UNIX text formatting tools.

## lptest

Generates the famous "ripple pattern" used to check printer quality:

```
localhost# lptest
!"#$%&'()*+,-./0123456789:;<=>?@ABCDEFGHIJKLMNOPQRSTUVWXYZ[\]^_`abcdefghijklmno
"#$%&'()*+,-./0123456789:;<=>?@ABCDEFGHIJKLMNOPQRSTUVWXYZ[\]^_`abcdefghijklmnop
#$%&'()*+,-./0123456789:;<=>?@ABCDEFGHIJKLMNOPQRSTUVWXYZ[\]^_`abcdefghijklmnopq
$%&'()*+,-./0123456789:;<=>?@ABCDEFGHIJKLMNOPQRSTUVWXYZ[\]^_`abcdefghijklmnopqr
%&'()*+,-./0123456789:;<=>?@ABCDEFGHIJKLMNOPQRSTUVWXYZ[\]^_`abcdefghijklmnopqrs
&'()*+,-./0123456789:;<=>?@ABCDEFGHIJKLMNOPQRSTUVWXYZ[\]^_`abcdefghijklmnopqrst
```

And so on, for many more lines. To see this slide from the Laser Printer, pipe it:

```
localhost# lptest | lpr
```

## ls

For "list files," one of the most common UNIX commands.

```
localhost# cd NextApps
localhost# ls
```

```
.list          InterfaceBuilder*   Preferences*   Terminal*
.places        Librarian.app/      Printer*       Webster*
BuildDisk*     Mail.app/           Quotations*    Workspace*
Edit*          Mathematica.app/    Shell*         WriteNow.app/
```

ls has many useful options, including:

-l      long listing,

-t      list by time modified, and

-s      list by size.

Ls is aliased to "ls -F" on NeXT, which prints trailing "/'s" after the names of directories.

## m4

A macro preprocessor for use with a variety of languages.

## mail

The traditional UNIX Mail program, radically enhanced on NeXT to become the Mail application.

## make

A programming utility, make works with the compiler to turn a disparate collection of source files and program "headers " into applications. To compile a program (possibly one of the example applications), use the Shell to set the current directory to the location of the program files, then enter "make." That's all that's needed. Make fires up the compiler...and the application is created.

## MAKEDEV

A utility to install new devices into the system. MAKE DEVice.

## map3270

A text file in /etc to map keyboard keys to IBM 3270 compatible definitions. A curiosity only, let's hope.

## md

For Make Dependencies. A programmer's utility. Interface Builder takes care of this automatically; it shouldn't be necessary to use md.

## mesg

A handy utility for when you want to be alone.

Mesg lets you permit or deny mail to be sent to your terminal. It works by denying write permission to everyone but yourself. Think of unplugging your telephone.

The syntax is "mesg n" to forbid mail, and "mesg y" to permit mail. With no arguments, mesg displays its current setting:

```
localhost# mesg
is y
```

The default is yes: Allow mail to be received.

## mkdir

Another often-used utility, mkdir is MaKeDIRectory. New directories are simply made:

```
localhost# mkdir mynewdirectory
localhost# ls
.NeXT/          .userdict       clients/        mynewdirectory/
.cshrc          .userdict~      dev/            odmach*
.editdict       Mailboxes/      doug/           personal/
.editdict~      Net/            etc/            phonelist
.hidden         NextApps/       lib/            private/
.list           NextDeveloper/  lost+found/     sdmach*
.login          NextLibrary/    mach@           tmp/
.places         TheBook/        mach man.edit   usr/
.profile        bin/            me/             vmUNIX@
```

There's the new directory: at the top of the rightmost column.

The counterpart of mkdir is rmdir, which removes directories. Unlike mkdir, rmdir has many options. See rmdir.

## mkdirs

A beefed-up version of mkdir, this one creates a number of nested directories. To
make a directory in a directory in a directory:

```
localhost# mkdirs /newdir/newdir2/newdir3
localhost# ls
.NeXT/      .profile      TheBook/      mach@ sdmach*
.cshrc      .userdict     bin/          mach man.edit tmp/
.editdict   .userdict~    clients/      me/ usr/
.editdict~  Mailboxes/    dev/          newdir/ vmUNIX@
.hidden     Net/          doug/         odmach*
.list       NextApps/     etc/          personal/
.login      NextDeveloper/ lib/         phonelist
.places     NextLibrary/  lost+found/ private/
localhost# cd newdir
localhost# ls
newdir2/
localhost# cd newdir2
localhost# ls
newdir3/
```

## mkfs

The "mk" prefix means "make." This command, mkfs, makes an entire file system.
The manual entry is interesting; read it and you'll know what file systems are composed of, and the options available to file system creators. But don't try it yourself.

## mknod

A specialized utility to create "special files" which represent new devices to be
mounted on the UNIX system.

## mkpasswd

Generates a hashed password table. NeXT takes care of this at a much higher level.

## mkproto

Used to make a new (or "prototype") file system, which is then bootstrapped onto the existing file system. As with the above entries, you won't ever use this utility (if you do, send me a copy of your UNIX book when it's finished), but browsing through the manual entries for the various "mk" utilities gives you valuable insight into the UNIX operating system.

## motd

Motd is "Message Of The Day." If your NeXT is on a network, the network administrator can change the contents of the file text /private/etc/motd. On boot-up, reading and displaying the message of the day is one of UNIX's most pleasurable chores. NeXT cubes, out of the box, contain only NeXT release version numbers. No snappy comments.

## mount

A fundamental UNIX command, mount places—mounts—a device or file system onto an existing directory. Once mounted, the device or file system can be accessed like any other. Mount's counterpart, umount, does what you'd guess.

## msgwrap

A low-level routine for generating Speaker and Listener classes. Don't look here for more information on speaking and listening; see the relevant Application Kit documentation instead.

## mtab

This one's interesting. Mtab is a text file table of currently mounted file systems. It's located in /etc:

```
localhost# cat /etc/mtab
/dev/sd0a / 4.3 rw,noquota,noauto 0 1
/dev/sd0b /clients 4.3 rw,noquota 0 2
```

The fields, somewhat cryptically, are:

```
fsname dir type opts freq passno
```

A look at the C structure behind this shows:

```
struct mntent {
        char  *mnt_fsname;  /* file system name */
        char  *mnt_dir;     /* file system path prefix
*/
        char  *mnt_type;    /* 4.2, nfs, swap, or
ignore */
        char  *mnt_opts;    /* ro, quota, etc. */
        int   mnt_freq;     /* dump frequency, in days
*/
        int   mnt_passno;   /* pass number on parallel
fsck */
    };
```

We can now decipher:

```
/dev/sd0a / 4.3 rw,noquota,noauto 0 1
/dev/sd0b /clients 4.3 rw,noquota 0 2
```

and find that currently, two file systems are mounted, both on the SCSI (sd) hard disk. The two partitions are sd0a and sd0b. The first partition is mounted on / —the root directory. The second is mounted in the /clients directory.

The "4.3" number tells UNIX to treat the mounted file systems as it would UNIX 4.3BSD file systems. Moving along, "rw" means both partitions are mounted for both reading and writing.

On both lines, "noquota" means that file system usage limits aren't in effect. (Network administrators, if they wish, can limit file system use, and often do.)

On the top line, "noauto" means the file system isn't automatically booted. (NeXT system software takes care of this elsewhere.) The "0's" on each line mean that auto file backup (or "dump") isn't implemented. (Amazing how much stuff is here, isn't it?) The final numbers are used by fsck, a utility for "file system checking, " which does low-level housekeeping and disk repair chores.

## mv

The UNIX command to move or rename a file. The syntax is:

```
mv [options] file1 file2
mv [options] file ... directory
```

The first method renames a file. Note that if "file2" exists, it's deleted before "file1" is moved. The second method moves a file to another directory. The most important option is -i, for interactive. With the -i option, you're prompted if mv will overwrite an existing file, and given the chance to change your mind.

Mv is the UNIX equivalent of The Workspace Manager's "drag an icon" moving method—The Workspace Manager, in fact, calls mv to do the actual file-system dirty work.

## neqn

One of three commands (the others are eqn and checkeq) used to typeset mathematics. The commands are used with troff, a text formatting preprocessor. Mathematica is a better way to go.

## netgroup

A text database containing information about network group members.

## networks

Contains network information and network addresses.

```
localhost# cat /etc/networks
#
# NeXT customer networks
# NOTE: This file is never consulted if NetInfo or Yellow
Pages is running
#
loopback      127        loopback-net software-loopback-net
next-default  192.42.172         NeXTether ethernet
localnet
#
# Internet networks
#
arpanet       10         arpa
ucb-ether     46         ucbether
```

## newaliases

A command to rebuild the database of mail aliases. The file that's rebuilt is /usr/lib /aliases. First you change /usr/lib/aliases, then you run the newaliases command, which requires no options.

## newclient

Used to build /private directories for clients on a local cube.

## newfs

Creates a new file system. Mach uses this command in the BuildDisk application.

## nice

UNIX commands which run at a low priority give more time to other active processes—they're "nice" to other processes. They take longer to run, but they don't bog down other running programs. The simplest way to run a UNIX command nicely is to end the command with "&."

The Find command is a good candidate for niceness:

```
localhost# find . -name 'Util*' -print&
[1] 197
localhost#
```

Appending the command with "&" and hitting Return sends it on its way. To alert you that it is, indeed, running, the command's process number is given; here, it's 197. The Shell prompt appears immediately, and you can continue Shelling while the commands runs, nicely, in the background. (I'm actually typing this description while the find command is scurrying through my hard disk.)

Sometime later...

```
./NextApps/Mathematica.app/Kernel/Utilities
./NextApps/Copy_of_NextApps/Mathematica.app/Kernel/Utilities
./TB/Backmatter/UtilAppendix.al
./TB/Backmatter/UtilAppendix.mz
./TB/Backmatter/UtilAppendix.al~
./TB/Backmatter/UtilAppendix.mz~
```

```
./TB/Backmatter/UtilAppendix.BU
[1]    Done                    find . -name Util* -print
localhost#
```

The command displays its output. For even more control, the syntax:

```
nice [ -number ] command [ arguments ]
```

lets you specify "niceness" as a number. Higher numbers result in lower priorities (wouldn't you know) up to a maximum of 20. The default nice, using "&", is 10.

If you're *really* in a hurry, negative nice numbers run commands at *higher* than normal priority.

# nidump
# niload
# niutil

Let's take these three commands as an excuse to learn about "how to learn about UNIX commands."

First, all three commands are probably similar—they all begin with "ni." Let's use the man command to glance at the first command:

```
localhost# man nidump
NIDUMP(1)              UNIX Programmer's Manual
NIDUMP(1)NAME
     nidump - extract a UNIX-format file out of NetInfo
SYNOPSIS
     nidump format domain
DESCRIPTION
     nidump reads the given NetInfo domain and dumps a UNIX for-
     mat file to standard output.
```

There's more, but that's enough. The key word here seems to be "NetInfo." Okay, let's use the man -k option to see where else NetInfo appears:

```
localhost# man -k netinfo
netinfo (3N)     - library routines for NetInfo calls
netinfod (8)     - NetInfo daemon
nibindd (8)      - NetInfo binder
nidomain (8      - NetInfo domain utility
nidump (1)       - extract a UNIX-format file out of NetInfo
```

```
niload (1)        - load UNIX-format file into NetInfo
niutil (1)        - NetInfo utility
```

There they are: all three of the commands in question—nidump, niload, and niutil. We could now use the man command (without the -k option) to elucidate each individual command. Or, curiosity piqued, we could continue to rummage around, possibly looking for all files beginning with "net. " Like this:

```
localhost# find . -name 'net*' -print
./usr/template/client/etc/networks
./usr/template/client/etc/netgroup
./usr/template/client/etc/netinfo
./usr/etc/netinfod
./usr/ucb/netstat
./usr/include/netdb.h
./usr/include/netname_defs.h
./usr/include/netinfo
./usr/include/servers/netname.h
./usr/include/net
./usr/include/net/netisr.h
./usr/include/netimp
./usr/include/netinet
./usr/include/netns
./private/etc/networks
./private/etc/netgroup
./private/etc/netinfo
./NextLibrary/Documentation/UNIX/ManPages/cat1/netstat.1
./NextLibrary/Documentation/UNIX/ManPages/cat3/netinfo.3n
./NextLibrary/Documentation/UNIX/ManPages/cat3/network.3n
./NextLibrary/Documentation/UNIX/ManPages/cat4/networking.4n
./NextLibrary/Documentation/UNIX/ManPages/cat5/netgroup.5
./NextLibrary/Documentation/UNIX/ManPages/cat5/networks.5
./NextLibrary/Documentation/UNIX/ManPages/cat8/netinfod.8
./NextLibrary/Documentation/UNIX/ManPages/man1/netstat.1
./NextLibrary/Documentation/UNIX/ManPages/man3/netinfo.3n
./NextLibrary/Documentation/UNIX/ManPages/man3/network.3n
./NextLibrary/Documentation/UNIX/ManPages/man4/networking.4n
./NextLibrary/Documentation/UNIX/ManPages/man5/netgroup.5
./NextLibrary/Documentation/UNIX/ManPages/man5/networks.5
./NextLibrary/Documentation/UNIX/ManPages/man8/netinfod.8
./NextLibrary/References/Webster-
Dictionary/pictures/netsuke.tiff
```

Now what? Use man again? Or use a text editor to read those network-related files?

In case you're annoyed with this lack of specificity, here's a brief explanation of each "ni" utility:

Niload allows you to load UNIX files into NetInfo, NeXT's network management software. The UNIX files are then known and used by their simpler NetInfo names. These are the files in question:

| UNIX file | NetInfo name |
| --- | --- |
| /etc/passwd | users |
| /etc/hosts | machines |
| /etc/printcap | printers |
| /etc/fstab | mounts |
| /etc/networks | networks |
| /etc/services | services |
| /etc/protocols | protocols |
| /etc/rpc | rpcs |
| /usr/lib/aliases | aliases |

As you can see, NetInfo simplifies some of the UNIX names.

Nidump converts NetInfo domain data into standard UNIX file format.

Niutil is used for arbitrary reads and writes in a NetInfo domain.

These commands, as you've probably guessed, won't typically be used by non-systems administrators.

## nm

A programmer's utility to print the symbol table of a compiled object file.

## nmserver

A server containing names of machines on a network.

# nohup

Nohup? It's from "NO Hang UP." It makes commands (usually running in the background) immune to having their processes killed. In the C Shell, running a command "nicely" or with an "&" appended automatically invokes nohup. The command comes from the need to make sure that certain processes finish their work before system shutdown.

# nppower

Want to turn the NeXT Laser Printer on and off from the Shell? This is the command:

```
localhost# nppower off
```

turns off the Laser Printer and:

```
localhost# nppower on
```

turns it on. Why do this? For fun. To save power: Every watt counts.

# nroff

A less powerful version of troff (see the troff entry), used for printing formatted documents on typewriter-like printers.

# nu

For New User. Used to manage user accounts on networks. NeXT's NetInfo does this more gracefully, but nu is straightforward, and somewhat fun to use (I've obviously been working with this stuff too long).

You might use nu if, for instance, you're not on a network, but wish to make your cube available to users calling in by modem. Once you've set up the new user account, they can "dial you up" and log in, provided they know their password. Here's a typical nu session:

```
localhost# nu
usage:  nu -a                      add new accounts
        nu -m                      modify existing accounts
        nu -d                      delete existing accounts
        nu -k user1 user2 ...      kill old accounts
```

```
localhost# nu -a
nu NeXT-1.0 [12 July 1989] (localhost:/etc/nu.cf)
Login name? (1-8 alphanumerics) [no default] steve
Passwords are very important to system security. When you are
entering a new password, make sure that it is at least 6 characters
long and that it contains at least one character that is not a letter.
Enter password:
Retype password, please:
Enter actual user name: Steve Wozniak
User id number? (small integer)  [21]
Which user group? (name or number; ? for list) [other] ?
        daemon  sys  bin  uucp
        kmem  news  tty  operator
        staff  other  wheel  ingres
Which user group? (name or number; ? for list) [other] wheel
Login directory?  [/steve]
Enter Shell [/bin/csh]
    1)  login ...... steve
    2)  password ... cwT7MHmTpj2G6 (encrypted)
    3)  name ....... Steve Wozniak
    4)  userid ..... 21
    5)  groupid .... 0 (wheel)
    6)  login dir .. /steve
    7)  login sh ... /bin/csh
Are these values OK? (y or n)   [y]
Account added to NetInfo.
Do you wish to add more new users? (y or n)   [y] n
localhost#
```

## on

Used to execute a command on a remote system. Forgoing options, the syntax is:

```
on host command [ argument ] ...
```

A good grounding in uucp commands is a recommended prelude to use of this command.

## open

One of the bedrock UNIX "system calls." Not a command; this is used in C programs.

## otool

This command prints portions of object files or libraries. It has many options, and some must be specified. With the -d option:

```
otool -d someobjectfile
```

otool prints the _data section of an object file.

## pagesize

Returns the size of one memory page in bytes.

```
localhost# pagesize
8192
```

## passwd

Changes or installs password information. NeXT provides high-level tools for these tasks. Still, to give Bruce a new password from the Shell:

```
localhost# passwd bruce
New password:
Retype new password:
localhost#
```

The new password isn't displayed as it's entered; hence the need to retype to confirm.

## pft

A bare-bones program that lets you communicate with The Window Server from the Shell. Pft has four options:

"pft -host hostname" connects The Window Server on machine "hostname,"

"pft -f filename" sends filename directory to The Window Server. A fast way to test Window Server code from the Shell,

An -s option, when used with the -f option, causes pft to exit after the file has been processed. The usage would be: "pft -s -f filename,"

"pft -PSName file" sets a string for pft to use in determining which Window

Server to connect with. This also sets the name that the Window Server uses to register with the network name server.

## ping

A networking testing utility. The name comes—guessing here—from ships' sonar that "pinged" for the presence of enemy submarines.

Ping does essentially that: It pings across a network, to see if hosts are indeed "there. " If they're not, it's probably due to hardware problems.

## playscore

Plays a NeXT scorefile from the Shell

```
playscore <filename>
```

is all that's needed. Try:

```
playscore Gamelan
```

for a treat that shows off the Music Kit and the NeXT sound capabilities.

## prebuild

Takes a binary description of a font and builds a PostScript representation for use by The Window Server.

## printcap

A file containing printer characteristics. Similar, but simpler, than the termcap file. Each entry describes one printer.

```
localhost# cat /etc/printcap
#
#       /etc/printcap
#
# PostScript printer driven by TranScript software
# PostScript and TranScript are trademarks of Adobe Systems
# Incorporated
#
# NOTE: This file is never consulted by printing software if NetInfo
```

```
# is running.
#
# np is a local NeXT printer
#
#np|LocalPrinter:\
#        :lp=/dev/null:\
#        :sd=/usr/spool/np:\
#        :re:mf:\
#        :if=/usr/lib/NextPrinter/npcomm:\
#        :ty=NeXT 400 dpi Laser Printer:
#
# netnp is a NeXT printer on machine remotehost.
# The logical /etc/hosts.equiv file on remotehost must allow your
# machine to talk to remotehost.  You might have to reboot after
# changing that file for it to take effect.
#
#NetNextPrinter|netnp:\
#        :lp=:rm=remotehost:rp=np:sd=/usr/spool/np:\
#        :ty=NeXT 400 dpi Laser Printer:
#
# lp is a LaserWriter on serial port a.  You might have to check
# the transmision rate is right for the device.
# The spool file need not be /usr/spool/lw, but it must exist
# (mkdir it) and it is best to have each printer have its own
# spool file.  Copy the directory permissions and owner/group of
# the existing ones:       drwxrwx--  daemon   daemon
# NEEDS null modem cable between NeXT cube and printer.
#
# LaserWriter is a trademark of Apple Computer, Inc.
#
#LaserWriter|lw:\
#        :lp=/dev/ttya:\
#        :sd=/usr/spool/lw:\
#        :tr=^D:\
#        :lf=/usr/adm/lw-log:\
#        :af=/usr/adm/lw.acct:\
#        :br#9600:rw:\
#        :fc#0000374:\
#        :fs#0000003:\
#        :xc#0:\
#        :xs#0040040:\
```

```
#           :mx#0:sf:sb:\
#           :if=/usr/lib/transcript/psif:\
#           :of=/usr/lib/transcript/psof:\
#           :gf=/usr/lib/transcript/psof:\
#           :nf=/usr/lib/transcript/psnf:\
#           :tf=/usr/lib/transcript/psnf:\
#           :vf=/usr/lib/transcript/pstf:\
#           :gf=/usr/lib/transcript/pscf:\
#           :df=/usr/lib/transcript/psgf:\
#           :ty=LaserWriter:
#
# netlw is a LaserWriter printer on the net somewhere. The
# hosts.equivcomment in the netnp section above applies here too.
# The printcap file on remotehost must have a PostScript entry.
#NetLaserWriter|netlw:\
#           :lp=:rm=remotehost:rp=PostScript:sd=/usr/spool/lpd:pl#66:\
#           :ty=LaserWriter:
localhost#
```

## profile.std

This is an empty "template" file:

```
cat /usr/template/client/etc/profile.std
#
# Standard sh login profile
# sh will source this file before the home .profile
#
```

As the man says, the profile.std file is checked by sh (Shell) before checking the
.profile file. Here's where you'd add custom profile information.

## protocols

A file containing "last resort" network information:

```
localhost# cat /private/etc/protocols
#
# Internet (IP) protocols
#
# NOTE: This file is never consulted if NetInfo or Yellow Pages
is running.
#
```

```
ip        0    IP        # internet protocol, pseudo protocol number
icmp      1    ICMP      # internet control message protocol
ggp       3    GGP       # gateway-gateway protocol
tcp       6    TCP       # transmission control protocol
egp       8    EGP       # exterior gateway protocol
pup       12   PUP       # PARC universal packet protocol
udp       17   UDP       # user datagram protocol
hmp       20   HMP       # host monitoring protocol
xns-idp   22   XNS-IDP   # Xerox NS IDP
rdp       27   RDP       # "reliable datagram" protocol
```

# ps
# ps4014
# ps630
# pscat
# pscatmap
# psdit
# psplot
# psrev
# psroff
# pswrap
# ptroff

Files beginning with "ps" are PostScript-related. Ptroff, obviously, is misnamed. The only file above you can't use is "ps," a binary file used by The Window Server. The others?

Ps4014 and ps630 convert Tektronix 4014 files and Diablo 630 files, respectively, to PostScript format. Pscat does the same to C/A/T files.

Pscatmap builds PostScript width tables for use by ptroff. Ptroff, itself, is a version of troff, a text formatter. Ptroff is a "PostScript troff." Psdit is similar: It converts ditroff format to PostScript format.

Another converter, psplot, converts plot(5) files to PostScript format.

Psrev is a good one. It lets you select or reverse the order of a PostScript file.

Psroff is a Shell script that runs diroff or troff to print PostScript files.

Pswrap creates C code from PostScript language mutterings.

## ptx

Creates permutated indexes of text files, usually for the purpose of making real indexes. Many options. Until word processors come along that do indexing, you can use this, with some effort.

## pwd

A vital, must-know, UNIX command. Present Working Directory. Type pwd in the Shell to see where you are. Then use cd (see entry) to change your location in the directory hierarchy.

## pword

Another amazing text utility. If you like words, and can suffer through the process of learning UNIX, you can frolic for years with these things. This one displays the "peculiar words" in a document. Options? Hah!

```
pword [-c] [-p] [-f] [-w] [-S] [-m #] [-P #] [-n #] [-t #]
[-s #] [-i #] [files ...]
```

Who could resist?

```
localhost# pword Mach.chap
1.000000 mach
0.861308 multiprocessing
0.861308 froman
0.484486 nuemann
0.484486 microprocessor
0.484486 bottleneck
0.484486 carnegie
0.484486 mellon
0.215327 themselve
0.215327 alway
0.215327 gigabyte
```

Yes, there *are* some peculiar words there—and some misspellings, also! The number at left is the "peculiarity index." The higher the number, the odder the word. Here, mach is the most peculiar word found, multiprocessing is the next most peculiar word, and so on. Only a portion of the output is shown.

## quot

Quot gives ownership statistics for file systems, by counting the disk blocks "owned" by each user. Why? Because in UNIX, it's possible (and frequent) to limit disk usage based on "quotas."

## quotacheck

Checks actual disk space used by users against allowable use quotas found in the file /etc/rc.local.

## quotaon
## quotaoff

Two commands to enable or disable quotas on disk use. See above entries.

## rc.boot

A Shell script that sets up a cube to function as a single-user machine.

```
localhost# cat /etc/rc.boot
```

displays the file. It's a recommended read.

## rc.local

A text file containing commands set at system start-up. It calls another file, etc/hostconfig, which sets Shell variables used in still other scripts. Both files are worth a glance.

## rcp

For Remote Copy Procedure. A low-level utility for file transfer on networks.

## rdump

The Remote Dump command is used to "dump" file systems across a network, usually for backup purposes.

## reboot

Reboot shuts everything down, then starts it up again. Unlike "Log out" in The Workspace Manager, reboot completely shuts down, then restarts the cube. As a result, all the startup operations are performed: checking disks, starting daemons, and more. Reboot is useful if you're having problems with your cube (bizarre drawing onscreen, for example), and nothing else has worked. At the least, rebooting cleans things up (the technical term) in the system. Can't hurt.

## refer

A preprocessor for nroff and troff, used to insert and format references (hence its name) in documents.

## remote

A text file containing descriptions of remote computer hosts. You should be familiar with this file if you're planning to telecommunicate using TIP or CU.

## renice

The nice command (see entry) sets the priority of processes. Renice lets you change the priority of processes *while* they're running. What will they think of next?

## repquota

Displays a summary of quotas and actual disk use. See the "quota..." entries.

## rev

Reverses the lines in a file. I don't know what it's for either.

## rexecd

A remote execution server.

## rlogind

A remote login server.

## rm

An often-used command, rm "removes" a file. What does MS-DOS call this, these days? del? Something like that. There's not much to it:

```
rm file
```

Rm is powerful and typically unforgiving. Use the black hole, instead, unless you're confident. Or use the -i option, which gives you a chance to back out, before the file is deleted.

## rmail

Handles remote mail that comes from uucp transmissions.

## rmdir

Like rm, but this one removes directories.

## route

Use this command to manually change the network routing tables. You don't want to do this.

## rpc

For "Remote Procedure Call." The calls allow programs to perform procedures on remote machines.

## rpcgen

A compiler for remote procedure calls.

## rrestore

Restores information from a backup device: a tape unit in traditional UNIX setups.

## rsh

A remote shell, used to run a command on another machine. The syntax is:

```
rsh host [ -l username ] [ -n ] command
host [ -l username ] [ -n ] command
```

Basically, you name the host you wish to connect with, and give the command to run, and rsh does the rest.

## rshd

For Remote Shell server. The "d" means Daemon. The rshd server waits for rsh requests (see entry above) and executes them.

## sed

For "Stream EDitor." To understand the acronym, know that "ed" is the old-shoe, bare-bones editor that thousands of UNIXheads take for granted.

The sed utility, then, is a "batch" editor. It allows you to throw ed commands at files without first opening them for editing. Sed is useful, to a point. For true power manipulation, look into awk, a text-processing language.

## services

A database of services available on Internet. Not used if NetInfo or Yellow Pages are running. Notice, way at the bottom, that the cube offers up its Window Server (NSWS) to other computers.

```
localhost# cat /private/etc/services
#       @(#)services   1.16 (Berkeley) 86/04/20
#
# Network services, Internet style
#
# NOTE: This file is never consulted if NetInfo or Yellow
Pages is running
```

```
#
echo           7/tcp
echo           7/udp
discard        9/tcp       sink null
discard        9/udp       sink null
systat        11/tcp       users
daytime       13/tcp
daytime       13/udp
netstat       15/tcp
qotd          17/tcp       quote
chargen       19/tcp       ttytst source
chargen       19/udp       ttytst source
ftp           21/tcp
telnet        23/tcp
smtp          25/tcp       mail
time          37/tcp       timserver
time          37/udp       timserver
rlp           39/udp       resource          # resource location
nameserver    42/tcp       name              # IEN 116
whois         43/tcp       nicname
domain        53/tcp       nameserver        # name-domain server
domain        53/udp       nameserver
mtp           57/tcp                         # deprecated
tftp          69/udp
rje           77/tcp       netrjs
finger        79/tcp
link          87/tcp       ttylink
supdup        95/tcp
hostnames    101/tcp       hostname          # usually from sri-nic
#csnet-cs    105/?
pop          109/tcp       postoffice
sunrpc       111/tcp
sunrpc       111/udp
auth         113/tcp       authentication
sftp         115/tcp
uucp-path    117/tcp
nntp         119/tcp       readnews untp     # USENET News
Transfer Protocol
ntp          123/udp
#
```

```
# UNIX specific services
#
exec        512/tcp
biff        512/udp    comsat
login       513/tcp
who         513/udp    whod
shell       514/tcp    cmd                  # no passwords used
syslog      514/udp
printer     515/tcp    spooler              # line printer spooler
talk        517/udp
ntalk       518/udp
efs         520/tcp                         # for LucasFilm
route       520/udp    router routed
timed       525/udp    timeserver
tempo       526/tcp    newdate
courier     530/tcp    rpc
conference  531/tcp    chat
netnews     532/tcp    readnews
netwall     533/udp                         # -for
emergency broadcasts
uucp        540/tcp    uucpd                # uucp daemon
remotefs    556/tcp    rfs_server rfs  # Brunhoff
remote filesystem
#
ingreslock  1524/tcp
#
# NeXT specific services
#
NSWS        178/tcp
localhost#
```

## sh

There's a language embedded in Shell, and this is it. It reads and executes commands, handles piping and redirection, and much more: You can write scripts that the sh language interprets and performs.

On your way to learning the Shell, print out the manual entry for "sh." One way to do that is to fire up Edit, choose Source from the Utilities menu, enter sh, hit return, then print the manual listing that appears. It's about ten pages of must reading for novice Shellers.

## shutdown

The equivalent of hitting the power key to shut down your cube, but with many more options. Read the entertaining, informative manual entry.

## size

Reports on the size of an object (nontext) file. Let's look at the size of the "ed" editor:

```
localhost# size ed
text    data    bss     dec     hex
49152   8192    2792    60136   eae8
localhost# size -m ed
Segment __TEXT: 49152
        Section __text: 45616
        total 45616
Segment __DATA: 16384
        Section __data: 4576
        Section __bss: 6408
        total 10984
Segment __PAGEZERO: 8192
total 73728
```

The -m option shows the sizes of the various Mach segments.

## slattach

A low-level command to attach serial lines to network interfaces.

## sleep

Suspends the execution of a process: "puts it to sleep" for a specified number of seconds. Usually used to delay the execution of a command:

```
(sleep <how many seconds>; command)&
```

Also handy in Shell script loops, where commands can be run, put to sleep, run...

This command has a great bug entry in the manual:

```
BUGS
     Time must be less than 2,147,483,647 seconds.
```

# snd_register
# sndconvert
# sndinfo
# sndplay
# sndrecord

The "snd " commands deal with sound. Sndconvert converts between file types, sampling rates, and more. Sndinfo displays the headers of sound files:

```
localhost# sndinfo Breeble.snd
Filename: Breeble.snd
Size: 12264 bytes
Format: Music Kit DSP Image
SamplingRate: 44100.000 Hz
Channels: 2
```

Sndplay and sndrecord allow you to play or record from a Shell window.

# sort

A command you should know and use. Don't be intimidated by the manual entry synopsis:

```
SYNOPSIS
     sort [ -mubdfinrtx ] [ +pos1 [ -pos2 ] ] ... [ -o name ] [
     -T directory ] [ name ] ...
```

In general, sort sorts lines in a file, or sorts standard input.

```
localhost# ls
.NeXT/      .places      Net/          dev/
odmach*
.cshrc      .profile     NextApps/     doug/
private/
.editdict   .userdict    NextDeveloper/ etc/
sdmach*
.editdict~  .userdict~   NextLibrary/  lib/
tmp/
```

```
.hidden     DBook/      bin/         lost+found/
  usr/
.list       Mailboxes/  bruce/       mach@
vmUNIX@
.login      NeXTdocs/   clients/     me/
localhost# ls | sort
.NeXT/
.cshrc
.editdict
.editdict~
.hidden
.list
.login
.places
.profile
.userdict
.userdict~
DBook/
Mailboxes/
NeXTdocs/
Net/
NextApps/
NextDeveloper/
NextLibrary/
bin/
bruce/
clients/
dev/
doug/
etc/
lib/
lost+found/
mach@
me/
odmach*
private/
sdmach*
tmp/
usr/
vmUNIX@
```

If you use the Shell frequently, sort will come in handy time and again.

## sortbib

A specialized version of sort, to sort bibliography entries. UNIX has a raft of bibliographic-related commands and utilities. Among them: refer, addbib, roffbib, inxbib, and lookbib.

## spell

A nifty, but limited, spelling checker. Without options, it's:

```
spell <filename>
```

The spell command races through the file, collects words which may be misspelled, and displays the suspect word list. By default, the words in your document are checked against /usr/dict/words: a list of 24,259 words.

There are many useful options. You can specify a different, or additional, word list to check. You can specify that documents be checked for British spelling.

## spellin
## spellout

These are files used by the spell utility.

## spline

This command produces, as numerical output, the equivalent of smooth "spline" curves seen in programs like Adobe Illustrator. You give it a list of number pairs; it gives you another list, appropriately spaced.

## split

Splits one file into many files. The -n option lets you choose the number of files to create.

## strings

Another neat command. Boy, are there some neat commands in UNIX. This one finds strings in binary (object) files. A great way to snoop.

## strip

A programmer utility to compress object files by removing the symbol table and relocation bits.

## struct

Converts FORTRAN files into Ratfor ( "Rational FORTRAN") files.

## stty

For Set TTY: a utility to set terminal characteristics. Here, it sets characteristics for text in the Shell and Terminal windows. As is, the command shows current settings:

```
localhost# stty
new tty, speed 9600 baud; -tabs crt
pendin decctlq
```

The settings are toggles. A - prefix means "off " or "no." Above,

"-tabs" means replace tabs with spaces,

"crt" means set options for crt output,

"pendin" means

```
Input is pending after a switch from cbreak to
        cooked and will be re-input when a read becomes
        pending or more input arrives (internal state
        bit).
```

and, "decctlq" (for DEC ConTroL-Q) means suspended output can only be restarted with Control-Q.

A Control-S suspends output.

I wouldn't mess with these settings, with one exception: decctlq. This command:

```
localhost# stty -decctlq
```

allows any character typed to unsuspend the display. Which makes more sense to me. There's enough to remember.

# style

Allow me a personal note here.

I once created a program called "Doug Clapp's Word Tools." At the time, I'd never used UNIX; I knew absolutely nothing about UNIX.

When the product was released, I often heard comments such as "Word Tools. It's similar to Writer's Workbench, right?"

I'd heard of something called "Writer's Workbench," but I'd never used it, never seen it.

I have now. Writer's Workbench is a suite of programs to check and improve writing. The programs were created by Lorinda Cherry and include diction and style. Ms. Cherry is also the author of bc, dc, eqn, and bwk. (She probably has kids named Bbby, Jdy, and Sm.)

The portion of Writer's Workbench at hand is style. This is a great, great program—but then I'm biased: I love this kind of thing!

One way to use style is from the Shell:

```
localhost# style UNIX.History
  UNIX.History
readability grades:
        (Kincaid)  7.4  (auto)  6.7  (Coleman-Liau)  9.2  (Flesch)  8.6
  (63.9)
sentence info:
        no. sent 74 no. wds 918
        av sent leng 12.4 av word leng 4.66
        no. questions 0 no. imperatives 1
        no. nonfunc wds 560  61.0%   av leng 5.88
        short sent (<7) 23% (17) long sent (>22)  11% (8)
        longest sent 38 wds at sent 45; shortest sent 2 wds at sent 44
sentence types:
        simple  68% (50) complex  11% (8)
        compound  15% (11) compound-complex   7% (5)
word usage:
        verb types as % of total verbs
        tobe  36% (44) aux  12% (15) inf   8% (10)
        passives as % of non-inf verbs  12% (13)
        types as % of total
```

```
prep 9.7% (89) conj 3.8% (35) adv 4.6% (42)
noun 29.3% (269) adj 16.7% (153) pron 5.3% (49)
nominalizations   1 % (5)
```
sentence beginnings:
```
subject opener: noun (19) pron (7) pos (0) adj (9) art (17) tot  70%
prep   8% (6) adv   8% (6)
verb   1% (1)  sub_conj   3% (2) conj   7% (5)
expletives   3% (2)
```

To a writer, this information is priceless. Let's see...grade level could be lower (in general, the lower the reading level, the better). Sentence length is okay. Sentence types also looks good—simple sentences are easier to read, this sentence notwithstanding. It goes on. Wonderful utility; thank you, Ms. Cherry!

If you use Edit as a word processor, you can create a custom User menu that includes style and other writing utilities. See the Edit chapter for details.

## tail

Use tail to see the last few lines in a file.

```
localhost# tail -5 temp
Esc >   Move to end of  text
Control-N       Move down one line
Control-P       Move up one line
Esc-N   Move down one page
Esc-P   Move up one page
```

prints the last five lines in the file "temp."

## touch

One of the great utility names. Touch attempts to set the modified date of a file. If the file doesn't exist, touch creates a new file (unless told not to, by the -c option). So touch can be used to tickle a file to life.

```
localhost# touch junk
```

creates a new file named junk.

## tr

For "TRanslate." A compact, powerful, search-and-replace command. Input comes from standard input; output goes to standard output—so you'll most often use tr with pipes or redirection. Syntax:

```
tr <from> <to>
```

where <from> are the existing characters and <to> is the substitution you wish to make. You can use octal representations for "invisible characters" if you take care to place them in quotes.

```
Character               Octal
Backspace               10
Tab                     11
Linefeed (Newline)      12
Formfeed                14
Carriage Return         15
```

So converting all newlines in a file to carriage returns could be done like this:

```
cat theFile | tr '\012' '\015' > changedFile
```

The input is piped from theFile into tr, where the substitution is done. The output is redirected to changedFile.

To change all lowercase letters to uppercase:

```
localhost# cat someFile | tr '[a-z]' '[A-Z]'
```

Since no output is specified here, the results will be displayed on the screen: the standard output.

## troff

Text formatters have been a UNIX fixture since the early days. Troff (pronounced "tee-roff") is the standard formatter for use with phototypesetters. You type many arcane, hard to remember, text formatting codes into text, and troff translates the codes for the typesetter, which produces formatted documents containing bold-face, indents, headers, and so on.

Laser printers and WYSIWYG word processors have made troff and its siblings, nroff and droff, obsolete, but they're still widely in use. As are black-and-white TVs and character-oriented computer displays.

## true

Used when writing Shell scripts. Like false, true is nice to have around.

## tsort

A variation on the sort command. This performs a topological sort of pairs of entries.

## tty
## ttys

The discussion of tty and ttys grew so lengthy that it became a chapter: Terminal and Shell.

## ul

Interesting. The abbreviation is for "UnderLine." This command reads files and converts underlines into something more acceptable on your terminal. The basic use is:

```
ul filename
```

but options are available, not surprisingly.

## umount

The UNIX equivalent to the Unmount command in The Workspace Manager. The result is the same: The device, and all its directories, are unmounted—removed and forgotten. In the Shell, though, the options go on and on:

```
/etc/umount [ -t type ] [ -h host ]
/etc/umount -a[v]
/etc/umount [ -v ] fsname | dir
```

The options are interesting, but it's doubtful you'll use this command from the Shell.

## unexpand

Converts spaces to tabs. Its partner, expand, converts tabs to spaces.

## uniq

Finds repeated lines in a file. The repeated lines must be adjacent. Without options, uniq removes the second and subsequent repeated lines.

## units

A conversion program to convert between units of measurement.

## update

A command that calls another command, sync, every 30 seconds. The sync command makes sure the file system is updated. Once a file system is "sync'ed," the contents can be recovered if a crash occurs. The command isn't employed by users.

## users

Shows who's currently logged in. You can get this information with other commands. This is the basic version.

```
localhost# users
root
localhost#
```

## utmp

A file with information about who's currently using the system. If you're on a network, try:

```
localhost# cat /etc/utmp
```

# uucp
# uucp/
# uudecode
# uuencode
# uulog
# uuname
# uupoll
# uuq
# uusend
# uusnap
# uux

The "uu's." These are important commands. Know them well if your cube is connected to Internet, or otherwise connected to remote computers.

In general, the commands deal with copying files to remote systems, or directly using remote systems. Some, like uuname, which shows remote systems that your cube knows about, are straightforward. Others, like uux, which executes commands on remote systems, allow for wonderfully sophisticated computing events. The linchpin is uucp, for UNIX-to-UNIX copy. The UNIX manual pages, and the Further Reading appendix, can get you going. Here, let's just say that reading is one thing, using another. If you're connected to a remote system, try your hand at these commands. They have great utility.

# vipw

Used to edit password files.

# vm_stat

For a real-time look at how virtual memory works:

```
localhost# vm_stat
Mach Virtual Memory Statistics: (page size of 8192 bytes)
Pages free:                        35.
Pages active:                    1119.
Pages inactive:                   632.
```

```
Pages wired down:                    164.
"Translation faults":              40439.
Pages copy-on-write:               11976.
Pages zero filled:                  8304.
Pages reactivated:                 13653.
Pageins:                            2865.
Pageouts:                           1728.
Object cache: 2705 hits of 3292 lookups (82% hit rate)
```

What can we glean from this without delving into technical tomes on the design of the UNIX operating system? This, at least: The cube's speed is intimately tied to caching, in RAM, of objects. NeXT scientists, we can bet, spend much time trying to raise the cache "hit rate."

## vmmprint

To print virtual memory statistics. Not for mere users. Also allows for statistics on particular processes (the -p option).

```
localhost# vmmprint
Usage:  vmmprint [-a<hex. address>] [-n<map name>] [-p<pid>]
```

## vmoprint

Gives a detailed, lengthy (very lengthy) display of virtual memory object use. Again, not a command you need, except as a curiosity. Here's just a drib of the output:

```
localhost# vmoprint
Obj 0x40773f0: size=0x2000000, in=152, ref=162,
pager=(269043072,0x0), shadow=(0x0)+0x0
Obj 0x10008000: size=0x20000, in=16, ref=16, pager=(0,0x0),
shadow=(0x0)+0x0
Obj 0x10009490: size=0x2000, in=4, ref=1, pager=(0,0x0),
shadow=(0x0)+0x0
Obj 0x1000f970: size=0x0, in=0, ref=1, pager=(268499248,0x0)
copy=0x1000fba0
```

## w

The all-time terse UNIX command, this one tells you who's on the network, and what they're up to:

```
localhost# w
```

```
12:58am  up  3:58,  1 user,  load average: 0.79, 0.36, 0.34
User      tty       login@ idle   JCPU   PCPU  what
root      ttyp1     12:44am               39      1  w
```

## wall

Derived from "Write to ALL," this command sends a message to all users on the network.

## wfcomp

Creates files of word frequencies. Handy, if you're into low-level word analysis. From the manual:

```
WFCOMP(1)          UNIX Programmer's Manual
WFCOMP(1)
NAME
       wfcomp - word frequency table compiler
SYNOPSIS
       wfcomp [ file ] name
DESCRIPTION
       Wfcomp reads word frequency data of the form
              word frequency
              .br
              ...
from file or from the standard input, and generates:
  (1) a C file called name.c containing a word frequency
  table declaration;
  (2) a .wf data file, containing the same data suitable for
  loading by readWFTable().
EXAMPLE
  wfcomp histogram AmericanEnglish
  creates a file called AmericanEnglish.c containing a
  WFTable structure called AmericanEnglish, and a data file
  called AmericanEnglish.wf.
```

## who

A version of the whoami command.

```
localhost# who
```

```
root      ttyp1   Aug 18 16:00    (localhost)
localhost# whoami
root
```

## whoami

Requires no explanation. Just an example:

```
localhost# whoami
root
localhost# whoareyou
whoareyou: Command not found.
```

## whereis

Used to locate source files, binary files, or UNIX manual entries:

```
localhost# whereis whereis
whereis: /usr/ucb/whereis /usr/man/man1/whereis.1
localhost# whereis mach
mach: /usr/include/mach.h
```

## xargs

A complex, many-optioned command used to create argument lists, then execute a specific command one or more times.

## xget
## xsend

These two commands implement an encrypted means to send "secret mail." Also see "enroll," which needs to be called first. Enroll asks you for a password; from then on xsend sends protected mail.

## yacc

A compiler compiler. The name comes from "Yet Another Compiler Compiler." The "Yet Another" prefix is a running UNIX joke: an acknowledgment of the many versions of many types of utilities.

Yacc has stood the test of time, though. Briefly, you give yacc rules as input, and yacc creates a compiler for the new language. Objective-C, during its inception, was created using yacc.

# ypcat
# ypmatch
# yppasswd
# ypwhich

These are NFS "Yellow Pages" commands. By default, the cube doesn't use Yellow Pages, although the Yellow Pages services are available.

# Appendix E

# Files in the NeXT 1.0 Software Release

This appendix contains the complete listing of files in the NeXT 1.0 Software Release.

Why was this appendix included? Here's a story:

A few years back, my wife and I wanted to buy a car. A small car, an inexpensive car, but a *new* car. So we began watching car commercials on TV. (That *is* the way it's done, right?)

Well, we saw lots of things. We saw cute commercials, and commercials with "high production values." We saw accomplished actors performing engaging skits. Once in a while, we even saw things that were probably cars—but they were usually speeding by, or speeding off, often with appropriate whizzy effects.

But I just wanted to look at some *cars,* you know? What do they look like? Show me a picture of the car's dashboard, will ya!?

I wanted to see *The Thing Itself.*

With The NeXT Computer, a good bit of The Thing Itself are the files included with the cube.

So here they are. Get ready.

There's no explanation here of "what's what." But if you've read to here (and bless you if you have!), you should be able to wade through this listing and get the general idea. That's the most to hope for. Nobody understands *all the files* contained herein.

And here it is:

```
.
./lost+found
./mach
./.places
./.hidden
./.login
./.cshrc
./.profile
./.NeXT
./.NeXT/.dock
./.NeXT/.places
./.NeXT/.NeXTdefaults.D
./.NeXT/.NeXTdefaults.L
./.NeXT/.NeXTtrash
./.NeXT/.NeXTtrash/.places
./.NeXT/targets
./.NeXT/targets/targetFile
./.NeXT/targets/Targets1.0
./.NeXT/targets/.places
./etc
./dev
./tmp
./Net
./usr
./usr/template
./usr/template/user
./usr/template/user/Apps
./usr/template/user/Apps/README.wn
./usr/template/user/Apps/.places
./usr/template/user/.NeXT
./usr/template/user/.NeXT/.dock
./usr/template/user/.NeXT/.places
./usr/template/user/Mailboxes
./usr/template/user/Mailboxes/.places
./usr/template/user/.cshrc
./usr/template/user/.mailrc
./usr/template/user/.logout
./usr/template/user/.plan
./usr/template/user/.profile
./usr/template/user/.login
./usr/template/user/.places
./usr/template/client
./usr/template/client/tmp
./usr/template/client/tmp/.places
./usr/template/client/preserve
./usr/template/client/preserve/.places
./usr/template/client/Net
./usr/template/client/Net/.places
./usr/template/client/adm
./usr/template/client/adm/daily
./usr/template/client/adm/monthly
./usr/template/client/adm/weekly
./usr/template/client/adm/daily.log
./usr/template/client/adm/weekly.log
./usr/template/client/adm/monthly.log
./usr/template/client/adm/lpd-errs
./usr/template/client/adm/messages
./usr/template/client/adm/msgbuf
./usr/template/client/adm/wtmp
./usr/template/client/adm/lastlog
./usr/template/client/adm/aculog
./usr/template/client/adm/.places
./usr/template/client/dev
./usr/template/client/dev/MAKEDEV
./usr/template/client/dev/MAKEDEV.local
./usr/template/client/dev/.places
./usr/template/client/etc
./usr/template/client/etc/fstab.client
./usr/template/client/etc/fstab.od
./usr/template/client/etc/fstab.sd330
./usr/template/client/etc/fstab.sd660
./usr/template/client/etc/rc
./usr/template/client/etc/rc.boot
./usr/template/client/etc/rc.swap
./usr/template/client/etc/crontab
./usr/template/client/etc/exports.example
./usr/template/client/etc/group
./usr/template/client/etc/hostconfig
./usr/template/client/etc/hosts
./usr/template/client/etc/networks
./usr/template/client/etc/passwd
./usr/template/client/etc/protocols
./usr/template/client/etc/printcap
./usr/template/client/etc/rc.local
./usr/template/client/etc/rpc
./usr/template/client/etc/services
./usr/template/client/etc/shells
./usr/template/client/etc/termcap
./usr/template/client/etc/ttys
./usr/template/client/etc/dumpdates
./usr/template/client/etc/find.codes
./usr/template/client/etc/hosts.equiv
./usr/template/client/etc/hosts.lpd
./usr/template/client/etc/motd
./usr/template/client/etc/netgroup
./usr/template/client/etc/rmtab
./usr/template/client/etc/syslog.pid
./usr/template/client/etc/utmp
./usr/template/client/etc/xtab
./usr/template/client/etc/mtab
./usr/template/client/etc/yp
./usr/template/client/etc/yp/makedbm
```

```
./usr/template/client/etc/yp/revnetgroup
./usr/template/client/etc/yp/stdhosts
./usr/template/client/etc/yp/yppoll
./usr/template/client/etc/yp/yppush
./usr/template/client/etc/yp/ypset
./usr/template/client/etc/yp/ypxfr
./usr/template/client/etc/yp/ypinit
./usr/template/client/etc/yp/ypxfr_1perday
./usr/template/client/etc/yp/ypxfr_2perday
./usr/template/client/etc/yp/ypxfr_1perhour
./usr/template/client/etc/yp/Makefile
./usr/template/client/etc/yp/.places
./usr/template/client/etc/bootptab
./usr/template/client/etc/BLD.od
./usr/template/client/etc/BLD.sd330
./usr/template/client/etc/BLD.sd660
./usr/template/client/etc/disktab
./usr/template/client/etc/ftpusers
./usr/template/client/etc/gettytab
./usr/template/client/etc/localgateways
./usr/template/client/etc/localhost
./usr/template/client/etc/localnetworks
./usr/template/client/etc/inetd.conf
./usr/template/client/etc/nulib
./usr/template/client/etc/nulib/nu1.sh
./usr/template/client/etc/nulib/nu2.sh
./usr/template/client/etc/nulib/nu3.sh
./usr/template/client/etc/nulib/nu4.sh
./usr/template/client/etc/nulib/.places
./usr/template/client/etc/nu.cf
./usr/template/client/etc/syslog.conf
./usr/template/client/etc/zoneinfo
./usr/template/client/etc/zoneinfo/Japan
./usr/template/client/etc/zoneinfo/Singapore
./usr/template/client/etc/zoneinfo/Australia
./usr/template/client/etc/zoneinfo/Australia/Tasmania
./usr/template/client/etc/zoneinfo/Australia/Queensland
./usr/template/client/etc/zoneinfo/Australia/North
./usr/template/client/etc/zoneinfo/Australia/West
./usr/template/client/etc/zoneinfo/Australia/South
./usr/template/client/etc/zoneinfo/Australia/Victoria
./usr/template/client/etc/zoneinfo/Australia/NSW
./usr/template/client/etc/zoneinfo/Australia/.places
./usr/template/client/etc/zoneinfo/NZ
./usr/template/client/etc/zoneinfo/GB-Eire
./usr/template/client/etc/zoneinfo/WET
./usr/template/client/etc/zoneinfo/Iceland
./usr/template/client/etc/zoneinfo/MET
./usr/template/client/etc/zoneinfo/Poland
./usr/template/client/etc/zoneinfo/EET
./usr/template/client/etc/zoneinfo/Turkey

./usr/template/client/etc/zoneinfo/W-SU
./usr/template/client/etc/zoneinfo/GMT
./usr/template/client/etc/zoneinfo/GMT-12
./usr/template/client/etc/zoneinfo/GMT-11
./usr/template/client/etc/zoneinfo/GMT-10
./usr/template/client/etc/zoneinfo/GMT-9
./usr/template/client/etc/zoneinfo/GMT-8
./usr/template/client/etc/zoneinfo/GMT-7
./usr/template/client/etc/zoneinfo/GMT-6
./usr/template/client/etc/zoneinfo/GMT-5
./usr/template/client/etc/zoneinfo/GMT-4
./usr/template/client/etc/zoneinfo/GMT-3
./usr/template/client/etc/zoneinfo/GMT-2
./usr/template/client/etc/zoneinfo/GMT-1
./usr/template/client/etc/zoneinfo/GMT+1
./usr/template/client/etc/zoneinfo/GMT+2
./usr/template/client/etc/zoneinfo/GMT+3
./usr/template/client/etc/zoneinfo/GMT+4
./usr/template/client/etc/zoneinfo/GMT+5
./usr/template/client/etc/zoneinfo/GMT+6
./usr/template/client/etc/zoneinfo/GMT+7
./usr/template/client/etc/zoneinfo/GMT+8
./usr/template/client/etc/zoneinfo/GMT+9
./usr/template/client/etc/zoneinfo/GMT+10
./usr/template/client/etc/zoneinfo/GMT+11
./usr/template/client/etc/zoneinfo/GMT+12
./usr/template/client/etc/zoneinfo/GMT+13
./usr/template/client/etc/zoneinfo/US
./usr/template/client/etc/zoneinfo/US/Eastern
./usr/template/client/etc/zoneinfo/US/Central
./usr/template/client/etc/zoneinfo/US/Mountain
./usr/template/client/etc/zoneinfo/US/Pacific
./usr/template/client/etc/zoneinfo/US/Yukon
./usr/template/client/etc/zoneinfo/US/East-Indiana
./usr/template/client/etc/zoneinfo/US/Arizona
./usr/template/client/etc/zoneinfo/US/Hawaii
./usr/template/client/etc/zoneinfo/US/Pacific-New
./usr/template/client/etc/zoneinfo/US/.places
./usr/template/client/etc/zoneinfo/Canada
./usr/template/client/etc/zoneinfo/Canada/Newfoundland
./usr/template/client/etc/zoneinfo/Canada/Atlantic
./usr/template/client/etc/zoneinfo/Canada/Eastern
./usr/template/client/etc/zoneinfo/Canada/Central
./usr/template/client/etc/zoneinfo/Canada/East-Saskatchewan
./usr/template/client/etc/zoneinfo/Canada/Mountain
./usr/template/client/etc/zoneinfo/Canada/Pacific
./usr/template/client/etc/zoneinfo/Canada/Yukon
./usr/template/client/etc/zoneinfo/Canada/.places
./usr/template/client/etc/zoneinfo/SystemV
./usr/template/client/etc/zoneinfo/SystemV/AST4ADT
./usr/template/client/etc/zoneinfo/SystemV/EST5EDT
```

```
./usr/template/client/etc/zoneinfo/SystemV/CST6CDT
./usr/template/client/etc/zoneinfo/SystemV/MST7MDT
./usr/template/client/etc/zoneinfo/SystemV/PST8PDT
./usr/template/client/etc/zoneinfo/SystemV/YST9YDT
./usr/template/client/etc/zoneinfo/SystemV/AST4
./usr/template/client/etc/zoneinfo/SystemV/EST5
./usr/template/client/etc/zoneinfo/SystemV/CST6
./usr/template/client/etc/zoneinfo/SystemV/MST7
./usr/template/client/etc/zoneinfo/SystemV/PST8
./usr/template/client/etc/zoneinfo/SystemV/YST9
./usr/template/client/etc/zoneinfo/SystemV/HST10
./usr/template/client/etc/zoneinfo/SystemV/.places
./usr/template/client/etc/zoneinfo/CET
./usr/template/client/etc/zoneinfo/UTC
./usr/template/client/etc/zoneinfo/UCT
./usr/template/client/etc/zoneinfo/Universal
./usr/template/client/etc/zoneinfo/Greenwich
./usr/template/client/etc/zoneinfo/EST5EDT
./usr/template/client/etc/zoneinfo/CST6CDT
./usr/template/client/etc/zoneinfo/MST7MDT
./usr/template/client/etc/zoneinfo/PST8PDT
./usr/template/client/etc/zoneinfo/EST
./usr/template/client/etc/zoneinfo/MST
./usr/template/client/etc/zoneinfo/HST
./usr/template/client/etc/zoneinfo/localtime
./usr/template/client/etc/zoneinfo/.places
./usr/template/client/etc/catman
./usr/template/client/etc/chown
./usr/template/client/etc/disk
./usr/template/client/etc/dump
./usr/template/client/etc/rdump
./usr/template/client/etc/edquota
./usr/template/client/etc/fsirand
./usr/template/client/etc/halt
./usr/template/client/etc/ifconfig
./usr/template/client/etc/inetd
./usr/template/client/etc/init
./usr/template/client/etc/mkfs
./usr/template/client/etc/mkhosts
./usr/template/client/etc/mklost+found
./usr/template/client/etc/mknod
./usr/template/client/etc/mkpasswd
./usr/template/client/etc/mkplaces
./usr/template/client/etc/mkproto
./usr/template/client/etc/mount
./usr/template/client/etc/newclient
./usr/template/client/etc/newfs
./usr/template/client/etc/nu
./usr/template/client/etc/ping
./usr/template/client/etc/quot
./usr/template/client/etc/quotacheck
./usr/template/client/etc/quotaon
./usr/template/client/etc/reboot
./usr/template/client/etc/renice
./usr/template/client/etc/repquota
./usr/template/client/etc/restore
./usr/template/client/etc/rrestore
./usr/template/client/etc/rexecd
./usr/template/client/etc/rlogind
./usr/template/client/etc/rmt
./usr/template/client/etc/route
./usr/template/client/etc/rshd
./usr/template/client/etc/rwhod
./usr/template/client/etc/shutdown
./usr/template/client/etc/umount
./usr/template/client/etc/update
./usr/template/client/etc/vipw
./usr/template/client/etc/Mail.rc
./usr/template/client/etc/sendmail
./usr/template/client/etc/sendmail/sendmail.mailhost.cf
./usr/template/client/etc/sendmail/sendmail.subsidiary.cf
./usr/template/client/etc/sendmail/aliases
./usr/template/client/etc/sendmail/sendmail.sharedsubsidiary.cf
./usr/template/client/etc/sendmail/sendmail.cf
./usr/template/client/etc/sendmail/aliases.dir
./usr/template/client/etc/sendmail/aliases.pag
./usr/template/client/etc/sendmail/.places
./usr/template/client/etc/map3270
./usr/template/client/etc/remote
./usr/template/client/etc/uucp
./usr/template/client/etc/uucp/UUAIDS
./usr/template/client/etc/uucp/UUAIDS/L-devices
./usr/template/client/etc/uucp/UUAIDS/L-devices.samples
./usr/template/client/etc/uucp/UUAIDS/L-dialcodes
./usr/template/client/etc/uucp/UUAIDS/L-dialcodes.samples
./usr/template/client/etc/uucp/UUAIDS/L.aliases
./usr/template/client/etc/uucp/UUAIDS/L.aliases.samples
./usr/template/client/etc/uucp/UUAIDS/L.cmds
./usr/template/client/etc/uucp/UUAIDS/L.cmds.samples
./usr/template/client/etc/uucp/UUAIDS/L.sys
./usr/template/client/etc/uucp/UUAIDS/L.sys.samples
./usr/template/client/etc/uucp/UUAIDS/READ_ME
./usr/template/client/etc/uucp/UUAIDS/SEQF
./usr/template/client/etc/uucp/UUAIDS/USERFILE
./usr/template/client/etc/uucp/UUAIDS/uu.daily
./usr/template/client/etc/uucp/UUAIDS/uu.daily.seismo
./usr/template/client/etc/uucp/UUAIDS/uu.hourly
./usr/template/client/etc/uucp/UUAIDS/uu.weekly
./usr/template/client/etc/uucp/UUAIDS/uucp.daily
./usr/template/client/etc/uucp/UUAIDS/uucp.day.sh
./usr/template/client/etc/uucp/UUAIDS/uucpsrv.c
./usr/template/client/etc/uucp/UUAIDS/uucpsummary
```

```
./usr/template/client/etc/uucp/UUAIDS/uucpsummary.monthly
./usr/template/client/etc/uucp/UUAIDS/uurate
./usr/template/client/etc/uucp/UUAIDS/uutbl
./usr/template/client/etc/uucp/UUAIDS/uuusage
./usr/template/client/etc/uucp/UUAIDS/.places
./usr/template/client/etc/uucp/USERFILE
./usr/template/client/etc/uucp/L.aliases
./usr/template/client/etc/uucp/L.sys
./usr/template/client/etc/uucp/L.cmds
./usr/template/client/etc/uucp/L-devices
./usr/template/client/etc/uucp/L-dialcodes
./usr/template/client/etc/uucp/uucp.day.sh
./usr/template/client/etc/uucp/.places
./usr/template/client/etc/swaptab
./usr/template/client/etc/nmserver
./usr/template/client/etc/NETMSG_CONFIG
./usr/template/client/etc/bootparams
./usr/template/client/etc/mach_init
./usr/template/client/etc/BLD.swapdisk
./usr/template/client/etc/BLD.sd200app
./usr/template/client/etc/BLD.sd200dev
./usr/template/client/etc/MAKEDEV
./usr/template/client/etc/netinfo
./usr/template/client/etc/netinfo/local.nidb
./usr/template/client/etc/netinfo/local.nidb/collection
./usr/template/client/etc/netinfo/local.nidb/.places
./usr/template/client/etc/netinfo/.places
./usr/template/client/etc/cshrc.std
./usr/template/client/etc/login.std
./usr/template/client/etc/logout.std
./usr/template/client/etc/profile.std
./usr/template/client/etc/kern_loader.conf
./usr/template/client/etc/.places
./usr/template/client/spool
./usr/template/client/spool/lpd
./usr/template/client/spool/lpd/.places
./usr/template/client/spool/np
./usr/template/client/spool/np/.places
./usr/template/client/spool/appkit
./usr/template/client/spool/appkit/.places
./usr/template/client/spool/mail
./usr/template/client/spool/mail/.places
./usr/template/client/spool/mqueue
./usr/template/client/spool/mqueue/syslog
./usr/template/client/spool/mqueue/.places
./usr/template/client/spool/at
./usr/template/client/spool/at/past
./usr/template/client/spool/at/past/.places
./usr/template/client/spool/at/lasttimedone
./usr/template/client/spool/at/.places
./usr/template/client/spool/uucp
./usr/template/client/spool/uucp/CORRUPT
./usr/template/client/spool/uucp/CORRUPT/.places
./usr/template/client/spool/uucp/AUDIT
./usr/template/client/spool/uucp/AUDIT/.places
./usr/template/client/spool/uucp/STST
./usr/template/client/spool/uucp/STST/.places
./usr/template/client/spool/uucp/C.
./usr/template/client/spool/uucp/C./.places
./usr/template/client/spool/uucp/X.
./usr/template/client/spool/uucp/X./.places
./usr/template/client/spool/uucp/TM.
./usr/template/client/spool/uucp/TM./.places
./usr/template/client/spool/uucp/LCK
./usr/template/client/spool/uucp/LCK/.places
./usr/template/client/spool/uucp/STATS
./usr/template/client/spool/uucp/STATS/.places
./usr/template/client/spool/uucp/ERRLOG
./usr/template/client/spool/uucp/D.
./usr/template/client/spool/uucp/D./.places
./usr/template/client/spool/uucp/.places
./usr/template/client/spool/uucppublic
./usr/template/client/spool/uucppublic/.hushlogin
./usr/template/client/spool/uucppublic/.places
./usr/template/client/spool/.places
./usr/template/client/tftpboot
./usr/template/client/tftpboot/private
./usr/template/client/tftpboot/private/tftpboot
./usr/template/client/tftpboot/private/.places
./usr/template/client/tftpboot/.places
./usr/template/client/vm
./usr/template/client/vm/swapfile
./usr/template/client/vm/.places
./usr/template/client/.places
./usr/template/.places
./usr/etc
./usr/etc/ac
./usr/etc/accton
./usr/etc/arp
./usr/etc/autodiskmount
./usr/etc/biod
./usr/etc/bootpd
./usr/etc/builddisk
./usr/etc/catman
./usr/etc/clri
./usr/etc/comsat
./usr/etc/cron
./usr/etc/dcheck
./usr/etc/disk
./usr/etc/dmesg
./usr/etc/dump
./usr/etc/rdump
```

./usr/etc/dumpfs
./usr/etc/edquota
./usr/etc/fingerd
./usr/etc/fsck
./usr/etc/fsirand
./usr/etc/ftpd
./usr/etc/gettable
./usr/etc/getty
./usr/etc/halt
./usr/etc/htable
./usr/etc/icheck
./usr/etc/ifconfig
./usr/etc/inetd
./usr/etc/init
./usr/etc/kgmon
./usr/etc/mkfs
./usr/etc/mkhosts
./usr/etc/mklost+found
./usr/etc/mknod
./usr/etc/mkpasswd
./usr/etc/mkplaces
./usr/etc/mkproto
./usr/etc/mount
./usr/etc/named
./usr/etc/ncheck
./usr/etc/newclient
./usr/etc/newfs
./usr/etc/nfsd
./usr/etc/nppower
./usr/etc/nu
./usr/etc/ping
./usr/etc/portmap
./usr/etc/quot
./usr/etc/quotacheck
./usr/etc/quotaon
./usr/etc/reboot
./usr/etc/renice
./usr/etc/repquota
./usr/etc/restore
./usr/etc/rrestore
./usr/etc/rexecd
./usr/etc/rlogind
./usr/etc/rmt
./usr/etc/route
./usr/etc/routed
./usr/etc/rpc.statd
./usr/etc/rshd
./usr/etc/rwhod
./usr/etc/sa
./usr/etc/scsimodes
./usr/etc/shutdown

./usr/etc/snd_register
./usr/etc/syslogd
./usr/etc/talkd
./usr/etc/ntalkd
./usr/etc/telnetd
./usr/etc/tftpd
./usr/etc/timed
./usr/etc/timedc
./usr/etc/tunefs
./usr/etc/zic
./usr/etc/umount
./usr/etc/update
./usr/etc/vipw
./usr/etc/vmmprint
./usr/etc/vmoprint
./usr/etc/ypbind
./usr/etc/zprint
./usr/etc/mconnect
./usr/etc/mailstats
./usr/etc/uucpd
./usr/etc/autonfsmount
./usr/etc/checkswap
./usr/etc/exportfs
./usr/etc/mach_swapon
./usr/etc/mkfile
./usr/etc/nfsstat
./usr/etc/nmserver
./usr/etc/rexd
./usr/etc/rpc.bootparamd
./usr/etc/rpc.mountd
./usr/etc/rpc.rquotad
./usr/etc/rpc.rstatd
./usr/etc/rpc.rusersd
./usr/etc/rpc.rwalld
./usr/etc/rpc.sprayd
./usr/etc/rpc.yppasswdd
./usr/etc/rpcinfo
./usr/etc/rwall
./usr/etc/mach_init
./usr/etc/showmount
./usr/etc/spray
./usr/etc/yp
./usr/etc/yp/makedbm
./usr/etc/yp/revnetgroup
./usr/etc/yp/stdhosts
./usr/etc/yp/yppoll
./usr/etc/yp/yppush
./usr/etc/yp/ypset
./usr/etc/yp/ypxfr
./usr/etc/yp/.places
./usr/etc/ypserv

```
./usr/etc/MAKEDEV                       ./usr/lib/me/local.me
./usr/etc/nidomain                      ./usr/lib/me/null.me
./usr/etc/nibindd                       ./usr/lib/me/refer.me
./usr/etc/netinfod                      ./usr/lib/me/sh.me
./usr/etc/lookupd                       ./usr/lib/me/tbl.me
./usr/etc/chown                         ./usr/lib/me/thesis.me
./usr/etc/restore0.9                    ./usr/lib/me/revisions
./usr/etc/pbs                           ./usr/lib/me/.places
./usr/etc/kern_loader                   ./usr/lib/tmac
./usr/etc/kl_util                       ./usr/lib/tmac/tmac.e
./usr/etc/lpc                           ./usr/lib/tmac/tmac.a
./usr/etc/pac                           ./usr/lib/tmac/tmac.an
./usr/etc/.places                       ./usr/lib/tmac/tmac.an.new
./usr/shlib                             ./usr/lib/tmac/tmac.an6n
./usr/shlib/libsys_s.B.shlib            ./usr/lib/tmac/tmac.an6t
./usr/shlib/libdsp_s.A.shlib            ./usr/lib/tmac/tmac.ayday
./usr/shlib/libNeXT_s.C.shlib           ./usr/lib/tmac/tmac.cp
./usr/shlib/.places                     ./usr/lib/tmac/tmac.imagen
./usr/lib                               ./usr/lib/tmac/tmac.os
./usr/lib/NextStep                      ./usr/lib/tmac/tmac.r
./usr/lib/NextStep/NSWSd                ./usr/lib/tmac/tmac.s
./usr/lib/NextStep/printPackage1.0.ps   ./usr/lib/tmac/tmac.scover
./usr/lib/NextStep/windowPackage1.0.ps  ./usr/lib/tmac/tmac.sdisp
./usr/lib/NextStep/AlertPanel.nib       ./usr/lib/tmac/tmac.skeep
./usr/lib/NextStep/FontPanel.nib        ./usr/lib/tmac/tmac.srefs
./usr/lib/NextStep/PageLayout.nib       ./usr/lib/tmac/tmac.vcat
./usr/lib/NextStep/PrintPanel.nib       ./usr/lib/tmac/tmac.vgrind
./usr/lib/NextStep/SavePanel.nib        ./usr/lib/tmac/tmac.bib
./usr/lib/NextStep/ChoosePrinter.nib    ./usr/lib/tmac/tmac.syb
./usr/lib/NextStep/loginwindow          ./usr/lib/tmac/tmac.Franz
./usr/lib/NextStep/nextlogin.tiff       ./usr/lib/tmac/.places
./usr/lib/NextStep/WindowServer         ./usr/lib/ms
./usr/lib/NextStep/PS.VM                ./usr/lib/ms/README
./usr/lib/NextStep/Workspace            ./usr/lib/ms/end.awk
./usr/lib/NextStep/.places              ./usr/lib/ms/endnote
./usr/lib/crontab                       ./usr/lib/ms/s.acc
./usr/lib/Mail.rc                       ./usr/lib/ms/s.cov
./usr/lib/bootimages                    ./usr/lib/ms/s.eqn
./usr/lib/bootimages/systemfiles.eps    ./usr/lib/ms/s.ref
./usr/lib/bootimages/fsck.eps           ./usr/lib/ms/s.tbl
./usr/lib/bootimages/nfsmount.eps       ./usr/lib/ms/s.ths
./usr/lib/bootimages/ifconfig.eps       ./usr/lib/ms/s.toc
./usr/lib/bootimages/.places            ./usr/lib/ms/swapacc
./usr/lib/me                            ./usr/lib/ms/.places
./usr/lib/me/acm.me                     ./usr/lib/tabset
./usr/lib/me/chars.me                   ./usr/lib/tabset/3101
./usr/lib/me/deltext.me                 ./usr/lib/tabset/aa
./usr/lib/me/eqn.me                     ./usr/lib/tabset/aed512
./usr/lib/me/float.me                   ./usr/lib/tabset/beehive
./usr/lib/me/footnote.me                ./usr/lib/tabset/diablo
./usr/lib/me/index.me                   ./usr/lib/tabset/dtc382
```

```
./usr/lib/tabset/ibm3101                    ./usr/lib/term/tabqume
./usr/lib/tabset/std                        ./usr/lib/term/tabqume12
./usr/lib/tabset/stdcrt                     ./usr/lib/term/tabxerox
./usr/lib/tabset/tandem653                  ./usr/lib/term/tabxerox12
./usr/lib/tabset/teleray                    ./usr/lib/term/tabx-ecs
./usr/lib/tabset/vt100                      ./usr/lib/term/tabx-ecs12
./usr/lib/tabset/wyse-adds                  ./usr/lib/term/tabtn300
./usr/lib/tabset/xerox1720                  ./usr/lib/term/tabcrt
./usr/lib/tabset/xerox1730                  ./usr/lib/term/tab300s
./usr/lib/tabset/xerox1730-lm               ./usr/lib/term/tab300s-12
./usr/lib/tabset/zenith29                   ./usr/lib/term/tabdtc
./usr/lib/tabset/.places                    ./usr/lib/term/tabdtc12
./usr/lib/gprof.flat                        ./usr/lib/term/tabipsi
./usr/lib/gprof.callg                       ./usr/lib/term/tabipsi12
./usr/lib/diffh                             ./usr/lib/term/README
./usr/lib/Mail.help                         ./usr/lib/term/.places
./usr/lib/Mail.tildehelp                    ./usr/lib/merge
./usr/lib/more.help                         ./usr/lib/spell
./usr/lib/sendmail.hf                       ./usr/lib/struct
./usr/lib/sendmail                          ./usr/lib/struct/structure
./usr/lib/vfontedpr                         ./usr/lib/struct/beautify
./usr/lib/vgrindefs                         ./usr/lib/struct/.places
./usr/lib/atrun                             ./usr/lib/units
./usr/lib/calendar                          ./usr/lib/uucp
./usr/lib/style1                            ./usr/lib/uucp/uucico
./usr/lib/style2                            ./usr/lib/uucp/uuclean
./usr/lib/style3                            ./usr/lib/uucp/uuxqt
./usr/lib/dprog                             ./usr/lib/uucp/.places
./usr/lib/dict.d                            ./usr/lib/emacs
./usr/lib/explain.d                         ./usr/lib/emacs/etc
./usr/lib/diff3                             ./usr/lib/emacs/etc/ctags
./usr/lib/term                              ./usr/lib/emacs/etc/cvtmail
./usr/lib/term/tab37                        ./usr/lib/emacs/etc/digest-doc
./usr/lib/term/tablpr                       ./usr/lib/emacs/etc/emacsclient
./usr/lib/term/tab300                       ./usr/lib/emacs/etc/env
./usr/lib/term/tab300-12                    ./usr/lib/emacs/etc/fakemail
./usr/lib/term/tab302                       ./usr/lib/emacs/etc/loadst
./usr/lib/term/tab302-12                    ./usr/lib/emacs/etc/make-docfile
./usr/lib/term/tab382                       ./usr/lib/emacs/etc/movemail
./usr/lib/term/tab382-12                    ./usr/lib/emacs/etc/server
./usr/lib/term/tab450                       ./usr/lib/emacs/etc/sorted-doc
./usr/lib/term/tab450-12                    ./usr/lib/emacs/etc/test-distrib
./usr/lib/term/tab833                       ./usr/lib/emacs/etc/yow
./usr/lib/term/tab833-12                    ./usr/lib/emacs/etc/DOC-18.53.11
./usr/lib/term/tabepson                     ./usr/lib/emacs/etc/.places
./usr/lib/term/tabitoh                      ./usr/lib/emacs/info
./usr/lib/term/tabitoh12                    ./usr/lib/emacs/info/COPYING
./usr/lib/term/tabnec                       ./usr/lib/emacs/info/dir
./usr/lib/term/tabnec12                     ./usr/lib/emacs/info/emacs
./usr/lib/term/tabnec-t                     ./usr/lib/emacs/info/emacs-1
./usr/lib/term/tabnec25-t                   ./usr/lib/emacs/info/emacs-10
```

```
./usr/lib/emacs/info/emacs-11
./usr/lib/emacs/info/emacs-12
./usr/lib/emacs/info/emacs-13
./usr/lib/emacs/info/emacs-2
./usr/lib/emacs/info/emacs-3
./usr/lib/emacs/info/emacs-4
./usr/lib/emacs/info/emacs-5
./usr/lib/emacs/info/emacs-6
./usr/lib/emacs/info/emacs-7
./usr/lib/emacs/info/emacs-8
./usr/lib/emacs/info/emacs-9
./usr/lib/emacs/info/gcc
./usr/lib/emacs/info/gcc.info-1
./usr/lib/emacs/info/gcc.info-2
./usr/lib/emacs/info/gcc.info-3
./usr/lib/emacs/info/gcc.info-4
./usr/lib/emacs/info/gcc.info-5
./usr/lib/emacs/info/gcc.info-6
./usr/lib/emacs/info/gcc.info-7
./usr/lib/emacs/info/gcc.info-8
./usr/lib/emacs/info/gdb
./usr/lib/emacs/info/gdb-1
./usr/lib/emacs/info/gdb-2
./usr/lib/emacs/info/gdb-3
./usr/lib/emacs/info/gnus
./usr/lib/emacs/info/gnus-1
./usr/lib/emacs/info/gnus-2
./usr/lib/emacs/info/gnus-3
./usr/lib/emacs/info/info
./usr/lib/emacs/info/termcap
./usr/lib/emacs/info/termcap-1
./usr/lib/emacs/info/termcap-2
./usr/lib/emacs/info/termcap-3
./usr/lib/emacs/info/texinfo
./usr/lib/emacs/info/texinfo-1
./usr/lib/emacs/info/texinfo-2
./usr/lib/emacs/info/texinfo-3
./usr/lib/emacs/info/texinfo-4
./usr/lib/emacs/info/vip
./usr/lib/emacs/info/.places
./usr/lib/emacs/lisp
./usr/lib/emacs/lisp/COPYING
./usr/lib/emacs/lisp/ChangeLog
./usr/lib/emacs/lisp/abbrev.el
./usr/lib/emacs/lisp/abbrevlist.el
./usr/lib/emacs/lisp/ada.el
./usr/lib/emacs/lisp/add-log.el
./usr/lib/emacs/lisp/autoinsert.el
./usr/lib/emacs/lisp/backquote.el
./usr/lib/emacs/lisp/bibtex.el
./usr/lib/emacs/lisp/blackbox.el
./usr/lib/emacs/lisp/buff-menu.el
./usr/lib/emacs/lisp/bytecomp.el
./usr/lib/emacs/lisp/c-fill.el
./usr/lib/emacs/lisp/c-mode.el
./usr/lib/emacs/lisp/cal.el
./usr/lib/emacs/lisp/chistory.el
./usr/lib/emacs/lisp/cl-indent.el
./usr/lib/emacs/lisp/cl.el
./usr/lib/emacs/lisp/cmacexp.el
./usr/lib/emacs/lisp/compare-w.el
./usr/lib/emacs/lisp/compile.el
./usr/lib/emacs/lisp/dabbrev.el
./usr/lib/emacs/lisp/dbx.el
./usr/lib/emacs/lisp/debug.el
./usr/lib/emacs/lisp/dired.el
./usr/lib/emacs/lisp/disass.el
./usr/lib/emacs/lisp/dissociate.el
./usr/lib/emacs/lisp/doctex.el
./usr/lib/emacs/lisp/doctor.el
./usr/lib/emacs/lisp/ebuff-menu.el
./usr/lib/emacs/lisp/echistory.el
./usr/lib/emacs/lisp/edt-doc.el
./usr/lib/emacs/lisp/edt.el
./usr/lib/emacs/lisp/ehelp.el
./usr/lib/emacs/lisp/electric.el
./usr/lib/emacs/lisp/emacsbug.el
./usr/lib/emacs/lisp/files.el
./usr/lib/emacs/lisp/fill.el
./usr/lib/emacs/lisp/flame.el
./usr/lib/emacs/lisp/float.el
./usr/lib/emacs/lisp/fortran.el
./usr/lib/emacs/lisp/ftp.el
./usr/lib/emacs/lisp/gdb.el
./usr/lib/emacs/lisp/gosmacs.el
./usr/lib/emacs/lisp/grow-vers.el
./usr/lib/emacs/lisp/hanoi.el
./usr/lib/emacs/lisp/help.el
./usr/lib/emacs/lisp/helper.el
./usr/lib/emacs/lisp/hideif.el
./usr/lib/emacs/lisp/icon.el
./usr/lib/emacs/lisp/inc-vers.el
./usr/lib/emacs/lisp/indent.el
./usr/lib/emacs/lisp/info.el
./usr/lib/emacs/lisp/informat.el
./usr/lib/emacs/lisp/isearch.el
./usr/lib/emacs/lisp/kermit.el
./usr/lib/emacs/lisp/keypad.el
./usr/lib/emacs/lisp/ledit.el
./usr/lib/emacs/lisp/life.el
./usr/lib/emacs/lisp/lisp-mode.el
./usr/lib/emacs/lisp/lisp.el
```

./usr/lib/emacs/lisp/loaddefs.el

./usr/lib/emacs/lisp/loadup.el

./usr/lib/emacs/lisp/lpr.el

./usr/lib/emacs/lisp/macros.el

./usr/lib/emacs/lisp/mail-utils.el

./usr/lib/emacs/lisp/mailalias.el

./usr/lib/emacs/lisp/mailpost.el

./usr/lib/emacs/lisp/makesum.el

./usr/lib/emacs/lisp/man.el

./usr/lib/emacs/lisp/medit.el

./usr/lib/emacs/lisp/meese.el

./usr/lib/emacs/lisp/mh-e.el

./usr/lib/emacs/lisp/mim-mode.el

./usr/lib/emacs/lisp/mim-syntax.el

./usr/lib/emacs/lisp/modula2.el

./usr/lib/emacs/lisp/mlconvert.el

./usr/lib/emacs/lisp/mlsupport.el

./usr/lib/emacs/lisp/novice.el

./usr/lib/emacs/lisp/nroff-mode.el

./usr/lib/emacs/lisp/options.el

./usr/lib/emacs/lisp/outline.el

./usr/lib/emacs/lisp/page.el

./usr/lib/emacs/lisp/paragraphs.el

./usr/lib/emacs/lisp/paths.el

./usr/lib/emacs/lisp/picture.el

./usr/lib/emacs/lisp/prolog.el

./usr/lib/emacs/lisp/rect.el

./usr/lib/emacs/lisp/register.el

./usr/lib/emacs/lisp/replace.el

./usr/lib/emacs/lisp/rfc822.el

./usr/lib/emacs/lisp/rmail.el

./usr/lib/emacs/lisp/rmailedit.el

./usr/lib/emacs/lisp/rmailkwd.el

./usr/lib/emacs/lisp/rmailmsc.el

./usr/lib/emacs/lisp/rmailout.el

./usr/lib/emacs/lisp/rmailsum.el

./usr/lib/emacs/lisp/rnews.el

./usr/lib/emacs/lisp/rnewspost.el

./usr/lib/emacs/lisp/saveconf.el

./usr/lib/emacs/lisp/sort.el

./usr/lib/emacs/lisp/scheme.el

./usr/lib/emacs/lisp/scribe.el

./usr/lib/emacs/lisp/sendmail.el

./usr/lib/emacs/lisp/server.el

./usr/lib/emacs/lisp/shell.el

./usr/lib/emacs/lisp/simple.el

./usr/lib/emacs/lisp/simula.el

./usr/lib/emacs/lisp/spell.el

./usr/lib/emacs/lisp/spook.el

./usr/lib/emacs/lisp/startup.el

./usr/lib/emacs/lisp/studly.el

./usr/lib/emacs/lisp/subr.el

./usr/lib/emacs/lisp/sun-cursors.el

./usr/lib/emacs/lisp/sun-fns.el

./usr/lib/emacs/lisp/sun-keys.el

./usr/lib/emacs/lisp/sun-mouse.el

./usr/lib/emacs/lisp/sup-mouse.el

./usr/lib/emacs/lisp/tabify.el

./usr/lib/emacs/lisp/tags.el

./usr/lib/emacs/lisp/telnet.el

./usr/lib/emacs/lisp/terminal.el

./usr/lib/emacs/lisp/tex-mode.el

./usr/lib/emacs/lisp/tex-start.el

./usr/lib/emacs/lisp/texinfmt.el

./usr/lib/emacs/lisp/texinfo.el

./usr/lib/emacs/lisp/text-mode.el

./usr/lib/emacs/lisp/time.el

./usr/lib/emacs/lisp/uncompress.el

./usr/lib/emacs/lisp/underline.el

./usr/lib/emacs/lisp/undigest.el

./usr/lib/emacs/lisp/unused.el

./usr/lib/emacs/lisp/userlock.el

./usr/lib/emacs/lisp/version.el

./usr/lib/emacs/lisp/vi.el

./usr/lib/emacs/lisp/view.el

./usr/lib/emacs/lisp/vip.el

./usr/lib/emacs/lisp/vms-patch.el

./usr/lib/emacs/lisp/vmsproc.el

./usr/lib/emacs/lisp/window.el

./usr/lib/emacs/lisp/x-menu.el

./usr/lib/emacs/lisp/x-mouse.el

./usr/lib/emacs/lisp/xscheme.el

./usr/lib/emacs/lisp/yow.el

./usr/lib/emacs/lisp/simula.defns

./usr/lib/emacs/lisp/abbrev.elc

./usr/lib/emacs/lisp/abbrevlist.elc

./usr/lib/emacs/lisp/ada.elc

./usr/lib/emacs/lisp/add-log.elc

./usr/lib/emacs/lisp/backquote.elc

./usr/lib/emacs/lisp/bibtex.elc

./usr/lib/emacs/lisp/fi

./usr/lib/emacs/lisp/fi/Makefile

./usr/lib/emacs/lisp/fi/README

./usr/lib/emacs/lisp/fi/clman.data

./usr/lib/emacs/lisp/fi/clman.el

./usr/lib/emacs/lisp/fi/clman.elc

./usr/lib/emacs/lisp/fi/docompile.sh

./usr/lib/emacs/lisp/fi/dot.clinit

./usr/lib/emacs/lisp/fi/dot.emacs

./usr/lib/emacs/lisp/fi/dot.emacsX11

./usr/lib/emacs/lisp/fi/emacs.cl

./usr/lib/emacs/lisp/fi/filec.el

```
./usr/lib/emacs/lisp/fi/filec.elc          ./usr/lib/emacs/lisp/flame.elc
./usr/lib/emacs/lisp/fi/indent.el          ./usr/lib/emacs/lisp/float.elc
./usr/lib/emacs/lisp/fi/indent.elc         ./usr/lib/emacs/lisp/fortran.elc
./usr/lib/emacs/lisp/fi/ipc.cl             ./usr/lib/emacs/lisp/ftp.elc
./usr/lib/emacs/lisp/fi/keys.el            ./usr/lib/emacs/lisp/gdb.elc
./usr/lib/emacs/lisp/fi/keys.elc           ./usr/lib/emacs/lisp/hanoi.elc
./usr/lib/emacs/lisp/fi/ltags.el           ./usr/lib/emacs/lisp/help.elc
./usr/lib/emacs/lisp/fi/ltags.elc          ./usr/lib/emacs/lisp/helper.elc
./usr/lib/emacs/lisp/fi/modes.el           ./usr/lib/emacs/lisp/hideif.elc
./usr/lib/emacs/lisp/fi/modes.elc          ./usr/lib/emacs/lisp/icon.elc
./usr/lib/emacs/lisp/fi/ring.el            ./usr/lib/emacs/lisp/indent.elc
./usr/lib/emacs/lisp/fi/ring.elc           ./usr/lib/emacs/lisp/info.elc
./usr/lib/emacs/lisp/fi/rlogin.el          ./usr/lib/emacs/lisp/informat.elc
./usr/lib/emacs/lisp/fi/rlogin.elc         ./usr/lib/emacs/lisp/isearch.elc
./usr/lib/emacs/lisp/fi/shell.el           ./usr/lib/emacs/lisp/keypad.elc
./usr/lib/emacs/lisp/fi/shell.elc          ./usr/lib/emacs/lisp/life.elc
./usr/lib/emacs/lisp/fi/site-init.el       ./usr/lib/emacs/lisp/lisp-mode.elc
./usr/lib/emacs/lisp/fi/spec.out           ./usr/lib/emacs/lisp/lisp.elc
./usr/lib/emacs/lisp/fi/sublisp.el         ./usr/lib/emacs/lisp/lpr.elc
./usr/lib/emacs/lisp/fi/sublisp.elc        ./usr/lib/emacs/lisp/macros.elc
./usr/lib/emacs/lisp/fi/subproc.el         ./usr/lib/emacs/lisp/mail-utils.elc
./usr/lib/emacs/lisp/fi/subproc.elc        ./usr/lib/emacs/lisp/mailalias.elc
./usr/lib/emacs/lisp/fi/tcplisp.el         ./usr/lib/emacs/lisp/makesum.elc
./usr/lib/emacs/lisp/fi/tcplisp.elc        ./usr/lib/emacs/lisp/man.elc
./usr/lib/emacs/lisp/fi/utils.el           ./usr/lib/emacs/lisp/medit.elc
./usr/lib/emacs/lisp/fi/utils.elc          ./usr/lib/emacs/lisp/vi.elc
./usr/lib/emacs/lisp/fi/.places            ./usr/lib/emacs/lisp/mh-e.elc
./usr/lib/emacs/lisp/blackbox.elc          ./usr/lib/emacs/lisp/mim-mode.elc
./usr/lib/emacs/lisp/buff-menu.elc         ./usr/lib/emacs/lisp/mim-syntax.elc
./usr/lib/emacs/lisp/bytecomp.elc          ./usr/lib/emacs/lisp/mlconvert.elc
./usr/lib/emacs/lisp/c-fill.elc            ./usr/lib/emacs/lisp/mlsupport.elc
./usr/lib/emacs/lisp/c-mode.elc            ./usr/lib/emacs/lisp/modula2.elc
./usr/lib/emacs/lisp/chistory.elc          ./usr/lib/emacs/lisp/nroff-mode.elc
./usr/lib/emacs/lisp/cl-indent.elc         ./usr/lib/emacs/lisp/options.elc
./usr/lib/emacs/lisp/cl.elc                ./usr/lib/emacs/lisp/outline.elc
./usr/lib/emacs/lisp/compare-w.elc         ./usr/lib/emacs/lisp/page.elc
./usr/lib/emacs/lisp/compile.elc           ./usr/lib/emacs/lisp/paragraphs.elc
./usr/lib/emacs/lisp/dabbrev.elc           ./usr/lib/emacs/lisp/picture.elc
./usr/lib/emacs/lisp/dbx.elc               ./usr/lib/emacs/lisp/prolog.elc
./usr/lib/emacs/lisp/debug.elc             ./usr/lib/emacs/lisp/rect.elc
./usr/lib/emacs/lisp/dired.elc             ./usr/lib/emacs/lisp/register.elc
./usr/lib/emacs/lisp/disass.elc            ./usr/lib/emacs/lisp/replace.elc
./usr/lib/emacs/lisp/dissociate.elc        ./usr/lib/emacs/lisp/rfc822.elc
./usr/lib/emacs/lisp/doctor.elc            ./usr/lib/emacs/lisp/rmail.elc
./usr/lib/emacs/lisp/ebuff-menu.elc        ./usr/lib/emacs/lisp/rmailedit.elc
./usr/lib/emacs/lisp/echistory.elc         ./usr/lib/emacs/lisp/rmailkwd.elc
./usr/lib/emacs/lisp/edt.elc               ./usr/lib/emacs/lisp/rmailmsc.elc
./usr/lib/emacs/lisp/ehelp.elc             ./usr/lib/emacs/lisp/rmailout.elc
./usr/lib/emacs/lisp/electric.elc          ./usr/lib/emacs/lisp/rmailsum.elc
./usr/lib/emacs/lisp/files.elc             ./usr/lib/emacs/lisp/rnews.elc
./usr/lib/emacs/lisp/fill.elc              ./usr/lib/emacs/lisp/rnewspost.elc
```

```
./usr/lib/emacs/lisp/scheme.elc
./usr/lib/emacs/lisp/scribe.elc
./usr/lib/emacs/lisp/sendmail.elc
./usr/lib/emacs/lisp/server.elc
./usr/lib/emacs/lisp/shell.elc
./usr/lib/emacs/lisp/simple.elc
./usr/lib/emacs/lisp/simula.elc
./usr/lib/emacs/lisp/sort.elc
./usr/lib/emacs/lisp/spell.elc
./usr/lib/emacs/lisp/startup.elc
./usr/lib/emacs/lisp/studly.elc
./usr/lib/emacs/lisp/subr.elc
./usr/lib/emacs/lisp/sun-fns.elc
./usr/lib/emacs/lisp/sun-mouse.elc
./usr/lib/emacs/lisp/sup-mouse.elc
./usr/lib/emacs/lisp/tabify.elc
./usr/lib/emacs/lisp/tags.elc
./usr/lib/emacs/lisp/telnet.elc
./usr/lib/emacs/lisp/terminal.elc
./usr/lib/emacs/lisp/tex-mode.elc
./usr/lib/emacs/lisp/texinfmt.elc
./usr/lib/emacs/lisp/texinfo.elc
./usr/lib/emacs/lisp/text-mode.elc
./usr/lib/emacs/lisp/time.elc
./usr/lib/emacs/lisp/underline.elc
./usr/lib/emacs/lisp/undigest.elc
./usr/lib/emacs/lisp/userlock.elc
./usr/lib/emacs/lisp/view.elc
./usr/lib/emacs/lisp/vip.elc
./usr/lib/emacs/lisp/vms-patch.elc
./usr/lib/emacs/lisp/vmsproc.elc
./usr/lib/emacs/lisp/window.elc
./usr/lib/emacs/lisp/x-menu.elc
./usr/lib/emacs/lisp/x-mouse.elc
./usr/lib/emacs/lisp/xscheme.elc
./usr/lib/emacs/lisp/yow.elc
./usr/lib/emacs/lisp/term
./usr/lib/emacs/lisp/term/COPYING
./usr/lib/emacs/lisp/term/apollo.el
./usr/lib/emacs/lisp/term/bobcat.el
./usr/lib/emacs/lisp/term/s4.el
./usr/lib/emacs/lisp/term/sun.el
./usr/lib/emacs/lisp/term/supdup.el
./usr/lib/emacs/lisp/term/unixpc.el
./usr/lib/emacs/lisp/term/vt100.el
./usr/lib/emacs/lisp/term/vt125.el
./usr/lib/emacs/lisp/term/vt200.el
./usr/lib/emacs/lisp/term/vt220.el
./usr/lib/emacs/lisp/term/vt240.el
./usr/lib/emacs/lisp/term/x-win.el
./usr/lib/emacs/lisp/term/.places
./usr/lib/emacs/lisp/.places
./usr/lib/emacs/man
./usr/lib/emacs/man/ChangeLog
./usr/lib/emacs/man/README
./usr/lib/emacs/man/cl.texinfo
./usr/lib/emacs/man/emacs.aux
./usr/lib/emacs/man/emacs.cps
./usr/lib/emacs/man/emacs.fns
./usr/lib/emacs/man/emacs.kys
./usr/lib/emacs/man/emacs.pgs
./usr/lib/emacs/man/emacs.tex
./usr/lib/emacs/man/emacs.tps
./usr/lib/emacs/man/emacs.vrs
./usr/lib/emacs/man/gdb.aux
./usr/lib/emacs/man/gdb.cps
./usr/lib/emacs/man/gdb.fns
./usr/lib/emacs/man/gdb.kys
./usr/lib/emacs/man/gdb.pgs
./usr/lib/emacs/man/gdb.texinfo
./usr/lib/emacs/man/gdb.tps
./usr/lib/emacs/man/gdb.vrs
./usr/lib/emacs/man/split-man
./usr/lib/emacs/man/termcap.aux
./usr/lib/emacs/man/termcap.cps
./usr/lib/emacs/man/termcap.fns
./usr/lib/emacs/man/termcap.kys
./usr/lib/emacs/man/termcap.pgs
./usr/lib/emacs/man/termcap.texinfo
./usr/lib/emacs/man/termcap.tps
./usr/lib/emacs/man/termcap.vrs
./usr/lib/emacs/man/texindex.c
./usr/lib/emacs/man/texinfo.aux
./usr/lib/emacs/man/texinfo.cps
./usr/lib/emacs/man/texinfo.fns
./usr/lib/emacs/man/texinfo.kys
./usr/lib/emacs/man/texinfo.pgs
./usr/lib/emacs/man/texinfo.tex
./usr/lib/emacs/man/texinfo.texinfo
./usr/lib/emacs/man/texinfo.tps
./usr/lib/emacs/man/texinfo.vrs
./usr/lib/emacs/man/vip.texinfo
./usr/lib/emacs/man/.places
./usr/lib/emacs/.places
./usr/lib/libcs.a
./usr/lib/database
./usr/lib/database/dbCatenate
./usr/lib/database/dbCompare
./usr/lib/database/dbCompress
./usr/lib/database/dbCopy
./usr/lib/database/dbDescribe
./usr/lib/database/dbExpand
```

```
./usr/lib/database/.places
./usr/lib/libm.a
./usr/lib/libnm.a
./usr/lib/libm_p.a
./usr/lib/libnm_p.a
./usr/lib/lib.b
./usr/lib/libcurses.a
./usr/lib/libcurses_p.a
./usr/lib/libdbm.a
./usr/lib/libdbm_p.a
./usr/lib/libg.a
./usr/lib/libl.a
./usr/lib/libl_p.a
./usr/lib/libln.a
./usr/lib/libmp.a
./usr/lib/libmp_p.a
./usr/lib/libtermlib.a
./usr/lib/libtermlib_p.a
./usr/lib/libtermcap.a
./usr/lib/liby.a
./usr/lib/liby_p.a
./usr/lib/librpcsvc.a
./usr/lib/makewhatis
./usr/lib/getNAME
./usr/lib/makekey
./usr/lib/find
./usr/lib/find/code
./usr/lib/find/bigram
./usr/lib/find/updatedb
./usr/lib/find/.places
./usr/lib/lex
./usr/lib/lex/ncform
./usr/lib/lex/nrform
./usr/lib/lex/.places
./usr/lib/migcom
./usr/lib/refer
./usr/lib/refer/mkey
./usr/lib/refer/inv
./usr/lib/refer/hunt
./usr/lib/refer/.places
./usr/lib/yaccpar
./usr/lib/ex3.7recover
./usr/lib/ex3.7preserve
./usr/lib/sound
./usr/lib/sound/booter.snd
./usr/lib/sound/codec.snd
./usr/lib/sound/mulawcodec.snd
./usr/lib/sound/mono.snd
./usr/lib/sound/monobyte.snd
./usr/lib/sound/dsprecord.snd
./usr/lib/sound/encodemulawsquelch.snd
```

```
./usr/lib/sound/mulawcodecsquelch.snd
./usr/lib/sound/decodemulawsquelch.snd
./usr/lib/sound/.places
./usr/lib/libix_p.a
./usr/lib/indexing
./usr/lib/indexing/files
./usr/lib/indexing/files/wf
./usr/lib/indexing/files/wf/DefaultEnglish.wf
./usr/lib/indexing/files/wf/.places
./usr/lib/indexing/files/fileTypeTable
./usr/lib/indexing/files/.places
./usr/lib/indexing/ixBuild
./usr/lib/indexing/ixClean
./usr/lib/indexing/ixDump
./usr/lib/indexing/ixFind
./usr/lib/indexing/ixRemove
./usr/lib/indexing/ixRepair
./usr/lib/indexing/ixStat
./usr/lib/indexing/fileType
./usr/lib/indexing/rtf-ascii
./usr/lib/indexing/rtf-desc
./usr/lib/indexing/shakes-desc
./usr/lib/indexing/rtf-keys
./usr/lib/indexing/sh-keys
./usr/lib/indexing/psw-keys
./usr/lib/indexing/mail-keys
./usr/lib/indexing/man-desc
./usr/lib/indexing/man-keys
./usr/lib/indexing/doc-desc
./usr/lib/indexing/findFile
./usr/lib/indexing/roff-desc
./usr/lib/indexing/wn-desc
./usr/lib/indexing/english-desc
./usr/lib/indexing/frame-desc
./usr/lib/indexing/csh-keys
./usr/lib/indexing/doc-keys
./usr/lib/indexing/english-keys
./usr/lib/indexing/roff-keys
./usr/lib/indexing/wn-keys
./usr/lib/indexing/c-keys
./usr/lib/indexing/frame-keys
./usr/lib/indexing/name-keys
./usr/lib/indexing/no-keys
./usr/lib/indexing/lexer
./usr/lib/indexing/search
./usr/lib/indexing/FrameToAscii
./usr/lib/indexing/.places
./usr/lib/indexing/lispdoc-desc
./usr/lib/indexing/lispdoc-desc-sed
./usr/lib/indexing/lispdoc-keys
./usr/lib/indexing/lispdoc-sed
```

```
./usr/lib/libtext.a
./usr/lib/dsp
./usr/lib/dsp/apman
./usr/lib/dsp/apman/AP_MACROS_SUMMARY
./usr/lib/dsp/apman/AP_CALL_SUMMARY
./usr/lib/dsp/apman/AP_FUNCTION_DOC
./usr/lib/dsp/apman/.places
./usr/lib/dsp/apbin
./usr/lib/dsp/apbin/cvcombine.dsp
./usr/lib/dsp/apbin/cvconjugate.dsp
./usr/lib/dsp/apbin/cvfill.dsp
./usr/lib/dsp/apbin/cvfilli.dsp
./usr/lib/dsp/apbin/cvmandelbrot.dsp
./usr/lib/dsp/apbin/cvmcv.dsp
./usr/lib/dsp/apbin/cvmove.dsp
./usr/lib/dsp/apbin/cvnegate.dsp
./usr/lib/dsp/apbin/cvpcv.dsp
./usr/lib/dsp/apbin/cvreal.dsp
./usr/lib/dsp/apbin/cvtcv.dsp
./usr/lib/dsp/apbin/fftr2a.dsp
./usr/lib/dsp/apbin/maxmagv.dsp
./usr/lib/dsp/apbin/maxv.dsp
./usr/lib/dsp/apbin/minmagv.dsp
./usr/lib/dsp/apbin/minv.dsp
./usr/lib/dsp/apbin/mtm.dsp
./usr/lib/dsp/apbin/sumv.dsp
./usr/lib/dsp/apbin/sumvmag.dsp
./usr/lib/dsp/apbin/sumvnolim.dsp
./usr/lib/dsp/apbin/sumvsq.dsp
./usr/lib/dsp/apbin/sumvsquares.dsp
./usr/lib/dsp/apbin/vabs.dsp
./usr/lib/dsp/apbin/vand.dsp
./usr/lib/dsp/apbin/vasl.dsp
./usr/lib/dsp/apbin/vasr.dsp
./usr/lib/dsp/apbin/vclear.dsp
./usr/lib/dsp/apbin/veor.dsp
./usr/lib/dsp/apbin/vfill.dsp
./usr/lib/dsp/apbin/vfilli.dsp
./usr/lib/dsp/apbin/vimag.dsp
./usr/lib/dsp/apbin/vlsl.dsp
./usr/lib/dsp/apbin/vlsr.dsp
./usr/lib/dsp/apbin/vmax.dsp
./usr/lib/dsp/apbin/vmin.dsp
./usr/lib/dsp/apbin/vmove.dsp
./usr/lib/dsp/apbin/vmoveb.dsp
./usr/lib/dsp/apbin/vmovebr.dsp
./usr/lib/dsp/apbin/vmv.dsp
./usr/lib/dsp/apbin/vnegate.dsp
./usr/lib/dsp/apbin/vor.dsp
./usr/lib/dsp/apbin/vps.dsp
./usr/lib/dsp/apbin/vpsi.dsp
./usr/lib/dsp/apbin/vpv.dsp
./usr/lib/dsp/apbin/vpvnolim.dsp
./usr/lib/dsp/apbin/vramp.dsp
./usr/lib/dsp/apbin/vrampi.dsp
./usr/lib/dsp/apbin/vrand.dsp
./usr/lib/dsp/apbin/vreal.dsp
./usr/lib/dsp/apbin/vreverse.dsp
./usr/lib/dsp/apbin/vsquare.dsp
./usr/lib/dsp/apbin/vssq.dsp
./usr/lib/dsp/apbin/vswap.dsp
./usr/lib/dsp/apbin/vts.dsp
./usr/lib/dsp/apbin/vtsi.dsp
./usr/lib/dsp/apbin/vtsmv.dsp
./usr/lib/dsp/apbin/vtspv.dsp
./usr/lib/dsp/apbin/vtv.dsp
./usr/lib/dsp/apbin/vtvms.dsp
./usr/lib/dsp/apbin/vtvmvtv.dsp
./usr/lib/dsp/apbin/vtvps.dsp
./usr/lib/dsp/apbin/vtvpv.dsp
./usr/lib/dsp/apbin/vtvpvtv.dsp
./usr/lib/dsp/apbin/.places
./usr/lib/dsp/apsrc
./usr/lib/dsp/apsrc/cvcombine.asm
./usr/lib/dsp/apsrc/cvconjugate.asm
./usr/lib/dsp/apsrc/cvfill.asm
./usr/lib/dsp/apsrc/cvfilli.asm
./usr/lib/dsp/apsrc/cvmandelbrot.asm
./usr/lib/dsp/apsrc/cvmcv.asm
./usr/lib/dsp/apsrc/cvmove.asm
./usr/lib/dsp/apsrc/cvnegate.asm
./usr/lib/dsp/apsrc/cvpcv.asm
./usr/lib/dsp/apsrc/cvreal.asm
./usr/lib/dsp/apsrc/cvtcv.asm
./usr/lib/dsp/apsrc/fftr2a.asm
./usr/lib/dsp/apsrc/maxmagv.asm
./usr/lib/dsp/apsrc/maxv.asm
./usr/lib/dsp/apsrc/minmagv.asm
./usr/lib/dsp/apsrc/minv.asm
./usr/lib/dsp/apsrc/mtm.asm
./usr/lib/dsp/apsrc/sumv.asm
./usr/lib/dsp/apsrc/sumvmag.asm
./usr/lib/dsp/apsrc/sumvnolim.asm
./usr/lib/dsp/apsrc/sumvsq.asm
./usr/lib/dsp/apsrc/sumvsquares.asm
./usr/lib/dsp/apsrc/vabs.asm
./usr/lib/dsp/apsrc/vand.asm
./usr/lib/dsp/apsrc/vasl.asm
./usr/lib/dsp/apsrc/vasr.asm
./usr/lib/dsp/apsrc/vclear.asm
./usr/lib/dsp/apsrc/veor.asm
./usr/lib/dsp/apsrc/vfill.asm
```

./usr/lib/dsp/apsrc/vfilli.asm
./usr/lib/dsp/apsrc/vimag.asm
./usr/lib/dsp/apsrc/vlsl.asm
./usr/lib/dsp/apsrc/vlsr.asm
./usr/lib/dsp/apsrc/vmax.asm
./usr/lib/dsp/apsrc/vmin.asm
./usr/lib/dsp/apsrc/vmove.asm
./usr/lib/dsp/apsrc/vmoveb.asm
./usr/lib/dsp/apsrc/vmovebr.asm
./usr/lib/dsp/apsrc/vmv.asm
./usr/lib/dsp/apsrc/vnegate.asm
./usr/lib/dsp/apsrc/vor.asm
./usr/lib/dsp/apsrc/vps.asm
./usr/lib/dsp/apsrc/vpsi.asm
./usr/lib/dsp/apsrc/vpv.asm
./usr/lib/dsp/apsrc/vpvnolim.asm
./usr/lib/dsp/apsrc/vramp.asm
./usr/lib/dsp/apsrc/vrampi.asm
./usr/lib/dsp/apsrc/vrand.asm
./usr/lib/dsp/apsrc/vreal.asm
./usr/lib/dsp/apsrc/vreverse.asm
./usr/lib/dsp/apsrc/vsquare.asm
./usr/lib/dsp/apsrc/vssq.asm
./usr/lib/dsp/apsrc/vswap.asm
./usr/lib/dsp/apsrc/vts.asm
./usr/lib/dsp/apsrc/vtsi.asm
./usr/lib/dsp/apsrc/vtsmv.asm
./usr/lib/dsp/apsrc/vtspv.asm
./usr/lib/dsp/apsrc/vtv.asm
./usr/lib/dsp/apsrc/vtvms.asm
./usr/lib/dsp/apsrc/vtvmvtv.asm
./usr/lib/dsp/apsrc/vtvps.asm
./usr/lib/dsp/apsrc/vtvpv.asm
./usr/lib/dsp/apsrc/vtvpvtv.asm
./usr/lib/dsp/apsrc/.places
./usr/lib/dsp/monitor
./usr/lib/dsp/monitor/degnext.lod
./usr/lib/dsp/monitor/mkmon8k.lod
./usr/lib/dsp/monitor/apmon8k.lod
./usr/lib/dsp/monitor/mkmon8k.dsp
./usr/lib/dsp/monitor/apmon8k.dsp
./usr/lib/dsp/monitor/mkmon8k.mem
./usr/lib/dsp/monitor/apmon8k.mem
./usr/lib/dsp/monitor/.places
./usr/lib/dsp/smsrc
./usr/lib/dsp/smsrc/sys_messages.asm
./usr/lib/dsp/smsrc/sys_memory_map_ap.asm
./usr/lib/dsp/smsrc/sys_memory_map_mk.asm
./usr/lib/dsp/smsrc/allocsys.asm
./usr/lib/dsp/smsrc/hmdispatch.asm
./usr/lib/dsp/smsrc/allocusr.asm
./usr/lib/dsp/smsrc/hmlib.asm
./usr/lib/dsp/smsrc/hmlib_mk.asm
./usr/lib/dsp/smsrc/verrev.asm
./usr/lib/dsp/smsrc/jsrlib.asm
./usr/lib/dsp/smsrc/sys_li.asm
./usr/lib/dsp/smsrc/beginend.asm
./usr/lib/dsp/smsrc/memmap.asm
./usr/lib/dsp/smsrc/misc.asm
./usr/lib/dsp/smsrc/sys_xe.asm
./usr/lib/dsp/smsrc/config.asm
./usr/lib/dsp/smsrc/mkmon8k.asm
./usr/lib/dsp/smsrc/apmon8k.asm
./usr/lib/dsp/smsrc/sys_ye.asm
./usr/lib/dsp/smsrc/defines.asm
./usr/lib/dsp/smsrc/reg_defines.asm
./usr/lib/dsp/smsrc/reset_boot.asm
./usr/lib/dsp/smsrc/vectors.asm
./usr/lib/dsp/smsrc/iv_decl.asm
./usr/lib/dsp/smsrc/dspmsgs.asm
./usr/lib/dsp/smsrc/handlers.asm
./usr/lib/dsp/smsrc/music_macros.asm
./usr/lib/dsp/smsrc/ap_macros.asm
./usr/lib/dsp/smsrc/degnext.asm
./usr/lib/dsp/smsrc/degmon.asm
./usr/lib/dsp/smsrc/degmon_vectors.asm
./usr/lib/dsp/smsrc/ioequ.asm
./usr/lib/dsp/smsrc/README
./usr/lib/dsp/smsrc/mkmon8k.mem
./usr/lib/dsp/smsrc/apmon8k.mem
./usr/lib/dsp/smsrc/include_dirs.asm
./usr/lib/dsp/smsrc/.places
./usr/lib/dsp/umsrc
./usr/lib/dsp/umsrc/test
./usr/lib/dsp/umsrc/test/tcosine_sum.asm
./usr/lib/dsp/umsrc/test/.places
./usr/lib/dsp/umsrc/ditfft.asm
./usr/lib/dsp/umsrc/harmonic_sum.asm
./usr/lib/dsp/umsrc/power2.asm
./usr/lib/dsp/umsrc/unsign.asm
./usr/lib/dsp/umsrc/codec.asm
./usr/lib/dsp/umsrc/sind.asm
./usr/lib/dsp/umsrc/unsigny.asm
./usr/lib/dsp/umsrc/cosine_sum.asm
./usr/lib/dsp/umsrc/sinewave.asm
./usr/lib/dsp/umsrc/template
./usr/lib/dsp/umsrc/README
./usr/lib/dsp/umsrc/.places
./usr/lib/dsp/ugsrc
./usr/lib/dsp/ugsrc/test
./usr/lib/dsp/ugsrc/test/tscale.asm
./usr/lib/dsp/ugsrc/test/toscg5.asm

```
./usr/lib/dsp/ugsrc/test/.places
./usr/lib/dsp/ugsrc/delay.asm
./usr/lib/dsp/ugsrc/oscgaf.asm
./usr/lib/dsp/ugsrc/oscgafi.asm
./usr/lib/dsp/ugsrc/out2sum.asm
./usr/lib/dsp/ugsrc/dswitch.asm
./usr/lib/dsp/ugsrc/oscg.asm
./usr/lib/dsp/ugsrc/mul2.asm
./usr/lib/dsp/ugsrc/add2.asm
./usr/lib/dsp/ugsrc/onezero.asm
./usr/lib/dsp/ugsrc/allpass1.asm
./usr/lib/dsp/ugsrc/onepole.asm
./usr/lib/dsp/ugsrc/unoise.asm
./usr/lib/dsp/ugsrc/scale.asm
./usr/lib/dsp/ugsrc/asymp.asm
./usr/lib/dsp/ugsrc/constant.asm
./usr/lib/dsp/ugsrc/orchloopbegin.asm
./usr/lib/dsp/ugsrc/orchloopend.asm
./usr/lib/dsp/ugsrc/biquad.asm
./usr/lib/dsp/ugsrc/osci.asm
./usr/lib/dsp/ugsrc/oscs.asm
./usr/lib/dsp/ugsrc/oscgf.asm
./usr/lib/dsp/ugsrc/oscw.asm
./usr/lib/dsp/ugsrc/sawtooth.asm
./usr/lib/dsp/ugsrc/slpdur.asm
./usr/lib/dsp/ugsrc/twopole.asm
./usr/lib/dsp/ugsrc/unoisehp.asm
./usr/lib/dsp/ugsrc/delayticks.asm
./usr/lib/dsp/ugsrc/impulses.asm
./usr/lib/dsp/ugsrc/sclladd2.asm
./usr/lib/dsp/ugsrc/patch.asm
./usr/lib/dsp/ugsrc/ramp.asm
./usr/lib/dsp/ugsrc/readticks.asm
./usr/lib/dsp/ugsrc/README
./usr/lib/dsp/ugsrc/.places
./usr/lib/dsp/test
./usr/lib/dsp/test/README
./usr/lib/dsp/test/mk_ex1.asm
./usr/lib/dsp/test/mk_ex2.asm
./usr/lib/dsp/test/mk_ex3.asm
./usr/lib/dsp/test/ap_ex1.asm
./usr/lib/dsp/test/config_standalone.asm
./usr/lib/dsp/test/dspasm
./usr/lib/dsp/test/dspasm1
./usr/lib/dsp/test/.places
./usr/lib/dsp/.places
./usr/lib/libarrayproc.a
./usr/lib/libarrayproc_p.a
./usr/lib/.gdbinit
./usr/lib/libdpsops.a
./usr/lib/libdsp_s.a
./usr/lib/libdsp_p.a
./usr/lib/libNeXT_s.a
./usr/lib/libNeXT_p.a
./usr/lib/libmidi.a
./usr/lib/libmidi_p.a
./usr/lib/kern_loader
./usr/lib/kern_loader/Midi
./usr/lib/kern_loader/Midi/midi_reloc
./usr/lib/kern_loader/Midi/midi.kern_server
./usr/lib/kern_loader/Midi/.places
./usr/lib/kern_loader/.places
./usr/lib/libmusickit_p.a
./usr/lib/libmusickit.a
./usr/lib/nib
./usr/lib/nib/AlignPref.nib
./usr/lib/nib/AutosizeInspector.nib
./usr/lib/nib/BitmapInspector.nib
./usr/lib/nib/BoxInspector.nib
./usr/lib/nib/BrowserInspector.nib
./usr/lib/nib/ButtonInspector.nib
./usr/lib/nib/CellInspector.nib
./usr/lib/nib/ClassInspector.nib
./usr/lib/nib/ConnectInspector.nib
./usr/lib/nib/CustomObjectInspector.nib
./usr/lib/nib/CustomViewInspector.nib
./usr/lib/nib/Dimensions.nib
./usr/lib/nib/FormInspector.nib
./usr/lib/nib/IB.nib
./usr/lib/nib/Info.nib
./usr/lib/nib/InspectDriver.nib
./usr/lib/nib/MatrixInspector.nib
./usr/lib/nib/Menus.nib
./usr/lib/nib/MenusData.nib
./usr/lib/nib/NibClassManager.nib
./usr/lib/nib/NibDebug.nib
./usr/lib/nib/NibEditor.nib
./usr/lib/nib/NibManager.nib
./usr/lib/nib/NibNew.nib
./usr/lib/nib/NoInspector.nib
./usr/lib/nib/Palette.nib
./usr/lib/nib/ProjectInspector.nib
./usr/lib/nib/ScrollTextInspector.nib
./usr/lib/nib/SliderInspector.nib
./usr/lib/nib/SoundInspector.nib
./usr/lib/nib/TextFieldInspector.nib
./usr/lib/nib/Views.nib
./usr/lib/nib/WindowInspector.nib
./usr/lib/nib/Windows.nib
./usr/lib/nib/classes.nib
./usr/lib/nib/images.nib
./usr/lib/nib/newapp.nib
```

```
./usr/lib/nib/newobject.nib
./usr/lib/nib/.places
./usr/lib/nib/InterfaceBuilder.h
./usr/lib/nib/Makefile.common
./usr/lib/nib/Makefile.libinterfaces
./usr/lib/nib/default_app_icon.tiff
./usr/lib/nib/libnib.o
./usr/lib/transcript
./usr/lib/transcript/psbanner
./usr/lib/transcript/pscomm
./usr/lib/transcript/psrv
./usr/lib/transcript/pstext
./usr/lib/transcript/enscript
./usr/lib/transcript/ps4014
./usr/lib/transcript/ps630
./usr/lib/transcript/pscat
./usr/lib/transcript/pscatmap
./usr/lib/transcript/psdit
./usr/lib/transcript/psplot
./usr/lib/transcript/psrev
./usr/lib/transcript/banner.pro
./usr/lib/transcript/enscript.pro
./usr/lib/transcript/pstext.pro
./usr/lib/transcript/ps4014.pro
./usr/lib/transcript/ps630.pro
./usr/lib/transcript/pscat.pro
./usr/lib/transcript/psplot.pro
./usr/lib/transcript/psdit.pro
./usr/lib/transcript/ehandler.ps
./usr/lib/transcript/uartpatch.ps
./usr/lib/transcript/bogusmsg.ps
./usr/lib/transcript/font.map
./usr/lib/transcript/Notice
./usr/lib/transcript/psint.sh
./usr/lib/transcript/psbad.sh
./usr/lib/transcript/AvantGarde-Book.afm
./usr/lib/transcript/AvantGarde-BookOblique.afm
./usr/lib/transcript/AvantGarde-Demi.afm
./usr/lib/transcript/AvantGarde-DemiOblique.afm
./usr/lib/transcript/Bookman-Demi.afm
./usr/lib/transcript/Bookman-DemiItalic.afm
./usr/lib/transcript/Bookman-Light.afm
./usr/lib/transcript/Bookman-LightItalic.afm
./usr/lib/transcript/Courier-Bold.afm
./usr/lib/transcript/Courier-BoldOblique.afm
./usr/lib/transcript/Courier-Oblique.afm
./usr/lib/transcript/Courier.afm
./usr/lib/transcript/DIThacks.afm
./usr/lib/transcript/Garamond-Bold.afm
./usr/lib/transcript/Garamond-BoldItalic.afm
./usr/lib/transcript/Garamond-Light.afm

./usr/lib/transcript/Helvetica.afm
./usr/lib/transcript/Garamond-LightItalic.afm
./usr/lib/transcript/Helvetica-Bold.afm
./usr/lib/transcript/Helvetica-BoldOblique.afm
./usr/lib/transcript/Helvetica-Narrow-Bold.afm
./usr/lib/transcript/Helvetica-Narrow-BoldOblique.afm
./usr/lib/transcript/Helvetica-Narrow-Oblique.afm
./usr/lib/transcript/Helvetica-Narrow.afm
./usr/lib/transcript/Helvetica-Oblique.afm
./usr/lib/transcript/LubalinGraph-Book.afm
./usr/lib/transcript/LubalinGraph-BookOblique.afm
./usr/lib/transcript/LubalinGraph-Demi.afm
./usr/lib/transcript/LubalinGraph-DemiOblique.afm
./usr/lib/transcript/NewCenturySchlbk-Bold.afm
./usr/lib/transcript/NewCenturySchlbk-BoldItalic.afm
./usr/lib/transcript/NewCenturySchlbk-Italic.afm
./usr/lib/transcript/NewCenturySchlbk-Roman.afm
./usr/lib/transcript/Optima-Bold.afm
./usr/lib/transcript/Optima-BoldOblique.afm
./usr/lib/transcript/Optima-Oblique.afm
./usr/lib/transcript/Optima.afm
./usr/lib/transcript/Palatino-Bold.afm
./usr/lib/transcript/Palatino-BoldItalic.afm
./usr/lib/transcript/Palatino-Italic.afm
./usr/lib/transcript/Palatino-Roman.afm
./usr/lib/transcript/Souvenir-Demi.afm
./usr/lib/transcript/Souvenir-DemiItalic.afm
./usr/lib/transcript/Souvenir-Light.afm
./usr/lib/transcript/Souvenir-LightItalic.afm
./usr/lib/transcript/Symbol.afm
./usr/lib/transcript/Times-Bold.afm
./usr/lib/transcript/Times-BoldItalic.afm
./usr/lib/transcript/Times-Italic.afm
./usr/lib/transcript/Times-Roman.afm
./usr/lib/transcript/ZapfChancery-MediumItalic.afm
./usr/lib/transcript/ZapfDingbats.afm
./usr/lib/transcript/psif
./usr/lib/transcript/psof
./usr/lib/transcript/psnf
./usr/lib/transcript/pstf
./usr/lib/transcript/psgf
./usr/lib/transcript/psvf
./usr/lib/transcript/psdf
./usr/lib/transcript/pscf
./usr/lib/transcript/psrf
./usr/lib/transcript/psbad
./usr/lib/transcript/troff.font
./usr/lib/transcript/troff.font/AvantGarde.map
./usr/lib/transcript/troff.font/Bookman.map
./usr/lib/transcript/troff.font/Courier.map
./usr/lib/transcript/troff.font/Garamond.map
```

```
./usr/lib/transcript/troff.font/HelvNarrow.map            ./usr/lib/transcript/ditroff.font/AG.map
./usr/lib/transcript/troff.font/Helvetica.map             ./usr/lib/transcript/ditroff.font/Ag.map
./usr/lib/transcript/troff.font/Lubalin.map               ./usr/lib/transcript/ditroff.font/B.map
./usr/lib/transcript/troff.font/Makefile                  ./usr/lib/transcript/ditroff.font/BI.map
./usr/lib/transcript/troff.font/Makefile.sysv             ./usr/lib/transcript/ditroff.font/BO.map
./usr/lib/transcript/troff.font/NewCentury.map            ./usr/lib/transcript/ditroff.font/Bo.map
./usr/lib/transcript/troff.font/Optima.map                ./usr/lib/transcript/ditroff.font/C.map
./usr/lib/transcript/troff.font/Palatino.map              ./usr/lib/transcript/ditroff.font/CB.map
./usr/lib/transcript/troff.font/Souvenir.map              ./usr/lib/transcript/ditroff.font/CD.map
./usr/lib/transcript/troff.font/Times.map                 ./usr/lib/transcript/ditroff.font/CO.map
./usr/lib/transcript/troff.font/Zapf.map                  ./usr/lib/transcript/ditroff.font/GA.map
./usr/lib/transcript/troff.font/chartab.inc               ./usr/lib/transcript/ditroff.font/Ga.map
./usr/lib/transcript/troff.font/doto.awk                  ./usr/lib/transcript/ditroff.font/H.map
./usr/lib/transcript/troff.font/font.head                 ./usr/lib/transcript/ditroff.font/HB.map
./usr/lib/transcript/troff.font/makefontdir               ./usr/lib/transcript/ditroff.font/HD.map
./usr/lib/transcript/troff.font/makefontdir.sysv          ./usr/lib/transcript/ditroff.font/HN.map
./usr/lib/transcript/troff.font/Times                     ./usr/lib/transcript/ditroff.font/HO.map
./usr/lib/transcript/troff.font/Times/font.ct             ./usr/lib/transcript/ditroff.font/Hn.map
./usr/lib/transcript/troff.font/Times/font.head           ./usr/lib/transcript/ditroff.font/I.map
./usr/lib/transcript/troff.font/Times/ftTR                ./usr/lib/transcript/ditroff.font/LU.map
./usr/lib/transcript/troff.font/Times/ftTI                ./usr/lib/transcript/ditroff.font/Lu.map
./usr/lib/transcript/troff.font/Times/ftTB                ./usr/lib/transcript/ditroff.font/Make.family
./usr/lib/transcript/troff.font/Times/ftS                 ./usr/lib/transcript/ditroff.font/Makefile
./usr/lib/transcript/troff.font/Times/ftR                 ./usr/lib/transcript/ditroff.font/Makefile.sysv
./usr/lib/transcript/troff.font/Times/ftI                 ./usr/lib/transcript/ditroff.font/NC.map
./usr/lib/transcript/troff.font/Times/ftB                 ./usr/lib/transcript/ditroff.font/Nc.map
./usr/lib/transcript/troff.font/Times/.places             ./usr/lib/transcript/ditroff.font/OP.map
./usr/lib/transcript/troff.font/Helvetica                 ./usr/lib/transcript/ditroff.font/Op.map
./usr/lib/transcript/troff.font/Helvetica/font.ct         ./usr/lib/transcript/ditroff.font/PA.map
./usr/lib/transcript/troff.font/Helvetica/font.head       ./usr/lib/transcript/ditroff.font/PB.map
./usr/lib/transcript/troff.font/Helvetica/ftH             ./usr/lib/transcript/ditroff.font/PI.map
./usr/lib/transcript/troff.font/Helvetica/ftHO            ./usr/lib/transcript/ditroff.font/PX.map
./usr/lib/transcript/troff.font/Helvetica/ftHB            ./usr/lib/transcript/ditroff.font/R.map
./usr/lib/transcript/troff.font/Helvetica/ftS             ./usr/lib/transcript/ditroff.font/README
./usr/lib/transcript/troff.font/Helvetica/ftR             ./usr/lib/transcript/ditroff.font/S.map
./usr/lib/transcript/troff.font/Helvetica/ftI             ./usr/lib/transcript/ditroff.font/SS.map
./usr/lib/transcript/troff.font/Helvetica/ftB             ./usr/lib/transcript/ditroff.font/SV.map
./usr/lib/transcript/troff.font/Helvetica/.places         ./usr/lib/transcript/ditroff.font/Sv.map
./usr/lib/transcript/troff.font/Courier                   ./usr/lib/transcript/ditroff.font/TB.map
./usr/lib/transcript/troff.font/Courier/font.ct           ./usr/lib/transcript/ditroff.font/TD.map
./usr/lib/transcript/troff.font/Courier/font.head         ./usr/lib/transcript/ditroff.font/TI.map
./usr/lib/transcript/troff.font/Courier/ftC               ./usr/lib/transcript/ditroff.font/TR.map
./usr/lib/transcript/troff.font/Courier/ftCO              ./usr/lib/transcript/ditroff.font/ZC.map
./usr/lib/transcript/troff.font/Courier/ftCB              ./usr/lib/transcript/ditroff.font/aG.map
./usr/lib/transcript/troff.font/Courier/ftS               ./usr/lib/transcript/ditroff.font/afmdit
./usr/lib/transcript/troff.font/Courier/ftR               ./usr/lib/transcript/ditroff.font/afmdit.awk
./usr/lib/transcript/troff.font/Courier/ftI               ./usr/lib/transcript/ditroff.font/afmdit.sysv
./usr/lib/transcript/troff.font/Courier/ftB               ./usr/lib/transcript/ditroff.font/ag.map
./usr/lib/transcript/troff.font/Courier/.places           ./usr/lib/transcript/ditroff.font/bO.map
./usr/lib/transcript/troff.font/.places                   ./usr/lib/transcript/ditroff.font/bo.map
./usr/lib/transcript/troff.font/ditroff.font              ./usr/lib/transcript/ditroff.font/charset
```

```
./usr/lib/transcript/ditroff.font/devspecs        ./usr/adm
./usr/lib/transcript/ditroff.font/gA.map          ./usr/preserve
./usr/lib/transcript/ditroff.font/ga.map          ./usr/spool
./usr/lib/transcript/ditroff.font/hN.map          ./usr/tmp
./usr/lib/transcript/ditroff.font/hn.map          ./usr/dict
./usr/lib/transcript/ditroff.font/lU.map          ./usr/dict/connectives
./usr/lib/transcript/ditroff.font/lu.map          ./usr/dict/web2
./usr/lib/transcript/ditroff.font/makefamily      ./usr/dict/web2a
./usr/lib/transcript/ditroff.font/makeout         ./usr/dict/papers
./usr/lib/transcript/ditroff.font/nC.map          ./usr/dict/papers/Rbstjissue
./usr/lib/transcript/ditroff.font/nc.map          ./usr/dict/papers/Rv7man
./usr/lib/transcript/ditroff.font/oP.map          ./usr/dict/papers/runinv
./usr/lib/transcript/ditroff.font/op.map          ./usr/dict/papers/Ind.ia
./usr/lib/transcript/ditroff.font/sV.map          ./usr/dict/papers/Ind.ib
./usr/lib/transcript/ditroff.font/sv.map          ./usr/dict/papers/Ind.ic
./usr/lib/transcript/ditroff.font/.places         ./usr/dict/papers/.places
./usr/lib/transcript/.places                      ./usr/dict/words
./usr/lib/NextPrinter                             ./usr/dict/hlist
./usr/lib/NextPrinter/npcomm                      ./usr/dict/hlista
./usr/lib/NextPrinter/comm                        ./usr/dict/hlistb
./usr/lib/NextPrinter/psif                        ./usr/dict/hstop
./usr/lib/NextPrinter/psnf                        ./usr/dict/.places
./usr/lib/NextPrinter/pstf                        ./usr/pub
./usr/lib/NextPrinter/psgf                        ./usr/pub/ascii
./usr/lib/NextPrinter/psplot                      ./usr/pub/eqnchar
./usr/lib/NextPrinter/psvf                        ./usr/pub/greek
./usr/lib/NextPrinter/pscf                        ./usr/pub/.places
./usr/lib/NextPrinter/psdf                        ./usr/ucb
./usr/lib/NextPrinter/psrf                        ./usr/ucb/gprof
./usr/lib/NextPrinter/npd                         ./usr/ucb/Mail
./usr/lib/NextPrinter/Inform                      ./usr/ucb/mail
./usr/lib/NextPrinter/pdf                         ./usr/ucb/fmt
./usr/lib/NextPrinter/pdf/L100_380.pdf            ./usr/ucb/apply
./usr/lib/NextPrinter/pdf/LaserWriter_Plus.pdf    ./usr/ucb/biff
./usr/lib/NextPrinter/pdf/NeXT_400_dpi_Laser_Printer.pdf  ./usr/ucb/checknr
./usr/lib/NextPrinter/pdf/.places                 ./usr/ucb/clear
./usr/lib/NextPrinter/manualfeed.snd              ./usr/ucb/colcrt
./usr/lib/NextPrinter/nopaper.snd                 ./usr/ucb/colrm
./usr/lib/NextPrinter/paperjam.snd                ./usr/ucb/compress
./usr/lib/NextPrinter/printeropen.snd             ./usr/ucb/uncompress
./usr/lib/NextPrinter/testpage.ps                 ./usr/ucb/zcat
./usr/lib/NextPrinter/.places                     ./usr/ucb/error
./usr/lib/lpd                                     ./usr/ucb/expand
./usr/lib/lpf                                     ./usr/ucb/finger
./usr/lib/necf                                    ./usr/ucb/fold
./usr/lib/libsynthpatches_p.a                     ./usr/ucb/from
./usr/lib/libsynthpatches.a                       ./usr/ucb/ftp
./usr/lib/libunitgenerators_p.a                   ./usr/ucb/grep
./usr/lib/libunitgenerators.a                     ./usr/ucb/groups
./usr/lib/.places                                 ./usr/ucb/head
./usr/man                                         ./usr/ucb/indent
```

```
./usr/ucb/last                          ./usr/ucb/yes
./usr/ucb/lastcomm                      ./usr/ucb/ctags
./usr/ucb/leave                         ./usr/ucb/ptags
./usr/ucb/lock                          ./usr/ucb/ctree
./usr/ucb/logger                        ./usr/ucb/cfunc
./usr/ucb/man                           ./usr/ucb/ex
./usr/ucb/apropos                       ./usr/ucb/edit
./usr/ucb/whatis                        ./usr/ucb/vi
./usr/ucb/mkstr                         ./usr/ucb/view
./usr/ucb/more                          ./usr/ucb/lpr
./usr/ucb/page                          ./usr/ucb/lpq
./usr/ucb/msgs                          ./usr/ucb/lprm
./usr/ucb/netstat                       ./usr/ucb/lptest
./usr/ucb/printenv                      ./usr/ucb/.places
./usr/ucb/quota                         ./usr/include
./usr/ucb/rcp                           ./usr/include/ldsyms.h
./usr/ucb/rdist                         ./usr/include/reloc.h
./usr/ucb/rlogin                        ./usr/include/acc.h
./usr/ucb/rsh                           ./usr/include/access.h
./usr/ucb/rup                           ./usr/include/aliasdb.h
./usr/ucb/ruptime                       ./usr/include/ansi.h
./usr/ucb/rusers                        ./usr/include/ar.h
./usr/ucb/rwho                          ./usr/include/assert.h
./usr/ucb/script                        ./usr/include/c.h
./usr/ucb/praliases                     ./usr/include/ci.h
./usr/ucb/vacation                      ./usr/include/cthread_internals.h
./usr/ucb/soelim                        ./usr/include/cthreads.h
./usr/ucb/sysline                       ./usr/include/ctype.h
./usr/ucb/tail                          ./usr/include/dbm.h
./usr/ucb/talk                          ./usr/include/del.h
./usr/ucb/tcopy                         ./usr/include/disktab.h
./usr/ucb/telnet                        ./usr/include/errno.h
./usr/ucb/tftp                          ./usr/include/exc.h
./usr/ucb/tn3270                        ./usr/include/exportent.h
./usr/ucb/mset                          ./usr/include/fcntl.h
./usr/ucb/tset                          ./usr/include/float.h
./usr/ucb/reset                         ./usr/include/fstab.h
./usr/ucb/ul                            ./usr/include/grp.h
./usr/ucb/unexpand                      ./usr/include/key_defs.h
./usr/ucb/unifdef                       ./usr/include/lastlog.h
./usr/ucb/users                         ./usr/include/libc.h
./usr/ucb/vgrind                        ./usr/include/limits.h
./usr/ucb/w                             ./usr/include/locale.h
./usr/ucb/uptime                        ./usr/include/ls_defs.h
./usr/ucb/wc                            ./usr/include/mach.h
./usr/ucb/what                          ./usr/include/mach_error.h
./usr/ucb/whereis                       ./usr/include/mach_exception.h
./usr/ucb/which                         ./usr/include/mach_extra.h
./usr/ucb/whoami                        ./usr/include/mach_init.h
./usr/ucb/whois                         ./usr/include/mach_types.h
./usr/ucb/xstr                          ./usr/include/math.h
```

./usr/include/memory.h
./usr/include/mntent.h
./usr/include/mp.h
./usr/include/msg_type.h
./usr/include/mtab.h
./usr/include/ndbm.h
./usr/include/netdb.h
./usr/include/netname_defs.h
./usr/include/nlist.h
./usr/include/nm_defs.h
./usr/include/pager.h
./usr/include/pcc.h
./usr/include/printerdb.h
./usr/include/pwd.h
./usr/include/ranlib.h
./usr/include/regex.h
./usr/include/resolv.h
./usr/include/setjmp.h
./usr/include/sgtty.h
./usr/include/signal.h
./usr/include/stab.h
./usr/include/stdarg.h
./usr/include/stddef.h
./usr/include/stdio.h
./usr/include/stdlib.h
./usr/include/string.h
./usr/include/strings.h
./usr/include/struct.h
./usr/include/syscall.h
./usr/include/sysexits.h
./usr/include/syslog.h
./usr/include/time.h
./usr/include/ttyent.h
./usr/include/ttyloc.h
./usr/include/tzfile.h
./usr/include/utmp.h
./usr/include/varargs.h
./usr/include/vfont.h
./usr/include/std_types.defs
./usr/include/mach.defs
./usr/include/pager.defs
./usr/include/exc.defs
./usr/include/servers
./usr/include/servers/km.defs
./usr/include/servers/logstat.defs
./usr/include/servers/env_mgr.defs
./usr/include/servers/ipcx.defs
./usr/include/servers/service.defs
./usr/include/servers/netname.defs
./usr/include/servers/emdefs.h
./usr/include/servers/env_mgr.h

./usr/include/servers/ipcx.h
./usr/include/servers/ipcx_types.h
./usr/include/servers/km.h
./usr/include/servers/logstat.h
./usr/include/servers/netname.h
./usr/include/servers/service.h
./usr/include/servers/.places
./usr/include/arpa
./usr/include/arpa/ftp.h
./usr/include/arpa/inet.h
./usr/include/arpa/nameser.h
./usr/include/arpa/telnet.h
./usr/include/arpa/tftp.h
./usr/include/arpa/.places
./usr/include/netinfo
./usr/include/netinfo/_lu_types.x
./usr/include/netinfo/lookup_types.h
./usr/include/netinfo/ni.h
./usr/include/netinfo/ni_prot.h
./usr/include/netinfo/ni_prot.x
./usr/include/netinfo/ni_util.h
./usr/include/netinfo/nibind_prot.h
./usr/include/netinfo/nibind_prot.x
./usr/include/netinfo/lookup.defs
./usr/include/netinfo/.places
./usr/include/next
./usr/include/next/cthreads.h
./usr/include/next/DEFAULT.h
./usr/include/next/FEATURES.h
./usr/include/next/boolean.h
./usr/include/next/cframe.h
./usr/include/next/clock.h
./usr/include/next/cons.h
./usr/include/next/cpu.h
./usr/include/next/event_meter.h
./usr/include/next/eventc.h
./usr/include/next/exception.h
./usr/include/next/fpc.h
./usr/include/next/ipl_meas.h
./usr/include/next/kern_return.h
./usr/include/next/machparam.h
./usr/include/next/mem.h
./usr/include/next/mmu.h
./usr/include/next/mtio.h
./usr/include/next/param.h
./usr/include/next/pcb.h
./usr/include/next/pmap.h
./usr/include/next/printf.h
./usr/include/next/psl.h
./usr/include/next/reboot.h
./usr/include/next/reg.h

```
./usr/include/next/scb.h
./usr/include/next/sched_param.h
./usr/include/next/scr.h
./usr/include/next/signal.h
./usr/include/next/spl.h
./usr/include/next/spl_measured.h
./usr/include/next/syscall_sw.h
./usr/include/next/table.h
./usr/include/next/thread.h
./usr/include/next/thread_status.h
./usr/include/next/time_stamp.h
./usr/include/next/timer.h
./usr/include/next/trap.h
./usr/include/next/unix_traps.h
./usr/include/next/user.h
./usr/include/next/vm_param.h
./usr/include/next/vm_types.h
./usr/include/next/vmparam.h
./usr/include/next/xpr.h
./usr/include/next/.places
./usr/include/protocols
./usr/include/protocols/dumprestore.h
./usr/include/protocols/routed.h
./usr/include/protocols/rwhod.h
./usr/include/protocols/talkd.h
./usr/include/protocols/timed.h
./usr/include/protocols/.places
./usr/include/rpc
./usr/include/rpc/auth.h
./usr/include/rpc/auth_unix.h
./usr/include/rpc/clnt.h
./usr/include/rpc/pmap_clnt.h
./usr/include/rpc/pmap_prot.h
./usr/include/rpc/pmap_rmt.h
./usr/include/rpc/rpc.h
./usr/include/rpc/rpc_msg.h
./usr/include/rpc/svc.h
./usr/include/rpc/svc_auth.h
./usr/include/rpc/types.h
./usr/include/rpc/xdr.h
./usr/include/rpc/.places
./usr/include/rpcsvc
./usr/include/rpcsvc/bootparam.h
./usr/include/rpcsvc/ether.h
./usr/include/rpcsvc/klm_prot.h
./usr/include/rpcsvc/mount.h
./usr/include/rpcsvc/nlm_prot.h
./usr/include/rpcsvc/rex.h
./usr/include/rpcsvc/rquota.h
./usr/include/rpcsvc/rstat.h
./usr/include/rpcsvc/rusers.h

./usr/include/rpcsvc/rwall.h
./usr/include/rpcsvc/sm_inter.h
./usr/include/rpcsvc/spray.h
./usr/include/rpcsvc/yp_prot.h
./usr/include/rpcsvc/ypclnt.h
./usr/include/rpcsvc/yppasswd.h
./usr/include/rpcsvc/ypv1_prot.h
./usr/include/rpcsvc/.places
./usr/include/udp
./usr/include/udp/udp.h
./usr/include/udp/.places
./usr/include/machine
./usr/include/db
./usr/include/db/db.h
./usr/include/db/.places
./usr/include/curses.h
./usr/include/mon
./usr/include/mon/animate.h
./usr/include/mon/assym.h
./usr/include/mon/bootp.h
./usr/include/mon/cursor.h
./usr/include/mon/global.h
./usr/include/mon/kmreg.h
./usr/include/mon/monparam.h
./usr/include/mon/msgbuf.h
./usr/include/mon/nvram.h
./usr/include/mon/region.h
./usr/include/mon/reglist.h
./usr/include/mon/sio.h
./usr/include/mon/tftp.h
./usr/include/mon/.places
./usr/include/net
./usr/include/net/af.h
./usr/include/net/dli_var.h
./usr/include/net/if.h
./usr/include/net/if_arp.h
./usr/include/net/netisr.h
./usr/include/net/raw_cb.h
./usr/include/net/route.h
./usr/include/net/.places
./usr/include/netimp
./usr/include/netimp/if_imp.h
./usr/include/netimp/if_imphost.h
./usr/include/netimp/.places
./usr/include/netinet
./usr/include/netinet/icmp_var.h
./usr/include/netinet/if_ether.h
./usr/include/netinet/in.h
./usr/include/netinet/in_pcb.h
./usr/include/netinet/in_systm.h
./usr/include/netinet/in_var.h
```

./usr/include/netinet/ip.h
./usr/include/netinet/ip_icmp.h
./usr/include/netinet/ip_var.h
./usr/include/netinet/pcbheadsw.h
./usr/include/netinet/tcp.h
./usr/include/netinet/tcp_debug.h
./usr/include/netinet/tcp_fsm.h
./usr/include/netinet/tcp_seq.h
./usr/include/netinet/tcp_timer.h
./usr/include/netinet/tcp_var.h
./usr/include/netinet/tcpip.h
./usr/include/netinet/udp.h
./usr/include/netinet/udp_var.h
./usr/include/netinet/.places
./usr/include/netns
./usr/include/netns/idp.h
./usr/include/netns/idp_var.h
./usr/include/netns/ns.h
./usr/include/netns/ns_error.h
./usr/include/netns/ns_if.h
./usr/include/netns/ns_pcb.h
./usr/include/netns/sp.h
./usr/include/netns/spidp.h
./usr/include/netns/spp_debug.h
./usr/include/netns/spp_timer.h
./usr/include/netns/spp_var.h
./usr/include/netns/.places
./usr/include/nextdev
./usr/include/nextdev/busvar.h
./usr/include/nextdev/canon.h
./usr/include/nextdev/disk.h
./usr/include/nextdev/dma.h
./usr/include/nextdev/ev_vars.h
./usr/include/nextdev/event.h
./usr/include/nextdev/event_interface.h
./usr/include/nextdev/evio.h
./usr/include/nextdev/evsio.h
./usr/include/nextdev/font8x10.h
./usr/include/nextdev/ifs.h
./usr/include/nextdev/keycodes.h
./usr/include/nextdev/kmreg.h
./usr/include/nextdev/ldd.h
./usr/include/nextdev/monreg.h
./usr/include/nextdev/nbicreg.h
./usr/include/nextdev/np_buddy.h
./usr/include/nextdev/npio.h
./usr/include/nextdev/npreg.h
./usr/include/nextdev/npvar.h
./usr/include/nextdev/odreg.h
./usr/include/nextdev/odvar.h
./usr/include/nextdev/ohlfs12.h

./usr/include/nextdev/screg.h
./usr/include/nextdev/scsireg.h
./usr/include/nextdev/scsivar.h
./usr/include/nextdev/scvar.h
./usr/include/nextdev/sdvar.h
./usr/include/nextdev/sgvar.h
./usr/include/nextdev/slot.h
./usr/include/nextdev/snd_dsp.h
./usr/include/nextdev/snd_dspreg.h
./usr/include/nextdev/snd_msgs.h
./usr/include/nextdev/snd_snd.h
./usr/include/nextdev/snd_var.h
./usr/include/nextdev/stvar.h
./usr/include/nextdev/td.h
./usr/include/nextdev/video.h
./usr/include/nextdev/zscom.h
./usr/include/nextdev/zsreg.h
./usr/include/nextdev/.places
./usr/include/nextif
./usr/include/nextif/if_bus.h
./usr/include/nextif/if_enreg.h
./usr/include/nextif/.places
./usr/include/sys
./usr/include/sys/acct.h
./usr/include/sys/assert.h
./usr/include/sys/bkmac.h
./usr/include/sys/boolean.h
./usr/include/sys/buf.h
./usr/include/sys/callout.h
./usr/include/sys/clist.h
./usr/include/sys/conf.h
./usr/include/sys/dir.h
./usr/include/sys/disktab.h
./usr/include/sys/dk.h
./usr/include/sys/dkbad.h
./usr/include/sys/dnlc.h
./usr/include/sys/domain.h
./usr/include/sys/errno.h
./usr/include/sys/exception.h
./usr/include/sys/fcntl.h
./usr/include/sys/features.h
./usr/include/sys/file.h
./usr/include/sys/qprof.h
./usr/include/sys/ioctl.h
./usr/include/sys/kalloc.h
./usr/include/sys/kern_msg.h
./usr/include/sys/kern_obj.h
./usr/include/sys/kern_port.h
./usr/include/sys/kern_return.h
./usr/include/sys/kern_set.h
./usr/include/sys/kernel.h

./usr/include/sys/loader.h

./usr/include/sys/lock.h

./usr/include/sys/mach_extra.h

./usr/include/sys/mach_param.h

./usr/include/sys/mach_swapon.h

./usr/include/sys/machine.h

./usr/include/sys/mbuf.h

./usr/include/sys/message.h

./usr/include/sys/metalink.h

./usr/include/sys/mfs.h

./usr/include/sys/miq_errors.h

./usr/include/sys/mman.h

./usr/include/sys/mount.h

./usr/include/sys/msg_queue.h

./usr/include/sys/msg_type.h

./usr/include/sys/msgbuf.h

./usr/include/sys/mtio.h

./usr/include/sys/notify.h

./usr/include/sys/param.h

./usr/include/sys/pathname.h

./usr/include/sys/port.h

./usr/include/sys/port_object.h

./usr/include/sys/proc.h

./usr/include/sys/protosw.h

./usr/include/sys/ptrace.h

./usr/include/sys/queue.h

./usr/include/sys/quota.h

./usr/include/sys/reboot.h

./usr/include/sys/resource.h

./usr/include/sys/sched.h

./usr/include/sys/sched_prim.h

./usr/include/sys/sched_prim_macros.h

./usr/include/sys/signal.h

./usr/include/sys/socket.h

./usr/include/sys/socketvar.h

./usr/include/sys/stat.h

./usr/include/sys/syslog.h

./usr/include/sys/sysmacros.h

./usr/include/sys/systm.h

./usr/include/sys/table.h

./usr/include/sys/task.h

./usr/include/sys/task_info.h

./usr/include/sys/task_special_ports.h

./usr/include/sys/thread.h

./usr/include/sys/thread_info.h

./usr/include/sys/thread_modes.h

./usr/include/sys/thread_special_ports.h

./usr/include/sys/thread_status.h

./usr/include/sys/thread_swap.h

./usr/include/sys/time.h

./usr/include/sys/time_stamp.h

./usr/include/sys/time_value.h

./usr/include/sys/timeb.h

./usr/include/sys/timer.h

./usr/include/sys/times.h

./usr/include/sys/trace.h

./usr/include/sys/tty.h

./usr/include/sys/ttychars.h

./usr/include/sys/ttydev.h

./usr/include/sys/types.h

./usr/include/sys/uio.h

./usr/include/sys/un.h

./usr/include/sys/unpcb.h

./usr/include/sys/user.h

./usr/include/sys/utime.h

./usr/include/sys/ux_exception.h

./usr/include/sys/vadvise.h

./usr/include/sys/version.h

./usr/include/sys/vfs.h

./usr/include/sys/vlimit.h

./usr/include/sys/vm.h

./usr/include/sys/vmmac.h

./usr/include/sys/vmmeter.h

./usr/include/sys/vmparam.h

./usr/include/sys/vmsystm.h

./usr/include/sys/vnode.h

./usr/include/sys/wait.h

./usr/include/sys/xpr.h

./usr/include/sys/zalloc.h

./usr/include/sys/.places

./usr/include/ufs

./usr/include/ufs/fs.h

./usr/include/ufs/fsdir.h

./usr/include/ufs/inode.h

./usr/include/ufs/mount.h

./usr/include/ufs/quotas.h

./usr/include/ufs/.places

./usr/include/nfs

./usr/include/nfs/export.h

./usr/include/nfs/nfs.h

./usr/include/nfs/nfs_clnt.h

./usr/include/nfs/nfs_mount.h

./usr/include/nfs/rnode.h

./usr/include/nfs/.places

./usr/include/kern

./usr/include/kern/exc.h

./usr/include/kern/ipc_basics.h

./usr/include/kern/ipc_cache.h

./usr/include/kern/ipc_copyin.h

./usr/include/kern/ipc_copyout.h

./usr/include/kern/ipc_globals.h

./usr/include/kern/ipc_hash.h

```
./usr/include/kern/ipc_kmesg.h
./usr/include/kern/ipc_mports.h
./usr/include/kern/ipc_netport.h
./usr/include/kern/ipc_pobj.h
./usr/include/kern/ipc_prims.h
./usr/include/kern/ipc_ptraps.h
./usr/include/kern/ipc_signal.h
./usr/include/kern/ipc_statistics.h
./usr/include/kern/ipc_tt.h
./usr/include/kern/mach.h
./usr/include/kern/mach_ipc_defs.h
./usr/include/kern/mach_redefines.h
./usr/include/kern/mach_traps.h
./usr/include/kern/mach_types.h
./usr/include/kern/mach_user_internal.h
./usr/include/kern/macro_help.h
./usr/include/kern/pager.h
./usr/include/kern/pager_default.h
./usr/include/kern/parallel.h
./usr/include/kern/syscall_sw.h
./usr/include/kern/.places
./usr/include/vm
./usr/include/vm/device_pager.h
./usr/include/vm/memory_object.h
./usr/include/vm/pmap.h
./usr/include/vm/vm_fault.h
./usr/include/vm/vm_inherit.h
./usr/include/vm/vm_kern.h
./usr/include/vm/vm_map.h
./usr/include/vm/vm_object.h
./usr/include/vm/vm_page.h
./usr/include/vm/vm_pageout.h
./usr/include/vm/vm_pager.h
./usr/include/vm/vm_param.h
./usr/include/vm/vm_prot.h
./usr/include/vm/vm_statistics.h
./usr/include/vm/vm_user.h
./usr/include/vm/vnode_pager.h
./usr/include/vm/.places
./usr/include/objc
./usr/include/objc/Object.h
./usr/include/objc/HashTable.h
./usr/include/objc/List.h
./usr/include/objc/Storage.h
./usr/include/objc/StreamTable.h
./usr/include/objc/objc-runtime.h
./usr/include/objc/objc-class.h
./usr/include/objc/objc.h
./usr/include/objc/vectors.h
./usr/include/objc/hashtable.h
./usr/include/objc/typedstream.h
./usr/include/objc/.places
./usr/include/mig_errors.h
./usr/include/sound
./usr/include/sound/sound.h
./usr/include/sound/soundstruct.h
./usr/include/sound/sounderror.h
./usr/include/sound/utilsound.h
./usr/include/sound/filesound.h
./usr/include/sound/editsound.h
./usr/include/sound/sounddriver.h
./usr/include/sound/accesssound.h
./usr/include/sound/convertsound.h
./usr/include/sound/performsound.h
./usr/include/sound/.places
./usr/include/streams
./usr/include/streams/streams.h
./usr/include/streams/streamsimpl.h
./usr/include/streams/error.h
./usr/include/streams/.places
./usr/include/text
./usr/include/text/fileutil.h
./usr/include/text/text.h
./usr/include/text/pathutil.h
./usr/include/text/search.h
./usr/include/text/spell.h
./usr/include/text/strutil.h
./usr/include/text/webster.h
./usr/include/text/wftable.h
./usr/include/text/ix.h
./usr/include/text/.places
./usr/include/dsp
./usr/include/dsp/arrayproc.h
./usr/include/dsp/dsp.h
./usr/include/dsp/dsp_errno.h
./usr/include/dsp/dsp_structs.h
./usr/include/dsp/libdsp.h
./usr/include/dsp/DSPMessage.h
./usr/include/dsp/DSPTransfer.h
./usr/include/dsp/DSPControl.h
./usr/include/dsp/DSPConversion.h
./usr/include/dsp/DSPStructMisc.h
./usr/include/dsp/DSPObject.h
./usr/include/dsp/DSPError.h
./usr/include/dsp/dsp_messages.h
./usr/include/dsp/dsp_memory_map_mk.h
./usr/include/dsp/dsp_memory_map_ap.h
./usr/include/dsp/.places
./usr/include/appkit
./usr/include/appkit/ActionCell.h
./usr/include/appkit/Application.h
./usr/include/appkit/Bitmap.h
```

```
./usr/include/appkit/Box.h
./usr/include/appkit/Button.h
./usr/include/appkit/ButtonCell.h
./usr/include/appkit/Cell.h
./usr/include/appkit/ChoosePrinter.h
./usr/include/appkit/ClipView.h
./usr/include/appkit/Control.h
./usr/include/appkit/Cursor.h
./usr/include/appkit/Font.h
./usr/include/appkit/FontPanel.h
./usr/include/appkit/FontManager.h
./usr/include/appkit/Form.h
./usr/include/appkit/FormCell.h
./usr/include/appkit/Listener.h
./usr/include/appkit/Matrix.h
./usr/include/appkit/Menu.h
./usr/include/appkit/MenuCell.h
./usr/include/appkit/OpenPanel.h
./usr/include/appkit/PageLayout.h
./usr/include/appkit/Panel.h
./usr/include/appkit/Pasteboard.h
./usr/include/appkit/PopUpList.h
./usr/include/appkit/PrintInfo.h
./usr/include/appkit/PrintPanel.h
./usr/include/appkit/Responder.h
./usr/include/appkit/SavePanel.h
./usr/include/appkit/ScrollView.h
./usr/include/appkit/Scroller.h
./usr/include/appkit/SelectionCell.h
./usr/include/appkit/Slider.h
./usr/include/appkit/SliderCell.h
./usr/include/appkit/Speaker.h
./usr/include/appkit/Text.h
./usr/include/appkit/TextField.h
./usr/include/appkit/TextFieldCell.h
./usr/include/appkit/View.h
./usr/include/appkit/Window.h
./usr/include/appkit/appkit.h
./usr/include/appkit/afm.h
./usr/include/appkit/chunk.h
./usr/include/appkit/defaults.h
./usr/include/appkit/errors.h
./usr/include/appkit/graphics.h
./usr/include/appkit/nextstd.h
./usr/include/appkit/timer.h
./usr/include/appkit/tiff.h
./usr/include/appkit/.places
./usr/include/appkit/publicWraps.h
./usr/include/dpsclient
./usr/include/dpsclient/dpsNeXT.h
./usr/include/dpsclient/dpsclient.h
```

```
./usr/include/dpsclient/dpsfriends.h
./usr/include/dpsclient/event.h
./usr/include/dpsclient/psops.h
./usr/include/dpsclient/wraps.h
./usr/include/dpsclient/dpswraps.h
./usr/include/dpsclient/dpsops.h
./usr/include/dpsclient/.places
./usr/include/midi
./usr/include/midi/midi_types.h
./usr/include/midi/midi_error.h
./usr/include/midi/midi_timer_error.h
./usr/include/midi/midi_reply_handler.h
./usr/include/midi/midi_timer_reply_handler.h
./usr/include/midi/midi_server.h
./usr/include/midi/midi_timer.h
./usr/include/midi/.places
./usr/include/musickit
./usr/include/musickit/Conductor.h
./usr/include/musickit/Midi.h
./usr/include/musickit/FilePerformer.h
./usr/include/musickit/Envelope.h
./usr/include/musickit/PartPerformer.h
./usr/include/musickit/FileWriter.h
./usr/include/musickit/Instrument.h
./usr/include/musickit/Note.h
./usr/include/musickit/NoteFilter.h
./usr/include/musickit/NoteReceiver.h
./usr/include/musickit/NoteSender.h
./usr/include/musickit/Orchestra.h
./usr/include/musickit/Part.h
./usr/include/musickit/PatchTemplate.h
./usr/include/musickit/PartRecorder.h
./usr/include/musickit/ScorePerformer.h
./usr/include/musickit/Performer.h
./usr/include/musickit/Score.h
./usr/include/musickit/ScorefilePerformer.h
./usr/include/musickit/ScoreRecorder.h
./usr/include/musickit/ScorefileWriter.h
./usr/include/musickit/SynthData.h
./usr/include/musickit/SynthInstrument.h
./usr/include/musickit/SynthPatch.h
./usr/include/musickit/TuningSystem.h
./usr/include/musickit/UnitGenerator.h
./usr/include/musickit/Partials.h
./usr/include/musickit/WaveTable.h
./usr/include/musickit/Samples.h
./usr/include/musickit/musickit.h
./usr/include/musickit/timeunits.h
./usr/include/musickit/devstatus.h
./usr/include/musickit/orch.h
./usr/include/musickit/dspwrap.h
```

```
./usr/include/musickit/errors.h
./usr/include/musickit/pitches.h
./usr/include/musickit/keynums.h
./usr/include/musickit/scorefileobject.h
./usr/include/musickit/params.h
./usr/include/musickit/synthpatches
./usr/include/musickit/synthpatches/Simp.h
./usr/include/musickit/synthpatches/DBWave1vi.h
./usr/include/musickit/synthpatches/Wave1i.h
./usr/include/musickit/synthpatches/Wave1vi.h
./usr/include/musickit/synthpatches/Fm1i.h
./usr/include/musickit/synthpatches/Fm1vi.h
./usr/include/musickit/synthpatches/DBWave1v.h
./usr/include/musickit/synthpatches/Wave1.h
./usr/include/musickit/synthpatches/Wave1v.h
./usr/include/musickit/synthpatches/Fm1.h
./usr/include/musickit/synthpatches/Fm1v.h
./usr/include/musickit/synthpatches/Fm2pnvi.h
./usr/include/musickit/synthpatches/Fm2pvi.h
./usr/include/musickit/synthpatches/Fm2cnvi.h
./usr/include/musickit/synthpatches/Fm2cvi.h
./usr/include/musickit/synthpatches/DBFm1vi.h
./usr/include/musickit/synthpatches/DBWave2vi.h
./usr/include/musickit/synthpatches/Pluck.h
./usr/include/musickit/synthpatches/synthpatches.h
./usr/include/musickit/synthpatches/.places
./usr/include/musickit/unitgenerators
./usr/include/musickit/unitgenerators/Add2UG.h
./usr/include/musickit/unitgenerators/Add2UGxxx.h
./usr/include/musickit/unitgenerators/Add2UGxxy.h
./usr/include/musickit/unitgenerators/Add2UGxyx.h
./usr/include/musickit/unitgenerators/Add2UGxyy.h
./usr/include/musickit/unitgenerators/Add2UGyxx.h
./usr/include/musickit/unitgenerators/Add2UGyxy.h
./usr/include/musickit/unitgenerators/Add2UGyyx.h
./usr/include/musickit/unitgenerators/Add2UGyyy.h
./usr/include/musickit/unitgenerators/Allpass1UG.h
./usr/include/musickit/unitgenerators/Allpass1UGxx.h
./usr/include/musickit/unitgenerators/Allpass1UGxy.h
./usr/include/musickit/unitgenerators/Allpass1UGyx.h
./usr/include/musickit/unitgenerators/Allpass1UGyy.h
./usr/include/musickit/unitgenerators/AsympUG.h
./usr/include/musickit/unitgenerators/AsympUGx.h
./usr/include/musickit/unitgenerators/AsympUGy.h
./usr/include/musickit/unitgenerators/ConstantUG.h
./usr/include/musickit/unitgenerators/ConstantUGx.h
./usr/include/musickit/unitgenerators/ConstantUGy.h
./usr/include/musickit/unitgenerators/DelayUG.h
./usr/include/musickit/unitgenerators/DelayUGxxx.h
./usr/include/musickit/unitgenerators/DelayUGxxy.h
./usr/include/musickit/unitgenerators/DelayUGxyx.h
```

```
./usr/include/musickit/unitgenerators/DelayUGxyy.h
./usr/include/musickit/unitgenerators/DelayUGyxx.h
./usr/include/musickit/unitgenerators/DelayUGyxy.h
./usr/include/musickit/unitgenerators/DelayUGyyx.h
./usr/include/musickit/unitgenerators/DelayUGyyy.h
./usr/include/musickit/unitgenerators/DswitchUG.h
./usr/include/musickit/unitgenerators/DswitchUGxx.h
./usr/include/musickit/unitgenerators/DswitchUGxy.h
./usr/include/musickit/unitgenerators/DswitchUGyx.h
./usr/include/musickit/unitgenerators/DswitchUGyy.h
./usr/include/musickit/unitgenerators/DswitchtUG.h
./usr/include/musickit/unitgenerators/DswitchtUGxx.h
./usr/include/musickit/unitgenerators/DswitchtUGxy.h
./usr/include/musickit/unitgenerators/DswitchtUGyx.h
./usr/include/musickit/unitgenerators/DswitchtUGyy.h
./usr/include/musickit/unitgenerators/InterpUG.h
./usr/include/musickit/unitgenerators/InterpUGxxxx.h
./usr/include/musickit/unitgenerators/InterpUGxxxy.h
./usr/include/musickit/unitgenerators/InterpUGxxyx.h
./usr/include/musickit/unitgenerators/InterpUGxxyy.h
./usr/include/musickit/unitgenerators/InterpUGxyxx.h
./usr/include/musickit/unitgenerators/InterpUGxyxy.h
./usr/include/musickit/unitgenerators/InterpUGxyyx.h
./usr/include/musickit/unitgenerators/InterpUGxyyy.h
./usr/include/musickit/unitgenerators/InterpUGyxxx.h
./usr/include/musickit/unitgenerators/InterpUGyxxy.h
./usr/include/musickit/unitgenerators/InterpUGyxyx.h
./usr/include/musickit/unitgenerators/InterpUGyxyy.h
./usr/include/musickit/unitgenerators/InterpUGyyxx.h
./usr/include/musickit/unitgenerators/InterpUGyyxy.h
./usr/include/musickit/unitgenerators/InterpUGyyyx.h
./usr/include/musickit/unitgenerators/InterpUGyyyy.h
./usr/include/musickit/unitgenerators/Mul1add2UG.h
./usr/include/musickit/unitgenerators/Mul1add2UGxxxx.h
./usr/include/musickit/unitgenerators/Mul1add2UGxxxy.h
./usr/include/musickit/unitgenerators/Mul1add2UGxxyx.h
./usr/include/musickit/unitgenerators/Mul1add2UGxxyy.h
./usr/include/musickit/unitgenerators/Mul1add2UGxyxx.h
./usr/include/musickit/unitgenerators/Mul1add2UGxyxy.h
./usr/include/musickit/unitgenerators/Mul1add2UGxyyx.h
./usr/include/musickit/unitgenerators/Mul1add2UGxyyy.h
./usr/include/musickit/unitgenerators/Mul1add2UGyxxx.h
./usr/include/musickit/unitgenerators/Mul1add2UGyxxy.h
./usr/include/musickit/unitgenerators/Mul1add2UGyxyx.h
./usr/include/musickit/unitgenerators/Mul1add2UGyxyy.h
./usr/include/musickit/unitgenerators/Mul1add2UGyyxx.h
./usr/include/musickit/unitgenerators/Mul1add2UGyyxy.h
./usr/include/musickit/unitgenerators/Mul1add2UGyyyx.h
./usr/include/musickit/unitgenerators/Mul1add2UGyyyy.h
./usr/include/musickit/unitgenerators/Mul2UG.h
./usr/include/musickit/unitgenerators/Mul2UGxxx.h
```

```
./usr/include/musickit/unitgenerators/Mul2UGxxy.h            ./usr/include/musickit/unitgenerators/OscgafiUGyxxy.h
./usr/include/musickit/unitgenerators/Mul2UGxyx.h            ./usr/include/musickit/unitgenerators/OscgafiUGyxyx.h
./usr/include/musickit/unitgenerators/Mul2UGxyy.h            ./usr/include/musickit/unitgenerators/OscgafiUGyxyy.h
./usr/include/musickit/unitgenerators/Mul2UGyxx.h            ./usr/include/musickit/unitgenerators/OscgafiUGyyxx.h
./usr/include/musickit/unitgenerators/Mul2UGyxy.h            ./usr/include/musickit/unitgenerators/OscgafiUGyyxy.h
./usr/include/musickit/unitgenerators/Mul2UGyyx.h            ./usr/include/musickit/unitgenerators/OscgafiUGyyyx.h
./usr/include/musickit/unitgenerators/Mul2UGyyy.h            ./usr/include/musickit/unitgenerators/OscgafiUGyyyy.h
./usr/include/musickit/unitgenerators/OnepoleUG.h            ./usr/include/musickit/unitgenerators/Out1aUG.h
./usr/include/musickit/unitgenerators/OnepoleUGxy.h          ./usr/include/musickit/unitgenerators/Out1aUGx.h
./usr/include/musickit/unitgenerators/OnepoleUGyx.h          ./usr/include/musickit/unitgenerators/Out1aUGy.h
./usr/include/musickit/unitgenerators/.places               ./usr/include/musickit/unitgenerators/Out1bUG.h
./usr/include/musickit/unitgenerators/OnepoleUGyy.h          ./usr/include/musickit/unitgenerators/Out1bUGx.h
./usr/include/musickit/unitgenerators/OnepoleUGxx.h          ./usr/include/musickit/unitgenerators/Out1bUGy.h
./usr/include/musickit/unitgenerators/OnezeroUG.h            ./usr/include/musickit/unitgenerators/Out2sumUG.h
./usr/include/musickit/unitgenerators/OnezeroUGxy.h          ./usr/include/musickit/unitgenerators/Out2sumUGx.h
./usr/include/musickit/unitgenerators/OnezeroUGyx.h          ./usr/include/musickit/unitgenerators/Out2sumUGy.h
./usr/include/musickit/unitgenerators/OnezeroUGyy.h          ./usr/include/musickit/unitgenerators/ScaleUG.h
./usr/include/musickit/unitgenerators/OnezeroUGxx.h          ./usr/include/musickit/unitgenerators/ScaleUGxy.h
./usr/include/musickit/unitgenerators/OscgUG.h               ./usr/include/musickit/unitgenerators/ScaleUGyx.h
./usr/include/musickit/unitgenerators/OscgUGxy.h             ./usr/include/musickit/unitgenerators/ScaleUGyy.h
./usr/include/musickit/unitgenerators/OscgUGyx.h             ./usr/include/musickit/unitgenerators/ScaleUGxx.h
./usr/include/musickit/unitgenerators/OscgUGyy.h             ./usr/include/musickit/unitgenerators/Scl1add2UG.h
./usr/include/musickit/unitgenerators/OscgUGxx.h             ./usr/include/musickit/unitgenerators/Scl1add2UGxxx.h
./usr/include/musickit/unitgenerators/OscgafUGs.h            ./usr/include/musickit/unitgenerators/Scl1add2UGxxy.h
./usr/include/musickit/unitgenerators/OscgafUG.h             ./usr/include/musickit/unitgenerators/Scl1add2UGxyx.h
./usr/include/musickit/unitgenerators/OscgafiUG.h            ./usr/include/musickit/unitgenerators/Scl1add2UGxyy.h
./usr/include/musickit/unitgenerators/OscgafUGxxxx.h         ./usr/include/musickit/unitgenerators/Scl1add2UGyxx.h
./usr/include/musickit/unitgenerators/OscgafUGxxxy.h         ./usr/include/musickit/unitgenerators/Scl1add2UGyxy.h
./usr/include/musickit/unitgenerators/OscgafUGxxyx.h         ./usr/include/musickit/unitgenerators/Scl1add2UGyyx.h
./usr/include/musickit/unitgenerators/OscgafUGxxyy.h         ./usr/include/musickit/unitgenerators/Scl1add2UGyyy.h
./usr/include/musickit/unitgenerators/OscgafUGxyxx.h         ./usr/include/musickit/unitgenerators/Scl2add2UG.h
./usr/include/musickit/unitgenerators/OscgafUGxyxy.h         ./usr/include/musickit/unitgenerators/Scl2add2UGxxx.h
./usr/include/musickit/unitgenerators/OscgafUGxyyx.h         ./usr/include/musickit/unitgenerators/Scl2add2UGxxy.h
./usr/include/musickit/unitgenerators/OscgafUGxyyy.h         ./usr/include/musickit/unitgenerators/Scl2add2UGxyx.h
./usr/include/musickit/unitgenerators/OscgafUGyxxx.h         ./usr/include/musickit/unitgenerators/Scl2add2UGxyy.h
./usr/include/musickit/unitgenerators/OscgatUGyxxy.h         ./usr/include/musickit/unitgenerators/Scl2add2UGyxx.h
./usr/include/musickit/unitgenerators/OscgafUGyxyx.h         ./usr/include/musickit/unitgenerators/Scl2add2UGyxy.h
./usr/include/musickit/unitgenerators/OscgafUGyxyy.h         ./usr/include/musickit/unitgenerators/Scl2add2UGyyx.h
./usr/include/musickit/unitgenerators/OscgafUGyyxx.h         ./usr/include/musickit/unitgenerators/Scl2add2UGyyy.h
./usr/include/musickit/unitgenerators/OscgafUGyyxy.h         ./usr/include/musickit/unitgenerators/SnoiseUG.h
./usr/include/musickit/unitgenerators/OscgafUGyyyx.h         ./usr/include/musickit/unitgenerators/SnoiseUGx.h
./usr/include/musickit/unitgenerators/OscgafUGyyyy.h         ./usr/include/musickit/unitgenerators/SnoiseUGy.h
./usr/include/musickit/unitgenerators/OscgafiUGxxxx.h        ./usr/include/musickit/unitgenerators/UnoiseUG.h
./usr/include/musickit/unitgenerators/OscgafiUGxxxy.h        ./usr/include/musickit/unitgenerators/UnoiseUGx.h
./usr/include/musickit/unitgenerators/OscgafiUGxxyx.h        ./usr/include/musickit/unitgenerators/UnoiseUGy.h
./usr/include/musickit/unitgenerators/OscgafiUGxxyy.h        ./usr/include/musickit/unitgenerators/unitgenerators.h
./usr/include/musickit/unitgenerators/OscgafiUGxyxx.h        ./usr/include/musickit/.places
./usr/include/musickit/unitgenerators/OscgafiUGxyxy.h        ./usr/include/nib
./usr/include/musickit/unitgenerators/OscgafiUGxyyx.h        ./usr/include/nib/InterfaceBuilder.h
./usr/include/musickit/unitgenerators/OscgafiUGxyyy.h        ./usr/include/nib/.places
./usr/include/musickit/unitgenerators/OscgafiUGyxxx.h        ./usr/include/soundkit
```

```
./usr/include/soundkit/soundkit.h          ./usr/bin/sleep
./usr/include/soundkit/Sound.h             ./usr/bin/spellout
./usr/include/soundkit/SoundView.h         ./usr/bin/spellin
./usr/include/soundkit/SoundMeter.h        ./usr/bin/spell
./usr/include/soundkit/.places             ./usr/bin/spline
./usr/include/.places                      ./usr/bin/split
./usr/bin                                  ./usr/bin/struct
./usr/bin/newaliases                       ./usr/bin/sum
./usr/bin/mailq                            ./usr/bin/tabs
./usr/bin/arll                             ./usr/bin/tbl
./usr/bin/atq                              ./usr/bin/tc
./usr/bin/at                               ./usr/bin/tip
./usr/bin/atrm                             ./usr/bin/cu
./usr/bin/bc                               ./usr/bin/tk
./usr/bin/blit                             ./usr/bin/troff
./usr/bin/bm                               ./usr/bin/tty
./usr/bin/cal                              ./usr/bin/units
./usr/bin/calendar                         ./usr/bin/uucp
./usr/bin/cb                               ./usr/bin/uux
./usr/bin/checkeq                          ./usr/bin/uulog
./usr/bin/col                              ./usr/bin/uuname
./usr/bin/comm                             ./usr/bin/uusnap
./usr/bin/crypt                            ./usr/bin/uupoll
./usr/bin/dc                               ./usr/bin/uuq
./usr/bin/deroff                           ./usr/bin/uusend
./usr/bin/style                            ./usr/bin/ruusend
./usr/bin/diction                          ./usr/bin/uuencode
./usr/bin/explain                          ./usr/bin/uudecode
./usr/bin/diff3                            ./usr/bin/vm_stat
./usr/bin/egrep                            ./usr/bin/wh
./usr/bin/eqn                              ./usr/bin/xargs
./usr/bin/fgrep                            ./usr/bin/enroll
./usr/bin/hostinfo                         ./usr/bin/xget
./usr/bin/iostat                           ./usr/bin/xsend
./usr/bin/less                             ./usr/bin/ypcat
./usr/bin/look                             ./usr/bin/ypmatch
./usr/bin/mesg                             ./usr/bin/yppasswd
./usr/bin/neqn                             ./usr/bin/ypwhich
./usr/bin/nohup                            ./usr/bin/on
./usr/bin/nroff                            ./usr/bin/etags
./usr/bin/ptx                              ./usr/bin/emacs
./usr/bin/ratfor                           ./usr/bin/niload
./usr/bin/ci                               ./usr/bin/nidump
./usr/bin/co                               ./usr/bin/niutil
./usr/bin/ident                            ./usr/bin/basename
./usr/bin/rcs                              ./usr/bin/find
./usr/bin/rcsdiff                          ./usr/bin/install
./usr/bin/rcsmerge                         ./usr/bin/join
./usr/bin/rlog                             ./usr/bin/lex
./usr/bin/sccstorcs                        ./usr/bin/lorder
./usr/bin/rev                              ./usr/bin/m4
```

```
./usr/bin/md                           ./usr/bin/enscript
./usr/bin/mig                          ./usr/bin/ps4014
./usr/bin/refer                        ./usr/bin/ps630
./usr/bin/addbib                       ./usr/bin/pscat
./usr/bin/sortbib                      ./usr/bin/pscatmap
./usr/bin/roffbib                      ./usr/bin/psdit
./usr/bin/indxbib                      ./usr/bin/psplot
./usr/bin/lookbib                      ./usr/bin/psrev
./usr/bin/rpcgen                       ./usr/bin/ptroff
./usr/bin/sort                         ./usr/bin/psroff
./usr/bin/touch                        ./usr/bin/pswrap
./usr/bin/tr                           ./usr/bin/playscore
./usr/bin/tsort                        ./usr/bin/Install_TeX
./usr/bin/uniq                         ./usr/bin/tex
./usr/bin/vers_string                  ./usr/bin/.places
./usr/bin/yacc                         ./usr/standalone
./usr/bin/sndinfo                      ./usr/standalone/boot
./usr/bin/sndplay                      ./usr/standalone/.places
./usr/bin/sndconvert                   ./usr/cl
./usr/bin/sndrecord                    ./usr/cl/README
./usr/bin/jot                          ./usr/cl/bm
./usr/bin/math                         ./usr/cl/bm/DISCLAIMER
./usr/bin/mathremote                   ./usr/cl/bm/README
./usr/bin/ixBuild                      ./usr/cl/bm/boyer.cl.Z
./usr/bin/installman                   ./usr/cl/bm/browse.cl.Z
./usr/bin/wfcomp                       ./usr/cl/bm/ctak.cl.Z
./usr/bin/pword                        ./usr/cl/bm/dderiv.cl.Z
./usr/bin/pft                          ./usr/cl/bm/deriv.cl.Z
./usr/bin/buildafmdir                  ./usr/cl/bm/destru.cl.Z
./usr/bin/copy                         ./usr/cl/bm/div2.cl.Z
./usr/bin/paste                        ./usr/cl/bm/fft.cl.Z
./usr/bin/msgwrap                      ./usr/cl/bm/fprint.cl.Z
./usr/bin/dread                        ./usr/cl/bm/fread.cl.Z
./usr/bin/dremove                      ./usr/cl/bm/frpoly.cl.Z
./usr/bin/dwrite                       ./usr/cl/bm/puzzle.cl.Z
./usr/bin/dspimg                       ./usr/cl/bm/stak.cl.Z
./usr/bin/dspmsg                       ./usr/cl/bm/tak.cl.Z
./usr/bin/dsptest                      ./usr/cl/bm/tak1.cl.Z
./usr/bin/dspbeep                      ./usr/cl/bm/tprint.cl.Z
./usr/bin/dspabort                     ./usr/cl/bm/traverse.cl.Z
./usr/bin/asm56000                     ./usr/cl/bm/triang.cl.Z
./usr/bin/lib56000                     ./usr/cl/bm/Makefile.Z
./usr/bin/lnk56000                     ./usr/cl/bm/control.cl.Z
./usr/bin/dspwrap                      ./usr/cl/bm/takr.cl.Z
./usr/bin/dsploadwrap                  ./usr/cl/bm/.places
./usr/bin/editFilter                   ./usr/cl/build
./usr/bin/openfile                     ./usr/cl/build/bin
./usr/bin/open                         ./usr/cl/build/bin/cl_help
./usr/bin/prebuild                     ./usr/cl/build/bin/dirname
./usr/bin/screenafm                    ./usr/cl/build/bin/read_number
./usr/bin/cl                           ./usr/cl/build/bin/read_size
```

```
./usr/cl/build/bin/read_string
./usr/cl/build/bin/yes_or_no_p
./usr/cl/build/bin/yesp
./usr/cl/build/bin/size_convert
./usr/cl/build/bin/cpt
./usr/cl/build/bin/faslcvt
./usr/cl/build/bin/.places
./usr/cl/build/config
./usr/cl/build/custom.cl
./usr/cl/build/installtest.cl
./usr/cl/build/inst_lib.sh
./usr/cl/build/inst_bin.sh
./usr/cl/build/files.bu
./usr/cl/build/crt0.o
./usr/cl/build/ucl.o
./usr/cl/build/static.o
./usr/cl/build/static2.o
./usr/cl/build/static2.c
./usr/cl/build/update
./usr/cl/build/update/.places
./usr/cl/build/.places
./usr/cl/examples
./usr/cl/examples/objc
./usr/cl/examples/objc/Calculator.cl
./usr/cl/examples/objc/Evaluator.cl
./usr/cl/examples/objc/.places
./usr/cl/examples/.places
./usr/cl/lib
./usr/cl/lib/misc
./usr/cl/lib/misc/lisp.h
./usr/cl/lib/misc/.places
./usr/cl/lib/code
./usr/cl/lib/code/loop.cl
./usr/cl/lib/code/defsys.fasl
./usr/cl/lib/code/trace.fasl
./usr/cl/lib/code/step.fasl
./usr/cl/lib/code/inspect.fasl
./usr/cl/lib/code/loop.fasl
./usr/cl/lib/code/foreign.fasl
./usr/cl/lib/code/process.fasl
./usr/cl/lib/code/mdproc.fasl
./usr/cl/lib/code/cstructs.fasl
./usr/cl/lib/code/defctype.fasl
./usr/cl/lib/code/sigio.fasl
./usr/cl/lib/code/disass68.fasl
./usr/cl/lib/code/emacs.fasl
./usr/cl/lib/code/ipc.fasl
./usr/cl/lib/code/objc.fasl
./usr/cl/lib/code/objc.o
./usr/cl/lib/code/pcl.fasl
./usr/cl/lib/code/prof.doc
```

```
./usr/cl/lib/code/.places
./usr/cl/lib/objc
./usr/cl/lib/objc/Evaluator.nib
./usr/cl/lib/objc/.places
./usr/cl/lib/.places
./usr/cl/ops5
./usr/cl/ops5/mab.cl.Z
./usr/cl/ops5/README
./usr/cl/ops5/Makefile.Z
./usr/cl/ops5/ops.cl.Z
./usr/cl/ops5/.places
./usr/cl/pcl
./usr/cl/pcl/3-19-87-notes.text.Z
./usr/cl/pcl/4-21-87-notes.text.Z
./usr/cl/pcl/7debug.cl.Z
./usr/cl/pcl/5-22-87-notes.text.Z
./usr/cl/pcl/8-28-88-notes.text.Z
./usr/cl/pcl/boot.cl.Z
./usr/cl/pcl/get-pcl.text.Z
./usr/cl/pcl/braid1.cl.Z
./usr/cl/pcl/README
./usr/cl/pcl/cmu-low.cl.Z
./usr/cl/pcl/combin-test.cl.Z
./usr/cl/pcl/combin.cl.Z
./usr/cl/pcl/compat.cl.Z
./usr/cl/pcl/construct.cl.Z
./usr/cl/pcl/coral-low.cl.Z
./usr/cl/pcl/dcode.cl.Z
./usr/cl/pcl/defclass.cl.Z
./usr/cl/pcl/defs.cl.Z
./usr/cl/pcl/defsys.cl.Z
./usr/cl/pcl/env.cl.Z
./usr/cl/pcl/fin.cl.Z
./usr/cl/pcl/fixup.cl.Z
./usr/cl/pcl/fsc.cl.Z
./usr/cl/pcl/gcl-patches.cl.Z
./usr/cl/pcl/gold-low.cl.Z
./usr/cl/pcl/kcl-mods.text.Z
./usr/cl/pcl/high.cl.Z
./usr/cl/pcl/ibcl-low.cl.Z
./usr/cl/pcl/ibcl-patches.cl.Z
./usr/cl/pcl/init.cl.Z
./usr/cl/pcl/iterate.cl.Z
./usr/cl/pcl/kcl-patches.cl.Z
./usr/cl/pcl/notes.text.Z
./usr/cl/pcl/lap.cl.Z
./usr/cl/pcl/low.cl.Z
./usr/cl/pcl/macros.cl.Z
./usr/cl/pcl/make.cl.Z
./usr/cl/pcl/medley-pcl-env.cl.Z
./usr/cl/pcl/methods.cl.Z
```

```
./usr/cl/pcl/pcl-env.cl.Z                    ./usr/sybase/bin/defncopy
./usr/cl/pcl/pkg.cl.Z                        ./usr/sybase/bin/isql
./usr/cl/pcl/precom1.cl.Z                    ./usr/sybase/bin/probe
./usr/cl/pcl/precom2.cl.Z                    ./usr/sybase/bin/syman
./usr/cl/pcl/precom3.cl.Z                    ./usr/sybase/bin/dataserver
./usr/cl/pcl/precom4.cl.Z                    ./usr/sybase/bin/buildmaster
./usr/cl/pcl/pyr-patches.cl.Z                ./usr/sybase/bin/.places
./usr/cl/pcl/rel-7-2-patches.cl.Z            ./usr/sybase/doc
./usr/cl/pcl/slots.cl.Z                      ./usr/sybase/doc/abort.man
./usr/cl/pcl/std-class.cl.Z                  ./usr/sybase/doc/abort_xact.man
./usr/cl/pcl/test.cl.Z                       ./usr/sybase/doc/addalias.man
./usr/cl/pcl/ti-low.cl.Z                     ./usr/sybase/doc/addgroup.man
./usr/cl/pcl/ti-patches.cl.Z                 ./usr/sybase/doc/addlogin.man
./usr/cl/pcl/vaxl-low.cl.Z                   ./usr/sybase/doc/addremotelogin.man
./usr/cl/pcl/vector.cl.Z                     ./usr/sybase/doc/addsegment.man
./usr/cl/pcl/walk.cl.Z                       ./usr/sybase/doc/addserver.man
./usr/cl/pcl/xerox-patches.cl.Z              ./usr/sybase/doc/addtype.man
./usr/cl/pcl/12-7-88-notes.text.Z            ./usr/sybase/doc/addumpdevice.man
./usr/cl/pcl/Makefile.Z                      ./usr/sybase/doc/adduser.man
./usr/cl/pcl/3600-low.cl.Z                   ./usr/sybase/doc/append.man
./usr/cl/pcl/excl-low.cl.Z                   ./usr/sybase/doc/bcp.man
./usr/cl/pcl/hp-low.cl.Z                      ./usr/sybase/doc/bcp_batch.man
./usr/cl/pcl/kcl-low.cl.Z                    ./usr/sybase/doc/bcp_bind.man
./usr/cl/pcl/lucid-low.cl.Z                  ./usr/sybase/doc/bcp_colfmt.man
./usr/cl/pcl/points.cl.Z                     ./usr/sybase/doc/bcp_collen.man
./usr/cl/pcl/pyr-low.cl.Z                    ./usr/sybase/doc/bcp_colptr.man
./usr/cl/pcl/xerox-low.cl.Z                  ./usr/sybase/doc/bcp_columns.man
./usr/cl/pcl/3-17-88-notes.text.Z            ./usr/sybase/doc/bcp_control.man
./usr/cl/pcl/4-29-87-notes.text.Z            ./usr/sybase/doc/bcp_done.man
./usr/cl/pcl/readme.text.Z                   ./usr/sybase/doc/bcp_exec.man
./usr/cl/pcl/.places                         ./usr/sybase/doc/bcp_init.man
./usr/cl/.places                             ./usr/sybase/doc/bcp_moretext.man
./usr/sybase                                 ./usr/sybase/doc/bcp_sendrow.man
./usr/sybase/Install                         ./usr/sybase/doc/bcp_setl.man
./usr/sybase/Install/SPR                     ./usr/sybase/doc/bindefault.man
./usr/sybase/Install/SPR/spr_ds              ./usr/sybase/doc/bindrule.man
./usr/sybase/Install/SPR/cpr_ds              ./usr/sybase/doc/break.man
./usr/sybase/Install/SPR/cpr_dblib           ./usr/sybase/doc/build_xact_string.man
./usr/sybase/Install/SPR/spr_dblib           ./usr/sybase/doc/buildmaster.man
./usr/sybase/Install/SPR/.places             ./usr/sybase/doc/builtin.man
./usr/sybase/Install/installserver           ./usr/sybase/doc/builtins.man
./usr/sybase/Install/showserver              ./usr/sybase/doc/call.man
./usr/sybase/Install/startserver             ./usr/sybase/doc/callextern.man
./usr/sybase/Install/stopserver              ./usr/sybase/doc/callform.man
./usr/sybase/Install/.places                 ./usr/sybase/doc/cancelform.man
./usr/sybase/Makefile                        ./usr/sybase/doc/changedbowner.man
./usr/sybase/ReleaseNote4.0.nr               ./usr/sybase/doc/changegroup.man
./usr/sybase/bin                             ./usr/sybase/doc/channel.man
./usr/sybase/bin/bcp                         ./usr/sybase/doc/closesql.man
./usr/sybase/bin/bcptrans                    ./usr/sybase/doc/close_commit.man
./usr/sybase/bin/console                     ./usr/sybase/doc/commit_xact.man
```

```
./usr/sybase/doc/commonkey.man
./usr/sybase/doc/configure.man
./usr/sybase/doc/connect.man
./usr/sybase/doc/console.man
./usr/sybase/doc/continue.man
./usr/sybase/doc/create.man
./usr/sybase/doc/dataserver.man
./usr/sybase/doc/dbadata.man
./usr/sybase/doc/dbadlen.man
./usr/sybase/doc/dbaltbind.man
./usr/sybase/doc/dbaltcolid.man
./usr/sybase/doc/dbaltlen.man
./usr/sybase/doc/dbaltop.man
./usr/sybase/doc/dbalttype.man
./usr/sybase/doc/dbbind.man
./usr/sybase/doc/dbbylist.man
./usr/sybase/doc/dbcancel.man
./usr/sybase/doc/dbcancel_a.man
./usr/sybase/doc/dbcanquery.man
./usr/sybase/doc/dbchange.man
./usr/sybase/doc/dbclose.man
./usr/sybase/doc/dbclrbuf.man
./usr/sybase/doc/dbclropt.man
./usr/sybase/doc/dbcmd.man
./usr/sybase/doc/dbcmdrow.man
./usr/sybase/doc/dbcolbrowse.man
./usr/sybase/doc/dbcollen.man
./usr/sybase/doc/dbcolname.man
./usr/sybase/doc/dbcolsource.man
./usr/sybase/doc/dbcoltype.man
./usr/sybase/doc/dbconvert.man
./usr/sybase/doc/dbcount.man
./usr/sybase/doc/dbcurcmd.man
./usr/sybase/doc/dbcurrow.man
./usr/sybase/doc/dbdata.man
./usr/sybase/doc/dbdatlen.man
./usr/sybase/doc/dbdead.man
./usr/sybase/doc/dberrhandle.man
./usr/sybase/doc/dbexit.man
./usr/sybase/doc/dbfcmd.man
./usr/sybase/doc/dbfirstrow.man
./usr/sybase/doc/dbfreebuf.man
./usr/sybase/doc/dbinit.man
./usr/sybase/doc/dbfreequal.man
./usr/sybase/doc/dbgetchar.man
./usr/sybase/doc/dbgetmaxprocs.man
./usr/sybase/doc/dbgetoff.man
./usr/sybase/doc/dbgetrow.man
./usr/sybase/doc/dbgettime.man
./usr/sybase/doc/dbgetuserdata.man
./usr/sybase/doc/dbhasretstat.man
```

```
./usr/sybase/doc/dbiordesc.man
./usr/sybase/doc/dbiowdesc.man
./usr/sybase/doc/dbisavail.man
./usr/sybase/doc/dbisopt.man
./usr/sybase/doc/dblastrow.man
./usr/sybase/doc/dblogin.man
./usr/sybase/doc/dbloginfree.man
./usr/sybase/doc/dbmorecmds.man
./usr/sybase/doc/dbmoretext.man
./usr/sybase/doc/dbmsghandle.man
./usr/sybase/doc/dbname.man
./usr/sybase/doc/dbnextrow.man
./usr/sybase/doc/dbnextrow_a.man
./usr/sybase/doc/dbnumalts.man
./usr/sybase/doc/dbnumcols.man
./usr/sybase/doc/dbnumcompute.man
./usr/sybase/doc/dbnumorders.man
./usr/sybase/doc/dbnumrets.man
./usr/sybase/doc/dbopen.man
./usr/sybase/doc/dbopen_a.man
./usr/sybase/doc/dboption.man
./usr/sybase/doc/dbordercol.man
./usr/sybase/doc/dbprhead.man
./usr/sybase/doc/dbprrow.man
./usr/sybase/doc/dbprtype.man
./usr/sybase/doc/dbqual.man
./usr/sybase/doc/dbrbuf.man
./usr/sybase/doc/dbreadpage.man
./usr/sybase/doc/dbresults.man
./usr/sybase/doc/dbresults_a.man
./usr/sybase/doc/dbretdata.man
./usr/sybase/doc/dbretlen.man
./usr/sybase/doc/dbretname.man
./usr/sybase/doc/dbretstatus.man
./usr/sybase/doc/dbrettype.man
./usr/sybase/doc/dbrows.man
./usr/sybase/doc/dbrowtype.man
./usr/sybase/doc/dbrpcinit.man
./usr/sybase/doc/dbrpcparam.man
./usr/sybase/doc/dbrpcsend.man
./usr/sybase/doc/dbrpwclr.man
./usr/sybase/doc/dbrpwset.man
./usr/sybase/doc/dbsetavail.man
./usr/sybase/doc/dbsetbusy.man
./usr/sybase/doc/dbsetconnect.man
./usr/sybase/doc/dbsetidle.man
./usr/sybase/doc/dbsetifile.man
./usr/sybase/doc/dbsetinterrupt.man
./usr/sybase/doc/dbsetlapp.man
./usr/sybase/doc/dbsetlhost.man
./usr/sybase/doc/dbsetlogintime.man
```

./usr/sybase/doc/dbsetlpwd.man
./usr/sybase/doc/dbsetluser.man
./usr/sybase/doc/dbsetmaxprocs.man
./usr/sybase/doc/dbsetnull.man
./usr/sybase/doc/dbsetopt.man
./usr/sybase/doc/dbsettime.man
./usr/sybase/doc/dbsetuserdata.man
./usr/sybase/doc/dbsqlexec.man
./usr/sybase/doc/dbsqlexec_a.man
./usr/sybase/doc/dbsqlok.man
./usr/sybase/doc/dbsqlsend.man
./usr/sybase/doc/dbstrcpy.man
./usr/sybase/doc/dbstrlen.man
./usr/sybase/doc/dbtabbrowse.man
./usr/sybase/doc/dbtabcount.man
./usr/sybase/doc/dbtabname.man
./usr/sybase/doc/dbtabsource.man
./usr/sybase/doc/dbtsnewlen.man
./usr/sybase/doc/dbtsnewval.man
./usr/sybase/doc/dbtsput.man
./usr/sybase/doc/dbtxptr.man
./usr/sybase/doc/dbtxtimestamp.man
./usr/sybase/doc/dbtxtsnewval.man
./usr/sybase/doc/dbtxtsput.man
./usr/sybase/doc/dbuse.man
./usr/sybase/doc/dbvarylen.man
./usr/sybase/doc/dbwillconvert.man
./usr/sybase/doc/dbwritepage.man
./usr/sybase/doc/dbwritetext.man
./usr/sybase/doc/defaultdb.man
./usr/sybase/doc/define.man
./usr/sybase/doc/defncopy.man
./usr/sybase/doc/delete.man
./usr/sybase/doc/depends.man
./usr/sybase/doc/disconnect.man
./usr/sybase/doc/diskdefault.man
./usr/sybase/doc/dropalias.man
./usr/sybase/doc/dropdevice.man
./usr/sybase/doc/dropgroup.man
./usr/sybase/doc/dropkey.man
./usr/sybase/doc/droplogin.man
./usr/sybase/doc/dropremotelogin.man
./usr/sybase/doc/dropsegment.man
./usr/sybase/doc/dropserver.man
./usr/sybase/doc/droptype.man
./usr/sybase/doc/dropuser.man
./usr/sybase/doc/entry.man
./usr/sybase/doc/errors.man
./usr/sybase/doc/exitform.man
./usr/sybase/doc/extendsegment.man
./usr/sybase/doc/fetchsql.man

./usr/sybase/doc/foreach.man
./usr/sybase/doc/foreignkey.man
./usr/sybase/doc/fsabort.man
./usr/sybase/doc/fscallform.man
./usr/sybase/doc/fscancelform.man
./usr/sybase/doc/fsclosescreen.man
./usr/sybase/doc/fsclrformflags.man
./usr/sybase/doc/fscopyobj.man
./usr/sybase/doc/fscurform.man
./usr/sybase/doc/fsdbenviron.man
./usr/sybase/doc/fsdblogin.man
./usr/sybase/doc/fsdbproc.man
./usr/sybase/doc/fsdbrec.man
./usr/sybase/doc/fsdcurddc.man
./usr/sybase/doc/fsdgetddc.man
./usr/sybase/doc/fsdgetid.man
./usr/sybase/doc/fsdgetinitstate.man
./usr/sybase/doc/fsdgetlen.man
./usr/sybase/doc/fsdgetmaxlen.man
./usr/sybase/doc/fsdgetprvval.man
./usr/sybase/doc/fsdgetstate.man
./usr/sybase/doc/fsdgetval.man
./usr/sybase/doc/fsdputinitstate.man
./usr/sybase/doc/fsdputstate.man
./usr/sybase/doc/fsdputval.man
./usr/sybase/doc/fsexitform.man
./usr/sybase/doc/fsfclrfldflags.man
./usr/sybase/doc/fsfcurfld.man
./usr/sybase/doc/fsfgetdefault.man
./usr/sybase/doc/fsfgetdtype.man
./usr/sybase/doc/fsfgetfld.man
./usr/sybase/doc/fsfgetid.man
./usr/sybase/doc/fsfgetinitfld.man
./usr/sybase/doc/fsfgetlen.man
./usr/sybase/doc/fsfgetname.man
./usr/sybase/doc/fsfgetrow.man
./usr/sybase/doc/fsfgettype.man
./usr/sybase/doc/fsfgetval.man
./usr/sybase/doc/fsfisfldmod.man
./usr/sybase/doc/fsformname.man
./usr/sybase/doc/fsformver.man
./usr/sybase/doc/fsfprvfld.man
./usr/sybase/doc/fsfputdefault.man
./usr/sybase/doc/fsfputval.man
./usr/sybase/doc/fsfreadval.man
./usr/sybase/doc/fsfreeform.man
./usr/sybase/doc/fsfsetcurfld.man
./usr/sybase/doc/fsfsetfldflags.man
./usr/sybase/doc/fsfsetinitfld.man
./usr/sybase/doc/fsfsetvalues.man
./usr/sybase/doc/fsftestfldflags.man

./usr/sybase/doc/fsfwriteval.man
./usr/sybase/doc/fsgaddrow.man
./usr/sybase/doc/fsgclrgrpflags.man
./usr/sybase/doc/fsgcopyindex.man
./usr/sybase/doc/fsgdelrow.man
./usr/sybase/doc/fsgetform.man
./usr/sybase/doc/fsggetgrp.man
./usr/sybase/doc/fsggetindex.man
./usr/sybase/doc/fsggetmaxrows.man
./usr/sybase/doc/fsggetparent.man
./usr/sybase/doc/fsggetusedrows.man
./usr/sybase/doc/fsgmoverow.man
./usr/sybase/doc/fsgscrollgrp.man
./usr/sybase/doc/fsgsetgrpflags.man
./usr/sybase/doc/fsgsetusedrows.man
./usr/sybase/doc/fsgtestgrpflags.man
./usr/sybase/doc/fsinstallkeys.man
./usr/sybase/doc/fsinstallproc.man
./usr/sybase/doc/fsioalloc.man
./usr/sybase/doc/fsiofree.man
./usr/sybase/doc/fsiogetform.man
./usr/sybase/doc/fsionxtddc.man
./usr/sybase/doc/fsionxtfld.man
./usr/sybase/doc/fsionxtrow.man
./usr/sybase/doc/fsiosetddc.man
./usr/sybase/doc/fsiosetfld.man
./usr/sybase/doc/fsisformmod.man
./usr/sybase/doc/fskeyargs.man
./usr/sybase/doc/fsmcurmenu.man
./usr/sybase/doc/fsmessage.man
./usr/sybase/doc/fsmoffmenu.man
./usr/sybase/doc/fsmonmenu.man
./usr/sybase/doc/fsopenscreen.man
./usr/sybase/doc/fsprint.man
./usr/sybase/doc/fsprocargs.man
./usr/sybase/doc/fsprocreturn.man
./usr/sybase/doc/fsresume.man
./usr/sybase/doc/fssetformflags.man
./usr/sybase/doc/fsseticon.man
./usr/sybase/doc/fssql.man
./usr/sybase/doc/fssuspend.man
./usr/sybase/doc/fstendcrit.man
./usr/sybase/doc/fstestformflags.man
./usr/sybase/doc/fstsetalarm.man
./usr/sybase/doc/fststartcrit.man
./usr/sybase/doc/functions.man
./usr/sybase/doc/group.man
./usr/sybase/doc/help.man
./usr/sybase/doc/helpdb.man
./usr/sybase/doc/helpdevice.man
./usr/sybase/doc/helpgroup.man

./usr/sybase/doc/helpindex.man
./usr/sybase/doc/helpjoins.man
./usr/sybase/doc/helpkey.man
./usr/sybase/doc/helplog.man
./usr/sybase/doc/helpremotelogin.man
./usr/sybase/doc/helpprotect.man
./usr/sybase/doc/helpsegment.man
./usr/sybase/doc/helpserver.man
./usr/sybase/doc/helptext.man
./usr/sybase/doc/helpuser.man
./usr/sybase/doc/if.man
./usr/sybase/doc/insert.man
./usr/sybase/doc/interruptsql.man
./usr/sybase/doc/isql.man
./usr/sybase/doc/lock.man
./usr/sybase/doc/logdevice.man
./usr/sybase/doc/mchoice.man
./usr/sybase/doc/menu.man
./usr/sybase/doc/monitor.man
./usr/sybase/doc/nextquery.man
./usr/sybase/doc/open_commit.man
./usr/sybase/doc/opensql.man
./usr/sybase/doc/options.man
./usr/sybase/doc/password.man
./usr/sybase/doc/perform.man
./usr/sybase/doc/placeobject.man
./usr/sybase/doc/positionform.man
./usr/sybase/doc/primarykey.man
./usr/sybase/doc/print.man
./usr/sybase/doc/printform.man
./usr/sybase/doc/rchoice.man
./usr/sybase/doc/remoteoption.man
./usr/sybase/doc/remove_xact.man
./usr/sybase/doc/rename.man
./usr/sybase/doc/renamedb.man
./usr/sybase/doc/reset.man
./usr/sybase/doc/return.man
./usr/sybase/doc/runrpt.man
./usr/sybase/doc/save.man
./usr/sybase/doc/scan_xact.man
./usr/sybase/doc/schoice.man
./usr/sybase/doc/serveroption.man
./usr/sybase/doc/showserver.man
./usr/sybase/doc/spaceused.man
./usr/sybase/doc/sqlrow.man
./usr/sybase/doc/start_xact.man
./usr/sybase/doc/startserver.man
./usr/sybase/doc/stat_xact.man
./usr/sybase/doc/submit.man
./usr/sybase/doc/syman.man
./usr/sybase/doc/symbconstants.man

```
./usr/sybase/doc/system.man                        ./usr/sybase/scripts/installmodel
./usr/sybase/doc/trace.man                         ./usr/sybase/scripts/CreateMaster
./usr/sybase/doc/transfer.man                      ./usr/sybase/scripts/SetVars
./usr/sybase/doc/trim.man                          ./usr/sybase/scripts/.places
./usr/sybase/doc/truncate.man                      ./usr/sybase/.places
./usr/sybase/doc/types.man                         ./usr/tex
./usr/sybase/doc/unbindefault.man                  ./usr/tex/TeXdist.tar.Z
./usr/sybase/doc/unbindrule.man                    ./usr/tex/README
./usr/sybase/doc/useform.man                       ./usr/tex/.places
./usr/sybase/doc/variable.man                      ./usr/.places
./usr/sybase/doc/while.man                         ./bin
./usr/sybase/doc/who.man                           ./bin/as-16
./usr/sybase/doc/.places                           ./bin/as
./usr/sybase/include                               ./bin/cc-16
./usr/sybase/include/sybdb.h                       ./bin/cc
./usr/sybase/include/sybdbtoken.h                  ./bin/ld-16
./usr/sybase/include/syberror.h                    ./bin/ld
./usr/sybase/include/sybfront.h                    ./bin/gdb-16
./usr/sybase/include/syblogin.h                    ./bin/gdb
./usr/sybase/include/.places                       ./bin/atom
./usr/sybase/interfaces                            ./bin/file
./usr/sybase/lib                                   ./bin/nm
./usr/sybase/lib/libsybdb.a                        ./bin/otool
./usr/sybase/lib/.places                           ./bin/size
./usr/sybase/msgs                                  ./bin/strip
./usr/sybase/msgs/copyright_dblib                  ./bin/ar
./usr/sybase/msgs/.places                          ./bin/strings
./usr/sybase/sample                                ./bin/ranlib
./usr/sybase/sample/dblibrary                      ./bin/dd
./usr/sybase/sample/dblibrary/makefile             ./bin/df
./usr/sybase/sample/dblibrary/README               ./bin/diff
./usr/sybase/sample/dblibrary/datafile             ./bin/domainname
./usr/sybase/sample/dblibrary/example1.c           ./bin/du
./usr/sybase/sample/dblibrary/example2.c           ./bin/echo
./usr/sybase/sample/dblibrary/example3.c           ./bin/false
./usr/sybase/sample/dblibrary/example4.c           ./bin/grep
./usr/sybase/sample/dblibrary/example5.c           ./bin/hostid
./usr/sybase/sample/dblibrary/example6.c           ./bin/hostname
./usr/sybase/sample/dblibrary/example7.c           ./bin/kill
./usr/sybase/sample/dblibrary/example8.c           ./bin/login
./usr/sybase/sample/dblibrary/example9.c           ./bin/mail
./usr/sybase/sample/dblibrary/twophase.c           ./bin/mt
./usr/sybase/sample/dblibrary/makefile_share       ./bin/nice
./usr/sybase/sample/dblibrary/makefile_unshare     ./bin/od
./usr/sybase/sample/dblibrary/.places              ./bin/pagesize
./usr/sybase/sample/.places                        ./bin/passwd
./usr/sybase/scripts                               ./bin/pr
./usr/sybase/scripts/AddHost                       ./bin/ps
./usr/sybase/scripts/installmaster                 ./bin/rmail
./usr/sybase/scripts/installmaster2                ./bin/rmdir
./usr/sybase/scripts/installpubs                   ./bin/stty
```

```
./bin/su                                ./private/adm/lpd-errs
./bin/su.wheel                          ./private/adm/messages
./bin/sync                              ./private/adm/msgbuf
./bin/tar                               ./private/adm/wtmp
./bin/tee                               ./private/adm/lastlog
./bin/test                              ./private/adm/aculog
./bin/[                                 ./private/adm/.places
./bin/time                              ./private/adm/psout
./bin/tp                                ./private/adm/nu.log
./bin/true                              ./private/adm/messages.old
./bin/wall                              ./private/dev
./bin/who                               ./private/dev/MAKEDEV
./bin/write                             ./private/dev/MAKEDEV.local
./bin/awk                               ./private/dev/.places
./bin/cat                               ./private/dev/console
./bin/chgrp                             ./private/dev/drum
./bin/chmod                             ./private/dev/mem
./bin/cmp                               ./private/dev/kmem
./bin/csh                               ./private/dev/null
./bin/cp                                ./private/dev/dsp
./bin/date                              ./private/dev/tty
./bin/ed                                ./private/dev/ttya
./bin/expr                              ./private/dev/ttyb
./bin/ln                                ./private/dev/ttyda
./bin/ls                                ./private/dev/ttydb
./bin/make                              ./private/dev/cua
./bin/mkdir                             ./private/dev/cub
./bin/mkdirs                            ./private/dev/klog
./bin/mv                                ./private/dev/sound
./bin/pwd                               ./private/dev/odc0
./bin/rm                                ./private/dev/od0a
./bin/sed                               ./private/dev/od0b
./bin/sh                                ./private/dev/od0c
./bin/jsh                               ./private/dev/od0g
./bin/.places                           ./private/dev/rod0a
./private                               ./private/dev/rod0b
./private/tmp                           ./private/dev/rod0c
./private/tmp/k_load000095              ./private/dev/rod0g
./private/tmp/console.log               ./private/dev/od0d
./private/tmp/WorkspaceTypeTable        ./private/dev/od0e
./private/tmp/Edit.socket.root          ./private/dev/od0f
./private/preserve                      ./private/dev/od0h
./private/Net                           ./private/dev/rod0d
./private/Net/.places                   ./private/dev/rod0e
./private/adm                           ./private/dev/rod0f
./private/adm/daily                     ./private/dev/rod0h
./private/adm/monthly                   ./private/dev/od1a
./private/adm/weekly                    ./private/dev/od1b
./private/adm/daily.log                 ./private/dev/od1c
./private/adm/weekly.log                ./private/dev/od1g
./private/adm/monthly.log               ./private/dev/rod1a
```

```
./private/dev/rod1b                          ./private/dev/od4d
./private/dev/rod1c                          ./private/dev/od4e
./private/dev/rod1g                          ./private/dev/od4f
./private/dev/od1d                           ./private/dev/od4h
./private/dev/od1e                           ./private/dev/rod4d
./private/dev/od1f                           ./private/dev/rod4e
./private/dev/od1h                           ./private/dev/rod4f
./private/dev/rod1d                          ./private/dev/rod4h
./private/dev/rod1e                          ./private/dev/od5a
./private/dev/rod1f                          ./private/dev/od5b
./private/dev/rod1h                          ./private/dev/od5c
./private/dev/od2a                           ./private/dev/od5g
./private/dev/od2b                           ./private/dev/rod5a
./private/dev/od2c                           ./private/dev/rod5b
./private/dev/od2g                           ./private/dev/rod5c
./private/dev/rod2a                          ./private/dev/rod5g
./private/dev/rod2b                          ./private/dev/od5d
./private/dev/rod2c                          ./private/dev/od5e
./private/dev/rod2g                          ./private/dev/od5f
./private/dev/od2d                           ./private/dev/od5h
./private/dev/od2e                           ./private/dev/rod5d
./private/dev/od2f                           ./private/dev/rod5e
./private/dev/od2h                           ./private/dev/rod5f
./private/dev/rod2d                          ./private/dev/rod5h
./private/dev/rod2e                          ./private/dev/od6a
./private/dev/rod2f                          ./private/dev/od6b
./private/dev/rod2h                          ./private/dev/od6c
./private/dev/od3a                           ./private/dev/od6g
./private/dev/od3b                           ./private/dev/rod6a
./private/dev/od3c                           ./private/dev/rod6b
./private/dev/od3g                           ./private/dev/rod6c
./private/dev/rod3a                          ./private/dev/rod6g
./private/dev/rod3b                          ./private/dev/od6d
./private/dev/rod3c                          ./private/dev/od6e
./private/dev/rod3g                          ./private/dev/od6f
./private/dev/od3d                           ./private/dev/od6h
./private/dev/od3e                           ./private/dev/rod6d
./private/dev/od3f                           ./private/dev/rod6e
./private/dev/od3h                           ./private/dev/rod6f
./private/dev/rod3d                          ./private/dev/rod6h
./private/dev/rod3e                          ./private/dev/od7a
./private/dev/rod3f                          ./private/dev/od7b
./private/dev/rod3h                          ./private/dev/od7c
./private/dev/od4a                           ./private/dev/od7g
./private/dev/od4b                           ./private/dev/rod7a
./private/dev/od4c                           ./private/dev/rod7b
./private/dev/od4g                           ./private/dev/rod7c
./private/dev/rod4a                          ./private/dev/rod7g
./private/dev/rod4b                          ./private/dev/od7d
./private/dev/rod4c                          ./private/dev/od7e
./private/dev/rod4g                          ./private/dev/od7f
```

./private/dev/od7h
./private/dev/rod7d
./private/dev/rod7e
./private/dev/rod7f
./private/dev/rod7h
./private/dev/sd0a
./private/dev/sd0b
./private/dev/sd0c
./private/dev/sd0g
./private/dev/rsd0a
./private/dev/rsd0b
./private/dev/rsd0c
./private/dev/rsd0g
./private/dev/sd0d
./private/dev/sd0e
./private/dev/sd0f
./private/dev/sd0h
./private/dev/rsd0d
./private/dev/rsd0e
./private/dev/rsd0f
./private/dev/rsd0h
./private/dev/sd1a
./private/dev/sd1b
./private/dev/sd1c
./private/dev/sd1g
./private/dev/rsd1a
./private/dev/rsd1b
./private/dev/rsd1c
./private/dev/rsd1g
./private/dev/sd1d
./private/dev/sd1e
./private/dev/sd1f
./private/dev/sd1h
./private/dev/rsd1d
./private/dev/rsd1e
./private/dev/rsd1f
./private/dev/rsd1h
./private/dev/sd2a
./private/dev/sd2b
./private/dev/sd2c
./private/dev/sd2g
./private/dev/rsd2a
./private/dev/rsd2b
./private/dev/rsd2c
./private/dev/rsd2g
./private/dev/sd2d
./private/dev/sd2e
./private/dev/sd2f
./private/dev/sd2h
./private/dev/rsd2d
./private/dev/rsd2e

./private/dev/rsd2f
./private/dev/rsd2h
./private/dev/sd3a
./private/dev/sd3b
./private/dev/sd3c
./private/dev/sd3g
./private/dev/rsd3a
./private/dev/rsd3b
./private/dev/rsd3c
./private/dev/rsd3g
./private/dev/sd3d
./private/dev/sd3e
./private/dev/sd3f
./private/dev/sd3h
./private/dev/rsd3d
./private/dev/rsd3e
./private/dev/rsd3f
./private/dev/rsd3h
./private/dev/sd4a
./private/dev/sd4b
./private/dev/sd4c
./private/dev/sd4g
./private/dev/rsd4a
./private/dev/rsd4b
./private/dev/rsd4c
./private/dev/rsd4g
./private/dev/sd4d
./private/dev/sd4e
./private/dev/sd4f
./private/dev/sd4h
./private/dev/rsd4d
./private/dev/rsd4e
./private/dev/rsd4f
./private/dev/rsd4h
./private/dev/sd5a
./private/dev/sd5b
./private/dev/sd5c
./private/dev/sd5g
./private/dev/rsd5a
./private/dev/rsd5b
./private/dev/rsd5c
./private/dev/rsd5g
./private/dev/sd5d
./private/dev/sd5e
./private/dev/sd5f
./private/dev/sd5h
./private/dev/rsd5d
./private/dev/rsd5e
./private/dev/rsd5f
./private/dev/rsd5h
./private/dev/sd6a

```
./private/dev/sd6b                    ./private/dev/ptypd
./private/dev/sd6c                    ./private/dev/ttype
./private/dev/sd6g                    ./private/dev/ptype
./private/dev/rsd6a                   ./private/dev/ttypf
./private/dev/rsd6b                   ./private/dev/ptypf
./private/dev/rsd6c                   ./private/dev/ttyq0
./private/dev/rsd6g                   ./private/dev/ptyq0
./private/dev/sd6d                    ./private/dev/ttyq1
./private/dev/sd6e                    ./private/dev/ptyq1
./private/dev/sd6f                    ./private/dev/ttyq2
./private/dev/sd6h                    ./private/dev/ptyq2
./private/dev/rsd6d                   ./private/dev/ttyq3
./private/dev/rsd6e                   ./private/dev/ptyq3
./private/dev/rsd6f                   ./private/dev/ttyq4
./private/dev/rsd6h                   ./private/dev/ptyq4
./private/dev/sg0                     ./private/dev/ttyq5
./private/dev/rst0                    ./private/dev/ptyq5
./private/dev/nrst0                   ./private/dev/ttyq6
./private/dev/rxt0                    ./private/dev/ptyq6
./private/dev/nrxt0                   ./private/dev/ttyq7
./private/dev/rst1                    ./private/dev/ptyq7
./private/dev/nrst1                   ./private/dev/ttyq8
./private/dev/rxt1                    ./private/dev/ptyq8
./private/dev/nrxt1                   ./private/dev/ttyq9
./private/dev/ttyp0                   ./private/dev/ptyq9
./private/dev/ptyp0                   ./private/dev/ttyqa
./private/dev/ttyp1                   ./private/dev/ptyqa
./private/dev/ptyp1                   ./private/dev/ttyqb
./private/dev/ttyp2                   ./private/dev/ptyqb
./private/dev/ptyp2                   ./private/dev/ttyqc
./private/dev/ttyp3                   ./private/dev/ptyqc
./private/dev/ptyp3                   ./private/dev/ttyqd
./private/dev/ttyp4                   ./private/dev/ptyqd
./private/dev/ptyp4                   ./private/dev/ttyqe
./private/dev/ttyp5                   ./private/dev/ptyqe
./private/dev/ptyp5                   ./private/dev/ttyqf
./private/dev/ttyp6                   ./private/dev/ptyqf
./private/dev/ptyp6                   ./private/dev/vid0
./private/dev/ttyp7                   ./private/dev/ev0
./private/dev/ptyp7                   ./private/dev/evs0
./private/dev/ttyp8                   ./private/dev/np0
./private/dev/ptyp8                   ./private/dev/nps0
./private/dev/ttyp9                   ./private/dev/log
./private/dev/ptyp9                   ./private/dev/printer
./private/dev/ttypa                   ./private/etc
./private/dev/ptypa                   ./private/etc/fstab.client
./private/dev/ttypb                   ./private/etc/fstab.od
./private/dev/ptypb                   ./private/etc/fstab.sd330
./private/dev/ttypc                   ./private/etc/fstab.sd660
./private/dev/ptypc                   ./private/etc/rc
./private/dev/ttypd                   ./private/etc/rc.boot
```

```
./private/etc/rc.swap                      ./private/etc/inetd.conf
./private/etc/crontab                      ./private/etc/nulib
./private/etc/exports.example              ./private/etc/nulib/nu1.sh
./private/etc/group                        ./private/etc/nulib/nu2.sh
./private/etc/hostconfig                   ./private/etc/nulib/nu3.sh
./private/etc/hosts                        ./private/etc/nulib/nu4.sh
./private/etc/networks                     ./private/etc/nulib/.places
./private/etc/passwd                       ./private/etc/nu.cf
./private/etc/protocols                    ./private/etc/syslog.conf
./private/etc/printcap                     ./private/etc/zoneinfo
./private/etc/rc.local                     ./private/etc/zoneinfo/Japan
./private/etc/rpc                          ./private/etc/zoneinfo/Singapore
./private/etc/services                     ./private/etc/zoneinfo/Australia
./private/etc/shells                       ./private/etc/zoneinfo/Australia/Tasmania
./private/etc/termcap                      ./private/etc/zoneinfo/Australia/Queensland
./private/etc/ttys                         ./private/etc/zoneinfo/Australia/North
./private/etc/dumpdates                    ./private/etc/zoneinfo/Australia/West
./private/etc/find.codes                   ./private/etc/zoneinfo/Australia/South
./private/etc/hosts.equiv                  ./private/etc/zoneinfo/Australia/Victoria
./private/etc/hosts.lpd                    ./private/etc/zoneinfo/Australia/NSW
./private/etc/motd                         ./private/etc/zoneinfo/Australia/.places
./private/etc/netgroup                     ./private/etc/zoneinfo/NZ
./private/etc/rmtab                        ./private/etc/zoneinfo/GB-Eire
./private/etc/syslog.pid                   ./private/etc/zoneinfo/WET
./private/etc/utmp                         ./private/etc/zoneinfo/Iceland
./private/etc/xtab                         ./private/etc/zoneinfo/MET
./private/etc/mtab                         ./private/etc/zoneinfo/Poland
./private/etc/yp                           ./private/etc/zoneinfo/EET
./private/etc/yp/makedbm                   ./private/etc/zoneinfo/Turkey
./private/etc/yp/revnetgroup               ./private/etc/zoneinfo/W-SU
./private/etc/yp/stdhosts                  ./private/etc/zoneinfo/GMT
./private/etc/yp/yppoll                    ./private/etc/zoneinfo/GMT-12
./private/etc/yp/yppush                    ./private/etc/zoneinfo/GMT-11
./private/etc/yp/ypset                     ./private/etc/zoneinfo/GMT-10
./private/etc/yp/ypxfr                     ./private/etc/zoneinfo/GMT-9
./private/etc/yp/ypinit                    ./private/etc/zoneinfo/GMT-8
./private/etc/yp/ypxfr_1perday             ./private/etc/zoneinfo/GMT-7
./private/etc/yp/ypxfr_2perday             ./private/etc/zoneinfo/GMT-6
./private/etc/yp/ypxfr_1perhour            ./private/etc/zoneinfo/GMT-5
./private/etc/yp/Makefile                  ./private/etc/zoneinfo/GMT-4
./private/etc/yp/.places                   ./private/etc/zoneinfo/GMT-3
./private/etc/bootptab                     ./private/etc/zoneinfo/GMT-2
./private/etc/BLD.od                       ./private/etc/zoneinfo/GMT-1
./private/etc/BLD.sd330                     ./private/etc/zoneinfo/GMT+1
./private/etc/BLD.sd660                     ./private/etc/zoneinfo/GMT+2
./private/etc/disktab                      ./private/etc/zoneinfo/GMT+3
./private/etc/ftpusers                     ./private/etc/zoneinfo/GMT+4
./private/etc/gettytab                     ./private/etc/zoneinfo/GMT+5
./private/etc/localgateways                ./private/etc/zoneinfo/GMT+6
./private/etc/localhost                    ./private/etc/zoneinfo/GMT+7
./private/etc/localnetworks                ./private/etc/zoneinfo/GMT+8
```

```
./private/etc/zoneinfo/GMT+9                          ./private/etc/zoneinfo/MST
./private/etc/zoneinfo/GMT+10                         ./private/etc/zoneinfo/HST
./private/etc/zoneinfo/GMT+11                         ./private/etc/zoneinfo/localtime
./private/etc/zoneinfo/GMT+12                         ./private/etc/zoneinfo/.places
./private/etc/zoneinfo/GMT+13                         ./private/etc/catman
./private/etc/zoneinfo/US                             ./private/etc/chown
./private/etc/zoneinfo/US/Eastern                     ./private/etc/disk
./private/etc/zoneinfo/US/Central                     ./private/etc/dump
./private/etc/zoneinfo/US/Mountain                    ./private/etc/rdump
./private/etc/zoneinfo/US/Pacific                     ./private/etc/edquota
./private/etc/zoneinfo/US/Yukon                       ./private/etc/fsirand
./private/etc/zoneinfo/US/East-Indiana                ./private/etc/halt
./private/etc/zoneinfo/US/Arizona                     ./private/etc/ifconfig
./private/etc/zoneinfo/US/Hawaii                      ./private/etc/inetd
./private/etc/zoneinfo/US/Pacific-New                 ./private/etc/init
./private/etc/zoneinfo/US/.places                     ./private/etc/mkfs
./private/etc/zoneinfo/Canada                         ./private/etc/mkhosts
./private/etc/zoneinfo/Canada/Newfoundland            ./private/etc/mklost+found
./private/etc/zoneinfo/Canada/Atlantic                ./private/etc/mknod
./private/etc/zoneinfo/Canada/Eastern                 ./private/etc/mkpasswd
./private/etc/zoneinfo/Canada/Central                 ./private/etc/mkplaces
./private/etc/zoneinfo/Canada/East-Saskatchewan       ./private/etc/mkproto
./private/etc/zoneinfo/Canada/Mountain                ./private/etc/mount
./private/etc/zoneinfo/Canada/Pacific                 ./private/etc/newclient
./private/etc/zoneinfo/Canada/Yukon                   ./private/etc/newfs
./private/etc/zoneinfo/Canada/.places                 ./private/etc/nu
./private/etc/zoneinfo/SystemV                        ./private/etc/ping
./private/etc/zoneinfo/SystemV/AST4ADT                ./private/etc/quot
./private/etc/zoneinfo/SystemV/EST5EDT                ./private/etc/quotacheck
./private/etc/zoneinfo/SystemV/CST6CDT                ./private/etc/quotaon
./private/etc/zoneinfo/SystemV/MST7MDT                ./private/etc/reboot
./private/etc/zoneinfo/SystemV/PST8PDT                ./private/etc/renice
./private/etc/zoneinfo/SystemV/YST9YDT                ./private/etc/repquota
./private/etc/zoneinfo/SystemV/AST4                   ./private/etc/restore
./private/etc/zoneinfo/SystemV/EST5                   ./private/etc/rrestore
./private/etc/zoneinfo/SystemV/CST6                   ./private/etc/rexecd
./private/etc/zoneinfo/SystemV/MST7                   ./private/etc/rlogind
./private/etc/zoneinfo/SystemV/PST8                   ./private/etc/rmt
./private/etc/zoneinfo/SystemV/YST9                   ./private/etc/route
./private/etc/zoneinfo/SystemV/HST10                  ./private/etc/rshd
./private/etc/zoneinfo/SystemV/.places                ./private/etc/rwhod
./private/etc/zoneinfo/CET                            ./private/etc/shutdown
./private/etc/zoneinfo/UTC                            ./private/etc/umount
./private/etc/zoneinfo/UCT                            ./private/etc/update
./private/etc/zoneinfo/Universal                      ./private/etc/vipw
./private/etc/zoneinfo/Greenwich                      ./private/etc/Mail.rc
./private/etc/zoneinfo/EST5EDT                        ./private/etc/sendmail
./private/etc/zoneinfo/CST6CDT                        ./private/etc/sendmail/sendmail.mailhost.cf
./private/etc/zoneinfo/MST7MDT                        ./private/etc/sendmail/sendmail.subsidiary.cf
./private/etc/zoneinfo/PST8PDT                        ./private/etc/sendmail/aliases
./private/etc/zoneinfo/EST                            ./private/etc/sendmail/sendmail.sharedsubsidiary.cf
```

```
./private/etc/sendmail/sendmail.cf
./private/etc/sendmail/aliases.dir
./private/etc/sendmail/aliases.pag
./private/etc/sendmail/.places
./private/etc/map3270
./private/etc/remote
./private/etc/uucp
./private/etc/uucp/UUAIDS
./private/etc/uucp/UUAIDS/L-devices
./private/etc/uucp/UUAIDS/L-devices.samples
./private/etc/uucp/UUAIDS/L-dialcodes
./private/etc/uucp/UUAIDS/L-dialcodes.samples
./private/etc/uucp/UUAIDS/L.aliases
./private/etc/uucp/UUAIDS/L.aliases.samples
./private/etc/uucp/UUAIDS/L.cmds
./private/etc/uucp/UUAIDS/L.cmds.samples
./private/etc/uucp/UUAIDS/L.sys
./private/etc/uucp/UUAIDS/L.sys.samples
./private/etc/uucp/UUAIDS/READ_ME
./private/etc/uucp/UUAIDS/SEQF
./private/etc/uucp/UUAIDS/USERFILE
./private/etc/uucp/UUAIDS/uu.daily
./private/etc/uucp/UUAIDS/uu.daily.seismo
./private/etc/uucp/UUAIDS/uu.hourly
./private/etc/uucp/UUAIDS/uu.weekly
./private/etc/uucp/UUAIDS/uucp.daily
./private/etc/uucp/UUAIDS/uucp.day.sh
./private/etc/uucp/UUAIDS/uucpsrv.c
./private/etc/uucp/UUAIDS/uucpsummary
./private/etc/uucp/UUAIDS/uucpsummary.monthly
./private/etc/uucp/UUAIDS/uurate
./private/etc/uucp/UUAIDS/uutbl
./private/etc/uucp/UUAIDS/uuusage
./private/etc/uucp/UUAIDS/.places
./private/etc/uucp/USERFILE
./private/etc/uucp/L.aliases
./private/etc/uucp/L.sys
./private/etc/uucp/L.cmds
./private/etc/uucp/L-devices
./private/etc/uucp/L-dialcodes
./private/etc/uucp/uucp.day.sh
./private/etc/uucp/.places
./private/etc/swaptab
./private/etc/nmserver
./private/etc/NETMSG_CONFIG
./private/etc/bootparams
./private/etc/mach_init
./private/etc/BLD.swapdisk
./private/etc/BLD.sd200app
./private/etc/BLD.sd200dev
./private/etc/MAKEDEV

./private/etc/netinfo
./private/etc/netinfo/local.nidb
./private/etc/netinfo/local.nidb/collection
./private/etc/netinfo/local.nidb/.places
./private/etc/netinfo/local.nidb/extension_132
./private/etc/netinfo/.places
./private/etc/cshrc.std
./private/etc/login.std
./private/etc/logout.std
./private/etc/profile.std
./private/etc/kern_loader.conf
./private/etc/.places
./private/etc/fstab
./private/spool
./private/spool/lpd
./private/spool/lpd/.places
./private/spool/np
./private/spool/np/.places
./private/spool/np/.seq
./private/spool/np/lock
./private/spool/np/status
./private/spool/appkit
./private/spool/appkit/.places
./private/spool/mail
./private/spool/mail/.places
./private/spool/mail/root
./private/spool/mqueue
./private/spool/mqueue/syslog
./private/spool/mqueue/.places
./private/spool/at
./private/spool/at/past
./private/spool/at/past/.places
./private/spool/at/lasttimedone
./private/spool/at/.places
./private/spool/uucp
./private/spool/uucp/CORRUPT
./private/spool/uucp/CORRUPT/.places
./private/spool/uucp/AUDIT
./private/spool/uucp/AUDIT/.places
./private/spool/uucp/STST
./private/spool/uucp/STST/.places
./private/spool/uucp/C.
./private/spool/uucp/C./.places
./private/spool/uucp/X.
./private/spool/uucp/X./.places
./private/spool/uucp/TM.
./private/spool/uucp/TM./.places
./private/spool/uucp/LCK
./private/spool/uucp/LCK/.places
./private/spool/uucp/STATS
./private/spool/uucp/STATS/.places
```

```
./private/spool/uucp/ERRLOG
./private/spool/uucp/D.
./private/spool/uucp/D./.places
./private/spool/uucp/.places
./private/spool/uucppublic
./private/spool/uucppublic/.hushlogin
./private/spool/uucppublic/.places
./private/spool/.places
./private/spool/lpd.lock
./private/spool/NeXT
./private/tftpboot
./private/tftpboot/private
./private/tftpboot/private/tftpboot
./private/tftpboot/private/.places
./private/tftpboot/.places
./private/vm
./private/vm/swapfile
./private/vm/.places
./private/.places
./NextApps
./NextApps/Librarian.app
./NextApps/Librarian.app/Librarian
./NextApps/Librarian.app/images
./NextApps/Librarian.app/images/ascii.tiff
./NextApps/Librarian.app/images/c.tiff
./NextApps/Librarian.app/images/cat.tiff
./NextApps/Librarian.app/images/csh.tiff
./NextApps/Librarian.app/images/cshH.tiff
./NextApps/Librarian.app/images/directory.tiff
./NextApps/Librarian.app/images/directoryH.tiff
./NextApps/Librarian.app/images/english.tiff
./NextApps/Librarian.app/images/eps.tiff
./NextApps/Librarian.app/images/epsH.tiff
./NextApps/Librarian.app/images/find.tiff
./NextApps/Librarian.app/images/findH.tiff
./NextApps/Librarian.app/images/link.tiff
./NextApps/Librarian.app/images/linkH.tiff
./NextApps/Librarian.app/images/mail.tiff
./NextApps/Librarian.app/images/man.tiff
./NextApps/Librarian.app/images/next.tiff
./NextApps/Librarian.app/images/nextH.tiff
./NextApps/Librarian.app/images/nib.tiff
./NextApps/Librarian.app/images/nob.tiff
./NextApps/Librarian.app/images/nobH.tiff
./NextApps/Librarian.app/images/prev.tiff
./NextApps/Librarian.app/images/prevH.tiff
./NextApps/Librarian.app/images/ps.tiff
./NextApps/Librarian.app/images/psH.tiff
./NextApps/Librarian.app/images/psw.tiff
./NextApps/Librarian.app/images/roff.tiff
./NextApps/Librarian.app/images/rtf.tiff

./NextApps/Librarian.app/images/rtfH.tiff
./NextApps/Librarian.app/images/search.tiff
./NextApps/Librarian.app/images/searchH.tiff
./NextApps/Librarian.app/images/sh.tiff
./NextApps/Librarian.app/images/shH.tiff
./NextApps/Librarian.app/images/stop.tiff
./NextApps/Librarian.app/images/tiff.tiff
./NextApps/Librarian.app/images/unknown.tiff
./NextApps/Librarian.app/images/wn.tiff
./NextApps/Librarian.app/images/.places
./NextApps/Librarian.app/targets
./NextApps/Librarian.app/targets/targetFile
./NextApps/Librarian.app/targets/Targets1.0
./NextApps/Librarian.app/targets/.places
./NextApps/Librarian.app/aux
./NextApps/Librarian.app/aux/help
./NextApps/Librarian.app/aux/.places
./NextApps/Librarian.app/.places
./NextApps/Mathematica.app
./NextApps/Mathematica.app/PrefsFile.mb
./NextApps/Mathematica.app/.places
./NextApps/Mathematica.app/.list
./NextApps/Mathematica.app/MathematicaHelp.mb
./NextApps/Mathematica.app/ApplicationResources.mb
./NextApps/Mathematica.app/MathematicaHelp.ma
./NextApps/Mathematica.app/Mathematica
./NextApps/Mathematica.app/Kernel
./NextApps/Mathematica.app/Kernel/NeXT
./NextApps/Mathematica.app/Kernel/NeXT/mathexe
./NextApps/Mathematica.app/Kernel/NeXT/StartUp
./NextApps/Mathematica.app/Kernel/NeXT/StartUp/Attributes.m
./NextApps/Mathematica.app/Kernel/NeXT/StartUp/Digits.m
./NextApps/Mathematica.app/Kernel/NeXT/StartUp/Edit.m
./NextApps/Mathematica.app/Kernel/NeXT/StartUp/Elliptic.m
./NextApps/Mathematica.app/Kernel/NeXT/StartUp/Formats.m
./NextApps/Mathematica.app/Kernel/NeXT/StartUp/GroebnerBasis.m
./NextApps/Mathematica.app/Kernel/NeXT/StartUp/IntegralTables.m
./NextApps/Mathematica.app/Kernel/NeXT/StartUp/InverseFunctions.m
./NextApps/Mathematica.app/Kernel/NeXT/StartUp/LinearProgramming.m
./NextApps/Mathematica.app/Kernel/NeXT/StartUp/README
./NextApps/Mathematica.app/Kernel/NeXT/StartUp/RunThrough.m
./NextApps/Mathematica.app/Kernel/NeXT/StartUp/Series.m
./NextApps/Mathematica.app/Kernel/NeXT/StartUp/ValueQ.m
./NextApps/Mathematica.app/Kernel/NeXT/StartUp/sysinit.m
./NextApps/Mathematica.app/Kernel/NeXT/StartUp/msg.m
./NextApps/Mathematica.app/Kernel/NeXT/StartUp/info.m
./NextApps/Mathematica.app/Kernel/NeXT/StartUp/.places
./NextApps/Mathematica.app/Kernel/NeXT/.places
./NextApps/Mathematica.app/Kernel/MathTalk
./NextApps/Mathematica.app/Kernel/MathTalk/control
./NextApps/Mathematica.app/Kernel/MathTalk/leftcrc
```

```
./NextApps/Mathematica.app/Kernel/MathTalk/leftend
./NextApps/Mathematica.app/Kernel/MathTalk/rightcrc
./NextApps/Mathematica.app/Kernel/MathTalk/rightend
./NextApps/Mathematica.app/Kernel/MathTalk/twoway
./NextApps/Mathematica.app/Kernel/MathTalk/.places
./NextApps/Mathematica.app/Kernel/InitFiles
./NextApps/Mathematica.app/Kernel/InitFiles/FileGraphics.m
./NextApps/Mathematica.app/Kernel/InitFiles/PSDirect.m
./NextApps/Mathematica.app/Kernel/InitFiles/README
./NextApps/Mathematica.app/Kernel/InitFiles/Tek.m
./NextApps/Mathematica.app/Kernel/InitFiles/Terminal.m
./NextApps/Mathematica.app/Kernel/InitFiles/end.m
./NextApps/Mathematica.app/Kernel/InitFiles/init.m
./NextApps/Mathematica.app/Kernel/InitFiles/.places
./NextApps/Mathematica.app/Kernel/Utilities
./NextApps/Mathematica.app/Kernel/Utilities/mathlink.c
./NextApps/Mathematica.app/Kernel/Utilities/mathlink.h
./NextApps/Mathematica.app/Kernel/Utilities/mdefs.h
./NextApps/Mathematica.app/Kernel/Utilities/psfix
./NextApps/Mathematica.app/Kernel/Utilities/tekps
./NextApps/Mathematica.app/Kernel/Utilities/ttyps
./NextApps/Mathematica.app/Kernel/Utilities/.places
./NextApps/Mathematica.app/Kernel/.places
./NextApps/Mathematica.app/Kernel/math
./NextApps/Mathematica.app/Kernel/mathremote
./NextApps/Mathematica.app/Kernel/mathnext
./NextApps/Quotations
./NextApps/Webster
./NextApps/BuildDisk
./NextApps/Edit
./NextApps/Mail.app
./NextApps/Mail.app/Mail
./NextApps/Mail.app/Mail Help
./NextApps/Mail.app/Mail Help/.places
./NextApps/Mail.app/Mail Help/2. Reading Mail
./NextApps/Mail.app/Mail Help/2. Reading Mail/.places
./NextApps/Mail.app/Mail Help/2. Reading Mail/2. Deleting Mail
./NextApps/Mail.app/Mail Help/2. Reading Mail/3. Printing
./NextApps/Mail.app/Mail Help/2. Reading Mail/1. The Mailbox Window
./NextApps/Mail.app/Mail Help/8. Trouble
./NextApps/Mail.app/Mail Help/8. Trouble/.places
./NextApps/Mail.app/Mail Help/8. Trouble/1. Trouble
./NextApps/Mail.app/Mail Help/3. Sending Mail
./NextApps/Mail.app/Mail Help/3. Sending Mail/.places
./NextApps/Mail.app/Mail Help/3. Sending Mail/1. Send Window
./NextApps/Mail.app/Mail Help/3. Sending Mail/2. Replying
./NextApps/Mail.app/Mail Help/3. Sending Mail/3. Forwarding
./NextApps/Mail.app/Mail Help/3. Sending Mail/4. Addresses
./NextApps/Mail.app/Mail Help/4. Mailboxes
./NextApps/Mail.app/Mail Help/4. Mailboxes/.places
./NextApps/Mail.app/Mail Help/4. Mailboxes/1. Managing

./NextApps/Mail.app/Mail Help/1. Getting Started
./NextApps/Mail.app/Mail Help/1. Getting Started/.places
./NextApps/Mail.app/Mail Help/1. Getting Started/2. Starting Mail
./NextApps/Mail.app/Mail Help/1. Getting Started/1. Before You Start
./NextApps/Mail.app/Mail Help/6. Attachments
./NextApps/Mail.app/Mail Help/6. Attachments/.places
./NextApps/Mail.app/Mail Help/6. Attachments/1. Attachments
./NextApps/Mail.app/Mail Help/7. Advanced
./NextApps/Mail.app/Mail Help/7. Advanced/.places
./NextApps/Mail.app/Mail Help/7. Advanced/4. Pictures
./NextApps/Mail.app/Mail Help/7. Advanced/2. Conversion
./NextApps/Mail.app/Mail Help/7. Advanced/3. Index Files
./NextApps/Mail.app/Mail Help/7. Advanced/1. Mail Defaults
./NextApps/Mail.app/Mail Help/7. Advanced/5. Mail File Format
./NextApps/Mail.app/Mail Help/7. Advanced/6. Protocol
./NextApps/Mail.app/Mail Help/5. Sound Recordings
./NextApps/Mail.app/Mail Help/5. Sound Recordings/.places
./NextApps/Mail.app/Mail Help/5. Sound Recordings/1. Recording Sound
./NextApps/Mail.app/Mail Help/5. Sound Recordings/2. Listening
./NextApps/Mail.app/Mail Help/0.Table of Contents
./NextApps/Mail.app/decode
./NextApps/Mail.app/MailConvert
./NextApps/Mail.app/.places
./NextApps/InterfaceBuilder
./NextApps/Preferences
./NextApps/Preview
./NextApps/PrintManager
./NextApps/Shell
./NextApps/Terminal
./NextApps/WriteNow.app
./NextApps/WriteNow.app/WriteNow
./NextApps/WriteNow.app/wn2rtf
./NextApps/WriteNow.app/rtf2wn
./NextApps/WriteNow.app/WNDictionary.wndict
./NextApps/WriteNow.app/WNEmptyDictionary.wndict
./NextApps/WriteNow.app/.places
./NextApps/.places
./lib
./lib/cc1-16
./lib/cpp-16
./lib/cc1
./lib/cpp
./lib/libc.a
./lib/crt0.o
./lib/mcrt0.o
./lib/gcrt0.o
./lib/libsys_s.a
./lib/libsys_p.a
./lib/.places
./NextDeveloper
./NextDeveloper/Apps
```

```
./NextDeveloper/Apps/Bug56.app
./NextDeveloper/Apps/Bug56.app/Bug56
./NextDeveloper/Apps/Bug56.app/HELP
./NextDeveloper/Apps/Bug56.app/HELP/.places
./NextDeveloper/Apps/Bug56.app/HELP/resetProc.rtf
./NextDeveloper/Apps/Bug56.app/HELP/ipr.rtf
./NextDeveloper/Apps/Bug56.app/HELP/basics.rtf
./NextDeveloper/Apps/Bug56.app/HELP/loadErase.rtf
./NextDeveloper/Apps/Bug56.app/HELP/loadAppend.rtf
./NextDeveloper/Apps/Bug56.app/HELP/loadSymOnly.rtf
./NextDeveloper/Apps/Bug56.app/HELP/AppendSymOnly.rtf
./NextDeveloper/Apps/Bug56.app/HELP/symbolState.rtf
./NextDeveloper/Apps/Bug56.app/HELP/rasmPasm.rtf
./NextDeveloper/Apps/Bug56.app/HELP/hostCommand.rtf
./NextDeveloper/Apps/Bug56.app/HELP/pxyEditors.rtf
./NextDeveloper/Apps/Bug56.app/HELP/hostPortWrite.rtf
./NextDeveloper/Apps/Bug56.app/HELP/hostFlags.rtf
./NextDeveloper/Apps/Bug56.app/HELP/quikVu.rtf
./NextDeveloper/Apps/Bug56.app/HELP/stackPanel.rtf
./NextDeveloper/Apps/Bug56.app/HELP/dataAluPanel.rtf
./NextDeveloper/Apps/Bug56.app/HELP/addrAluPanel.rtf
./NextDeveloper/Apps/Bug56.app/HELP/pcrPanel.rtf
./NextDeveloper/Apps/Bug56.app/HELP/bpstateSw.rtf
./NextDeveloper/Apps/Bug56.app/HELP/dataROMsw.rtf
./NextDeveloper/Apps/Bug56.app/HELP/runModeButtons.rtf
./NextDeveloper/Apps/Bug56.app/HELP/bpOnlySw.rtf
./NextDeveloper/Apps/Bug56.app/HELP/hostHandlerSw.rtf
./NextDeveloper/Apps/Bug56.app/HELP/hostRecircSw.rtf
./NextDeveloper/Apps/Bug56.app/HELP/intInhSw.rtf
./NextDeveloper/Apps/Bug56.app/HELP/useSyms.rtf
./NextDeveloper/Apps/Bug56.app/HELP/iprMaskSw.rtf
./NextDeveloper/Apps/Bug56.app/HELP/tracePtSw.rtf
./NextDeveloper/Apps/Bug56.app/HELP/resetHpH.rtf
./NextDeveloper/Apps/Bug56.app/HELP/grab.rtf
./NextDeveloper/Apps/Bug56.app/HELP/sstep.rtf
./NextDeveloper/Apps/Bug56.app/HELP/clrAll.rtf
./NextDeveloper/Apps/Bug56.app/HELP/clrAlu.rtf
./NextDeveloper/Apps/Bug56.app/HELP/ssFinish.rtf
./NextDeveloper/Apps/Bug56.app/HELP/ssAuto.rtf
./NextDeveloper/Apps/Bug56.app/HELP/autoUpdate.rtf
./NextDeveloper/Apps/Bug56.app/HELP/manUpdate.rtf
./NextDeveloper/Apps/Bug56.app/HELP/ignoreToSw.rtf
./NextDeveloper/Apps/Bug56.app/HELP/ignoreFromSw.rtf
./NextDeveloper/Apps/Bug56.app/HELP/clrFromSw.rtf
./NextDeveloper/Apps/Bug56.app/HELP/clrToSw.rtf
./NextDeveloper/Apps/Bug56.app/HELP/bpPanel.rtf
./NextDeveloper/Apps/Bug56.app/HELP/.list
./NextDeveloper/Apps/Bug56.app/HELP/sciPanel.rtf
./NextDeveloper/Apps/Bug56.app/HELP/allRegs.rtf
./NextDeveloper/Apps/Bug56.app/HELP/HostPanel.rtf
./NextDeveloper/Apps/Bug56.app/HELP/ssiPanel.rtf
./NextDeveloper/Apps/Bug56.app/HELP/controlPanel.rtf
./NextDeveloper/Apps/Bug56.app/HELP/PortcPanel.rtf
./NextDeveloper/Apps/Bug56.app/HELP/DSPeek.rtf
./NextDeveloper/Apps/Bug56.app/HELP/eventLogger.rtf
./NextDeveloper/Apps/Bug56.app/HELP/tpPanel.rtf
./NextDeveloper/Apps/Bug56.app/HELP/symWindow.rtf
./NextDeveloper/Apps/Bug56.app/HELP/export.rtf
./NextDeveloper/Apps/Bug56.app/HELP/import.rtf
./NextDeveloper/Apps/Bug56.app/HELP/searcher.rtf
./NextDeveloper/Apps/Bug56.app/HELP/fillMem.rtf
./NextDeveloper/Apps/Bug56.app/HELP/moveMem.rtf
./NextDeveloper/Apps/Bug56.app/.places
./NextDeveloper/Apps/.places
./NextDeveloper/Demos
./NextDeveloper/Demos/README.wn
./NextDeveloper/Demos/DataViz
./NextDeveloper/Demos/.places
./NextDeveloper/Demos/TopologyLab.app
./NextDeveloper/Demos/TopologyLab.app/TopologyLab
./NextDeveloper/Demos/TopologyLab.app/gaussian.top
./NextDeveloper/Demos/TopologyLab.app/ribbon.top
./NextDeveloper/Demos/TopologyLab.app/diffraction.top
./NextDeveloper/Demos/TopologyLab.app/.places
./NextDeveloper/Demos/CircuitBuilder.app
./NextDeveloper/Demos/CircuitBuilder.app/CircuitBuilder
./NextDeveloper/Demos/CircuitBuilder.app/passive.ckt
./NextDeveloper/Demos/CircuitBuilder.app/lowpass.ckt
./NextDeveloper/Demos/CircuitBuilder.app/acamplifier.ckt
./NextDeveloper/Demos/CircuitBuilder.app/chargepump.ckt
./NextDeveloper/Demos/CircuitBuilder.app/lowpass.ma
./NextDeveloper/Demos/CircuitBuilder.app/lowpass.mb
./NextDeveloper/Demos/CircuitBuilder.app/.places
./NextDeveloper/Demos/Mandelbrot
./NextDeveloper/Demos/BreakApp
./NextDeveloper/Demos/Stealth.app
./NextDeveloper/Demos/Stealth.app/Stealth
./NextDeveloper/Demos/Stealth.app/atcFacilities
./NextDeveloper/Demos/Stealth.app/coeff
./NextDeveloper/Demos/Stealth.app/fastScene.st
./NextDeveloper/Demos/Stealth.app/fullScene.st
./NextDeveloper/Demos/Stealth.app/scene.st
./NextDeveloper/Demos/Stealth.app/screw.ps
./NextDeveloper/Demos/Stealth.app/stealthDoc
./NextDeveloper/Demos/Stealth.app/vors
./NextDeveloper/Demos/Stealth.app/farm.snd
./NextDeveloper/Demos/Stealth.app/crunch.snd
./NextDeveloper/Demos/Stealth.app/approach.snd
./NextDeveloper/Demos/Stealth.app/atis.snd
./NextDeveloper/Demos/Stealth.app/cDeparture.snd
./NextDeveloper/Demos/Stealth.app/ctower.snd
./NextDeveloper/Demos/Stealth.app/departure.snd
```

./NextDeveloper/Demos/Stealth.app/take-off.snd
./NextDeveloper/Demos/Stealth.app/.places
./NextDeveloper/Demos/ScorePlayer
./NextDeveloper/Demos/Synthesizer.app
./NextDeveloper/Demos/Synthesizer.app/Synthesizer
./NextDeveloper/Demos/Synthesizer.app/helpText.rtf
./NextDeveloper/Demos/Synthesizer.app/.places
./NextDeveloper/Demos/Chess
./NextDeveloper/Demos/MonsterScope
./NextDeveloper/Demos/Poker
./NextDeveloper/Demos/Balancer.app
./NextDeveloper/Demos/Balancer.app/Balancer
./NextDeveloper/Demos/Balancer.app/Sound2.snd
./NextDeveloper/Demos/Balancer.app/InfoText.rtf
./NextDeveloper/Demos/Balancer.app/Networks
./NextDeveloper/Demos/Balancer.app/Networks/Network_0100_0.wgts
./NextDeveloper/Demos/Balancer.app/Networks/Network_0500_0.wgts
./NextDeveloper/Demos/Balancer.app/Networks/Network_0900_0.wgts
./NextDeveloper/Demos/Balancer.app/Networks/Network_0200_0.wgts
./NextDeveloper/Demos/Balancer.app/Networks/Network_0600_0.wgts
./NextDeveloper/Demos/Balancer.app/Networks/Network_1000_0.wgts
./NextDeveloper/Demos/Balancer.app/Networks/Network_0300_0.wgts
./NextDeveloper/Demos/Balancer.app/Networks/Network_0700_0.wgts
./NextDeveloper/Demos/Balancer.app/Networks/Network_0400_0.wgts
./NextDeveloper/Demos/Balancer.app/Networks/Network_0800_0.wgts
./NextDeveloper/Demos/Balancer.app/Networks/.places
./NextDeveloper/Demos/Balancer.app/seal1.tiff
./NextDeveloper/Demos/Balancer.app/seal2.tiff
./NextDeveloper/Demos/Balancer.app/seal3.tiff
./NextDeveloper/Demos/Balancer.app/oops.snd
./NextDeveloper/Demos/Balancer.app/sorry.snd
./NextDeveloper/Demos/Balancer.app/.places
./NextDeveloper/Demos/Saturn.app
./NextDeveloper/Demos/Saturn.app/Saturn
./NextDeveloper/Demos/Saturn.app/satellite0.tiff
./NextDeveloper/Demos/Saturn.app/satellite1.tiff
./NextDeveloper/Demos/Saturn.app/satellite2.tiff
./NextDeveloper/Demos/Saturn.app/satellite3.tiff
./NextDeveloper/Demos/Saturn.app/satellite4.tiff
./NextDeveloper/Demos/Saturn.app/satellite5.tiff
./NextDeveloper/Demos/Saturn.app/satellite6.tiff
./NextDeveloper/Demos/Saturn.app/satellite7.tiff
./NextDeveloper/Demos/Saturn.app/satellite8.tiff
./NextDeveloper/Demos/Saturn.app/satellite9.tiff
./NextDeveloper/Demos/Saturn.app/satellite10.tiff
./NextDeveloper/Demos/Saturn.app/satellite11.tiff
./NextDeveloper/Demos/Saturn.app/satellite12.tiff
./NextDeveloper/Demos/Saturn.app/satellite13.tiff
./NextDeveloper/Demos/Saturn.app/satellite14.tiff
./NextDeveloper/Demos/Saturn.app/satellite15.tiff
./NextDeveloper/Demos/Saturn.app/satellite16.tiff

./NextDeveloper/Demos/Saturn.app/satellite17.tiff
./NextDeveloper/Demos/Saturn.app/satellite18.tiff
./NextDeveloper/Demos/Saturn.app/satellite19.tiff
./NextDeveloper/Demos/Saturn.app/.places
./NextDeveloper/Demos/Billiards.app
./NextDeveloper/Demos/Billiards.app/Billiards
./NextDeveloper/Demos/Billiards.app/ball22.snd
./NextDeveloper/Demos/Billiards.app/cue22.snd
./NextDeveloper/Demos/Billiards.app/pocket22.snd
./NextDeveloper/Demos/Billiards.app/rail22.snd
./NextDeveloper/Demos/Billiards.app/gong22.snd
./NextDeveloper/Demos/Billiards.app/.places
./NextDeveloper/Demos/StatLab.app
./NextDeveloper/Demos/StatLab.app/StatLab
./NextDeveloper/Demos/StatLab.app/signal.fdat
./NextDeveloper/Demos/StatLab.app/lorenz.fdat
./NextDeveloper/Demos/StatLab.app/gray.fdat
./NextDeveloper/Demos/StatLab.app/grades.fdat
./NextDeveloper/Demos/StatLab.app/.places
./NextDeveloper/Demos/Molecule.app
./NextDeveloper/Demos/Molecule.app/Molecule
./NextDeveloper/Demos/Molecule.app/TNT.mol
./NextDeveloper/Demos/Molecule.app/cyclopropane.mol
./NextDeveloper/Demos/Molecule.app/nbutane.mol
./NextDeveloper/Demos/Molecule.app/aspirin.mol
./NextDeveloper/Demos/Molecule.app/ethanol.mol
./NextDeveloper/Demos/Molecule.app/nitroglycerin.mol
./NextDeveloper/Demos/Molecule.app/benzene.mol
./NextDeveloper/Demos/Molecule.app/methane.mol
./NextDeveloper/Demos/Molecule.app/octane.mol
./NextDeveloper/Demos/Molecule.app/cyclohexane.mol
./NextDeveloper/Demos/Molecule.app/methanol.mol
./NextDeveloper/Demos/Molecule.app/water.mol
./NextDeveloper/Demos/Molecule.app/cyclohexane.tiff
./NextDeveloper/Demos/Molecule.app/.places
./NextDeveloper/Demos/Yap
./NextDeveloper/Demos/Draw
./NextDeveloper/Demos/SoundPlayer
./NextDeveloper/Demos/Ray.app
./NextDeveloper/Demos/Ray.app/Ray
./NextDeveloper/Demos/Ray.app/balls.nff
./NextDeveloper/Demos/Ray.app/gears.nff
./NextDeveloper/Demos/Ray.app/mountain.nff
./NextDeveloper/Demos/Ray.app/rings.nff
./NextDeveloper/Demos/Ray.app/slantballs.nff
./NextDeveloper/Demos/Ray.app/tetra.nff
./NextDeveloper/Demos/Ray.app/tree.nff
./NextDeveloper/Demos/Ray.app/MTV_ray_engine
./NextDeveloper/Demos/Ray.app/.places
./NextDeveloper/Demos/FrameMaker.app
./NextDeveloper/Demos/FrameMaker.app/.fminit2.0

```
./NextDeveloper/Demos/FrameMaker.app/.fminit2.0/langdir
./NextDeveloper/Demos/FrameMaker.app/.fminit2.0/langdir/eng.env
./NextDeveloper/Demos/FrameMaker.app/.fminit2.0/langdir/eng.hyp
./NextDeveloper/Demos/FrameMaker.app/.fminit2.0/langdir/eng.lex
./NextDeveloper/Demos/FrameMaker.app/.fminit2.0/langdir/eng12.clx
./NextDeveloper/Demos/FrameMaker.app/.fminit2.0/langdir/engphon.env
./NextDeveloper/Demos/FrameMaker.app/.fminit2.0/langdir/hyphens.eng
./NextDeveloper/Demos/FrameMaker.app/.fminit2.0/langdir/.places
./NextDeveloper/Demos/FrameMaker.app/.fminit2.0/wntomif
./NextDeveloper/Demos/FrameMaker.app/.fminit2.0/english
./NextDeveloper/Demos/FrameMaker.app/.fminit2.0/english/dbre
./NextDeveloper/Demos/FrameMaker.app/.fminit2.0/english/dbre/arrowhead.dbre
./NextDeveloper/Demos/FrameMaker.app/.fminit2.0/english/dbre/book_kit.dbre
./NextDeveloper/Demos/FrameMaker.app/.fminit2.0/english/dbre/changebar.dbre
./NextDeveloper/Demos/FrameMaker.app/.fminit2.0/english/dbre/column_connect.dbre
./NextDeveloper/Demos/FrameMaker.app/.fminit2.0/english/dbre
        /dictionary_browser.dbre
./NextDeveloper/Demos/FrameMaker.app/.fminit2.0/english/dbre/doc_bitmap.dbre
./NextDeveloper/Demos/FrameMaker.app/.fminit2.0/english/dbre/doc_capture.dbre
./NextDeveloper/Demos/FrameMaker.app/.fminit2.0/english/dbre/doc_custom.dbre
./NextDeveloper/Demos/FrameMaker.app/.fminit2.0/english/dbre
        /doc_file_locked1.dbre
./NextDeveloper/Demos/FrameMaker.app/.fminit2.0/english/dbre
        /doc_file_locked2.dbre
./NextDeveloper/Demos/FrameMaker.app/.fminit2.0/english/dbre/doc_import.dbre
./NextDeveloper/Demos/FrameMaker.app/.fminit2.0/english/dbre/doc_info.dbre
./NextDeveloper/Demos/FrameMaker.app/.fminit2.0/english/dbre/doc_keyboard.dbre
./NextDeveloper/Demos/FrameMaker.app/.fminit2.0/english/dbre/doc_open.dbre
./NextDeveloper/Demos/FrameMaker.app/.fminit2.0/english/dbre/doc_open_text.dbre
./NextDeveloper/Demos/FrameMaker.app/.fminit2.0/english/dbre/doc_print.dbre
./NextDeveloper/Demos/FrameMaker.app/.fminit2.0/english/dbre/doc_properties.dbre
./NextDeveloper/Demos/FrameMaker.app/.fminit2.0/english/dbre/doc_quit.dbre
./NextDeveloper/Demos/FrameMaker.app/.fminit2.0/english/dbre/doc_raster_dpi.dbre
./NextDeveloper/Demos/FrameMaker.app/.fminit2.0/english/dbre/doc_save.dbre
./NextDeveloper/Demos/FrameMaker.app/.fminit2.0/english/dbre/doc_save_text.dbre
./NextDeveloper/Demos/FrameMaker.app/.fminit2.0/english/dbre/doc_template.dbre
./NextDeveloper/Demos/FrameMaker.app/.fminit2.0/english/dbre
        /edit_anchored_frame.dbre
./NextDeveloper/Demos/FrameMaker.app/.fminit2.0/english/dbre
        /edit_dictionaries.dbre
./NextDeveloper/Demos/FrameMaker.app/.fminit2.0/english/dbre/edit_markers.dbre
./NextDeveloper/Demos/FrameMaker.app/.fminit2.0/english/dbre/edit_search.dbre
./NextDeveloper/Demos/FrameMaker.app/.fminit2.0/english/dbre/edit_set_search.dbre
./NextDeveloper/Demos/FrameMaker.app/.fminit2.0/english/dbre/edit_spell.dbre
./NextDeveloper/Demos/FrameMaker.app/.fminit2.0/english/dbre/editors.dbre
./NextDeveloper/Demos/FrameMaker.app/.fminit2.0/english/dbre/equation.dbre
./NextDeveloper/Demos/FrameMaker.app/.fminit2.0/english/dbre/flow_properties.dbre
./NextDeveloper/Demos/FrameMaker.app/.fminit2.0/english/dbre/fmbook_add.dbre
./NextDeveloper/Demos/FrameMaker.app/.fminit2.0/english/dbre/fmbook_define.dbre
./NextDeveloper/Demos/FrameMaker.app/.fminit2.0/english/dbre
        /fmbook_definefile.dbre
./NextDeveloper/Demos/FrameMaker.app/.fminit2.0/english/dbre
        /fmbook_definegenerate.dbre
./NextDeveloper/Demos/FrameMaker.app/.fminit2.0/english/dbre/fmbook_edit.dbre
./NextDeveloper/Demos/FrameMaker.app/.fminit2.0/english/dbre/fmbook_generate.dbre
./NextDeveloper/Demos/FrameMaker.app/.fminit2.0/english/dbre/fmbook_print.dbre
./NextDeveloper/Demos/FrameMaker.app/.fminit2.0/english/dbre
        /fmbook_printfile.dbre
./NextDeveloper/Demos/FrameMaker.app/.fminit2.0/english/dbre/fmbook_save.dbre
./NextDeveloper/Demos/FrameMaker.app/.fminit2.0/english/dbre/fmbook_update.dbre
./NextDeveloper/Demos/FrameMaker.app/.fminit2.0/english/dbre/fmbook_usefmt.dbre
./NextDeveloper/Demos/FrameMaker.app/.fminit2.0/english/dbre/font_catalog.dbre
./NextDeveloper/Demos/FrameMaker.app/.fminit2.0/english/dbre/font_kit.dbre
./NextDeveloper/Demos/FrameMaker.app/.fminit2.0/english/dbre/fontdesign.dbre
./NextDeveloper/Demos/FrameMaker.app/.fminit2.0/english/dbre/fontsearch.dbre
./NextDeveloper/Demos/FrameMaker.app/.fminit2.0/english/dbre/footnote.dbre
./NextDeveloper/Demos/FrameMaker.app/.fminit2.0/english/dbre/format_capital.dbre
./NextDeveloper/Demos/FrameMaker.app/.fminit2.0/english/dbre/frame_name.dbre
./NextDeveloper/Demos/FrameMaker.app/.fminit2.0/english/dbre/hard_heap_full.dbre
./NextDeveloper/Demos/FrameMaker.app/.fminit2.0/english/dbre/layout_page.dbre
./NextDeveloper/Demos/FrameMaker.app/.fminit2.0/english/dbre/license.dbre
./NextDeveloper/Demos/FrameMaker.app/.fminit2.0/english/dbre/license_failed.dbre
./NextDeveloper/Demos/FrameMaker.app/.fminit2.0/english/dbre/linewidth.dbre
./NextDeveloper/Demos/FrameMaker.app/.fminit2.0/english/dbre/math_equ.dbre
./NextDeveloper/Demos/FrameMaker.app/.fminit2.0/english/dbre/obj_prop_arc.dbre
./NextDeveloper/Demos/FrameMaker.app/.fminit2.0/english/dbre/obj_prop_frame.dbre
./NextDeveloper/Demos/FrameMaker.app/.fminit2.0/english/dbre/obj_prop_group.dbre
./NextDeveloper/Demos/FrameMaker.app/.fminit2.0/english/dbre/obj_prop_inset.dbre
./NextDeveloper/Demos/FrameMaker.app/.fminit2.0/english/dbre/obj_prop_line.dbre
./NextDeveloper/Demos/FrameMaker.app/.fminit2.0/english/dbre/obj_prop_math.dbre
./NextDeveloper/Demos/FrameMaker.app/.fminit2.0/english/dbre/obj_prop_object.dbre
./NextDeveloper/Demos/FrameMaker.app/.fminit2.0/english/dbre/obj_prop_rrect.dbre
./NextDeveloper/Demos/FrameMaker.app/.fminit2.0/english/dbre/obj_prop_text.dbre
./NextDeveloper/Demos/FrameMaker.app/.fminit2.0/english/dbre/page_add.dbre
./NextDeveloper/Demos/FrameMaker.app/.fminit2.0/english/dbre/page_delete.dbre
./NextDeveloper/Demos/FrameMaker.app/.fminit2.0/english/dbre/page_goto.dbre
./NextDeveloper/Demos/FrameMaker.app/.fminit2.0/english/dbre/page_name.dbre
./NextDeveloper/Demos/FrameMaker.app/.fminit2.0/english/dbre/page_properties.dbre
./NextDeveloper/Demos/FrameMaker.app/.fminit2.0/english/dbre/pagination.dbre
./NextDeveloper/Demos/FrameMaker.app/.fminit2.0/english/dbre/pgf_catalog.dbre
./NextDeveloper/Demos/FrameMaker.app/.fminit2.0/english/dbre/pgf_kit.dbre
./NextDeveloper/Demos/FrameMaker.app/.fminit2.0/english/dbre/pgfadvance.dbre
./NextDeveloper/Demos/FrameMaker.app/.fminit2.0/english/dbre/pgfbasic.dbre
./NextDeveloper/Demos/FrameMaker.app/.fminit2.0/english/dbre/pgffont.dbre
./NextDeveloper/Demos/FrameMaker.app/.fminit2.0/english/dbre/pgfnum.dbre
./NextDeveloper/Demos/FrameMaker.app/.fminit2.0/english/dbre/pgfswitch.dbre
./NextDeveloper/Demos/FrameMaker.app/.fminit2.0/english/dbre/pgftab.dbre
./NextDeveloper/Demos/FrameMaker.app/.fminit2.0/english/dbre/quick_catalog.dbre
./NextDeveloper/Demos/FrameMaker.app/.fminit2.0/english/dbre/separation.dbre
./NextDeveloper/Demos/FrameMaker.app/.fminit2.0/english/dbre/session_pref.dbre
./NextDeveloper/Demos/FrameMaker.app/.fminit2.0/english/dbre/soft_heap_full.dbre
./NextDeveloper/Demos/FrameMaker.app/.fminit2.0/english/dbre/spell_options.dbre
./NextDeveloper/Demos/FrameMaker.app/.fminit2.0/english/dbre/tools_align.dbre
```

./NextDeveloper/Demos/FrameMaker.app/.fminit2.0/english/dbre
    /tools_distribute.dbre
./NextDeveloper/Demos/FrameMaker.app/.fminit2.0/english/dbre/tools_scale.dbre
./NextDeveloper/Demos/FrameMaker.app/.fminit2.0/english/dbre/tools_sides.dbre
./NextDeveloper/Demos/FrameMaker.app/.fminit2.0/english/dbre/usefmt.dbre
./NextDeveloper/Demos/FrameMaker.app/.fminit2.0/english/dbre/var_deref.dbre
./NextDeveloper/Demos/FrameMaker.app/.fminit2.0/english/dbre/var_main.dbre
./NextDeveloper/Demos/FrameMaker.app/.fminit2.0/english/dbre/var_sys_edit.dbre
./NextDeveloper/Demos/FrameMaker.app/.fminit2.0/english/dbre/var_user_edit.dbre
./NextDeveloper/Demos/FrameMaker.app/.fminit2.0/english/dbre
    /var_xref_textdef.dbre
./NextDeveloper/Demos/FrameMaker.app/.fminit2.0/english/dbre/view.dbre
./NextDeveloper/Demos/FrameMaker.app/.fminit2.0/english/dbre/xref_deref.dbre
./NextDeveloper/Demos/FrameMaker.app/.fminit2.0/english/dbre/xref_findfile.dbre
./NextDeveloper/Demos/FrameMaker.app/.fminit2.0/english/dbre/xref_format.dbre
./NextDeveloper/Demos/FrameMaker.app/.fminit2.0/english/dbre/xref_main.dbre
./NextDeveloper/Demos/FrameMaker.app/.fminit2.0/english/dbre/xref_unresolve.dbre
./NextDeveloper/Demos/FrameMaker.app/.fminit2.0/english/dbre/xref_update.dbre
./NextDeveloper/Demos/FrameMaker.app/.fminit2.0/english/dbre/zoomfactor.dbre
./NextDeveloper/Demos/FrameMaker.app/.fminit2.0/english/dbre/.places
./NextDeveloper/Demos/FrameMaker.app/.fminit2.0/english/srre
./NextDeveloper/Demos/FrameMaker.app/.fminit2.0/english/srre/core.srre
./NextDeveloper/Demos/FrameMaker.app/.fminit2.0/english/srre/coredb.srre
./NextDeveloper/Demos/FrameMaker.app/.fminit2.0/english/srre/dd.srre
./NextDeveloper/Demos/FrameMaker.app/.fminit2.0/english/srre/fmprintdriver.srre
./NextDeveloper/Demos/FrameMaker.app/.fminit2.0/english/srre/languages.srre
./NextDeveloper/Demos/FrameMaker.app/.fminit2.0/english/srre/menus.srre
./NextDeveloper/Demos/FrameMaker.app/.fminit2.0/english/srre/mif.srre
./NextDeveloper/Demos/FrameMaker.app/.fminit2.0/english/srre/mml.srre
./NextDeveloper/Demos/FrameMaker.app/.fminit2.0/english/srre/next.srre
./NextDeveloper/Demos/FrameMaker.app/.fminit2.0/english/srre/nextdb.srre
./NextDeveloper/Demos/FrameMaker.app/.fminit2.0/english/srre/sun.srre
./NextDeveloper/Demos/FrameMaker.app/.fminit2.0/english/srre/sundb.srre
./NextDeveloper/Demos/FrameMaker.app/.fminit2.0/english/srre/unix.srre
./NextDeveloper/Demos/FrameMaker.app/.fminit2.0/english/srre/unixdb.srre
./NextDeveloper/Demos/FrameMaker.app/.fminit2.0/english/srre/errors.srre
./NextDeveloper/Demos/FrameMaker.app/.fminit2.0/english/srre/.places
./NextDeveloper/Demos/FrameMaker.app/.fminit2.0/english/helpdir
./NextDeveloper/Demos/FrameMaker.app/.fminit2.0/english/helpdir/HelpIndex.doc
./NextDeveloper/Demos/FrameMaker.app/.fminit2.0/english/helpdir/helpbuttons.doc
./NextDeveloper/Demos/FrameMaker.app/.fminit2.0/english/helpdir/helpmouse.doc
./NextDeveloper/Demos/FrameMaker.app/.fminit2.0/english/helpdir/helptools.doc
./NextDeveloper/Demos/FrameMaker.app/.fminit2.0/english/helpdir/helptools2.doc
./NextDeveloper/Demos/FrameMaker.app/.fminit2.0/english/helpdir/helpusing.doc
./NextDeveloper/Demos/FrameMaker.app/.fminit2.0/english/helpdir/rfiles
./NextDeveloper/Demos/FrameMaker.app/.fminit2.0/english/helpdir/rfiles
    /OneOptionButton.rf
./NextDeveloper/Demos/FrameMaker.app/.fminit2.0/english/helpdir/rfiles
    /ScrollList.rf
./NextDeveloper/Demos/FrameMaker.app/.fminit2.0/english/helpdir/rfiles
    /TextSymbols.rf
./NextDeveloper/Demos/FrameMaker.app/.fminit2.0/english/helpdir/rfiles/bitpat.rf

./NextDeveloper/Demos/FrameMaker.app/.fminit2.0/english/helpdir/rfiles/bitpat2.rf
./NextDeveloper/Demos/FrameMaker.app/.fminit2.0/english/helpdir/rfiles/buttons.rf
./NextDeveloper/Demos/FrameMaker.app/.fminit2.0/english/helpdir/rfiles
    /buttons1.rf
./NextDeveloper/Demos/FrameMaker.app/.fminit2.0/english/helpdir/rfiles
    /buttons2.rf
./NextDeveloper/Demos/FrameMaker.app/.fminit2.0/english/helpdir/rfiles
    /buttons3.rf
./NextDeveloper/Demos/FrameMaker.app/.fminit2.0/english/helpdir/rfiles
    /charcaticon.rf
./NextDeveloper/Demos/FrameMaker.app/.fminit2.0/english/helpdir/rfiles/cross.rf
./NextDeveloper/Demos/FrameMaker.app/.fminit2.0/english/helpdir/rfiles/eqnicon.rf
./NextDeveloper/Demos/FrameMaker.app/.fminit2.0/english/helpdir/rfiles/eqnobj.rf
./NextDeveloper/Demos/FrameMaker.app/.fminit2.0/english/helpdir/rfiles
    /fcaticon.rf
./NextDeveloper/Demos/FrameMaker.app/.fminit2.0/english/helpdir/rfiles/graypat.rf
./NextDeveloper/Demos/FrameMaker.app/.fminit2.0/english/helpdir/rfiles
    /graypat2.rf
./NextDeveloper/Demos/FrameMaker.app/.fminit2.0/english/helpdir/rfiles/ibeam.rf
./NextDeveloper/Demos/FrameMaker.app/.fminit2.0/english/helpdir/rfiles/icons.rf
./NextDeveloper/Demos/FrameMaker.app/.fminit2.0/english/helpdir/rfiles/marker.rf
./NextDeveloper/Demos/FrameMaker.app/.fminit2.0/english/helpdir/rfiles
    /paracaticon.rf
./NextDeveloper/Demos/FrameMaker.app/.fminit2.0/english/helpdir/rfiles
    /pcaticon.rf
./NextDeveloper/Demos/FrameMaker.app/.fminit2.0/english/helpdir/rfiles/popup.rf
./NextDeveloper/Demos/FrameMaker.app/.fminit2.0/english/helpdir/rfiles
    /printsep.rf
./NextDeveloper/Demos/FrameMaker.app/.fminit2.0/english/helpdir/rfiles/ruler.rf
./NextDeveloper/Demos/FrameMaker.app/.fminit2.0/english/helpdir/rfiles
    /toolicon.rf
./NextDeveloper/Demos/FrameMaker.app/.fminit2.0/english/helpdir/rfiles/tools.rf
./NextDeveloper/Demos/FrameMaker.app/.fminit2.0/english/helpdir/rfiles
    /toolwindow.rf
./NextDeveloper/Demos/FrameMaker.app/.fminit2.0/english/helpdir/rfiles
    /windowicons.rf
./NextDeveloper/Demos/FrameMaker.app/.fminit2.0/english/helpdir/rfiles/.places
./NextDeveloper/Demos/FrameMaker.app/.fminit2.0/english/helpdir/rfiles/xyz.rf
./NextDeveloper/Demos/FrameMaker.app/.fminit2.0/english/helpdir/rfiles
    /NeXTbuttons.help.rf
./NextDeveloper/Demos/FrameMaker.app/.fminit2.0/english/helpdir/.places
./NextDeveloper/Demos/FrameMaker.app/.fminit2.0/english/Equations
./NextDeveloper/Demos/FrameMaker.app/.fminit2.0/english/custom.doc
./NextDeveloper/Demos/FrameMaker.app/.fminit2.0/english/Donotdelete.frame
./NextDeveloper/Demos/FrameMaker.app/.fminit2.0/english/markers
./NextDeveloper/Demos/FrameMaker.app/.fminit2.0/english/kbmap
./NextDeveloper/Demos/FrameMaker.app/.fminit2.0/english/tabs
./NextDeveloper/Demos/FrameMaker.app/.fminit2.0/english/.places
./NextDeveloper/Demos/FrameMaker.app/.fminit2.0/english/doclanguages
./NextDeveloper/Demos/FrameMaker.app/.fminit2.0/english/DonotdeleteTOC.frame
./NextDeveloper/Demos/FrameMaker.app/.fminit2.0/english/rfiles
./NextDeveloper/Demos/FrameMaker.app/.fminit2.0/english/rfiles/.places
./NextDeveloper/Demos/FrameMaker.app/.fminit2.0/english/rfiles/catalog2.tiff

```
./NextDeveloper/Demos/FrameMaker.app/.fminit2.0/english/rfiles/fcat.tiff
./NextDeveloper/Demos/FrameMaker.app/.fminit2.0/english/rfiles/arc.tiff
./NextDeveloper/Demos/FrameMaker.app/.fminit2.0/english/rfiles/lines.tiff
./NextDeveloper/Demos/FrameMaker.app/.fminit2.0/english/rfiles/spell.tiff
./NextDeveloper/Demos/FrameMaker.app/.fminit2.0/english/rfiles/ruler.tiff
./NextDeveloper/Demos/FrameMaker.app/.fminit2.0/english/rfiles/pcat.tiff
./NextDeveloper/Demos/FrameMaker.app/.fminit2.0/english/rfiles/pagenxt.tiff
./NextDeveloper/Demos/FrameMaker.app/.fminit2.0/english/rfiles/catalog.tiff
./NextDeveloper/Demos/FrameMaker.app/.fminit2.0/english/rfiles/dock.tiff
./NextDeveloper/Demos/FrameMaker.app/.fminit2.0/english/rfiles/flow.tiff
./NextDeveloper/Demos/FrameMaker.app/.fminit2.0/english/rfiles/pglo.tiff
./NextDeveloper/Demos/FrameMaker.app/.fminit2.0/english/rfiles/tools.tiff
./NextDeveloper/Demos/FrameMaker.app/.fminit2.0/english/rfiles/eq.tiff
./NextDeveloper/Demos/FrameMaker.app/.fminit2.0/english/rfiles/arrows.tiff
./NextDeveloper/Demos/FrameMaker.app/.fminit2.0/english/rfiles/NeXT.eps
./NextDeveloper/Demos/FrameMaker.app/.fminit2.0/english/rfiles/options.tiff
./NextDeveloper/Demos/FrameMaker.app/.fminit2.0/english/sndfiles
./NextDeveloper/Demos/FrameMaker.app/.fminit2.0/english/sndfiles/.places
./NextDeveloper/Demos/FrameMaker.app/.fminit2.0/english/sndfiles/welcome.snd
./NextDeveloper/Demos/FrameMaker.app/.fminit2.0/english/sndfiles/titanic.snd
./NextDeveloper/Demos/FrameMaker.app/.fminit2.0/english/sndfiles/costs.snd
./NextDeveloper/Demos/FrameMaker.app/.fminit2.0/english/sndfiles/margin.snd
./NextDeveloper/Demos/FrameMaker.app/.fminit2.0/spelling
./NextDeveloper/Demos/FrameMaker.app/.fminit2.0/rtftomif
./NextDeveloper/Demos/FrameMaker.app/.fminit2.0/display
./NextDeveloper/Demos/FrameMaker.app/.fminit2.0/next
./NextDeveloper/Demos/FrameMaker.app/.fminit2.0/next/makerbegin.ps
./NextDeveloper/Demos/FrameMaker.app/.fminit2.0/next/palette.nib
./NextDeveloper/Demos/FrameMaker.app/.fminit2.0/next/InfoPanel.nib
./NextDeveloper/Demos/FrameMaker.app/.fminit2.0/next/makerprint.ps
./NextDeveloper/Demos/FrameMaker.app/.fminit2.0/next/preference.nib
./NextDeveloper/Demos/FrameMaker.app/.fminit2.0/next/.places
./NextDeveloper/Demos/FrameMaker.app/.fminit2.0/patterns
./NextDeveloper/Demos/FrameMaker.app/.fminit2.0/.places
./NextDeveloper/Demos/FrameMaker.app/.fminit2.0/widths
./NextDeveloper/Demos/FrameMaker.app/.fminit2.0/bitmaps
./NextDeveloper/Demos/FrameMaker.app/.fminit2.0/suffixlist
./NextDeveloper/Demos/FrameMaker.app/.fminit2.0/txttomif.m4
./NextDeveloper/Demos/FrameMaker.app/.fminit2.0/mouse
./NextDeveloper/Demos/FrameMaker.app/.fminit2.0/maker.rc
./NextDeveloper/Demos/FrameMaker.app/.fminit2.0/zoom
./NextDeveloper/Demos/FrameMaker.app/.fminit2.0/dictionaries
./NextDeveloper/Demos/FrameMaker.app/.fminit2.0/site.dict
./NextDeveloper/Demos/FrameMaker.app/.fminit2.0/MifWrite
./NextDeveloper/Demos/FrameMaker.app/.fminit2.0/languages
./NextDeveloper/Demos/FrameMaker.app/.fminit2.0/MifRead
./NextDeveloper/Demos/FrameMaker.app/.fminit2.0/preferences
./NextDeveloper/Demos/FrameMaker.app/.fminit2.0/.makerinit
./NextDeveloper/Demos/FrameMaker.app/.fminit2.0/.makerinit/english
./NextDeveloper/Demos/FrameMaker.app/.fminit2.0/.makerinit/english/srre
./NextDeveloper/Demos/FrameMaker.app/.fminit2.0/.makerinit/english/srre
    /errors.srre
./NextDeveloper/Demos/FrameMaker.app/.fminit2.0/.makerinit/english/srre/mml.srre
./NextDeveloper/Demos/FrameMaker.app/.fminit2.0/.makerinit/english/srre/.places
./NextDeveloper/Demos/FrameMaker.app/.fminit2.0/.makerinit/english/doclanguages
./NextDeveloper/Demos/FrameMaker.app/.fminit2.0/.makerinit/english/markers
./NextDeveloper/Demos/FrameMaker.app/.fminit2.0/.makerinit/english/.places
./NextDeveloper/Demos/FrameMaker.app/.fminit2.0/.makerinit/fontdir
./NextDeveloper/Demos/FrameMaker.app/.fminit2.0/.makerinit/fontdir/fontlist
./NextDeveloper/Demos/FrameMaker.app/.fminit2.0/.makerinit/fontdir
    /fontlist.lwpstd
./NextDeveloper/Demos/FrameMaker.app/.fminit2.0/.makerinit/fontdir/fontlist.lwstd
./NextDeveloper/Demos/FrameMaker.app/.fminit2.0/.makerinit/fontdir/.places
./NextDeveloper/Demos/FrameMaker.app/.fminit2.0/.makerinit/languages
./NextDeveloper/Demos/FrameMaker.app/.fminit2.0/.makerinit/CHARGEN.DAT
./NextDeveloper/Demos/FrameMaker.app/.fminit2.0/.makerinit/DEVICES.TEXT
./NextDeveloper/Demos/FrameMaker.app/.fminit2.0/.makerinit/.places
./NextDeveloper/Demos/FrameMaker.app/.fminit2.0/magic
./NextDeveloper/Demos/FrameMaker.app/.fminit2.0/tifficons
./NextDeveloper/Demos/FrameMaker.app/.fminit2.0/tifficons/allselect
./NextDeveloper/Demos/FrameMaker.app/.fminit2.0/tifficons/arc
./NextDeveloper/Demos/FrameMaker.app/.fminit2.0/tifficons/arrow
./NextDeveloper/Demos/FrameMaker.app/.fminit2.0/tifficons/arrow120.16.12.filled
./NextDeveloper/Demos/FrameMaker.app/.fminit2.0/tifficons/arrow70.16.12.filled
./NextDeveloper/Demos/FrameMaker.app/.fminit2.0/tifficons/arrow90.16.12.filled
./NextDeveloper/Demos/FrameMaker.app/.fminit2.0/tifficons/arrow90.16.12.hollow
./NextDeveloper/Demos/FrameMaker.app/.fminit2.0/tifficons/arrow90.16.12.stick
./NextDeveloper/Demos/FrameMaker.app/.fminit2.0/tifficons/arrow90.30.6.filled
./NextDeveloper/Demos/FrameMaker.app/.fminit2.0/tifficons/arrow90.30.6.stick
./NextDeveloper/Demos/FrameMaker.app/.fminit2.0/tifficons/arrow90.30.8.filled
./NextDeveloper/Demos/FrameMaker.app/.fminit2.0/tifficons/baseangle1
./NextDeveloper/Demos/FrameMaker.app/.fminit2.0/tifficons/baseangle2
./NextDeveloper/Demos/FrameMaker.app/.fminit2.0/tifficons/buttcap
./NextDeveloper/Demos/FrameMaker.app/.fminit2.0/tifficons/circle
./NextDeveloper/Demos/FrameMaker.app/.fminit2.0/tifficons/ctab
./NextDeveloper/Demos/FrameMaker.app/.fminit2.0/tifficons/dnarrow
./NextDeveloper/Demos/FrameMaker.app/.fminit2.0/tifficons/dopoint_cursor.tiff
./NextDeveloper/Demos/FrameMaker.app/.fminit2.0/tifficons/draw_cursor.tiff
./NextDeveloper/Demos/FrameMaker.app/.fminit2.0/tifficons/dtab
./NextDeveloper/Demos/FrameMaker.app/.fminit2.0/tifficons/ellipse
./NextDeveloper/Demos/FrameMaker.app/.fminit2.0/tifficons/escf8.tiff
./NextDeveloper/Demos/FrameMaker.app/.fminit2.0/tifficons/fill
./NextDeveloper/Demos/FrameMaker.app/.fminit2.0/tifficons/findent
./NextDeveloper/Demos/FrameMaker.app/.fminit2.0/tifficons/font
./NextDeveloper/Demos/FrameMaker.app/.fminit2.0/tifficons/frame
./NextDeveloper/Demos/FrameMaker.app/.fminit2.0/tifficons/freehand
./NextDeveloper/Demos/FrameMaker.app/.fminit2.0/tifficons/grey25
./NextDeveloper/Demos/FrameMaker.app/.fminit2.0/tifficons/hollow
./NextDeveloper/Demos/FrameMaker.app/.fminit2.0/tifficons/hollow_cursor.tiff
./NextDeveloper/Demos/FrameMaker.app/.fminit2.0/tifficons/ip
./NextDeveloper/Demos/FrameMaker.app/.fminit2.0/tifficons/leftarrow
./NextDeveloper/Demos/FrameMaker.app/.fminit2.0/tifficons/lindent
```

./NextDeveloper/Demos/FrameMaker.app/.fminit2.0/tifficons/line
./NextDeveloper/Demos/FrameMaker.app/.fminit2.0/tifficons/ltab
./NextDeveloper/Demos/FrameMaker.app/.fminit2.0/tifficons/ltab.2bits
./NextDeveloper/Demos/FrameMaker.app/.fminit2.0/tifficons/maker
./NextDeveloper/Demos/FrameMaker.app/.fminit2.0/tifficons/math
./NextDeveloper/Demos/FrameMaker.app/.fminit2.0/tifficons/none
./NextDeveloper/Demos/FrameMaker.app/.fminit2.0/tifficons/objselect
./NextDeveloper/Demos/FrameMaker.app/.fminit2.0/tifficons/option.tiff
./NextDeveloper/Demos/FrameMaker.app/.fminit2.0/tifficons/pagebackward
./NextDeveloper/Demos/FrameMaker.app/.fminit2.0/tifficons/pageforward
./NextDeveloper/Demos/FrameMaker.app/.fminit2.0/tifficons/pattern
./NextDeveloper/Demos/FrameMaker.app/.fminit2.0/tifficons/patternnone
./NextDeveloper/Demos/FrameMaker.app/.fminit2.0/tifficons/pgf
./NextDeveloper/Demos/FrameMaker.app/.fminit2.0/tifficons/polygon
./NextDeveloper/Demos/FrameMaker.app/.fminit2.0/tifficons/polyline
./NextDeveloper/Demos/FrameMaker.app/.fminit2.0/tifficons/rectangle
./NextDeveloper/Demos/FrameMaker.app/.fminit2.0/tifficons/resize
./NextDeveloper/Demos/FrameMaker.app/.fminit2.0/tifficons/reshape_cursor.tiff
./NextDeveloper/Demos/FrameMaker.app/.fminit2.0/tifficons/rightarrow
./NextDeveloper/Demos/FrameMaker.app/.fminit2.0/tifficons/rindent
./NextDeveloper/Demos/FrameMaker.app/.fminit2.0/tifficons/rootgrey
./NextDeveloper/Demos/FrameMaker.app/.fminit2.0/tifficons/rotatebmp
./NextDeveloper/Demos/FrameMaker.app/.fminit2.0/tifficons/roundcap
./NextDeveloper/Demos/FrameMaker.app/.fminit2.0/tifficons/roundrect
./NextDeveloper/Demos/FrameMaker.app/.fminit2.0/tifficons/rtab
./NextDeveloper/Demos/FrameMaker.app/.fminit2.0/tifficons/sound.tiff
./NextDeveloper/Demos/FrameMaker.app/.fminit2.0/tifficons/square
./NextDeveloper/Demos/FrameMaker.app/.fminit2.0/tifficons/squarecap
./NextDeveloper/Demos/FrameMaker.app/.fminit2.0/tifficons/stick
./NextDeveloper/Demos/FrameMaker.app/.fminit2.0/tifficons/text
./NextDeveloper/Demos/FrameMaker.app/.fminit2.0/tifficons/tipangle1
./NextDeveloper/Demos/FrameMaker.app/.fminit2.0/tifficons/tipangle2
./NextDeveloper/Demos/FrameMaker.app/.fminit2.0/tifficons/tool
./NextDeveloper/Demos/FrameMaker.app/.fminit2.0/tifficons/trect
./NextDeveloper/Demos/FrameMaker.app/.fminit2.0/tifficons/uparrow
./NextDeveloper/Demos/FrameMaker.app/.fminit2.0/tifficons/zoomin
./NextDeveloper/Demos/FrameMaker.app/.fminit2.0/tifficons/zoomout
./NextDeveloper/Demos/FrameMaker.app/.fminit2.0/tifficons/eqsizes
./NextDeveloper/Demos/FrameMaker.app/.fminit2.0/tifficons/.places
./NextDeveloper/Demos/FrameMaker.app/.fminit2.0/fontdir
./NextDeveloper/Demos/FrameMaker.app/.fminit2.0/fontdir/fontlist
./NextDeveloper/Demos/FrameMaker.app/.fminit2.0/fontdir/.places
./NextDeveloper/Demos/FrameMaker.app/.fminit2.0/ASCIITemplate.doc
./NextDeveloper/Demos/FrameMaker.app/FrameMaker
./NextDeveloper/Demos/FrameMaker.app/bin
./NextDeveloper/Demos/FrameMaker.app/bin/fmtemplates
./NextDeveloper/Demos/FrameMaker.app/bin/fmtemplates/Books
./NextDeveloper/Demos/FrameMaker.app/bin/fmtemplates/Books/.places
./NextDeveloper/Demos/FrameMaker.app/bin/fmtemplates/Books/Chapter.frame
./NextDeveloper/Demos/FrameMaker.app/bin/fmtemplates/LettersAndMemos
./NextDeveloper/Demos/FrameMaker.app/bin/fmtemplates/LettersAndMemos

/Letter1.frame
./NextDeveloper/Demos/FrameMaker.app/bin/fmtemplates/LettersAndMemos
/Letter2.frame
./NextDeveloper/Demos/FrameMaker.app/bin/fmtemplates/LettersAndMemos/Memo2.frame
./NextDeveloper/Demos/FrameMaker.app/bin/fmtemplates/LettersAndMemos/.places
./NextDeveloper/Demos/FrameMaker.app/bin/fmtemplates/Newsletters
./NextDeveloper/Demos/FrameMaker.app/bin/fmtemplates/Newsletters
/Newsletter1.frame
./NextDeveloper/Demos/FrameMaker.app/bin/fmtemplates/Newsletters/.places
./NextDeveloper/Demos/FrameMaker.app/bin/fmtemplates/Reports
./NextDeveloper/Demos/FrameMaker.app/bin/fmtemplates/Reports/Report2.frame
./NextDeveloper/Demos/FrameMaker.app/bin/fmtemplates/Reports/Report3.frame
./NextDeveloper/Demos/FrameMaker.app/bin/fmtemplates/Reports/Report4.frame
./NextDeveloper/Demos/FrameMaker.app/bin/fmtemplates/Reports/.places
./NextDeveloper/Demos/FrameMaker.app/bin/fmtemplates/Viewgraphs
./NextDeveloper/Demos/FrameMaker.app/bin/fmtemplates/Viewgraphs
/ViewgraphTall2.frame
./NextDeveloper/Demos/FrameMaker.app/bin/fmtemplates/Viewgraphs/.places
./NextDeveloper/Demos/FrameMaker.app/bin/fmtemplates/Viewgraphs
/ViewgraphWide2.frame
./NextDeveloper/Demos/FrameMaker.app/bin/fmtemplates/.places
./NextDeveloper/Demos/FrameMaker.app/bin/fmtemplates/BlankPaper
./NextDeveloper/Demos/FrameMaker.app/bin/fmtemplates/BlankPaper/.places
./NextDeveloper/Demos/FrameMaker.app/bin/fmtemplates/BlankPaper
/BlankLandscape.frame
./NextDeveloper/Demos/FrameMaker.app/bin/fmtemplates/BlankPaper
/BlankPortrait.frame
./NextDeveloper/Demos/FrameMaker.app/bin/.places
./NextDeveloper/Demos/FrameMaker.app/.places
./NextDeveloper/Demos/FrameMaker.app/FrameDemo
./NextDeveloper/Demos/FrameMaker.app/FrameDemo/.places
./NextDeveloper/Demos/FrameMaker.app/FrameDemo/FrameDemo.frame
./NextDeveloper/Demos/FrameMaker.app/FrameDemo/FrameDemoIX.frame
./NextDeveloper/Demos/FrameMaker.app/FrameDemo/NeXT.eps
./NextDeveloper/Demos/FrameMaker.app/FrameDemo/greatjob.snd
./NextDeveloper/Demos/Icon
./NextDeveloper/Demos/Scene
./NextDeveloper/Demos/RealTimeAlgebra
./NextDeveloper/Examples
./NextDeveloper/Examples/Clock
./NextDeveloper/Examples/Clock/AnalogClock.m
./NextDeveloper/Examples/Clock/ClockApp.m
./NextDeveloper/Examples/Clock/AnalogClock.h
./NextDeveloper/Examples/Clock/ClockApp.h
./NextDeveloper/Examples/Clock/Clock.nib
./NextDeveloper/Examples/Clock/Clock.tiff
./NextDeveloper/Examples/Clock/Clock_main.m
./NextDeveloper/Examples/Clock/AnalogClockPS.psw
./NextDeveloper/Examples/Clock/IB.proj
./NextDeveloper/Examples/Clock/Makefile
./NextDeveloper/Examples/Clock/Clock.iconheader
./NextDeveloper/Examples/Clock/.places

```
./NextDeveloper/Examples/Calculator
./NextDeveloper/Examples/Calculator/Calculator.m
./NextDeveloper/Examples/Calculator/Calculator.h
./NextDeveloper/Examples/Calculator/Calc.nib
./NextDeveloper/Examples/Calculator/Calc.tiff
./NextDeveloper/Examples/Calculator/Calc_main.m
./NextDeveloper/Examples/Calculator/IB.proj
./NextDeveloper/Examples/Calculator/Makefile
./NextDeveloper/Examples/Calculator/Calc.iconheader
./NextDeveloper/Examples/Calculator/.places
./NextDeveloper/Examples/CompositeLab
./NextDeveloper/Examples/CompositeLab/CompositeView.m
./NextDeveloper/Examples/CompositeLab/CompositeView.h
./NextDeveloper/Examples/CompositeLab/CompositeLab.nib
./NextDeveloper/Examples/CompositeLab/CompositeLab.tiff
./NextDeveloper/Examples/CompositeLab/CompositeLab_main.m
./NextDeveloper/Examples/CompositeLab/IB.proj
./NextDeveloper/Examples/CompositeLab/Makefile
./NextDeveloper/Examples/CompositeLab/CompositeLab.iconheader
./NextDeveloper/Examples/CompositeLab/.places
./NextDeveloper/Examples/EventLab
./NextDeveloper/Examples/EventLab/AnalogGauge.m
./NextDeveloper/Examples/EventLab/Animator.m
./NextDeveloper/Examples/EventLab/DigitalGauge.m
./NextDeveloper/Examples/EventLab/EventLab.m
./NextDeveloper/Examples/EventLab/MyView.m
./NextDeveloper/Examples/EventLab/AnalogGauge.h
./NextDeveloper/Examples/EventLab/Animator.h
./NextDeveloper/Examples/EventLab/DigitalGauge.h
./NextDeveloper/Examples/EventLab/EventLab.h
./NextDeveloper/Examples/EventLab/MyView.h
./NextDeveloper/Examples/EventLab/EventLab.tiff
./NextDeveloper/Examples/EventLab/EventLab_main.m
./NextDeveloper/Examples/EventLab/Gauge.psw
./NextDeveloper/Examples/EventLab/README
./NextDeveloper/Examples/EventLab/IB.proj
./NextDeveloper/Examples/EventLab/Makefile
./NextDeveloper/Examples/EventLab/EventLab.iconheader
./NextDeveloper/Examples/EventLab/.places
./NextDeveloper/Examples/EventLab/obj
./NextDeveloper/Examples/EventLab/obj/Gauge.o
./NextDeveloper/Examples/EventLab/obj/AnalogGauge.o
./NextDeveloper/Examples/EventLab/obj/Animator.o
./NextDeveloper/Examples/EventLab/obj/DigitalGauge.o
./NextDeveloper/Examples/EventLab/obj/EventLab.o
./NextDeveloper/Examples/EventLab/obj/MyView.o
./NextDeveloper/Examples/EventLab/obj/EventLab_main.o
./NextDeveloper/Examples/EventLab/Gauge.c
./NextDeveloper/Examples/EventLab/Gauge.h
./NextDeveloper/Examples/EventLab/EventLab
./NextDeveloper/Examples/Lines
```

```
./NextDeveloper/Examples/Lines/LinesView.m
./NextDeveloper/Examples/Lines/LinesView.h
./NextDeveloper/Examples/Lines/Lines.nib
./NextDeveloper/Examples/Lines/Lines.tiff
./NextDeveloper/Examples/Lines/Lines_main.m
./NextDeveloper/Examples/Lines/IB.proj
./NextDeveloper/Examples/Lines/Makefile
./NextDeveloper/Examples/Lines/Lines.iconheader
./NextDeveloper/Examples/Lines/.places
./NextDeveloper/Examples/Lines/obj
./NextDeveloper/Examples/Lines/obj/LinesView.o
./NextDeveloper/Examples/Lines/obj/Lines_main.o
./NextDeveloper/Examples/Lines/Lines
./NextDeveloper/Examples/Patch
./NextDeveloper/Examples/Patch/BinaryFile.m
./NextDeveloper/Examples/Patch/MyApp.m
./NextDeveloper/Examples/Patch/BinaryFile.h
./NextDeveloper/Examples/Patch/MyApp.h
./NextDeveloper/Examples/Patch/BinaryFile.nib
./NextDeveloper/Examples/Patch/Patch.nib
./NextDeveloper/Examples/Patch/Patch.tiff
./NextDeveloper/Examples/Patch/Patch_main.m
./NextDeveloper/Examples/Patch/IB.proj
./NextDeveloper/Examples/Patch/Makefile
./NextDeveloper/Examples/Patch/Patch.iconheader
./NextDeveloper/Examples/Patch/.places
./NextDeveloper/Examples/Stopwatch
./NextDeveloper/Examples/Stopwatch/Animator.m
./NextDeveloper/Examples/Stopwatch/StopwatchView.m
./NextDeveloper/Examples/Stopwatch/Animator.h
./NextDeveloper/Examples/Stopwatch/StopwatchView.h
./NextDeveloper/Examples/Stopwatch/Stopwatch.nib
./NextDeveloper/Examples/Stopwatch/Stopwatch.tiff
./NextDeveloper/Examples/Stopwatch/Stopwatch_main.m
./NextDeveloper/Examples/Stopwatch/README
./NextDeveloper/Examples/Stopwatch/StopwatchI.nib
./NextDeveloper/Examples/Stopwatch/StopwatchII.nib
./NextDeveloper/Examples/Stopwatch/IB.proj
./NextDeveloper/Examples/Stopwatch/Makefile
./NextDeveloper/Examples/Stopwatch/Stopwatch.iconheader
./NextDeveloper/Examples/Stopwatch/.places
./NextDeveloper/Examples/Sound
./NextDeveloper/Examples/Sound/playtest.c
./NextDeveloper/Examples/Sound/recordtest.c
./NextDeveloper/Examples/Sound/chaintest.c
./NextDeveloper/Examples/Sound/converttest.c
./NextDeveloper/Examples/Sound/hosttest.c
./NextDeveloper/Examples/Sound/README
./NextDeveloper/Examples/Sound/Makefile
./NextDeveloper/Examples/Sound/.places
./NextDeveloper/Examples/DSP
```

```
./NextDeveloper/Examples/DSP/ArrayProcessing
./NextDeveloper/Examples/DSP/ArrayProcessing/apsound
./NextDeveloper/Examples/DSP/ArrayProcessing/apsound/apreverse.c
./NextDeveloper/Examples/DSP/ArrayProcessing/apsound/README
./NextDeveloper/Examples/DSP/ArrayProcessing/apsound/Makefile
./NextDeveloper/Examples/DSP/ArrayProcessing/apsound/.places
./NextDeveloper/Examples/DSP/ArrayProcessing/fdfilter
./NextDeveloper/Examples/DSP/ArrayProcessing/fdfilter/fdfilter.c
./NextDeveloper/Examples/DSP/ArrayProcessing/fdfilter/README
./NextDeveloper/Examples/DSP/ArrayProcessing/fdfilter/Makefile
./NextDeveloper/Examples/DSP/ArrayProcessing/fdfilter/.places
./NextDeveloper/Examples/DSP/ArrayProcessing/matrix
./NextDeveloper/Examples/DSP/ArrayProcessing/matrix/matrix.c
./NextDeveloper/Examples/DSP/ArrayProcessing/matrix/README
./NextDeveloper/Examples/DSP/ArrayProcessing/matrix/Makefile
./NextDeveloper/Examples/DSP/ArrayProcessing/matrix/.places
./NextDeveloper/Examples/DSP/ArrayProcessing/fuse
./NextDeveloper/Examples/DSP/ArrayProcessing/fuse/vpvtvpv.asm
./NextDeveloper/Examples/DSP/ArrayProcessing/fuse/tvpvtvpv.asm
./NextDeveloper/Examples/DSP/ArrayProcessing/fuse/config_standalone.asm
./NextDeveloper/Examples/DSP/ArrayProcessing/fuse/DSPAPvpvtvpvI.h
./NextDeveloper/Examples/DSP/ArrayProcessing/fuse/DSPAPvpvtvpvI.c
./NextDeveloper/Examples/DSP/ArrayProcessing/fuse/ctest.c
./NextDeveloper/Examples/DSP/ArrayProcessing/fuse/README
./NextDeveloper/Examples/DSP/ArrayProcessing/fuse/Makefile
./NextDeveloper/Examples/DSP/ArrayProcessing/fuse/.places
./NextDeveloper/Examples/DSP/ArrayProcessing/libap
./NextDeveloper/Examples/DSP/ArrayProcessing/libap/myvnot.asm
./NextDeveloper/Examples/DSP/ArrayProcessing/libap/mytest.c
./NextDeveloper/Examples/DSP/ArrayProcessing/libap/README
./NextDeveloper/Examples/DSP/ArrayProcessing/libap/Makefile
./NextDeveloper/Examples/DSP/ArrayProcessing/libap/.places
./NextDeveloper/Examples/DSP/ArrayProcessing/.places
./NextDeveloper/Examples/DSP/SoundDSPDriver
./NextDeveloper/Examples/DSP/SoundDSPDriver/dsp_example_1
./NextDeveloper/Examples/DSP/SoundDSPDriver/dsp_example_1/dsp_example_1.c
./NextDeveloper/Examples/DSP/SoundDSPDriver/dsp_example_1/dsp_example_1.asm
./NextDeveloper/Examples/DSP/SoundDSPDriver/dsp_example_1/ioequ.asm
./NextDeveloper/Examples/DSP/SoundDSPDriver/dsp_example_1/Makefile
./NextDeveloper/Examples/DSP/SoundDSPDriver/dsp_example_1/.places
./NextDeveloper/Examples/DSP/SoundDSPDriver/dsp_example_2
./NextDeveloper/Examples/DSP/SoundDSPDriver/dsp_example_2/dsp_example_2.c
./NextDeveloper/Examples/DSP/SoundDSPDriver/dsp_example_2/dsp_example_2.asm
./NextDeveloper/Examples/DSP/SoundDSPDriver/dsp_example_2/ioequ.asm
./NextDeveloper/Examples/DSP/SoundDSPDriver/dsp_example_2/Makefile
./NextDeveloper/Examples/DSP/SoundDSPDriver/dsp_example_2/.places
./NextDeveloper/Examples/DSP/SoundDSPDriver/dsp_example_3
./NextDeveloper/Examples/DSP/SoundDSPDriver/dsp_example_3/dsp_example_3.c
./NextDeveloper/Examples/DSP/SoundDSPDriver/dsp_example_3/dsp_example_3.asm
./NextDeveloper/Examples/DSP/SoundDSPDriver/dsp_example_3/ioequ.asm
./NextDeveloper/Examples/DSP/SoundDSPDriver/dsp_example_3/Makefile
./NextDeveloper/Examples/DSP/SoundDSPDriver/dsp_example_3/.places
./NextDeveloper/Examples/DSP/SoundDSPDriver/dsp_example_4
./NextDeveloper/Examples/DSP/SoundDSPDriver/dsp_example_4/dsp_example_4.c
./NextDeveloper/Examples/DSP/SoundDSPDriver/dsp_example_4/dsp_example_4.asm
./NextDeveloper/Examples/DSP/SoundDSPDriver/dsp_example_4/dspstream.asm
./NextDeveloper/Examples/DSP/SoundDSPDriver/dsp_example_4/ioequ.asm
./NextDeveloper/Examples/DSP/SoundDSPDriver/dsp_example_4/Makefile
./NextDeveloper/Examples/DSP/SoundDSPDriver/dsp_example_4/.places
./NextDeveloper/Examples/DSP/SoundDSPDriver/.places
./NextDeveloper/Examples/DSP/.places
./NextDeveloper/Examples/CustomIBDemo
./NextDeveloper/Examples/CustomIBDemo/Graphic.m
./NextDeveloper/Examples/CustomIBDemo/GraphicView.m
./NextDeveloper/Examples/CustomIBDemo/Group.m
./NextDeveloper/Examples/CustomIBDemo/PSGraphic.m
./NextDeveloper/Examples/CustomIBDemo/Rectangle.m
./NextDeveloper/Examples/CustomIBDemo/Tiff.m
./NextDeveloper/Examples/CustomIBDemo/Graphic.h
./NextDeveloper/Examples/CustomIBDemo/GraphicView.h
./NextDeveloper/Examples/CustomIBDemo/Group.h
./NextDeveloper/Examples/CustomIBDemo/PSGraphic.h
./NextDeveloper/Examples/CustomIBDemo/Rectangle.h
./NextDeveloper/Examples/CustomIBDemo/Tiff.h
./NextDeveloper/Examples/CustomIBDemo/DrawPalette.nib
./NextDeveloper/Examples/CustomIBDemo/DrawIB_main.m
./NextDeveloper/Examples/CustomIBDemo/draw.psw
./NextDeveloper/Examples/CustomIBDemo/README
./NextDeveloper/Examples/CustomIBDemo/hand.tiff
./NextDeveloper/Examples/CustomIBDemo/IB.proj
./NextDeveloper/Examples/CustomIBDemo/Makefile
./NextDeveloper/Examples/CustomIBDemo/DrawIB.iconheader
./NextDeveloper/Examples/CustomIBDemo/.places
./NextDeveloper/Examples/Draw
./NextDeveloper/Examples/Draw/Circle.m
./NextDeveloper/Examples/Draw/Curve.m
./NextDeveloper/Examples/Draw/DrawApp.m
./NextDeveloper/Examples/Draw/DrawDocument.m
./NextDeveloper/Examples/Draw/DrawPageLayout.m
./NextDeveloper/Examples/Draw/Graphic.m
./NextDeveloper/Examples/Draw/GraphicView.m
./NextDeveloper/Examples/Draw/GridView.m
./NextDeveloper/Examples/Draw/Group.m
./NextDeveloper/Examples/Draw/InspectorPanel.m
./NextDeveloper/Examples/Draw/Line.m
./NextDeveloper/Examples/Draw/PSGraphic.m
./NextDeveloper/Examples/Draw/Polygon.m
./NextDeveloper/Examples/Draw/Rectangle.m
./NextDeveloper/Examples/Draw/Scribble.m
./NextDeveloper/Examples/Draw/TextGraphic.m
./NextDeveloper/Examples/Draw/Tiff.m
./NextDeveloper/Examples/Draw/Circle.h
```

```
./NextDeveloper/Examples/Draw/Curve.h                      ./NextDeveloper/Examples/BreakApp/BackGround.h
./NextDeveloper/Examples/Draw/DrawApp.h                    ./NextDeveloper/Examples/BreakApp/Ball.h
./NextDeveloper/Examples/Draw/DrawDocument.h               ./NextDeveloper/Examples/BreakApp/BreakApp.h
./NextDeveloper/Examples/Draw/DrawPageLayout.h             ./NextDeveloper/Examples/BreakApp/BreakView.h
./NextDeveloper/Examples/Draw/Graphic.h                    ./NextDeveloper/Examples/BreakApp/MovingPiece.h
./NextDeveloper/Examples/Draw/GraphicView.h                ./NextDeveloper/Examples/BreakApp/Paddle.h
./NextDeveloper/Examples/Draw/GridView.h                   ./NextDeveloper/Examples/BreakApp/Piece.h
./NextDeveloper/Examples/Draw/Group.h                      ./NextDeveloper/Examples/BreakApp/QuickText.h
./NextDeveloper/Examples/Draw/InspectorPanel.h             ./NextDeveloper/Examples/BreakApp/SoundGenerator.h
./NextDeveloper/Examples/Draw/Line.h                       ./NextDeveloper/Examples/BreakApp/ToughTile.h
./NextDeveloper/Examples/Draw/PSGraphic.h                  ./NextDeveloper/Examples/BreakApp/ViciousTile.h
./NextDeveloper/Examples/Draw/Polygon.h                    ./NextDeveloper/Examples/BreakApp/WimpyTile.h
./NextDeveloper/Examples/Draw/Rectangle.h                  ./NextDeveloper/Examples/BreakApp/BreakApp.nib
./NextDeveloper/Examples/Draw/Scribble.h                   ./NextDeveloper/Examples/BreakApp/BreakApp.tiff
./NextDeveloper/Examples/Draw/TextGraphic.h                ./NextDeveloper/Examples/BreakApp/BreakApp_main.m
./NextDeveloper/Examples/Draw/Tiff.h                       ./NextDeveloper/Examples/BreakApp/BackGroundPS.psw
./NextDeveloper/Examples/Draw/Draw.nib                     ./NextDeveloper/Examples/BreakApp/Makefile.preamble
./NextDeveloper/Examples/Draw/GridView.nib                 ./NextDeveloper/Examples/BreakApp/IB.proj
./NextDeveloper/Examples/Draw/InfoPanel.nib                ./NextDeveloper/Examples/BreakApp/Makefile
./NextDeveloper/Examples/Draw/InspectorPanel.nib           ./NextDeveloper/Examples/BreakApp/BreakApp.iconheader
./NextDeveloper/Examples/Draw/draw.tiff                    ./NextDeveloper/Examples/BreakApp/.places
./NextDeveloper/Examples/Draw/drawdoc.tiff                 ./NextDeveloper/Examples/MidiDriver
./NextDeveloper/Examples/Draw/Draw_main.m                  ./NextDeveloper/Examples/MidiDriver/BayBlue.midi
./NextDeveloper/Examples/Draw/draw.psw                     ./NextDeveloper/Examples/MidiDriver/Clockworks.midi
./NextDeveloper/Examples/Draw/DrawPalette.tiff             ./NextDeveloper/Examples/MidiDriver/DrugsAreDeath.midi
./NextDeveloper/Examples/Draw/DrawPaletteH.tiff            ./NextDeveloper/Examples/MidiDriver/BigArm.midi
./NextDeveloper/Examples/Draw/Makefile.preamble            ./NextDeveloper/Examples/MidiDriver/DoomInTheBathroom.midi
./NextDeveloper/Examples/Draw/README.wn                    ./NextDeveloper/Examples/MidiDriver/recordmidifile.c
./NextDeveloper/Examples/Draw/help.draw                    ./NextDeveloper/Examples/MidiDriver/playmidifile.c
./NextDeveloper/Examples/Draw/cross.tiff                   ./NextDeveloper/Examples/MidiDriver/midifile.c
./NextDeveloper/Examples/Draw/hand.tiff                    ./NextDeveloper/Examples/MidiDriver/midifile.h
./NextDeveloper/Examples/Draw/pencil.tiff                  ./NextDeveloper/Examples/MidiDriver/Makefile
./NextDeveloper/Examples/Draw/IB.proj                      ./NextDeveloper/Examples/MidiDriver/README
./NextDeveloper/Examples/Draw/Makefile                     ./NextDeveloper/Examples/MidiDriver/.places
./NextDeveloper/Examples/Draw/Draw.iconheader              ./NextDeveloper/Examples/Yap
./NextDeveloper/Examples/Draw/.places                      ./NextDeveloper/Examples/Yap/PSText.m
./NextDeveloper/Examples/BreakApp                          ./NextDeveloper/Examples/Yap/YapApp.m
./NextDeveloper/Examples/BreakApp/Animator.m               ./NextDeveloper/Examples/Yap/YapDocument.m
./NextDeveloper/Examples/BreakApp/BackGround.m             ./NextDeveloper/Examples/Yap/YapOutput.m
./NextDeveloper/Examples/BreakApp/Ball.m                   ./NextDeveloper/Examples/Yap/PSText.h
./NextDeveloper/Examples/BreakApp/BreakApp.m               ./NextDeveloper/Examples/Yap/YapApp.h
./NextDeveloper/Examples/BreakApp/BreakView.m              ./NextDeveloper/Examples/Yap/YapDocument.h
./NextDeveloper/Examples/BreakApp/MovingPiece.m            ./NextDeveloper/Examples/Yap/YapOutput.h
./NextDeveloper/Examples/BreakApp/Paddle.m                 ./NextDeveloper/Examples/Yap/Yap.nib
./NextDeveloper/Examples/BreakApp/Piece.m                  ./NextDeveloper/Examples/Yap/YapDocument.nib
./NextDeveloper/Examples/BreakApp/QuickText.m              ./NextDeveloper/Examples/Yap/Yap.tiff
./NextDeveloper/Examples/BreakApp/SoundGenerator.m         ./NextDeveloper/Examples/Yap/ps.tiff
./NextDeveloper/Examples/BreakApp/ToughTile.m              ./NextDeveloper/Examples/Yap/eps.tiff
./NextDeveloper/Examples/BreakApp/ViciousTile.m            ./NextDeveloper/Examples/Yap/Yap_main.m
./NextDeveloper/Examples/BreakApp/WimpyTile.m              ./NextDeveloper/Examples/Yap/YapWrap.psw
./NextDeveloper/Examples/BreakApp/Animator.h               ./NextDeveloper/Examples/Yap/IB.proj
```

```
./NextDeveloper/Examples/Yap/Makefile
./NextDeveloper/Examples/Yap/Yap.iconheader
./NextDeveloper/Examples/Yap/.places
./NextDeveloper/Examples/MusicKit
./NextDeveloper/Examples/MusicKit/exampsynthpatch
./NextDeveloper/Examples/MusicKit/exampsynthpatch/Envy.m
./NextDeveloper/Examples/MusicKit/exampsynthpatch/Simplicity.m
./NextDeveloper/Examples/MusicKit/exampsynthpatch/playscorefile2.m
./NextDeveloper/Examples/MusicKit/exampsynthpatch/Envy.h
./NextDeveloper/Examples/MusicKit/exampsynthpatch/Simplicity.h
./NextDeveloper/Examples/MusicKit/exampsynthpatch/Simplicity.score
./NextDeveloper/Examples/MusicKit/exampsynthpatch/Envy.score
./NextDeveloper/Examples/MusicKit/exampsynthpatch/Makefile
./NextDeveloper/Examples/MusicKit/exampsynthpatch/README
./NextDeveloper/Examples/MusicKit/exampsynthpatch/.places
./NextDeveloper/Examples/MusicKit/mixsounds
./NextDeveloper/Examples/MusicKit/mixsounds/mixsounds.m
./NextDeveloper/Examples/MusicKit/mixsounds/MixInstrument.m
./NextDeveloper/Examples/MusicKit/mixsounds/MixInstrument.h
./NextDeveloper/Examples/MusicKit/mixsounds/testMix.score
./NextDeveloper/Examples/MusicKit/mixsounds/testMix2.score
./NextDeveloper/Examples/MusicKit/mixsounds/testMix3.score
./NextDeveloper/Examples/MusicKit/mixsounds/Makefile
./NextDeveloper/Examples/MusicKit/mixsounds/README
./NextDeveloper/Examples/MusicKit/mixsounds/.places
./NextDeveloper/Examples/MusicKit/mixscorefiles
./NextDeveloper/Examples/MusicKit/mixscorefiles/mixscorefiles.m
./NextDeveloper/Examples/MusicKit/mixscorefiles/Makefile
./NextDeveloper/Examples/MusicKit/mixscorefiles/README
./NextDeveloper/Examples/MusicKit/mixscorefiles/.places
./NextDeveloper/Examples/MusicKit/playscorefile
./NextDeveloper/Examples/MusicKit/playscorefile/playscorefile.m
./NextDeveloper/Examples/MusicKit/playscorefile/Makefile
./NextDeveloper/Examples/MusicKit/playscorefile/README
./NextDeveloper/Examples/MusicKit/playscorefile/.places
./NextDeveloper/Examples/MusicKit/playscorefile2
./NextDeveloper/Examples/MusicKit/playscorefile2/playscorefile2.m
./NextDeveloper/Examples/MusicKit/playscorefile2/Makefile
./NextDeveloper/Examples/MusicKit/playscorefile2/README
./NextDeveloper/Examples/MusicKit/playscorefile2/.places
./NextDeveloper/Examples/MusicKit/playpart
./NextDeveloper/Examples/MusicKit/playpart/playpart.m
./NextDeveloper/Examples/MusicKit/playpart/Makefile
./NextDeveloper/Examples/MusicKit/playpart/README
./NextDeveloper/Examples/MusicKit/playpart/.places
./NextDeveloper/Examples/MusicKit/MidiEcho
./NextDeveloper/Examples/MusicKit/MidiEcho/MidiEcho.m
./NextDeveloper/Examples/MusicKit/MidiEcho/MyApp.m
./NextDeveloper/Examples/MusicKit/MidiEcho/EchoFilter.m
./NextDeveloper/Examples/MusicKit/MidiEcho/MyApp.h
./NextDeveloper/Examples/MusicKit/MidiEcho/EchoFilter.h
./NextDeveloper/Examples/MusicKit/MidiEcho/MidiEcho.nib
./NextDeveloper/Examples/MusicKit/MidiEcho/Makefile
./NextDeveloper/Examples/MusicKit/MidiEcho/README
./NextDeveloper/Examples/MusicKit/MidiEcho/.places
./NextDeveloper/Examples/MusicKit/MidiLoop
./NextDeveloper/Examples/MusicKit/MidiLoop/MidiLoop.m
./NextDeveloper/Examples/MusicKit/MidiLoop/MyApp.m
./NextDeveloper/Examples/MusicKit/MidiLoop/MyApp.h
./NextDeveloper/Examples/MusicKit/MidiLoop/MidiLoop.nib
./NextDeveloper/Examples/MusicKit/MidiLoop/Makefile
./NextDeveloper/Examples/MusicKit/MidiLoop/README
./NextDeveloper/Examples/MusicKit/MidiLoop/.places
./NextDeveloper/Examples/MusicKit/MidiPlay
./NextDeveloper/Examples/MusicKit/MidiPlay/MidiPlay.m
./NextDeveloper/Examples/MusicKit/MidiPlay/MyApp.m
./NextDeveloper/Examples/MusicKit/MidiPlay/MyApp.h
./NextDeveloper/Examples/MusicKit/MidiPlay/MidiPlay.nib
./NextDeveloper/Examples/MusicKit/MidiPlay/Makefile
./NextDeveloper/Examples/MusicKit/MidiPlay/README
./NextDeveloper/Examples/MusicKit/MidiPlay/.places
./NextDeveloper/Examples/MusicKit/MidiRecord
./NextDeveloper/Examples/MusicKit/MidiRecord/MidiRecord.m
./NextDeveloper/Examples/MusicKit/MidiRecord/MyApp.m
./NextDeveloper/Examples/MusicKit/MidiRecord/MyApp.h
./NextDeveloper/Examples/MusicKit/MidiRecord/MidiRecord.nib
./NextDeveloper/Examples/MusicKit/MidiRecord/Makefile
./NextDeveloper/Examples/MusicKit/MidiRecord/README
./NextDeveloper/Examples/MusicKit/MidiRecord/.places
./NextDeveloper/Examples/MusicKit/PlayNote
./NextDeveloper/Examples/MusicKit/PlayNote/PlayNote.m
./NextDeveloper/Examples/MusicKit/PlayNote/ExampApp.m
./NextDeveloper/Examples/MusicKit/PlayNote/ExampApp.h
./NextDeveloper/Examples/MusicKit/PlayNote/PlayNote.nib
./NextDeveloper/Examples/MusicKit/PlayNote/Makefile
./NextDeveloper/Examples/MusicKit/PlayNote/README
./NextDeveloper/Examples/MusicKit/PlayNote/.places
./NextDeveloper/Examples/MusicKit/PlayNote/PlayNote.o
./NextDeveloper/Examples/MusicKit/PlayNote/ExampApp.o
./NextDeveloper/Examples/MusicKit/PlayNote/PlayNote
./NextDeveloper/Examples/MusicKit/PerformerExample
./NextDeveloper/Examples/MusicKit/PerformerExample/PerformerExample.m
./NextDeveloper/Examples/MusicKit/PerformerExample/PerformerController.m
./NextDeveloper/Examples/MusicKit/PerformerExample/RandomPerformer.m
./NextDeveloper/Examples/MusicKit/PerformerExample/PerformerController.h
./NextDeveloper/Examples/MusicKit/PerformerExample/RandomPerformer.h
./NextDeveloper/Examples/MusicKit/PerformerExample/PerformerExample.nib
./NextDeveloper/Examples/MusicKit/PerformerExample/Makefile
./NextDeveloper/Examples/MusicKit/PerformerExample/README
./NextDeveloper/Examples/MusicKit/PerformerExample/.places
./NextDeveloper/Examples/MusicKit/PerformerExample/PerformerExample.o
./NextDeveloper/Examples/MusicKit/PerformerExample/PerformerController.o
```

```
./NextDeveloper/Examples/MusicKit/PerformerExample/RandomPerformer.o
./NextDeveloper/Examples/MusicKit/PerformerExample/PerformerExample
./NextDeveloper/Examples/MusicKit/playscorefilemidi
./NextDeveloper/Examples/MusicKit/playscorefilemidi/playscorefilemidi.m
./NextDeveloper/Examples/MusicKit/playscorefilemidi/Makefile
./NextDeveloper/Examples/MusicKit/playscorefilemidi/README
./NextDeveloper/Examples/MusicKit/playscorefilemidi/.places
./NextDeveloper/Examples/MusicKit/README
./NextDeveloper/Examples/MusicKit/.places
./NextDeveloper/Examples/SoundEditor
./NextDeveloper/Examples/SoundEditor/ScrollingSound.m
./NextDeveloper/Examples/SoundEditor/SoundController.m
./NextDeveloper/Examples/SoundEditor/SoundDocument.m
./NextDeveloper/Examples/SoundEditor/ScrollingSound.h
./NextDeveloper/Examples/SoundEditor/SoundController.h
./NextDeveloper/Examples/SoundEditor/SoundDocument.h
./NextDeveloper/Examples/SoundEditor/SoundDocument.nib
./NextDeveloper/Examples/SoundEditor/SoundEditor.nib
./NextDeveloper/Examples/SoundEditor/sndapp.tiff
./NextDeveloper/Examples/SoundEditor/SoundEditor_main.m
./NextDeveloper/Examples/SoundEditor/IB.proj
./NextDeveloper/Examples/SoundEditor/Makefile
./NextDeveloper/Examples/SoundEditor/SoundEditor.iconheader
./NextDeveloper/Examples/SoundEditor/.places
./NextDeveloper/Examples/SoundEditor/obj
./NextDeveloper/Examples/SoundEditor/obj/ScrollingSound.o
./NextDeveloper/Examples/SoundEditor/obj/SoundController.o
./NextDeveloper/Examples/SoundEditor/obj/SoundDocument.o
./NextDeveloper/Examples/SoundEditor/obj/SoundEditor_main.o
./NextDeveloper/Examples/SoundEditor/SoundEditor
./NextDeveloper/Examples/README.wn
./NextDeveloper/Examples/IBTutorial
./NextDeveloper/Examples/IBTutorial/Sounds
./NextDeveloper/Examples/IBTutorial/Sounds/drum1.snd
./NextDeveloper/Examples/IBTutorial/Sounds/drum2.snd
./NextDeveloper/Examples/IBTutorial/Sounds/drum3.snd
./NextDeveloper/Examples/IBTutorial/Sounds/.places
./NextDeveloper/Examples/IBTutorial/Images
./NextDeveloper/Examples/IBTutorial/Images/willy.tiff
./NextDeveloper/Examples/IBTutorial/Images/.places
./NextDeveloper/Examples/IBTutorial/.places
./NextDeveloper/Examples/Little
./NextDeveloper/Examples/Little/makefile
./NextDeveloper/Examples/Little/little.iconheader
./NextDeveloper/Examples/Little/little.m
./NextDeveloper/Examples/Little/.places
./NextDeveloper/Examples/Little/little.o
./NextDeveloper/Examples/Little/little
./NextDeveloper/Examples/PostScript
./NextDeveloper/Examples/PostScript/Bounce.ps
./NextDeveloper/Examples/PostScript/Tree.ps
./NextDeveloper/Examples/PostScript/Rays.ps
./NextDeveloper/Examples/PostScript/Rectangle.ps
./NextDeveloper/Examples/PostScript/ShadedName.ps
./NextDeveloper/Examples/PostScript/Stanford.ps
./NextDeveloper/Examples/PostScript/Logo.eps
./NextDeveloper/Examples/PostScript/Compositing.ps
./NextDeveloper/Examples/PostScript/.places
./NextDeveloper/Examples/SCSI
./NextDeveloper/Examples/SCSI/Makefile
./NextDeveloper/Examples/SCSI/sg_example.c
./NextDeveloper/Examples/SCSI/.places
./NextDeveloper/Examples/.places
./NextDeveloper/.places
./NextAdmin
./NextAdmin/NetInfoManager
./NextAdmin/MailManager
./NextAdmin/NetManager
./NextAdmin/PrinterTester
./NextAdmin/UserManager
./NextAdmin/.places
./NextLibrary
./NextLibrary/Documentation
./NextLibrary/Documentation/Unix
./NextLibrary/Documentation/Unix/ManPages
./NextLibrary/Documentation/Unix/ManPages/cat1
./NextLibrary/Documentation/Unix/ManPages/cat1/.places
./NextLibrary/Documentation/Unix/ManPages/cat1/ls.1
./NextLibrary/Documentation/Unix/ManPages/cat1/gprof.1
./NextLibrary/Documentation/Unix/ManPages/cat1/dread.1
./NextLibrary/Documentation/Unix/ManPages/cat1/dwrite.1
./NextLibrary/Documentation/Unix/ManPages/cat1/dremove.1
./NextLibrary/Documentation/Unix/ManPages/cat1/bm.1
./NextLibrary/Documentation/Unix/ManPages/cat1/tip.1c
./NextLibrary/Documentation/Unix/ManPages/cat1/time.1
./NextLibrary/Documentation/Unix/ManPages/cat1/talk.1
./NextLibrary/Documentation/Unix/ManPages/cat1/rm.1
./NextLibrary/Documentation/Unix/ManPages/cat1/whoami.1
./NextLibrary/Documentation/Unix/ManPages/cat1/find.1
./NextLibrary/Documentation/Unix/ManPages/cat2
./NextLibrary/Documentation/Unix/ManPages/cat2/.places
./NextLibrary/Documentation/Unix/ManPages/cat3
./NextLibrary/Documentation/Unix/ManPages/cat3/.places
./NextLibrary/Documentation/Unix/ManPages/cat3/netinfo.3n
./NextLibrary/Documentation/Unix/ManPages/cat3/inet.3n
./NextLibrary/Documentation/Unix/ManPages/cat4
./NextLibrary/Documentation/Unix/ManPages/cat4/.places
./NextLibrary/Documentation/Unix/ManPages/cat4/tcp.4p
./NextLibrary/Documentation/Unix/ManPages/cat4/evs.4
./NextLibrary/Documentation/Unix/ManPages/cat5
./NextLibrary/Documentation/Unix/ManPages/cat5/.places
./NextLibrary/Documentation/Unix/ManPages/cat6
```

```
./NextLibrary/Documentation/Unix/ManPages/cat6/.places
./NextLibrary/Documentation/Unix/ManPages/cat7
./NextLibrary/Documentation/Unix/ManPages/cat7/.places
./NextLibrary/Documentation/Unix/ManPages/cat8
./NextLibrary/Documentation/Unix/ManPages/cat8/.places
./NextLibrary/Documentation/Unix/ManPages/cat8/kgmon.8
./NextLibrary/Documentation/Unix/ManPages/cat8/routed.8c
./NextLibrary/Documentation/Unix/ManPages/cat8/nppower.8
./NextLibrary/Documentation/Unix/ManPages/cat9
./NextLibrary/Documentation/Unix/ManPages/cat9/.places
./NextLibrary/Documentation/Unix/ManPages/cat1
./NextLibrary/Documentation/Unix/ManPages/cat1/.places
./NextLibrary/Documentation/Unix/ManPages/catn
./NextLibrary/Documentation/Unix/ManPages/catn/.places
./NextLibrary/Documentation/Unix/ManPages/man1
./NextLibrary/Documentation/Unix/ManPages/man1/BuildDisk.1
./NextLibrary/Documentation/Unix/ManPages/man1/DigitalLibrarian.1
./NextLibrary/Documentation/Unix/ManPages/man1/DigitalQuotations.1
./NextLibrary/Documentation/Unix/ManPages/man1/DigitalWebster.1
./NextLibrary/Documentation/Unix/ManPages/man1/Edit.1
./NextLibrary/Documentation/Unix/ManPages/man1/IB.1
./NextLibrary/Documentation/Unix/ManPages/man1/Install_TeX.1
./NextLibrary/Documentation/Unix/ManPages/man1/InterfaceBuilder.1
./NextLibrary/Documentation/Unix/ManPages/man1/Librarian.1
./NextLibrary/Documentation/Unix/ManPages/man1/Mail.1
./NextLibrary/Documentation/Unix/ManPages/man1/Mathematica.1
./NextLibrary/Documentation/Unix/ManPages/man1/NIB.1
./NextLibrary/Documentation/Unix/ManPages/man1/NeXTApps.1
./NextLibrary/Documentation/Unix/ManPages/man1/NetInfoManager.1
./NextLibrary/Documentation/Unix/ManPages/man1/NetManager.1
./NextLibrary/Documentation/Unix/ManPages/man1/Preferences.1
./NextLibrary/Documentation/Unix/ManPages/man1/Preview.1
./NextLibrary/Documentation/Unix/ManPages/man1/PrintManager.1
./NextLibrary/Documentation/Unix/ManPages/man1/PrinterTester.1
./NextLibrary/Documentation/Unix/ManPages/man1/Quotations.1
./NextLibrary/Documentation/Unix/ManPages/man1/Shell.1
./NextLibrary/Documentation/Unix/ManPages/man1/TeXview.1
./NextLibrary/Documentation/Unix/ManPages/man1/TechReport.1
./NextLibrary/Documentation/Unix/ManPages/man1/Terminal.1
./NextLibrary/Documentation/Unix/ManPages/man1/UserManager.1
./NextLibrary/Documentation/Unix/ManPages/man1/Webster.1
./NextLibrary/Documentation/Unix/ManPages/man1/WriteNow.1
./NextLibrary/Documentation/Unix/ManPages/man1/addbib.1
./NextLibrary/Documentation/Unix/ManPages/man1/apply.1
./NextLibrary/Documentation/Unix/ManPages/man1/ar.1
./NextLibrary/Documentation/Unix/ManPages/man1/as.1
./NextLibrary/Documentation/Unix/ManPages/man1/asm56000.1
./NextLibrary/Documentation/Unix/ManPages/man1/at.1
./NextLibrary/Documentation/Unix/ManPages/man1/atom.1
./NextLibrary/Documentation/Unix/ManPages/man1/atq.1
./NextLibrary/Documentation/Unix/ManPages/man1/atrm.1
./NextLibrary/Documentation/Unix/ManPages/man1/awk.1
./NextLibrary/Documentation/Unix/ManPages/man1/basename.1
./NextLibrary/Documentation/Unix/ManPages/man1/bc.1
./NextLibrary/Documentation/Unix/ManPages/man1/bibtex.1
./NextLibrary/Documentation/Unix/ManPages/man1/biff.1
./NextLibrary/Documentation/Unix/ManPages/man1/binmail.1
./NextLibrary/Documentation/Unix/ManPages/man1/bison.1
./NextLibrary/Documentation/Unix/ManPages/man1/bm.1
./NextLibrary/Documentation/Unix/ManPages/man1/buildafmdir.1
./NextLibrary/Documentation/Unix/ManPages/man1/cal.1
./NextLibrary/Documentation/Unix/ManPages/man1/calendar.1
./NextLibrary/Documentation/Unix/ManPages/man1/case.1
./NextLibrary/Documentation/Unix/ManPages/man1/cat.1
./NextLibrary/Documentation/Unix/ManPages/man1/cb.1
./NextLibrary/Documentation/Unix/ManPages/man1/cc.1
./NextLibrary/Documentation/Unix/ManPages/man1/cd.1
./NextLibrary/Documentation/Unix/ManPages/man1/checkeq.1
./NextLibrary/Documentation/Unix/ManPages/man1/checknr.1
./NextLibrary/Documentation/Unix/ManPages/man1/chfn.1
./NextLibrary/Documentation/Unix/ManPages/man1/chgrp.1
./NextLibrary/Documentation/Unix/ManPages/man1/chmod.1
./NextLibrary/Documentation/Unix/ManPages/man1/chsh.1
./NextLibrary/Documentation/Unix/ManPages/man1/ci.1
./NextLibrary/Documentation/Unix/ManPages/man1/cl.1
./NextLibrary/Documentation/Unix/ManPages/man1/clear.1
./NextLibrary/Documentation/Unix/ManPages/man1/cmp.1
./NextLibrary/Documentation/Unix/ManPages/man1/co.1
./NextLibrary/Documentation/Unix/ManPages/man1/col.1
./NextLibrary/Documentation/Unix/ManPages/man1/colcrt.1
./NextLibrary/Documentation/Unix/ManPages/man1/colrm.1
./NextLibrary/Documentation/Unix/ManPages/man1/comm.1
./NextLibrary/Documentation/Unix/ManPages/man1/compress.1
./NextLibrary/Documentation/Unix/ManPages/man1/copy.1
./NextLibrary/Documentation/Unix/ManPages/man1/cp.1
./NextLibrary/Documentation/Unix/ManPages/man1/crypt.1
./NextLibrary/Documentation/Unix/ManPages/man1/csh.1
./NextLibrary/Documentation/Unix/ManPages/man1/ctags.1
./NextLibrary/Documentation/Unix/ManPages/man1/ctree.1
./NextLibrary/Documentation/Unix/ManPages/man1/cu.1c
./NextLibrary/Documentation/Unix/ManPages/man1/date.1
./NextLibrary/Documentation/Unix/ManPages/man1/dbCatenate.1
./NextLibrary/Documentation/Unix/ManPages/man1/dc.1
./NextLibrary/Documentation/Unix/ManPages/man1/dd.1
./NextLibrary/Documentation/Unix/ManPages/man1/deroff.1
./NextLibrary/Documentation/Unix/ManPages/man1/df.1
./NextLibrary/Documentation/Unix/ManPages/man1/diction.1
./NextLibrary/Documentation/Unix/ManPages/man1/diff.1
./NextLibrary/Documentation/Unix/ManPages/man1/diff3.1
./NextLibrary/Documentation/Unix/ManPages/man1/diffh.1
./NextLibrary/Documentation/Unix/ManPages/man1/domainname.1
./NextLibrary/Documentation/Unix/ManPages/man1/dread.1
```

```
./NextLibrary/Documentation/Unix/ManPages/man1/dremove.1        ./NextLibrary/Documentation/Unix/ManPages/man1/intro.1
./NextLibrary/Documentation/Unix/ManPages/man1/dspabort.1       ./NextLibrary/Documentation/Unix/ManPages/man1/iostat.1
./NextLibrary/Documentation/Unix/ManPages/man1/dspbeep.1        ./NextLibrary/Documentation/Unix/ManPages/man1/ixBuild.1
./NextLibrary/Documentation/Unix/ManPages/man1/dspimg.1         ./NextLibrary/Documentation/Unix/ManPages/man1/ixClean.1
./NextLibrary/Documentation/Unix/ManPages/man1/dsploadwrap.1    ./NextLibrary/Documentation/Unix/ManPages/man1/join.1
./NextLibrary/Documentation/Unix/ManPages/man1/dspmsg.1         ./NextLibrary/Documentation/Unix/ManPages/man1/jot.1
./NextLibrary/Documentation/Unix/ManPages/man1/dsptest.1        ./NextLibrary/Documentation/Unix/ManPages/man1/kill.1
./NextLibrary/Documentation/Unix/ManPages/man1/dspwrap.1        ./NextLibrary/Documentation/Unix/ManPages/man1/last.1
./NextLibrary/Documentation/Unix/ManPages/man1/du.1             ./NextLibrary/Documentation/Unix/ManPages/man1/lastcomm.1
./NextLibrary/Documentation/Unix/ManPages/man1/dvips.1          ./NextLibrary/Documentation/Unix/ManPages/man1/ld.1
./NextLibrary/Documentation/Unix/ManPages/man1/dwrite.1         ./NextLibrary/Documentation/Unix/ManPages/man1/leave.1
./NextLibrary/Documentation/Unix/ManPages/man1/echo.1           ./NextLibrary/Documentation/Unix/ManPages/man1/less.1
./NextLibrary/Documentation/Unix/ManPages/man1/ed.1             ./NextLibrary/Documentation/Unix/ManPages/man1/lex.1
./NextLibrary/Documentation/Unix/ManPages/man1/edit.1           ./NextLibrary/Documentation/Unix/ManPages/man1/lib56000.1
./NextLibrary/Documentation/Unix/ManPages/man1/egrep.1          ./NextLibrary/Documentation/Unix/ManPages/man1/ln.1
./NextLibrary/Documentation/Unix/ManPages/man1/emacs.1          ./NextLibrary/Documentation/Unix/ManPages/man1/lnk56000.1
./NextLibrary/Documentation/Unix/ManPages/man1/enroll.1         ./NextLibrary/Documentation/Unix/ManPages/man1/lock.1
./NextLibrary/Documentation/Unix/ManPages/man1/enscript.1       ./NextLibrary/Documentation/Unix/ManPages/man1/logger.1
./NextLibrary/Documentation/Unix/ManPages/man1/eqn.1            ./NextLibrary/Documentation/Unix/ManPages/man1/login.1
./NextLibrary/Documentation/Unix/ManPages/man1/error.1          ./NextLibrary/Documentation/Unix/ManPages/man1/look.1
./NextLibrary/Documentation/Unix/ManPages/man1/ex.1             ./NextLibrary/Documentation/Unix/ManPages/man1/lookbib.1
./NextLibrary/Documentation/Unix/ManPages/man1/expand.1         ./NextLibrary/Documentation/Unix/ManPages/man1/lorder.1
./NextLibrary/Documentation/Unix/ManPages/man1/explain.1        ./NextLibrary/Documentation/Unix/ManPages/man1/lpq.1
./NextLibrary/Documentation/Unix/ManPages/man1/expr.1           ./NextLibrary/Documentation/Unix/ManPages/man1/lpr.1
./NextLibrary/Documentation/Unix/ManPages/man1/false.1          ./NextLibrary/Documentation/Unix/ManPages/man1/lprm.1
./NextLibrary/Documentation/Unix/ManPages/man1/fgrep.1          ./NextLibrary/Documentation/Unix/ManPages/man1/lptest.1
./NextLibrary/Documentation/Unix/ManPages/man1/file.1           ./NextLibrary/Documentation/Unix/ManPages/man1/ls.1
./NextLibrary/Documentation/Unix/ManPages/man1/find.1           ./NextLibrary/Documentation/Unix/ManPages/man1/m4.1
./NextLibrary/Documentation/Unix/ManPages/man1/finger.1         ./NextLibrary/Documentation/Unix/ManPages/man1/mail.1
./NextLibrary/Documentation/Unix/ManPages/man1/fmt.1            ./NextLibrary/Documentation/Unix/ManPages/man1/make.1
./NextLibrary/Documentation/Unix/ManPages/man1/fold.1           ./NextLibrary/Documentation/Unix/ManPages/man1/man.1
./NextLibrary/Documentation/Unix/ManPages/man1/for.1            ./NextLibrary/Documentation/Unix/ManPages/man1/math.1
./NextLibrary/Documentation/Unix/ManPages/man1/from.1           ./NextLibrary/Documentation/Unix/ManPages/man1/mathremote.1
./NextLibrary/Documentation/Unix/ManPages/man1/ftp.1c           ./NextLibrary/Documentation/Unix/ManPages/man1/merge.1
./NextLibrary/Documentation/Unix/ManPages/man1/gcc.1            ./NextLibrary/Documentation/Unix/ManPages/man1/mesg.1
./NextLibrary/Documentation/Unix/ManPages/man1/gdb.1            ./NextLibrary/Documentation/Unix/ManPages/man1/mf.1
./NextLibrary/Documentation/Unix/ManPages/man1/gftopk.1         ./NextLibrary/Documentation/Unix/ManPages/man1/mig.1
./NextLibrary/Documentation/Unix/ManPages/man1/gftype.1         ./NextLibrary/Documentation/Unix/ManPages/man1/mkdir.1
./NextLibrary/Documentation/Unix/ManPages/man1/gprof.1          ./NextLibrary/Documentation/Unix/ManPages/man1/mkdirs.1
./NextLibrary/Documentation/Unix/ManPages/man1/grep.1           ./NextLibrary/Documentation/Unix/ManPages/man1/mkstr.1
./NextLibrary/Documentation/Unix/ManPages/man1/groups.1         ./NextLibrary/Documentation/Unix/ManPages/man1/more.1
./NextLibrary/Documentation/Unix/ManPages/man1/head.1           ./NextLibrary/Documentation/Unix/ManPages/man1/mset.1
./NextLibrary/Documentation/Unix/ManPages/man1/hostid.1         ./NextLibrary/Documentation/Unix/ManPages/man1/msgs.1
./NextLibrary/Documentation/Unix/ManPages/man1/hostinfo.1       ./NextLibrary/Documentation/Unix/ManPages/man1/mt.1
./NextLibrary/Documentation/Unix/ManPages/man1/hostname.1       ./NextLibrary/Documentation/Unix/ManPages/man1/mv.1
./NextLibrary/Documentation/Unix/ManPages/man1/ident.1          ./NextLibrary/Documentation/Unix/ManPages/man1/neqn.1
./NextLibrary/Documentation/Unix/ManPages/man1/if.1             ./NextLibrary/Documentation/Unix/ManPages/man1/netstat.1
./NextLibrary/Documentation/Unix/ManPages/man1/indent.1         ./NextLibrary/Documentation/Unix/ManPages/man1/newaliases.1
./NextLibrary/Documentation/Unix/ManPages/man1/indxbib.1        ./NextLibrary/Documentation/Unix/ManPages/man1/nice.1
./NextLibrary/Documentation/Unix/ManPages/man1/install.1        ./NextLibrary/Documentation/Unix/ManPages/man1/nidump.1
./NextLibrary/Documentation/Unix/ManPages/man1/installman.1     ./NextLibrary/Documentation/Unix/ManPages/man1/niload.1
```

```
./NextLibrary/Documentation/Unix/ManPages/man1/niutil.1
./NextLibrary/Documentation/Unix/ManPages/man1/nm.1
./NextLibrary/Documentation/Unix/ManPages/man1/nmcontrol.1
./NextLibrary/Documentation/Unix/ManPages/man1/nmtest.1
./NextLibrary/Documentation/Unix/ManPages/man1/nmtime.1
./NextLibrary/Documentation/Unix/ManPages/man1/nmxlog.1
./NextLibrary/Documentation/Unix/ManPages/man1/nohup.1
./NextLibrary/Documentation/Unix/ManPages/man1/nroff.1
./NextLibrary/Documentation/Unix/ManPages/man1/od.1
./NextLibrary/Documentation/Unix/ManPages/man1/on.1c
./NextLibrary/Documentation/Unix/ManPages/man1/open.1
./NextLibrary/Documentation/Unix/ManPages/man1/openfile.1
./NextLibrary/Documentation/Unix/ManPages/man1/otool.1
./NextLibrary/Documentation/Unix/ManPages/man1/page.1
./NextLibrary/Documentation/Unix/ManPages/man1/pagesize.1
./NextLibrary/Documentation/Unix/ManPages/man1/passwd.1
./NextLibrary/Documentation/Unix/ManPages/man1/paste.1
./NextLibrary/Documentation/Unix/ManPages/man1/pft.1
./NextLibrary/Documentation/Unix/ManPages/man1/pktogf.1
./NextLibrary/Documentation/Unix/ManPages/man1/pktype.1
./NextLibrary/Documentation/Unix/ManPages/man1/playscore.1
./NextLibrary/Documentation/Unix/ManPages/man1/pr.1
./NextLibrary/Documentation/Unix/ManPages/man1/prebuild.1
./NextLibrary/Documentation/Unix/ManPages/man1/printenv.1
./NextLibrary/Documentation/Unix/ManPages/man1/ps.1
./NextLibrary/Documentation/Unix/ManPages/man1/ps4014.1
./NextLibrary/Documentation/Unix/ManPages/man1/ps630.1
./NextLibrary/Documentation/Unix/ManPages/man1/pscat.1
./NextLibrary/Documentation/Unix/ManPages/man1/psdit.1
./NextLibrary/Documentation/Unix/ManPages/man1/psfix.1
./NextLibrary/Documentation/Unix/ManPages/man1/psfonts.1
./NextLibrary/Documentation/Unix/ManPages/man1/psplot.1
./NextLibrary/Documentation/Unix/ManPages/man1/psrev.1
./NextLibrary/Documentation/Unix/ManPages/man1/psroff.1
./NextLibrary/Documentation/Unix/ManPages/man1/w.1
./NextLibrary/Documentation/Unix/ManPages/man1/pssymbols.1
./NextLibrary/Documentation/Unix/ManPages/man1/pswrap.1
./NextLibrary/Documentation/Unix/ManPages/man1/ptags.1
./NextLibrary/Documentation/Unix/ManPages/man1/ptroff.1
./NextLibrary/Documentation/Unix/ManPages/man1/ptx.1
./NextLibrary/Documentation/Unix/ManPages/man1/pwd.1
./NextLibrary/Documentation/Unix/ManPages/man1/pword.1
./NextLibrary/Documentation/Unix/ManPages/man1/ranlib.1
./NextLibrary/Documentation/Unix/ManPages/man1/ratfor.1
./NextLibrary/Documentation/Unix/ManPages/man1/rcp.1c
./NextLibrary/Documentation/Unix/ManPages/man1/rcs.1
./NextLibrary/Documentation/Unix/ManPages/man1/rcsdiff.1
./NextLibrary/Documentation/Unix/ManPages/man1/rcsintro.1
./NextLibrary/Documentation/Unix/ManPages/man1/rcsmerge.1
./NextLibrary/Documentation/Unix/ManPages/man1/rdist.1
./NextLibrary/Documentation/Unix/ManPages/man1/refer.1
./NextLibrary/Documentation/Unix/ManPages/man1/reset.1
./NextLibrary/Documentation/Unix/ManPages/man1/rev.1
./NextLibrary/Documentation/Unix/ManPages/man1/rlog.1
./NextLibrary/Documentation/Unix/ManPages/man1/rlogin.1c
./NextLibrary/Documentation/Unix/ManPages/man1/rm.1
./NextLibrary/Documentation/Unix/ManPages/man1/rmail.1
./NextLibrary/Documentation/Unix/ManPages/man1/rmdir.1
./NextLibrary/Documentation/Unix/ManPages/man1/roffbib.1
./NextLibrary/Documentation/Unix/ManPages/man1/rpcgen.1
./NextLibrary/Documentation/Unix/ManPages/man1/rsh.1c
./NextLibrary/Documentation/Unix/ManPages/man1/rup.1c
./NextLibrary/Documentation/Unix/ManPages/man1/ruptime.1c
./NextLibrary/Documentation/Unix/ManPages/man1/rusers.1c
./NextLibrary/Documentation/Unix/ManPages/man1/rwho.1c
./NextLibrary/Documentation/Unix/ManPages/man1/sccstorcs.1
./NextLibrary/Documentation/Unix/ManPages/man1/screenafm.1
./NextLibrary/Documentation/Unix/ManPages/man1/script.1
./NextLibrary/Documentation/Unix/ManPages/man1/sed.1
./NextLibrary/Documentation/Unix/ManPages/man1/segedit.1
./NextLibrary/Documentation/Unix/ManPages/man1/sh.1
./NextLibrary/Documentation/Unix/ManPages/man1/size.1
./NextLibrary/Documentation/Unix/ManPages/man1/sleep.1
./NextLibrary/Documentation/Unix/ManPages/man1/sndconvert.1
./NextLibrary/Documentation/Unix/ManPages/man1/sndinfo.1
./NextLibrary/Documentation/Unix/ManPages/man1/sndplay.1
./NextLibrary/Documentation/Unix/ManPages/man1/sndrecord.1
./NextLibrary/Documentation/Unix/ManPages/man1/soelim.1
./NextLibrary/Documentation/Unix/ManPages/man1/sort.1
./NextLibrary/Documentation/Unix/ManPages/man1/sortbib.1
./NextLibrary/Documentation/Unix/ManPages/man1/spell.1
./NextLibrary/Documentation/Unix/ManPages/man1/spellin.1
./NextLibrary/Documentation/Unix/ManPages/man1/spellout.1
./NextLibrary/Documentation/Unix/ManPages/man1/spline.1g
./NextLibrary/Documentation/Unix/ManPages/man1/split.1
./NextLibrary/Documentation/Unix/ManPages/man1/strings.1
./NextLibrary/Documentation/Unix/ManPages/man1/strip.1
./NextLibrary/Documentation/Unix/ManPages/man1/struct.1
./NextLibrary/Documentation/Unix/ManPages/man1/stty.1
./NextLibrary/Documentation/Unix/ManPages/man1/style.1
./NextLibrary/Documentation/Unix/ManPages/man1/su.1
./NextLibrary/Documentation/Unix/ManPages/man1/su.wheel.1
./NextLibrary/Documentation/Unix/ManPages/man1/sum.1
./NextLibrary/Documentation/Unix/ManPages/man1/sysline.1
./NextLibrary/Documentation/Unix/ManPages/man1/tabs.1
./NextLibrary/Documentation/Unix/ManPages/man1/tail.1
./NextLibrary/Documentation/Unix/ManPages/man1/talk.1
./NextLibrary/Documentation/Unix/ManPages/man1/tar.1
./NextLibrary/Documentation/Unix/ManPages/man1/tbl.1
./NextLibrary/Documentation/Unix/ManPages/man1/tc.1
./NextLibrary/Documentation/Unix/ManPages/man1/tcopy.1
./NextLibrary/Documentation/Unix/ManPages/man1/tee.1
```

./NextLibrary/Documentation/Unix/ManPages/man1/telnet.1c
./NextLibrary/Documentation/Unix/ManPages/man1/test.1
./NextLibrary/Documentation/Unix/ManPages/man1/tex.1
./NextLibrary/Documentation/Unix/ManPages/man1/texview.1
./NextLibrary/Documentation/Unix/ManPages/man1/tftp.1c
./NextLibrary/Documentation/Unix/ManPages/man1/time.1
./NextLibrary/Documentation/Unix/ManPages/man1/tip.1c
./NextLibrary/Documentation/Unix/ManPages/man1/tk.1
./NextLibrary/Documentation/Unix/ManPages/man1/tn3270.1
./NextLibrary/Documentation/Unix/ManPages/man1/touch.1
./NextLibrary/Documentation/Unix/ManPages/man1/tp.1
./NextLibrary/Documentation/Unix/ManPages/man1/tr.1
./NextLibrary/Documentation/Unix/ManPages/man1/transcript.1
./NextLibrary/Documentation/Unix/ManPages/man1/troff.1
./NextLibrary/Documentation/Unix/ManPages/man1/true.1
./NextLibrary/Documentation/Unix/ManPages/man1/tset.1
./NextLibrary/Documentation/Unix/ManPages/man1/tsort.1
./NextLibrary/Documentation/Unix/ManPages/man1/tty.1
./NextLibrary/Documentation/Unix/ManPages/man1/ul.1
./NextLibrary/Documentation/Unix/ManPages/man1/uncompress.1
./NextLibrary/Documentation/Unix/ManPages/man1/unexpand.1
./NextLibrary/Documentation/Unix/ManPages/man1/unifdef.1
./NextLibrary/Documentation/Unix/ManPages/man1/uniq.1
./NextLibrary/Documentation/Unix/ManPages/man1/units.1
./NextLibrary/Documentation/Unix/ManPages/man1/users.1
./NextLibrary/Documentation/Unix/ManPages/man1/uucp.1c
./NextLibrary/Documentation/Unix/ManPages/man1/uudecode.1c
./NextLibrary/Documentation/Unix/ManPages/man1/uuencode.1c
./NextLibrary/Documentation/Unix/ManPages/man1/uulog.1c
./NextLibrary/Documentation/Unix/ManPages/man1/uuname.1c
./NextLibrary/Documentation/Unix/ManPages/man1/uuq.1c
./NextLibrary/Documentation/Unix/ManPages/man1/uusend.1c
./NextLibrary/Documentation/Unix/ManPages/man1/uux.1c
./NextLibrary/Documentation/Unix/ManPages/man1/vacation.1
./NextLibrary/Documentation/Unix/ManPages/man1/vers_string.1
./NextLibrary/Documentation/Unix/ManPages/man1/vgrind.1
./NextLibrary/Documentation/Unix/ManPages/man1/vi.1
./NextLibrary/Documentation/Unix/ManPages/man1/view.1
./NextLibrary/Documentation/Unix/ManPages/man1/vm_stat.1
./NextLibrary/Documentation/Unix/ManPages/man1/wait.1
./NextLibrary/Documentation/Unix/ManPages/man1/wall.1
./NextLibrary/Documentation/Unix/ManPages/man1/wc.1
./NextLibrary/Documentation/Unix/ManPages/man1/wfcomp.1
./NextLibrary/Documentation/Unix/ManPages/man1/what.1
./NextLibrary/Documentation/Unix/ManPages/man1/whereis.1
./NextLibrary/Documentation/Unix/ManPages/man1/which.1
./NextLibrary/Documentation/Unix/ManPages/man1/while.1
./NextLibrary/Documentation/Unix/ManPages/man1/who.1
./NextLibrary/Documentation/Unix/ManPages/man1/whoami.1
./NextLibrary/Documentation/Unix/ManPages/man1/whois.1
./NextLibrary/Documentation/Unix/ManPages/man1/window.1

./NextLibrary/Documentation/Unix/ManPages/man1/xargs.1
./NextLibrary/Documentation/Unix/ManPages/man1/xget.1
./NextLibrary/Documentation/Unix/ManPages/man1/xsend.1
./NextLibrary/Documentation/Unix/ManPages/man1/xstr.1
./NextLibrary/Documentation/Unix/ManPages/man1/yacc.1
./NextLibrary/Documentation/Unix/ManPages/man1/yes.1
./NextLibrary/Documentation/Unix/ManPages/man1/ypcat.1
./NextLibrary/Documentation/Unix/ManPages/man1/ypmatch.1
./NextLibrary/Documentation/Unix/ManPages/man1/yppasswd.1
./NextLibrary/Documentation/Unix/ManPages/man1/ypwhich.1
./NextLibrary/Documentation/Unix/ManPages/man1/zcat.1
./NextLibrary/Documentation/Unix/ManPages/man1/.places
./NextLibrary/Documentation/Unix/ManPages/man2
./NextLibrary/Documentation/Unix/ManPages/man2/accept.2
./NextLibrary/Documentation/Unix/ManPages/man2/access.2
./NextLibrary/Documentation/Unix/ManPages/man2/acct.2
./NextLibrary/Documentation/Unix/ManPages/man2/adjtime.2
./NextLibrary/Documentation/Unix/ManPages/man2/async_daemon.2
./NextLibrary/Documentation/Unix/ManPages/man2/bind.2
./NextLibrary/Documentation/Unix/ManPages/man2/brk.2
./NextLibrary/Documentation/Unix/ManPages/man2/chdir.2
./NextLibrary/Documentation/Unix/ManPages/man2/chmod.2
./NextLibrary/Documentation/Unix/ManPages/man2/chown.2
./NextLibrary/Documentation/Unix/ManPages/man2/chroot.2
./NextLibrary/Documentation/Unix/ManPages/man2/close.2
./NextLibrary/Documentation/Unix/ManPages/man2/connect.2
./NextLibrary/Documentation/Unix/ManPages/man2/creat.2
./NextLibrary/Documentation/Unix/ManPages/man2/dup.2
./NextLibrary/Documentation/Unix/ManPages/man2/dup2.2
./NextLibrary/Documentation/Unix/ManPages/man2/execve.2
./NextLibrary/Documentation/Unix/ManPages/man2/exit.2
./NextLibrary/Documentation/Unix/ManPages/man2/fchmod.2
./NextLibrary/Documentation/Unix/ManPages/man2/fchown.2
./NextLibrary/Documentation/Unix/ManPages/man2/fcntl.2
./NextLibrary/Documentation/Unix/ManPages/man2/flock.2
./NextLibrary/Documentation/Unix/ManPages/man2/fork.2
./NextLibrary/Documentation/Unix/ManPages/man2/fstat.2
./NextLibrary/Documentation/Unix/ManPages/man2/fsync.2
./NextLibrary/Documentation/Unix/ManPages/man2/ftruncate.2
./NextLibrary/Documentation/Unix/ManPages/man2/getdirentries.2
./NextLibrary/Documentation/Unix/ManPages/man2/getdomainname.2
./NextLibrary/Documentation/Unix/ManPages/man2/getdtablesize.2
./NextLibrary/Documentation/Unix/ManPages/man2/getegid.2
./NextLibrary/Documentation/Unix/ManPages/man2/geteuid.2
./NextLibrary/Documentation/Unix/ManPages/man2/getgid.2
./NextLibrary/Documentation/Unix/ManPages/man2/getgroups.2
./NextLibrary/Documentation/Unix/ManPages/man2/gethostid.2
./NextLibrary/Documentation/Unix/ManPages/man2/gethostname.2
./NextLibrary/Documentation/Unix/ManPages/man2/getitimer.2
./NextLibrary/Documentation/Unix/ManPages/man2/getpagesize.2
./NextLibrary/Documentation/Unix/ManPages/man2/getpeername.2

./NextLibrary/Documentation/Unix/ManPages/man2/getpgrp.2
./NextLibrary/Documentation/Unix/ManPages/man2/getpid.2
./NextLibrary/Documentation/Unix/ManPages/man2/getppid.2
./NextLibrary/Documentation/Unix/ManPages/man2/getpriority.2
./NextLibrary/Documentation/Unix/ManPages/man2/getrlimit.2
./NextLibrary/Documentation/Unix/ManPages/man2/getrusage.2
./NextLibrary/Documentation/Unix/ManPages/man2/getsockname.2
./NextLibrary/Documentation/Unix/ManPages/man2/getsockopt.2
./NextLibrary/Documentation/Unix/ManPages/man2/gettimeofday.2
./NextLibrary/Documentation/Unix/ManPages/man2/getuid.2
./NextLibrary/Documentation/Unix/ManPages/man2/host_into.2
./NextLibrary/Documentation/Unix/ManPages/man2/intro.2
./NextLibrary/Documentation/Unix/ManPages/man2/ioctl.2
./NextLibrary/Documentation/Unix/ManPages/man2/kern_timestamp.2
./NextLibrary/Documentation/Unix/ManPages/man2/kill.2
./NextLibrary/Documentation/Unix/ManPages/man2/killpg.2
./NextLibrary/Documentation/Unix/ManPages/man2/link.2
./NextLibrary/Documentation/Unix/ManPages/man2/listen.2
./NextLibrary/Documentation/Unix/ManPages/man2/lseek.2
./NextLibrary/Documentation/Unix/ManPages/man2/lstat.2
./NextLibrary/Documentation/Unix/ManPages/man2/mach_swapon.2
./NextLibrary/Documentation/Unix/ManPages/man2/mkdir.2
./NextLibrary/Documentation/Unix/ManPages/man2/mknod.2
./NextLibrary/Documentation/Unix/ManPages/man2/mount.2
./NextLibrary/Documentation/Unix/ManPages/man2/nfssvc.2
./NextLibrary/Documentation/Unix/ManPages/man2/open.2
./NextLibrary/Documentation/Unix/ManPages/man2/pipe.2
./NextLibrary/Documentation/Unix/ManPages/man2/profil.2
./NextLibrary/Documentation/Unix/ManPages/man2/ptrace.2
./NextLibrary/Documentation/Unix/ManPages/man2/read.2
./NextLibrary/Documentation/Unix/ManPages/man2/readlink.2
./NextLibrary/Documentation/Unix/ManPages/man2/readv.2
./NextLibrary/Documentation/Unix/ManPages/man2/reboot.2
./NextLibrary/Documentation/Unix/ManPages/man2/recv.2
./NextLibrary/Documentation/Unix/ManPages/man2/recvfrom.2
./NextLibrary/Documentation/Unix/ManPages/man2/recvmsg.2
./NextLibrary/Documentation/Unix/ManPages/man2/rename.2
./NextLibrary/Documentation/Unix/ManPages/man2/rmdir.2
./NextLibrary/Documentation/Unix/ManPages/man2/sbrk.2
./NextLibrary/Documentation/Unix/ManPages/man2/select.2
./NextLibrary/Documentation/Unix/ManPages/man2/send.2
./NextLibrary/Documentation/Unix/ManPages/man2/sendmsg.2
./NextLibrary/Documentation/Unix/ManPages/man2/sendto.2
./NextLibrary/Documentation/Unix/ManPages/man2/setdomainname.2
./NextLibrary/Documentation/Unix/ManPages/man2/setgroups.2
./NextLibrary/Documentation/Unix/ManPages/man2/sethostid.2
./NextLibrary/Documentation/Unix/ManPages/man2/sethostname.2
./NextLibrary/Documentation/Unix/ManPages/man2/setitimer.2
./NextLibrary/Documentation/Unix/ManPages/man2/setpgrp.2
./NextLibrary/Documentation/Unix/ManPages/man2/setpriority.2
./NextLibrary/Documentation/Unix/ManPages/man2/setregid.2

./NextLibrary/Documentation/Unix/ManPages/man2/setreuid.2
./NextLibrary/Documentation/Unix/ManPages/man2/setrlimit.2
./NextLibrary/Documentation/Unix/ManPages/man2/setsockopt.2
./NextLibrary/Documentation/Unix/ManPages/man2/settimeofday.2
./NextLibrary/Documentation/Unix/ManPages/man2/shutdown.2
./NextLibrary/Documentation/Unix/ManPages/man2/sigblock.2
./NextLibrary/Documentation/Unix/ManPages/man2/sigpause.2
./NextLibrary/Documentation/Unix/ManPages/man2/sigreturn.2
./NextLibrary/Documentation/Unix/ManPages/man2/sigsetmask.2
./NextLibrary/Documentation/Unix/ManPages/man2/sigstack.2
./NextLibrary/Documentation/Unix/ManPages/man2/sigvec.2
./NextLibrary/Documentation/Unix/ManPages/man2/slot_info.2
./NextLibrary/Documentation/Unix/ManPages/man2/socket.2
./NextLibrary/Documentation/Unix/ManPages/man2/socketpair.2
./NextLibrary/Documentation/Unix/ManPages/man2/stat.2
./NextLibrary/Documentation/Unix/ManPages/man2/statfs.2
./NextLibrary/Documentation/Unix/ManPages/man2/swapon.2
./NextLibrary/Documentation/Unix/ManPages/man2/symlink.2
./NextLibrary/Documentation/Unix/ManPages/man2/sync.2
./NextLibrary/Documentation/Unix/ManPages/man2/syscall.2
./NextLibrary/Documentation/Unix/ManPages/man2/truncate.2
./NextLibrary/Documentation/Unix/ManPages/man2/umask.2
./NextLibrary/Documentation/Unix/ManPages/man2/unlink.2
./NextLibrary/Documentation/Unix/ManPages/man2/unmount.2
./NextLibrary/Documentation/Unix/ManPages/man2/utimes.2
./NextLibrary/Documentation/Unix/ManPages/man2/vfork.2
./NextLibrary/Documentation/Unix/ManPages/man2/vhangup.2
./NextLibrary/Documentation/Unix/ManPages/man2/wait.2
./NextLibrary/Documentation/Unix/ManPages/man2/wait3.2
./NextLibrary/Documentation/Unix/ManPages/man2/write.2
./NextLibrary/Documentation/Unix/ManPages/man2/writev.2
./NextLibrary/Documentation/Unix/ManPages/man2/.places
./NextLibrary/Documentation/Unix/ManPages/man3
./NextLibrary/Documentation/Unix/ManPages/man3/ArrayFromFile.3
./NextLibrary/Documentation/Unix/ManPages/man3/_longjmp.3
./NextLibrary/Documentation/Unix/ManPages/man3/_setjmp.3
./NextLibrary/Documentation/Unix/ManPages/man3/abort.3
./NextLibrary/Documentation/Unix/ManPages/man3/abs.3
./NextLibrary/Documentation/Unix/ManPages/man3/acos.3m
./NextLibrary/Documentation/Unix/ManPages/man3/acosh.3m
./NextLibrary/Documentation/Unix/ManPages/man3/addr.3n
./NextLibrary/Documentation/Unix/ManPages/man3/alarm.3c
./NextLibrary/Documentation/Unix/ManPages/man3/aliasdb.3
./NextLibrary/Documentation/Unix/ManPages/man3/alloca.3
./NextLibrary/Documentation/Unix/ManPages/man3/alphasort.3
./NextLibrary/Documentation/Unix/ManPages/man3/arc.3x
./NextLibrary/Documentation/Unix/ManPages/man3/asctime.3
./NextLibrary/Documentation/Unix/ManPages/man3/asin.3m
./NextLibrary/Documentation/Unix/ManPages/man3/asinh.3m
./NextLibrary/Documentation/Unix/ManPages/man3/assert.3
./NextLibrary/Documentation/Unix/ManPages/man3/atan.3m

./NextLibrary/Documentation/Unix/ManPages/man3/atan2.3m
./NextLibrary/Documentation/Unix/ManPages/man3/atanh.3m
./NextLibrary/Documentation/Unix/ManPages/man3/atof.3
./NextLibrary/Documentation/Unix/ManPages/man3/atoh.3
./NextLibrary/Documentation/Unix/ManPages/man3/atoi.3
./NextLibrary/Documentation/Unix/ManPages/man3/atol.3
./NextLibrary/Documentation/Unix/ManPages/man3/atoo.3
./NextLibrary/Documentation/Unix/ManPages/man3/bcmp.3
./NextLibrary/Documentation/Unix/ManPages/man3/bcopy.3
./NextLibrary/Documentation/Unix/ManPages/man3/bindresvport.3n
./NextLibrary/Documentation/Unix/ManPages/man3/bootparam.3r
./NextLibrary/Documentation/Unix/ManPages/man3/bstring.3
./NextLibrary/Documentation/Unix/ManPages/man3/byteorder.3n
./NextLibrary/Documentation/Unix/ManPages/man3/bzero.3
./NextLibrary/Documentation/Unix/ManPages/man3/cabs.3m
./NextLibrary/Documentation/Unix/ManPages/man3/calloc.3
./NextLibrary/Documentation/Unix/ManPages/man3/cbrt.3m
./NextLibrary/Documentation/Unix/ManPages/man3/ceil.3m
./NextLibrary/Documentation/Unix/ManPages/man3/cfree.3
./NextLibrary/Documentation/Unix/ManPages/man3/circle.3x
./NextLibrary/Documentation/Unix/ManPages/man3/clearerr.3s
./NextLibrary/Documentation/Unix/ManPages/man3/closedir.3
./NextLibrary/Documentation/Unix/ManPages/man3/closelog.3
./NextLibrary/Documentation/Unix/ManPages/man3/comp.3
./NextLibrary/Documentation/Unix/ManPages/man3/cont.3x
./NextLibrary/Documentation/Unix/ManPages/man3/convert_ts_to_tv.3
./NextLibrary/Documentation/Unix/ManPages/man3/copysign.3m
./NextLibrary/Documentation/Unix/ManPages/man3/cos.3m
./NextLibrary/Documentation/Unix/ManPages/man3/cosh.3m
./NextLibrary/Documentation/Unix/ManPages/man3/crypt.3
./NextLibrary/Documentation/Unix/ManPages/man3/ctime.3
./NextLibrary/Documentation/Unix/ManPages/man3/ctype.3
./NextLibrary/Documentation/Unix/ManPages/man3/curses.3x
./NextLibrary/Documentation/Unix/ManPages/man3/db.3
./NextLibrary/Documentation/Unix/ManPages/man3/dbm.3x
./NextLibrary/Documentation/Unix/ManPages/man3/dbm_clearerr.3
./NextLibrary/Documentation/Unix/ManPages/man3/dbm_close.3
./NextLibrary/Documentation/Unix/ManPages/man3/dbm_delete.3
./NextLibrary/Documentation/Unix/ManPages/man3/dbm_error.3
./NextLibrary/Documentation/Unix/ManPages/man3/dbm_fetch.3
./NextLibrary/Documentation/Unix/ManPages/man3/dbm_firstkey.3
./NextLibrary/Documentation/Unix/ManPages/man3/dbm_nextkey.3
./NextLibrary/Documentation/Unix/ManPages/man3/dbm_open.3
./NextLibrary/Documentation/Unix/ManPages/man3/dbm_store.3
./NextLibrary/Documentation/Unix/ManPages/man3/dbminit.3x
./NextLibrary/Documentation/Unix/ManPages/man3/delete.3x
./NextLibrary/Documentation/Unix/ManPages/man3/directory.3
./NextLibrary/Documentation/Unix/ManPages/man3/drem.3m
./NextLibrary/Documentation/Unix/ManPages/man3/ecvt.3
./NextLibrary/Documentation/Unix/ManPages/man3/edata.3
./NextLibrary/Documentation/Unix/ManPages/man3/encrypt.3

./NextLibrary/Documentation/Unix/ManPages/man3/end.3
./NextLibrary/Documentation/Unix/ManPages/man3/endfsent.3
./NextLibrary/Documentation/Unix/ManPages/man3/endgrent.3
./NextLibrary/Documentation/Unix/ManPages/man3/endhostent.3n
./NextLibrary/Documentation/Unix/ManPages/man3/endnetent.3n
./NextLibrary/Documentation/Unix/ManPages/man3/endprotoent.3n
./NextLibrary/Documentation/Unix/ManPages/man3/endpwent.3
./NextLibrary/Documentation/Unix/ManPages/man3/endservent.3n
./NextLibrary/Documentation/Unix/ManPages/man3/endttyent.3
./NextLibrary/Documentation/Unix/ManPages/man3/endusershell.3
./NextLibrary/Documentation/Unix/ManPages/man3/environ.3
./NextLibrary/Documentation/Unix/ManPages/man3/erase.3x
./NextLibrary/Documentation/Unix/ManPages/man3/erf.3m
./NextLibrary/Documentation/Unix/ManPages/man3/erfc.3m
./NextLibrary/Documentation/Unix/ManPages/man3/errlist.3
./NextLibrary/Documentation/Unix/ManPages/man3/etext.3
./NextLibrary/Documentation/Unix/ManPages/man3/ethers.3n
./NextLibrary/Documentation/Unix/ManPages/man3/execl.3
./NextLibrary/Documentation/Unix/ManPages/man3/execle.3
./NextLibrary/Documentation/Unix/ManPages/man3/execlp.3
./NextLibrary/Documentation/Unix/ManPages/man3/exect.3
./NextLibrary/Documentation/Unix/ManPages/man3/execv.3
./NextLibrary/Documentation/Unix/ManPages/man3/execve.3
./NextLibrary/Documentation/Unix/ManPages/man3/execvp.3
./NextLibrary/Documentation/Unix/ManPages/man3/exit.3
./NextLibrary/Documentation/Unix/ManPages/man3/exp.3m
./NextLibrary/Documentation/Unix/ManPages/man3/expm1.3m
./NextLibrary/Documentation/Unix/ManPages/man3/exportent.3
./NextLibrary/Documentation/Unix/ManPages/man3/fabs.3m
./NextLibrary/Documentation/Unix/ManPages/man3/fclose.3s
./NextLibrary/Documentation/Unix/ManPages/man3/fcvt.3
./NextLibrary/Documentation/Unix/ManPages/man3/fdopen.3s
./NextLibrary/Documentation/Unix/ManPages/man3/feof.3s
./NextLibrary/Documentation/Unix/ManPages/man3/ferror.3s
./NextLibrary/Documentation/Unix/ManPages/man3/fetch.3x
./NextLibrary/Documentation/Unix/ManPages/man3/fflush.3s
./NextLibrary/Documentation/Unix/ManPages/man3/ffs.3
./NextLibrary/Documentation/Unix/ManPages/man3/free.3
./NextLibrary/Documentation/Unix/ManPages/man3/fgetc.3s
./NextLibrary/Documentation/Unix/ManPages/man3/fgets.3s
./NextLibrary/Documentation/Unix/ManPages/man3/fileno.3s
./NextLibrary/Documentation/Unix/ManPages/man3/fileutil.3
./NextLibrary/Documentation/Unix/ManPages/man3/finite.3m
./NextLibrary/Documentation/Unix/ManPages/man3/firstkey.3x
./NextLibrary/Documentation/Unix/ManPages/man3/floor.3m
./NextLibrary/Documentation/Unix/ManPages/man3/fopen.3s
./NextLibrary/Documentation/Unix/ManPages/man3/fprintf.3s
./NextLibrary/Documentation/Unix/ManPages/man3/fputc.3s
./NextLibrary/Documentation/Unix/ManPages/man3/fputs.3s
./NextLibrary/Documentation/Unix/ManPages/man3/fread.3s
./NextLibrary/Documentation/Unix/ManPages/man3/freopen.3s

./NextLibrary/Documentation/Unix/ManPages/man3/frexp.3
./NextLibrary/Documentation/Unix/ManPages/man3/fscanf.3s
./NextLibrary/Documentation/Unix/ManPages/man3/fseek.3s
./NextLibrary/Documentation/Unix/ManPages/man3/ftell.3s
./NextLibrary/Documentation/Unix/ManPages/man3/ftime.3c
./NextLibrary/Documentation/Unix/ManPages/man3/fwrite.3s
./NextLibrary/Documentation/Unix/ManPages/man3/gamma.3m
./NextLibrary/Documentation/Unix/ManPages/man3/gcvt.3
./NextLibrary/Documentation/Unix/ManPages/man3/getc.3s
./NextLibrary/Documentation/Unix/ManPages/man3/getchar.3s
./NextLibrary/Documentation/Unix/ManPages/man3/getdisk.3
./NextLibrary/Documentation/Unix/ManPages/man3/getdiskbydev.3
./NextLibrary/Documentation/Unix/ManPages/man3/getdiskbyname.3
./NextLibrary/Documentation/Unix/ManPages/man3/getenv.3
./NextLibrary/Documentation/Unix/ManPages/man3/getfsent.3
./NextLibrary/Documentation/Unix/ManPages/man3/getfsfile.3
./NextLibrary/Documentation/Unix/ManPages/man3/getfsspec.3
./NextLibrary/Documentation/Unix/ManPages/man3/getfstype.3
./NextLibrary/Documentation/Unix/ManPages/man3/getgrent.3
./NextLibrary/Documentation/Unix/ManPages/man3/getgrgid.3
./NextLibrary/Documentation/Unix/ManPages/man3/getgrnam.3
./NextLibrary/Documentation/Unix/ManPages/man3/gethostbyaddr.3n
./NextLibrary/Documentation/Unix/ManPages/man3/gethostbyname.3n
./NextLibrary/Documentation/Unix/ManPages/man3/gethostent.3n
./NextLibrary/Documentation/Unix/ManPages/man3/getlogin.3
./NextLibrary/Documentation/Unix/ManPages/man3/getmachheaders.3
./NextLibrary/Documentation/Unix/ManPages/man3/getmntent.3
./NextLibrary/Documentation/Unix/ManPages/man3/getnetbyaddr.3n
./NextLibrary/Documentation/Unix/ManPages/man3/getnetbyname.3n
./NextLibrary/Documentation/Unix/ManPages/man3/getnetent.3n
./NextLibrary/Documentation/Unix/ManPages/man3/getopt.3
./NextLibrary/Documentation/Unix/ManPages/man3/getpass.3
./NextLibrary/Documentation/Unix/ManPages/man3/getprotobyname.3n
./NextLibrary/Documentation/Unix/ManPages/man3/getprotobynumber.3n
./NextLibrary/Documentation/Unix/ManPages/man3/getprotoent.3n
./NextLibrary/Documentation/Unix/ManPages/man3/getpw.3c
./NextLibrary/Documentation/Unix/ManPages/man3/getpwent.3
./NextLibrary/Documentation/Unix/ManPages/man3/getpwnam.3
./NextLibrary/Documentation/Unix/ManPages/man3/getpwuid.3
./NextLibrary/Documentation/Unix/ManPages/man3/getrpcbyname.3n
./NextLibrary/Documentation/Unix/ManPages/man3/getrpcbynumber.3n
./NextLibrary/Documentation/Unix/ManPages/man3/getrpcent.3n
./NextLibrary/Documentation/Unix/ManPages/man3/getrpcport.3r
./NextLibrary/Documentation/Unix/ManPages/man3/gets.3s
./NextLibrary/Documentation/Unix/ManPages/man3/getsectbyname.3
./NextLibrary/Documentation/Unix/ManPages/man3/getsectbynamefromheader.3
./NextLibrary/Documentation/Unix/ManPages/man3/getsectdata.3
./NextLibrary/Documentation/Unix/ManPages/man3/getsectdatafromheader.3
./NextLibrary/Documentation/Unix/ManPages/man3/getsectdatafromlib.3
./NextLibrary/Documentation/Unix/ManPages/man3/getsegbyname.3
./NextLibrary/Documentation/Unix/ManPages/man3/getservbyname.3n

./NextLibrary/Documentation/Unix/ManPages/man3/getservbyport.3n
./NextLibrary/Documentation/Unix/ManPages/man3/getservent.3n
./NextLibrary/Documentation/Unix/ManPages/man3/getttyent.3
./NextLibrary/Documentation/Unix/ManPages/man3/getttynam.3
./NextLibrary/Documentation/Unix/ManPages/man3/getusershell.3
./NextLibrary/Documentation/Unix/ManPages/man3/getw.3s
./NextLibrary/Documentation/Unix/ManPages/man3/getwd.3
./NextLibrary/Documentation/Unix/ManPages/man3/gmtime.3
./NextLibrary/Documentation/Unix/ManPages/man3/gtty.3c
./NextLibrary/Documentation/Unix/ManPages/man3/htonl.3n
./NextLibrary/Documentation/Unix/ManPages/man3/htons.3n
./NextLibrary/Documentation/Unix/ManPages/man3/hypot.3m
./NextLibrary/Documentation/Unix/ManPages/man3/ieee.3m
./NextLibrary/Documentation/Unix/ManPages/man3/index.3
./NextLibrary/Documentation/Unix/ManPages/man3/inet.3n
./NextLibrary/Documentation/Unix/ManPages/man3/inet_addr.3n
./NextLibrary/Documentation/Unix/ManPages/man3/inet_lnaof.3n
./NextLibrary/Documentation/Unix/ManPages/man3/inet_makeaddr.3n
./NextLibrary/Documentation/Unix/ManPages/man3/inet_netof.3n
./NextLibrary/Documentation/Unix/ManPages/man3/inet_network.3n
./NextLibrary/Documentation/Unix/ManPages/man3/inet_ntoa.3n
./NextLibrary/Documentation/Unix/ManPages/man3/initgroups.3
./NextLibrary/Documentation/Unix/ManPages/man3/initstate.3
./NextLibrary/Documentation/Unix/ManPages/man3/insque.3
./NextLibrary/Documentation/Unix/ManPages/man3/intro.3
./NextLibrary/Documentation/Unix/ManPages/man3/intro.3r
./NextLibrary/Documentation/Unix/ManPages/man3/isalnum.3
./NextLibrary/Documentation/Unix/ManPages/man3/isalpha.3
./NextLibrary/Documentation/Unix/ManPages/man3/isascii.3
./NextLibrary/Documentation/Unix/ManPages/man3/isatty.3
./NextLibrary/Documentation/Unix/ManPages/man3/iscntrl.3
./NextLibrary/Documentation/Unix/ManPages/man3/isdigit.3
./NextLibrary/Documentation/Unix/ManPages/man3/islower.3
./NextLibrary/Documentation/Unix/ManPages/man3/isprint.3
./NextLibrary/Documentation/Unix/ManPages/man3/ispunct.3
./NextLibrary/Documentation/Unix/ManPages/man3/isspace.3
./NextLibrary/Documentation/Unix/ManPages/man3/isupper.3
./NextLibrary/Documentation/Unix/ManPages/man3/isxdigit.3
./NextLibrary/Documentation/Unix/ManPages/man3/ix.3
./NextLibrary/Documentation/Unix/ManPages/man3/j0.3m
./NextLibrary/Documentation/Unix/ManPages/man3/j1.3m
./NextLibrary/Documentation/Unix/ManPages/man3/jn.3m
./NextLibrary/Documentation/Unix/ManPages/man3/label.3x
./NextLibrary/Documentation/Unix/ManPages/man3/ldexp.3
./NextLibrary/Documentation/Unix/ManPages/man3/lgamma.3m
./NextLibrary/Documentation/Unix/ManPages/man3/lib2648.3x
./NextLibrary/Documentation/Unix/ManPages/man3/libudp.3
./NextLibrary/Documentation/Unix/ManPages/man3/line.3x
./NextLibrary/Documentation/Unix/ManPages/man3/linemod.3x
./NextLibrary/Documentation/Unix/ManPages/man3/localtime.3
./NextLibrary/Documentation/Unix/ManPages/man3/log.3m

./NextLibrary/Documentation/Unix/ManPages/man3/log10.3m
./NextLibrary/Documentation/Unix/ManPages/man3/log1p.3m
./NextLibrary/Documentation/Unix/ManPages/man3/logb.3m
./NextLibrary/Documentation/Unix/ManPages/man3/longjmp.3
./NextLibrary/Documentation/Unix/ManPages/man3/mach_error.3
./NextLibrary/Documentation/Unix/ManPages/man3/mach_init.3
./NextLibrary/Documentation/Unix/ManPages/man3/malloc.3
./NextLibrary/Documentation/Unix/ManPages/man3/malloc_debug.3
./NextLibrary/Documentation/Unix/ManPages/man3/malloc_error.3
./NextLibrary/Documentation/Unix/ManPages/man3/malloc_good_size.3
./NextLibrary/Documentation/Unix/ManPages/man3/malloc_size.3
./NextLibrary/Documentation/Unix/ManPages/man3/math.3m
./NextLibrary/Documentation/Unix/ManPages/man3/mkstemp.3
./NextLibrary/Documentation/Unix/ManPages/man3/mktemp.3
./NextLibrary/Documentation/Unix/ManPages/man3/modf.3
./NextLibrary/Documentation/Unix/ManPages/man3/moncontrol.3
./NextLibrary/Documentation/Unix/ManPages/man3/monitor.3
./NextLibrary/Documentation/Unix/ManPages/man3/monstartup.3
./NextLibrary/Documentation/Unix/ManPages/man3/mount.3r
./NextLibrary/Documentation/Unix/ManPages/man3/move.3x
./NextLibrary/Documentation/Unix/ManPages/man3/mp.3x
./NextLibrary/Documentation/Unix/ManPages/man3/mstats.3
./NextLibrary/Documentation/Unix/ManPages/man3/ndbm.3
./NextLibrary/Documentation/Unix/ManPages/man3/netinfo.3n
./NextLibrary/Documentation/Unix/ManPages/man3/network.3n
./NextLibrary/Documentation/Unix/ManPages/man3/nextkey.3x
./NextLibrary/Documentation/Unix/ManPages/man3/nice.3c
./NextLibrary/Documentation/Unix/ManPages/man3/nlist.3
./NextLibrary/Documentation/Unix/ManPages/man3/ns.3n
./NextLibrary/Documentation/Unix/ManPages/man3/ns_addr.3n
./NextLibrary/Documentation/Unix/ManPages/man3/ns_ntoa.3n
./NextLibrary/Documentation/Unix/ManPages/man3/ntoa.3n
./NextLibrary/Documentation/Unix/ManPages/man3/ntohl.3n
./NextLibrary/Documentation/Unix/ManPages/man3/ntohs.3n
./NextLibrary/Documentation/Unix/ManPages/man3/opendir.3
./NextLibrary/Documentation/Unix/ManPages/man3/openlog.3
./NextLibrary/Documentation/Unix/ManPages/man3/openpl.3x
./NextLibrary/Documentation/Unix/ManPages/man3/pathutil.3
./NextLibrary/Documentation/Unix/ManPages/man3/pause.3c
./NextLibrary/Documentation/Unix/ManPages/man3/pclose.3
./NextLibrary/Documentation/Unix/ManPages/man3/perror.3s
./NextLibrary/Documentation/Unix/ManPages/man3/plot.3x
./NextLibrary/Documentation/Unix/ManPages/man3/point.3x
./NextLibrary/Documentation/Unix/ManPages/man3/popen.3
./NextLibrary/Documentation/Unix/ManPages/man3/pow.3m
./NextLibrary/Documentation/Unix/ManPages/man3/printerdb.3
./NextLibrary/Documentation/Unix/ManPages/man3/printf.3s
./NextLibrary/Documentation/Unix/ManPages/man3/psignal.3
./NextLibrary/Documentation/Unix/ManPages/man3/putc.3s
./NextLibrary/Documentation/Unix/ManPages/man3/putchar.3s
./NextLibrary/Documentation/Unix/ManPages/man3/puts.3s

./NextLibrary/Documentation/Unix/ManPages/man3/putw.3s
./NextLibrary/Documentation/Unix/ManPages/man3/qsort.3
./NextLibrary/Documentation/Unix/ManPages/man3/quit.3
./NextLibrary/Documentation/Unix/ManPages/man3/rand.3c
./NextLibrary/Documentation/Unix/ManPages/man3/random.3
./NextLibrary/Documentation/Unix/ManPages/man3/rcmd.3
./NextLibrary/Documentation/Unix/ManPages/man3/re_comp.3
./NextLibrary/Documentation/Unix/ManPages/man3/re_exec.3
./NextLibrary/Documentation/Unix/ManPages/man3/readdir.3
./NextLibrary/Documentation/Unix/ManPages/man3/realloc.3
./NextLibrary/Documentation/Unix/ManPages/man3/regex.3
./NextLibrary/Documentation/Unix/ManPages/man3/remove.3s
./NextLibrary/Documentation/Unix/ManPages/man3/remque.3
./NextLibrary/Documentation/Unix/ManPages/man3/resolver.3
./NextLibrary/Documentation/Unix/ManPages/man3/rewind.3s
./NextLibrary/Documentation/Unix/ManPages/man3/rewinddir.3
./NextLibrary/Documentation/Unix/ManPages/man3/rex.3r
./NextLibrary/Documentation/Unix/ManPages/man3/rexec.3
./NextLibrary/Documentation/Unix/ManPages/man3/rindex.3
./NextLibrary/Documentation/Unix/ManPages/man3/rint.3m
./NextLibrary/Documentation/Unix/ManPages/man3/rnusers.3r
./NextLibrary/Documentation/Unix/ManPages/man3/rpc.3n
./NextLibrary/Documentation/Unix/ManPages/man3/rresvport.3
./NextLibrary/Documentation/Unix/ManPages/man3/ruserok.3
./NextLibrary/Documentation/Unix/ManPages/man3/rusers.3r
./NextLibrary/Documentation/Unix/ManPages/man3/rwall.3r
./NextLibrary/Documentation/Unix/ManPages/man3/scalb.3m
./NextLibrary/Documentation/Unix/ManPages/man3/scandir.3
./NextLibrary/Documentation/Unix/ManPages/man3/scanf.3s
./NextLibrary/Documentation/Unix/ManPages/man3/search.3
./NextLibrary/Documentation/Unix/ManPages/man3/seekdir.3
./NextLibrary/Documentation/Unix/ManPages/man3/service_checkin.3
./NextLibrary/Documentation/Unix/ManPages/man3/setbuf.3s
./NextLibrary/Documentation/Unix/ManPages/man3/setbuffer.3s
./NextLibrary/Documentation/Unix/ManPages/man3/setegid.3
./NextLibrary/Documentation/Unix/ManPages/man3/seteuid.3
./NextLibrary/Documentation/Unix/ManPages/man3/setfsent.3
./NextLibrary/Documentation/Unix/ManPages/man3/setgid.3
./NextLibrary/Documentation/Unix/ManPages/man3/setgrent.3
./NextLibrary/Documentation/Unix/ManPages/man3/sethostent.3n
./NextLibrary/Documentation/Unix/ManPages/man3/sethostfile.3n
./NextLibrary/Documentation/Unix/ManPages/man3/setjmp.3
./NextLibrary/Documentation/Unix/ManPages/man3/setkey.3
./NextLibrary/Documentation/Unix/ManPages/man3/setlinebuf.3s
./NextLibrary/Documentation/Unix/ManPages/man3/setlogmask.3
./NextLibrary/Documentation/Unix/ManPages/man3/setnetent.3n
./NextLibrary/Documentation/Unix/ManPages/man3/setprotoent.3n
./NextLibrary/Documentation/Unix/ManPages/man3/setpwent.3
./NextLibrary/Documentation/Unix/ManPages/man3/setpwfile.3
./NextLibrary/Documentation/Unix/ManPages/man3/setrgid.3
./NextLibrary/Documentation/Unix/ManPages/man3/setruid.3

./NextLibrary/Documentation/Unix/ManPages/man3/setservent.3n
./NextLibrary/Documentation/Unix/ManPages/man3/setstate.3
./NextLibrary/Documentation/Unix/ManPages/man3/setttyent.3
./NextLibrary/Documentation/Unix/ManPages/man3/setuid.3
./NextLibrary/Documentation/Unix/ManPages/man3/setusershell.3
./NextLibrary/Documentation/Unix/ManPages/man3/setvbuf.3s
./NextLibrary/Documentation/Unix/ManPages/man3/siginterrupt.3
./NextLibrary/Documentation/Unix/ManPages/man3/signal.3c
./NextLibrary/Documentation/Unix/ManPages/man3/sin.3m
./NextLibrary/Documentation/Unix/ManPages/man3/sinh.3m
./NextLibrary/Documentation/Unix/ManPages/man3/sleep.3
./NextLibrary/Documentation/Unix/ManPages/man3/sopen.3
./NextLibrary/Documentation/Unix/ManPages/man3/space.3x
./NextLibrary/Documentation/Unix/ManPages/man3/spell.3
./NextLibrary/Documentation/Unix/ManPages/man3/sprintf.3s
./NextLibrary/Documentation/Unix/ManPages/man3/sqrt.3m
./NextLibrary/Documentation/Unix/ManPages/man3/srand.3c
./NextLibrary/Documentation/Unix/ManPages/man3/srandom.3
./NextLibrary/Documentation/Unix/ManPages/man3/sscanf.3s
./NextLibrary/Documentation/Unix/ManPages/man3/stdio.3s
./NextLibrary/Documentation/Unix/ManPages/man3/store.3x
./NextLibrary/Documentation/Unix/ManPages/man3/strcat.3
./NextLibrary/Documentation/Unix/ManPages/man3/strcmp.3
./NextLibrary/Documentation/Unix/ManPages/man3/strcpy.3
./NextLibrary/Documentation/Unix/ManPages/man3/strerror.3
./NextLibrary/Documentation/Unix/ManPages/man3/string.3
./NextLibrary/Documentation/Unix/ManPages/man3/strlen.3
./NextLibrary/Documentation/Unix/ManPages/man3/strncat.3
./NextLibrary/Documentation/Unix/ManPages/man3/strncmp.3
./NextLibrary/Documentation/Unix/ManPages/man3/strncpy.3
./NextLibrary/Documentation/Unix/ManPages/man3/strutil.3
./NextLibrary/Documentation/Unix/ManPages/man3/stty.3c
./NextLibrary/Documentation/Unix/ManPages/man3/swab.3
./NextLibrary/Documentation/Unix/ManPages/man3/sys.3
./NextLibrary/Documentation/Unix/ManPages/man3/sys_errlist.3
./NextLibrary/Documentation/Unix/ManPages/man3/sys_nerr.3
./NextLibrary/Documentation/Unix/ManPages/man3/sys_siglist.3
./NextLibrary/Documentation/Unix/ManPages/man3/syslog.3
./NextLibrary/Documentation/Unix/ManPages/man3/system.3
./NextLibrary/Documentation/Unix/ManPages/man3/tan.3m
./NextLibrary/Documentation/Unix/ManPages/man3/tanh.3m
./NextLibrary/Documentation/Unix/ManPages/man3/telldir.3
./NextLibrary/Documentation/Unix/ManPages/man3/termcap.3x
./NextLibrary/Documentation/Unix/ManPages/man3/text.3
./NextLibrary/Documentation/Unix/ManPages/man3/tgetent.3x
./NextLibrary/Documentation/Unix/ManPages/man3/tgetflag.3x
./NextLibrary/Documentation/Unix/ManPages/man3/tgetnum.3x
./NextLibrary/Documentation/Unix/ManPages/man3/tgetstr.3x
./NextLibrary/Documentation/Unix/ManPages/man3/tgoto.3x
./NextLibrary/Documentation/Unix/ManPages/man3/threads.3
./NextLibrary/Documentation/Unix/ManPages/man3/time.3c

./NextLibrary/Documentation/Unix/ManPages/man3/times.3c
./NextLibrary/Documentation/Unix/ManPages/man3/timezone.3
./NextLibrary/Documentation/Unix/ManPages/man3/tmpfile.3s
./NextLibrary/Documentation/Unix/ManPages/man3/tmpnam.3s
./NextLibrary/Documentation/Unix/ManPages/man3/toascii.3
./NextLibrary/Documentation/Unix/ManPages/man3/tolower.3
./NextLibrary/Documentation/Unix/ManPages/man3/toupper.3
./NextLibrary/Documentation/Unix/ManPages/man3/tputs.3x
./NextLibrary/Documentation/Unix/ManPages/man3/ttyname.3
./NextLibrary/Documentation/Unix/ManPages/man3/ttyslot.3
./NextLibrary/Documentation/Unix/ManPages/man3/ualarm.3
./NextLibrary/Documentation/Unix/ManPages/man3/ungetc.3s
./NextLibrary/Documentation/Unix/ManPages/man3/usleep.3
./NextLibrary/Documentation/Unix/ManPages/man3/utime.3c
./NextLibrary/Documentation/Unix/ManPages/man3/valloc.3c
./NextLibrary/Documentation/Unix/ManPages/man3/varargs.3
./NextLibrary/Documentation/Unix/ManPages/man3/vfprintf.3s
./NextLibrary/Documentation/Unix/ManPages/man3/vfree.3
./NextLibrary/Documentation/Unix/ManPages/man3/vlimit.3c
./NextLibrary/Documentation/Unix/ManPages/man3/vprintf.3s
./NextLibrary/Documentation/Unix/ManPages/man3/vsprintf.3s
./NextLibrary/Documentation/Unix/ManPages/man3/vtimes.3c
./NextLibrary/Documentation/Unix/ManPages/man3/webster.3
./NextLibrary/Documentation/Unix/ManPages/man3/wftable.3
./NextLibrary/Documentation/Unix/ManPages/man3/xdr.3n
./NextLibrary/Documentation/Unix/ManPages/man3/y0.3m
./NextLibrary/Documentation/Unix/ManPages/man3/y1.3m
./NextLibrary/Documentation/Unix/ManPages/man3/yn.3m
./NextLibrary/Documentation/Unix/ManPages/man3/yp_all.3n
./NextLibrary/Documentation/Unix/ManPages/man3/yp_bind.3n
./NextLibrary/Documentation/Unix/ManPages/man3/yp_first.3n
./NextLibrary/Documentation/Unix/ManPages/man3/yp_get_default_domain.3n
./NextLibrary/Documentation/Unix/ManPages/man3/yp_master.3n
./NextLibrary/Documentation/Unix/ManPages/man3/yp_match.3n
./NextLibrary/Documentation/Unix/ManPages/man3/yp_next.3n
./NextLibrary/Documentation/Unix/ManPages/man3/yp_order.3n
./NextLibrary/Documentation/Unix/ManPages/man3/yp_unbind.3n
./NextLibrary/Documentation/Unix/ManPages/man3/ypclnt.3n
./NextLibrary/Documentation/Unix/ManPages/man3/yperr_string.3n
./NextLibrary/Documentation/Unix/ManPages/man3/yppasswd.3r
./NextLibrary/Documentation/Unix/ManPages/man3/ypprot_err.3n
./NextLibrary/Documentation/Unix/ManPages/man3/.places
./NextLibrary/Documentation/Unix/ManPages/man4
./NextLibrary/Documentation/Unix/ManPages/man4/arp.4p
./NextLibrary/Documentation/Unix/ManPages/man4/bk.4
./NextLibrary/Documentation/Unix/ManPages/man4/en.4
./NextLibrary/Documentation/Unix/ManPages/man4/evs.4
./NextLibrary/Documentation/Unix/ManPages/man4/icmp.4p
./NextLibrary/Documentation/Unix/ManPages/man4/if.4n
./NextLibrary/Documentation/Unix/ManPages/man4/inet.4f
./NextLibrary/Documentation/Unix/ManPages/man4/intro.4

```
./NextLibrary/Documentation/Unix/ManPages/man4/intro.4n          ./NextLibrary/Documentation/Unix/ManPages/man5/mtab.5
./NextLibrary/Documentation/Unix/ManPages/man4/ip.4p             ./NextLibrary/Documentation/Unix/ManPages/man5/netgroup.5
./NextLibrary/Documentation/Unix/ManPages/man4/kmem.4            ./NextLibrary/Documentation/Unix/ManPages/man5/netinfo.5
./NextLibrary/Documentation/Unix/ManPages/man4/lo.4             ./NextLibrary/Documentation/Unix/ManPages/man5/networks.5
./NextLibrary/Documentation/Unix/ManPages/man4/mem.4            ./NextLibrary/Documentation/Unix/ManPages/man5/passwd.5
./NextLibrary/Documentation/Unix/ManPages/man4/midi.4           ./NextLibrary/Documentation/Unix/ManPages/man5/phones.5
./NextLibrary/Documentation/Unix/ManPages/man4/midi_timer.4      ./NextLibrary/Documentation/Unix/ManPages/man5/plot.5
./NextLibrary/Documentation/Unix/ManPages/man4/networking.4n     ./NextLibrary/Documentation/Unix/ManPages/man5/printcap.5
./NextLibrary/Documentation/Unix/ManPages/man4/nfs.4p           ./NextLibrary/Documentation/Unix/ManPages/man5/protocols.5
./NextLibrary/Documentation/Unix/ManPages/man4/np.4             ./NextLibrary/Documentation/Unix/ManPages/man5/rcsfile.5
./NextLibrary/Documentation/Unix/ManPages/man4/null.4           ./NextLibrary/Documentation/Unix/ManPages/man5/remote.5
./NextLibrary/Documentation/Unix/ManPages/man4/pty.4            ./NextLibrary/Documentation/Unix/ManPages/man5/resolver.5
./NextLibrary/Documentation/Unix/ManPages/man4/sd.4            ./NextLibrary/Documentation/Unix/ManPages/man5/rmtab.5
./NextLibrary/Documentation/Unix/ManPages/man4/sg.4            ./NextLibrary/Documentation/Unix/ManPages/man5/rpc.5
./NextLibrary/Documentation/Unix/ManPages/man4/sound.4          ./NextLibrary/Documentation/Unix/ManPages/man5/services.5
./NextLibrary/Documentation/Unix/ManPages/man4/st.4            ./NextLibrary/Documentation/Unix/ManPages/man5/stab.5
./NextLibrary/Documentation/Unix/ManPages/man4/tb.4            ./NextLibrary/Documentation/Unix/ManPages/man5/swaptab.5
./NextLibrary/Documentation/Unix/ManPages/man4/tcp.4p           ./NextLibrary/Documentation/Unix/ManPages/man5/tar.5
./NextLibrary/Documentation/Unix/ManPages/man4/tty.4           ./NextLibrary/Documentation/Unix/ManPages/man5/termcap.5
./NextLibrary/Documentation/Unix/ManPages/man4/udp.4p           ./NextLibrary/Documentation/Unix/ManPages/man5/tp.5
./NextLibrary/Documentation/Unix/ManPages/man4/zs.4            ./NextLibrary/Documentation/Unix/ManPages/man5/ttys.5
./NextLibrary/Documentation/Unix/ManPages/man4/.places         ./NextLibrary/Documentation/Unix/ManPages/man5/types.5
./NextLibrary/Documentation/Unix/ManPages/man5               ./NextLibrary/Documentation/Unix/ManPages/man5/tzfile.5
./NextLibrary/Documentation/Unix/ManPages/man5/L-devices.5      ./NextLibrary/Documentation/Unix/ManPages/man5/utmp.5
./NextLibrary/Documentation/Unix/ManPages/man5/L-dialcodes.5     ./NextLibrary/Documentation/Unix/ManPages/man5/uuencode.5
./NextLibrary/Documentation/Unix/ManPages/man5/L.aliases.5      ./NextLibrary/Documentation/Unix/ManPages/man5/vfont.5
./NextLibrary/Documentation/Unix/ManPages/man5/L.cmds.5        ./NextLibrary/Documentation/Unix/ManPages/man5/vgrindefs.5
./NextLibrary/Documentation/Unix/ManPages/man5/L.sys.5         ./NextLibrary/Documentation/Unix/ManPages/man5/wtmp.5
./NextLibrary/Documentation/Unix/ManPages/man5/Mach-0.5        ./NextLibrary/Documentation/Unix/ManPages/man5/ypfiles.5
./NextLibrary/Documentation/Unix/ManPages/man5/USERFILE.5      ./NextLibrary/Documentation/Unix/ManPages/man5/.places
./NextLibrary/Documentation/Unix/ManPages/man5/a.out.5         ./NextLibrary/Documentation/Unix/ManPages/man6
./NextLibrary/Documentation/Unix/ManPages/man5/acct.5         ./NextLibrary/Documentation/Unix/ManPages/man6/.places
./NextLibrary/Documentation/Unix/ManPages/man5/aliases.5       ./NextLibrary/Documentation/Unix/ManPages/man7
./NextLibrary/Documentation/Unix/ManPages/man5/ar.5          ./NextLibrary/Documentation/Unix/ManPages/man7/afm.7
./NextLibrary/Documentation/Unix/ManPages/man5/bootparams.5     ./NextLibrary/Documentation/Unix/ManPages/man7/ascii.7
./NextLibrary/Documentation/Unix/ManPages/man5/dbx.5          ./NextLibrary/Documentation/Unix/ManPages/man7/environ.7
./NextLibrary/Documentation/Unix/ManPages/man5/dir.5          ./NextLibrary/Documentation/Unix/ManPages/man7/eqnchar.7
./NextLibrary/Documentation/Unix/ManPages/man5/disktab.5       ./NextLibrary/Documentation/Unix/ManPages/man7/hier.7
./NextLibrary/Documentation/Unix/ManPages/man5/dump.5         ./NextLibrary/Documentation/Unix/ManPages/man7/intro.7
./NextLibrary/Documentation/Unix/ManPages/man5/dumpdates.5      ./NextLibrary/Documentation/Unix/ManPages/man7/mailaddr.7
./NextLibrary/Documentation/Unix/ManPages/man5/ethers.5        ./NextLibrary/Documentation/Unix/ManPages/man7/man.7
./NextLibrary/Documentation/Unix/ManPages/man5/exports.5       ./NextLibrary/Documentation/Unix/ManPages/man7/me.7
./NextLibrary/Documentation/Unix/ManPages/man5/fs.5          ./NextLibrary/Documentation/Unix/ManPages/man7/ms.7
./NextLibrary/Documentation/Unix/ManPages/man5/fstab.5        ./NextLibrary/Documentation/Unix/ManPages/man7/postscript.7
./NextLibrary/Documentation/Unix/ManPages/man5/gettytab.5      ./NextLibrary/Documentation/Unix/ManPages/man7/term.7
./NextLibrary/Documentation/Unix/ManPages/man5/group.5        ./NextLibrary/Documentation/Unix/ManPages/man7/.places
./NextLibrary/Documentation/Unix/ManPages/man5/hosts.5        ./NextLibrary/Documentation/Unix/ManPages/man8
./NextLibrary/Documentation/Unix/ManPages/man5/hosts.equiv.5    ./NextLibrary/Documentation/Unix/ManPages/man8/NSWSd.8c
./NextLibrary/Documentation/Unix/ManPages/man5/inode.5        ./NextLibrary/Documentation/Unix/ManPages/man8/ac.8
./NextLibrary/Documentation/Unix/ManPages/man5/map3270.5      ./NextLibrary/Documentation/Unix/ManPages/man8/accton.8
./NextLibrary/Documentation/Unix/ManPages/man5/mntent.5       ./NextLibrary/Documentation/Unix/ManPages/man8/adduser.8
```

./NextLibrary/Documentation/Unix/ManPages/man8/arp.8c
./NextLibrary/Documentation/Unix/ManPages/man8/autodiskmount.8
./NextLibrary/Documentation/Unix/ManPages/man8/biod.8
./NextLibrary/Documentation/Unix/ManPages/man8/bootparamd.8
./NextLibrary/Documentation/Unix/ManPages/man8/bootpd.8
./NextLibrary/Documentation/Unix/ManPages/man8/bugfiler.8
./NextLibrary/Documentation/Unix/ManPages/man8/catman.8
./NextLibrary/Documentation/Unix/ManPages/man8/checkswap.8
./NextLibrary/Documentation/Unix/ManPages/man8/chown.8
./NextLibrary/Documentation/Unix/ManPages/man8/clri.8
./NextLibrary/Documentation/Unix/ManPages/man8/comsat.8c
./NextLibrary/Documentation/Unix/ManPages/man8/cron.8
./NextLibrary/Documentation/Unix/ManPages/man8/dcheck.8
./NextLibrary/Documentation/Unix/ManPages/man8/disk.8
./NextLibrary/Documentation/Unix/ManPages/man8/drtest.8
./NextLibrary/Documentation/Unix/ManPages/man8/dump.8
./NextLibrary/Documentation/Unix/ManPages/man8/dumpfs.8
./NextLibrary/Documentation/Unix/ManPages/man8/exportfs.8
./NextLibrary/Documentation/Unix/ManPages/man8/fingerd.8c
./NextLibrary/Documentation/Unix/ManPages/man8/fsck.8
./NextLibrary/Documentation/Unix/ManPages/man8/fsirand.8
./NextLibrary/Documentation/Unix/ManPages/man8/ftpd.8c
./NextLibrary/Documentation/Unix/ManPages/man8/getty.8
./NextLibrary/Documentation/Unix/ManPages/man8/halt.8
./NextLibrary/Documentation/Unix/ManPages/man8/icheck.8
./NextLibrary/Documentation/Unix/ManPages/man8/ifconfig.8c
./NextLibrary/Documentation/Unix/ManPages/man8/inetd.8
./NextLibrary/Documentation/Unix/ManPages/man8/init.8
./NextLibrary/Documentation/Unix/ManPages/man8/intro.8
./NextLibrary/Documentation/Unix/ManPages/man8/kern_loader.8
./NextLibrary/Documentation/Unix/ManPages/man8/kgmon.8
./NextLibrary/Documentation/Unix/ManPages/man8/kl_util.8
./NextLibrary/Documentation/Unix/ManPages/man8/lookupd.8
./NextLibrary/Documentation/Unix/ManPages/man8/lpc.8
./NextLibrary/Documentation/Unix/ManPages/man8/lpd.8
./NextLibrary/Documentation/Unix/ManPages/man8/mach_swapon.8
./NextLibrary/Documentation/Unix/ManPages/man8/mailq.8
./NextLibrary/Documentation/Unix/ManPages/man8/makedbm.8
./NextLibrary/Documentation/Unix/ManPages/man8/makedev.8
./NextLibrary/Documentation/Unix/ManPages/man8/makekey.8
./NextLibrary/Documentation/Unix/ManPages/man8/md.8
./NextLibrary/Documentation/Unix/ManPages/man8/mkfile.8
./NextLibrary/Documentation/Unix/ManPages/man8/mkfs.8
./NextLibrary/Documentation/Unix/ManPages/man8/mkhosts.8
./NextLibrary/Documentation/Unix/ManPages/man8/mklost+found.8
./NextLibrary/Documentation/Unix/ManPages/man8/mknod.8
./NextLibrary/Documentation/Unix/ManPages/man8/mkpasswd.8
./NextLibrary/Documentation/Unix/ManPages/man8/mkproto.8
./NextLibrary/Documentation/Unix/ManPages/man8/mount.8
./NextLibrary/Documentation/Unix/ManPages/man8/mountd.8c
./NextLibrary/Documentation/Unix/ManPages/man8/msgwrap.8

./NextLibrary/Documentation/Unix/ManPages/man8/named.8
./NextLibrary/Documentation/Unix/ManPages/man8/ncheck.8
./NextLibrary/Documentation/Unix/ManPages/man8/netinfod.8
./NextLibrary/Documentation/Unix/ManPages/man8/newclient.8
./NextLibrary/Documentation/Unix/ManPages/man8/newfs.8
./NextLibrary/Documentation/Unix/ManPages/man8/nfsd.8
./NextLibrary/Documentation/Unix/ManPages/man8/nfsstat.8
./NextLibrary/Documentation/Unix/ManPages/man8/nibindd.8
./NextLibrary/Documentation/Unix/ManPages/man8/nidomain.8
./NextLibrary/Documentation/Unix/ManPages/man8/nmserver.8
./NextLibrary/Documentation/Unix/ManPages/man8/nppower.8
./NextLibrary/Documentation/Unix/ManPages/man8/nu.8
./NextLibrary/Documentation/Unix/ManPages/man8/pac.8
./NextLibrary/Documentation/Unix/ManPages/man8/ping.8
./NextLibrary/Documentation/Unix/ManPages/man8/portmap.8c
./NextLibrary/Documentation/Unix/ManPages/man8/pscatmap.8
./NextLibrary/Documentation/Unix/ManPages/man8/pscomm.8
./NextLibrary/Documentation/Unix/ManPages/man8/rc.8
./NextLibrary/Documentation/Unix/ManPages/man8/rc.boot.8
./NextLibrary/Documentation/Unix/ManPages/man8/rc.local.8
./NextLibrary/Documentation/Unix/ManPages/man8/rdump.8c
./NextLibrary/Documentation/Unix/ManPages/man8/reboot.8
./NextLibrary/Documentation/Unix/ManPages/man8/renice.8
./NextLibrary/Documentation/Unix/ManPages/man8/restore.8
./NextLibrary/Documentation/Unix/ManPages/man8/rexd.8c
./NextLibrary/Documentation/Unix/ManPages/man8/rexecd.8c
./NextLibrary/Documentation/Unix/ManPages/man8/rlogind.8c
./NextLibrary/Documentation/Unix/ManPages/man8/rmt.8c
./NextLibrary/Documentation/Unix/ManPages/man8/route.8c
./NextLibrary/Documentation/Unix/ManPages/man8/routed.8c
./NextLibrary/Documentation/Unix/ManPages/man8/rpc.bootparamd.8
./NextLibrary/Documentation/Unix/ManPages/man8/rpc.mountd.8c
./NextLibrary/Documentation/Unix/ManPages/man8/rpc.rstatd.8c
./NextLibrary/Documentation/Unix/ManPages/man8/rpc.rusersd.8c
./NextLibrary/Documentation/Unix/ManPages/man8/rpc.rwalld.8c
./NextLibrary/Documentation/Unix/ManPages/man8/rpc.sprayd.8c
./NextLibrary/Documentation/Unix/ManPages/man8/rpc.yppasswdd.8c
./NextLibrary/Documentation/Unix/ManPages/man8/rpcinfo.8
./NextLibrary/Documentation/Unix/ManPages/man8/rpcinfo.8c
./NextLibrary/Documentation/Unix/ManPages/man8/rrestore.8c
./NextLibrary/Documentation/Unix/ManPages/man8/rshd.8c
./NextLibrary/Documentation/Unix/ManPages/man8/rstatd.8c
./NextLibrary/Documentation/Unix/ManPages/man8/rusersd.8c
./NextLibrary/Documentation/Unix/ManPages/man8/rwalld.8c
./NextLibrary/Documentation/Unix/ManPages/man8/rwhod.8c
./NextLibrary/Documentation/Unix/ManPages/man8/sa.8
./NextLibrary/Documentation/Unix/ManPages/man8/sendmail.8
./NextLibrary/Documentation/Unix/ManPages/man8/showmount.8
./NextLibrary/Documentation/Unix/ManPages/man8/shutdown.8
./NextLibrary/Documentation/Unix/ManPages/man8/slattach.8c
./NextLibrary/Documentation/Unix/ManPages/man8/snd_register.8

```
./NextLibrary/Documentation/Unix/ManPages/man8/sprayd.8c
./NextLibrary/Documentation/Unix/ManPages/man8/sticky.8
./NextLibrary/Documentation/Unix/ManPages/man8/sync.8
./NextLibrary/Documentation/Unix/ManPages/man8/syslogd.8
./NextLibrary/Documentation/Unix/ManPages/man8/talkd.8c
./NextLibrary/Documentation/Unix/ManPages/man8/telnetd.8c
./NextLibrary/Documentation/Unix/ManPages/man8/tftpd.8c
./NextLibrary/Documentation/Unix/ManPages/man8/timed.8
./NextLibrary/Documentation/Unix/ManPages/man8/timedc.8
./NextLibrary/Documentation/Unix/ManPages/man8/tnamed.8c
./NextLibrary/Documentation/Unix/ManPages/man8/trpt.8c
./NextLibrary/Documentation/Unix/ManPages/man8/trsp.8c
./NextLibrary/Documentation/Unix/ManPages/man8/tunefs.8
./NextLibrary/Documentation/Unix/ManPages/man8/umount.8
./NextLibrary/Documentation/Unix/ManPages/man8/update.8
./NextLibrary/Documentation/Unix/ManPages/man8/uucico.8c
./NextLibrary/Documentation/Unix/ManPages/man8/uuclean.8c
./NextLibrary/Documentation/Unix/ManPages/man8/uucpd.8c
./NextLibrary/Documentation/Unix/ManPages/man8/uupoll.8c
./NextLibrary/Documentation/Unix/ManPages/man8/uusnap.8c
./NextLibrary/Documentation/Unix/ManPages/man8/uuxqt.8c
./NextLibrary/Documentation/Unix/ManPages/man8/vipw.8
./NextLibrary/Documentation/Unix/ManPages/man8/ypbind.8
./NextLibrary/Documentation/Unix/ManPages/man8/ypinit.8
./NextLibrary/Documentation/Unix/ManPages/man8/ypmake.8
./NextLibrary/Documentation/Unix/ManPages/man8/yppasswdd.8c
./NextLibrary/Documentation/Unix/ManPages/man8/yppoll.8
./NextLibrary/Documentation/Unix/ManPages/man8/yppush.8
./NextLibrary/Documentation/Unix/ManPages/man8/ypserv.8
./NextLibrary/Documentation/Unix/ManPages/man8/ypset.8
./NextLibrary/Documentation/Unix/ManPages/man8/ypwhich.8
./NextLibrary/Documentation/Unix/ManPages/man8/ypxfr.8
./NextLibrary/Documentation/Unix/ManPages/man8/ypxfr_1perday.8
./NextLibrary/Documentation/Unix/ManPages/man8/ypxfr_1perhour.8
./NextLibrary/Documentation/Unix/ManPages/man8/ypxfr_2perday.8
./NextLibrary/Documentation/Unix/ManPages/man8/.places
./NextLibrary/Documentation/Unix/ManPages/man1
./NextLibrary/Documentation/Unix/ManPages/man1/.places
./NextLibrary/Documentation/Unix/ManPages/whatis
./NextLibrary/Documentation/Unix/ManPages/.index
./NextLibrary/Documentation/Unix/ManPages/.index/index
./NextLibrary/Documentation/Unix/ManPages/.index/index.D
./NextLibrary/Documentation/Unix/ManPages/.index/index.L
./NextLibrary/Documentation/Unix/ManPages/.index/index.Registry.D
./NextLibrary/Documentation/Unix/ManPages/.index/index.Registry.L
./NextLibrary/Documentation/Unix/ManPages/.index/icon.tiff
./NextLibrary/Documentation/Unix/ManPages/.index/.roffArgs
./NextLibrary/Documentation/Unix/ManPages/.index/.places
./NextLibrary/Documentation/Unix/ManPages/.places
./NextLibrary/Documentation/Unix/.places
./NextLibrary/Documentation/NeXT
```

```
./NextLibrary/Documentation/NeXT/RelNotes
./NextLibrary/Documentation/NeXT/RelNotes/SybaseNotes.wn
./NextLibrary/Documentation/NeXT/RelNotes/SybaseNotes.wn/WNDocument.wn
./NextLibrary/Documentation/NeXT/RelNotes/SybaseNotes.wn/WNGraphic.104598.eps
./NextLibrary/Documentation/NeXT/RelNotes/SybaseNotes.wn/WNGraphic.760153.eps
./NextLibrary/Documentation/NeXT/RelNotes/SybaseNotes.wn/WNGraphic.801232.eps
./NextLibrary/Documentation/NeXT/RelNotes/SybaseNotes.wn/WNGraphic.840236.eps
./NextLibrary/Documentation/NeXT/RelNotes/SybaseNotes.wn/WNGraphic.927868.eps
./NextLibrary/Documentation/NeXT/RelNotes/SybaseNotes.wn/.places
./NextLibrary/Documentation/NeXT/RelNotes/.index
./NextLibrary/Documentation/NeXT/RelNotes/.index/icon.tiff
./NextLibrary/Documentation/NeXT/RelNotes/.index/Copyright.rtf
./NextLibrary/Documentation/NeXT/RelNotes/.index/index
./NextLibrary/Documentation/NeXT/RelNotes/.index/index.D
./NextLibrary/Documentation/NeXT/RelNotes/.index/index.L
./NextLibrary/Documentation/NeXT/RelNotes/.index/index.Registry.D
./NextLibrary/Documentation/NeXT/RelNotes/.index/index.Registry.L
./NextLibrary/Documentation/NeXT/RelNotes/.index/.places
./NextLibrary/Documentation/NeXT/RelNotes/.macros
./NextLibrary/Documentation/NeXT/RelNotes/Contents.wn
./NextLibrary/Documentation/NeXT/RelNotes/ExampleNotes.wn
./NextLibrary/Documentation/NeXT/RelNotes/OSNotes.wn
./NextLibrary/Documentation/NeXT/RelNotes/FrameMakerNotes.wn
./NextLibrary/Documentation/NeXT/RelNotes/IBNotes.wn
./NextLibrary/Documentation/NeXT/RelNotes/IndexingNotes.wn
./NextLibrary/Documentation/NeXT/RelNotes/AppKitNotes.wn
./NextLibrary/Documentation/NeXT/RelNotes/BSDNotes.wn
./NextLibrary/Documentation/NeXT/RelNotes/CNotes.wn
./NextLibrary/Documentation/NeXT/RelNotes/ClientLibNotes.wn
./NextLibrary/Documentation/NeXT/RelNotes/DSPDebugNotes.wn
./NextLibrary/Documentation/NeXT/RelNotes/DSPNotes.wn
./NextLibrary/Documentation/NeXT/RelNotes/DatabaseNotes.wn
./NextLibrary/Documentation/NeXT/RelNotes/MathematicaNotes.wn
./NextLibrary/Documentation/NeXT/RelNotes/WorkspaceNotes.wn
./NextLibrary/Documentation/NeXT/RelNotes/IndexingPaper.wn
./NextLibrary/Documentation/NeXT/RelNotes/LTBCNotes.wn
./NextLibrary/Documentation/NeXT/RelNotes/LibrarianNotes.wn
./NextLibrary/Documentation/NeXT/RelNotes/LispNotes.wn
./NextLibrary/Documentation/NeXT/RelNotes/LoginwindowNotes.wn
./NextLibrary/Documentation/NeXT/RelNotes/MailNotes.wn
./NextLibrary/Documentation/NeXT/RelNotes/MusicKitNotes.wn
./NextLibrary/Documentation/NeXT/RelNotes/PreferencesNotes.wn
./NextLibrary/Documentation/NeXT/RelNotes/PrintMgrNotes.wn
./NextLibrary/Documentation/NeXT/RelNotes/QuotationsNotes.wn
./NextLibrary/Documentation/NeXT/RelNotes/ServerNotes.wn
./NextLibrary/Documentation/NeXT/RelNotes/ShellNotes.wn
./NextLibrary/Documentation/NeXT/RelNotes/SoundNotes.wn
./NextLibrary/Documentation/NeXT/RelNotes/StreamsNotes.wn
./NextLibrary/Documentation/NeXT/RelNotes/TeXNotes.wn
./NextLibrary/Documentation/NeXT/RelNotes/WebsterNotes.wn
./NextLibrary/Documentation/NeXT/RelNotes/TerminalNotes.wn
```

```
./NextLibrary/Documentation/NeXT/RelNotes/UserManagerNotes.wn
./NextLibrary/Documentation/NeXT/RelNotes/WriteNowNotes.wn
./NextLibrary/Documentation/NeXT/RelNotes/WriteNowNotes.wn/WNDocument.wn
./NextLibrary/Documentation/NeXT/RelNotes/WriteNowNotes.wn/.places
./NextLibrary/Documentation/NeXT/RelNotes/.places
./NextLibrary/Documentation/NeXT/RelNotes/EditNotes.wn
./NextLibrary/Documentation/NeXT/RelNotes/EditNotes.wn/WNDocument.wn
./NextLibrary/Documentation/NeXT/RelNotes/EditNotes.wn/textmenu.404423.eps
./NextLibrary/Documentation/NeXT/RelNotes/EditNotes.wn/mini.182541.eps
./NextLibrary/Documentation/NeXT/RelNotes/EditNotes.wn/minih.369557.eps
./NextLibrary/Documentation/NeXT/RelNotes/EditNotes.wn/x.477359.eps
./NextLibrary/Documentation/NeXT/RelNotes/EditNotes.wn/activate.799896.eps
./NextLibrary/Documentation/NeXT/RelNotes/EditNotes.wn/wrap.675063.eps
./NextLibrary/Documentation/NeXT/RelNotes/EditNotes.wn/pref.503742.eps
./NextLibrary/Documentation/NeXT/RelNotes/EditNotes.wn/dict.183877.eps
./NextLibrary/Documentation/NeXT/SysRefMan
./NextLibrary/Documentation/NeXT/SysRefMan/Cover.wn
./NextLibrary/Documentation/NeXT/SysRefMan/Cover.wn/Logo.eps
./NextLibrary/Documentation/NeXT/SysRefMan/Cover.wn/WNDocument.wn
./NextLibrary/Documentation/NeXT/SysRefMan/Cover.wn/.places
./NextLibrary/Documentation/NeXT/SysRefMan/02_UserIntf.wn
./NextLibrary/Documentation/NeXT/SysRefMan/02_UserIntf.wn/Rubberband.eps
./NextLibrary/Documentation/NeXT/SysRefMan/02_UserIntf.wn/Keyboard.eps
./NextLibrary/Documentation/NeXT/SysRefMan/02_UserIntf.wn/Panels.eps
./NextLibrary/Documentation/NeXT/SysRefMan/02_UserIntf.wn/Window.eps
./NextLibrary/Documentation/NeXT/SysRefMan/02_UserIntf.wn/PopUpList.eps
./NextLibrary/Documentation/NeXT/SysRefMan/02_UserIntf.wn/Ibeam_Sub3.473753.eps
./NextLibrary/Documentation/NeXT/SysRefMan/02_UserIntf.wn/SampleCom.eps
./NextLibrary/Documentation/NeXT/SysRefMan/02_UserIntf.wn/Slider.eps
./NextLibrary/Documentation/NeXT/SysRefMan/02_UserIntf.wn/1StateBut.eps
./NextLibrary/Documentation/NeXT/SysRefMan/02_UserIntf.wn/TextFieldForm.eps
./NextLibrary/Documentation/NeXT/SysRefMan/02_UserIntf.wn/ScrollableDoc.eps
./NextLibrary/Documentation/NeXT/SysRefMan/02_UserIntf.wn/VertScroller.eps
./NextLibrary/Documentation/NeXT/SysRefMan/02_UserIntf.wn/2StateButtons.eps
./NextLibrary/Documentation/NeXT/SysRefMan/02_UserIntf.wn/EditMenu.199507.eps
./NextLibrary/Documentation/NeXT/SysRefMan/02_UserIntf.wn/ThreeAttMenu.763292.eps
./NextLibrary/Documentation/NeXT/SysRefMan/02_UserIntf.wn/TopLevelDir4.407562.eps
./NextLibrary/Documentation/NeXT/SysRefMan/02_UserIntf.wn/CloseCommands.eps
./NextLibrary/Documentation/NeXT/SysRefMan/02_UserIntf.wn/CopyAs.eps
./NextLibrary/Documentation/NeXT/SysRefMan/02_UserIntf.wn/FindMenu.eps
./NextLibrary/Documentation/NeXT/SysRefMan/02_UserIntf.wn/KeyWin.eps
./NextLibrary/Documentation/NeXT/SysRefMan/02_UserIntf.wn/MainWin.eps
./NextLibrary/Documentation/NeXT/SysRefMan/02_UserIntf.wn/StandWin.eps
./NextLibrary/Documentation/NeXT/SysRefMan/02_UserIntf.wn/WindowMenu.eps
./NextLibrary/Documentation/NeXT/SysRefMan/02_UserIntf.wn/SelectTextGraph.eps
./NextLibrary/Documentation/NeXT/SysRefMan/02_UserIntf.wn/MenuFour.767767.eps
./NextLibrary/Documentation/NeXT/SysRefMan/02_UserIntf.wn/WNDocument.wn
./NextLibrary/Documentation/NeXT/SysRefMan/02_UserIntf.wn/ExtShiftKey.eps
./NextLibrary/Documentation/NeXT/SysRefMan/02_UserIntf.wn/MiniaturizedWin.eps
./NextLibrary/Documentation/NeXT/SysRefMan/02_UserIntf.wn/FreeIcon.eps
./NextLibrary/Documentation/NeXT/SysRefMan/02_UserIntf.wn/Buttons.eps

./NextLibrary/Documentation/NeXT/SysRefMan/02_UserIntf.wn/PopUp_Sub2.eps
./NextLibrary/Documentation/NeXT/SysRefMan/02_UserIntf.wn/PullDown_Sub1.eps
./NextLibrary/Documentation/NeXT/SysRefMan/02_UserIntf.wn/Submenu_Sub1.eps
./NextLibrary/Documentation/NeXT/SysRefMan/02_UserIntf.wn/Return_Sub3.eps
./NextLibrary/Documentation/NeXT/SysRefMan/02_UserIntf.wn
    /BrightVolKeys.393735.eps
./NextLibrary/Documentation/NeXT/SysRefMan/02_UserIntf.wn/ExtAltKey.643803.eps
./NextLibrary/Documentation/NeXT/SysRefMan/02_UserIntf.wn
    /PullDownListAction.329684.eps
./NextLibrary/Documentation/NeXT/SysRefMan/02_UserIntf.wn/TitleBarBtns.028523.eps
./NextLibrary/Documentation/NeXT/SysRefMan/02_UserIntf.wn
    /AttschSubmenu.608470.eps
./NextLibrary/Documentation/NeXT/SysRefMan/02_UserIntf.wn/AttachedCopy.000337.eps
./NextLibrary/Documentation/NeXT/SysRefMan/02_UserIntf.wn/MainMenuName.421454.eps
./NextLibrary/Documentation/NeXT/SysRefMan/02_UserIntf.wn/FontMenu.616953.eps
./NextLibrary/Documentation/NeXT/SysRefMan/02_UserIntf.wn/RequestMenu.786471.eps
./NextLibrary/Documentation/NeXT/SysRefMan/02_UserIntf.wn/AttnPanel.581555.eps
./NextLibrary/Documentation/NeXT/SysRefMan/02_UserIntf.wn/.places
./NextLibrary/Documentation/NeXT/SysRefMan/09_UIObjects.wn
./NextLibrary/Documentation/NeXT/SysRefMan/09_UIObjects.wn/WNDocument.wn
./NextLibrary/Documentation/NeXT/SysRefMan/09_UIObjects.wn/TitlePos.eps
./NextLibrary/Documentation/NeXT/SysRefMan/09_UIObjects.wn/BorderTypes.eps
./NextLibrary/Documentation/NeXT/SysRefMan/09_UIObjects.wn/LayoutRectBox.eps
./NextLibrary/Documentation/NeXT/SysRefMan/09_UIObjects.wn/TypicalBox.eps
./NextLibrary/Documentation/NeXT/SysRefMan/09_UIObjects.wn/LineCharMet.eps
./NextLibrary/Documentation/NeXT/SysRefMan/09_UIObjects.wn/TextLayout.eps
./NextLibrary/Documentation/NeXT/SysRefMan/09_UIObjects.wn/.places
./NextLibrary/Documentation/NeXT/SysRefMan/12_Music.wn
./NextLibrary/Documentation/NeXT/SysRefMan/12_Music.wn/WNDocument.wn
./NextLibrary/Documentation/NeXT/SysRefMan/12_Music.wn
    /MusicDataRepClasses.347182.eps
./NextLibrary/Documentation/NeXT/SysRefMan/12_Music.wn/EarlyNoteOffB.314054.eps
./NextLibrary/Documentation/NeXT/SysRefMan/12_Music.wn/EarlyNoteOffC.916311.eps
./NextLibrary/Documentation/NeXT/SysRefMan/12_Music.wn/PianoEnvelope.776652.eps
./NextLibrary/Documentation/NeXT/SysRefMan/12_Music.wn/SimpleEnvelope.250470.eps
./NextLibrary/Documentation/NeXT/SysRefMan/12_Music.wn
    /TypicalEnvelopesA.069265.eps
./NextLibrary/Documentation/NeXT/SysRefMan/12_Music.wn
    /TypicalEnvelopesB.454984.eps
./NextLibrary/Documentation/NeXT/SysRefMan/12_Music.wn
    /TypicalEnvelopesC.303703.eps
./NextLibrary/Documentation/NeXT/SysRefMan/12_Music.wn
    /BreakptEnvelopesA.668383.eps
./NextLibrary/Documentation/NeXT/SysRefMan/12_Music.wn
    /BreakptEnvelopesB.367689.eps
./NextLibrary/Documentation/NeXT/SysRefMan/12_Music.wn
    /BreakptEnvelopesC.754342.eps
./NextLibrary/Documentation/NeXT/SysRefMan/12_Music.wn
    /ScaledAmpEnv.864349.eps
./NextLibrary/Documentation/NeXT/SysRefMan/12_Music.wn
    /SimulatedPiano.513626.eps
./NextLibrary/Documentation/NeXT/SysRefMan/12_Music.wn
    /BasicPerformanceClasses.684947.eps
```

./NextLibrary/Documentation/NeXT/SysRefMan/12_Music.wn/LinearInterp.804436.eps
./NextLibrary/Documentation/NeXT/SysRefMan/12_Music.wn/EnvWStikptA.726558.eps
./NextLibrary/Documentation/NeXT/SysRefMan/12_Music.wn/EnvWStikptB.378040.eps
./NextLibrary/Documentation/NeXT/SysRefMan/12_Music.wn/EnvWStikptC.257682.eps
./NextLibrary/Documentation/NeXT/SysRefMan/12_Music.wn/AttackRelease.221882.eps
./NextLibrary/Documentation/NeXT/SysRefMan/12_Music.wn/EnvWthAttRelA.261223.eps
./NextLibrary/Documentation/NeXT/SysRefMan/12_Music.wn/EnvWthAttRelB.331889.eps
./NextLibrary/Documentation/NeXT/SysRefMan/12_Music.wn/EnvWthAttRelC.431273.eps
./NextLibrary/Documentation/NeXT/SysRefMan/12_Music.wn/EarlyNoteOffA.575809.eps
./NextLibrary/Documentation/NeXT/SysRefMan/12_Music.wn/EnvelopeWSmooth.323406.eps
./NextLibrary/Documentation/NeXT/SysRefMan/12_Music.wn/PXYChartA.737778.eps
./NextLibrary/Documentation/NeXT/SysRefMan/12_Music.wn/SineRomChartA.527453.eps
./NextLibrary/Documentation/NeXT/SysRefMan/12_Music.wn/.places
./NextLibrary/Documentation/NeXT/SysRefMan/12_Music.wn/SineRomChartB.496193.eps
./NextLibrary/Documentation/NeXT/SysRefMan/12_Music.wn/SineRomChartC.654491.eps
./NextLibrary/Documentation/NeXT/SysRefMan/12_Music.wn
    /SynthesisClasses.896543.eps
./NextLibrary/Documentation/NeXT/SysRefMan/10_Support.wn
./NextLibrary/Documentation/NeXT/SysRefMan/README.wn
./NextLibrary/Documentation/NeXT/SysRefMan/18_Tools.wn
./NextLibrary/Documentation/NeXT/SysRefMan/22_ClassSpecs
./NextLibrary/Documentation/NeXT/SysRefMan/22_ClassSpecs/MusicKit
./NextLibrary/Documentation/NeXT/SysRefMan/22_ClassSpecs/MusicKit/Conductor.wn
./NextLibrary/Documentation/NeXT/SysRefMan/22_ClassSpecs/MusicKit/Envelope.wn
./NextLibrary/Documentation/NeXT/SysRefMan/22_ClassSpecs/MusicKit
    /FilePerformer.wn
./NextLibrary/Documentation/NeXT/SysRefMan/22_ClassSpecs/MusicKit/FileWriter.wn
./NextLibrary/Documentation/NeXT/SysRefMan/22_ClassSpecs/MusicKit/Instrument.wn
./NextLibrary/Documentation/NeXT/SysRefMan/22_ClassSpecs/MusicKit/Orchestra.wn
./NextLibrary/Documentation/NeXT/SysRefMan/22_ClassSpecs/MusicKit/Note.wn
./NextLibrary/Documentation/NeXT/SysRefMan/22_ClassSpecs/MusicKit/NoteFilter.wn
./NextLibrary/Documentation/NeXT/SysRefMan/22_ClassSpecs/MusicKit/NoteReceiver.wn
./NextLibrary/Documentation/NeXT/SysRefMan/22_ClassSpecs/MusicKit/Midi.wn
./NextLibrary/Documentation/NeXT/SysRefMan/22_ClassSpecs/MusicKit/NoteSender.wn
./NextLibrary/Documentation/NeXT/SysRefMan/22_ClassSpecs/MusicKit/Part.wn
./NextLibrary/Documentation/NeXT/SysRefMan/22_ClassSpecs/MusicKit
    /PartPerformer.wn
./NextLibrary/Documentation/NeXT/SysRefMan/22_ClassSpecs/MusicKit/PartRecorder.wn
./NextLibrary/Documentation/NeXT/SysRefMan/22_ClassSpecs/MusicKit
    /PatchTemplate.wn
./NextLibrary/Documentation/NeXT/SysRefMan/22_ClassSpecs/MusicKit/Performer.wn
./NextLibrary/Documentation/NeXT/SysRefMan/22_ClassSpecs/MusicKit/Samples.wn
./NextLibrary/Documentation/NeXT/SysRefMan/22_ClassSpecs/MusicKit/Score.wn
./NextLibrary/Documentation/NeXT/SysRefMan/22_ClassSpecs/MusicKit
    /ScorePerformer.wn
./NextLibrary/Documentation/NeXT/SysRefMan/22_ClassSpecs/MusicKit
    /ScorefilePerformer.wn
./NextLibrary/Documentation/NeXT/SysRefMan/22_ClassSpecs/MusicKit/TuningSystem.wn
./NextLibrary/Documentation/NeXT/SysRefMan/22_ClassSpecs/MusicKit
    /SynthInstrument.wn
./NextLibrary/Documentation/NeXT/SysRefMan/22_ClassSpecs/MusicKit
    /UnitGenerator.wn

./NextLibrary/Documentation/NeXT/SysRefMan/22_ClassSpecs/MusicKit/SynthData.wn
./NextLibrary/Documentation/NeXT/SysRefMan/22_ClassSpecs/MusicKit/Partials.wn
./NextLibrary/Documentation/NeXT/SysRefMan/22_ClassSpecs/MusicKit/WaveTable.wn
./NextLibrary/Documentation/NeXT/SysRefMan/22_ClassSpecs/MusicKit/SynthPatch.wn
./NextLibrary/Documentation/NeXT/SysRefMan/22_ClassSpecs/MusicKit
    /ScorefileWriter.wn
./NextLibrary/Documentation/NeXT/SysRefMan/22_ClassSpecs/MusicKit
    /ScoreRecorder.wn
./NextLibrary/Documentation/NeXT/SysRefMan/22_ClassSpecs/MusicKit/.places
./NextLibrary/Documentation/NeXT/SysRefMan/22_ClassSpecs/SoundKitIntro.wn
./NextLibrary/Documentation/NeXT/SysRefMan/22_ClassSpecs/AppKitIntro.wn
./NextLibrary/Documentation/NeXT/SysRefMan/22_ClassSpecs/AppKitIntro.wn
    /InheritanceHier.eps
./NextLibrary/Documentation/NeXT/SysRefMan/22_ClassSpecs/AppKitIntro.wn
    /WNDocument.wn
./NextLibrary/Documentation/NeXT/SysRefMan/22_ClassSpecs/AppKitIntro.wn/.places
./NextLibrary/Documentation/NeXT/SysRefMan/22_ClassSpecs/CommonClasses
./NextLibrary/Documentation/NeXT/SysRefMan/22_ClassSpecs/CommonClasses/List.wn
./NextLibrary/Documentation/NeXT/SysRefMan/22_ClassSpecs/CommonClasses/Object.wn
./NextLibrary/Documentation/NeXT/SysRefMan/22_ClassSpecs/CommonClasses
    /HashTable.wn
./NextLibrary/Documentation/NeXT/SysRefMan/22_ClassSpecs/CommonClasses/Storage.wn
./NextLibrary/Documentation/NeXT/SysRefMan/22_ClassSpecs/CommonClasses
    /StreamTable.wn
./NextLibrary/Documentation/NeXT/SysRefMan/22_ClassSpecs/CommonClasses/.places
./NextLibrary/Documentation/NeXT/SysRefMan/22_ClassSpecs/AppKit
./NextLibrary/Documentation/NeXT/SysRefMan/22_ClassSpecs/AppKit/ActionCell.wn
./NextLibrary/Documentation/NeXT/SysRefMan/22_ClassSpecs/AppKit/Application.wn
./NextLibrary/Documentation/NeXT/SysRefMan/22_ClassSpecs/AppKit/Bitmap.wn
./NextLibrary/Documentation/NeXT/SysRefMan/22_ClassSpecs/AppKit/Box.wn
./NextLibrary/Documentation/NeXT/SysRefMan/22_ClassSpecs/AppKit/Button.wn
./NextLibrary/Documentation/NeXT/SysRefMan/22_ClassSpecs/AppKit/ButtonCell.wn
./NextLibrary/Documentation/NeXT/SysRefMan/22_ClassSpecs/AppKit/Cell.wn
./NextLibrary/Documentation/NeXT/SysRefMan/22_ClassSpecs/AppKit/ChoosePrinter.wn
./NextLibrary/Documentation/NeXT/SysRefMan/22_ClassSpecs/AppKit/ClipView.wn
./NextLibrary/Documentation/NeXT/SysRefMan/22_ClassSpecs/AppKit/Control.wn
./NextLibrary/Documentation/NeXT/SysRefMan/22_ClassSpecs/AppKit/Cursor.wn
./NextLibrary/Documentation/NeXT/SysRefMan/22_ClassSpecs/AppKit/Font.wn
./NextLibrary/Documentation/NeXT/SysRefMan/22_ClassSpecs/AppKit/FontManager.wn
./NextLibrary/Documentation/NeXT/SysRefMan/22_ClassSpecs/AppKit/FontPanel.wn
./NextLibrary/Documentation/NeXT/SysRefMan/22_ClassSpecs/AppKit/Form.wn
./NextLibrary/Documentation/NeXT/SysRefMan/22_ClassSpecs/AppKit/FormCell.wn
./NextLibrary/Documentation/NeXT/SysRefMan/22_ClassSpecs/AppKit/Listener.wn
./NextLibrary/Documentation/NeXT/SysRefMan/22_ClassSpecs/AppKit/Matrix.wn
./NextLibrary/Documentation/NeXT/SysRefMan/22_ClassSpecs/AppKit/Menu.wn
./NextLibrary/Documentation/NeXT/SysRefMan/22_ClassSpecs/AppKit/MenuCell.wn
./NextLibrary/Documentation/NeXT/SysRefMan/22_ClassSpecs/AppKit/OpenPanel.wn
./NextLibrary/Documentation/NeXT/SysRefMan/22_ClassSpecs/AppKit/PageLayout.wn
./NextLibrary/Documentation/NeXT/SysRefMan/22_ClassSpecs/AppKit/Panel.wn
./NextLibrary/Documentation/NeXT/SysRefMan/22_ClassSpecs/AppKit/Pasteboard.wn
./NextLibrary/Documentation/NeXT/SysRefMan/22_ClassSpecs/AppKit/PopUpList.wn
./NextLibrary/Documentation/NeXT/SysRefMan/22_ClassSpecs/AppKit/PrintInfo.wn

```
./NextLibrary/Documentation/NeXT/SysRefMan/22_ClassSpecs/AppKit/PrintPanel.wn
./NextLibrary/Documentation/NeXT/SysRefMan/22_ClassSpecs/AppKit/Responder.wn
./NextLibrary/Documentation/NeXT/SysRefMan/22_ClassSpecs/AppKit/SavePanel.wn
./NextLibrary/Documentation/NeXT/SysRefMan/22_ClassSpecs/AppKit/ScrollView.wn
./NextLibrary/Documentation/NeXT/SysRefMan/22_ClassSpecs/AppKit/Scroller.wn
./NextLibrary/Documentation/NeXT/SysRefMan/22_ClassSpecs/AppKit/SelectionCell.wn
./NextLibrary/Documentation/NeXT/SysRefMan/22_ClassSpecs/AppKit/Slider.wn
./NextLibrary/Documentation/NeXT/SysRefMan/22_ClassSpecs/AppKit/SliderCell.wn
./NextLibrary/Documentation/NeXT/SysRefMan/22_ClassSpecs/AppKit/Speaker.wn
./NextLibrary/Documentation/NeXT/SysRefMan/22_ClassSpecs/AppKit/TextField.wn
./NextLibrary/Documentation/NeXT/SysRefMan/22_ClassSpecs/AppKit/TextFieldCell.wn
./NextLibrary/Documentation/NeXT/SysRefMan/22_ClassSpecs/AppKit/Text.wn
./NextLibrary/Documentation/NeXT/SysRefMan/22_ClassSpecs/AppKit/View.wn
./NextLibrary/Documentation/NeXT/SysRefMan/22_ClassSpecs/AppKit/Window.wn
./NextLibrary/Documentation/NeXT/SysRefMan/22_ClassSpecs/AppKit/.places
./NextLibrary/Documentation/NeXT/SysRefMan/22_ClassSpecs/SoundKit
./NextLibrary/Documentation/NeXT/SysRefMan/22_ClassSpecs/SoundKit/Sound.wn
./NextLibrary/Documentation/NeXT/SysRefMan/22_ClassSpecs/SoundKit/SoundView.wn
./NextLibrary/Documentation/NeXT/SysRefMan/22_ClassSpecs/SoundKit/SoundMeter.wn
./NextLibrary/Documentation/NeXT/SysRefMan/22_ClassSpecs/SoundKit/.places
./NextLibrary/Documentation/NeXT/SysRefMan/22_ClassSpecs/MusicKitIntro.wn
./NextLibrary/Documentation/NeXT/SysRefMan/22_ClassSpecs/CommonClassesIntro.wn
./NextLibrary/Documentation/NeXT/SysRefMan/22_ClassSpecs/CommonClassesIntro.wn
    /BasicObjCClass.eps
./NextLibrary/Documentation/NeXT/SysRefMan/22_ClassSpecs/CommonClassesIntro.wn
    /WNDocument.wn
./NextLibrary/Documentation/NeXT/SysRefMan/22_ClassSpecs/CommonClassesIntro.wn
    /.places
./NextLibrary/Documentation/NeXT/SysRefMan/22_ClassSpecs/Intro.wn
./NextLibrary/Documentation/NeXT/SysRefMan/22_ClassSpecs/Intro.wn/WNDocument.wn
./NextLibrary/Documentation/NeXT/SysRefMan/22_ClassSpecs/Intro.wn/.places
./NextLibrary/Documentation/NeXT/SysRefMan/22_ClassSpecs/.places
./NextLibrary/Documentation/NeXT/SysRefMan/ApC_CFuncSummary.wn
./NextLibrary/Documentation/NeXT/SysRefMan/Pt1_Concepts.wn
./NextLibrary/Documentation/NeXT/SysRefMan/.macros
./NextLibrary/Documentation/NeXT/SysRefMan/03_ObjC.wn
./NextLibrary/Documentation/NeXT/SysRefMan/03_ObjC.wn/SomeAppKitClass.eps
./NextLibrary/Documentation/NeXT/SysRefMan/03_ObjC.wn/Messaging.693897.eps
./NextLibrary/Documentation/NeXT/SysRefMan/03_ObjC.wn/WNDocument.wn
./NextLibrary/Documentation/NeXT/SysRefMan/03_ObjC.wn/.places
./NextLibrary/Documentation/NeXT/SysRefMan/04_Drawing.wn
./NextLibrary/Documentation/NeXT/SysRefMan/04_Drawing.wn/Rectangle.eps
./NextLibrary/Documentation/NeXT/SysRefMan/04_Drawing.wn/WNDocument.wn
./NextLibrary/Documentation/NeXT/SysRefMan/04_Drawing.wn/HalftoneBWPix.eps
./NextLibrary/Documentation/NeXT/SysRefMan/04_Drawing.wn/HalftoneGWPix.eps
./NextLibrary/Documentation/NeXT/SysRefMan/04_Drawing.wn/ScreenCoordSys.eps
./NextLibrary/Documentation/NeXT/SysRefMan/04_Drawing.wn/PointsPixels.eps
./NextLibrary/Documentation/NeXT/SysRefMan/04_Drawing.wn/WindowCorner.eps
./NextLibrary/Documentation/NeXT/SysRefMan/04_Drawing.wn/RotXAxis.eps
./NextLibrary/Documentation/NeXT/SysRefMan/04_Drawing.wn/PSExecCont.eps
./NextLibrary/Documentation/NeXT/SysRefMan/04_Drawing.wn/WindowBuff.eps

./NextLibrary/Documentation/NeXT/SysRefMan/04_Drawing.wn/PathOutline.eps
./NextLibrary/Documentation/NeXT/SysRefMan/04_Drawing.wn/SecWhiteCircle.eps
./NextLibrary/Documentation/NeXT/SysRefMan/04_Drawing.wn/FilledRect.eps
./NextLibrary/Documentation/NeXT/SysRefMan/04_Drawing.wn/PathBelowPixMid.eps
./NextLibrary/Documentation/NeXT/SysRefMan/04_Drawing.wn/PixDisplayPts.eps
./NextLibrary/Documentation/NeXT/SysRefMan/04_Drawing.wn/ZeroWidthLines.eps
./NextLibrary/Documentation/NeXT/SysRefMan/04_Drawing.wn/ChoosingPix.eps
./NextLibrary/Documentation/NeXT/SysRefMan/04_Drawing.wn/ZeroWthLnRec.eps
./NextLibrary/Documentation/NeXT/SysRefMan/04_Drawing.wn/ClipPathBtnPix.eps
./NextLibrary/Documentation/NeXT/SysRefMan/04_Drawing.wn/ClipPathXPix.eps
./NextLibrary/Documentation/NeXT/SysRefMan/04_Drawing.wn/ClipZeroRecLn.eps
./NextLibrary/Documentation/NeXT/SysRefMan/04_Drawing.wn/UnionIntrsctRec.eps
./NextLibrary/Documentation/NeXT/SysRefMan/04_Drawing.wn/03_GraphStates.eps
./NextLibrary/Documentation/NeXT/SysRefMan/04_Drawing.wn/NonRectRect.eps
./NextLibrary/Documentation/NeXT/SysRefMan/04_Drawing.wn/PathAtMidpt.eps
./NextLibrary/Documentation/NeXT/SysRefMan/04_Drawing.wn/PermPixVals.eps
./NextLibrary/Documentation/NeXT/SysRefMan/04_Drawing.wn/Compositing.eps
./NextLibrary/Documentation/NeXT/SysRefMan/04_Drawing.wn/WindowAndView2.eps
./NextLibrary/Documentation/NeXT/SysRefMan/04_Drawing.wn/MixPaint.eps
./NextLibrary/Documentation/NeXT/SysRefMan/04_Drawing.wn
    /StrkAdjPathBelowPixMdpt.eps
./NextLibrary/Documentation/NeXT/SysRefMan/04_Drawing.wn/PntngWithTrans.eps
./NextLibrary/Documentation/NeXT/SysRefMan/04_Drawing.wn/CompositeOper.941293.eps
./NextLibrary/Documentation/NeXT/SysRefMan/04_Drawing.wn/.places
./NextLibrary/Documentation/NeXT/SysRefMan/05_Events.wn
./NextLibrary/Documentation/NeXT/SysRefMan/05_Events.wn/WNDocument.wn
./NextLibrary/Documentation/NeXT/SysRefMan/05_Events.wn/EventFlags.eps
./NextLibrary/Documentation/NeXT/SysRefMan/05_Events.wn/.places
./NextLibrary/Documentation/NeXT/SysRefMan/07_ProgDynam.wn
./NextLibrary/Documentation/NeXT/SysRefMan/07_ProgDynam.wn/ResizeSubview.eps
./NextLibrary/Documentation/NeXT/SysRefMan/07_ProgDynam.wn/Little.753408.eps
./NextLibrary/Documentation/NeXT/SysRefMan/07_ProgDynam.wn/4TextObjWin.eps
./NextLibrary/Documentation/NeXT/SysRefMan/07_ProgDynam.wn/OverLapSubVw.eps
./NextLibrary/Documentation/NeXT/SysRefMan/07_ProgDynam.wn/RespondChain.eps
./NextLibrary/Documentation/NeXT/SysRefMan/07_ProgDynam.wn/DefCoordUnRotVw.eps
./NextLibrary/Documentation/NeXT/SysRefMan/07_ProgDynam.wn/FlippedCoord.eps
./NextLibrary/Documentation/NeXT/SysRefMan/07_ProgDynam.wn/RotBoundRec.eps
./NextLibrary/Documentation/NeXT/SysRefMan/07_ProgDynam.wn/DrawSuperCoord.eps
./NextLibrary/Documentation/NeXT/SysRefMan/07_ProgDynam.wn/DrawFlipSuper.eps
./NextLibrary/Documentation/NeXT/SysRefMan/07_ProgDynam.wn/UpdateRect.eps
./NextLibrary/Documentation/NeXT/SysRefMan/07_ProgDynam.wn/ResizeConstants.eps
./NextLibrary/Documentation/NeXT/SysRefMan/07_ProgDynam.wn/SearchPath.652688.eps
./NextLibrary/Documentation/NeXT/SysRefMan/07_ProgDynam.wn/WNDocument.wn
./NextLibrary/Documentation/NeXT/SysRefMan/07_ProgDynam.wn
    /CursorLocation.024113.eps
./NextLibrary/Documentation/NeXT/SysRefMan/07_ProgDynam.wn
    /RotatedVisibleRect.345314.eps
./NextLibrary/Documentation/NeXT/SysRefMan/07_ProgDynam.wn/.places
./NextLibrary/Documentation/NeXT/SysRefMan/11_Sound.wn
./NextLibrary/Documentation/NeXT/SysRefMan/11_Sound.wn/WNDocument.wn
./NextLibrary/Documentation/NeXT/SysRefMan/11_Sound.wn/AirPressWave.eps
```

```
./NextLibrary/Documentation/NeXT/SysRefMan/11_Sound.wn/SamplWavForm.eps
./NextLibrary/Documentation/NeXT/SysRefMan/11_Sound.wn/3BitQuant.eps
./NextLibrary/Documentation/NeXT/SysRefMan/11_Sound.wn/.places
./NextLibrary/Documentation/NeXT/SysRefMan/13_ArrayProc.wn
./NextLibrary/Documentation/NeXT/SysRefMan/16_Mach.wn
./NextLibrary/Documentation/NeXT/SysRefMan/17_ROM.wn
./NextLibrary/Documentation/NeXT/SysRefMan/24_PostOps.wn
./NextLibrary/Documentation/NeXT/SysRefMan/24_PostOps.wn/CompositeOper.597250.eps
./NextLibrary/Documentation/NeXT/SysRefMan/24_PostOps.wn/Placewindow.eps
./NextLibrary/Documentation/NeXT/SysRefMan/24_PostOps.wn/WNDocument.wn
./NextLibrary/Documentation/NeXT/SysRefMan/24_PostOps.wn/.places
./NextLibrary/Documentation/NeXT/SysRefMan/01_SysOver.wn
./NextLibrary/Documentation/NeXT/SysRefMan/01_SysOver.wn/SysOver.eps
./NextLibrary/Documentation/NeXT/SysRefMan/01_SysOver.wn/WNDocument.wn
./NextLibrary/Documentation/NeXT/SysRefMan/01_SysOver.wn/NextStep.eps
./NextLibrary/Documentation/NeXT/SysRefMan/01_SysOver.wn/WinSysData.eps
./NextLibrary/Documentation/NeXT/SysRefMan/01_SysOver.wn/WinServeApp.eps
./NextLibrary/Documentation/NeXT/SysRefMan/01_SysOver.wn/MusSoundComp.eps
./NextLibrary/Documentation/NeXT/SysRefMan/01_SysOver.wn/.places
./NextLibrary/Documentation/NeXT/SysRefMan/ApF_MusicTables.wn
./NextLibrary/Documentation/NeXT/SysRefMan/Glossary.wn
./NextLibrary/Documentation/NeXT/SysRefMan/23_CFunctions.wn
./NextLibrary/Documentation/NeXT/SysRefMan/23_CFunctions.wn/InOffRect.eps
./NextLibrary/Documentation/NeXT/SysRefMan/23_CFunctions.wn/RectBorders.eps
./NextLibrary/Documentation/NeXT/SysRefMan/23_CFunctions.wn/PlaneMeshConfig.eps
./NextLibrary/Documentation/NeXT/SysRefMan/23_CFunctions.wn/WNDocument.wn
./NextLibrary/Documentation/NeXT/SysRefMan/23_CFunctions.wn/.places
./NextLibrary/Documentation/NeXT/SysRefMan/06_ProgStruct.wn
./NextLibrary/Documentation/NeXT/SysRefMan/06_ProgStruct.wn/ConnectVwHier.eps
./NextLibrary/Documentation/NeXT/SysRefMan/06_ProgStruct.wn
        /DefaultCoordCroc.345314.eps
./NextLibrary/Documentation/NeXT/SysRefMan/06_ProgStruct.wn/DisplacedFrRec.eps
./NextLibrary/Documentation/NeXT/SysRefMan/06_ProgStruct.wn/ConnectWin.eps
./NextLibrary/Documentation/NeXT/SysRefMan/06_ProgStruct.wn
        /ScrollingAView.808444.eps
./NextLibrary/Documentation/NeXT/SysRefMan/06_ProgStruct.wn
        /EventDrivenApp.404825.eps
./NextLibrary/Documentation/NeXT/SysRefMan/06_ProgStruct.wn
        /ViewFrameRot.548894.eps
./NextLibrary/Documentation/NeXT/SysRefMan/06_ProgStruct.wn/MoveWindow.eps
./NextLibrary/Documentation/NeXT/SysRefMan/06_ProgStruct.wn/PlaceWindow.eps
./NextLibrary/Documentation/NeXT/SysRefMan/06_ProgStruct.wn/WNDocument.wn
./NextLibrary/Documentation/NeXT/SysRefMan/06_ProgStruct.wn
        /InheritanceHier.092574.eps
./NextLibrary/Documentation/NeXT/SysRefMan/06_ProgStruct.wn
        /PrincAppKitClass.655827.eps
./NextLibrary/Documentation/NeXT/SysRefMan/06_ProgStruct.wn
        /FrameRecViewHier.507348.eps
./NextLibrary/Documentation/NeXT/SysRefMan/06_ProgStruct.wn
        /ViewHierarchy.601725.eps
./NextLibrary/Documentation/NeXT/SysRefMan/06_ProgStruct.wn/.places
./NextLibrary/Documentation/NeXT/SysRefMan/08_IntfBuilder.wn
```

```
./NextLibrary/Documentation/NeXT/SysRefMan/08_IntfBuilder.wn/FileMenu.eps
./NextLibrary/Documentation/NeXT/SysRefMan/08_IntfBuilder.wn/EditMenu.eps
./NextLibrary/Documentation/NeXT/SysRefMan/08_IntfBuilder.wn/WindowsMenu.eps
./NextLibrary/Documentation/NeXT/SysRefMan/08_IntfBuilder.wn/PalettesWindow.eps
./NextLibrary/Documentation/NeXT/SysRefMan/08_IntfBuilder.wn/SoundsWindow.eps
./NextLibrary/Documentation/NeXT/SysRefMan/08_IntfBuilder.wn/ClassesWindow.eps
./NextLibrary/Documentation/NeXT/SysRefMan/08_IntfBuilder.wn/FileWindow.eps
./NextLibrary/Documentation/NeXT/SysRefMan/08_IntfBuilder.wn/Text.eps
./NextLibrary/Documentation/NeXT/SysRefMan/08_IntfBuilder.wn/button.eps
./NextLibrary/Documentation/NeXT/SysRefMan/08_IntfBuilder.wn/title.eps
./NextLibrary/Documentation/NeXT/SysRefMan/08_IntfBuilder.wn/switch.eps
./NextLibrary/Documentation/NeXT/SysRefMan/08_IntfBuilder.wn/radio.eps
./NextLibrary/Documentation/NeXT/SysRefMan/08_IntfBuilder.wn/field.eps
./NextLibrary/Documentation/NeXT/SysRefMan/08_IntfBuilder.wn/hslider.eps
./NextLibrary/Documentation/NeXT/SysRefMan/08_IntfBuilder.wn/CustomView.eps
./NextLibrary/Documentation/NeXT/SysRefMan/08_IntfBuilder.wn/item.eps
./NextLibrary/Documentation/NeXT/SysRefMan/08_IntfBuilder.wn/submenu.eps
./NextLibrary/Documentation/NeXT/SysRefMan/08_IntfBuilder.wn/window.eps
./NextLibrary/Documentation/NeXT/SysRefMan/08_IntfBuilder.wn/edit.eps
./NextLibrary/Documentation/NeXT/SysRefMan/08_IntfBuilder.wn/font.eps
./NextLibrary/Documentation/NeXT/SysRefMan/08_IntfBuilder.wn/AtCustomView.eps
./NextLibrary/Documentation/NeXT/SysRefMan/08_IntfBuilder.wn/AtBoxTitle.eps
./NextLibrary/Documentation/NeXT/SysRefMan/08_IntfBuilder.wn/AtBoxBorder.eps
./NextLibrary/Documentation/NeXT/SysRefMan/08_IntfBuilder.wn/AtFormCell.eps
./NextLibrary/Documentation/NeXT/SysRefMan/08_IntfBuilder.wn/AtTextFieldAlign.eps
./NextLibrary/Documentation/NeXT/SysRefMan/08_IntfBuilder.wn
        /AtTextFieldBgrndGray.eps
./NextLibrary/Documentation/NeXT/SysRefMan/08_IntfBuilder.wn/AtTextFieldBordr.eps
./NextLibrary/Documentation/NeXT/SysRefMan/08_IntfBuilder.wn/AtTextFieldTag.eps
./NextLibrary/Documentation/NeXT/SysRefMan/08_IntfBuilder.wn
        /AtTextFieldTextGry.eps
./NextLibrary/Documentation/NeXT/SysRefMan/08_IntfBuilder.wn/AtButtonAlign.eps
./NextLibrary/Documentation/NeXT/SysRefMan/08_IntfBuilder.wn/AtButtonAlt.eps
./NextLibrary/Documentation/NeXT/SysRefMan/08_IntfBuilder.wn/AtButtonOptions.eps
./NextLibrary/Documentation/NeXT/SysRefMan/08_IntfBuilder.wn/resize.eps
./NextLibrary/Documentation/NeXT/SysRefMan/08_IntfBuilder.wn
        /AtMatrixBgrndGray.eps
./NextLibrary/Documentation/NeXT/SysRefMan/08_IntfBuilder.wn/AtMatrixMode.eps
./NextLibrary/Documentation/NeXT/SysRefMan/08_IntfBuilder.wn
        /AtMatrixPrototype.eps
./NextLibrary/Documentation/NeXT/SysRefMan/08_IntfBuilder.wn/AtMatrixTag.eps
./NextLibrary/Documentation/NeXT/SysRefMan/08_IntfBuilder.wn/AtFormBgrndGray.eps
./NextLibrary/Documentation/NeXT/SysRefMan/08_IntfBuilder.wn/AtFormOptions.eps
./NextLibrary/Documentation/NeXT/SysRefMan/08_IntfBuilder.wn/AtFormTag.eps
./NextLibrary/Documentation/NeXT/SysRefMan/08_IntfBuilder.wn/AtFormText.eps
./NextLibrary/Documentation/NeXT/SysRefMan/08_IntfBuilder.wn/AtFormTitle.eps
./NextLibrary/Documentation/NeXT/SysRefMan/08_IntfBuilder.wn/AtBoxHorzOff.eps
./NextLibrary/Documentation/NeXT/SysRefMan/08_IntfBuilder.wn/AtBoxVertOff.eps
./NextLibrary/Documentation/NeXT/SysRefMan/08_IntfBuilder.wn/AtSliderValues.eps
./NextLibrary/Documentation/NeXT/SysRefMan/08_IntfBuilder.wn/AtSliderOptions.eps
./NextLibrary/Documentation/NeXT/SysRefMan/08_IntfBuilder.wn/AtSliderTag.eps
```

./NextLibrary/Documentation/NeXT/SysRefMan/08_IntfBuilder.wn
    /AtScrollViewBgrndGray.eps
./NextLibrary/Documentation/NeXT/SysRefMan/08_IntfBuilder.wn
    /AtScrollViewTextGray.eps
./NextLibrary/Documentation/NeXT/SysRefMan/08_IntfBuilder.wn
    /AtScrollViewBordr.eps
./NextLibrary/Documentation/NeXT/SysRefMan/08_IntfBuilder.wn/AtWindowBacking.eps
./NextLibrary/Documentation/NeXT/SysRefMan/08_IntfBuilder.wn/Autosizing.eps
./NextLibrary/Documentation/NeXT/SysRefMan/08_IntfBuilder.wn
    /AtButtonIconPosition.eps
./NextLibrary/Documentation/NeXT/SysRefMan/08_IntfBuilder.wn/AtMenuCell.eps
./NextLibrary/Documentation/NeXT/SysRefMan/08_IntfBuilder.wn/WindowTitle.eps
./NextLibrary/Documentation/NeXT/SysRefMan/08_IntfBuilder.wn/WindowOptions.eps
./NextLibrary/Documentation/NeXT/SysRefMan/08_IntfBuilder.wn/WindowControls.eps
./NextLibrary/Documentation/NeXT/SysRefMan/08_IntfBuilder.wn/WindowClass.eps
./NextLibrary/Documentation/NeXT/SysRefMan/08_IntfBuilder.wn/resizeButton.eps
./NextLibrary/Documentation/NeXT/SysRefMan/08_IntfBuilder.wn/BuildApp.eps
./NextLibrary/Documentation/NeXT/SysRefMan/08_IntfBuilder.wn/ModulePanel.eps
./NextLibrary/Documentation/NeXT/SysRefMan/08_IntfBuilder.wn/IconWindow.eps
./NextLibrary/Documentation/NeXT/SysRefMan/08_IntfBuilder.wn/ClInstantiate.eps
./NextLibrary/Documentation/NeXT/SysRefMan/08_IntfBuilder.wn/ClParse.eps
./NextLibrary/Documentation/NeXT/SysRefMan/08_IntfBuilder.wn/ClUnparse.eps
./NextLibrary/Documentation/NeXT/SysRefMan/08_IntfBuilder.wn/ClSubclass.eps
./NextLibrary/Documentation/NeXT/SysRefMan/08_IntfBuilder.wn/AtTextFieldOps.eps
./NextLibrary/Documentation/NeXT/SysRefMan/08_IntfBuilder.wn/AtMatrixOps.eps
./NextLibrary/Documentation/NeXT/SysRefMan/08_IntfBuilder.wn/AtSounds.eps
./NextLibrary/Documentation/NeXT/SysRefMan/08_IntfBuilder.wn/ClassInspector.eps
./NextLibrary/Documentation/NeXT/SysRefMan/08_IntfBuilder.wn/WNGraphic.265231.eps
./NextLibrary/Documentation/NeXT/SysRefMan/08_IntfBuilder.wn/AtProjectTypes.eps
./NextLibrary/Documentation/NeXT/SysRefMan/08_IntfBuilder.wn/MainMenu.eps
./NextLibrary/Documentation/NeXT/SysRefMan/08_IntfBuilder.wn/AtProjectOptions.eps
./NextLibrary/Documentation/NeXT/SysRefMan/08_IntfBuilder.wn/AtScrollViewOpts.eps
./NextLibrary/Documentation/NeXT/SysRefMan/08_IntfBuilder.wn
    /FormConnections.028523.eps
./NextLibrary/Documentation/NeXT/SysRefMan/08_IntfBuilder.wn/AtFilesOwner.eps
./NextLibrary/Documentation/NeXT/SysRefMan/08_IntfBuilder.wn/AtIcons.eps
./NextLibrary/Documentation/NeXT/SysRefMan/08_IntfBuilder.wn/bigSwitch.184746.eps
./NextLibrary/Documentation/NeXT/SysRefMan/08_IntfBuilder.wn
    /TWindowInspector.282664.eps
./NextLibrary/Documentation/NeXT/SysRefMan/08_IntfBuilder.wn
    /ProjectFiles.712731.eps
./NextLibrary/Documentation/NeXT/SysRefMan/08_IntfBuilder.wn
    /Miscellaneous.028186.eps
./NextLibrary/Documentation/NeXT/SysRefMan/08_IntfBuilder.wn/WNGraphic.996861.eps
./NextLibrary/Documentation/NeXT/SysRefMan/08_IntfBuilder.wn/WNDocument.wn
./NextLibrary/Documentation/NeXT/SysRefMan/08_IntfBuilder.wn/WNGraphic.075608.eps
./NextLibrary/Documentation/NeXT/SysRefMan/08_IntfBuilder.wn/WNGraphic.863013.eps
./NextLibrary/Documentation/NeXT/SysRefMan/08_IntfBuilder.wn/WNGraphic.320799.eps
./NextLibrary/Documentation/NeXT/SysRefMan/08_IntfBuilder.wn/WNGraphic.649212.eps
./NextLibrary/Documentation/NeXT/SysRefMan/08_IntfBuilder.wn/WNGraphic.917180.eps
./NextLibrary/Documentation/NeXT/SysRefMan/08_IntfBuilder.wn/WNGraphic.514495.eps
./NextLibrary/Documentation/NeXT/SysRefMan/08_IntfBuilder.wn/SampleButtons2.eps

./NextLibrary/Documentation/NeXT/SysRefMan/08_IntfBuilder.wn/WNGraphic.977158.eps
./NextLibrary/Documentation/NeXT/SysRefMan/08_IntfBuilder.wn/WNGraphic.765964.eps
./NextLibrary/Documentation/NeXT/SysRefMan/08_IntfBuilder.wn/alignment.987911.eps
./NextLibrary/Documentation/NeXT/SysRefMan/08_IntfBuilder.wn/WNGraphic.325209.eps
./NextLibrary/Documentation/NeXT/SysRefMan/08_IntfBuilder.wn/WNGraphic.974486.eps
./NextLibrary/Documentation/NeXT/SysRefMan/08_IntfBuilder.wn/WNGraphic.064790.eps
./NextLibrary/Documentation/NeXT/SysRefMan/08_IntfBuilder.wn/WNGraphic.850924.eps
./NextLibrary/Documentation/NeXT/SysRefMan/08_IntfBuilder.wn/WNGraphic.040612.eps
./NextLibrary/Documentation/NeXT/SysRefMan/08_IntfBuilder.wn
    /ProjInspectFiles.097918.286737.eps
./NextLibrary/Documentation/NeXT/SysRefMan/08_IntfBuilder.wn/WNGraphic.809378.eps
./NextLibrary/Documentation/NeXT/SysRefMan/08_IntfBuilder.wn/FontMenu.811985.eps
./NextLibrary/Documentation/NeXT/SysRefMan/08_IntfBuilder.wn/WNGraphic.730566.eps
./NextLibrary/Documentation/NeXT/SysRefMan/08_IntfBuilder.wn/WNGraphic.162838.eps
./NextLibrary/Documentation/NeXT/SysRefMan/08_IntfBuilder.wn/TextEditor.eps
./NextLibrary/Documentation/NeXT/SysRefMan/08_IntfBuilder.wn/AppDesIntFill.eps
./NextLibrary/Documentation/NeXT/SysRefMan/08_IntfBuilder.wn/WNGraphic.136857.eps
./NextLibrary/Documentation/NeXT/SysRefMan/08_IntfBuilder.wn/WNGraphic.398612.eps
./NextLibrary/Documentation/NeXT/SysRefMan/08_IntfBuilder.wn/WNGraphic.481769.eps
./NextLibrary/Documentation/NeXT/SysRefMan/08_IntfBuilder.wn/.places
./NextLibrary/Documentation/NeXT/SysRefMan/08_IntfBuilder.wn/WNGraphic.251871.eps
./NextLibrary/Documentation/NeXT/SysRefMan/14_ProgDSP.wn
./NextLibrary/Documentation/NeXT/SysRefMan/15_WinServer.wn
./NextLibrary/Documentation/NeXT/SysRefMan/19_CompilerDebugger.wn
./NextLibrary/Documentation/NeXT/SysRefMan/21_Header.wn
./NextLibrary/Documentation/NeXT/SysRefMan/25_ScoreFileRef.wn
./NextLibrary/Documentation/NeXT/SysRefMan/27_MachFunctions.wn
./NextLibrary/Documentation/NeXT/SysRefMan/28_DataFormats.wn
./NextLibrary/Documentation/NeXT/SysRefMan/About.wn
./NextLibrary/Documentation/NeXT/SysRefMan/ApA_ObjCSummary.wn
./NextLibrary/Documentation/NeXT/SysRefMan/ApD_OpSummary.wn
./NextLibrary/Documentation/NeXT/SysRefMan/ApE_SFileSummary.wn
./NextLibrary/Documentation/NeXT/SysRefMan/ApH_DSPDetails.wn
./NextLibrary/Documentation/NeXT/SysRefMan/ApH_DSPDetails.wn/WNDocument.wn
./NextLibrary/Documentation/NeXT/SysRefMan/ApH_DSPDetails.wn/DSPConInterface.eps
./NextLibrary/Documentation/NeXT/SysRefMan/ApH_DSPDetails.wn
    /ApH_DSPDetails.wn.prv
./NextLibrary/Documentation/NeXT/SysRefMan/ApH_DSPDetails.wn/.places
./NextLibrary/Documentation/NeXT/SysRefMan/ApI_MachSummary.wn
./NextLibrary/Documentation/NeXT/SysRefMan/ApJ_UNIXDiffs.wn
./NextLibrary/Documentation/NeXT/SysRefMan/ApK_KeyInfo.wn
./NextLibrary/Documentation/NeXT/SysRefMan/ApK_KeyInfo.wn/KeyCodes.eps
./NextLibrary/Documentation/NeXT/SysRefMan/ApK_KeyInfo.wn/WNDocument.wn
./NextLibrary/Documentation/NeXT/SysRefMan/ApK_KeyInfo.wn/StandEncodVect.eps
./NextLibrary/Documentation/NeXT/SysRefMan/ApK_KeyInfo.wn/SymbEncodVect.eps
./NextLibrary/Documentation/NeXT/SysRefMan/ApK_KeyInfo.wn/.places
./NextLibrary/Documentation/NeXT/SysRefMan/ApL_SysBitmaps.wn
./NextLibrary/Documentation/NeXT/SysRefMan/ApL_SysBitmaps.wn/WNDocument.wn
./NextLibrary/Documentation/NeXT/SysRefMan/ApL_SysBitmaps.wn/PortraitH.eps
./NextLibrary/Documentation/NeXT/SysRefMan/ApL_SysBitmaps.wn/Portrait.eps
./NextLibrary/Documentation/NeXT/SysRefMan/ApL_SysBitmaps.wn/LandscapeH.eps

```
./NextLibrary/Documentation/NeXT/SysRefMan/ApL_SysBitmaps.wn/Landscape.eps
./NextLibrary/Documentation/NeXT/SysRefMan/ApL_SysBitmaps.wn/ChooseH.eps
./NextLibrary/Documentation/NeXT/SysRefMan/ApL_SysBitmaps.wn/Choose.eps
./NextLibrary/Documentation/NeXT/SysRefMan/ApL_SysBitmaps.wn/Manual.eps
./NextLibrary/Documentation/NeXT/SysRefMan/ApL_SysBitmaps.wn/Auto.eps
./NextLibrary/Documentation/NeXT/SysRefMan/ApL_SysBitmaps.wn/MiniWorld.eps
./NextLibrary/Documentation/NeXT/SysRefMan/ApL_SysBitmaps.wn/MiniWindow.eps
./NextLibrary/Documentation/NeXT/SysRefMan/ApL_SysBitmaps.wn/DefaultIcon.eps
./NextLibrary/Documentation/NeXT/SysRefMan/ApL_SysBitmaps.wn/DefaultAppIcon.eps
./NextLibrary/Documentation/NeXT/SysRefMan/ApL_SysBitmaps.wn/ScrollMenuUpH.eps
./NextLibrary/Documentation/NeXT/SysRefMan/ApL_SysBitmaps.wn/ScrollMenuUpD.eps
./NextLibrary/Documentation/NeXT/SysRefMan/ApL_SysBitmaps.wn/ScrollMenuUp.eps
./NextLibrary/Documentation/NeXT/SysRefMan/ApL_SysBitmaps.wn/ScrollMenuRightH.eps
./NextLibrary/Documentation/NeXT/SysRefMan/ApL_SysBitmaps.wn/ScrollMenuRightD.eps
./NextLibrary/Documentation/NeXT/SysRefMan/ApL_SysBitmaps.wn/ScrollMenuRight.eps
./NextLibrary/Documentation/NeXT/SysRefMan/ApL_SysBitmaps.wn/ScrollMenuLeftH.eps
./NextLibrary/Documentation/NeXT/SysRefMan/ApL_SysBitmaps.wn/ScrollMenuLeftD.eps
./NextLibrary/Documentation/NeXT/SysRefMan/ApL_SysBitmaps.wn/ScrollMenuLeft.eps
./NextLibrary/Documentation/NeXT/SysRefMan/ApL_SysBitmaps.wn/ScrollMenuDownH.eps
./NextLibrary/Documentation/NeXT/SysRefMan/ApL_SysBitmaps.wn/ScrollMenuDownD.eps
./NextLibrary/Documentation/NeXT/SysRefMan/ApL_SysBitmaps.wn/ScrollMenuDown.eps
./NextLibrary/Documentation/NeXT/SysRefMan/ApL_SysBitmaps.wn/ScrollUpH.eps
./NextLibrary/Documentation/NeXT/SysRefMan/ApL_SysBitmaps.wn/ScrollUp.eps
./NextLibrary/Documentation/NeXT/SysRefMan/ApL_SysBitmaps.wn/ScrollRightH.eps
./NextLibrary/Documentation/NeXT/SysRefMan/ApL_SysBitmaps.wn/ScrollRight.eps
./NextLibrary/Documentation/NeXT/SysRefMan/ApL_SysBitmaps.wn/ScrollLeftH.eps
./NextLibrary/Documentation/NeXT/SysRefMan/ApL_SysBitmaps.wn/ScrollLeft.eps
./NextLibrary/Documentation/NeXT/SysRefMan/ApL_SysBitmaps.wn/ScrollDownH.eps
./NextLibrary/Documentation/NeXT/SysRefMan/ApL_SysBitmaps.wn/ScrollDown.eps
./NextLibrary/Documentation/NeXT/SysRefMan/ApL_SysBitmaps.wn/ScrollKnob.eps
./NextLibrary/Documentation/NeXT/SysRefMan/ApL_SysBitmaps.wn/PullDownH.eps
./NextLibrary/Documentation/NeXT/SysRefMan/ApL_SysBitmaps.wn/PullDown.eps
./NextLibrary/Documentation/NeXT/SysRefMan/ApL_SysBitmaps.wn/MenuArrowH.eps
./NextLibrary/Documentation/NeXT/SysRefMan/ApL_SysBitmaps.wn/MenuArrow.eps
./NextLibrary/Documentation/NeXT/SysRefMan/ApL_SysBitmaps.wn/VSliderKnob.eps
./NextLibrary/Documentation/NeXT/SysRefMan/ApL_SysBitmaps.wn/.places
./NextLibrary/Documentation/NeXT/SysRefMan/ApL_SysBitmaps.wn/ReturnSign.eps
./NextLibrary/Documentation/NeXT/SysRefMan/ApL_SysBitmaps.wn/RadioH.eps
./NextLibrary/Documentation/NeXT/SysRefMan/ApL_SysBitmaps.wn/Radio.eps
./NextLibrary/Documentation/NeXT/SysRefMan/ApL_SysBitmaps.wn/PopUpH.eps
./NextLibrary/Documentation/NeXT/SysRefMan/ApL_SysBitmaps.wn/PopUp.eps
./NextLibrary/Documentation/NeXT/SysRefMan/ApL_SysBitmaps.wn/IconifyH.eps
./NextLibrary/Documentation/NeXT/SysRefMan/ApL_SysBitmaps.wn/Iconify.eps
./NextLibrary/Documentation/NeXT/SysRefMan/ApL_SysBitmaps.wn/Editing.eps
./NextLibrary/Documentation/NeXT/SysRefMan/ApL_SysBitmaps.wn/CloseH.eps
./NextLibrary/Documentation/NeXT/SysRefMan/ApL_SysBitmaps.wn/Close.eps
./NextLibrary/Documentation/NeXT/SysRefMan/ApL_SysBitmaps.wn/SwitchH.eps
./NextLibrary/Documentation/NeXT/SysRefMan/ApL_SysBitmaps.wn/Switch.eps
./NextLibrary/Documentation/NeXT/SysRefMan/ApL_SysBitmaps.wn/Square16H.eps
./NextLibrary/Documentation/NeXT/SysRefMan/ApL_SysBitmaps.wn/Square16.eps
./NextLibrary/Documentation/NeXT/SysRefMan/ApL_SysBitmaps.wn/HsliderKnob.eps
./NextLibrary/Documentation/NeXT/SysRefMan/ApL_SysBitmaps.wn/NXArrowGray.eps
./NextLibrary/Documentation/NeXT/SysRefMan/ApL_SysBitmaps.wn/NXIBeamGray.eps
./NextLibrary/Documentation/NeXT/SysRefMan/ApL_SysBitmaps.wn/NXWaitGray.eps
./NextLibrary/Documentation/NeXT/SysRefMan/Contents.wn
./NextLibrary/Documentation/NeXT/SysRefMan/Pt2_Reference.wn
./NextLibrary/Documentation/NeXT/SysRefMan/PtAppendices.wn
./NextLibrary/Documentation/NeXT/SysRefMan/Reading.wn
./NextLibrary/Documentation/NeXT/SysRefMan/.places
./NextLibrary/Documentation/NeXT/SysRefNotes
./NextLibrary/Documentation/NeXT/SysRefNotes/15_WinServer
./NextLibrary/Documentation/NeXT/SysRefNotes/15_WinServer/statusdict
./NextLibrary/Documentation/NeXT/SysRefNotes/15_WinServer/Fonts.wn
./NextLibrary/Documentation/NeXT/SysRefNotes/15_WinServer/Events
./NextLibrary/Documentation/NeXT/SysRefNotes/15_WinServer/Packages
./NextLibrary/Documentation/NeXT/SysRefNotes/15_WinServer/MessageProtocol.wn
./NextLibrary/Documentation/NeXT/SysRefNotes/15_WinServer/WindowManagement
./NextLibrary/Documentation/NeXT/SysRefNotes/15_WinServer/.places
./NextLibrary/Documentation/NeXT/SysRefNotes/16_Mach
./NextLibrary/Documentation/NeXT/SysRefNotes/16_Mach/Drivers
./NextLibrary/Documentation/NeXT/SysRefNotes/16_Mach/Drivers/SoundDriver.wn
./NextLibrary/Documentation/NeXT/SysRefNotes/16_Mach/Drivers/MidiDriver.wn
./NextLibrary/Documentation/NeXT/SysRefNotes/16_Mach/Drivers/MidiDriver.wn/WNDocument.wn
./NextLibrary/Documentation/NeXT/SysRefNotes/16_Mach/Drivers/MidiDriver.wn/WNGraphic.266165.eps
./NextLibrary/Documentation/NeXT/SysRefNotes/16_Mach/Drivers/MidiDriver.wn/.places
./NextLibrary/Documentation/NeXT/SysRefNotes/16_Mach/Drivers/.places
./NextLibrary/Documentation/NeXT/SysRefNotes/16_Mach/.places
./NextLibrary/Documentation/NeXT/SysRefNotes/24_PostOps
./NextLibrary/Documentation/NeXT/SysRefNotes/24_PostOps/statusdictOps
./NextLibrary/Documentation/NeXT/SysRefNotes/24_PostOps/.places
./NextLibrary/Documentation/NeXT/SysRefNotes/ApC_CFuncSummary
./NextLibrary/Documentation/NeXT/SysRefNotes/ApC_CFuncSummary/MusicKitFunctions
./NextLibrary/Documentation/NeXT/SysRefNotes/ApC_CFuncSummary/.places
./NextLibrary/Documentation/NeXT/SysRefNotes/Contents.wn
./NextLibrary/Documentation/NeXT/SysRefNotes/.places
./NextLibrary/Documentation/NeXT/SysAdmin
./NextLibrary/Documentation/NeXT/SysAdmin/About.wn
./NextLibrary/Documentation/NeXT/SysAdmin/ApA_BootSequence.wn
./NextLibrary/Documentation/NeXT/SysAdmin/ApB_Lpd.wn
./NextLibrary/Documentation/NeXT/SysAdmin/Bibliography.wn
./NextLibrary/Documentation/NeXT/SysAdmin/ApC_Sendmail.wn
./NextLibrary/Documentation/NeXT/SysAdmin/Contents.wn
./NextLibrary/Documentation/NeXT/SysAdmin/03_FileSystems.wn
./NextLibrary/Documentation/NeXT/SysAdmin/04_AdminServices.wn
./NextLibrary/Documentation/NeXT/SysAdmin/07_Printing.wn
./NextLibrary/Documentation/NeXT/SysAdmin/07_Printing.wn/WNDocument.wn
./NextLibrary/Documentation/NeXT/SysAdmin/07_Printing.wn/PrintManagerIcon.065257.eps
./NextLibrary/Documentation/NeXT/SysAdmin/07_Printing.wn/PMPanel.eps
```

```
./NextLibrary/Documentation/NeXT/SysAdmin/07_Printing.wn
    /ConfigurePrinterPanel.815591.eps
./NextLibrary/Documentation/NeXT/SysAdmin/07_Printing.wn
    /SelectDomainFinal.348985.eps
./NextLibrary/Documentation/NeXT/SysAdmin/07_Printing.wn/.places
./NextLibrary/Documentation/NeXT/SysAdmin/08_Maintenance.wn
./NextLibrary/Documentation/NeXT/SysAdmin/08_Maintenance.wn/WNDocument.wn
./NextLibrary/Documentation/NeXT/SysAdmin/08_Maintenance.wn/BuildDiskWindow.eps
./NextLibrary/Documentation/NeXT/SysAdmin/08_Maintenance.wn/BuildDiskIcon.eps
./NextLibrary/Documentation/NeXT/SysAdmin/08_Maintenance.wn/.places
./NextLibrary/Documentation/NeXT/SysAdmin/ApD_BIND.wn
./NextLibrary/Documentation/NeXT/SysAdmin/ApE_Security.wn
./NextLibrary/Documentation/NeXT/SysAdmin/ApF_UUCP.wn
./NextLibrary/Documentation/NeXT/SysAdmin/ApG_Fsck.wn
./NextLibrary/Documentation/NeXT/SysAdmin/ApH_NetInfoManager.wn
./NextLibrary/Documentation/NeXT/SysAdmin/ApH_NetInfoManager.wn/NIM.eps
./NextLibrary/Documentation/NeXT/SysAdmin/ApH_NetInfoManager.wn/Browser.eps
./NextLibrary/Documentation/NeXT/SysAdmin/ApH_NetInfoManager.wn/PropEdit.eps
./NextLibrary/Documentation/NeXT/SysAdmin/ApH_NetInfoManager.wn/ViewBy.eps
./NextLibrary/Documentation/NeXT/SysAdmin/ApH_NetInfoManager.wn/BD.eps
./NextLibrary/Documentation/NeXT/SysAdmin/ApH_NetInfoManager.wn/WNDocument.wn
./NextLibrary/Documentation/NeXT/SysAdmin/ApH_NetInfoManager.wn/.places
./NextLibrary/Documentation/NeXT/SysAdmin/Cover.wn
./NextLibrary/Documentation/NeXT/SysAdmin/Cover.wn/Logo.eps
./NextLibrary/Documentation/NeXT/SysAdmin/Cover.wn/WNDocument.wn
./NextLibrary/Documentation/NeXT/SysAdmin/Cover.wn/.places
./NextLibrary/Documentation/NeXT/SysAdmin/.places
./NextLibrary/Documentation/NeXT/.index
./NextLibrary/Documentation/NeXT/.index/icon.tiff
./NextLibrary/Documentation/NeXT/.index/Copyright.rtf
./NextLibrary/Documentation/NeXT/.index/index
./NextLibrary/Documentation/NeXT/.index/index.D
./NextLibrary/Documentation/NeXT/.index/index.L
./NextLibrary/Documentation/NeXT/.index/index.Registry.D
./NextLibrary/Documentation/NeXT/.index/index.Registry.L
./NextLibrary/Documentation/NeXT/.index/.places
./NextLibrary/Documentation/NeXT/Examples
./NextLibrary/Documentation/NeXT/Examples/WNDataDoc.wn
./NextLibrary/Documentation/NeXT/Examples/WNTemplate.wn
./NextLibrary/Documentation/NeXT/Examples/.places
./NextLibrary/Documentation/NeXT/.macros
./NextLibrary/Documentation/NeXT/.places
./NextLibrary/Documentation/Adobe
./NextLibrary/Documentation/Adobe/Perspective.ps
./NextLibrary/Documentation/Adobe/pswrap.ps
./NextLibrary/Documentation/Adobe/ClientLibrary.ps
./NextLibrary/Documentation/Adobe/CharBitmap.ps
./NextLibrary/Documentation/Adobe/EPSFiles.ps
./NextLibrary/Documentation/Adobe/ColorExtensions.ps
./NextLibrary/Documentation/Adobe/DocStructConv.ps
./NextLibrary/Documentation/Adobe/FontMetricFiles.ps
./NextLibrary/Documentation/Adobe/DPSExtensions.ps
./NextLibrary/Documentation/Adobe/.places
./NextLibrary/Documentation/Ariel
./NextLibrary/Documentation/Ariel/.index
./NextLibrary/Documentation/Ariel/.index/index
./NextLibrary/Documentation/Ariel/.index/index.D
./NextLibrary/Documentation/Ariel/.index/index.L
./NextLibrary/Documentation/Ariel/.index/index.Registry.D
./NextLibrary/Documentation/Ariel/.index/index.Registry.L
./NextLibrary/Documentation/Ariel/.index/.places
./NextLibrary/Documentation/Ariel/Bug56Reference.wn
./NextLibrary/Documentation/Ariel/Bug56Reference.wn/WNDocument.wn
./NextLibrary/Documentation/Ariel/Bug56Reference.wn/WNGraphic.918049.eps
./NextLibrary/Documentation/Ariel/Bug56Reference.wn/WNGraphic.755613.eps
./NextLibrary/Documentation/Ariel/Bug56Reference.wn/WNGraphic.425397.eps
./NextLibrary/Documentation/Ariel/Bug56Reference.wn/WNGraphic.801232.eps
./NextLibrary/Documentation/Ariel/Bug56Reference.wn/WNGraphic.571334.eps
./NextLibrary/Documentation/Ariel/Bug56Reference.wn/WNGraphic.942694.eps
./NextLibrary/Documentation/Ariel/Bug56Reference.wn/WNGraphic.368221.eps
./NextLibrary/Documentation/Ariel/Bug56Reference.wn/WNGraphic.093443.eps
./NextLibrary/Documentation/Ariel/Bug56Reference.wn/WNGraphic.328815.eps
./NextLibrary/Documentation/Ariel/Bug56Reference.wn/WNGraphic.833893.eps
./NextLibrary/Documentation/Ariel/Bug56Reference.wn/WNGraphic.994526.eps
./NextLibrary/Documentation/Ariel/Bug56Reference.wn/WNGraphic.285401.eps
./NextLibrary/Documentation/Ariel/Bug56Reference.wn/WNGraphic.344510.eps
./NextLibrary/Documentation/Ariel/Bug56Reference.wn/WNGraphic.451845.eps
./NextLibrary/Documentation/Ariel/Bug56Reference.wn/WNGraphic.552500.eps
./NextLibrary/Documentation/Ariel/Bug56Reference.wn/WNGraphic.814255.eps
./NextLibrary/Documentation/Ariel/Bug56Reference.wn/WNGraphic.832155.eps
./NextLibrary/Documentation/Ariel/Bug56Reference.wn/WNGraphic.762358.eps
./NextLibrary/Documentation/Ariel/Bug56Reference.wn/WNGraphic.647811.eps
./NextLibrary/Documentation/Ariel/Bug56Reference.wn/WNGraphic.804371.eps
./NextLibrary/Documentation/Ariel/Bug56Reference.wn/WNGraphic.464803.eps
./NextLibrary/Documentation/Ariel/Bug56Reference.wn/WNGraphic.541280.eps
./NextLibrary/Documentation/Ariel/Bug56Reference.wn/WNGraphic.781127.eps
./NextLibrary/Documentation/Ariel/Bug56Reference.wn/WNGraphic.179337.eps
./NextLibrary/Documentation/Ariel/Bug56Reference.wn/WNGraphic.348453.eps
./NextLibrary/Documentation/Ariel/Bug56Reference.wn/WNGraphic.595045.eps
./NextLibrary/Documentation/Ariel/Bug56Reference.wn/WNGraphic.719878.eps
./NextLibrary/Documentation/Ariel/Bug56Reference.wn/WNGraphic.182074.eps
./NextLibrary/Documentation/Ariel/Bug56Reference.wn/WNGraphic.381179.eps
./NextLibrary/Documentation/Ariel/Bug56Reference.wn/WNGraphic.877839.eps
./NextLibrary/Documentation/Ariel/Bug56Reference.wn/.places
./NextLibrary/Documentation/Ariel/Bug56Reference.wn/WNGraphic.104598.eps
./NextLibrary/Documentation/Ariel/Bug56Reference.wn/WNGraphic.732836.eps
./NextLibrary/Documentation/Ariel/Bug56Reference.wn/WNGraphic.493923.eps
./NextLibrary/Documentation/Ariel/Bug56Reference.wn/WNGraphic.710863.eps
./NextLibrary/Documentation/Ariel/Bug56Reference.wn/WNGraphic.124366.eps
./NextLibrary/Documentation/Ariel/Bug56Reference.wn/WNGraphic.323471.eps
./NextLibrary/Documentation/Ariel/Bug56Reference.wn/WNGraphic.696167.eps
./NextLibrary/Documentation/Ariel/Bug56Reference.wn/WNGraphic.909099.eps
```

./NextLibrary/Documentation/Ariel/Bug56Reference.wn/WNGraphic.308178.eps

./NextLibrary/Documentation/Ariel/degnext.asm

./NextLibrary/Documentation/Ariel/.places

./NextLibrary/Documentation/CommonLisp

./NextLibrary/Documentation/CommonLisp/.index

./NextLibrary/Documentation/CommonLisp/.index/.roffArgs

./NextLibrary/Documentation/CommonLisp/.index/tmac.Franz

./NextLibrary/Documentation/CommonLisp/.index/index

./NextLibrary/Documentation/CommonLisp/.index/index.D

./NextLibrary/Documentation/CommonLisp/.index/index.L

./NextLibrary/Documentation/CommonLisp/.index/index.Registry.D

./NextLibrary/Documentation/CommonLisp/.index/index.Registry.L

./NextLibrary/Documentation/CommonLisp/.index/.places

./NextLibrary/Documentation/CommonLisp/CLUserMan

./NextLibrary/Documentation/CommonLisp/CLUserMan/abouts

./NextLibrary/Documentation/CommonLisp/CLUserMan/abouts/aboutHbuildingHlisp.lispd

./NextLibrary/Documentation/CommonLisp/CLUserMan/abouts/aboutHcstructs.lispd

./NextLibrary/Documentation/CommonLisp/CLUserMan/abouts/aboutHdataHtypes.lispd

./NextLibrary/Documentation/CommonLisp/CLUserMan/abouts/aboutHdebugging.lispd

./NextLibrary/Documentation/CommonLisp/CLUserMan/abouts/aboutHdeclarations.lispd

./NextLibrary/Documentation/CommonLisp/CLUserMan/abouts/aboutHfiletypes.lispd

./NextLibrary/Documentation/CommonLisp/CLUserMan/abouts/aboutHforeign.lispd

./NextLibrary/Documentation/CommonLisp/CLUserMan/abouts/aboutHhelp.lispd

./NextLibrary/Documentation/CommonLisp/CLUserMan/abouts/aboutHinitialization.lispd

./NextLibrary/Documentation/CommonLisp/CLUserMan/abouts/aboutHmp.lispd

./NextLibrary/Documentation/CommonLisp/CLUserMan/abouts/aboutHobjectiveHc.lispd

./NextLibrary/Documentation/CommonLisp/CLUserMan/abouts/aboutHpackages.lispd

./NextLibrary/Documentation/CommonLisp/CLUserMan/abouts/aboutHpassingHvalues.lispd

./NextLibrary/Documentation/CommonLisp/CLUserMan/abouts/aboutHpathnames.lispd

./NextLibrary/Documentation/CommonLisp/CLUserMan/abouts/aboutHcaseHmodes.lispd

./NextLibrary/Documentation/CommonLisp/CLUserMan/abouts/aboutHprocHdynHenv.lispd

./NextLibrary/Documentation/CommonLisp/CLUserMan/abouts/aboutHprocessHlocks.lispd

./NextLibrary/Documentation/CommonLisp/CLUserMan/abouts/aboutHprofiling.lispd

./NextLibrary/Documentation/CommonLisp/CLUserMan/abouts/aboutHscheduler.lispd

./NextLibrary/Documentation/CommonLisp/CLUserMan/abouts/aboutHsearchHlists.lispd

./NextLibrary/Documentation/CommonLisp/CLUserMan/abouts/aboutHstackHgroups.lispd

./NextLibrary/Documentation/CommonLisp/CLUserMan/abouts/aboutHstepping.lispd

./NextLibrary/Documentation/CommonLisp/CLUserMan/abouts/aboutHtoplevel.lispd

./NextLibrary/Documentation/CommonLisp/CLUserMan/abouts/aboutHtracing.lispd

./NextLibrary/Documentation/CommonLisp/CLUserMan/abouts/aboutHcHtypes.lispd

./NextLibrary/Documentation/CommonLisp/CLUserMan/abouts/aboutHinspecting.lispd

./NextLibrary/Documentation/CommonLisp/CLUserMan/abouts/aboutHadvice.lispd

./NextLibrary/Documentation/CommonLisp/CLUserMan/abouts/aboutHautoloading.lispd

./NextLibrary/Documentation/CommonLisp/CLUserMan/abouts/aboutHcompiling.lispd

./NextLibrary/Documentation/CommonLisp/CLUserMan/abouts/aboutHgarbageHcollecting.lispd

./NextLibrary/Documentation/CommonLisp/CLUserMan/abouts/.places

./NextLibrary/Documentation/CommonLisp/CLUserMan/abouts/aboutHportability.lispd

./NextLibrary/Documentation/CommonLisp/CLUserMan/abouts/aboutHsourceHfileHrecording.lispd

./NextLibrary/Documentation/CommonLisp/CLUserMan/clroff

./NextLibrary/Documentation/CommonLisp/CLUserMan/compiler

./NextLibrary/Documentation/CommonLisp/CLUserMan/compiler/explain.lispd

./NextLibrary/Documentation/CommonLisp/CLUserMan/compiler/generateHcallHcountHcodeHswitch.lispd

./NextLibrary/Documentation/CommonLisp/CLUserMan/compiler/saveHlocalHnamesHswitch.lispd

./NextLibrary/Documentation/CommonLisp/CLUserMan/compiler/tailHmergeHswitch.lispd

./NextLibrary/Documentation/CommonLisp/CLUserMan/compiler/targetHfpp.lispd

./NextLibrary/Documentation/CommonLisp/CLUserMan/compiler/trustHdeclarationsHswitch.lispd

./NextLibrary/Documentation/CommonLisp/CLUserMan/compiler/verifyHargumentHcountHswitch.lispd

./NextLibrary/Documentation/CommonLisp/CLUserMan/compiler/verifyHcarHcdrHswitch.lispd

./NextLibrary/Documentation/CommonLisp/CLUserMan/compiler/verifyHnonHgenericHswitch.lispd

./NextLibrary/Documentation/CommonLisp/CLUserMan/compiler/verifyHsymbolHvalueHisHboundHswitch.lispd

./NextLibrary/Documentation/CommonLisp/CLUserMan/compiler/generateHinterruptHchecksHswitch.lispd

./NextLibrary/Documentation/CommonLisp/CLUserMan/compiler/declaredHfixnumsHremainHfixnumsHswitch.lispd

./NextLibrary/Documentation/CommonLisp/CLUserMan/compiler/.places

./NextLibrary/Documentation/CommonLisp/CLUserMan/excl

./NextLibrary/Documentation/CommonLisp/CLUserMan/excl/SclearHinputHonHerrorS.lispd

./NextLibrary/Documentation/CommonLisp/CLUserMan/excl/ScompileHadviceS.lispd

./NextLibrary/Documentation/CommonLisp/CLUserMan/excl/SdefaultHlispHlistenerHbindingsS.lispd

./NextLibrary/Documentation/CommonLisp/CLUserMan/excl/SexclHpackageS.lispd

./NextLibrary/Documentation/CommonLisp/CLUserMan/excl/SfaslHdefaultHtypeS.lispd

./NextLibrary/Documentation/CommonLisp/CLUserMan/excl/SgcHafterHhookS.lispd

./NextLibrary/Documentation/CommonLisp/CLUserMan/excl/SglobalHgcHbehaviorS.lispd

./NextLibrary/Documentation/CommonLisp/CLUserMan/excl/SignoreHpackageHnameHcaseS.lispd

./NextLibrary/Documentation/CommonLisp/CLUserMan/excl/SinternHallowsHsymbolS.lispd

./NextLibrary/Documentation/CommonLisp/CLUserMan/excl/SkeywordHpackageS.lispd

./NextLibrary/Documentation/CommonLisp/CLUserMan/excl/SlispHpackageS.lispd

./NextLibrary/Documentation/CommonLisp/CLUserMan/excl/SopenHrenameHprefixS.lispd

./NextLibrary/Documentation/CommonLisp/CLUserMan/excl/advise.lispd

./NextLibrary/Documentation/CommonLisp/CLUserMan/excl/adviseH1.lispd

./NextLibrary/Documentation/CommonLisp/CLUserMan/excl/SprintHnicknameS.lispd

./NextLibrary/Documentation/CommonLisp/CLUserMan/excl/SprintHstructuresS.lispd

./NextLibrary/Documentation/CommonLisp/CLUserMan/excl/SrecordHsourceHfilesS.lispd

./NextLibrary/Documentation/CommonLisp/CLUserMan/excl/SredefinitionHwarningsS.lispd

./NextLibrary/Documentation/CommonLisp/CLUserMan/excl/SrestartHactionsS.lispd

./NextLibrary/Documentation/CommonLisp/CLUserMan/excl/SsourceHpathnameS.lispd

./NextLibrary/Documentation/CommonLisp/CLUserMan/excl/SstepHprintHlengthS.lispd

./NextLibrary/Documentation/CommonLisp/CLUserMan/excl/SstepHprintHlevelS.lispd

./NextLibrary/Documentation/CommonLisp/CLUserMan/excl/SsystemHpackageS.lispd
./NextLibrary/Documentation/CommonLisp/CLUserMan/excl/StraceHprintHlengthS.lispd
./NextLibrary/Documentation/CommonLisp/CLUserMan/excl/StraceHprintHlevelS.lispd
./NextLibrary/Documentation/CommonLisp/CLUserMan/excl/advisedHfunctions.lispd
./NextLibrary/Documentation/CommonLisp/CLUserMan/excl/arglist.lispd
./NextLibrary/Documentation/CommonLisp/CLUserMan/excl/bignump.lispd
./NextLibrary/Documentation/CommonLisp/CLUserMan/excl/chdir.lispd
./NextLibrary/Documentation/CommonLisp/CLUserMan/excl/compileHadvice.lispd
./NextLibrary/Documentation/CommonLisp/CLUserMan/excl
    /compileHfileHifHneeded.lispd
./NextLibrary/Documentation/CommonLisp/CLUserMan/excl/currentHdirectory.lispd
./NextLibrary/Documentation/CommonLisp/CLUserMan/excl
    /defHfunctionHspecHhandler.lispd
./NextLibrary/Documentation/CommonLisp/CLUserMan/excl/defadvice.lispd
./NextLibrary/Documentation/CommonLisp/CLUserMan/excl/describeHadvice.lispd
./NextLibrary/Documentation/CommonLisp/CLUserMan/excl
    /discardHallHsourceHfileHinfo.lispd
./NextLibrary/Documentation/CommonLisp/CLUserMan/excl/dribbleHbug.lispd
./NextLibrary/Documentation/CommonLisp/CLUserMan/excl/dumplisp.lispd
./NextLibrary/Documentation/CommonLisp/CLUserMan/excl/errorset.lispd
./NextLibrary/Documentation/CommonLisp/CLUserMan/excl/exit.lispd
./NextLibrary/Documentation/CommonLisp/CLUserMan/excl/fixnump.lispd
./NextLibrary/Documentation/CommonLisp/CLUserMan/excl/functionHcallHclear.lispd
./NextLibrary/Documentation/CommonLisp/CLUserMan/excl/functionHcallHcount.lispd
./NextLibrary/Documentation/CommonLisp/CLUserMan/excl/functionHcallHlist.lispd
./NextLibrary/Documentation/CommonLisp/CLUserMan/excl/functionHcallHrun.lispd
./NextLibrary/Documentation/CommonLisp/CLUserMan/excl/gc.lispd
./NextLibrary/Documentation/CommonLisp/CLUserMan/excl/ifS.lispd
./NextLibrary/Documentation/CommonLisp/CLUserMan/excl
    /generateHlibraryHpathnames.lispd
./NextLibrary/Documentation/CommonLisp/CLUserMan/excl
    /getHandHzeroHcallHcount.lispd
./NextLibrary/Documentation/CommonLisp/CLUserMan/excl/getHfunction.lispd
./NextLibrary/Documentation/CommonLisp/CLUserMan/excl/instancep.lispd
./NextLibrary/Documentation/CommonLisp/CLUserMan/excl/lispHsleep.lispd
./NextLibrary/Documentation/CommonLisp/CLUserMan/excl/pp.lispd
./NextLibrary/Documentation/CommonLisp/CLUserMan/excl/ratiop.lispd
./NextLibrary/Documentation/CommonLisp/CLUserMan/excl/runHshellHcommand.lispd
./NextLibrary/Documentation/CommonLisp/CLUserMan/excl/setHcaseHmode.lispd
./NextLibrary/Documentation/CommonLisp/CLUserMan/excl/shell.lispd
./NextLibrary/Documentation/CommonLisp/CLUserMan/excl/sourceHfile.lispd
./NextLibrary/Documentation/CommonLisp/CLUserMan/excl/unadvise.lispd
./NextLibrary/Documentation/CommonLisp/CLUserMan/excl/unadviseH1.lispd
./NextLibrary/Documentation/CommonLisp/CLUserMan/excl/uncompile.lispd
./NextLibrary/Documentation/CommonLisp/CLUserMan/excl
    /SclHdefaultHspecialHbindingsS.lispd
./NextLibrary/Documentation/CommonLisp/CLUserMan/excl/ScurrentHcaseHmodeS.lispd
./NextLibrary/Documentation/CommonLisp/CLUserMan/excl
    /SopenHrenameHfunctionS.lispd
./NextLibrary/Documentation/CommonLisp/CLUserMan/excl/SopenHrenameHsuffixS.lispd
./NextLibrary/Documentation/CommonLisp/CLUserMan/excl/StenuredHbytesHlimitS.lispd
./NextLibrary/Documentation/CommonLisp/CLUserMan/excl/fileHolderHp.lispd

./NextLibrary/Documentation/CommonLisp/CLUserMan/excl/functionHcallHreport.lispd
./NextLibrary/Documentation/CommonLisp/CLUserMan/excl/singleHfloatHp.lispd
./NextLibrary/Documentation/CommonLisp/CLUserMan/excl
    /usernameHtoHhomeHdirectory.lispd
./NextLibrary/Documentation/CommonLisp/CLUserMan/excl/.places
./NextLibrary/Documentation/CommonLisp/CLUserMan/foreign
./NextLibrary/Documentation/CommonLisp/CLUserMan/foreign/Carguments.lispd
./NextLibrary/Documentation/CommonLisp/CLUserMan/foreign/CconvertHsymbol.lispd
./NextLibrary/Documentation/CommonLisp/CLUserMan/foreign/CentryHpoint.lispd
./NextLibrary/Documentation/CommonLisp/CLUserMan/foreign/CforeignHfiles.lispd
./NextLibrary/Documentation/CommonLisp/CLUserMan/foreign/Clanguage.lispd
./NextLibrary/Documentation/CommonLisp/CLUserMan/foreign/Cprint.lispd
./NextLibrary/Documentation/CommonLisp/CLUserMan/foreign/CrememberHaddress.lispd
./NextLibrary/Documentation/CommonLisp/CLUserMan/foreign/CreturnHtype.lispd
./NextLibrary/Documentation/CommonLisp/CLUserMan/foreign/CsystemHlibraries.lispd
./NextLibrary/Documentation/CommonLisp/CLUserMan/foreign/convertHtoHlang.lispd
./NextLibrary/Documentation/CommonLisp/CLUserMan/foreign/defHcHtype.lispd
./NextLibrary/Documentation/CommonLisp/CLUserMan/foreign/defHcHtypedef.lispd
./NextLibrary/Documentation/CommonLisp/CLUserMan/foreign/defforeign.lispd
./NextLibrary/Documentation/CommonLisp/CLUserMan/foreign/defunHcHcallable.lispd
./NextLibrary/Documentation/CommonLisp/CLUserMan/foreign/foreignHargument.lispd
./NextLibrary/Documentation/CommonLisp/CLUserMan/foreign/freeHcstruct.lispd
./NextLibrary/Documentation/CommonLisp/CLUserMan/foreign/lispHvalue.lispd
./NextLibrary/Documentation/CommonLisp/CLUserMan/foreign/makeHcstruct.lispd
./NextLibrary/Documentation/CommonLisp/CLUserMan/foreign/mallocHcstruct.lispd
./NextLibrary/Documentation/CommonLisp/CLUserMan/foreign/registerHfunction.lispd
./NextLibrary/Documentation/CommonLisp/CLUserMan/foreign/registerHvalue.lispd
./NextLibrary/Documentation/CommonLisp/CLUserMan/foreign/defcstruct.lispd
./NextLibrary/Documentation/CommonLisp/CLUserMan/foreign/removeHentryHpoint.lispd
./NextLibrary/Documentation/CommonLisp/CLUserMan/foreign
    /resetHentryHpointHtable.lispd
./NextLibrary/Documentation/CommonLisp/CLUserMan/foreign/Caddress.lispd
./NextLibrary/Documentation/CommonLisp/CLUserMan/foreign/CargHchecking.lispd
./NextLibrary/Documentation/CommonLisp/CLUserMan/foreign/CpassHtypes.lispd
./NextLibrary/Documentation/CommonLisp/CLUserMan/foreign
    /CunreferencedHlibHnames.lispd
./NextLibrary/Documentation/CommonLisp/CLUserMan/foreign/defforeignHlist.lispd
./NextLibrary/Documentation/CommonLisp/CLUserMan/foreign/getHentryHpoints.lispd
./NextLibrary/Documentation/CommonLisp/CLUserMan/foreign/.places
./NextLibrary/Documentation/CommonLisp/CLUserMan/mp
./NextLibrary/Documentation/CommonLisp/CLUserMan/mp/globalHsymbolHvalue.lispd
./NextLibrary/Documentation/CommonLisp/CLUserMan/mp/makeHprocess.lispd
./NextLibrary/Documentation/CommonLisp/CLUserMan/mp/makeHprocessHlock.lispd
./NextLibrary/Documentation/CommonLisp/CLUserMan/mp/makeHstackHgroup.lispd
./NextLibrary/Documentation/CommonLisp/CLUserMan/mp/processHactiveHp.lispd
./NextLibrary/Documentation/CommonLisp/CLUserMan/mp/processHaddHrunHreason.lispd
./NextLibrary/Documentation/CommonLisp/CLUserMan/mp/processHallowHschedule.lispd
./NextLibrary/Documentation/CommonLisp/CLUserMan/mp/processHarrestHreasons.lispd
./NextLibrary/Documentation/CommonLisp/CLUserMan/mp/processHdisable.lispd
./NextLibrary/Documentation/CommonLisp/CLUserMan/mp/processHenable.lispd
./NextLibrary/Documentation/CommonLisp/CLUserMan/mp/processHflush.lispd

./NextLibrary/Documentation/CommonLisp/CLUserMan/mp
    /processHinitialHbindings.lispd

./NextLibrary/Documentation/CommonLisp/CLUserMan/mp/processHinitialHform.lispd

./NextLibrary/Documentation/CommonLisp/CLUserMan/mp/processHinterrupt.lispd

./NextLibrary/Documentation/CommonLisp/CLUserMan/mp/processHkill.lispd

./NextLibrary/Documentation/CommonLisp/CLUserMan/mp/processHlockHlocker.lispd

./NextLibrary/Documentation/CommonLisp/CLUserMan/mp/processHname.lispd

./NextLibrary/Documentation/CommonLisp/CLUserMan/mp/processHpreset.lispd

./NextLibrary/Documentation/CommonLisp/CLUserMan/mp/processHpriority.lispd

./NextLibrary/Documentation/CommonLisp/CLUserMan/mp/processHquantum.lispd

./NextLibrary/Documentation/CommonLisp/CLUserMan/mp/processHreset.lispd

./NextLibrary/Documentation/CommonLisp/CLUserMan/mp/processHresumeHhook.lispd

./NextLibrary/Documentation/CommonLisp/CLUserMan/mp
    /processHrevokeHarrestHreason.lispd

./NextLibrary/Documentation/CommonLisp/CLUserMan/mp
    /processHrevokeHrunHreason.lispd

./NextLibrary/Documentation/CommonLisp/CLUserMan/mp/processHrunHfunction.lispd

./NextLibrary/Documentation/CommonLisp/CLUserMan/mp/processHrunHreasons.lispd

./NextLibrary/Documentation/CommonLisp/CLUserMan/mp/processHrunnableHp.lispd

./NextLibrary/Documentation/CommonLisp/CLUserMan/mp/processHsleep.lispd

./NextLibrary/Documentation/CommonLisp/CLUserMan/mp/processHstackHgroup.lispd

./NextLibrary/Documentation/CommonLisp/CLUserMan/mp/processHsuspendHhook.lispd

./NextLibrary/Documentation/CommonLisp/CLUserMan/mp/processHunlock.lispd

./NextLibrary/Documentation/CommonLisp/CLUserMan/mp/processHwait.lispd

./NextLibrary/Documentation/CommonLisp/CLUserMan/mp/processHwaitHargs.lispd

./NextLibrary/Documentation/CommonLisp/CLUserMan/mp/processHwaitHfunction.lispd

./NextLibrary/Documentation/CommonLisp/CLUserMan/mp
    /processHwaitHwithHtimeout.lispd

./NextLibrary/Documentation/CommonLisp/CLUserMan/mp/processHwhostate.lispd

./NextLibrary/Documentation/CommonLisp/CLUserMan/mp/stackHgroupHfuncall.lispd

./NextLibrary/Documentation/CommonLisp/CLUserMan/mp/stackHgroupHname.lispd

./NextLibrary/Documentation/CommonLisp/CLUserMan/mp/stackHgroupHresume.lispd

./NextLibrary/Documentation/CommonLisp/CLUserMan/mp/stackHgroupHresumer.lispd

./NextLibrary/Documentation/CommonLisp/CLUserMan/mp/stackHgroupHreturn.lispd

./NextLibrary/Documentation/CommonLisp/CLUserMan/mp/stackHgroupHstate.lispd

./NextLibrary/Documentation/CommonLisp/CLUserMan/mp/startHscheduler.lispd

./NextLibrary/Documentation/CommonLisp/CLUserMan/mp/withoutHscheduling.lispd

./NextLibrary/Documentation/CommonLisp/CLUserMan/mp/withHprocessHlock.lispd

./NextLibrary/Documentation/CommonLisp/CLUserMan/mp/withHtimeout.lispd

./NextLibrary/Documentation/CommonLisp/CLUserMan/mp/SallHprocessesS.lispd

./NextLibrary/Documentation/CommonLisp/CLUserMan/mp/ScurrentHprocessS.lispd

./NextLibrary/Documentation/CommonLisp/CLUserMan/mp
    /processHaddHarrestHreason.lispd

./NextLibrary/Documentation/CommonLisp/CLUserMan/mp/processHlock.lispd

./NextLibrary/Documentation/CommonLisp/CLUserMan/mp/processHpropertyHlist.lispd

./NextLibrary/Documentation/CommonLisp/CLUserMan/mp
    /processHrunHrestartableHfunction.lispd

./NextLibrary/Documentation/CommonLisp/CLUserMan/mp/stackHgroupHpreset.lispd

./NextLibrary/Documentation/CommonLisp/CLUserMan/mp/symevalHinHstackHgroup.lispd

./NextLibrary/Documentation/CommonLisp/CLUserMan/mp/.places

./NextLibrary/Documentation/CommonLisp/CLUserMan/next-intro.lispd

./NextLibrary/Documentation/CommonLisp/CLUserMan/objc

./NextLibrary/Documentation/CommonLisp/CLUserMan/objc/cmd.lispd

./NextLibrary/Documentation/CommonLisp/CLUserMan/objc/defHobjcHclass.lispd

./NextLibrary/Documentation/CommonLisp/CLUserMan/objc/defHobjcHmethod.lispd

./NextLibrary/Documentation/CommonLisp/CLUserMan/objc/findHclass.lispd

./NextLibrary/Documentation/CommonLisp/CLUserMan/objc/isa.lispd

./NextLibrary/Documentation/CommonLisp/CLUserMan/objc/iv.lispd

./NextLibrary/Documentation/CommonLisp/CLUserMan/objc/makeHapplication.lispd

./NextLibrary/Documentation/CommonLisp/CLUserMan/objc/methodHnameHtoHnumber.lispd

./NextLibrary/Documentation/CommonLisp/CLUserMan/objc/objcHinstanceHp.lispd

./NextLibrary/Documentation/CommonLisp/CLUserMan/objc/objcHmethod.lispd

./NextLibrary/Documentation/CommonLisp/CLUserMan/objc/printHclassHivars.lispd

./NextLibrary/Documentation/CommonLisp/CLUserMan/objc/printHclassHmethods.lispd

./NextLibrary/Documentation/CommonLisp/CLUserMan/objc/printHinstance.lispd

./NextLibrary/Documentation/CommonLisp/CLUserMan/objc/publicHiv.lispd

./NextLibrary/Documentation/CommonLisp/CLUserMan/objc/self.lispd

./NextLibrary/Documentation/CommonLisp/CLUserMan/objc/send.lispd

./NextLibrary/Documentation/CommonLisp/CLUserMan/objc/sendHsuper.lispd

./NextLibrary/Documentation/CommonLisp/CLUserMan/objc/simpleHprintHinstance.lispd

./NextLibrary/Documentation/CommonLisp/CLUserMan/objc/stringHtoHcharS.lispd

./NextLibrary/Documentation/CommonLisp/CLUserMan/objc/objcHclassHmethod.lispd

./NextLibrary/Documentation/CommonLisp/CLUserMan/objc/printHclass.lispd

./NextLibrary/Documentation/CommonLisp/CLUserMan/objc/SallHclassesS.lispd

./NextLibrary/Documentation/CommonLisp/CLUserMan/objc/charSHtoHstring.lispd

./NextLibrary/Documentation/CommonLisp/CLUserMan/objc/defHobjcHclassHmethod.lispd

./NextLibrary/Documentation/CommonLisp/CLUserMan/objc/methodHnumberHtoHname.lispd

./NextLibrary/Documentation/CommonLisp/CLUserMan/objc/simpleHprintHclass.lispd

./NextLibrary/Documentation/CommonLisp/CLUserMan/objc/.places

./NextLibrary/Documentation/CommonLisp/CLUserMan/supp

./NextLibrary/Documentation/CommonLisp/CLUserMan/supp/load.lispd

./NextLibrary/Documentation/CommonLisp/CLUserMan/supp/inspect.lispd

./NextLibrary/Documentation/CommonLisp/CLUserMan/supp/.places

./NextLibrary/Documentation/CommonLisp/CLUserMan/sys

./NextLibrary/Documentation/CommonLisp/CLUserMan/sys
    /CexpansionHfreeHpercentHnew.lispd

./NextLibrary/Documentation/CommonLisp/CLUserMan/sys
    /CexpansionHfreeHpercentHold.lispd

./NextLibrary/Documentation/CommonLisp/CLUserMan/sys/CfreeHbytesHnewHother.lispd

./NextLibrary/Documentation/CommonLisp/CLUserMan/sys/CfreeHbytesHnewHpages.lispd

./NextLibrary/Documentation/CommonLisp/CLUserMan/sys/CfreeHpercentHnew.lispd

./NextLibrary/Documentation/CommonLisp/CLUserMan/sys/CgenerationHspread.lispd

./NextLibrary/Documentation/CommonLisp/CLUserMan/sys/ChookHafterHgc.lispd

./NextLibrary/Documentation/CommonLisp/CLUserMan/sys/Cprint-sys.lispd

./NextLibrary/Documentation/CommonLisp/CLUserMan/sys/Cquantum.lispd

./NextLibrary/Documentation/CommonLisp/CLUserMan/sys/Cstats.lispd

./NextLibrary/Documentation/CommonLisp/CLUserMan/sys/CtenureHlimit.lispd

./NextLibrary/Documentation/CommonLisp/CLUserMan/sys
    /ScurrentHstackHgroupHresumerS.lispd

./NextLibrary/Documentation/CommonLisp/CLUserMan/sys/ScurrentHstackHgroupS.lispd

./NextLibrary/Documentation/CommonLisp/CLUserMan/sys/SloadHsearchHlistS.lispd

./NextLibrary/Documentation/CommonLisp/CLUserMan/sys/SsourceHfileHtypesS.lispd

./NextLibrary/Documentation/CommonLisp/CLUserMan/sys/commandHlineHargument.lispd

./NextLibrary/Documentation/CommonLisp/CLUserMan/sys
    /commandHlineHargumentHcount.lispd
./NextLibrary/Documentation/CommonLisp/CLUserMan/sys/commandHlineHarguments.lispd
./NextLibrary/Documentation/CommonLisp/CLUserMan/sys/getenv.lispd
./NextLibrary/Documentation/CommonLisp/CLUserMan/sys/gsgcHparameter.lispd
./NextLibrary/Documentation/CommonLisp/CLUserMan/sys/gsgcHparameters.lispd
./NextLibrary/Documentation/CommonLisp/CLUserMan/sys/gsgcHstepHgeneration.lispd
./NextLibrary/Documentation/CommonLisp/CLUserMan/sys/gsgcHswitch.lispd
./NextLibrary/Documentation/CommonLisp/CLUserMan/sys/osHwait.lispd
./NextLibrary/Documentation/CommonLisp/CLUserMan/sys/CautoHstep.lispd
./NextLibrary/Documentation/CommonLisp/CLUserMan/sys/CcurrentHgeneration.lispd
./NextLibrary/Documentation/CommonLisp/CLUserMan/sys/CnextHgcHisHglobal.lispd
./NextLibrary/Documentation/CommonLisp/CLUserMan/sys/SrequireHsearchHlistS.lispd
./NextLibrary/Documentation/CommonLisp/CLUserMan/sys/.places
./NextLibrary/Documentation/CommonLisp/CLUserMan/toplevel
./NextLibrary/Documentation/CommonLisp/CLUserMan/toplevel/Call.lispd
./NextLibrary/Documentation/CommonLisp/CLUserMan/toplevel/Carrest.lispd
./NextLibrary/Documentation/CommonLisp/CLUserMan/toplevel/CbreakHafter.lispd
./NextLibrary/Documentation/CommonLisp/CLUserMan/toplevel/CbreakHall.lispd
./NextLibrary/Documentation/CommonLisp/CLUserMan/toplevel/CbreakHbefore.lispd
./NextLibrary/Documentation/CommonLisp/CLUserMan/toplevel/Ccf.lispd
./NextLibrary/Documentation/CommonLisp/CLUserMan/toplevel/Ccload.lispd
./NextLibrary/Documentation/CommonLisp/CLUserMan/toplevel/Ccontinue.lispd
./NextLibrary/Documentation/CommonLisp/CLUserMan/toplevel/Ccurrent.lispd
./NextLibrary/Documentation/CommonLisp/CLUserMan/toplevel/Cdn.lispd
./NextLibrary/Documentation/CommonLisp/CLUserMan/toplevel/Cerror.lispd
./NextLibrary/Documentation/CommonLisp/CLUserMan/toplevel/Cexit.lispd
./NextLibrary/Documentation/CommonLisp/CLUserMan/toplevel/Cfind.lispd
./NextLibrary/Documentation/CommonLisp/CLUserMan/toplevel/Chelp.lispd
./NextLibrary/Documentation/CommonLisp/CLUserMan/toplevel/Chide.lispd
./NextLibrary/Documentation/CommonLisp/CLUserMan/toplevel/Chistory.lispd
./NextLibrary/Documentation/CommonLisp/CLUserMan/toplevel/Cinside.lispd
./NextLibrary/Documentation/CommonLisp/CLUserMan/toplevel/Cinspect.lispd
./NextLibrary/Documentation/CommonLisp/CLUserMan/toplevel/Ckill.lispd
./NextLibrary/Documentation/CommonLisp/CLUserMan/toplevel/Clocal.lispd
./NextLibrary/Documentation/CommonLisp/CLUserMan/toplevel/Cmacroexpand.lispd
./NextLibrary/Documentation/CommonLisp/CLUserMan/toplevel/Coptimize.lispd
./NextLibrary/Documentation/CommonLisp/CLUserMan/toplevel/Cpop.lispd
./NextLibrary/Documentation/CommonLisp/CLUserMan/toplevel/CprintHafter.lispd
./NextLibrary/Documentation/CommonLisp/CLUserMan/toplevel/CprintHall.lispd
./NextLibrary/Documentation/CommonLisp/CLUserMan/toplevel/CprintHbefore.lispd
./NextLibrary/Documentation/CommonLisp/CLUserMan/toplevel/Cprocesses.lispd
./NextLibrary/Documentation/CommonLisp/CLUserMan/toplevel/Cprt.lispd
./NextLibrary/Documentation/CommonLisp/CLUserMan/toplevel/Creset.lispd
./NextLibrary/Documentation/CommonLisp/CLUserMan/toplevel/Crestart.lispd
./NextLibrary/Documentation/CommonLisp/CLUserMan/toplevel/Creturn.lispd
./NextLibrary/Documentation/CommonLisp/CLUserMan/toplevel/Cscont.lispd
./NextLibrary/Documentation/CommonLisp/CLUserMan/toplevel/CsetHlocal.lispd
./NextLibrary/Documentation/CommonLisp/CLUserMan/toplevel/Csover.lispd
./NextLibrary/Documentation/CommonLisp/CLUserMan/toplevel/Cstep.lispd
./NextLibrary/Documentation/CommonLisp/CLUserMan/toplevel/Ctop.lispd

./NextLibrary/Documentation/CommonLisp/CLUserMan/toplevel/Cunarrest.lispd
./NextLibrary/Documentation/CommonLisp/CLUserMan/toplevel/Cunhide.lispd
./NextLibrary/Documentation/CommonLisp/CLUserMan/toplevel/Cuntrace.lispd
./NextLibrary/Documentation/CommonLisp/CLUserMan/toplevel/Cup.lispd
./NextLibrary/Documentation/CommonLisp/CLUserMan/toplevel/Czoom.lispd
./NextLibrary/Documentation/CommonLisp/CLUserMan/toplevel/SexitHonHeofS.lispd
./NextLibrary/Documentation/CommonLisp/CLUserMan/toplevel/SevalS.lispd
./NextLibrary/Documentation/CommonLisp/CLUserMan/toplevel/ShistoryS.lispd
./NextLibrary/Documentation/CommonLisp/CLUserMan/toplevel/SprintHlengthS.lispd
./NextLibrary/Documentation/CommonLisp/CLUserMan/toplevel/SprintHlevelS.lispd
./NextLibrary/Documentation/CommonLisp/CLUserMan/toplevel/SprintS.lispd
./NextLibrary/Documentation/CommonLisp/CLUserMan/toplevel/SpromptS.lispd
./NextLibrary/Documentation/CommonLisp/CLUserMan/toplevel/SreadS.lispd
./NextLibrary/Documentation/CommonLisp/CLUserMan/toplevel/SresetHookS.lispd
./NextLibrary/Documentation/CommonLisp/CLUserMan/toplevel/alias.lispd
./NextLibrary/Documentation/CommonLisp/CLUserMan/toplevel/doHcommand.lispd
./NextLibrary/Documentation/CommonLisp/CLUserMan/toplevel/C.lispd
./NextLibrary/Documentation/CommonLisp/CLUserMan/toplevel
    /SzoomHprintHlevelS.lispd
./NextLibrary/Documentation/CommonLisp/CLUserMan/toplevel
    /SzoomHprintHspecialHbndsS.lispd
./NextLibrary/Documentation/CommonLisp/CLUserMan/toplevel
    /topHlevelHrepHloop.lispd
./NextLibrary/Documentation/CommonLisp/CLUserMan/toplevel/removeHalias.lispd
./NextLibrary/Documentation/CommonLisp/CLUserMan/toplevel/setqHdefault.lispd
./NextLibrary/Documentation/CommonLisp/CLUserMan/toplevel
    /startHinteractiveHtl.lispd
./NextLibrary/Documentation/CommonLisp/CLUserMan/toplevel/CC.lispd
./NextLibrary/Documentation/CommonLisp/CLUserMan/toplevel/Cbottom.lispd
./NextLibrary/Documentation/CommonLisp/CLUserMan/toplevel/SzoomHdisplayS.lispd
./NextLibrary/Documentation/CommonLisp/CLUserMan/toplevel/Ccondition.lispd
./NextLibrary/Documentation/CommonLisp/CLUserMan/toplevel/Cfocus.lispd
./NextLibrary/Documentation/CommonLisp/CLUserMan/toplevel/Cld.lispd
./NextLibrary/Documentation/CommonLisp/CLUserMan/toplevel/Cpackage.lispd
./NextLibrary/Documentation/CommonLisp/CLUserMan/toplevel
    /CprinterHvariables.lispd
./NextLibrary/Documentation/CommonLisp/CLUserMan/toplevel/Ctrace.lispd
./NextLibrary/Documentation/CommonLisp/CLUserMan/toplevel/SautoHzoomS.lispd
./NextLibrary/Documentation/CommonLisp/CLUserMan/toplevel/ScommandHcharS.lispd
./NextLibrary/Documentation/CommonLisp/CLUserMan/toplevel
    /StplHrepHloopHwrapperS.lispd
./NextLibrary/Documentation/CommonLisp/CLUserMan/toplevel
    /SzoomHprintHlengthS.lispd
./NextLibrary/Documentation/CommonLisp/CLUserMan/toplevel/.places
./NextLibrary/Documentation/CommonLisp/CLUserMan/.places
./NextLibrary/Documentation/CommonLisp/README.wn
./NextLibrary/Documentation/CommonLisp/.places
./NextLibrary/Documentation/Mathematica
./NextLibrary/Documentation/Mathematica/.index
./NextLibrary/Documentation/Mathematica/.index/Copyright.rtf
./NextLibrary/Documentation/Mathematica/.index/index
./NextLibrary/Documentation/Mathematica/.index/index.D

```
./NextLibrary/Documentation/Mathematica/.index/index.L
./NextLibrary/Documentation/Mathematica/.index/index.Registry.D
./NextLibrary/Documentation/Mathematica/.index/index.Registry.L
./NextLibrary/Documentation/Mathematica/.index/.places
./NextLibrary/Documentation/Mathematica/NewFeatures.wn
./NextLibrary/Documentation/Mathematica/UnixSummary.wn
./NextLibrary/Documentation/Mathematica/FrontEndSummary.wn
./NextLibrary/Documentation/Mathematica/FrontEndSummary.wn/WNDocument.wn
./NextLibrary/Documentation/Mathematica/FrontEndSummary.wn/image.b.149815.eps
./NextLibrary/Documentation/Mathematica/FrontEndSummary.wn/fig12.535936.eps
./NextLibrary/Documentation/Mathematica/FrontEndSummary.wn/fig13.885388.eps
./NextLibrary/Documentation/Mathematica/FrontEndSummary.wn/fig14.255477.eps
./NextLibrary/Documentation/Mathematica/FrontEndSummary.wn/fig1.903288.eps
./NextLibrary/Documentation/Mathematica/FrontEndSummary.wn/fig2.799494.eps
./NextLibrary/Documentation/Mathematica/FrontEndSummary.wn/fig3.885855.eps
./NextLibrary/Documentation/Mathematica/FrontEndSummary.wn/fig7.915377.eps
./NextLibrary/Documentation/Mathematica/FrontEndSummary.wn/fig8.612880.eps
./NextLibrary/Documentation/Mathematica/FrontEndSummary.wn/fig9.666580.eps
./NextLibrary/Documentation/Mathematica/FrontEndSummary.wn/fig10.861210.eps
./NextLibrary/Documentation/Mathematica/FrontEndSummary.wn
    /image.cellbrackets.125170.eps
./NextLibrary/Documentation/Mathematica/FrontEndSummary.wn/fig15.815189.eps
./NextLibrary/Documentation/Mathematica/FrontEndSummary.wn/fig16.621428.eps
./NextLibrary/Documentation/Mathematica/FrontEndSummary.wn/fig17.633517.eps
./NextLibrary/Documentation/Mathematica/FrontEndSummary.wn/fig18.931007.eps
./NextLibrary/Documentation/Mathematica/FrontEndSummary.wn/fig19.737311.eps
./NextLibrary/Documentation/Mathematica/FrontEndSummary.wn
    /fig21(teensy).394137.eps
./NextLibrary/Documentation/Mathematica/FrontEndSummary.wn/fig22.510422.eps
./NextLibrary/Documentation/Mathematica/FrontEndSummary.wn/.places
./NextLibrary/Documentation/Mathematica/Contexts.wn
./NextLibrary/Documentation/Mathematica/.places
./NextLibrary/Documentation/Motorola
./NextLibrary/Documentation/Motorola/dsp_assembler_manual.txt
./NextLibrary/Documentation/Motorola/.index
./NextLibrary/Documentation/Motorola/.index/index
./NextLibrary/Documentation/Motorola/.index/index.D
./NextLibrary/Documentation/Motorola/.index/index.L
./NextLibrary/Documentation/Motorola/.index/index.Registry.D
./NextLibrary/Documentation/Motorola/.index/index.Registry.L
./NextLibrary/Documentation/Motorola/.index/.places
./NextLibrary/Documentation/Motorola/.places
./NextLibrary/Documentation/NFS
./NextLibrary/Documentation/NFS/README
./NextLibrary/Documentation/NFS/c0.cover.PS.Z
./NextLibrary/Documentation/NFS/c1.net.svcs.PS.Z
./NextLibrary/Documentation/NFS/c2.rpc.prog.PS.Z
./NextLibrary/Documentation/NFS/c3.xdr.spec.PS.Z
./NextLibrary/Documentation/NFS/c4.rpc.spec.PS.Z
./NextLibrary/Documentation/NFS/c5.nfs.spec.PS.Z
./NextLibrary/Documentation/NFS/c6.yp.spec.PS.Z

./NextLibrary/Documentation/NFS/c7.ipc.prim.PS.Z
./NextLibrary/Documentation/NFS/c8.net.impl.PS.Z
./NextLibrary/Documentation/NFS/rpcgen.guide.PS.Z
./NextLibrary/Documentation/NFS/system.admin.PS.Z
./NextLibrary/Documentation/NFS/xdr.notes.PS.Z
./NextLibrary/Documentation/NFS/.places
./NextLibrary/Documentation/Sybase
./NextLibrary/Documentation/Sybase/Appendices
./NextLibrary/Documentation/Sybase/Appendices/pubsdb
./NextLibrary/Documentation/Sybase/Appendices/systables
./NextLibrary/Documentation/Sybase/Appendices/gloss.40
./NextLibrary/Documentation/Sybase/Appendices/.places
./NextLibrary/Documentation/Sybase/COMREF
./NextLibrary/Documentation/Sybase/COMREF/SPROCS
./NextLibrary/Documentation/Sybase/COMREF/SPROCS/sp_addalias.nr
./NextLibrary/Documentation/Sybase/COMREF/SPROCS/sp_addgroup.nr
./NextLibrary/Documentation/Sybase/COMREF/SPROCS/sp_addlogin.nr
./NextLibrary/Documentation/Sybase/COMREF/SPROCS/sp_addremotelogin.nr
./NextLibrary/Documentation/Sybase/COMREF/SPROCS/sp_addsegment.nr
./NextLibrary/Documentation/Sybase/COMREF/SPROCS/sp_addserver.nr
./NextLibrary/Documentation/Sybase/COMREF/SPROCS/sp_addtype.nr
./NextLibrary/Documentation/Sybase/COMREF/SPROCS/sp_addumpdevice.nr
./NextLibrary/Documentation/Sybase/COMREF/SPROCS/sp_adduser.nr
./NextLibrary/Documentation/Sybase/COMREF/SPROCS/sp_bindefault.nr
./NextLibrary/Documentation/Sybase/COMREF/SPROCS/sp_bindrule.nr
./NextLibrary/Documentation/Sybase/COMREF/SPROCS/sp_changedbowner.nr
./NextLibrary/Documentation/Sybase/COMREF/SPROCS/sp_changegroup.nr
./NextLibrary/Documentation/Sybase/COMREF/SPROCS/sp_commonkey.nr
./NextLibrary/Documentation/Sybase/COMREF/SPROCS/sp_configure.nr
./NextLibrary/Documentation/Sybase/COMREF/SPROCS/sp_dboption.nr
./NextLibrary/Documentation/Sybase/COMREF/SPROCS/sp_defaultdb.nr
./NextLibrary/Documentation/Sybase/COMREF/SPROCS/sp_depends.nr
./NextLibrary/Documentation/Sybase/COMREF/SPROCS/sp_diskdefault.nr
./NextLibrary/Documentation/Sybase/COMREF/SPROCS/sp_dropalias.nr
./NextLibrary/Documentation/Sybase/COMREF/SPROCS/sp_dropdevice.nr
./NextLibrary/Documentation/Sybase/COMREF/SPROCS/sp_dropgroup.nr
./NextLibrary/Documentation/Sybase/COMREF/SPROCS/sp_dropkey.nr
./NextLibrary/Documentation/Sybase/COMREF/SPROCS/sp_droplogin.nr
./NextLibrary/Documentation/Sybase/COMREF/SPROCS/sp_dropremotelogin.nr
./NextLibrary/Documentation/Sybase/COMREF/SPROCS/sp_dropsegment.nr
./NextLibrary/Documentation/Sybase/COMREF/SPROCS/sp_dropserver.nr
./NextLibrary/Documentation/Sybase/COMREF/SPROCS/sp_droptype.nr
./NextLibrary/Documentation/Sybase/COMREF/SPROCS/sp_dropuser.nr
./NextLibrary/Documentation/Sybase/COMREF/SPROCS/sp_extendsegment.nr
./NextLibrary/Documentation/Sybase/COMREF/SPROCS/sp_foreignkey.nr
./NextLibrary/Documentation/Sybase/COMREF/SPROCS/sp_help.nr
./NextLibrary/Documentation/Sybase/COMREF/SPROCS/sp_helpdb.nr
./NextLibrary/Documentation/Sybase/COMREF/SPROCS/sp_helpdevice.nr
./NextLibrary/Documentation/Sybase/COMREF/SPROCS/sp_helpgroup.nr
./NextLibrary/Documentation/Sybase/COMREF/SPROCS/sp_helpindex.nr
./NextLibrary/Documentation/Sybase/COMREF/SPROCS/sp_helpjoins.nr
```

```
./NextLibrary/Documentation/Sybase/COMREF/SPROCS/sp_helpsegment.nr
./NextLibrary/Documentation/Sybase/COMREF/SPROCS/sp_helpserver.nr
./NextLibrary/Documentation/Sybase/COMREF/SPROCS/sp_helptext.nr
./NextLibrary/Documentation/Sybase/COMREF/SPROCS/sp_helpuser.nr
./NextLibrary/Documentation/Sybase/COMREF/SPROCS/sp_lock.nr
./NextLibrary/Documentation/Sybase/COMREF/SPROCS/sp_logdevice.nr
./NextLibrary/Documentation/Sybase/COMREF/SPROCS/sp_monitor.nr
./NextLibrary/Documentation/Sybase/COMREF/SPROCS/sp_password.nr
./NextLibrary/Documentation/Sybase/COMREF/SPROCS/sp_placeobject.nr
./NextLibrary/Documentation/Sybase/COMREF/SPROCS/sp_primarykey.nr
./NextLibrary/Documentation/Sybase/COMREF/SPROCS/sp_remoteoption.nr
./NextLibrary/Documentation/Sybase/COMREF/SPROCS/sp_rename.nr
./NextLibrary/Documentation/Sybase/COMREF/SPROCS/sp_renamedb.nr
./NextLibrary/Documentation/Sybase/COMREF/SPROCS/sp_serveroption.nr
./NextLibrary/Documentation/Sybase/COMREF/SPROCS/sp_spaceused.nr
./NextLibrary/Documentation/Sybase/COMREF/SPROCS/sp_unbindefault.nr
./NextLibrary/Documentation/Sybase/COMREF/SPROCS/sp_unbindrule.nr
./NextLibrary/Documentation/Sybase/COMREF/SPROCS/new.tit
./NextLibrary/Documentation/Sybase/COMREF/SPROCS/sp_who.nr
./NextLibrary/Documentation/Sybase/COMREF/SPROCS/intro3
./NextLibrary/Documentation/Sybase/COMREF/SPROCS/.places
./NextLibrary/Documentation/Sybase/COMREF/UTILITIES
./NextLibrary/Documentation/Sybase/COMREF/UTILITIES/Generic
./NextLibrary/Documentation/Sybase/COMREF/UTILITIES/Generic/bcp.nr
./NextLibrary/Documentation/Sybase/COMREF/UTILITIES/Generic/bldmastr.nr
./NextLibrary/Documentation/Sybase/COMREF/UTILITIES/Generic/console.nr
./NextLibrary/Documentation/Sybase/COMREF/UTILITIES/Generic/defncopy.nr
./NextLibrary/Documentation/Sybase/COMREF/UTILITIES/Generic/isql.nr
./NextLibrary/Documentation/Sybase/COMREF/UTILITIES/Generic/runrpt.nr
./NextLibrary/Documentation/Sybase/COMREF/UTILITIES/Generic/showserver.nr
./NextLibrary/Documentation/Sybase/COMREF/UTILITIES/Generic/sqlservr.nr
./NextLibrary/Documentation/Sybase/COMREF/UTILITIES/Generic/startsql.nr
./NextLibrary/Documentation/Sybase/COMREF/UTILITIES/Generic/syman.nr
./NextLibrary/Documentation/Sybase/COMREF/UTILITIES/Generic/halftit.u
./NextLibrary/Documentation/Sybase/COMREF/UTILITIES/Generic/utils.tit
./NextLibrary/Documentation/Sybase/COMREF/UTILITIES/Generic/.places
./NextLibrary/Documentation/Sybase/COMREF/UTILITIES/.places
./NextLibrary/Documentation/Sybase/COMREF/comref.a
./NextLibrary/Documentation/Sybase/COMREF/comref.c
./NextLibrary/Documentation/Sybase/COMREF/comref.d
./NextLibrary/Documentation/Sybase/COMREF/comref.e
./NextLibrary/Documentation/Sybase/COMREF/comref.n
./NextLibrary/Documentation/Sybase/COMREF/comref.preface
./NextLibrary/Documentation/Sybase/COMREF/comref.t
./NextLibrary/Documentation/Sybase/COMREF/four.tit
./NextLibrary/Documentation/Sybase/COMREF/vno
./NextLibrary/Documentation/Sybase/COMREF/two.tit
./NextLibrary/Documentation/Sybase/COMREF/titpage
./NextLibrary/Documentation/Sybase/COMREF/relno
./NextLibrary/Documentation/Sybase/COMREF/one.tit
./NextLibrary/Documentation/Sybase/COMREF/halftit.2
```

```
./NextLibrary/Documentation/Sybase/COMREF/disclaimer
./NextLibrary/Documentation/Sybase/COMREF/halftit.3
./NextLibrary/Documentation/Sybase/COMREF/docid
./NextLibrary/Documentation/Sybase/COMREF/author
./NextLibrary/Documentation/Sybase/COMREF/ap.a.tit
./NextLibrary/Documentation/Sybase/COMREF/ap.b.tit
./NextLibrary/Documentation/Sybase/COMREF/.places
./NextLibrary/Documentation/Sybase/DBLIB
./NextLibrary/Documentation/Sybase/DBLIB/Section2
./NextLibrary/Documentation/Sybase/DBLIB/Section2/dbadata.nr
./NextLibrary/Documentation/Sybase/DBLIB/Section2/dbadlen.nr
./NextLibrary/Documentation/Sybase/DBLIB/Section2/dbaltbind.nr
./NextLibrary/Documentation/Sybase/DBLIB/Section2/dbaltcolid.nr
./NextLibrary/Documentation/Sybase/DBLIB/Section2/dbaltlen.nr
./NextLibrary/Documentation/Sybase/DBLIB/Section2/dbaltop.nr
./NextLibrary/Documentation/Sybase/DBLIB/Section2/dbalttype.nr
./NextLibrary/Documentation/Sybase/DBLIB/Section2/dbbind.nr
./NextLibrary/Documentation/Sybase/DBLIB/Section2/dbbylist.nr
./NextLibrary/Documentation/Sybase/DBLIB/Section2/dbcancel.nr
./NextLibrary/Documentation/Sybase/DBLIB/Section2/dbcancel_a.nr
./NextLibrary/Documentation/Sybase/DBLIB/Section2/dbcanquery.nr
./NextLibrary/Documentation/Sybase/DBLIB/Section2/dbchange.nr
./NextLibrary/Documentation/Sybase/DBLIB/Section2/dbclose.nr
./NextLibrary/Documentation/Sybase/DBLIB/Section2/dbclrbuf.nr
./NextLibrary/Documentation/Sybase/DBLIB/Section2/dbclropt.nr
./NextLibrary/Documentation/Sybase/DBLIB/Section2/dbcmd.nr
./NextLibrary/Documentation/Sybase/DBLIB/Section2/dbcmdrow.nr
./NextLibrary/Documentation/Sybase/DBLIB/Section2/dbcolbrowse.nr
./NextLibrary/Documentation/Sybase/DBLIB/Section2/dbcollen.nr
./NextLibrary/Documentation/Sybase/DBLIB/Section2/dbcolname.nr
./NextLibrary/Documentation/Sybase/DBLIB/Section2/dbcolsource.nr
./NextLibrary/Documentation/Sybase/DBLIB/Section2/dbcoltype.nr
./NextLibrary/Documentation/Sybase/DBLIB/Section2/dbconvert.nr
./NextLibrary/Documentation/Sybase/DBLIB/Section2/dbcount.nr
./NextLibrary/Documentation/Sybase/DBLIB/Section2/dbcurcmd.nr
./NextLibrary/Documentation/Sybase/DBLIB/Section2/dbcurrow.nr
./NextLibrary/Documentation/Sybase/DBLIB/Section2/dbdata.nr
./NextLibrary/Documentation/Sybase/DBLIB/Section2/dbdatlen.nr
./NextLibrary/Documentation/Sybase/DBLIB/Section2/dbdead.nr
./NextLibrary/Documentation/Sybase/DBLIB/Section2/dberrhandle.nr
./NextLibrary/Documentation/Sybase/DBLIB/Section2/dbexit.nr
./NextLibrary/Documentation/Sybase/DBLIB/Section2/dbfcmd.nr
./NextLibrary/Documentation/Sybase/DBLIB/Section2/dbfirstrow.nr
./NextLibrary/Documentation/Sybase/DBLIB/Section2/dbfreebuf.nr
./NextLibrary/Documentation/Sybase/DBLIB/Section2/dbfreequal.nr
./NextLibrary/Documentation/Sybase/DBLIB/Section2/dbgetchar.nr
./NextLibrary/Documentation/Sybase/DBLIB/Section2/dbgetmaxprocs.nr
./NextLibrary/Documentation/Sybase/DBLIB/Section2/dbgetoff.nr
./NextLibrary/Documentation/Sybase/DBLIB/Section2/dbgetrow.nr
./NextLibrary/Documentation/Sybase/DBLIB/Section2/dbgettime.nr
./NextLibrary/Documentation/Sybase/DBLIB/Section2/dbgetuserdata.nr
```

```
./NextLibrary/Documentation/Sybase/DBLIB/Section2/dbhasretstat.nr
./NextLibrary/Documentation/Sybase/DBLIB/Section2/dbinit.nr
./NextLibrary/Documentation/Sybase/DBLIB/Section2/dbisopt.nr
./NextLibrary/Documentation/Sybase/DBLIB/Section2/.places
./NextLibrary/Documentation/Sybase/DBLIB/Section2/dbiordesc.nr
./NextLibrary/Documentation/Sybase/DBLIB/Section2/dbiowdesc.nr
./NextLibrary/Documentation/Sybase/DBLIB/Section2/dbisavail.nr
./NextLibrary/Documentation/Sybase/DBLIB/Section2/dblastrow.nr
./NextLibrary/Documentation/Sybase/DBLIB/Section2/dblogin.nr
./NextLibrary/Documentation/Sybase/DBLIB/Section2/dbloginfree.nr
./NextLibrary/Documentation/Sybase/DBLIB/Section2/dbmorecmds.nr
./NextLibrary/Documentation/Sybase/DBLIB/Section2/dbmoretext.nr
./NextLibrary/Documentation/Sybase/DBLIB/Section2/dbmsghandle.nr
./NextLibrary/Documentation/Sybase/DBLIB/Section2/dbname.nr
./NextLibrary/Documentation/Sybase/DBLIB/Section2/dbnextrow.nr
./NextLibrary/Documentation/Sybase/DBLIB/Section2/dbnextrow_a.nr
./NextLibrary/Documentation/Sybase/DBLIB/Section2/dbnumalts.nr
./NextLibrary/Documentation/Sybase/DBLIB/Section2/dbnumcols.nr
./NextLibrary/Documentation/Sybase/DBLIB/Section2/dbnumcompute.nr
./NextLibrary/Documentation/Sybase/DBLIB/Section2/dbnumorders.nr
./NextLibrary/Documentation/Sybase/DBLIB/Section2/dbnumrets.nr
./NextLibrary/Documentation/Sybase/DBLIB/Section2/dbopen.nr
./NextLibrary/Documentation/Sybase/DBLIB/Section2/dbordercol.nr
./NextLibrary/Documentation/Sybase/DBLIB/Section2/dbprhead.nr
./NextLibrary/Documentation/Sybase/DBLIB/Section2/dbprrow.nr
./NextLibrary/Documentation/Sybase/DBLIB/Section2/dbprtype.nr
./NextLibrary/Documentation/Sybase/DBLIB/Section2/dbqual.nr
./NextLibrary/Documentation/Sybase/DBLIB/Section2/dbrbuf.nr
./NextLibrary/Documentation/Sybase/DBLIB/Section2/dbreadpage.nr
./NextLibrary/Documentation/Sybase/DBLIB/Section2/dbresults.nr
./NextLibrary/Documentation/Sybase/DBLIB/Section2/dbresults_a.nr
./NextLibrary/Documentation/Sybase/DBLIB/Section2/dbretdata.nr
./NextLibrary/Documentation/Sybase/DBLIB/Section2/dbretlen.nr
./NextLibrary/Documentation/Sybase/DBLIB/Section2/dbretname.nr
./NextLibrary/Documentation/Sybase/DBLIB/Section2/dbretstatus.nr
./NextLibrary/Documentation/Sybase/DBLIB/Section2/dbrettype.nr
./NextLibrary/Documentation/Sybase/DBLIB/Section2/dbrows.nr
./NextLibrary/Documentation/Sybase/DBLIB/Section2/dbrowtype.nr
./NextLibrary/Documentation/Sybase/DBLIB/Section2/dbrpcinit.nr
./NextLibrary/Documentation/Sybase/DBLIB/Section2/dbrpcparam.nr
./NextLibrary/Documentation/Sybase/DBLIB/Section2/dbrpcsend.nr
./NextLibrary/Documentation/Sybase/DBLIB/Section2/dbrpwclr.nr
./NextLibrary/Documentation/Sybase/DBLIB/Section2/dbrpwset.nr
./NextLibrary/Documentation/Sybase/DBLIB/Section2/dbsetavail.nr
./NextLibrary/Documentation/Sybase/DBLIB/Section2/dbsetbusy.nr
./NextLibrary/Documentation/Sybase/DBLIB/Section2/dbsetconnect.nr
./NextLibrary/Documentation/Sybase/DBLIB/Section2/dbsetidle.nr
./NextLibrary/Documentation/Sybase/DBLIB/Section2/dbsetifile.nr
./NextLibrary/Documentation/Sybase/DBLIB/Section2/dbsetinterrupt.nr
./NextLibrary/Documentation/Sybase/DBLIB/Section2/dbsetlapp.nr
./NextLibrary/Documentation/Sybase/DBLIB/Section2/dbsetlhost.nr
./NextLibrary/Documentation/Sybase/DBLIB/Section2/dbsetlogintime.nr
./NextLibrary/Documentation/Sybase/DBLIB/Section2/dbsetlpwd.nr
./NextLibrary/Documentation/Sybase/DBLIB/Section2/dbsetluser.nr
./NextLibrary/Documentation/Sybase/DBLIB/Section2/dbsetmaxprocs.nr
./NextLibrary/Documentation/Sybase/DBLIB/Section2/dbsetnull.nr
./NextLibrary/Documentation/Sybase/DBLIB/Section2/dbsetopt.nr
./NextLibrary/Documentation/Sybase/DBLIB/Section2/dbsettime.nr
./NextLibrary/Documentation/Sybase/DBLIB/Section2/dbsetuserdata.nr
./NextLibrary/Documentation/Sybase/DBLIB/Section2/dbsqlexec.nr
./NextLibrary/Documentation/Sybase/DBLIB/Section2/dbsqlexec_a.nr
./NextLibrary/Documentation/Sybase/DBLIB/Section2/dbsqlok.nr
./NextLibrary/Documentation/Sybase/DBLIB/Section2/dbsqlsend.nr
./NextLibrary/Documentation/Sybase/DBLIB/Section2/dbstrcpy.nr
./NextLibrary/Documentation/Sybase/DBLIB/Section2/dbstrlen.nr
./NextLibrary/Documentation/Sybase/DBLIB/Section2/dbtabbrowse.nr
./NextLibrary/Documentation/Sybase/DBLIB/Section2/dbtabcount.nr
./NextLibrary/Documentation/Sybase/DBLIB/Section2/dbtabname.nr
./NextLibrary/Documentation/Sybase/DBLIB/Section2/dbtabsource.nr
./NextLibrary/Documentation/Sybase/DBLIB/Section2/dbtsnewlen.nr
./NextLibrary/Documentation/Sybase/DBLIB/Section2/dbtsnewval.nr
./NextLibrary/Documentation/Sybase/DBLIB/Section2/dbtsput.nr
./NextLibrary/Documentation/Sybase/DBLIB/Section2/dbtxptr.nr
./NextLibrary/Documentation/Sybase/DBLIB/Section2/dbtxtimestamp.nr
./NextLibrary/Documentation/Sybase/DBLIB/Section2/dbtxtsnewval.nr
./NextLibrary/Documentation/Sybase/DBLIB/Section2/dbtxtsput.nr
./NextLibrary/Documentation/Sybase/DBLIB/Section2/dbuse.nr
./NextLibrary/Documentation/Sybase/DBLIB/Section2/dbvarylen.nr
./NextLibrary/Documentation/Sybase/DBLIB/Section2/dbwillconvert.nr
./NextLibrary/Documentation/Sybase/DBLIB/Section2/dbwritepage.nr
./NextLibrary/Documentation/Sybase/DBLIB/Section2/dbwritetext.nr
./NextLibrary/Documentation/Sybase/DBLIB/Section2/errors.nr
./NextLibrary/Documentation/Sybase/DBLIB/Section2/options.nr
./NextLibrary/Documentation/Sybase/DBLIB/Section2/types.nr
./NextLibrary/Documentation/Sybase/DBLIB/Section2/dbadata.ex
./NextLibrary/Documentation/Sybase/DBLIB/Section2/dbadlen.ex
./NextLibrary/Documentation/Sybase/DBLIB/Section2/dbaltbind.ex
./NextLibrary/Documentation/Sybase/DBLIB/Section2/dbbind.ex
./NextLibrary/Documentation/Sybase/DBLIB/Section2/dbcollen.ex
./NextLibrary/Documentation/Sybase/DBLIB/Section2/dbcolname.ex
./NextLibrary/Documentation/Sybase/DBLIB/Section2/dbcoltype.ex
./NextLibrary/Documentation/Sybase/DBLIB/Section2/dbconvert.ex
./NextLibrary/Documentation/Sybase/DBLIB/Section2/dbdata.ex
./NextLibrary/Documentation/Sybase/DBLIB/Section2/dbdatlen.ex
./NextLibrary/Documentation/Sybase/DBLIB/Section2/dberrhandle.ex
./NextLibrary/Documentation/Sybase/DBLIB/Section2/dbgetoff.ex
./NextLibrary/Documentation/Sybase/DBLIB/Section2/dblogin.ex
./NextLibrary/Documentation/Sybase/DBLIB/Section2/dbmsghandle.ex
./NextLibrary/Documentation/Sybase/DBLIB/Section2/dbnextrow.ex
./NextLibrary/Documentation/Sybase/DBLIB/Section2/dbnumcols.ex
./NextLibrary/Documentation/Sybase/DBLIB/Section2/dbopen.ex
./NextLibrary/Documentation/Sybase/DBLIB/Section2/dbresults.ex
```

```
./NextLibrary/Documentation/Sybase/DBLIB/Section2/dbsetconnect.ex
./NextLibrary/Documentation/Sybase/DBLIB/Section2/dbsetuserdata.ex
./NextLibrary/Documentation/Sybase/DBLIB/Section2/dbsqlexec.ex
./NextLibrary/Documentation/Sybase/DBLIB/Section2/section2.tit
./NextLibrary/Documentation/Sybase/DBLIB/Section3
./NextLibrary/Documentation/Sybase/DBLIB/Section3/bcp_batch.nr
./NextLibrary/Documentation/Sybase/DBLIB/Section3/bcp_bind.nr
./NextLibrary/Documentation/Sybase/DBLIB/Section3/bcp_colfmt.nr
./NextLibrary/Documentation/Sybase/DBLIB/Section3/bcp_collen.nr
./NextLibrary/Documentation/Sybase/DBLIB/Section3/bcp_colptr.nr
./NextLibrary/Documentation/Sybase/DBLIB/Section3/bcp_columns.nr
./NextLibrary/Documentation/Sybase/DBLIB/Section3/bcp_control.nr
./NextLibrary/Documentation/Sybase/DBLIB/Section3/bcp_done.nr
./NextLibrary/Documentation/Sybase/DBLIB/Section3/bcp_exec.nr
./NextLibrary/Documentation/Sybase/DBLIB/Section3/bcp_init.nr
./NextLibrary/Documentation/Sybase/DBLIB/Section3/bcp_moretext.nr
./NextLibrary/Documentation/Sybase/DBLIB/Section3/bcp_sendrow.nr
./NextLibrary/Documentation/Sybase/DBLIB/Section3/bcp_setl.nr
./NextLibrary/Documentation/Sybase/DBLIB/Section3/twophase
./NextLibrary/Documentation/Sybase/DBLIB/Section3/section3.tit
./NextLibrary/Documentation/Sybase/DBLIB/Section3/bcp.tit
./NextLibrary/Documentation/Sybase/DBLIB/Section3/distrib.tit
./NextLibrary/Documentation/Sybase/DBLIB/Section3/.places
./NextLibrary/Documentation/Sybase/DBLIB/Appendix
./NextLibrary/Documentation/Sybase/DBLIB/Appendix/aa
./NextLibrary/Documentation/Sybase/DBLIB/Appendix/.places
./NextLibrary/Documentation/Sybase/DBLIB/author
./NextLibrary/Documentation/Sybase/DBLIB/relno
./NextLibrary/Documentation/Sybase/DBLIB/title
./NextLibrary/Documentation/Sybase/DBLIB/version
./NextLibrary/Documentation/Sybase/DBLIB/docid
./NextLibrary/Documentation/Sybase/DBLIB/disclaimer
./NextLibrary/Documentation/Sybase/DBLIB/Intro
./NextLibrary/Documentation/Sybase/DBLIB/.index
./NextLibrary/Documentation/Sybase/DBLIB/.index/index
./NextLibrary/Documentation/Sybase/DBLIB/.index/index.D
./NextLibrary/Documentation/Sybase/DBLIB/.index/index.L
./NextLibrary/Documentation/Sybase/DBLIB/.index/.places
./NextLibrary/Documentation/Sybase/DBLIB/.places
./NextLibrary/Documentation/Sybase/.index
./NextLibrary/Documentation/Sybase/.index/.roffArgs
./NextLibrary/Documentation/Sybase/.index/tmac.syb
./NextLibrary/Documentation/Sybase/.index/.roffArgs~
./NextLibrary/Documentation/Sybase/.index/.macros
./NextLibrary/Documentation/Sybase/.index/index
./NextLibrary/Documentation/Sybase/.index/index.D
./NextLibrary/Documentation/Sybase/.index/index.L
./NextLibrary/Documentation/Sybase/.index/index.Registry.D
./NextLibrary/Documentation/Sybase/.index/index.Registry.L
./NextLibrary/Documentation/Sybase/.index/.places
./NextLibrary/Documentation/Sybase/SAG
./NextLibrary/Documentation/Sybase/SAG/ap.a.tit
./NextLibrary/Documentation/Sybase/SAG/ap.b.tit
./NextLibrary/Documentation/Sybase/SAG/author
./NextLibrary/Documentation/Sybase/SAG/disclaimer
./NextLibrary/Documentation/Sybase/SAG/docid
./NextLibrary/Documentation/Sybase/SAG/relno
./NextLibrary/Documentation/Sybase/SAG/sag1
./NextLibrary/Documentation/Sybase/SAG/sag2
./NextLibrary/Documentation/Sybase/SAG/sag3
./NextLibrary/Documentation/Sybase/SAG/sag4
./NextLibrary/Documentation/Sybase/SAG/sag5
./NextLibrary/Documentation/Sybase/SAG/sag6
./NextLibrary/Documentation/Sybase/SAG/sag7
./NextLibrary/Documentation/Sybase/SAG/titpage.sag
./NextLibrary/Documentation/Sybase/SAG/vno
./NextLibrary/Documentation/Sybase/SAG/.places
./NextLibrary/Documentation/Sybase/SQLUG
./NextLibrary/Documentation/Sybase/SQLUG/sql01
./NextLibrary/Documentation/Sybase/SQLUG/sql02
./NextLibrary/Documentation/Sybase/SQLUG/sql03
./NextLibrary/Documentation/Sybase/SQLUG/sql04
./NextLibrary/Documentation/Sybase/SQLUG/sql05
./NextLibrary/Documentation/Sybase/SQLUG/sql06
./NextLibrary/Documentation/Sybase/SQLUG/sql07
./NextLibrary/Documentation/Sybase/SQLUG/sql08
./NextLibrary/Documentation/Sybase/SQLUG/sql09
./NextLibrary/Documentation/Sybase/SQLUG/sql10
./NextLibrary/Documentation/Sybase/SQLUG/sql11
./NextLibrary/Documentation/Sybase/SQLUG/sql12
./NextLibrary/Documentation/Sybase/SQLUG/sql13
./NextLibrary/Documentation/Sybase/SQLUG/sql14
./NextLibrary/Documentation/Sybase/SQLUG/sqlug_changes
./NextLibrary/Documentation/Sybase/SQLUG/vno
./NextLibrary/Documentation/Sybase/SQLUG/relno
./NextLibrary/Documentation/Sybase/SQLUG/docid
./NextLibrary/Documentation/Sybase/SQLUG/author
./NextLibrary/Documentation/Sybase/SQLUG/titpage.sqlug
./NextLibrary/Documentation/Sybase/SQLUG/disclaimer
./NextLibrary/Documentation/Sybase/SQLUG/ap.a.tit
./NextLibrary/Documentation/Sybase/SQLUG/ap.b.tit
./NextLibrary/Documentation/Sybase/SQLUG/.places
./NextLibrary/Documentation/Sybase/README.wn
./NextLibrary/Documentation/Sybase/.places
./NextLibrary/Documentation/.places
./NextLibrary/Sounds
./NextLibrary/Sounds/Bonk.snd
./NextLibrary/Sounds/Pop.snd
./NextLibrary/Sounds/Tink.snd
./NextLibrary/Sounds/Basso.snd
./NextLibrary/Sounds/Frog.snd
./NextLibrary/Sounds/Funk.snd
```

```
./NextLibrary/Sounds/Tink.snd
./NextLibrary/Sounds/Basso.snd
./NextLibrary/Sounds/Frog.snd
./NextLibrary/Sounds/Funk.snd
./NextLibrary/Sounds/SystemBeep.snd
./NextLibrary/Sounds/.places
./NextLibrary/Literature
./NextLibrary/Literature/Shakespeare
./NextLibrary/Literature/Shakespeare/Plays
./NextLibrary/Literature/Shakespeare/Plays/As_You_Like_It
./NextLibrary/Literature/Shakespeare/Plays/As_You_Like_It/2.1
./NextLibrary/Literature/Shakespeare/Plays/As_You_Like_It/1.1
./NextLibrary/Literature/Shakespeare/Plays/As_You_Like_It/1.2
./NextLibrary/Literature/Shakespeare/Plays/As_You_Like_It/1.3
./NextLibrary/Literature/Shakespeare/Plays/As_You_Like_It/2.2
./NextLibrary/Literature/Shakespeare/Plays/As_You_Like_It/2.3
./NextLibrary/Literature/Shakespeare/Plays/As_You_Like_It/2.4
./NextLibrary/Literature/Shakespeare/Plays/As_You_Like_It/2.5
./NextLibrary/Literature/Shakespeare/Plays/As_You_Like_It/2.6
./NextLibrary/Literature/Shakespeare/Plays/As_You_Like_It/2.7
./NextLibrary/Literature/Shakespeare/Plays/As_You_Like_It/3.1
./NextLibrary/Literature/Shakespeare/Plays/As_You_Like_It/3.2
./NextLibrary/Literature/Shakespeare/Plays/As_You_Like_It/3.3
./NextLibrary/Literature/Shakespeare/Plays/As_You_Like_It/3.4
./NextLibrary/Literature/Shakespeare/Plays/As_You_Like_It/3.5
./NextLibrary/Literature/Shakespeare/Plays/As_You_Like_It/4.1
./NextLibrary/Literature/Shakespeare/Plays/As_You_Like_It/4.2
./NextLibrary/Literature/Shakespeare/Plays/As_You_Like_It/4.3
./NextLibrary/Literature/Shakespeare/Plays/As_You_Like_It/5.1
./NextLibrary/Literature/Shakespeare/Plays/As_You_Like_It/5.2
./NextLibrary/Literature/Shakespeare/Plays/As_You_Like_It/5.3
./NextLibrary/Literature/Shakespeare/Plays/As_You_Like_It/5.4
./NextLibrary/Literature/Shakespeare/Plays/As_You_Like_It/Epilogue
./NextLibrary/Literature/Shakespeare/Plays/As_You_Like_It/Introduction
./NextLibrary/Literature/Shakespeare/Plays/As_You_Like_It/Players
./NextLibrary/Literature/Shakespeare/Plays/As_You_Like_It/.places
./NextLibrary/Literature/Shakespeare/Plays/Romeo_and_Juliet
./NextLibrary/Literature/Shakespeare/Plays/Romeo_and_Juliet/Prologue
./NextLibrary/Literature/Shakespeare/Plays/Romeo_and_Juliet/1.1
./NextLibrary/Literature/Shakespeare/Plays/Romeo_and_Juliet/1.2
./NextLibrary/Literature/Shakespeare/Plays/Romeo_and_Juliet/1.3
./NextLibrary/Literature/Shakespeare/Plays/Romeo_and_Juliet/1.4
./NextLibrary/Literature/Shakespeare/Plays/Romeo_and_Juliet/1.5
./NextLibrary/Literature/Shakespeare/Plays/Romeo_and_Juliet/2.0
./NextLibrary/Literature/Shakespeare/Plays/Romeo_and_Juliet/2.1
./NextLibrary/Literature/Shakespeare/Plays/Romeo_and_Juliet/2.2
./NextLibrary/Literature/Shakespeare/Plays/Romeo_and_Juliet/2.3
./NextLibrary/Literature/Shakespeare/Plays/Romeo_and_Juliet/2.4
./NextLibrary/Literature/Shakespeare/Plays/Romeo_and_Juliet/2.5
./NextLibrary/Literature/Shakespeare/Plays/Romeo_and_Juliet/3.1
./NextLibrary/Literature/Shakespeare/Plays/Romeo_and_Juliet/3.2
./NextLibrary/Literature/Shakespeare/Plays/Romeo_and_Juliet/3.3
./NextLibrary/Literature/Shakespeare/Plays/Romeo_and_Juliet/3.4
./NextLibrary/Literature/Shakespeare/Plays/Romeo_and_Juliet/3.5
./NextLibrary/Literature/Shakespeare/Plays/Romeo_and_Juliet/4.1
./NextLibrary/Literature/Shakespeare/Plays/Romeo_and_Juliet/4.2
./NextLibrary/Literature/Shakespeare/Plays/Romeo_and_Juliet/4.3
./NextLibrary/Literature/Shakespeare/Plays/Romeo_and_Juliet/4.4
./NextLibrary/Literature/Shakespeare/Plays/Romeo_and_Juliet/5.1
./NextLibrary/Literature/Shakespeare/Plays/Romeo_and_Juliet/5.2
./NextLibrary/Literature/Shakespeare/Plays/Romeo_and_Juliet/5.3
./NextLibrary/Literature/Shakespeare/Plays/Romeo_and_Juliet/Introduction
./NextLibrary/Literature/Shakespeare/Plays/Romeo_and_Juliet/Players
./NextLibrary/Literature/Shakespeare/Plays/Romeo_and_Juliet/.places
./NextLibrary/Literature/Shakespeare/Plays/The_Two_Gentlemen_of_Verona
./NextLibrary/Literature/Shakespeare/Plays/The_Two_Gentlemen_of_Verona/1.1
./NextLibrary/Literature/Shakespeare/Plays/The_Two_Gentlemen_of_Verona/1.2
./NextLibrary/Literature/Shakespeare/Plays/The_Two_Gentlemen_of_Verona/1.3
./NextLibrary/Literature/Shakespeare/Plays/The_Two_Gentlemen_of_Verona/2.1
./NextLibrary/Literature/Shakespeare/Plays/The_Two_Gentlemen_of_Verona/2.2
./NextLibrary/Literature/Shakespeare/Plays/The_Two_Gentlemen_of_Verona/2.3
./NextLibrary/Literature/Shakespeare/Plays/The_Two_Gentlemen_of_Verona/2.4
./NextLibrary/Literature/Shakespeare/Plays/The_Two_Gentlemen_of_Verona/2.5
./NextLibrary/Literature/Shakespeare/Plays/The_Two_Gentlemen_of_Verona/2.6
./NextLibrary/Literature/Shakespeare/Plays/The_Two_Gentlemen_of_Verona/2.7
./NextLibrary/Literature/Shakespeare/Plays/The_Two_Gentlemen_of_Verona/3.1
./NextLibrary/Literature/Shakespeare/Plays/The_Two_Gentlemen_of_Verona/3.2
./NextLibrary/Literature/Shakespeare/Plays/The_Two_Gentlemen_of_Verona/4.1
./NextLibrary/Literature/Shakespeare/Plays/The_Two_Gentlemen_of_Verona/4.2
./NextLibrary/Literature/Shakespeare/Plays/The_Two_Gentlemen_of_Verona/4.3
./NextLibrary/Literature/Shakespeare/Plays/The_Two_Gentlemen_of_Verona/4.4
./NextLibrary/Literature/Shakespeare/Plays/The_Two_Gentlemen_of_Verona/5.1
./NextLibrary/Literature/Shakespeare/Plays/The_Two_Gentlemen_of_Verona/5.2
./NextLibrary/Literature/Shakespeare/Plays/The_Two_Gentlemen_of_Verona/5.3
./NextLibrary/Literature/Shakespeare/Plays/The_Two_Gentlemen_of_Verona/5.4
./NextLibrary/Literature/Shakespeare/Plays/The_Two_Gentlemen_of_Verona
    /Introduction
./NextLibrary/Literature/Shakespeare/Plays/The_Two_Gentlemen_of_Verona/Players
./NextLibrary/Literature/Shakespeare/Plays/The_Two_Gentlemen_of_Verona/.places
./NextLibrary/Literature/Shakespeare/Plays/The_Taming_of_the_Shrew
./NextLibrary/Literature/Shakespeare/Plays/The_Taming_of_the_Shrew/Induction_1
./NextLibrary/Literature/Shakespeare/Plays/The_Taming_of_the_Shrew/Induction_2
./NextLibrary/Literature/Shakespeare/Plays/The_Taming_of_the_Shrew/1.1
./NextLibrary/Literature/Shakespeare/Plays/The_Taming_of_the_Shrew/1.2
./NextLibrary/Literature/Shakespeare/Plays/The_Taming_of_the_Shrew/2.1
./NextLibrary/Literature/Shakespeare/Plays/The_Taming_of_the_Shrew/3.1
./NextLibrary/Literature/Shakespeare/Plays/The_Taming_of_the_Shrew/3.2
./NextLibrary/Literature/Shakespeare/Plays/The_Taming_of_the_Shrew/3.3
./NextLibrary/Literature/Shakespeare/Plays/The_Taming_of_the_Shrew/4.1
./NextLibrary/Literature/Shakespeare/Plays/The_Taming_of_the_Shrew/4.2
./NextLibrary/Literature/Shakespeare/Plays/The_Taming_of_the_Shrew/4.3
./NextLibrary/Literature/Shakespeare/Plays/The_Taming_of_the_Shrew/4.4
```

./NextLibrary/Literature/Shakespeare/Plays/The_Taming_of_the_Shrew/4.5
./NextLibrary/Literature/Shakespeare/Plays/The_Taming_of_the_Shrew/4.6
./NextLibrary/Literature/Shakespeare/Plays/The_Taming_of_the_Shrew/5.1
./NextLibrary/Literature/Shakespeare/Plays/The_Taming_of_the_Shrew/5.2
./NextLibrary/Literature/Shakespeare/Plays/The_Taming_of_the_Shrew/Introduction
./NextLibrary/Literature/Shakespeare/Plays/The_Taming_of_the_Shrew/Players
./NextLibrary/Literature/Shakespeare/Plays/The_Taming_of_the_Shrew/Additional
./NextLibrary/Literature/Shakespeare/Plays/The_Taming_of_the_Shrew/.places
./NextLibrary/Literature/Shakespeare/Plays/Sir_Thomas_More
./NextLibrary/Literature/Shakespeare/Plays/Sir_Thomas_More/Add.II.D
./NextLibrary/Literature/Shakespeare/Plays/Sir_Thomas_More/Add.III
./NextLibrary/Literature/Shakespeare/Plays/Sir_Thomas_More/.places
./NextLibrary/Literature/Shakespeare/Plays/Richard_II
./NextLibrary/Literature/Shakespeare/Plays/Richard_II/1.1
./NextLibrary/Literature/Shakespeare/Plays/Richard_II/1.2
./NextLibrary/Literature/Shakespeare/Plays/Richard_II/1.3
./NextLibrary/Literature/Shakespeare/Plays/Richard_II/1.4
./NextLibrary/Literature/Shakespeare/Plays/Richard_II/2.1
./NextLibrary/Literature/Shakespeare/Plays/Richard_II/2.2
./NextLibrary/Literature/Shakespeare/Plays/Richard_II/2.3
./NextLibrary/Literature/Shakespeare/Plays/Richard_II/2.4
./NextLibrary/Literature/Shakespeare/Plays/Richard_II/3.1
./NextLibrary/Literature/Shakespeare/Plays/Richard_II/3.2
./NextLibrary/Literature/Shakespeare/Plays/Richard_II/3.3
./NextLibrary/Literature/Shakespeare/Plays/Richard_II/3.4
./NextLibrary/Literature/Shakespeare/Plays/Richard_II/4.1
./NextLibrary/Literature/Shakespeare/Plays/Richard_II/5.1
./NextLibrary/Literature/Shakespeare/Plays/Richard_II/5.2
./NextLibrary/Literature/Shakespeare/Plays/Richard_II/5.3
./NextLibrary/Literature/Shakespeare/Plays/Richard_II/5.4
./NextLibrary/Literature/Shakespeare/Plays/Richard_II/5.5
./NextLibrary/Literature/Shakespeare/Plays/Richard_II/5.6
./NextLibrary/Literature/Shakespeare/Plays/Richard_II/Introduction
./NextLibrary/Literature/Shakespeare/Plays/Richard_II/Players
./NextLibrary/Literature/Shakespeare/Plays/Richard_II/.places
./NextLibrary/Literature/Shakespeare/Plays/The_Winters_Tale
./NextLibrary/Literature/Shakespeare/Plays/The_Winters_Tale/1.1
./NextLibrary/Literature/Shakespeare/Plays/The_Winters_Tale/1.2
./NextLibrary/Literature/Shakespeare/Plays/The_Winters_Tale/2.1
./NextLibrary/Literature/Shakespeare/Plays/The_Winters_Tale/2.2
./NextLibrary/Literature/Shakespeare/Plays/The_Winters_Tale/2.3
./NextLibrary/Literature/Shakespeare/Plays/The_Winters_Tale/3.1
./NextLibrary/Literature/Shakespeare/Plays/The_Winters_Tale/3.2
./NextLibrary/Literature/Shakespeare/Plays/The_Winters_Tale/3.3
./NextLibrary/Literature/Shakespeare/Plays/The_Winters_Tale/4.1
./NextLibrary/Literature/Shakespeare/Plays/The_Winters_Tale/4.2
./NextLibrary/Literature/Shakespeare/Plays/The_Winters_Tale/4.3
./NextLibrary/Literature/Shakespeare/Plays/The_Winters_Tale/4.4
./NextLibrary/Literature/Shakespeare/Plays/The_Winters_Tale/5.1
./NextLibrary/Literature/Shakespeare/Plays/The_Winters_Tale/5.2
./NextLibrary/Literature/Shakespeare/Plays/The_Winters_Tale/5.3

./NextLibrary/Literature/Shakespeare/Plays/The_Winters_Tale/Introduction
./NextLibrary/Literature/Shakespeare/Plays/The_Winters_Tale/Players
./NextLibrary/Literature/Shakespeare/Plays/The_Winters_Tale/.places
./NextLibrary/Literature/Shakespeare/Plays/Hamlet
./NextLibrary/Literature/Shakespeare/Plays/Hamlet/1.1
./NextLibrary/Literature/Shakespeare/Plays/Hamlet/1.2
./NextLibrary/Literature/Shakespeare/Plays/Hamlet/1.3
./NextLibrary/Literature/Shakespeare/Plays/Hamlet/1.4
./NextLibrary/Literature/Shakespeare/Plays/Hamlet/1.5
./NextLibrary/Literature/Shakespeare/Plays/Hamlet/2.1
./NextLibrary/Literature/Shakespeare/Plays/Hamlet/2.2
./NextLibrary/Literature/Shakespeare/Plays/Hamlet/3.1
./NextLibrary/Literature/Shakespeare/Plays/Hamlet/3.2
./NextLibrary/Literature/Shakespeare/Plays/Hamlet/3.3
./NextLibrary/Literature/Shakespeare/Plays/Hamlet/3.4
./NextLibrary/Literature/Shakespeare/Plays/Hamlet/4.1
./NextLibrary/Literature/Shakespeare/Plays/Hamlet/4.2
./NextLibrary/Literature/Shakespeare/Plays/Hamlet/4.3
./NextLibrary/Literature/Shakespeare/Plays/Hamlet/4.4
./NextLibrary/Literature/Shakespeare/Plays/Hamlet/4.5
./NextLibrary/Literature/Shakespeare/Plays/Hamlet/4.6
./NextLibrary/Literature/Shakespeare/Plays/Hamlet/4.7
./NextLibrary/Literature/Shakespeare/Plays/Hamlet/5.1
./NextLibrary/Literature/Shakespeare/Plays/Hamlet/5.2
./NextLibrary/Literature/Shakespeare/Plays/Hamlet/Introduction
./NextLibrary/Literature/Shakespeare/Plays/Hamlet/Players
./NextLibrary/Literature/Shakespeare/Plays/Hamlet/Additional
./NextLibrary/Literature/Shakespeare/Plays/Hamlet/.places
./NextLibrary/Literature/Shakespeare/Plays/Othello
./NextLibrary/Literature/Shakespeare/Plays/Othello/1.3
./NextLibrary/Literature/Shakespeare/Plays/Othello/2.1
./NextLibrary/Literature/Shakespeare/Plays/Othello/2.2
./NextLibrary/Literature/Shakespeare/Plays/Othello/2.3
./NextLibrary/Literature/Shakespeare/Plays/Othello/3.1
./NextLibrary/Literature/Shakespeare/Plays/Othello/3.2
./NextLibrary/Literature/Shakespeare/Plays/Othello/3.3
./NextLibrary/Literature/Shakespeare/Plays/Othello/3.4
./NextLibrary/Literature/Shakespeare/Plays/Othello/4.1
./NextLibrary/Literature/Shakespeare/Plays/Othello/4.2
./NextLibrary/Literature/Shakespeare/Plays/Othello/4.3
./NextLibrary/Literature/Shakespeare/Plays/Othello/5.1
./NextLibrary/Literature/Shakespeare/Plays/Othello/5.2
./NextLibrary/Literature/Shakespeare/Plays/Othello/Introduction
./NextLibrary/Literature/Shakespeare/Plays/Othello/Players
./NextLibrary/Literature/Shakespeare/Plays/Othello/1.1
./NextLibrary/Literature/Shakespeare/Plays/Othello/1.2
./NextLibrary/Literature/Shakespeare/Plays/Othello/.places
./NextLibrary/Literature/Shakespeare/Plays/The_First_Part_of_the_Contention
./NextLibrary/Literature/Shakespeare/Plays/The_First_Part_of_the_Contention
      /.places
./NextLibrary/Literature/Shakespeare/Plays/The_First_Part_of_the_Contention

```
./NextLibrary/Literature/Shakespeare/Plays/The_First_Part_of_the_Contention/1.4
./NextLibrary/Literature/Shakespeare/Plays/The_First_Part_of_the_Contention/2.1
./NextLibrary/Literature/Shakespeare/Plays/The_First_Part_of_the_Contention/2.2
./NextLibrary/Literature/Shakespeare/Plays/The_First_Part_of_the_Contention/2.3
./NextLibrary/Literature/Shakespeare/Plays/The_First_Part_of_the_Contention/2.4
./NextLibrary/Literature/Shakespeare/Plays/The_First_Part_of_the_Contention/3.1
./NextLibrary/Literature/Shakespeare/Plays/The_First_Part_of_the_Contention/3.2
./NextLibrary/Literature/Shakespeare/Plays/The_First_Part_of_the_Contention/3.3
./NextLibrary/Literature/Shakespeare/Plays/The_First_Part_of_the_Contention/4.1
./NextLibrary/Literature/Shakespeare/Plays/The_First_Part_of_the_Contention/4.2
./NextLibrary/Literature/Shakespeare/Plays/The_First_Part_of_the_Contention/4.3
./NextLibrary/Literature/Shakespeare/Plays/The_First_Part_of_the_Contention/4.4
./NextLibrary/Literature/Shakespeare/Plays/The_First_Part_of_the_Contention/4.5
./NextLibrary/Literature/Shakespeare/Plays/The_First_Part_of_the_Contention/4.6
./NextLibrary/Literature/Shakespeare/Plays/The_First_Part_of_the_Contention/4.7
./NextLibrary/Literature/Shakespeare/Plays/The_First_Part_of_the_Contention/4.8
./NextLibrary/Literature/Shakespeare/Plays/The_First_Part_of_the_Contention/4.9
./NextLibrary/Literature/Shakespeare/Plays/The_First_Part_of_the_Contention/5.1
./NextLibrary/Literature/Shakespeare/Plays/The_First_Part_of_the_Contention/5.2
./NextLibrary/Literature/Shakespeare/Plays/The_First_Part_of_the_Contention/5.3
./NextLibrary/Literature/Shakespeare/Plays/The_First_Part_of_the_Contention/5.4
./NextLibrary/Literature/Shakespeare/Plays/The_First_Part_of_the_Contention/5.5
./NextLibrary/Literature/Shakespeare/Plays/The_First_Part_of_the_Contention/Addi-
    tional
./NextLibrary/Literature/Shakespeare/Plays/The_First_Part_of_the_Contention/In-
    troduction
./NextLibrary/Literature/Shakespeare/Plays/Titus_Andronicus
./NextLibrary/Literature/Shakespeare/Plays/Titus_Andronicus/1.1
./NextLibrary/Literature/Shakespeare/Plays/Titus_Andronicus/2.1
./NextLibrary/Literature/Shakespeare/Plays/Titus_Andronicus/2.2
./NextLibrary/Literature/Shakespeare/Plays/Titus_Andronicus/2.3
./NextLibrary/Literature/Shakespeare/Plays/Titus_Andronicus/2.4
./NextLibrary/Literature/Shakespeare/Plays/Titus_Andronicus/3.1
./NextLibrary/Literature/Shakespeare/Plays/Titus_Andronicus/3.2
./NextLibrary/Literature/Shakespeare/Plays/Titus_Andronicus/4.1
./NextLibrary/Literature/Shakespeare/Plays/Titus_Andronicus/4.2
./NextLibrary/Literature/Shakespeare/Plays/Titus_Andronicus/4.3
./NextLibrary/Literature/Shakespeare/Plays/Titus_Andronicus/4.4
./NextLibrary/Literature/Shakespeare/Plays/Titus_Andronicus/5.1
./NextLibrary/Literature/Shakespeare/Plays/Titus_Andronicus/5.2
./NextLibrary/Literature/Shakespeare/Plays/Titus_Andronicus/5.3
./NextLibrary/Literature/Shakespeare/Plays/Titus_Andronicus/Introduction
./NextLibrary/Literature/Shakespeare/Plays/Titus_Andronicus/Players
./NextLibrary/Literature/Shakespeare/Plays/Titus_Andronicus/Additional
./NextLibrary/Literature/Shakespeare/Plays/Titus_Andronicus/.places
./NextLibrary/Literature/Shakespeare/Plays/1_Henry_VI
./NextLibrary/Literature/Shakespeare/Plays/1_Henry_VI/1.1
./NextLibrary/Literature/Shakespeare/Plays/1_Henry_VI/1.2
./NextLibrary/Literature/Shakespeare/Plays/1_Henry_VI/1.3
./NextLibrary/Literature/Shakespeare/Plays/1_Henry_VI/1.4
./NextLibrary/Literature/Shakespeare/Plays/1_Henry_VI/1.5
./NextLibrary/Literature/Shakespeare/Plays/1_Henry_VI/1.6
./NextLibrary/Literature/Shakespeare/Plays/1_Henry_VI/1.7
./NextLibrary/Literature/Shakespeare/Plays/1_Henry_VI/1.8
./NextLibrary/Literature/Shakespeare/Plays/1_Henry_VI/2.1
./NextLibrary/Literature/Shakespeare/Plays/1_Henry_VI/2.2
./NextLibrary/Literature/Shakespeare/Plays/1_Henry_VI/2.3
./NextLibrary/Literature/Shakespeare/Plays/1_Henry_VI/2.4
./NextLibrary/Literature/Shakespeare/Plays/1_Henry_VI/2.5
./NextLibrary/Literature/Shakespeare/Plays/1_Henry_VI/3.1
./NextLibrary/Literature/Shakespeare/Plays/1_Henry_VI/3.2
./NextLibrary/Literature/Shakespeare/Plays/1_Henry_VI/3.3
./NextLibrary/Literature/Shakespeare/Plays/1_Henry_VI/3.4
./NextLibrary/Literature/Shakespeare/Plays/1_Henry_VI/3.5
./NextLibrary/Literature/Shakespeare/Plays/1_Henry_VI/3.6
./NextLibrary/Literature/Shakespeare/Plays/1_Henry_VI/3.7
./NextLibrary/Literature/Shakespeare/Plays/1_Henry_VI/3.8
./NextLibrary/Literature/Shakespeare/Plays/1_Henry_VI/4.1
./NextLibrary/Literature/Shakespeare/Plays/1_Henry_VI/4.2
./NextLibrary/Literature/Shakespeare/Plays/1_Henry_VI/4.3
./NextLibrary/Literature/Shakespeare/Plays/1_Henry_VI/4.4
./NextLibrary/Literature/Shakespeare/Plays/1_Henry_VI/4.5
./NextLibrary/Literature/Shakespeare/Plays/1_Henry_VI/4.6
./NextLibrary/Literature/Shakespeare/Plays/1_Henry_VI/4.7
./NextLibrary/Literature/Shakespeare/Plays/1_Henry_VI/5.1
./NextLibrary/Literature/Shakespeare/Plays/1_Henry_VI/5.2
./NextLibrary/Literature/Shakespeare/Plays/1_Henry_VI/5.3
./NextLibrary/Literature/Shakespeare/Plays/1_Henry_VI/5.4
./NextLibrary/Literature/Shakespeare/Plays/1_Henry_VI/5.5
./NextLibrary/Literature/Shakespeare/Plays/1_Henry_VI/5.6
./NextLibrary/Literature/Shakespeare/Plays/1_Henry_VI/5.7
./NextLibrary/Literature/Shakespeare/Plays/1_Henry_VI/Introduction
./NextLibrary/Literature/Shakespeare/Plays/1_Henry_VI/Players
./NextLibrary/Literature/Shakespeare/Plays/1_Henry_VI/.places
./NextLibrary/Literature/Shakespeare/Plays/Richard_Duke_of_York
./NextLibrary/Literature/Shakespeare/Plays/Richard_Duke_of_York/1.1
./NextLibrary/Literature/Shakespeare/Plays/Richard_Duke_of_York/1.2
./NextLibrary/Literature/Shakespeare/Plays/Richard_Duke_of_York/1.3
./NextLibrary/Literature/Shakespeare/Plays/Richard_Duke_of_York/1.4
./NextLibrary/Literature/Shakespeare/Plays/Richard_Duke_of_York/2.1
./NextLibrary/Literature/Shakespeare/Plays/Richard_Duke_of_York/2.2
./NextLibrary/Literature/Shakespeare/Plays/Richard_Duke_of_York/2.3
./NextLibrary/Literature/Shakespeare/Plays/Richard_Duke_of_York/2.4
./NextLibrary/Literature/Shakespeare/Plays/Richard_Duke_of_York/2.5
./NextLibrary/Literature/Shakespeare/Plays/Richard_Duke_of_York/2.6
./NextLibrary/Literature/Shakespeare/Plays/Richard_Duke_of_York/3.1
./NextLibrary/Literature/Shakespeare/Plays/Richard_Duke_of_York/3.2
./NextLibrary/Literature/Shakespeare/Plays/Richard_Duke_of_York/3.3
./NextLibrary/Literature/Shakespeare/Plays/Richard_Duke_of_York/4.1
./NextLibrary/Literature/Shakespeare/Plays/Richard_Duke_of_York/4.2
./NextLibrary/Literature/Shakespeare/Plays/Richard_Duke_of_York/4.3
./NextLibrary/Literature/Shakespeare/Plays/Richard_Duke_of_York/4.4
```

./NextLibrary/Literature/Shakespeare/Plays/Richard_Duke_of_York/4.5
./NextLibrary/Literature/Shakespeare/Plays/Richard_Duke_of_York/4.6
./NextLibrary/Literature/Shakespeare/Plays/Richard_Duke_of_York/4.7
./NextLibrary/Literature/Shakespeare/Plays/Richard_Duke_of_York/4.8
./NextLibrary/Literature/Shakespeare/Plays/Richard_Duke_of_York/4.9
./NextLibrary/Literature/Shakespeare/Plays/Richard_Duke_of_York/4.10
./NextLibrary/Literature/Shakespeare/Plays/Richard_Duke_of_York/5.1
./NextLibrary/Literature/Shakespeare/Plays/Richard_Duke_of_York/5.2
./NextLibrary/Literature/Shakespeare/Plays/Richard_Duke_of_York/5.3
./NextLibrary/Literature/Shakespeare/Plays/Richard_Duke_of_York/5.4
./NextLibrary/Literature/Shakespeare/Plays/Richard_Duke_of_York/5.5
./NextLibrary/Literature/Shakespeare/Plays/Richard_Duke_of_York/5.6
./NextLibrary/Literature/Shakespeare/Plays/Richard_Duke_of_York/5.7
./NextLibrary/Literature/Shakespeare/Plays/Richard_Duke_of_York/Introduction
./NextLibrary/Literature/Shakespeare/Plays/Richard_Duke_of_York/Players
./NextLibrary/Literature/Shakespeare/Plays/Richard_Duke_of_York/.places
./NextLibrary/Literature/Shakespeare/Plays/The_Comedy_of_Errors
./NextLibrary/Literature/Shakespeare/Plays/The_Comedy_of_Errors/1.1
./NextLibrary/Literature/Shakespeare/Plays/The_Comedy_of_Errors/1.2
./NextLibrary/Literature/Shakespeare/Plays/The_Comedy_of_Errors/2.1
./NextLibrary/Literature/Shakespeare/Plays/The_Comedy_of_Errors/2.2
./NextLibrary/Literature/Shakespeare/Plays/The_Comedy_of_Errors/3.1
./NextLibrary/Literature/Shakespeare/Plays/The_Comedy_of_Errors/3.2
./NextLibrary/Literature/Shakespeare/Plays/The_Comedy_of_Errors/4.1
./NextLibrary/Literature/Shakespeare/Plays/The_Comedy_of_Errors/4.2
./NextLibrary/Literature/Shakespeare/Plays/The_Comedy_of_Errors/4.3
./NextLibrary/Literature/Shakespeare/Plays/The_Comedy_of_Errors/4.4
./NextLibrary/Literature/Shakespeare/Plays/The_Comedy_of_Errors/5.1
./NextLibrary/Literature/Shakespeare/Plays/The_Comedy_of_Errors/Introduction
./NextLibrary/Literature/Shakespeare/Plays/The_Comedy_of_Errors/Players
./NextLibrary/Literature/Shakespeare/Plays/The_Comedy_of_Errors/.places
./NextLibrary/Literature/Shakespeare/Plays/Julius_Caesar
./NextLibrary/Literature/Shakespeare/Plays/Julius_Caesar/1.1
./NextLibrary/Literature/Shakespeare/Plays/Julius_Caesar/1.2
./NextLibrary/Literature/Shakespeare/Plays/Julius_Caesar/1.3
./NextLibrary/Literature/Shakespeare/Plays/Julius_Caesar/2.1
./NextLibrary/Literature/Shakespeare/Plays/Julius_Caesar/2.2
./NextLibrary/Literature/Shakespeare/Plays/Julius_Caesar/2.3
./NextLibrary/Literature/Shakespeare/Plays/Julius_Caesar/2.4
./NextLibrary/Literature/Shakespeare/Plays/Julius_Caesar/3.1
./NextLibrary/Literature/Shakespeare/Plays/Julius_Caesar/3.2
./NextLibrary/Literature/Shakespeare/Plays/Julius_Caesar/3.3
./NextLibrary/Literature/Shakespeare/Plays/Julius_Caesar/4.1
./NextLibrary/Literature/Shakespeare/Plays/Julius_Caesar/4.2
./NextLibrary/Literature/Shakespeare/Plays/Julius_Caesar/5.1
./NextLibrary/Literature/Shakespeare/Plays/Julius_Caesar/5.2
./NextLibrary/Literature/Shakespeare/Plays/Julius_Caesar/5.3
./NextLibrary/Literature/Shakespeare/Plays/Julius_Caesar/5.4
./NextLibrary/Literature/Shakespeare/Plays/Julius_Caesar/5.5
./NextLibrary/Literature/Shakespeare/Plays/Julius_Caesar/Introduction
./NextLibrary/Literature/Shakespeare/Plays/Julius_Caesar/Players
./NextLibrary/Literature/Shakespeare/Plays/Julius_Caesar/.places
./NextLibrary/Literature/Shakespeare/Plays/Much_Ado_About_Nothing
./NextLibrary/Literature/Shakespeare/Plays/Much_Ado_About_Nothing/1.1
./NextLibrary/Literature/Shakespeare/Plays/Much_Ado_About_Nothing/1.2
./NextLibrary/Literature/Shakespeare/Plays/Much_Ado_About_Nothing/1.3
./NextLibrary/Literature/Shakespeare/Plays/Much_Ado_About_Nothing/2.1
./NextLibrary/Literature/Shakespeare/Plays/Much_Ado_About_Nothing/2.2
./NextLibrary/Literature/Shakespeare/Plays/Much_Ado_About_Nothing/2.3
./NextLibrary/Literature/Shakespeare/Plays/Much_Ado_About_Nothing/3.1
./NextLibrary/Literature/Shakespeare/Plays/Much_Ado_About_Nothing/3.2
./NextLibrary/Literature/Shakespeare/Plays/Much_Ado_About_Nothing/3.3
./NextLibrary/Literature/Shakespeare/Plays/Much_Ado_About_Nothing/3.4
./NextLibrary/Literature/Shakespeare/Plays/Much_Ado_About_Nothing/3.5
./NextLibrary/Literature/Shakespeare/Plays/Much_Ado_About_Nothing/4.1
./NextLibrary/Literature/Shakespeare/Plays/Much_Ado_About_Nothing/4.2
./NextLibrary/Literature/Shakespeare/Plays/Much_Ado_About_Nothing/5.1
./NextLibrary/Literature/Shakespeare/Plays/Much_Ado_About_Nothing/5.2
./NextLibrary/Literature/Shakespeare/Plays/Much_Ado_About_Nothing/5.3
./NextLibrary/Literature/Shakespeare/Plays/Much_Ado_About_Nothing/5.4
./NextLibrary/Literature/Shakespeare/Plays/Much_Ado_About_Nothing/Introduction
./NextLibrary/Literature/Shakespeare/Plays/Much_Ado_About_Nothing/Players
./NextLibrary/Literature/Shakespeare/Plays/Much_Ado_About_Nothing/.places
./NextLibrary/Literature/Shakespeare/Plays/The_Tempest
./NextLibrary/Literature/Shakespeare/Plays/The_Tempest/1.1
./NextLibrary/Literature/Shakespeare/Plays/The_Tempest/1.2
./NextLibrary/Literature/Shakespeare/Plays/The_Tempest/2.1
./NextLibrary/Literature/Shakespeare/Plays/The_Tempest/2.2
./NextLibrary/Literature/Shakespeare/Plays/The_Tempest/3.1
./NextLibrary/Literature/Shakespeare/Plays/The_Tempest/3.2
./NextLibrary/Literature/Shakespeare/Plays/The_Tempest/3.3
./NextLibrary/Literature/Shakespeare/Plays/The_Tempest/4.1
./NextLibrary/Literature/Shakespeare/Plays/The_Tempest/5.1
./NextLibrary/Literature/Shakespeare/Plays/The_Tempest/Epilogue
./NextLibrary/Literature/Shakespeare/Plays/The_Tempest/Introduction
./NextLibrary/Literature/Shakespeare/Plays/The_Tempest/Players
./NextLibrary/Literature/Shakespeare/Plays/The_Tempest/.places
./NextLibrary/Literature/Shakespeare/Plays/Timon_of_Athens
./NextLibrary/Literature/Shakespeare/Plays/Timon_of_Athens/1.1
./NextLibrary/Literature/Shakespeare/Plays/Timon_of_Athens/1.2
./NextLibrary/Literature/Shakespeare/Plays/Timon_of_Athens/2.1
./NextLibrary/Literature/Shakespeare/Plays/Timon_of_Athens/2.2
./NextLibrary/Literature/Shakespeare/Plays/Timon_of_Athens/3.1
./NextLibrary/Literature/Shakespeare/Plays/Timon_of_Athens/3.2
./NextLibrary/Literature/Shakespeare/Plays/Timon_of_Athens/3.3
./NextLibrary/Literature/Shakespeare/Plays/Timon_of_Athens/3.4
./NextLibrary/Literature/Shakespeare/Plays/Timon_of_Athens/3.5
./NextLibrary/Literature/Shakespeare/Plays/Timon_of_Athens/3.6
./NextLibrary/Literature/Shakespeare/Plays/Timon_of_Athens/3.7
./NextLibrary/Literature/Shakespeare/Plays/Timon_of_Athens/4.1
./NextLibrary/Literature/Shakespeare/Plays/Timon_of_Athens/4.2
./NextLibrary/Literature/Shakespeare/Plays/Timon_of_Athens/4.3

./NextLibrary/Literature/Shakespeare/Plays/Timon_of_Athens/5.1
./NextLibrary/Literature/Shakespeare/Plays/Timon_of_Athens/5.2
./NextLibrary/Literature/Shakespeare/Plays/Timon_of_Athens/5.3
./NextLibrary/Literature/Shakespeare/Plays/Timon_of_Athens/5.4
./NextLibrary/Literature/Shakespeare/Plays/Timon_of_Athens/5.5
./NextLibrary/Literature/Shakespeare/Plays/Timon_of_Athens/Introduction
./NextLibrary/Literature/Shakespeare/Plays/Timon_of_Athens/Players
./NextLibrary/Literature/Shakespeare/Plays/Timon_of_Athens/.places
./NextLibrary/Literature/Shakespeare/Plays/Loves_Labours_Lost
./NextLibrary/Literature/Shakespeare/Plays/Loves_Labours_Lost/1.1
./NextLibrary/Literature/Shakespeare/Plays/Loves_Labours_Lost/1.2
./NextLibrary/Literature/Shakespeare/Plays/Loves_Labours_Lost/2.1
./NextLibrary/Literature/Shakespeare/Plays/Loves_Labours_Lost/3.1
./NextLibrary/Literature/Shakespeare/Plays/Loves_Labours_Lost/4.1
./NextLibrary/Literature/Shakespeare/Plays/Loves_Labours_Lost/4.2
./NextLibrary/Literature/Shakespeare/Plays/Loves_Labours_Lost/4.3
./NextLibrary/Literature/Shakespeare/Plays/Loves_Labours_Lost/5.1
./NextLibrary/Literature/Shakespeare/Plays/Loves_Labours_Lost/5.2
./NextLibrary/Literature/Shakespeare/Plays/Loves_Labours_Lost/Introduction
./NextLibrary/Literature/Shakespeare/Plays/Loves_Labours_Lost/Players
./NextLibrary/Literature/Shakespeare/Plays/Loves_Labours_Lost/Additional
./NextLibrary/Literature/Shakespeare/Plays/Loves_Labours_Lost/.places
./NextLibrary/Literature/Shakespeare/Plays/Richard_III
./NextLibrary/Literature/Shakespeare/Plays/Richard_III/1.1
./NextLibrary/Literature/Shakespeare/Plays/Richard_III/1.2
./NextLibrary/Literature/Shakespeare/Plays/Richard_III/1.3
./NextLibrary/Literature/Shakespeare/Plays/Richard_III/1.4
./NextLibrary/Literature/Shakespeare/Plays/Richard_III/2.1
./NextLibrary/Literature/Shakespeare/Plays/Richard_III/2.2
./NextLibrary/Literature/Shakespeare/Plays/Richard_III/2.3
./NextLibrary/Literature/Shakespeare/Plays/Richard_III/2.4
./NextLibrary/Literature/Shakespeare/Plays/Richard_III/3.1
./NextLibrary/Literature/Shakespeare/Plays/Richard_III/3.2
./NextLibrary/Literature/Shakespeare/Plays/Richard_III/3.3
./NextLibrary/Literature/Shakespeare/Plays/Richard_III/3.4
./NextLibrary/Literature/Shakespeare/Plays/Richard_III/3.5
./NextLibrary/Literature/Shakespeare/Plays/Richard_III/3.6
./NextLibrary/Literature/Shakespeare/Plays/Richard_III/3.7
./NextLibrary/Literature/Shakespeare/Plays/Richard_III/4.1
./NextLibrary/Literature/Shakespeare/Plays/Richard_III/4.2
./NextLibrary/Literature/Shakespeare/Plays/Richard_III/4.3
./NextLibrary/Literature/Shakespeare/Plays/Richard_III/4.4
./NextLibrary/Literature/Shakespeare/Plays/Richard_III/4.5
./NextLibrary/Literature/Shakespeare/Plays/Richard_III/5.1
./NextLibrary/Literature/Shakespeare/Plays/Richard_III/5.2
./NextLibrary/Literature/Shakespeare/Plays/Richard_III/5.3
./NextLibrary/Literature/Shakespeare/Plays/Richard_III/5.4
./NextLibrary/Literature/Shakespeare/Plays/Richard_III/5.5
./NextLibrary/Literature/Shakespeare/Plays/Richard_III/5.6
./NextLibrary/Literature/Shakespeare/Plays/Richard_III/5.7
./NextLibrary/Literature/Shakespeare/Plays/Richard_III/5.8

./NextLibrary/Literature/Shakespeare/Plays/Richard_III/Introduction
./NextLibrary/Literature/Shakespeare/Plays/Richard_III/Players
./NextLibrary/Literature/Shakespeare/Plays/Richard_III/.places
./NextLibrary/Literature/Shakespeare/Plays/1_Henry_IV
./NextLibrary/Literature/Shakespeare/Plays/1_Henry_IV/1.1
./NextLibrary/Literature/Shakespeare/Plays/1_Henry_IV/1.2
./NextLibrary/Literature/Shakespeare/Plays/1_Henry_IV/1.3
./NextLibrary/Literature/Shakespeare/Plays/1_Henry_IV/2.1
./NextLibrary/Literature/Shakespeare/Plays/1_Henry_IV/2.2
./NextLibrary/Literature/Shakespeare/Plays/1_Henry_IV/2.3
./NextLibrary/Literature/Shakespeare/Plays/1_Henry_IV/2.4
./NextLibrary/Literature/Shakespeare/Plays/1_Henry_IV/2.5
./NextLibrary/Literature/Shakespeare/Plays/1_Henry_IV/3.1
./NextLibrary/Literature/Shakespeare/Plays/1_Henry_IV/3.2
./NextLibrary/Literature/Shakespeare/Plays/1_Henry_IV/3.3
./NextLibrary/Literature/Shakespeare/Plays/1_Henry_IV/4.1
./NextLibrary/Literature/Shakespeare/Plays/1_Henry_IV/4.2
./NextLibrary/Literature/Shakespeare/Plays/1_Henry_IV/4.3
./NextLibrary/Literature/Shakespeare/Plays/1_Henry_IV/4.4
./NextLibrary/Literature/Shakespeare/Plays/1_Henry_IV/5.1
./NextLibrary/Literature/Shakespeare/Plays/1_Henry_IV/5.2
./NextLibrary/Literature/Shakespeare/Plays/1_Henry_IV/5.3
./NextLibrary/Literature/Shakespeare/Plays/1_Henry_IV/5.4
./NextLibrary/Literature/Shakespeare/Plays/1_Henry_IV/5.5
./NextLibrary/Literature/Shakespeare/Plays/1_Henry_IV/Introduction
./NextLibrary/Literature/Shakespeare/Plays/1_Henry_IV/Players
./NextLibrary/Literature/Shakespeare/Plays/1_Henry_IV/.places
./NextLibrary/Literature/Shakespeare/Plays/All_Is_True
./NextLibrary/Literature/Shakespeare/Plays/All_Is_True/Prologue
./NextLibrary/Literature/Shakespeare/Plays/All_Is_True/1.1
./NextLibrary/Literature/Shakespeare/Plays/All_Is_True/1.2
./NextLibrary/Literature/Shakespeare/Plays/All_Is_True/1.3
./NextLibrary/Literature/Shakespeare/Plays/All_Is_True/1.4
./NextLibrary/Literature/Shakespeare/Plays/All_Is_True/2.1
./NextLibrary/Literature/Shakespeare/Plays/All_Is_True/2.2
./NextLibrary/Literature/Shakespeare/Plays/All_Is_True/2.3
./NextLibrary/Literature/Shakespeare/Plays/All_Is_True/2.4
./NextLibrary/Literature/Shakespeare/Plays/All_Is_True/3.1
./NextLibrary/Literature/Shakespeare/Plays/All_Is_True/3.2
./NextLibrary/Literature/Shakespeare/Plays/All_Is_True/4.1
./NextLibrary/Literature/Shakespeare/Plays/All_Is_True/4.2
./NextLibrary/Literature/Shakespeare/Plays/All_Is_True/5.1
./NextLibrary/Literature/Shakespeare/Plays/All_Is_True/5.2
./NextLibrary/Literature/Shakespeare/Plays/All_Is_True/5.3
./NextLibrary/Literature/Shakespeare/Plays/All_Is_True/5.4
./NextLibrary/Literature/Shakespeare/Plays/All_Is_True/Epilogue
./NextLibrary/Literature/Shakespeare/Plays/All_Is_True/Introduction
./NextLibrary/Literature/Shakespeare/Plays/All_Is_True/Players
./NextLibrary/Literature/Shakespeare/Plays/All_Is_True/.places
./NextLibrary/Literature/Shakespeare/Plays/Alls_Well_That_Ends_Well
./NextLibrary/Literature/Shakespeare/Plays/Alls_Well_That_Ends_Well/1.1

./NextLibrary/Literature/Shakespeare/Plays/Alls_Well_That_Ends_Well/1.2
./NextLibrary/Literature/Shakespeare/Plays/Alls_Well_That_Ends_Well/1.3
./NextLibrary/Literature/Shakespeare/Plays/Alls_Well_That_Ends_Well/2.1
./NextLibrary/Literature/Shakespeare/Plays/Alls_Well_That_Ends_Well/2.2
./NextLibrary/Literature/Shakespeare/Plays/Alls_Well_That_Ends_Well/2.3
./NextLibrary/Literature/Shakespeare/Plays/Alls_Well_That_Ends_Well/2.4
./NextLibrary/Literature/Shakespeare/Plays/Alls_Well_That_Ends_Well/2.5
./NextLibrary/Literature/Shakespeare/Plays/Alls_Well_That_Ends_Well/3.1
./NextLibrary/Literature/Shakespeare/Plays/Alls_Well_That_Ends_Well/3.2
./NextLibrary/Literature/Shakespeare/Plays/Alls_Well_That_Ends_Well/3.3
./NextLibrary/Literature/Shakespeare/Plays/Alls_Well_That_Ends_Well/3.4
./NextLibrary/Literature/Shakespeare/Plays/Alls_Well_That_Ends_Well/3.5
./NextLibrary/Literature/Shakespeare/Plays/Alls_Well_That_Ends_Well/3.6
./NextLibrary/Literature/Shakespeare/Plays/Alls_Well_That_Ends_Well/3.7
./NextLibrary/Literature/Shakespeare/Plays/Alls_Well_That_Ends_Well/4.1
./NextLibrary/Literature/Shakespeare/Plays/Alls_Well_That_Ends_Well/4.2
./NextLibrary/Literature/Shakespeare/Plays/Alls_Well_That_Ends_Well/4.3
./NextLibrary/Literature/Shakespeare/Plays/Alls_Well_That_Ends_Well/4.4
./NextLibrary/Literature/Shakespeare/Plays/Alls_Well_That_Ends_Well/4.5
./NextLibrary/Literature/Shakespeare/Plays/Alls_Well_That_Ends_Well/5.1
./NextLibrary/Literature/Shakespeare/Plays/Alls_Well_That_Ends_Well/5.2
./NextLibrary/Literature/Shakespeare/Plays/Alls_Well_That_Ends_Well/5.3
./NextLibrary/Literature/Shakespeare/Plays/Alls_Well_That_Ends_Well/Epilogue
./NextLibrary/Literature/Shakespeare/Plays/Alls_Well_That_Ends_Well/Introduction
./NextLibrary/Literature/Shakespeare/Plays/Alls_Well_That_Ends_Well/Players
./NextLibrary/Literature/Shakespeare/Plays/Alls_Well_That_Ends_Well/.places
./NextLibrary/Literature/Shakespeare/Plays/The_Merchant_of_Venice
./NextLibrary/Literature/Shakespeare/Plays/The_Merchant_of_Venice/1.1
./NextLibrary/Literature/Shakespeare/Plays/The_Merchant_of_Venice/1.2
./NextLibrary/Literature/Shakespeare/Plays/The_Merchant_of_Venice/1.3
./NextLibrary/Literature/Shakespeare/Plays/The_Merchant_of_Venice/2.1
./NextLibrary/Literature/Shakespeare/Plays/The_Merchant_of_Venice/2.2
./NextLibrary/Literature/Shakespeare/Plays/The_Merchant_of_Venice/2.3
./NextLibrary/Literature/Shakespeare/Plays/The_Merchant_of_Venice/2.4
./NextLibrary/Literature/Shakespeare/Plays/The_Merchant_of_Venice/2.5
./NextLibrary/Literature/Shakespeare/Plays/The_Merchant_of_Venice/2.6
./NextLibrary/Literature/Shakespeare/Plays/The_Merchant_of_Venice/2.7
./NextLibrary/Literature/Shakespeare/Plays/The_Merchant_of_Venice/2.8
./NextLibrary/Literature/Shakespeare/Plays/The_Merchant_of_Venice/2.9
./NextLibrary/Literature/Shakespeare/Plays/The_Merchant_of_Venice/3.1
./NextLibrary/Literature/Shakespeare/Plays/The_Merchant_of_Venice/3.2
./NextLibrary/Literature/Shakespeare/Plays/The_Merchant_of_Venice/3.3
./NextLibrary/Literature/Shakespeare/Plays/The_Merchant_of_Venice/3.4
./NextLibrary/Literature/Shakespeare/Plays/The_Merchant_of_Venice/3.5
./NextLibrary/Literature/Shakespeare/Plays/The_Merchant_of_Venice/4.1
./NextLibrary/Literature/Shakespeare/Plays/The_Merchant_of_Venice/4.2
./NextLibrary/Literature/Shakespeare/Plays/The_Merchant_of_Venice/5.1
./NextLibrary/Literature/Shakespeare/Plays/The_Merchant_of_Venice/Introduction
./NextLibrary/Literature/Shakespeare/Plays/The_Merchant_of_Venice/Players
./NextLibrary/Literature/Shakespeare/Plays/The_Merchant_of_Venice/.places
./NextLibrary/Literature/Shakespeare/Plays/Measure_for_Measure

./NextLibrary/Literature/Shakespeare/Plays/Measure_for_Measure/1.1
./NextLibrary/Literature/Shakespeare/Plays/Measure_for_Measure/1.2
./NextLibrary/Literature/Shakespeare/Plays/Measure_for_Measure/1.3
./NextLibrary/Literature/Shakespeare/Plays/Measure_for_Measure/1.4
./NextLibrary/Literature/Shakespeare/Plays/Measure_for_Measure/2.1
./NextLibrary/Literature/Shakespeare/Plays/Measure_for_Measure/2.2
./NextLibrary/Literature/Shakespeare/Plays/Measure_for_Measure/2.3
./NextLibrary/Literature/Shakespeare/Plays/Measure_for_Measure/2.4
./NextLibrary/Literature/Shakespeare/Plays/Measure_for_Measure/3.1
./NextLibrary/Literature/Shakespeare/Plays/Measure_for_Measure/4.1
./NextLibrary/Literature/Shakespeare/Plays/Measure_for_Measure/4.2
./NextLibrary/Literature/Shakespeare/Plays/Measure_for_Measure/4.3
./NextLibrary/Literature/Shakespeare/Plays/Measure_for_Measure/4.4
./NextLibrary/Literature/Shakespeare/Plays/Measure_for_Measure/4.5
./NextLibrary/Literature/Shakespeare/Plays/Measure_for_Measure/4.6
./NextLibrary/Literature/Shakespeare/Plays/Measure_for_Measure/5.1
./NextLibrary/Literature/Shakespeare/Plays/Measure_for_Measure/Introduction
./NextLibrary/Literature/Shakespeare/Plays/Measure_for_Measure/Players
./NextLibrary/Literature/Shakespeare/Plays/Measure_for_Measure/Additional
./NextLibrary/Literature/Shakespeare/Plays/Measure_for_Measure/.places
./NextLibrary/Literature/Shakespeare/Plays/Henry_V
./NextLibrary/Literature/Shakespeare/Plays/Henry_V/Prologue
./NextLibrary/Literature/Shakespeare/Plays/Henry_V/1.1
./NextLibrary/Literature/Shakespeare/Plays/Henry_V/1.2
./NextLibrary/Literature/Shakespeare/Plays/Henry_V/2.0
./NextLibrary/Literature/Shakespeare/Plays/Henry_V/2.1
./NextLibrary/Literature/Shakespeare/Plays/Henry_V/2.2
./NextLibrary/Literature/Shakespeare/Plays/Henry_V/2.3
./NextLibrary/Literature/Shakespeare/Plays/Henry_V/2.4
./NextLibrary/Literature/Shakespeare/Plays/Henry_V/3.0
./NextLibrary/Literature/Shakespeare/Plays/Henry_V/3.1
./NextLibrary/Literature/Shakespeare/Plays/Henry_V/3.2
./NextLibrary/Literature/Shakespeare/Plays/Henry_V/3.3
./NextLibrary/Literature/Shakespeare/Plays/Henry_V/3.4
./NextLibrary/Literature/Shakespeare/Plays/Henry_V/3.5
./NextLibrary/Literature/Shakespeare/Plays/Henry_V/3.6
./NextLibrary/Literature/Shakespeare/Plays/Henry_V/3.7
./NextLibrary/Literature/Shakespeare/Plays/Henry_V/4.0
./NextLibrary/Literature/Shakespeare/Plays/Henry_V/4.1
./NextLibrary/Literature/Shakespeare/Plays/Henry_V/4.2
./NextLibrary/Literature/Shakespeare/Plays/Henry_V/4.3
./NextLibrary/Literature/Shakespeare/Plays/Henry_V/4.4
./NextLibrary/Literature/Shakespeare/Plays/Henry_V/4.5
./NextLibrary/Literature/Shakespeare/Plays/Henry_V/4.6
./NextLibrary/Literature/Shakespeare/Plays/Henry_V/4.7
./NextLibrary/Literature/Shakespeare/Plays/Henry_V/4.8
./NextLibrary/Literature/Shakespeare/Plays/Henry_V/5.0
./NextLibrary/Literature/Shakespeare/Plays/Henry_V/5.1
./NextLibrary/Literature/Shakespeare/Plays/Henry_V/5.2
./NextLibrary/Literature/Shakespeare/Plays/Henry_V/Epilogue
./NextLibrary/Literature/Shakespeare/Plays/Henry_V/Introduction

./NextLibrary/Literature/Shakespeare/Plays/Henry_V/Players
./NextLibrary/Literature/Shakespeare/Plays/Henry_V/.places
./NextLibrary/Literature/Shakespeare/Plays/Twelfth_Night_or_What_You_Will
./NextLibrary/Literature/Shakespeare/Plays/Twelfth_Night_or_What_You_Will/1.1
./NextLibrary/Literature/Shakespeare/Plays/Twelfth_Night_or_What_You_Will/1.2
./NextLibrary/Literature/Shakespeare/Plays/Twelfth_Night_or_What_You_Will/1.3
./NextLibrary/Literature/Shakespeare/Plays/Twelfth_Night_or_What_You_Will/1.4
./NextLibrary/Literature/Shakespeare/Plays/Twelfth_Night_or_What_You_Will/1.5
./NextLibrary/Literature/Shakespeare/Plays/Twelfth_Night_or_What_You_Will/2.1
./NextLibrary/Literature/Shakespeare/Plays/Twelfth_Night_or_What_You_Will/2.2
./NextLibrary/Literature/Shakespeare/Plays/Twelfth_Night_or_What_You_Will/2.3
./NextLibrary/Literature/Shakespeare/Plays/Twelfth_Night_or_What_You_Will/2.4
./NextLibrary/Literature/Shakespeare/Plays/Twelfth_Night_or_What_You_Will/2.5
./NextLibrary/Literature/Shakespeare/Plays/Twelfth_Night_or_What_You_Will/3.1
./NextLibrary/Literature/Shakespeare/Plays/Twelfth_Night_or_What_You_Will/3.2
./NextLibrary/Literature/Shakespeare/Plays/Twelfth_Night_or_What_You_Will/3.3
./NextLibrary/Literature/Shakespeare/Plays/Twelfth_Night_or_What_You_Will/3.4
./NextLibrary/Literature/Shakespeare/Plays/Twelfth_Night_or_What_You_Will/4.1
./NextLibrary/Literature/Shakespeare/Plays/Twelfth_Night_or_What_You_Will/4.2
./NextLibrary/Literature/Shakespeare/Plays/Twelfth_Night_or_What_You_Will/4.3
./NextLibrary/Literature/Shakespeare/Plays/Twelfth_Night_or_What_You_Will/5.1
./NextLibrary/Literature/Shakespeare/Plays/Twelfth_Night_or_What_You_Will/Intro-
    duction
./NextLibrary/Literature/Shakespeare/Plays/Twelfth_Night_or_What_You_Will/Players
./NextLibrary/Literature/Shakespeare/Plays/Twelfth_Night_or_What_You_Will/.places
./NextLibrary/Literature/Shakespeare/Plays/The_History_of_King_Lear
./NextLibrary/Literature/Shakespeare/Plays/The_History_of_King_Lear/Sc.1
./NextLibrary/Literature/Shakespeare/Plays/The_History_of_King_Lear/Sc.2
./NextLibrary/Literature/Shakespeare/Plays/The_History_of_King_Lear/Sc.3
./NextLibrary/Literature/Shakespeare/Plays/The_History_of_King_Lear/Sc.4
./NextLibrary/Literature/Shakespeare/Plays/The_History_of_King_Lear/Sc.5
./NextLibrary/Literature/Shakespeare/Plays/The_History_of_King_Lear/Sc.6
./NextLibrary/Literature/Shakespeare/Plays/The_History_of_King_Lear/Sc.7
./NextLibrary/Literature/Shakespeare/Plays/The_History_of_King_Lear/Sc.8
./NextLibrary/Literature/Shakespeare/Plays/The_History_of_King_Lear/Sc.9
./NextLibrary/Literature/Shakespeare/Plays/The_History_of_King_Lear/Sc.10
./NextLibrary/Literature/Shakespeare/Plays/The_History_of_King_Lear/Sc.11
./NextLibrary/Literature/Shakespeare/Plays/The_History_of_King_Lear/Sc.12
./NextLibrary/Literature/Shakespeare/Plays/The_History_of_King_Lear/Sc.13
./NextLibrary/Literature/Shakespeare/Plays/The_History_of_King_Lear/Sc.14
./NextLibrary/Literature/Shakespeare/Plays/The_History_of_King_Lear/Sc.15
./NextLibrary/Literature/Shakespeare/Plays/The_History_of_King_Lear/Sc.16
./NextLibrary/Literature/Shakespeare/Plays/The_History_of_King_Lear/Sc.17
./NextLibrary/Literature/Shakespeare/Plays/The_History_of_King_Lear/Sc.18
./NextLibrary/Literature/Shakespeare/Plays/The_History_of_King_Lear/Sc.19
./NextLibrary/Literature/Shakespeare/Plays/The_History_of_King_Lear/Sc.20
./NextLibrary/Literature/Shakespeare/Plays/The_History_of_King_Lear/Sc.21
./NextLibrary/Literature/Shakespeare/Plays/The_History_of_King_Lear/Sc.22
./NextLibrary/Literature/Shakespeare/Plays/The_History_of_King_Lear/Sc.23
./NextLibrary/Literature/Shakespeare/Plays/The_History_of_King_Lear/Sc.24
./NextLibrary/Literature/Shakespeare/Plays/The_History_of_King_Lear/Introduction

./NextLibrary/Literature/Shakespeare/Plays/The_History_of_King_Lear/Players
./NextLibrary/Literature/Shakespeare/Plays/The_History_of_King_Lear/.places
./NextLibrary/Literature/Shakespeare/Plays/Macbeth
./NextLibrary/Literature/Shakespeare/Plays/Macbeth/1.1
./NextLibrary/Literature/Shakespeare/Plays/Macbeth/1.2
./NextLibrary/Literature/Shakespeare/Plays/Macbeth/1.3
./NextLibrary/Literature/Shakespeare/Plays/Macbeth/1.4
./NextLibrary/Literature/Shakespeare/Plays/Macbeth/1.5
./NextLibrary/Literature/Shakespeare/Plays/Macbeth/1.6
./NextLibrary/Literature/Shakespeare/Plays/Macbeth/1.7
./NextLibrary/Literature/Shakespeare/Plays/Macbeth/2.1
./NextLibrary/Literature/Shakespeare/Plays/Macbeth/2.2
./NextLibrary/Literature/Shakespeare/Plays/Macbeth/2.3
./NextLibrary/Literature/Shakespeare/Plays/Macbeth/2.4
./NextLibrary/Literature/Shakespeare/Plays/Macbeth/3.1
./NextLibrary/Literature/Shakespeare/Plays/Macbeth/3.2
./NextLibrary/Literature/Shakespeare/Plays/Macbeth/3.3
./NextLibrary/Literature/Shakespeare/Plays/Macbeth/3.4
./NextLibrary/Literature/Shakespeare/Plays/Macbeth/3.5
./NextLibrary/Literature/Shakespeare/Plays/Macbeth/3.6
./NextLibrary/Literature/Shakespeare/Plays/Macbeth/4.1
./NextLibrary/Literature/Shakespeare/Plays/Macbeth/4.2
./NextLibrary/Literature/Shakespeare/Plays/Macbeth/4.3
./NextLibrary/Literature/Shakespeare/Plays/Macbeth/5.1
./NextLibrary/Literature/Shakespeare/Plays/Macbeth/5.2
./NextLibrary/Literature/Shakespeare/Plays/Macbeth/5.3
./NextLibrary/Literature/Shakespeare/Plays/Macbeth/5.4
./NextLibrary/Literature/Shakespeare/Plays/Macbeth/5.5
./NextLibrary/Literature/Shakespeare/Plays/Macbeth/5.6
./NextLibrary/Literature/Shakespeare/Plays/Macbeth/5.7
./NextLibrary/Literature/Shakespeare/Plays/Macbeth/5.8
./NextLibrary/Literature/Shakespeare/Plays/Macbeth/5.9
./NextLibrary/Literature/Shakespeare/Plays/Macbeth/5.10
./NextLibrary/Literature/Shakespeare/Plays/Macbeth/5.11
./NextLibrary/Literature/Shakespeare/Plays/Macbeth/Introduction
./NextLibrary/Literature/Shakespeare/Plays/Macbeth/Players
./NextLibrary/Literature/Shakespeare/Plays/Macbeth/.places
./NextLibrary/Literature/Shakespeare/Plays/The_Merry_Wives_of_Windsor
./NextLibrary/Literature/Shakespeare/Plays/The_Merry_Wives_of_Windsor/Players
./NextLibrary/Literature/Shakespeare/Plays/The_Merry_Wives_of_Windsor/1.1
./NextLibrary/Literature/Shakespeare/Plays/The_Merry_Wives_of_Windsor/1.2
./NextLibrary/Literature/Shakespeare/Plays/The_Merry_Wives_of_Windsor/1.3
./NextLibrary/Literature/Shakespeare/Plays/The_Merry_Wives_of_Windsor/1.4
./NextLibrary/Literature/Shakespeare/Plays/The_Merry_Wives_of_Windsor/2.1
./NextLibrary/Literature/Shakespeare/Plays/The_Merry_Wives_of_Windsor/2.2
./NextLibrary/Literature/Shakespeare/Plays/The_Merry_Wives_of_Windsor/2.3
./NextLibrary/Literature/Shakespeare/Plays/The_Merry_Wives_of_Windsor/3.1
./NextLibrary/Literature/Shakespeare/Plays/The_Merry_Wives_of_Windsor/3.2
./NextLibrary/Literature/Shakespeare/Plays/The_Merry_Wives_of_Windsor/3.3
./NextLibrary/Literature/Shakespeare/Plays/The_Merry_Wives_of_Windsor/3.4
./NextLibrary/Literature/Shakespeare/Plays/The_Merry_Wives_of_Windsor/3.5

```
./NextLibrary/Literature/Shakespeare/Plays/The_Merry_Wives_of_Windsor/4.1
./NextLibrary/Literature/Shakespeare/Plays/The_Merry_Wives_of_Windsor/4.2
./NextLibrary/Literature/Shakespeare/Plays/The_Merry_Wives_of_Windsor/4.3
./NextLibrary/Literature/Shakespeare/Plays/The_Merry_Wives_of_Windsor/4.4
./NextLibrary/Literature/Shakespeare/Plays/The_Merry_Wives_of_Windsor/4.5
./NextLibrary/Literature/Shakespeare/Plays/The_Merry_Wives_of_Windsor/4.6
./NextLibrary/Literature/Shakespeare/Plays/The_Merry_Wives_of_Windsor/5.1
./NextLibrary/Literature/Shakespeare/Plays/The_Merry_Wives_of_Windsor/5.2
./NextLibrary/Literature/Shakespeare/Plays/The_Merry_Wives_of_Windsor/5.3
./NextLibrary/Literature/Shakespeare/Plays/The_Merry_Wives_of_Windsor/5.4
./NextLibrary/Literature/Shakespeare/Plays/The_Merry_Wives_of_Windsor/5.5
./NextLibrary/Literature/Shakespeare/Plays/The_Merry_Wives_of_Windsor/Introduc-
    tion
./NextLibrary/Literature/Shakespeare/Plays/The_Merry_Wives_of_Windsor/.places
./NextLibrary/Literature/Shakespeare/Plays/The_Tragedy_of_King_Lear
./NextLibrary/Literature/Shakespeare/Plays/The_Tragedy_of_King_Lear/1.1
./NextLibrary/Literature/Shakespeare/Plays/The_Tragedy_of_King_Lear/1.2
./NextLibrary/Literature/Shakespeare/Plays/The_Tragedy_of_King_Lear/1.3
./NextLibrary/Literature/Shakespeare/Plays/The_Tragedy_of_King_Lear/1.4
./NextLibrary/Literature/Shakespeare/Plays/The_Tragedy_of_King_Lear/1.5
./NextLibrary/Literature/Shakespeare/Plays/The_Tragedy_of_King_Lear/2.1
./NextLibrary/Literature/Shakespeare/Plays/The_Tragedy_of_King_Lear/2.2
./NextLibrary/Literature/Shakespeare/Plays/The_Tragedy_of_King_Lear/3.1
./NextLibrary/Literature/Shakespeare/Plays/The_Tragedy_of_King_Lear/3.2
./NextLibrary/Literature/Shakespeare/Plays/The_Tragedy_of_King_Lear/3.3
./NextLibrary/Literature/Shakespeare/Plays/The_Tragedy_of_King_Lear/3.4
./NextLibrary/Literature/Shakespeare/Plays/The_Tragedy_of_King_Lear/3.5
./NextLibrary/Literature/Shakespeare/Plays/The_Tragedy_of_King_Lear/3.6
./NextLibrary/Literature/Shakespeare/Plays/The_Tragedy_of_King_Lear/3.7
./NextLibrary/Literature/Shakespeare/Plays/The_Tragedy_of_King_Lear/4.1
./NextLibrary/Literature/Shakespeare/Plays/The_Tragedy_of_King_Lear/4.2
./NextLibrary/Literature/Shakespeare/Plays/The_Tragedy_of_King_Lear/4.3
./NextLibrary/Literature/Shakespeare/Plays/The_Tragedy_of_King_Lear/4.4
./NextLibrary/Literature/Shakespeare/Plays/The_Tragedy_of_King_Lear/4.5
./NextLibrary/Literature/Shakespeare/Plays/The_Tragedy_of_King_Lear/4.6
./NextLibrary/Literature/Shakespeare/Plays/The_Tragedy_of_King_Lear/5.1
./NextLibrary/Literature/Shakespeare/Plays/The_Tragedy_of_King_Lear/5.2
./NextLibrary/Literature/Shakespeare/Plays/The_Tragedy_of_King_Lear/5.3
./NextLibrary/Literature/Shakespeare/Plays/The_Tragedy_of_King_Lear/Introduction
./NextLibrary/Literature/Shakespeare/Plays/The_Tragedy_of_King_Lear/Players
./NextLibrary/Literature/Shakespeare/Plays/The_Tragedy_of_King_Lear/.places
./NextLibrary/Literature/Shakespeare/Plays/A_Midsummer_Nights_Dream
./NextLibrary/Literature/Shakespeare/Plays/A_Midsummer_Nights_Dream/1.1
./NextLibrary/Literature/Shakespeare/Plays/A_Midsummer_Nights_Dream/1.2
./NextLibrary/Literature/Shakespeare/Plays/A_Midsummer_Nights_Dream/2.1
./NextLibrary/Literature/Shakespeare/Plays/A_Midsummer_Nights_Dream/2.2
./NextLibrary/Literature/Shakespeare/Plays/A_Midsummer_Nights_Dream/3.1
./NextLibrary/Literature/Shakespeare/Plays/A_Midsummer_Nights_Dream/3.2
./NextLibrary/Literature/Shakespeare/Plays/A_Midsummer_Nights_Dream/3.3
./NextLibrary/Literature/Shakespeare/Plays/A_Midsummer_Nights_Dream/4.1
./NextLibrary/Literature/Shakespeare/Plays/A_Midsummer_Nights_Dream/4.2
./NextLibrary/Literature/Shakespeare/Plays/A_Midsummer_Nights_Dream/5.1
./NextLibrary/Literature/Shakespeare/Plays/A_Midsummer_Nights_Dream/5.2
./NextLibrary/Literature/Shakespeare/Plays/A_Midsummer_Nights_Dream/Epilogue
./NextLibrary/Literature/Shakespeare/Plays/A_Midsummer_Nights_Dream/Additional
./NextLibrary/Literature/Shakespeare/Plays/A_Midsummer_Nights_Dream/Introduction
./NextLibrary/Literature/Shakespeare/Plays/A_Midsummer_Nights_Dream/Players
./NextLibrary/Literature/Shakespeare/Plays/A_Midsummer_Nights_Dream/.places
./NextLibrary/Literature/Shakespeare/Plays/Antony_and_Cleopatra
./NextLibrary/Literature/Shakespeare/Plays/Antony_and_Cleopatra/1.1
./NextLibrary/Literature/Shakespeare/Plays/Antony_and_Cleopatra/1.2
./NextLibrary/Literature/Shakespeare/Plays/Antony_and_Cleopatra/1.3
./NextLibrary/Literature/Shakespeare/Plays/Antony_and_Cleopatra/1.4
./NextLibrary/Literature/Shakespeare/Plays/Antony_and_Cleopatra/1.5
./NextLibrary/Literature/Shakespeare/Plays/Antony_and_Cleopatra/2.1
./NextLibrary/Literature/Shakespeare/Plays/Antony_and_Cleopatra/2.2
./NextLibrary/Literature/Shakespeare/Plays/Antony_and_Cleopatra/2.3
./NextLibrary/Literature/Shakespeare/Plays/Antony_and_Cleopatra/2.4
./NextLibrary/Literature/Shakespeare/Plays/Antony_and_Cleopatra/2.5
./NextLibrary/Literature/Shakespeare/Plays/Antony_and_Cleopatra/2.6
./NextLibrary/Literature/Shakespeare/Plays/Antony_and_Cleopatra/2.7
./NextLibrary/Literature/Shakespeare/Plays/Antony_and_Cleopatra/3.1
./NextLibrary/Literature/Shakespeare/Plays/Antony_and_Cleopatra/3.2
./NextLibrary/Literature/Shakespeare/Plays/Antony_and_Cleopatra/3.3
./NextLibrary/Literature/Shakespeare/Plays/Antony_and_Cleopatra/3.4
./NextLibrary/Literature/Shakespeare/Plays/Antony_and_Cleopatra/3.5
./NextLibrary/Literature/Shakespeare/Plays/Antony_and_Cleopatra/3.6
./NextLibrary/Literature/Shakespeare/Plays/Antony_and_Cleopatra/3.7
./NextLibrary/Literature/Shakespeare/Plays/Antony_and_Cleopatra/3.8
./NextLibrary/Literature/Shakespeare/Plays/Antony_and_Cleopatra/3.9
./NextLibrary/Literature/Shakespeare/Plays/Antony_and_Cleopatra/3.10
./NextLibrary/Literature/Shakespeare/Plays/Antony_and_Cleopatra/3.11
./NextLibrary/Literature/Shakespeare/Plays/Antony_and_Cleopatra/3.12
./NextLibrary/Literature/Shakespeare/Plays/Antony_and_Cleopatra/3.13
./NextLibrary/Literature/Shakespeare/Plays/Antony_and_Cleopatra/4.1
./NextLibrary/Literature/Shakespeare/Plays/Antony_and_Cleopatra/4.2
./NextLibrary/Literature/Shakespeare/Plays/Antony_and_Cleopatra/4.3
./NextLibrary/Literature/Shakespeare/Plays/Antony_and_Cleopatra/4.4
./NextLibrary/Literature/Shakespeare/Plays/Antony_and_Cleopatra/4.5
./NextLibrary/Literature/Shakespeare/Plays/Antony_and_Cleopatra/4.6
./NextLibrary/Literature/Shakespeare/Plays/Antony_and_Cleopatra/4.7
./NextLibrary/Literature/Shakespeare/Plays/Antony_and_Cleopatra/4.8
./NextLibrary/Literature/Shakespeare/Plays/Antony_and_Cleopatra/4.9
./NextLibrary/Literature/Shakespeare/Plays/Antony_and_Cleopatra/4.10
./NextLibrary/Literature/Shakespeare/Plays/Antony_and_Cleopatra/4.11
./NextLibrary/Literature/Shakespeare/Plays/Antony_and_Cleopatra/4.12
./NextLibrary/Literature/Shakespeare/Plays/Antony_and_Cleopatra/4.13
./NextLibrary/Literature/Shakespeare/Plays/Antony_and_Cleopatra/4.14
./NextLibrary/Literature/Shakespeare/Plays/Antony_and_Cleopatra/4.15
./NextLibrary/Literature/Shakespeare/Plays/Antony_and_Cleopatra/4.16
./NextLibrary/Literature/Shakespeare/Plays/Antony_and_Cleopatra/5.1
./NextLibrary/Literature/Shakespeare/Plays/Antony_and_Cleopatra/5.2
```

```
./NextLibrary/Literature/Shakespeare/Plays/Antony_and_Cleopatra/Introduction
./NextLibrary/Literature/Shakespeare/Plays/Antony_and_Cleopatra/Players
./NextLibrary/Literature/Shakespeare/Plays/Antony_and_Cleopatra/.places
./NextLibrary/Literature/Shakespeare/Plays/Pericles_Prince_of_Tyre
./NextLibrary/Literature/Shakespeare/Plays/Pericles_Prince_of_Tyre/Sc.1
./NextLibrary/Literature/Shakespeare/Plays/Pericles_Prince_of_Tyre/Sc.2
./NextLibrary/Literature/Shakespeare/Plays/Pericles_Prince_of_Tyre/Sc.3
./NextLibrary/Literature/Shakespeare/Plays/Pericles_Prince_of_Tyre/Sc.4
./NextLibrary/Literature/Shakespeare/Plays/Pericles_Prince_of_Tyre/Sc.5
./NextLibrary/Literature/Shakespeare/Plays/Pericles_Prince_of_Tyre/Sc.6
./NextLibrary/Literature/Shakespeare/Plays/Pericles_Prince_of_Tyre/Sc.7
./NextLibrary/Literature/Shakespeare/Plays/Pericles_Prince_of_Tyre/Sc.8
./NextLibrary/Literature/Shakespeare/Plays/Pericles_Prince_of_Tyre/Sc.8a
./NextLibrary/Literature/Shakespeare/Plays/Pericles_Prince_of_Tyre/Sc.9
./NextLibrary/Literature/Shakespeare/Plays/Pericles_Prince_of_Tyre/Sc.10
./NextLibrary/Literature/Shakespeare/Plays/Pericles Prince_of_Tyre/Sc.11
./NextLibrary/Literature/Shakespeare/Plays/Pericles_Prince_of_Tyre/Sc.12
./NextLibrary/Literature/Shakespeare/Plays/Pericles_Prince_of_Tyre/Sc.13
./NextLibrary/Literature/Shakespeare/Plays/Pericles_Prince_of_Tyre/Sc.14
./NextLibrary/Literature/Shakespeare/Plays/Pericles_Prince_of_Tyre/Sc.15
./NextLibrary/Literature/Shakespeare/Plays/Pericles_Prince_of_Tyre/Sc.16
./NextLibrary/Literature/Shakespeare/Plays/Pericles_Prince_of_Tyre/Sc.17
./NextLibrary/Literature/Shakespeare/Plays/Pericles_Prince_of_Tyre/Sc.18
./NextLibrary/Literature/Shakespeare/Plays/Pericles_Prince_of_Tyre/Sc.19
./NextLibrary/Literature/Shakespeare/Plays/Pericles_Prince_of_Tyre/Sc.20
./NextLibrary/Literature/Shakespeare/Plays/Pericles_Prince_of_Tyre/Sc.21
./NextLibrary/Literature/Shakespeare/Plays/Pericles_Prince_of_Tyre/Sc.22
./NextLibrary/Literature/Shakespeare/Plays/Pericles_Prince_of_Tyre/Additional
./NextLibrary/Literature/Shakespeare/Plays/Pericles_Prince_of_Tyre/Introduction
./NextLibrary/Literature/Shakespeare/Plays/Pericles_Prince_of_Tyre/Players
./NextLibrary/Literature/Shakespeare/Plays/Pericles_Prince_of_Tyre/.places
./NextLibrary/Literature/Shakespeare/Plays/King_John
./NextLibrary/Literature/Shakespeare/Plays/King_John/1.1
./NextLibrary/Literature/Shakespeare/Plays/King_John/2.1
./NextLibrary/Literature/Shakespeare/Plays/King_John/2.2
./NextLibrary/Literature/Shakespeare/Plays/King_John/3.1
./NextLibrary/Literature/Shakespeare/Plays/King_John/3.2
./NextLibrary/Literature/Shakespeare/Plays/King_John/3.3
./NextLibrary/Literature/Shakespeare/Plays/King_John/3.4
./NextLibrary/Literature/Shakespeare/Plays/King_John/4.1
./NextLibrary/Literature/Shakespeare/Plays/King_John/4.2
./NextLibrary/Literature/Shakespeare/Plays/King_John/4.3
./NextLibrary/Literature/Shakespeare/Plays/King_John/5.1
./NextLibrary/Literature/Shakespeare/Plays/King_John/5.2
./NextLibrary/Literature/Shakespeare/Plays/King_John/5.3
./NextLibrary/Literature/Shakespeare/Plays/King_John/5.4
./NextLibrary/Literature/Shakespeare/Plays/King_John/5.5
./NextLibrary/Literature/Shakespeare/Plays/King_John/5.6
./NextLibrary/Literature/Shakespeare/Plays/King_John/5.7
./NextLibrary/Literature/Shakespeare/Plays/King_John/Introduction
./NextLibrary/Literature/Shakespeare/Plays/King_John/Players

./NextLibrary/Literature/Shakespeare/Plays/King_John/.places
./NextLibrary/Literature/Shakespeare/Plays/Cymbeline
./NextLibrary/Literature/Shakespeare/Plays/Cymbeline/1.1
./NextLibrary/Literature/Shakespeare/Plays/Cymbeline/1.2
./NextLibrary/Literature/Shakespeare/Plays/Cymbeline/1.3
./NextLibrary/Literature/Shakespeare/Plays/Cymbeline/1.4
./NextLibrary/Literature/Shakespeare/Plays/Cymbeline/1.5
./NextLibrary/Literature/Shakespeare/Plays/Cymbeline/1.6
./NextLibrary/Literature/Shakespeare/Plays/Cymbeline/2.1
./NextLibrary/Literature/Shakespeare/Plays/Cymbeline/2.2
./NextLibrary/Literature/Shakespeare/Plays/Cymbeline/2.3
./NextLibrary/Literature/Shakespeare/Plays/Cymbeline/2.4
./NextLibrary/Literature/Shakespeare/Plays/Cymbeline/2.5
./NextLibrary/Literature/Shakespeare/Plays/Cymbeline/3.1
./NextLibrary/Literature/Shakespeare/Plays/Cymbeline/3.2
./NextLibrary/Literature/Shakespeare/Plays/Cymbeline/3.3
./NextLibrary/Literature/Shakespeare/Plays/Cymbeline/3.4
./NextLibrary/Literature/Shakespeare/Plays/Cymbeline/3.5
./NextLibrary/Literature/Shakespeare/Plays/Cymbeline/3.6
./NextLibrary/Literature/Shakespeare/Plays/Cymbeline/3.7
./NextLibrary/Literature/Shakespeare/Plays/Cymbeline/4.1
./NextLibrary/Literature/Shakespeare/Plays/Cymbeline/4.2
./NextLibrary/Literature/Shakespeare/Plays/Cymbeline/4.3
./NextLibrary/Literature/Shakespeare/Plays/Cymbeline/4.4
./NextLibrary/Literature/Shakespeare/Plays/Cymbeline/5.1
./NextLibrary/Literature/Shakespeare/Plays/Cymbeline/5.2
./NextLibrary/Literature/Shakespeare/Plays/Cymbeline/5.3
./NextLibrary/Literature/Shakespeare/Plays/Cymbeline/5.4
./NextLibrary/Literature/Shakespeare/Plays/Cymbeline/5.5
./NextLibrary/Literature/Shakespeare/Plays/Cymbeline/5.6
./NextLibrary/Literature/Shakespeare/Plays/Cymbeline/.places
./NextLibrary/Literature/Shakespeare/Plays/.places
./NextLibrary/Literature/Shakespeare/Plays/Troilus_and_Cressida
./NextLibrary/Literature/Shakespeare/Plays/Troilus_and_Cressida/Prologue
./NextLibrary/Literature/Shakespeare/Plays/Troilus_and_Cressida/1.1
./NextLibrary/Literature/Shakespeare/Plays/Troilus_and_Cressida/1.2
./NextLibrary/Literature/Shakespeare/Plays/Troilus_and_Cressida/1.3
./NextLibrary/Literature/Shakespeare/Plays/Troilus_and_Cressida/2.1
./NextLibrary/Literature/Shakespeare/Plays/Troilus_and_Cressida/2.2
./NextLibrary/Literature/Shakespeare/Plays/Troilus_and_Cressida/2.3
./NextLibrary/Literature/Shakespeare/Plays/Troilus_and_Cressida/3.1
./NextLibrary/Literature/Shakespeare/Plays/Troilus_and_Cressida/3.2
./NextLibrary/Literature/Shakespeare/Plays/Troilus_and_Cressida/3.3
./NextLibrary/Literature/Shakespeare/Plays/Troilus_and_Cressida/4.1
./NextLibrary/Literature/Shakespeare/Plays/Troilus_and_Cressida/4.2
./NextLibrary/Literature/Shakespeare/Plays/Troilus_and_Cressida/4.3
./NextLibrary/Literature/Shakespeare/Plays/Troilus_and_Cressida/4.4
./NextLibrary/Literature/Shakespeare/Plays/Troilus_and_Cressida/4.5
./NextLibrary/Literature/Shakespeare/Plays/Troilus_and_Cressida/4.6
./NextLibrary/Literature/Shakespeare/Plays/Troilus_and_Cressida/4.7
./NextLibrary/Literature/Shakespeare/Plays/Troilus_and_Cressida/5.1
```

```
./NextLibrary/Literature/Shakespeare/Plays/Troilus_and_Cressida/5.2
./NextLibrary/Literature/Shakespeare/Plays/Troilus_and_Cressida/5.3
./NextLibrary/Literature/Shakespeare/Plays/Troilus_and_Cressida/5.4
./NextLibrary/Literature/Shakespeare/Plays/Troilus_and_Cressida/5.5
./NextLibrary/Literature/Shakespeare/Plays/Troilus_and_Cressida/5.6
./NextLibrary/Literature/Shakespeare/Plays/Troilus_and_Cressida/5.7
./NextLibrary/Literature/Shakespeare/Plays/Troilus_and_Cressida/5.8
./NextLibrary/Literature/Shakespeare/Plays/Troilus_and_Cressida/5.9
./NextLibrary/Literature/Shakespeare/Plays/Troilus_and_Cressida/5.10
./NextLibrary/Literature/Shakespeare/Plays/Troilus_and_Cressida/5.11
./NextLibrary/Literature/Shakespeare/Plays/Troilus_and_Cressida/Introduction
./NextLibrary/Literature/Shakespeare/Plays/Troilus_and_Cressida/Players
./NextLibrary/Literature/Shakespeare/Plays/Troilus_and_Cressida/Additional
./NextLibrary/Literature/Shakespeare/Plays/Troilus_and_Cressida/.places
./NextLibrary/Literature/Shakespeare/Plays/Coriolanus
./NextLibrary/Literature/Shakespeare/Plays/Coriolanus/1.1
./NextLibrary/Literature/Shakespeare/Plays/Coriolanus/1.2
./NextLibrary/Literature/Shakespeare/Plays/Coriolanus/1.3
./NextLibrary/Literature/Shakespeare/Plays/Coriolanus/1.4
./NextLibrary/Literature/Shakespeare/Plays/Coriolanus/1.5
./NextLibrary/Literature/Shakespeare/Plays/Coriolanus/1.6
./NextLibrary/Literature/Shakespeare/Plays/Coriolanus/1.7
./NextLibrary/Literature/Shakespeare/Plays/Coriolanus/1.8
./NextLibrary/Literature/Shakespeare/Plays/Coriolanus/1.9
./NextLibrary/Literature/Shakespeare/Plays/Coriolanus/1.10
./NextLibrary/Literature/Shakespeare/Plays/Coriolanus/1.11
./NextLibrary/Literature/Shakespeare/Plays/Coriolanus/2.1
./NextLibrary/Literature/Shakespeare/Plays/Coriolanus/2.2
./NextLibrary/Literature/Shakespeare/Plays/Coriolanus/2.3
./NextLibrary/Literature/Shakespeare/Plays/Coriolanus/3.1
./NextLibrary/Literature/Shakespeare/Plays/Coriolanus/3.2
./NextLibrary/Literature/Shakespeare/Plays/Coriolanus/3.3
./NextLibrary/Literature/Shakespeare/Plays/Coriolanus/4.1
./NextLibrary/Literature/Shakespeare/Plays/Coriolanus/4.2
./NextLibrary/Literature/Shakespeare/Plays/Coriolanus/4.3
./NextLibrary/Literature/Shakespeare/Plays/Coriolanus/4.4
./NextLibrary/Literature/Shakespeare/Plays/Coriolanus/4.5
./NextLibrary/Literature/Shakespeare/Plays/Coriolanus/4.6
./NextLibrary/Literature/Shakespeare/Plays/Coriolanus/4.7
./NextLibrary/Literature/Shakespeare/Plays/Coriolanus/5.1
./NextLibrary/Literature/Shakespeare/Plays/Coriolanus/5.2
./NextLibrary/Literature/Shakespeare/Plays/Coriolanus/5.3
./NextLibrary/Literature/Shakespeare/Plays/Coriolanus/5.4
./NextLibrary/Literature/Shakespeare/Plays/Coriolanus/5.5
./NextLibrary/Literature/Shakespeare/Plays/Coriolanus/5.6
./NextLibrary/Literature/Shakespeare/Plays/Coriolanus/Introduction
./NextLibrary/Literature/Shakespeare/Plays/Coriolanus/Players
./NextLibrary/Literature/Shakespeare/Plays/Coriolanus/.places
./NextLibrary/Literature/Shakespeare/Plays/The_Two_Noble_Kinsmen
./NextLibrary/Literature/Shakespeare/Plays/The_Two_Noble_Kinsmen/Prologue
./NextLibrary/Literature/Shakespeare/Plays/The_Two_Noble_Kinsmen/1.1
./NextLibrary/Literature/Shakespeare/Plays/The_Two_Noble_Kinsmen/1.2
./NextLibrary/Literature/Shakespeare/Plays/The_Two_Noble_Kinsmen/1.3
./NextLibrary/Literature/Shakespeare/Plays/The_Two_Noble_Kinsmen/1.4
./NextLibrary/Literature/Shakespeare/Plays/The_Two_Noble_Kinsmen/1.5
./NextLibrary/Literature/Shakespeare/Plays/The_Two_Noble_Kinsmen/2.1
./NextLibrary/Literature/Shakespeare/Plays/The_Two_Noble_Kinsmen/2.2
./NextLibrary/Literature/Shakespeare/Plays/The_Two_Noble_Kinsmen/2.3
./NextLibrary/Literature/Shakespeare/Plays/The_Two_Noble_Kinsmen/2.4
./NextLibrary/Literature/Shakespeare/Plays/The_Two_Noble_Kinsmen/2.5
./NextLibrary/Literature/Shakespeare/Plays/The_Two_Noble_Kinsmen/2.6
./NextLibrary/Literature/Shakespeare/Plays/The_Two_Noble_Kinsmen/3.1
./NextLibrary/Literature/Shakespeare/Plays/The_Two_Noble_Kinsmen/3.2
./NextLibrary/Literature/Shakespeare/Plays/The_Two_Noble_Kinsmen/3.3
./NextLibrary/Literature/Shakespeare/Plays/The_Two_Noble_Kinsmen/3.4
./NextLibrary/Literature/Shakespeare/Plays/The_Two_Noble_Kinsmen/3.5
./NextLibrary/Literature/Shakespeare/Plays/The_Two_Noble_Kinsmen/3.6
./NextLibrary/Literature/Shakespeare/Plays/The_Two_Noble_Kinsmen/4.1
./NextLibrary/Literature/Shakespeare/Plays/The_Two_Noble_Kinsmen/4.2
./NextLibrary/Literature/Shakespeare/Plays/The_Two_Noble_Kinsmen/4.3
./NextLibrary/Literature/Shakespeare/Plays/The_Two_Noble_Kinsmen/5.1
./NextLibrary/Literature/Shakespeare/Plays/The_Two_Noble_Kinsmen/5.2
./NextLibrary/Literature/Shakespeare/Plays/The_Two_Noble_Kinsmen/5.3
./NextLibrary/Literature/Shakespeare/Plays/The_Two_Noble_Kinsmen/5.4
./NextLibrary/Literature/Shakespeare/Plays/The_Two_Noble_Kinsmen/5.5
./NextLibrary/Literature/Shakespeare/Plays/The_Two_Noble_Kinsmen/5.6
./NextLibrary/Literature/Shakespeare/Plays/The_Two_Noble_Kinsmen/Epilogue
./NextLibrary/Literature/Shakespeare/Plays/The_Two_Noble_Kinsmen/Introduction
./NextLibrary/Literature/Shakespeare/Plays/The_Two_Noble_Kinsmen/Players
./NextLibrary/Literature/Shakespeare/Plays/The_Two_Noble_Kinsmen/.places
./NextLibrary/Literature/Shakespeare/Plays/2_Henry_IV
./NextLibrary/Literature/Shakespeare/Plays/2_Henry_IV/Induction
./NextLibrary/Literature/Shakespeare/Plays/2_Henry_IV/1.1
./NextLibrary/Literature/Shakespeare/Plays/2_Henry_IV/1.2
./NextLibrary/Literature/Shakespeare/Plays/2_Henry_IV/1.3
./NextLibrary/Literature/Shakespeare/Plays/2_Henry_IV/2.1
./NextLibrary/Literature/Shakespeare/Plays/2_Henry_IV/2.2
./NextLibrary/Literature/Shakespeare/Plays/2_Henry_IV/2.3
./NextLibrary/Literature/Shakespeare/Plays/2_Henry_IV/2.4
./NextLibrary/Literature/Shakespeare/Plays/2_Henry_IV/3.1
./NextLibrary/Literature/Shakespeare/Plays/2_Henry_IV/3.2
./NextLibrary/Literature/Shakespeare/Plays/2_Henry_IV/4.1
./NextLibrary/Literature/Shakespeare/Plays/2_Henry_IV/4.2
./NextLibrary/Literature/Shakespeare/Plays/2_Henry_IV/4.3
./NextLibrary/Literature/Shakespeare/Plays/2_Henry_IV/5.1
./NextLibrary/Literature/Shakespeare/Plays/2_Henry_IV/5.2
./NextLibrary/Literature/Shakespeare/Plays/2_Henry_IV/5.3
./NextLibrary/Literature/Shakespeare/Plays/2_Henry_IV/5.4
./NextLibrary/Literature/Shakespeare/Plays/2_Henry_IV/5.5
./NextLibrary/Literature/Shakespeare/Plays/2_Henry_IV/Epilogue
./NextLibrary/Literature/Shakespeare/Plays/2_Henry_IV/Additional
./NextLibrary/Literature/Shakespeare/Plays/2_Henry_IV/Introduction
```

```
./NextLibrary/Literature/Shakespeare/Plays/2_Henry_IV/Players
./NextLibrary/Literature/Shakespeare/Plays/2_Henry_IV/.places
./NextLibrary/Literature/Shakespeare/Sonnets_and_A_Lovers_Complaint
./NextLibrary/Literature/Shakespeare/Sonnets_and_A_Lovers_Complaint/Dedication
./NextLibrary/Literature/Shakespeare/Sonnets_and_A_Lovers_Complaint/1
./NextLibrary/Literature/Shakespeare/Sonnets_and_A_Lovers_Complaint/10
./NextLibrary/Literature/Shakespeare/Sonnets_and_A_Lovers_Complaint/100
./NextLibrary/Literature/Shakespeare/Sonnets_and_A_Lovers_Complaint/101
./NextLibrary/Literature/Shakespeare/Sonnets_and_A_Lovers_Complaint/102
./NextLibrary/Literature/Shakespeare/Sonnets_and_A_Lovers_Complaint/103
./NextLibrary/Literature/Shakespeare/Sonnets_and_A_Lovers_Complaint/104
./NextLibrary/Literature/Shakespeare/Sonnets_and_A_Lovers_Complaint/105
./NextLibrary/Literature/Shakespeare/Sonnets_and_A_Lovers_Complaint/106
./NextLibrary/Literature/Shakespeare/Sonnets_and_A_Lovers_Complaint/107
./NextLibrary/Literature/Shakespeare/Sonnets_and_A_Lovers_Complaint/108
./NextLibrary/Literature/Shakespeare/Sonnets_and_A_Lovers_Complaint/109
./NextLibrary/Literature/Shakespeare/Sonnets_and_A_Lovers_Complaint/11
./NextLibrary/Literature/Shakespeare/Sonnets_and_A_Lovers_Complaint/110
./NextLibrary/Literature/Shakespeare/Sonnets_and_A_Lovers_Complaint/111
./NextLibrary/Literature/Shakespeare/Sonnets_and_A_Lovers_Complaint/112
./NextLibrary/Literature/Shakespeare/Sonnets_and_A_Lovers_Complaint/113
./NextLibrary/Literature/Shakespeare/Sonnets_and_A_Lovers_Complaint/114
./NextLibrary/Literature/Shakespeare/Sonnets_and_A_Lovers_Complaint/115
./NextLibrary/Literature/Shakespeare/Sonnets_and_A_Lovers_Complaint/116
./NextLibrary/Literature/Shakespeare/Sonnets_and_A_Lovers_Complaint/117
./NextLibrary/Literature/Shakespeare/Sonnets_and_A_Lovers_Complaint/118
./NextLibrary/Literature/Shakespeare/Sonnets_and_A_Lovers_Complaint/119
./NextLibrary/Literature/Shakespeare/Sonnets_and_A_Lovers_Complaint/12
./NextLibrary/Literature/Shakespeare/Sonnets_and_A_Lovers_Complaint/120
./NextLibrary/Literature/Shakespeare/Sonnets_and_A_Lovers_Complaint/121
./NextLibrary/Literature/Shakespeare/Sonnets_and_A_Lovers_Complaint/122
./NextLibrary/Literature/Shakespeare/Sonnets_and_A_Lovers_Complaint/123
./NextLibrary/Literature/Shakespeare/Sonnets_and_A_Lovers_Complaint/124
./NextLibrary/Literature/Shakespeare/Sonnets_and_A_Lovers_Complaint/125
./NextLibrary/Literature/Shakespeare/Sonnets_and_A_Lovers_Complaint/126
./NextLibrary/Literature/Shakespeare/Sonnets_and_A_Lovers_Complaint/127
./NextLibrary/Literature/Shakespeare/Sonnets_and_A_Lovers_Complaint/128
./NextLibrary/Literature/Shakespeare/Sonnets_and_A_Lovers_Complaint/129
./NextLibrary/Literature/Shakespeare/Sonnets_and_A_Lovers_Complaint/13
./NextLibrary/Literature/Shakespeare/Sonnets_and_A_Lovers_Complaint/130
./NextLibrary/Literature/Shakespeare/Sonnets_and_A_Lovers_Complaint/131
./NextLibrary/Literature/Shakespeare/Sonnets_and_A_Lovers_Complaint/132
./NextLibrary/Literature/Shakespeare/Sonnets_and_A_Lovers_Complaint/133
./NextLibrary/Literature/Shakespeare/Sonnets_and_A_Lovers_Complaint/134
./NextLibrary/Literature/Shakespeare/Sonnets_and_A_Lovers_Complaint/135
./NextLibrary/Literature/Shakespeare/Sonnets_and_A_Lovers_Complaint/136
./NextLibrary/Literature/Shakespeare/Sonnets_and_A_Lovers_Complaint/137
./NextLibrary/Literature/Shakespeare/Sonnets_and_A_Lovers_Complaint/138
./NextLibrary/Literature/Shakespeare/Sonnets_and_A_Lovers_Complaint/139
./NextLibrary/Literature/Shakespeare/Sonnets_and_A_Lovers_Complaint/14
./NextLibrary/Literature/Shakespeare/Sonnets_and_A_Lovers_Complaint/140
./NextLibrary/Literature/Shakespeare/Sonnets_and_A_Lovers_Complaint/141
./NextLibrary/Literature/Shakespeare/Sonnets_and_A_Lovers_Complaint/142
./NextLibrary/Literature/Shakespeare/Sonnets_and_A_Lovers_Complaint/143
./NextLibrary/Literature/Shakespeare/Sonnets_and_A_Lovers_Complaint/144
./NextLibrary/Literature/Shakespeare/Sonnets_and_A_Lovers_Complaint/145
./NextLibrary/Literature/Shakespeare/Sonnets_and_A_Lovers_Complaint/146
./NextLibrary/Literature/Shakespeare/Sonnets_and_A_Lovers_Complaint/147
./NextLibrary/Literature/Shakespeare/Sonnets_and_A_Lovers_Complaint/148
./NextLibrary/Literature/Shakespeare/Sonnets_and_A_Lovers_Complaint/149
./NextLibrary/Literature/Shakespeare/Sonnets_and_A_Lovers_Complaint/15
./NextLibrary/Literature/Shakespeare/Sonnets_and_A_Lovers_Complaint/150
./NextLibrary/Literature/Shakespeare/Sonnets_and_A_Lovers_Complaint/151
./NextLibrary/Literature/Shakespeare/Sonnets_and_A_Lovers_Complaint/152
./NextLibrary/Literature/Shakespeare/Sonnets_and_A_Lovers_Complaint/153
./NextLibrary/Literature/Shakespeare/Sonnets_and_A_Lovers_Complaint/154
./NextLibrary/Literature/Shakespeare/Sonnets_and_A_Lovers_Complaint/16
./NextLibrary/Literature/Shakespeare/Sonnets_and_A_Lovers_Complaint/17
./NextLibrary/Literature/Shakespeare/Sonnets_and_A_Lovers_Complaint/18
./NextLibrary/Literature/Shakespeare/Sonnets_and_A_Lovers_Complaint/19
./NextLibrary/Literature/Shakespeare/Sonnets_and_A_Lovers_Complaint/2
./NextLibrary/Literature/Shakespeare/Sonnets_and_A_Lovers_Complaint/20
./NextLibrary/Literature/Shakespeare/Sonnets_and_A_Lovers_Complaint/21
./NextLibrary/Literature/Shakespeare/Sonnets_and_A_Lovers_Complaint/22
./NextLibrary/Literature/Shakespeare/Sonnets_and_A_Lovers_Complaint/23
./NextLibrary/Literature/Shakespeare/Sonnets_and_A_Lovers_Complaint/24
./NextLibrary/Literature/Shakespeare/Sonnets_and_A_Lovers_Complaint/25
./NextLibrary/Literature/Shakespeare/Sonnets_and_A_Lovers_Complaint/26
./NextLibrary/Literature/Shakespeare/Sonnets_and_A_Lovers_Complaint/27
./NextLibrary/Literature/Shakespeare/Sonnets_and_A_Lovers_Complaint/28
./NextLibrary/Literature/Shakespeare/Sonnets_and_A_Lovers_Complaint/29
./NextLibrary/Literature/Shakespeare/Sonnets_and_A_Lovers_Complaint/3
./NextLibrary/Literature/Shakespeare/Sonnets_and_A_Lovers_Complaint/30
./NextLibrary/Literature/Shakespeare/Sonnets_and_A_Lovers_Complaint/31
./NextLibrary/Literature/Shakespeare/Sonnets_and_A_Lovers_Complaint/32
./NextLibrary/Literature/Shakespeare/Sonnets_and_A_Lovers_Complaint/33
./NextLibrary/Literature/Shakespeare/Sonnets_and_A_Lovers_Complaint/34
./NextLibrary/Literature/Shakespeare/Sonnets_and_A_Lovers_Complaint/35
./NextLibrary/Literature/Shakespeare/Sonnets_and_A_Lovers_Complaint/36
./NextLibrary/Literature/Shakespeare/Sonnets_and_A_Lovers_Complaint/37
./NextLibrary/Literature/Shakespeare/Sonnets_and_A_Lovers_Complaint/38
./NextLibrary/Literature/Shakespeare/Sonnets_and_A_Lovers_Complaint/39
./NextLibrary/Literature/Shakespeare/Sonnets_and_A_Lovers_Complaint/4
./NextLibrary/Literature/Shakespeare/Sonnets_and_A_Lovers_Complaint/40
./NextLibrary/Literature/Shakespeare/Sonnets_and_A_Lovers_Complaint/41
./NextLibrary/Literature/Shakespeare/Sonnets_and_A_Lovers_Complaint/42
./NextLibrary/Literature/Shakespeare/Sonnets_and_A_Lovers_Complaint/43
./NextLibrary/Literature/Shakespeare/Sonnets_and_A_Lovers_Complaint/44
./NextLibrary/Literature/Shakespeare/Sonnets_and_A_Lovers_Complaint/45
./NextLibrary/Literature/Shakespeare/Sonnets_and_A_Lovers_Complaint/46
./NextLibrary/Literature/Shakespeare/Sonnets_and_A_Lovers_Complaint/47
./NextLibrary/Literature/Shakespeare/Sonnets_and_A_Lovers_Complaint/48
```

./NextLibrary/Literature/Shakespeare/Sonnets_and_A_Lovers_Complaint/45
./NextLibrary/Literature/Shakespeare/Sonnets_and_A_Lovers_Complaint/46
./NextLibrary/Literature/Shakespeare/Sonnets_and_A_Lovers_Complaint/47
./NextLibrary/Literature/Shakespeare/Sonnets_and_A_Lovers_Complaint/48
./NextLibrary/Literature/Shakespeare/Sonnets_and_A_Lovers_Complaint/49
./NextLibrary/Literature/Shakespeare/Sonnets_and_A_Lovers_Complaint/5
./NextLibrary/Literature/Shakespeare/Sonnets_and_A_Lovers_Complaint/50
./NextLibrary/Literature/Shakespeare/Sonnets_and_A_Lovers_Complaint/51
./NextLibrary/Literature/Shakespeare/Sonnets_and_A_Lovers_Complaint/52
./NextLibrary/Literature/Shakespeare/Sonnets_and_A_Lovers_Complaint/53
./NextLibrary/Literature/Shakespeare/Sonnets_and_A_Lovers_Complaint/54
./NextLibrary/Literature/Shakespeare/Sonnets_and_A_Lovers_Complaint/55
./NextLibrary/Literature/Shakespeare/Sonnets_and_A_Lovers_Complaint/56
./NextLibrary/Literature/Shakespeare/Sonnets_and_A_Lovers_Complaint/57
./NextLibrary/Literature/Shakespeare/Sonnets_and_A_Lovers_Complaint/58
./NextLibrary/Literature/Shakespeare/Sonnets_and_A_Lovers_Complaint/59
./NextLibrary/Literature/Shakespeare/Sonnets_and_A_Lovers_Complaint/6
./NextLibrary/Literature/Shakespeare/Sonnets_and_A_Lovers_Complaint/60
./NextLibrary/Literature/Shakespeare/Sonnets_and_A_Lovers_Complaint/61
./NextLibrary/Literature/Shakespeare/Sonnets_and_A_Lovers_Complaint/62
./NextLibrary/Literature/Shakespeare/Sonnets_and_A_Lovers_Complaint/63
./NextLibrary/Literature/Shakespeare/Sonnets_and_A_Lovers_Complaint/64
./NextLibrary/Literature/Shakespeare/Sonnets_and_A_Lovers_Complaint/65
./NextLibrary/Literature/Shakespeare/Sonnets_and_A_Lovers_Complaint/66
./NextLibrary/Literature/Shakespeare/Sonnets_and_A_Lovers_Complaint/67
./NextLibrary/Literature/Shakespeare/Sonnets_and_A_Lovers_Complaint/68
./NextLibrary/Literature/Shakespeare/Sonnets_and_A_Lovers_Complaint/69
./NextLibrary/Literature/Shakespeare/Sonnets_and_A_Lovers_Complaint/7
./NextLibrary/Literature/Shakespeare/Sonnets_and_A_Lovers_Complaint/70
./NextLibrary/Literature/Shakespeare/Sonnets_and_A_Lovers_Complaint/71
./NextLibrary/Literature/Shakespeare/Sonnets_and_A_Lovers_Complaint/72
./NextLibrary/Literature/Shakespeare/Sonnets_and_A_Lovers_Complaint/73
./NextLibrary/Literature/Shakespeare/Sonnets_and_A_Lovers_Complaint/74
./NextLibrary/Literature/Shakespeare/Sonnets_and_A_Lovers_Complaint/75
./NextLibrary/Literature/Shakespeare/Sonnets_and_A_Lovers_Complaint/76
./NextLibrary/Literature/Shakespeare/Sonnets_and_A_Lovers_Complaint/77
./NextLibrary/Literature/Shakespeare/Sonnets_and_A_Lovers_Complaint/78
./NextLibrary/Literature/Shakespeare/Sonnets_and_A_Lovers_Complaint/79
./NextLibrary/Literature/Shakespeare/Sonnets_and_A_Lovers_Complaint/8
./NextLibrary/Literature/Shakespeare/Sonnets_and_A_Lovers_Complaint/80
./NextLibrary/Literature/Shakespeare/Sonnets_and_A_Lovers_Complaint/81
./NextLibrary/Literature/Shakespeare/Sonnets_and_A_Lovers_Complaint/82
./NextLibrary/Literature/Shakespeare/Sonnets_and_A_Lovers_Complaint/83
./NextLibrary/Literature/Shakespeare/Sonnets_and_A_Lovers_Complaint/84
./NextLibrary/Literature/Shakespeare/Sonnets_and_A_Lovers_Complaint/85
./NextLibrary/Literature/Shakespeare/Sonnets_and_A_Lovers_Complaint/86
./NextLibrary/Literature/Shakespeare/Sonnets_and_A_Lovers_Complaint/87
./NextLibrary/Literature/Shakespeare/Sonnets_and_A_Lovers_Complaint/88
./NextLibrary/Literature/Shakespeare/Sonnets_and_A_Lovers_Complaint/89
./NextLibrary/Literature/Shakespeare/Sonnets_and_A_Lovers_Complaint/9
./NextLibrary/Literature/Shakespeare/Sonnets_and_A_Lovers_Complaint/90

./NextLibrary/Literature/Shakespeare/Sonnets_and_A_Lovers_Complaint/91
./NextLibrary/Literature/Shakespeare/Sonnets_and_A_Lovers_Complaint/92
./NextLibrary/Literature/Shakespeare/Sonnets_and_A_Lovers_Complaint/93
./NextLibrary/Literature/Shakespeare/Sonnets_and_A_Lovers_Complaint/94
./NextLibrary/Literature/Shakespeare/Sonnets_and_A_Lovers_Complaint/95
./NextLibrary/Literature/Shakespeare/Sonnets_and_A_Lovers_Complaint/96
./NextLibrary/Literature/Shakespeare/Sonnets_and_A_Lovers_Complaint/97
./NextLibrary/Literature/Shakespeare/Sonnets_and_A_Lovers_Complaint/98
./NextLibrary/Literature/Shakespeare/Sonnets_and_A_Lovers_Complaint/99
./NextLibrary/Literature/Shakespeare/Sonnets_and_A_Lovers_Complaint
    /A_Lovers_Complaint
./NextLibrary/Literature/Shakespeare/Sonnets_and_A_Lovers_Complaint
    /Alternative_Versions
./NextLibrary/Literature/Shakespeare/Sonnets_and_A_Lovers_Complaint/.places
./NextLibrary/Literature/Shakespeare/Various_Poems
./NextLibrary/Literature/Shakespeare/Various_Poems/A_Song
./NextLibrary/Literature/Shakespeare/Various_Poems/Epitaphs
./NextLibrary/Literature/Shakespeare/Various_Poems/Gloves
./NextLibrary/Literature/Shakespeare/Various_Poems/Sonnets_to_music
./NextLibrary/Literature/Shakespeare/Various_Poems/The_Passionate_Pilgrim
./NextLibrary/Literature/Shakespeare/Various_Poems/The_Phoenix_and_the_Turtle
./NextLibrary/Literature/Shakespeare/Various_Poems/The_Rape_of_Lucrece
./NextLibrary/Literature/Shakespeare/Various_Poems/Venus_and_Adonis
./NextLibrary/Literature/Shakespeare/Various_Poems/.places
./NextLibrary/Literature/Shakespeare/.index
./NextLibrary/Literature/Shakespeare/.index/index
./NextLibrary/Literature/Shakespeare/.index/index.D
./NextLibrary/Literature/Shakespeare/.index/.places
./NextLibrary/Literature/Shakespeare/.index/Copyright.ps
./NextLibrary/Literature/Shakespeare/.index/Copyright.rtf
./NextLibrary/Literature/Shakespeare/.index/icon.tiff
./NextLibrary/Literature/Shakespeare/.index/index.L
./NextLibrary/Literature/Shakespeare/.index/.descCommand
./NextLibrary/Literature/Shakespeare/.index/index.Registry.D
./NextLibrary/Literature/Shakespeare/.index/index.Registry.L
./NextLibrary/Literature/Shakespeare/.index/.upgrade
./NextLibrary/Literature/Shakespeare/.index/.upgrade.D
./NextLibrary/Literature/Shakespeare/.index/.upgrade.L
./NextLibrary/Literature/Shakespeare/.index/.upgrade.Registry.D
./NextLibrary/Literature/Shakespeare/.index/.upgrade.Registry.L
./NextLibrary/Literature/Shakespeare/Glossary
./NextLibrary/Literature/Shakespeare/Glossary/XYZ
./NextLibrary/Literature/Shakespeare/Glossary/A
./NextLibrary/Literature/Shakespeare/Glossary/B
./NextLibrary/Literature/Shakespeare/Glossary/C
./NextLibrary/Literature/Shakespeare/Glossary/D
./NextLibrary/Literature/Shakespeare/Glossary/E
./NextLibrary/Literature/Shakespeare/Glossary/F
./NextLibrary/Literature/Shakespeare/Glossary/G
./NextLibrary/Literature/Shakespeare/Glossary/H
./NextLibrary/Literature/Shakespeare/Glossary/I

```
./NextLibrary/Literature/Shakespeare/Glossary/N
./NextLibrary/Literature/Shakespeare/Glossary/O
./NextLibrary/Literature/Shakespeare/Glossary/P
./NextLibrary/Literature/Shakespeare/Glossary/Q
./NextLibrary/Literature/Shakespeare/Glossary/R
./NextLibrary/Literature/Shakespeare/Glossary/S
./NextLibrary/Literature/Shakespeare/Glossary/T
./NextLibrary/Literature/Shakespeare/Glossary/U
./NextLibrary/Literature/Shakespeare/Glossary/V
./NextLibrary/Literature/Shakespeare/Glossary/W
./NextLibrary/Literature/Shakespeare/Glossary/.places
./NextLibrary/Literature/Shakespeare/.list
./NextLibrary/Literature/Shakespeare/.places
./NextLibrary/Literature/Shakespeare/Commendatory_Poems_and_Prefaces
./NextLibrary/Literature/.places
./NextLibrary/Mathematica
./NextLibrary/Mathematica/.places
./NextLibrary/Mathematica/Packages
./NextLibrary/Mathematica/Packages/Algebra
./NextLibrary/Mathematica/Packages/Algebra/CountRoots.m
./NextLibrary/Mathematica/Packages/Algebra/GosperSum.m
./NextLibrary/Mathematica/Packages/Algebra/ReIm.m
./NextLibrary/Mathematica/Packages/Algebra/Trigonometry.m
./NextLibrary/Mathematica/Packages/Algebra/.places
./NextLibrary/Mathematica/Packages/Calculus
./NextLibrary/Mathematica/Packages/Calculus/DefiniteIntegrate.m
./NextLibrary/Mathematica/Packages/Calculus/InverseLaplace.m
./NextLibrary/Mathematica/Packages/Calculus/Laplace.m
./NextLibrary/Mathematica/Packages/Calculus/ODE.m
./NextLibrary/Mathematica/Packages/Calculus/VectorAnalysis.m
./NextLibrary/Mathematica/Packages/Calculus/.places
./NextLibrary/Mathematica/Packages/DataAnalysis
./NextLibrary/Mathematica/Packages/DataAnalysis/ConfidenceIntervals.m
./NextLibrary/Mathematica/Packages/DataAnalysis/ContinuousDistributions.m
./NextLibrary/Mathematica/Packages/DataAnalysis/DataManipulation.m
./NextLibrary/Mathematica/Packages/DataAnalysis/DescriptiveFunctions.m
./NextLibrary/Mathematica/Packages/DataAnalysis/DescriptiveStatistics.m
./NextLibrary/Mathematica/Packages/DataAnalysis/DiscreteDistributions.m
./NextLibrary/Mathematica/Packages/DataAnalysis/.places
./NextLibrary/Mathematica/Packages/DiscreteMath
./NextLibrary/Mathematica/Packages/DiscreteMath/ClebschGordan.m
./NextLibrary/Mathematica/Packages/DiscreteMath/CombinatorialFunctions.m
./NextLibrary/Mathematica/Packages/DiscreteMath/CombinatorialSimplification.m
./NextLibrary/Mathematica/Packages/DiscreteMath/Permutations.m
./NextLibrary/Mathematica/Packages/DiscreteMath/Tree.m
./NextLibrary/Mathematica/Packages/DiscreteMath/.places
./NextLibrary/Mathematica/Packages/Examples
./NextLibrary/Mathematica/Packages/Examples/CellularAutomata.m
./NextLibrary/Mathematica/Packages/Examples/CollatzProblem.m
./NextLibrary/Mathematica/Packages/Examples/CrystalStructure.m
./NextLibrary/Mathematica/Packages/Examples/EllipticCurves.m

./NextLibrary/Mathematica/Packages/Examples/Factor.m
./NextLibrary/Mathematica/Packages/Examples/FunctionalProgramming.m
./NextLibrary/Mathematica/Packages/Examples/ModularArithmetic.m
./NextLibrary/Mathematica/Packages/Examples/Mortgages.m
./NextLibrary/Mathematica/Packages/Examples/RingTheory.m
./NextLibrary/Mathematica/Packages/Examples/RungeKutta.m
./NextLibrary/Mathematica/Packages/Examples/.places
./NextLibrary/Mathematica/Packages/Geometry
./NextLibrary/Mathematica/Packages/Geometry/Polytopes.m
./NextLibrary/Mathematica/Packages/Geometry/Rotations.m
./NextLibrary/Mathematica/Packages/Geometry/.places
./NextLibrary/Mathematica/Packages/Graphics
./NextLibrary/Mathematica/Packages/Graphics/Colors.m
./NextLibrary/Mathematica/Packages/Graphics/Graphics.m
./NextLibrary/Mathematica/Packages/Graphics/ParametricPlot3D.m
./NextLibrary/Mathematica/Packages/Graphics/Polyhedra.m
./NextLibrary/Mathematica/Packages/Graphics/Shapes.m
./NextLibrary/Mathematica/Packages/Graphics/ThreeScript.m
./NextLibrary/Mathematica/Packages/Graphics/.places
./NextLibrary/Mathematica/Packages/LinearAlgebra
./NextLibrary/Mathematica/Packages/LinearAlgebra/Cross.m
./NextLibrary/Mathematica/Packages/LinearAlgebra/Vectors.m
./NextLibrary/Mathematica/Packages/LinearAlgebra/.places
./NextLibrary/Mathematica/Packages/Miscellaneous
./NextLibrary/Mathematica/Packages/Miscellaneous/PhysicalConstants.m
./NextLibrary/Mathematica/Packages/Miscellaneous/Units.m
./NextLibrary/Mathematica/Packages/Miscellaneous/.places
./NextLibrary/Mathematica/Packages/NumberTheory
./NextLibrary/Mathematica/Packages/NumberTheory/ContinuedFractions.m
./NextLibrary/Mathematica/Packages/NumberTheory/IntegerRoots.m
./NextLibrary/Mathematica/Packages/NumberTheory/Recognize.m
./NextLibrary/Mathematica/Packages/NumberTheory/.places
./NextLibrary/Mathematica/Packages/NumericalMath
./NextLibrary/Mathematica/Packages/NumericalMath/Approximations.m
./NextLibrary/Mathematica/Packages/NumericalMath/InverseStatisticalFunctions.m
./NextLibrary/Mathematica/Packages/NumericalMath/ListIntegrate.m
./NextLibrary/Mathematica/Packages/NumericalMath/RungeKutta.m
./NextLibrary/Mathematica/Packages/NumericalMath/.places
./NextLibrary/Mathematica/Packages/README
./NextLibrary/Mathematica/Packages/Utilities
./NextLibrary/Mathematica/Packages/Utilities/Record.m
./NextLibrary/Mathematica/Packages/Utilities/ShowTime.m
./NextLibrary/Mathematica/Packages/Utilities/.places
./NextLibrary/Mathematica/Packages/.places
./NextLibrary/Mathematica/Packages/.index
./NextLibrary/Mathematica/Packages/.index/.places
./NextLibrary/Mathematica/Notebooks
./NextLibrary/Mathematica/Notebooks/Animation.ma
./NextLibrary/Mathematica/Notebooks/Animation.mb
./NextLibrary/Mathematica/Notebooks/ComplexRoots.ma
./NextLibrary/Mathematica/Notebooks/.places
```

```
./NextLibrary/Mathematica/Notebooks/ComplexRoots.mb
./NextLibrary/Mathematica/Notebooks/HyperbolicIcosahedron.ma
./NextLibrary/Mathematica/Notebooks/HyperbolicIcosahedron.mb
./NextLibrary/Mathematica/Notebooks/MinimalSurface.ma
./NextLibrary/Mathematica/Notebooks/MinimalSurface.mb
./NextLibrary/Mathematica/Notebooks/PointPlots.ma
./NextLibrary/Mathematica/Notebooks/PointPlots.mb
./NextLibrary/Mathematica/Notebooks/TourOfMathematica.ma
./NextLibrary/Mathematica/Notebooks/TourOfMathematica.mb
./NextLibrary/Mathematica/Notebooks/tour.dat
./NextLibrary/Mathematica/Notebooks/.index
./NextLibrary/Mathematica/Notebooks/.index/.places
./NextLibrary/.places
./NextLibrary/References
./NextLibrary/References/OxfordQuotations
./NextLibrary/References/OxfordQuotations/.places
./NextLibrary/References/OxfordQuotations/tiff
./NextLibrary/References/OxfordQuotations/tiff/byQuote.tiff
./NextLibrary/References/OxfordQuotations/tiff/byQuoteH.tiff
./NextLibrary/References/OxfordQuotations/tiff/Quotations.tiff
./NextLibrary/References/OxfordQuotations/tiff/find.tiff
./NextLibrary/References/OxfordQuotations/tiff/findH.tiff
./NextLibrary/References/OxfordQuotations/tiff/stop.tiff
./NextLibrary/References/OxfordQuotations/tiff/search.tiff
./NextLibrary/References/OxfordQuotations/tiff/searchH.tiff
./NextLibrary/References/OxfordQuotations/tiff/nobH.tiff
./NextLibrary/References/OxfordQuotations/tiff/nob.tiff
./NextLibrary/References/OxfordQuotations/tiff/.places
./NextLibrary/References/OxfordQuotations/.list
./NextLibrary/References/OxfordQuotations/FrontMatter
./NextLibrary/References/OxfordQuotations/FrontMatter/HowToUse
./NextLibrary/References/OxfordQuotations/FrontMatter/preface
./NextLibrary/References/OxfordQuotations/FrontMatter/reader
./NextLibrary/References/OxfordQuotations/FrontMatter/introduction
./NextLibrary/References/OxfordQuotations/FrontMatter/help
./NextLibrary/References/OxfordQuotations/FrontMatter/copyright
./NextLibrary/References/OxfordQuotations/FrontMatter/.places
./NextLibrary/References/OxfordQuotations/FrontMatter/.list
./NextLibrary/References/OxfordQuotations/FrontMatter/Contents
./NextLibrary/References/OxfordQuotations/FrontMatter/noop
./NextLibrary/References/OxfordQuotations/FrontMatter/.index
./NextLibrary/References/OxfordQuotations/FrontMatter/.index/index
./NextLibrary/References/OxfordQuotations/FrontMatter/.index/index.D
./NextLibrary/References/OxfordQuotations/FrontMatter/.index/index.L
./NextLibrary/References/OxfordQuotations/FrontMatter/.index/index.Registry.D
./NextLibrary/References/OxfordQuotations/FrontMatter/.index/index.Registry.L
./NextLibrary/References/OxfordQuotations/FrontMatter/.index/.places
./NextLibrary/References/OxfordQuotations/.index
./NextLibrary/References/OxfordQuotations/.index/index
./NextLibrary/References/OxfordQuotations/.index/index.D
./NextLibrary/References/OxfordQuotations/.index/index.L
```

```
./NextLibrary/References/OxfordQuotations/.index/Copyright.ps
./NextLibrary/References/OxfordQuotations/.index/.places
./NextLibrary/References/.places
./NextLibrary/References/Webster-Dictionary
./NextLibrary/References/Webster-Dictionary/full-index
./NextLibrary/References/Webster-Dictionary/index
./NextLibrary/References/Webster-Dictionary/info
./NextLibrary/References/Webster-Dictionary/info/help
./NextLibrary/References/Webster-Dictionary/info/noop
./NextLibrary/References/Webster-Dictionary/info/preface-to-digital
./NextLibrary/References/Webster-Dictionary/info/preface
./NextLibrary/References/Webster-Dictionary/info/english-language
./NextLibrary/References/Webster-Dictionary/info/.list
./NextLibrary/References/Webster-Dictionary/info/style.1
./NextLibrary/References/Webster-Dictionary/info/notes.1
./NextLibrary/References/Webster-Dictionary/info/spelling
./NextLibrary/References/Webster-Dictionary/info/preface-to-thesaurus
./NextLibrary/References/Webster-Dictionary/info/intro-to-thesaurus
./NextLibrary/References/Webster-Dictionary/info/notes-to-thesaurus
./NextLibrary/References/Webster-Dictionary/info/staff
./NextLibrary/References/Webster-Dictionary/info/copyright
./NextLibrary/References/Webster-Dictionary/info/notes.10
./NextLibrary/References/Webster-Dictionary/info/notes.11
./NextLibrary/References/Webster-Dictionary/info/notes.12
./NextLibrary/References/Webster-Dictionary/info/notes.13
./NextLibrary/References/Webster-Dictionary/info/notes.14
./NextLibrary/References/Webster-Dictionary/info/notes.2
./NextLibrary/References/Webster-Dictionary/info/notes.3
./NextLibrary/References/Webster-Dictionary/info/notes.4
./NextLibrary/References/Webster-Dictionary/info/notes.5
./NextLibrary/References/Webster-Dictionary/info/notes.6
./NextLibrary/References/Webster-Dictionary/info/notes.7
./NextLibrary/References/Webster-Dictionary/info/notes.8
./NextLibrary/References/Webster-Dictionary/info/notes.9
./NextLibrary/References/Webster-Dictionary/info/style.2
./NextLibrary/References/Webster-Dictionary/info/style.3
./NextLibrary/References/Webster-Dictionary/info/style.4
./NextLibrary/References/Webster-Dictionary/info/style.5
./NextLibrary/References/Webster-Dictionary/info/style.6
./NextLibrary/References/Webster-Dictionary/info/Contents
./NextLibrary/References/Webster-Dictionary/info/.places
./NextLibrary/References/Webster-Dictionary/info/abbreviations.rtf
./NextLibrary/References/Webster-Dictionary/info/biographical.rtf
./NextLibrary/References/Webster-Dictionary/info/geographical.rtf
./NextLibrary/References/Webster-Dictionary/info/language.rtf
./NextLibrary/References/Webster-Dictionary/info/pronkey.rtf
./NextLibrary/References/Webster-Dictionary/info/guide-to-pron.rtf
./NextLibrary/References/Webster-Dictionary/info/pron-symbols.rtf
./NextLibrary/References/Webster-Dictionary/info/.index
./NextLibrary/References/Webster-Dictionary/info/.index/index
./NextLibrary/References/Webster-Dictionary/info/.index/index.D
```

./NextLibrary/References/Webster-Dictionary/info/pron-symbols.rtf
./NextLibrary/References/Webster-Dictionary/info/.index
./NextLibrary/References/Webster-Dictionary/info/.index/index
./NextLibrary/References/Webster-Dictionary/info/.index/index.D
./NextLibrary/References/Webster-Dictionary/info/.index/index.L
./NextLibrary/References/Webster-Dictionary/info/.index/index.Registry.D
./NextLibrary/References/Webster-Dictionary/info/.index/index.Registry.L
./NextLibrary/References/Webster-Dictionary/info/.index/.places
./NextLibrary/References/Webster-Dictionary/pictures
./NextLibrary/References/Webster-Dictionary/pictures/afro.tiff
./NextLibrary/References/Webster-Dictionary/pictures/aardwolf.tiff
./NextLibrary/References/Webster-Dictionary/pictures/asymptote.tiff
./NextLibrary/References/Webster-Dictionary/pictures/acanthus.tiff
./NextLibrary/References/Webster-Dictionary/pictures/accordion.tiff
./NextLibrary/References/Webster-Dictionary/pictures/adeliepenguin.tiff
./NextLibrary/References/Webster-Dictionary/pictures/afghanhound.tiff
./NextLibrary/References/Webster-Dictionary/pictures/agouti.tiff
./NextLibrary/References/Webster-Dictionary/pictures/airplane.tiff
./NextLibrary/References/Webster-Dictionary/pictures/alligator.tiff
./NextLibrary/References/Webster-Dictionary/pictures/alpaca.tiff
./NextLibrary/References/Webster-Dictionary/pictures/americansaddlehorse.tiff
./NextLibrary/References/Webster-Dictionary/pictures/amoeba.tiff
./NextLibrary/References/Webster-Dictionary/pictures/amphora.tiff
./NextLibrary/References/Webster-Dictionary/pictures/anaconda.tiff
./NextLibrary/References/Webster-Dictionary/pictures/anchor.tiff
./NextLibrary/References/Webster-Dictionary/pictures/angoragoat.tiff
./NextLibrary/References/Webster-Dictionary/pictures/ankh.tiff
./NextLibrary/References/Webster-Dictionary/pictures/anta.tiff
./NextLibrary/References/Webster-Dictionary/pictures/antbear.tiff
./NextLibrary/References/Webster-Dictionary/pictures/anticline.tiff
./NextLibrary/References/Webster-Dictionary/pictures/antlion.tiff
./NextLibrary/References/Webster-Dictionary/pictures/apogee.tiff
./NextLibrary/References/Webster-Dictionary/pictures/appaloosa.tiff
./NextLibrary/References/Webster-Dictionary/pictures/arabesque.tiff
./NextLibrary/References/Webster-Dictionary/pictures/arch.tiff
./NextLibrary/References/Webster-Dictionary/pictures/archimedesscrew.tiff
./NextLibrary/References/Webster-Dictionary/pictures/armadillo.tiff
./NextLibrary/References/Webster-Dictionary/pictures/armor.tiff
./NextLibrary/References/Webster-Dictionary/pictures/arrow.tiff
./NextLibrary/References/Webster-Dictionary/pictures/aspergillum.tiff
./NextLibrary/References/Webster-Dictionary/pictures/astrolabe.tiff
./NextLibrary/References/Webster-Dictionary/pictures/blockhouse.tiff
./NextLibrary/References/Webster-Dictionary/pictures/auk.tiff
./NextLibrary/References/Webster-Dictionary/pictures/australianterrier.tiff
./NextLibrary/References/Webster-Dictionary/pictures/avocet.tiff
./NextLibrary/References/Webster-Dictionary/pictures
    /azimuthalequidistantprojection.tiff
./NextLibrary/References/Webster-Dictionary/pictures/backhand.tiff
./NextLibrary/References/Webster-Dictionary/pictures/bagpipe.tiff
./NextLibrary/References/Webster-Dictionary/pictures/baldeagle.tiff
./NextLibrary/References/Webster-Dictionary/pictures/banjo.tiff

./NextLibrary/References/Webster-Dictionary/pictures/barnacle.tiff
./NextLibrary/References/Webster-Dictionary/pictures/base.tiff
./NextLibrary/References/Webster-Dictionary/pictures/basrelief.tiff
./NextLibrary/References/Webster-Dictionary/pictures/bassethound.tiff
./NextLibrary/References/Webster-Dictionary/pictures/battlement.tiff
./NextLibrary/References/Webster-Dictionary/pictures/abscissa.rtf
./NextLibrary/References/Webster-Dictionary/pictures/acanthus.rtf
./NextLibrary/References/Webster-Dictionary/pictures/agouti.rtf
./NextLibrary/References/Webster-Dictionary/pictures/airplane.rtf
./NextLibrary/References/Webster-Dictionary/pictures/alligator.rtf
./NextLibrary/References/Webster-Dictionary/pictures/alpaca.rtf
./NextLibrary/References/Webster-Dictionary/pictures/alternateangle.rtf
./NextLibrary/References/Webster-Dictionary/pictures/americansaddlehorse.rtf
./NextLibrary/References/Webster-Dictionary/pictures/amoeba.rtf
./NextLibrary/References/Webster-Dictionary/pictures/amphora.rtf
./NextLibrary/References/Webster-Dictionary/pictures/anchor.rtf
./NextLibrary/References/Webster-Dictionary/pictures/anticline.rtf
./NextLibrary/References/Webster-Dictionary/pictures/antlion.rtf
./NextLibrary/References/Webster-Dictionary/pictures/apogee.rtf
./NextLibrary/References/Webster-Dictionary/pictures/arabesque.rtf
./NextLibrary/References/Webster-Dictionary/pictures/arch.rtf
./NextLibrary/References/Webster-Dictionary/pictures/arrow.rtf
./NextLibrary/References/Webster-Dictionary/pictures/asymptote.rtf
./NextLibrary/References/Webster-Dictionary/pictures
    /azimuthalequidistantprojection.rtf
./NextLibrary/References/Webster-Dictionary/pictures/backhand.rtf
./NextLibrary/References/Webster-Dictionary/pictures/barnacle.rtf
./NextLibrary/References/Webster-Dictionary/pictures/base.rtf
./NextLibrary/References/Webster-Dictionary/pictures/battlement.rtf
./NextLibrary/References/Webster-Dictionary/pictures/anta.rtf
./NextLibrary/References/Webster-Dictionary/pictures/beef.rtf
./NextLibrary/References/Webster-Dictionary/pictures/beluga.rtf
./NextLibrary/References/Webster-Dictionary/pictures/bevel.rtf
./NextLibrary/References/Webster-Dictionary/pictures/bill.rtf
./NextLibrary/References/Webster-Dictionary/pictures/bird.rtf
./NextLibrary/References/Webster-Dictionary/pictures/blastula.rtf
./NextLibrary/References/Webster-Dictionary/pictures/blockhouse.rtf
./NextLibrary/References/Webster-Dictionary/pictures/boar.rtf
./NextLibrary/References/Webster-Dictionary/pictures/boss.rtf
./NextLibrary/References/Webster-Dictionary/pictures/brain.rtf
./NextLibrary/References/Webster-Dictionary/pictures/brazilnut.rtf
./NextLibrary/References/Webster-Dictionary/pictures/bridge.rtf
./NextLibrary/References/Webster-Dictionary/pictures/brilliant.rtf
./NextLibrary/References/Webster-Dictionary/pictures/buffalo.rtf
./NextLibrary/References/Webster-Dictionary/pictures/buoy.rtf
./NextLibrary/References/Webster-Dictionary/pictures/busby.rtf
./NextLibrary/References/Webster-Dictionary/pictures/caisson.rtf
./NextLibrary/References/Webster-Dictionary/pictures/camel.rtf
./NextLibrary/References/Webster-Dictionary/pictures/carpel.rtf
./NextLibrary/References/Webster-Dictionary/pictures/cat.rtf
./NextLibrary/References/Webster-Dictionary/pictures/cell.rtf

./NextLibrary/References/Webster-Dictionary/pictures/circle.rtf
./NextLibrary/References/Webster-Dictionary/pictures/clam.rtf
./NextLibrary/References/Webster-Dictionary/pictures/cloister.rtf
./NextLibrary/References/Webster-Dictionary/pictures/cloud.rtf
./NextLibrary/References/Webster-Dictionary/pictures/cock.rtf
./NextLibrary/References/Webster-Dictionary/pictures/coffee.rtf
./NextLibrary/References/Webster-Dictionary/pictures/column.rtf
./NextLibrary/References/Webster-Dictionary/pictures/commode.rtf
./NextLibrary/References/Webster-Dictionary/pictures/complement.rtf
./NextLibrary/References/Webster-Dictionary/pictures/cone.rtf
./NextLibrary/References/Webster-Dictionary/pictures/conicsection.rtf
./NextLibrary/References/Webster-Dictionary/pictures/copperhead.rtf
./NextLibrary/References/Webster-Dictionary/pictures/cornice.rtf
./NextLibrary/References/Webster-Dictionary/pictures/corymb.rtf
./NextLibrary/References/Webster-Dictionary/pictures/cow.rtf
./NextLibrary/References/Webster-Dictionary/pictures/crescendo.rtf
./NextLibrary/References/Webster-Dictionary/pictures/crocodile.rtf
./NextLibrary/References/Webster-Dictionary/pictures/cross.rtf
./NextLibrary/References/Webster-Dictionary/pictures/cuckoo.rtf
./NextLibrary/References/Webster-Dictionary/pictures/cuneiform.rtf
./NextLibrary/References/Webster-Dictionary/pictures/cusp.rtf
./NextLibrary/References/Webster-Dictionary/pictures/cycloid.rtf
./NextLibrary/References/Webster-Dictionary/pictures/dado.rtf
./NextLibrary/References/Webster-Dictionary/pictures/decrescendo.rtf
./NextLibrary/References/Webster-Dictionary/pictures/derby.rtf
./NextLibrary/References/Webster-Dictionary/pictures/devilfish.rtf
./NextLibrary/References/Webster-Dictionary/pictures/diaper.rtf
./NextLibrary/References/Webster-Dictionary/pictures/discbrake.rtf
./NextLibrary/References/Webster-Dictionary/pictures/distaff.rtf
./NextLibrary/References/Webster-Dictionary/pictures/dna.rtf
./NextLibrary/References/Webster-Dictionary/pictures/dog.rtf
./NextLibrary/References/Webster-Dictionary/pictures/dolphin.rtf
./NextLibrary/References/Webster-Dictionary/pictures/donjon.rtf
./NextLibrary/References/Webster-Dictionary/pictures/dovetail.rtf
./NextLibrary/References/Webster-Dictionary/pictures/drum.rtf
./NextLibrary/References/Webster-Dictionary/pictures/duck.rtf
./NextLibrary/References/Webster-Dictionary/pictures/ear.rtf
./NextLibrary/References/Webster-Dictionary/pictures/egg.rtf
./NextLibrary/References/Webster-Dictionary/pictures/ellipse.rtf
./NextLibrary/References/Webster-Dictionary/pictures/epaulet.rtf
./NextLibrary/References/Webster-Dictionary/pictures/elephant.rtf
./NextLibrary/References/Webster-Dictionary/pictures/embrasure.rtf
./NextLibrary/References/Webster-Dictionary/pictures/endocarp.rtf
./NextLibrary/References/Webster-Dictionary/pictures/entablature.rtf
./NextLibrary/References/Webster-Dictionary/pictures/equisetum.rtf
./NextLibrary/References/Webster-Dictionary/pictures/exteriorangle.rtf
./NextLibrary/References/Webster-Dictionary/pictures/eye.rtf
./NextLibrary/References/Webster-Dictionary/pictures/falcon.rtf
./NextLibrary/References/Webster-Dictionary/pictures/fault.rtf
./NextLibrary/References/Webster-Dictionary/pictures/feather.rtf
./NextLibrary/References/Webster-Dictionary/pictures/fig.rtf

./NextLibrary/References/Webster-Dictionary/pictures/fish.rtf
./NextLibrary/References/Webster-Dictionary/pictures/flower.rtf
./NextLibrary/References/Webster-Dictionary/pictures/flute.rtf
./NextLibrary/References/Webster-Dictionary/pictures/flyingbuttress.rtf
./NextLibrary/References/Webster-Dictionary/pictures/fret.rtf
./NextLibrary/References/Webster-Dictionary/pictures/gamelan.rtf
./NextLibrary/References/Webster-Dictionary/pictures/gargoyle.rtf
./NextLibrary/References/Webster-Dictionary/pictures/gerrymander.rtf
./NextLibrary/References/Webster-Dictionary/pictures/girandole.rtf
./NextLibrary/References/Webster-Dictionary/pictures/gnomon.rtf
./NextLibrary/References/Webster-Dictionary/pictures/graft.rtf
./NextLibrary/References/Webster-Dictionary/pictures/guitar.rtf
./NextLibrary/References/Webster-Dictionary/pictures/guppy.rtf
./NextLibrary/References/Webster-Dictionary/pictures/hackney.rtf
./NextLibrary/References/Webster-Dictionary/pictures/halter.rtf
./NextLibrary/References/Webster-Dictionary/pictures/hauberk.rtf
./NextLibrary/References/Webster-Dictionary/pictures/heart.rtf
./NextLibrary/References/Webster-Dictionary/pictures/honeybee.rtf
./NextLibrary/References/Webster-Dictionary/pictures/hoof.rtf
./NextLibrary/References/Webster-Dictionary/pictures/horse.rtf
./NextLibrary/References/Webster-Dictionary/pictures/hyperbola.rtf
./NextLibrary/References/Webster-Dictionary/pictures/hypotenuse.rtf
./NextLibrary/References/Webster-Dictionary/pictures/inflorescence.rtf
./NextLibrary/References/Webster-Dictionary/pictures/insect.rtf
./NextLibrary/References/Webster-Dictionary/pictures/interiorangle.rtf
./NextLibrary/References/Webster-Dictionary/pictures/involute.rtf
./NextLibrary/References/Webster-Dictionary/pictures/isometricprojection.rtf
./NextLibrary/References/Webster-Dictionary/pictures/knot.rtf
./NextLibrary/References/Webster-Dictionary/pictures/lamb.rtf
./NextLibrary/References/Webster-Dictionary/pictures/larynx.rtf
./NextLibrary/References/Webster-Dictionary/pictures/latitude.rtf
./NextLibrary/References/Webster-Dictionary/pictures/leaf.rtf
./NextLibrary/References/Webster-Dictionary/pictures/litter.rtf
./NextLibrary/References/Webster-Dictionary/pictures/loggia.rtf
./NextLibrary/References/Webster-Dictionary/pictures/.places
./NextLibrary/References/Webster-Dictionary/pictures/miter.rtf
./NextLibrary/References/Webster-Dictionary/pictures/longitude.rtf
./NextLibrary/References/Webster-Dictionary/pictures/metacenter.rtf
./NextLibrary/References/Webster-Dictionary/pictures/molding.rtf
./NextLibrary/References/Webster-Dictionary/pictures/netsuke.rtf
./NextLibrary/References/Webster-Dictionary/pictures/order.rtf
./NextLibrary/References/Webster-Dictionary/pictures/oriole.rtf
./NextLibrary/References/Webster-Dictionary/pictures/orthographicprojection.rtf
./NextLibrary/References/Webster-Dictionary/pictures/panda.rtf
./NextLibrary/References/Webster-Dictionary/pictures/parabola.rtf
./NextLibrary/References/Webster-Dictionary/pictures/peanut.rtf
./NextLibrary/References/Webster-Dictionary/pictures/pendentive.rtf
./NextLibrary/References/Webster-Dictionary/pictures/pestle.rtf
./NextLibrary/References/Webster-Dictionary/pictures/pick.rtf
./NextLibrary/References/Webster-Dictionary/pictures/pilaster.rtf
./NextLibrary/References/Webster-Dictionary/pictures/pinnacle.rtf

```
./NextLibrary/References/Webster-Dictionary/pictures/pitch.rtf
./NextLibrary/References/Webster-Dictionary/pictures/plimsollmark.rtf
./NextLibrary/References/Webster-Dictionary/pictures/poker.rtf
./NextLibrary/References/Webster-Dictionary/pictures/pork.rtf
./NextLibrary/References/Webster-Dictionary/pictures/ptarmigan.rtf
./NextLibrary/References/Webster-Dictionary/pictures/refraction.rtf
./NextLibrary/References/Webster-Dictionary/pictures/relief.rtf
./NextLibrary/References/Webster-Dictionary/pictures/remora.rtf
./NextLibrary/References/Webster-Dictionary/pictures/repeat.rtf
./NextLibrary/References/Webster-Dictionary/pictures/rest.rtf
./NextLibrary/References/Webster-Dictionary/pictures/ridgepole.rtf
./NextLibrary/References/Webster-Dictionary/pictures/roof.rtf
./NextLibrary/References/Webster-Dictionary/pictures/ruff.rtf
./NextLibrary/References/Webster-Dictionary/pictures/rune.rtf
./NextLibrary/References/Webster-Dictionary/pictures/sable.rtf
./NextLibrary/References/Webster-Dictionary/pictures/saddle.rtf
./NextLibrary/References/Webster-Dictionary/pictures/sail.rtf
./NextLibrary/References/Webster-Dictionary/pictures/scroll.rtf
./NextLibrary/References/Webster-Dictionary/pictures/semaphore.rtf
./NextLibrary/References/Webster-Dictionary/pictures/serif.rtf
./NextLibrary/References/Webster-Dictionary/pictures/shark.rtf
./NextLibrary/References/Webster-Dictionary/pictures/shroud.rtf
./NextLibrary/References/Webster-Dictionary/pictures/skeleton.rtf
./NextLibrary/References/Webster-Dictionary/pictures/spinnaker.rtf
./NextLibrary/References/Webster-Dictionary/pictures/sporran.rtf
./NextLibrary/References/Webster-Dictionary/pictures/timezone.rtf
./NextLibrary/References/Webster-Dictionary/pictures/tooth.rtf
./NextLibrary/References/Webster-Dictionary/pictures/transom.rtf
./NextLibrary/References/Webster-Dictionary/pictures/triangle.rtf
./NextLibrary/References/Webster-Dictionary/pictures/tympanum.rtf
./NextLibrary/References/Webster-Dictionary/pictures/veal.rtf
./NextLibrary/References/Webster-Dictionary/pictures/violin.rtf
./NextLibrary/References/Webster-Dictionary/pictures/undercarriage.rtf
./NextLibrary/References/Webster-Dictionary/pictures/varyinghare.rtf
./NextLibrary/References/Webster-Dictionary/pictures/venation.rtf
./NextLibrary/References/Webster-Dictionary/pictures/vertebra.rtf
./NextLibrary/References/Webster-Dictionary/pictures/vestment.rtf
./NextLibrary/References/Webster-Dictionary/pictures/visor.rtf
./NextLibrary/References/Webster-Dictionary/pictures/volva.rtf
./NextLibrary/References/Webster-Dictionary/pictures/welshcorgi.rtf
./NextLibrary/References/Webster-Dictionary/pictures/whiffletree.rtf
./NextLibrary/References/Webster-Dictionary/pictures/wing.rtf
./NextLibrary/References/Webster-Dictionary/pictures/civetcat.tiff
./NextLibrary/References/Webster-Dictionary/pictures/alternateangle.eps
./NextLibrary/References/Webster-Dictionary/pictures/beaufortscale.eps
./NextLibrary/References/Webster-Dictionary/pictures/beaver.tiff
./NextLibrary/References/Webster-Dictionary/pictures/beef.tiff
./NextLibrary/References/Webster-Dictionary/pictures/bell.eps
./NextLibrary/References/Webster-Dictionary/pictures/beluga.tiff
./NextLibrary/References/Webster-Dictionary/pictures/bevel.tiff
./NextLibrary/References/Webster-Dictionary/pictures/bighorn.tiff
./NextLibrary/References/Webster-Dictionary/pictures/bill.tiff
./NextLibrary/References/Webster-Dictionary/pictures/binomialtheorem.eps
./NextLibrary/References/Webster-Dictionary/pictures/bird.tiff
./NextLibrary/References/Webster-Dictionary/pictures/blackfootedferret.tiff
./NextLibrary/References/Webster-Dictionary/pictures/blastula.tiff
./NextLibrary/References/Webster-Dictionary/pictures/bluewhale.tiff
./NextLibrary/References/Webster-Dictionary/pictures/boar.tiff
./NextLibrary/References/Webster-Dictionary/pictures/bonsai.tiff
./NextLibrary/References/Webster-Dictionary/pictures/bootjack.tiff
./NextLibrary/References/Webster-Dictionary/pictures/boss.tiff
./NextLibrary/References/Webster-Dictionary/pictures/bouvierdesflandres.tiff
./NextLibrary/References/Webster-Dictionary/pictures/boxturtle.tiff
./NextLibrary/References/Webster-Dictionary/pictures/braille.tiff
./NextLibrary/References/Webster-Dictionary/pictures/brain.tiff
./NextLibrary/References/Webster-Dictionary/pictures/brazilnut.tiff
./NextLibrary/References/Webster-Dictionary/pictures/bridge.tiff
./NextLibrary/References/Webster-Dictionary/pictures/brilliant.tiff
./NextLibrary/References/Webster-Dictionary/pictures/bristleconepine.tiff
./NextLibrary/References/Webster-Dictionary/pictures/brusselsgriffon.tiff
./NextLibrary/References/Webster-Dictionary/pictures/buckboard.tiff
./NextLibrary/References/Webster-Dictionary/pictures/buffalo.tiff
./NextLibrary/References/Webster-Dictionary/pictures/bugle.tiff
./NextLibrary/References/Webster-Dictionary/pictures/rib.rtf
./NextLibrary/References/Webster-Dictionary/pictures/buoy.tiff
./NextLibrary/References/Webster-Dictionary/pictures/busby.tiff
./NextLibrary/References/Webster-Dictionary/pictures/caddisworm.tiff
./NextLibrary/References/Webster-Dictionary/pictures/caisson.tiff
./NextLibrary/References/Webster-Dictionary/pictures/californiacondor.tiff
./NextLibrary/References/Webster-Dictionary/pictures/camel.tiff
./NextLibrary/References/Webster-Dictionary/pictures/candelabrum.tiff
./NextLibrary/References/Webster-Dictionary/pictures/canopicjar.tiff
./NextLibrary/References/Webster-Dictionary/pictures/capstan.tiff
./NextLibrary/References/Webster-Dictionary/pictures/carboy.tiff
./NextLibrary/References/Webster-Dictionary/pictures/carpel.tiff
./NextLibrary/References/Webster-Dictionary/pictures/caryatid.tiff
./NextLibrary/References/Webster-Dictionary/pictures/cat.tiff
./NextLibrary/References/Webster-Dictionary/pictures/catfish.tiff
./NextLibrary/References/Webster-Dictionary/pictures/cell.tiff
./NextLibrary/References/Webster-Dictionary/pictures/cephalicindex.tiff
./NextLibrary/References/Webster-Dictionary/pictures/chalet.tiff
./NextLibrary/References/Webster-Dictionary/pictures/chasuble.tiff
./NextLibrary/References/Webster-Dictionary/pictures/cheetah.tiff
./NextLibrary/References/Webster-Dictionary/pictures/chihuahua.tiff
./NextLibrary/References/Webster-Dictionary/pictures/chlamys.tiff
./NextLibrary/References/Webster-Dictionary/pictures/chopstick.tiff
./NextLibrary/References/Webster-Dictionary/pictures/chowchow.tiff
./NextLibrary/References/Webster-Dictionary/pictures/chrysanthemum.tiff
./NextLibrary/References/Webster-Dictionary/pictures/circle.tiff
./NextLibrary/References/Webster-Dictionary/pictures/armor.rtf
./NextLibrary/References/Webster-Dictionary/pictures/clam.tiff
./NextLibrary/References/Webster-Dictionary/pictures/cloister.tiff
```

./NextLibrary/References/Webster-Dictionary/pictures/cloud.tiff
./NextLibrary/References/Webster-Dictionary/pictures/coati.tiff
./NextLibrary/References/Webster-Dictionary/pictures/cock.tiff
./NextLibrary/References/Webster-Dictionary/pictures/coffee.tiff
./NextLibrary/References/Webster-Dictionary/pictures/collie.tiff
./NextLibrary/References/Webster-Dictionary/pictures/column.tiff
./NextLibrary/References/Webster-Dictionary/pictures/commode.tiff
./NextLibrary/References/Webster-Dictionary/pictures/compasscard.tiff
./NextLibrary/References/Webster-Dictionary/pictures/complement.tiff
./NextLibrary/References/Webster-Dictionary/pictures/cone.tiff
./NextLibrary/References/Webster-Dictionary/pictures/conicsection.tiff
./NextLibrary/References/Webster-Dictionary/pictures/consoletable.tiff
./NextLibrary/References/Webster-Dictionary/pictures/contrabassoon.tiff
./NextLibrary/References/Webster-Dictionary/pictures/copperhead.tiff
./NextLibrary/References/Webster-Dictionary/pictures/cornice.tiff
./NextLibrary/References/Webster-Dictionary/pictures/corymb.tiff
./NextLibrary/References/Webster-Dictionary/pictures/cougar.tiff
./NextLibrary/References/Webster-Dictionary/pictures/cow.tiff
./NextLibrary/References/Webster-Dictionary/pictures/coyote.tiff
./NextLibrary/References/Webster-Dictionary/pictures/crescendo.tiff
./NextLibrary/References/Webster-Dictionary/pictures/crocodile.tiff
./NextLibrary/References/Webster-Dictionary/pictures/cross.tiff
./NextLibrary/References/Webster-Dictionary/pictures/crossbow.tiff
./NextLibrary/References/Webster-Dictionary/pictures/cuckoo.tiff
./NextLibrary/References/Webster-Dictionary/pictures/cuneiform.tiff
./NextLibrary/References/Webster-Dictionary/pictures/cusp.tiff
./NextLibrary/References/Webster-Dictionary/pictures/cycloid.tiff
./NextLibrary/References/Webster-Dictionary/pictures/dado.tiff
./NextLibrary/References/Webster-Dictionary/pictures/dandiedinmontterrier.tiff
./NextLibrary/References/Webster-Dictionary/pictures/davit.tiff
./NextLibrary/References/Webster-Dictionary/pictures/decagon.tiff
./NextLibrary/References/Webster-Dictionary/pictures/decrescendo.tiff
./NextLibrary/References/Webster-Dictionary/pictures/demijohn.tiff
./NextLibrary/References/Webster-Dictionary/pictures/derby.tiff
./NextLibrary/References/Webster-Dictionary/pictures/desmid.tiff
./NextLibrary/References/Webster-Dictionary/pictures/devilfish.tiff
./NextLibrary/References/Webster-Dictionary/pictures/diacritic.eps
./NextLibrary/References/Webster-Dictionary/pictures/diaper.tiff
./NextLibrary/References/Webster-Dictionary/pictures/dikdik.tiff
./NextLibrary/References/Webster-Dictionary/pictures/dingo.tiff
./NextLibrary/References/Webster-Dictionary/pictures/diptych.tiff
./NextLibrary/References/Webster-Dictionary/pictures/discbrake.tiff
./NextLibrary/References/Webster-Dictionary/pictures/discus.tiff
./NextLibrary/References/Webster-Dictionary/pictures/distaff.tiff
./NextLibrary/References/Webster-Dictionary/pictures/dna.tiff
./NextLibrary/References/Webster-Dictionary/pictures/dog.tiff
./NextLibrary/References/Webster-Dictionary/pictures/dolphin.tiff
./NextLibrary/References/Webster-Dictionary/pictures/donjon.tiff
./NextLibrary/References/Webster-Dictionary/pictures/doublebass.tiff
./NextLibrary/References/Webster-Dictionary/pictures/dovetail.tiff
./NextLibrary/References/Webster-Dictionary/pictures/dragonfly.tiff
./NextLibrary/References/Webster-Dictionary/pictures/dray.tiff
./NextLibrary/References/Webster-Dictionary/pictures/drum.tiff
./NextLibrary/References/Webster-Dictionary/pictures/duck.tiff
./NextLibrary/References/Webster-Dictionary/pictures/dugong.tiff
./NextLibrary/References/Webster-Dictionary/pictures/dutchdoor.tiff
./NextLibrary/References/Webster-Dictionary/pictures/ear.tiff
./NextLibrary/References/Webster-Dictionary/pictures/easter.eps
./NextLibrary/References/Webster-Dictionary/pictures/echidna.tiff
./NextLibrary/References/Webster-Dictionary/pictures/edelweiss.tiff
./NextLibrary/References/Webster-Dictionary/pictures/egg.tiff
./NextLibrary/References/Webster-Dictionary/pictures/eland.tiff
./NextLibrary/References/Webster-Dictionary/pictures/elephant.tiff
./NextLibrary/References/Webster-Dictionary/pictures/emu.tiff
./NextLibrary/References/Webster-Dictionary/pictures/ellipse.tiff
./NextLibrary/References/Webster-Dictionary/pictures/embrasure.tiff
./NextLibrary/References/Webster-Dictionary/pictures/endocarp.tiff
./NextLibrary/References/Webster-Dictionary/pictures/englishtoyspaniel.tiff
./NextLibrary/References/Webster-Dictionary/pictures/entablature.tiff
./NextLibrary/References/Webster-Dictionary/pictures/epaulet.tiff
./NextLibrary/References/Webster-Dictionary/pictures/equisetum.tiff
./NextLibrary/References/Webster-Dictionary/pictures/ermine.tiff
./NextLibrary/References/Webster-Dictionary/pictures/eskimocurlew.tiff
./NextLibrary/References/Webster-Dictionary/pictures/euphonium.tiff
./NextLibrary/References/Webster-Dictionary/pictures/ewer.tiff
./NextLibrary/References/Webster-Dictionary/pictures/exmoor.tiff
./NextLibrary/References/Webster-Dictionary/pictures/exteriorangle.tiff
./NextLibrary/References/Webster-Dictionary/pictures/eye.tiff
./NextLibrary/References/Webster-Dictionary/pictures/facade.tiff
./NextLibrary/References/Webster-Dictionary/pictures/falcon.tiff
./NextLibrary/References/Webster-Dictionary/pictures/fallowdeer.tiff
./NextLibrary/References/Webster-Dictionary/pictures/fantracery.tiff
./NextLibrary/References/Webster-Dictionary/pictures/fault.tiff
./NextLibrary/References/Webster-Dictionary/pictures/feather.tiff
./NextLibrary/References/Webster-Dictionary/pictures/felucca.tiff
./NextLibrary/References/Webster-Dictionary/pictures/fez.tiff
./NextLibrary/References/Webster-Dictionary/pictures/fig.tiff
./NextLibrary/References/Webster-Dictionary/pictures/figurehead.tiff
./NextLibrary/References/Webster-Dictionary/pictures/finback.tiff
./NextLibrary/References/Webster-Dictionary/pictures/fish.tiff
./NextLibrary/References/Webster-Dictionary/pictures/flagon.tiff
./NextLibrary/References/Webster-Dictionary/pictures/flamingo.tiff
./NextLibrary/References/Webster-Dictionary/pictures/fleurdelis.tiff
./NextLibrary/References/Webster-Dictionary/pictures/flower.tiff
./NextLibrary/References/Webster-Dictionary/pictures/flute.tiff
./NextLibrary/References/Webster-Dictionary/pictures/flyingbuttress.tiff
./NextLibrary/References/Webster-Dictionary/pictures/foolscap.tiff
./NextLibrary/References/Webster-Dictionary/pictures/forehand.tiff
./NextLibrary/References/Webster-Dictionary/pictures/forge.tiff
./NextLibrary/References/Webster-Dictionary/pictures/foxterrier.tiff
./NextLibrary/References/Webster-Dictionary/pictures/franklinstove.tiff
./NextLibrary/References/Webster-Dictionary/pictures/frenchhorn.tiff

./NextLibrary/References/Webster-Dictionary/pictures/fret.tiff
./NextLibrary/References/Webster-Dictionary/pictures/fruitbat.tiff
./NextLibrary/References/Webster-Dictionary/pictures/furseal.tiff
./NextLibrary/References/Webster-Dictionary/pictures/galago.tiff
./NextLibrary/References/Webster-Dictionary/pictures/gamelan.tiff
./NextLibrary/References/Webster-Dictionary/pictures/gargoyle.tiff
./NextLibrary/References/Webster-Dictionary/pictures/gaur.tiff
./NextLibrary/References/Webster-Dictionary/pictures/gemsbok.tiff
./NextLibrary/References/Webster-Dictionary/pictures/gerrymander.tiff
./NextLibrary/References/Webster-Dictionary/pictures/gibbon.tiff
./NextLibrary/References/Webster-Dictionary/pictures/gilamonster.tiff
./NextLibrary/References/Webster-Dictionary/pictures/girandole.tiff
./NextLibrary/References/Webster-Dictionary/pictures/glengarry.tiff
./NextLibrary/References/Webster-Dictionary/pictures/glockenspiel.tiff
./NextLibrary/References/Webster-Dictionary/pictures/gnomon.tiff
./NextLibrary/References/Webster-Dictionary/pictures/gnu.tiff
./NextLibrary/References/Webster-Dictionary/pictures/goldeneagle.tiff
./NextLibrary/References/Webster-Dictionary/pictures/goldenhamster.tiff
./NextLibrary/References/Webster-Dictionary/pictures/googolplex.eps
./NextLibrary/References/Webster-Dictionary/pictures/gordonsetter.tiff
./NextLibrary/References/Webster-Dictionary/pictures/graft.tiff
./NextLibrary/References/Webster-Dictionary/pictures/grandtouringcar.tiff
./NextLibrary/References/Webster-Dictionary/pictures/greatpyrenees.tiff
./NextLibrary/References/Webster-Dictionary/pictures/greyhound.tiff
./NextLibrary/References/Webster-Dictionary/pictures/groin.tiff
./NextLibrary/References/Webster-Dictionary/pictures/guan.tiff
./NextLibrary/References/Webster-Dictionary/pictures/guitar.tiff
./NextLibrary/References/Webster-Dictionary/pictures/guppy.tiff
./NextLibrary/References/Webster-Dictionary/pictures/gyrfalcon.tiff
./NextLibrary/References/Webster-Dictionary/pictures/hackney.tiff
./NextLibrary/References/Webster-Dictionary/pictures/haik.tiff
./NextLibrary/References/Webster-Dictionary/pictures/halter.tiff
./NextLibrary/References/Webster-Dictionary/pictures/hangglider.tiff
./NextLibrary/References/Webster-Dictionary/pictures/harlequin.tiff
./NextLibrary/References/Webster-Dictionary/pictures/harmonicseries.eps
./NextLibrary/References/Webster-Dictionary/pictures/hartebeest.tiff
./NextLibrary/References/Webster-Dictionary/pictures/hauberk.tiff
./NextLibrary/References/Webster-Dictionary/pictures/headdress.tiff
./NextLibrary/References/Webster-Dictionary/pictures/heart.tiff
./NextLibrary/References/Webster-Dictionary/pictures/hedgehog.tiff
./NextLibrary/References/Webster-Dictionary/pictures/helicon.tiff
./NextLibrary/References/Webster-Dictionary/pictures/hellbender.tiff
./NextLibrary/References/Webster-Dictionary/pictures/heptagon.tiff
./NextLibrary/References/Webster-Dictionary/pictures/hermaphroditebrig.tiff
./NextLibrary/References/Webster-Dictionary/pictures/pug.rtf
./NextLibrary/References/Webster-Dictionary/pictures/hexagram.tiff
./NextLibrary/References/Webster-Dictionary/pictures/hieroglyphic.tiff
./NextLibrary/References/Webster-Dictionary/pictures/hippopotamus.tiff
./NextLibrary/References/Webster-Dictionary/pictures/emu.rtf
./NextLibrary/References/Webster-Dictionary/pictures/hoatzin.tiff
./NextLibrary/References/Webster-Dictionary/pictures/hogan.tiff

./NextLibrary/References/Webster-Dictionary/pictures/honeybee.tiff
./NextLibrary/References/Webster-Dictionary/pictures/hoof.tiff
./NextLibrary/References/Webster-Dictionary/pictures/horse.tiff
./NextLibrary/References/Webster-Dictionary/pictures/hourglass.tiff
./NextLibrary/References/Webster-Dictionary/pictures/howlermonkey.tiff
./NextLibrary/References/Webster-Dictionary/pictures/humpbackwhale.tiff
./NextLibrary/References/Webster-Dictionary/pictures/hydrofoil.tiff
./NextLibrary/References/Webster-Dictionary/pictures/hyperbola.tiff
./NextLibrary/References/Webster-Dictionary/pictures/yawl.rtf
./NextLibrary/References/Webster-Dictionary/pictures/hypotenuse.tiff
./NextLibrary/References/Webster-Dictionary/pictures/hyrax.tiff
./NextLibrary/References/Webster-Dictionary/pictures/ibizanhound.tiff
./NextLibrary/References/Webster-Dictionary/pictures/iguana.tiff
./NextLibrary/References/Webster-Dictionary/pictures/imbrication.tiff
./NextLibrary/References/Webster-Dictionary/pictures/impala.tiff
./NextLibrary/References/Webster-Dictionary/pictures/imperialmoth.tiff
./NextLibrary/References/Webster-Dictionary/pictures/indeterminate.eps
./NextLibrary/References/Webster-Dictionary/pictures/indianpipe.tiff
./NextLibrary/References/Webster-Dictionary/pictures/inflorescence.tiff
./NextLibrary/References/Webster-Dictionary/pictures/inkycap.tiff
./NextLibrary/References/Webster-Dictionary/pictures/insect.tiff
./NextLibrary/References/Webster-Dictionary/pictures/intaglio.tiff
./NextLibrary/References/Webster-Dictionary/pictures/interiorangle.tiff
./NextLibrary/References/Webster-Dictionary/pictures/intersection.tiff
./NextLibrary/References/Webster-Dictionary/pictures/inverness.tiff
./NextLibrary/References/Webster-Dictionary/pictures/involute.tiff
./NextLibrary/References/Webster-Dictionary/pictures/irishwolfhound.tiff
./NextLibrary/References/Webster-Dictionary/pictures/isometricprojection.tiff
./NextLibrary/References/Webster-Dictionary/pictures/ivorybilledwoodpecker.tiff
./NextLibrary/References/Webster-Dictionary/pictures/jackinthepulpit.tiff
./NextLibrary/References/Webster-Dictionary/pictures/jaguar.tiff
./NextLibrary/References/Webster-Dictionary/pictures/jerboa.tiff
./NextLibrary/References/Webster-Dictionary/pictures/jewishcalendar.eps
./NextLibrary/References/Webster-Dictionary/pictures/pyramid.rtf
./NextLibrary/References/Webster-Dictionary/pictures/jewsharp.tiff
./NextLibrary/References/Webster-Dictionary/pictures/jodhpur.tiff
./NextLibrary/References/Webster-Dictionary/pictures/joshuatree.tiff
./NextLibrary/References/Webster-Dictionary/pictures/junk.tiff
./NextLibrary/References/Webster-Dictionary/pictures/karakul.tiff
./NextLibrary/References/Webster-Dictionary/pictures/kayak.tiff
./NextLibrary/References/Webster-Dictionary/pictures/ketch.tiff
./NextLibrary/References/Webster-Dictionary/pictures/kimono.tiff
./NextLibrary/References/Webster-Dictionary/pictures/kiwi.tiff
./NextLibrary/References/Webster-Dictionary/pictures/knot.tiff
./NextLibrary/References/Webster-Dictionary/pictures/kudu.tiff
./NextLibrary/References/Webster-Dictionary/pictures/labradorretriever.tiff
./NextLibrary/References/Webster-Dictionary/pictures/ladysslipper.tiff
./NextLibrary/References/Webster-Dictionary/pictures/lamb.tiff
./NextLibrary/References/Webster-Dictionary/pictures/language.eps
./NextLibrary/References/Webster-Dictionary/pictures/langur.tiff
./NextLibrary/References/Webster-Dictionary/pictures/laplacetransform.eps

./NextLibrary/References/Webster-Dictionary/pictures/larynx.tiff
./NextLibrary/References/Webster-Dictionary/pictures/latitude.tiff
./NextLibrary/References/Webster-Dictionary/pictures/leaf.tiff
./NextLibrary/References/Webster-Dictionary/pictures/leatherback.tiff
./NextLibrary/References/Webster-Dictionary/pictures/leopard.tiff
./NextLibrary/References/Webster-Dictionary/pictures/lhasaapso.tiff
./NextLibrary/References/Webster-Dictionary/pictures/lichen.tiff
./NextLibrary/References/Webster-Dictionary/pictures/lilyofthevalley.tiff
./NextLibrary/References/Webster-Dictionary/pictures/limpet.tiff
./NextLibrary/References/Webster-Dictionary/pictures/lionfish.tiff
./NextLibrary/References/Webster-Dictionary/pictures/litter.tiff
./NextLibrary/References/Webster-Dictionary/pictures/llama.tiff
./NextLibrary/References/Webster-Dictionary/pictures/loggia.tiff
./NextLibrary/References/Webster-Dictionary/pictures/longitude.tiff
./NextLibrary/References/Webster-Dictionary/pictures/loris.tiff
./NextLibrary/References/Webster-Dictionary/pictures/luge.tiff
./NextLibrary/References/Webster-Dictionary/pictures/lute.tiff
./NextLibrary/References/Webster-Dictionary/pictures/lyrebird.tiff
./NextLibrary/References/Webster-Dictionary/pictures/macaw.tiff
./NextLibrary/References/Webster-Dictionary/pictures/maclaurinsseries.eps
./NextLibrary/References/Webster-Dictionary/pictures/magendavid.tiff
./NextLibrary/References/Webster-Dictionary/pictures/magpie.tiff
./NextLibrary/References/Webster-Dictionary/pictures/maltese.tiff
./NextLibrary/References/Webster-Dictionary/pictures/mandrill.tiff
./NextLibrary/References/Webster-Dictionary/pictures/mantis.tiff
./NextLibrary/References/Webster-Dictionary/pictures/manualalphabet.tiff
./NextLibrary/References/Webster-Dictionary/pictures/marmoset.tiff
./NextLibrary/References/Webster-Dictionary/pictures/marshhawk.tiff
./NextLibrary/References/Webster-Dictionary/pictures/mastiff.tiff
./NextLibrary/References/Webster-Dictionary/pictures/meadowlark.tiff
./NextLibrary/References/Webster-Dictionary/pictures/megalith.tiff
./NextLibrary/References/Webster-Dictionary/pictures/menorah.tiff
./NextLibrary/References/Webster-Dictionary/pictures/mercatorprojection.tiff
./NextLibrary/References/Webster-Dictionary/pictures/metacenter.tiff
./NextLibrary/References/Webster-Dictionary/pictures/metricsystem.eps
./NextLibrary/References/Webster-Dictionary/pictures/metronome.tiff
./NextLibrary/References/Webster-Dictionary/pictures/milkwort.tiff
./NextLibrary/References/Webster-Dictionary/pictures/minaret.tiff
./NextLibrary/References/Webster-Dictionary/pictures/miniatureschnauzer.tiff
./NextLibrary/References/Webster-Dictionary/pictures/miter.tiff
./NextLibrary/References/Webster-Dictionary/pictures/mobiusstrip.tiff
./NextLibrary/References/Webster-Dictionary/pictures/molding.tiff
./NextLibrary/References/Webster-Dictionary/pictures/monarchbutterfly.tiff
./NextLibrary/References/Webster-Dictionary/pictures/mongoose.tiff
./NextLibrary/References/Webster-Dictionary/pictures/moose.tiff
./NextLibrary/References/Webster-Dictionary/pictures/morel.tiff
./NextLibrary/References/Webster-Dictionary/pictures/morsecode.eps
./NextLibrary/References/Webster-Dictionary/pictures/mortarboard.tiff
./NextLibrary/References/Webster-Dictionary/pictures/mouflon.tiff
./NextLibrary/References/Webster-Dictionary/pictures/muledeer.tiff
./NextLibrary/References/Webster-Dictionary/pictures/muntjac.tiff

./NextLibrary/References/Webster-Dictionary/pictures/mute.tiff
./NextLibrary/References/Webster-Dictionary/pictures/narwhal.tiff
./NextLibrary/References/Webster-Dictionary/pictures/nautilus.tiff
./NextLibrary/References/Webster-Dictionary/pictures/nene.tiff
./NextLibrary/References/Webster-Dictionary/pictures/netsuke.tiff
./NextLibrary/References/Webster-Dictionary/pictures/newfoundland.tiff
./NextLibrary/References/Webster-Dictionary/pictures/nighthawk.tiff
./NextLibrary/References/Webster-Dictionary/pictures/normaldistribution.eps
./NextLibrary/References/Webster-Dictionary/pictures/norwegianelkhound.tiff
./NextLibrary/References/Webster-Dictionary/pictures/notornis.tiff
./NextLibrary/References/Webster-Dictionary/pictures/nuthatch.tiff
./NextLibrary/References/Webster-Dictionary/pictures/obi.tiff
./NextLibrary/References/Webster-Dictionary/pictures/oboe.tiff
./NextLibrary/References/Webster-Dictionary/pictures/ocelot.tiff
./NextLibrary/References/Webster-Dictionary/pictures/okapi.tiff
./NextLibrary/References/Webster-Dictionary/pictures/onager.tiff
./NextLibrary/References/Webster-Dictionary/pictures/operaglass.tiff
./NextLibrary/References/Webster-Dictionary/pictures/opossum.tiff
./NextLibrary/References/Webster-Dictionary/pictures/orangutan.tiff
./NextLibrary/References/Webster-Dictionary/pictures/order.tiff
./NextLibrary/References/Webster-Dictionary/pictures/oriole.tiff
./NextLibrary/References/Webster-Dictionary/pictures/orthographicprojection.tiff
./NextLibrary/References/Webster-Dictionary/pictures/otter.tiff
./NextLibrary/References/Webster-Dictionary/pictures/ovenbird.tiff
./NextLibrary/References/Webster-Dictionary/pictures/oxbow.tiff
./NextLibrary/References/Webster-Dictionary/pictures/paca.tiff
./NextLibrary/References/Webster-Dictionary/pictures/pagoda.tiff
./NextLibrary/References/Webster-Dictionary/pictures/panda.tiff
./NextLibrary/References/Webster-Dictionary/pictures/pangolin.tiff
./NextLibrary/References/Webster-Dictionary/pictures/pantograph.tiff
./NextLibrary/References/Webster-Dictionary/pictures/parabola.tiff
./NextLibrary/References/Webster-Dictionary/pictures/parbuckle.tiff
./NextLibrary/References/Webster-Dictionary/pictures/partridge.tiff
./NextLibrary/References/Webster-Dictionary/pictures/passionflower.tiff
./NextLibrary/References/Webster-Dictionary/pictures/patchwork.tiff
./NextLibrary/References/Webster-Dictionary/pictures/peanut.tiff
./NextLibrary/References/Webster-Dictionary/pictures/pekingese.tiff
./NextLibrary/References/Webster-Dictionary/pictures/pendentive.tiff
./NextLibrary/References/Webster-Dictionary/pictures/peregrine.tiff
./NextLibrary/References/Webster-Dictionary/pictures/periodictable.eps
./NextLibrary/References/Webster-Dictionary/pictures/periscope.tiff
./NextLibrary/References/Webster-Dictionary/pictures/persianlamb.tiff
./NextLibrary/References/Webster-Dictionary/pictures/pestle.tiff
./NextLibrary/References/Webster-Dictionary/pictures/phoebe.tiff
./NextLibrary/References/Webster-Dictionary/pictures/phylactery.tiff
./NextLibrary/References/Webster-Dictionary/pictures/pick.tiff
./NextLibrary/References/Webster-Dictionary/pictures/pilaster.tiff
./NextLibrary/References/Webster-Dictionary/pictures/pinnacle.tiff
./NextLibrary/References/Webster-Dictionary/pictures/pinto.tiff
./NextLibrary/References/Webster-Dictionary/pictures/pitch.tiff
./NextLibrary/References/Webster-Dictionary/pictures/plane.tiff

./NextLibrary/References/Webster-Dictionary/pictures/planet.eps
./NextLibrary/References/Webster-Dictionary/pictures/platypus.tiff
./NextLibrary/References/Webster-Dictionary/pictures/plimsollmark.eps
./NextLibrary/References/Webster-Dictionary/pictures/pocketmouse.tiff
./NextLibrary/References/Webster-Dictionary/pictures/poker.tiff
./NextLibrary/References/Webster-Dictionary/pictures/polarbear.tiff
./NextLibrary/References/Webster-Dictionary/pictures/polonaise.tiff
./NextLibrary/References/Webster-Dictionary/pictures/pomegranate.tiff
./NextLibrary/References/Webster-Dictionary/pictures/pork.tiff
./NextLibrary/References/Webster-Dictionary/pictures/portcullis.tiff
./NextLibrary/References/Webster-Dictionary/pictures/portuguesemanofwar.tiff
./NextLibrary/References/Webster-Dictionary/pictures/wolverine.rtf
./NextLibrary/References/Webster-Dictionary/pictures/potterswheel.tiff
./NextLibrary/References/Webster-Dictionary/pictures/prairiechicken.tiff
./NextLibrary/References/Webster-Dictionary/pictures/pressuresuit.tiff
./NextLibrary/References/Webster-Dictionary/pictures/pricklypear.tiff
./NextLibrary/References/Webster-Dictionary/pictures/pronghorn.tiff
./NextLibrary/References/Webster-Dictionary/pictures/ptarmigan.tiff
./NextLibrary/References/Webster-Dictionary/pictures/pug.tiff
./NextLibrary/References/Webster-Dictionary/pictures/punchinello.tiff
./NextLibrary/References/Webster-Dictionary/pictures/punctuationmark.eps
./NextLibrary/References/Webster-Dictionary/pictures/puttee.tiff
./NextLibrary/References/Webster-Dictionary/pictures/pyramid.tiff
./NextLibrary/References/Webster-Dictionary/pictures/python.tiff
./NextLibrary/References/Webster-Dictionary/pictures/quadrant.tiff
./NextLibrary/References/Webster-Dictionary/pictures/quarterhorse.tiff
./NextLibrary/References/Webster-Dictionary/pictures/quetzal.tiff
./NextLibrary/References/Webster-Dictionary/pictures/quoin.tiff
./NextLibrary/References/Webster-Dictionary/pictures/raccoon.tiff
./NextLibrary/References/Webster-Dictionary/pictures/radiofrequency.eps
./NextLibrary/References/Webster-Dictionary/pictures/radiometer.tiff
./NextLibrary/References/Webster-Dictionary/pictures/rambouillet.tiff
./NextLibrary/References/Webster-Dictionary/pictures/rapier.tiff
./NextLibrary/References/Webster-Dictionary/pictures/raven.tiff
./NextLibrary/References/Webster-Dictionary/pictures/rebec.tiff
./NextLibrary/References/Webster-Dictionary/pictures/recorder.titt
./NextLibrary/References/Webster-Dictionary/pictures/redfox.tiff
./NextLibrary/References/Webster-Dictionary/pictures/reed.tiff
./NextLibrary/References/Webster-Dictionary/pictures/refraction.tiff
./NextLibrary/References/Webster-Dictionary/pictures/reindeer.tiff
./NextLibrary/References/Webster-Dictionary/pictures/relief.tiff
./NextLibrary/References/Webster-Dictionary/pictures/remora.tiff
./NextLibrary/References/Webster-Dictionary/pictures/repeat.tiff
./NextLibrary/References/Webster-Dictionary/pictures/rest.tiff
./NextLibrary/References/Webster-Dictionary/pictures/retort.tiff
./NextLibrary/References/Webster-Dictionary/pictures/rhea.tiff
./NextLibrary/References/Webster-Dictionary/pictures/rib.tiff
./NextLibrary/References/Webster-Dictionary/pictures/ridgepole.tiff
./NextLibrary/References/Webster-Dictionary/pictures/rightwhale.tiff
./NextLibrary/References/Webster-Dictionary/pictures/ringneckedpheasant.tiff
./NextLibrary/References/Webster-Dictionary/pictures/roof.tiff
./NextLibrary/References/Webster-Dictionary/pictures/roachback.tiff
./NextLibrary/References/Webster-Dictionary/pictures/roedeer.tiff
./NextLibrary/References/Webster-Dictionary/pictures/rook.tiff
./NextLibrary/References/Webster-Dictionary/pictures/rottweiler.tiff
./NextLibrary/References/Webster-Dictionary/pictures/ruff.tiff
./NextLibrary/References/Webster-Dictionary/pictures/rune.tiff
./NextLibrary/References/Webster-Dictionary/pictures/sable.tiff
./NextLibrary/References/Webster-Dictionary/pictures/saddle.tiff
./NextLibrary/References/Webster-Dictionary/pictures/sail.tiff
./NextLibrary/References/Webster-Dictionary/pictures/saluki.tiff
./NextLibrary/References/Webster-Dictionary/pictures/sanddollar.tiff
./NextLibrary/References/Webster-Dictionary/pictures/santagertrudis.tiff
./NextLibrary/References/Webster-Dictionary/pictures/sari.tiff
./NextLibrary/References/Webster-Dictionary/pictures/saxophone.tiff
./NextLibrary/References/Webster-Dictionary/pictures/scarab.tiff
./NextLibrary/References/Webster-Dictionary/pictures/schipperke.tiff
./NextLibrary/References/Webster-Dictionary/pictures/scimitar.tiff
./NextLibrary/References/Webster-Dictionary/pictures/scottishterrier.tiff
./NextLibrary/References/Webster-Dictionary/pictures/scroll.tiff
./NextLibrary/References/Webster-Dictionary/pictures/seahorse.tiff
./NextLibrary/References/Webster-Dictionary/pictures/secretarybird.tiff
./NextLibrary/References/Webster-Dictionary/pictures/segolily.tiff
./NextLibrary/References/Webster-Dictionary/pictures/semaphore.tiff
./NextLibrary/References/Webster-Dictionary/pictures/serif.tiff
./NextLibrary/References/Webster-Dictionary/pictures/serval.tiff
./NextLibrary/References/Webster-Dictionary/pictures/settle.tiff
./NextLibrary/References/Webster-Dictionary/pictures/sextant.tiff
./NextLibrary/References/Webster-Dictionary/pictures/shark.tiff
./NextLibrary/References/Webster-Dictionary/pictures/shire.tiff
./NextLibrary/References/Webster-Dictionary/pictures/shorthorn.tiff
./NextLibrary/References/Webster-Dictionary/pictures/shroud.tiff
./NextLibrary/References/Webster-Dictionary/pictures/sideboard.tiff
./NextLibrary/References/Webster-Dictionary/pictures/silkyterrier.tiff
./NextLibrary/References/Webster-Dictionary/pictures/sitar.tiff
./NextLibrary/References/Webster-Dictionary/pictures/skeleton.tiff
./NextLibrary/References/Webster-Dictionary/pictures/skunkcabbage.tiff
./NextLibrary/References/Webster-Dictionary/pictures/sleigh.tiff
./NextLibrary/References/Webster-Dictionary/pictures/sloop.tiff
./NextLibrary/References/Webster-Dictionary/pictures/sloth.tiff
./NextLibrary/References/Webster-Dictionary/pictures/snappingturtle.tiff
./NextLibrary/References/Webster-Dictionary/pictures/snowleopard.tiff
./NextLibrary/References/Webster-Dictionary/pictures/softshelledturtle.tiff
./NextLibrary/References/Webster-Dictionary/pictures/sombrero.tiff
./NextLibrary/References/Webster-Dictionary/pictures/sousaphone.tiff
./NextLibrary/References/Webster-Dictionary/pictures/spadix.tiff
./NextLibrary/References/Webster-Dictionary/pictures/spermwhale.tiff
./NextLibrary/References/Webster-Dictionary/pictures/spinnaker.tiff
./NextLibrary/References/Webster-Dictionary/pictures/splice.tiff
./NextLibrary/References/Webster-Dictionary/pictures/sporran.tiff
./NextLibrary/References/Webster-Dictionary/pictures/springbok.tiff
./NextLibrary/References/Webster-Dictionary/pictures/squarerigger.tiff

./NextLibrary/References/Webster-Dictionary/pictures/starnosedmole.tiff
./NextLibrary/References/Webster-Dictionary/pictures/staffordshirebullterrier.tiff
./NextLibrary/References/Webster-Dictionary/pictures/steelyard.tiff
./NextLibrary/References/Webster-Dictionary/pictures/stingray.tiff
./NextLibrary/References/Webster-Dictionary/pictures/stirlingsformula.eps
./NextLibrary/References/Webster-Dictionary/pictures/stonefish.tiff
./NextLibrary/References/Webster-Dictionary/pictures/stormpetrel.tiff
./NextLibrary/References/Webster-Dictionary/pictures/sturgeon.tiff
./NextLibrary/References/Webster-Dictionary/pictures/sugarbeet.tiff
./NextLibrary/References/Webster-Dictionary/pictures/sunbonnet.tiff
./NextLibrary/References/Webster-Dictionary/pictures/surrey.tiff
./NextLibrary/References/Webster-Dictionary/pictures/swallow.tiff
./NextLibrary/References/Webster-Dictionary/pictures/sweetgum.tiff
./NextLibrary/References/Webster-Dictionary/pictures/swordfish.tiff
./NextLibrary/References/Webster-Dictionary/pictures/syncline.tiff
./NextLibrary/References/Webster-Dictionary/pictures/tabla.tiff
./NextLibrary/References/Webster-Dictionary/pictures/tadpole.tiff
./NextLibrary/References/Webster-Dictionary/pictures/takin.tiff
./NextLibrary/References/Webster-Dictionary/pictures/tangram.eps
./NextLibrary/References/Webster-Dictionary/pictures/tapir.tiff
./NextLibrary/References/Webster-Dictionary/pictures/tasmanianwolf.tiff
./NextLibrary/References/Webster-Dictionary/pictures/tdistribution.eps
./NextLibrary/References/Webster-Dictionary/pictures/teasel.tiff
./NextLibrary/References/Webster-Dictionary/pictures/telamon.tiff
./NextLibrary/References/Webster-Dictionary/pictures/tennesseewalkinghorse.tiff
./NextLibrary/References/Webster-Dictionary/pictures/tepee.tiff
./NextLibrary/References/Webster-Dictionary/pictures/terrapin.tiff
./NextLibrary/References/Webster-Dictionary/pictures/tetrahedron.tiff
./NextLibrary/References/Webster-Dictionary/pictures/theodolite.tiff
./NextLibrary/References/Webster-Dictionary/pictures/thole.tiff
./NextLibrary/References/Webster-Dictionary/pictures/threespinedstickleback.tiff
./NextLibrary/References/Webster-Dictionary/pictures/tibetanterrier.tiff
./NextLibrary/References/Webster-Dictionary/pictures/tiger.tiff
./NextLibrary/References/Webster-Dictionary/pictures/timezone.tiff
./NextLibrary/References/Webster-Dictionary/pictures/titi.tiff
./NextLibrary/References/Webster-Dictionary/pictures/toga.tiff
./NextLibrary/References/Webster-Dictionary/pictures/tooth.tiff
./NextLibrary/References/Webster-Dictionary/pictures/torii.tiff
./NextLibrary/References/Webster-Dictionary/pictures/touringcar.tiff
./NextLibrary/References/Webster-Dictionary/pictures/toymanchesterterrier.tiff
./NextLibrary/References/Webster-Dictionary/pictures/transom.tiff
./NextLibrary/References/Webster-Dictionary/pictures/trapezoid.tiff
./NextLibrary/References/Webster-Dictionary/pictures/treeshrew.tiff
./NextLibrary/References/Webster-Dictionary/pictures/triangle.tiff
./NextLibrary/References/Webster-Dictionary/pictures/trillium.tiff
./NextLibrary/References/Webster-Dictionary/pictures/triskelion.tiff
./NextLibrary/References/Webster-Dictionary/pictures/tropicbird.tiff
./NextLibrary/References/Webster-Dictionary/pictures/trumpet.tiff
./NextLibrary/References/Webster-Dictionary/pictures/truthtable.eps
./NextLibrary/References/Webster-Dictionary/pictures/tuatara.tiff

./NextLibrary/References/Webster-Dictionary/pictures/turban.tiff
./NextLibrary/References/Webster-Dictionary/pictures/turnstone.tiff
./NextLibrary/References/Webster-Dictionary/pictures/tympanum.tiff
./NextLibrary/References/Webster-Dictionary/pictures/uncial.tiff
./NextLibrary/References/Webster-Dictionary/pictures/undercarriage.tiff
./NextLibrary/References/Webster-Dictionary/pictures/unicycle.tiff
./NextLibrary/References/Webster-Dictionary/pictures/universaljoint.tiff
./NextLibrary/References/Webster-Dictionary/pictures/uplandplover.tiff
./NextLibrary/References/Webster-Dictionary/pictures/vampire.tiff
./NextLibrary/References/Webster-Dictionary/pictures/varyinghare.tiff
./NextLibrary/References/Webster-Dictionary/pictures/veal.tiff
./NextLibrary/References/Webster-Dictionary/pictures/venation.tiff
./NextLibrary/References/Webster-Dictionary/pictures/venussflytrap.tiff
./NextLibrary/References/Webster-Dictionary/pictures/vertebra.tiff
./NextLibrary/References/Webster-Dictionary/pictures/vestment.tiff
./NextLibrary/References/Webster-Dictionary/pictures/vicuna.tiff
./NextLibrary/References/Webster-Dictionary/pictures/violin.tiff
./NextLibrary/References/Webster-Dictionary/pictures/viscacha.tiff
./NextLibrary/References/Webster-Dictionary/pictures/visor.tiff
./NextLibrary/References/Webster-Dictionary/pictures/volume.eps
./NextLibrary/References/Webster-Dictionary/pictures/volva.tiff
./NextLibrary/References/Webster-Dictionary/pictures/wallaby.tiff
./NextLibrary/References/Webster-Dictionary/pictures/warbonnet.tiff
./NextLibrary/References/Webster-Dictionary/pictures/warthog.tiff
./NextLibrary/References/Webster-Dictionary/pictures/waterbuffalo.tiff
./NextLibrary/References/Webster-Dictionary/pictures/waxwing.tiff
./NextLibrary/References/Webster-Dictionary/pictures/weasel.tiff
./NextLibrary/References/Webster-Dictionary/pictures/welshcorgi.tiff
./NextLibrary/References/Webster-Dictionary/pictures/whiffletree.tiff
./NextLibrary/References/Webster-Dictionary/pictures/whippoorwill.tiff
./NextLibrary/References/Webster-Dictionary/pictures/whitefootedmouse.tiff
./NextLibrary/References/Webster-Dictionary/pictures/whoopingcrane.tiff
./NextLibrary/References/Webster-Dictionary/pictures/wigwam.tiff
./NextLibrary/References/Webster-Dictionary/pictures/wimple.tiff
./NextLibrary/References/Webster-Dictionary/pictures/wing.tiff
./NextLibrary/References/Webster-Dictionary/pictures/wisent.tiff
./NextLibrary/References/Webster-Dictionary/pictures/wolverine.tiff
./NextLibrary/References/Webster-Dictionary/pictures/wormfence.tiff
./NextLibrary/References/Webster-Dictionary/pictures/wren.tiff
./NextLibrary/References/Webster-Dictionary/pictures/xebec.tiff
./NextLibrary/References/Webster-Dictionary/pictures/yawl.tiff
./NextLibrary/References/Webster-Dictionary/pictures/yurt.tiff
./NextLibrary/References/Webster-Dictionary/pictures/zebu.tiff
./NextLibrary/References/Webster-Dictionary/pictures/zither.tiff
./NextLibrary/References/Webster-Dictionary/pictures/zodiac.eps
./NextLibrary/References/Webster-Dictionary/pictures/poissondistribution.eps
./NextLibrary/References/Webster-Dictionary/pictures/hypergeometricdistribution.eps
./NextLibrary/References/Webster-Dictionary/pictures/wimple.rtf
./NextLibrary/References/Webster-Dictionary/pictures/weasel.rtf
./NextLibrary/References/Webster-Dictionary/pictures/vicuna.rtf

```
./NextLibrary/References/Webster-Dictionary/pictures/turban.rtf
./NextLibrary/References/Webster-Dictionary/pictures/trumpet.rtf
./NextLibrary/References/Webster-Dictionary/pictures/touringcar.rtf
./NextLibrary/References/Webster-Dictionary/pictures/tiger.rtf
./NextLibrary/References/Webster-Dictionary/pictures/thole.rtf
./NextLibrary/References/Webster-Dictionary/pictures/teasel.rtf
./NextLibrary/References/Webster-Dictionary/pictures/sweetgum.rtf
./NextLibrary/References/Webster-Dictionary/pictures/swallow.rtf
./NextLibrary/References/Webster-Dictionary/pictures/splice.rtf
./NextLibrary/References/Webster-Dictionary/pictures/spadix.rtf
./NextLibrary/References/Webster-Dictionary/pictures/snappingturtle.rtf
./NextLibrary/References/Webster-Dictionary/pictures/sloth.rtf
./NextLibrary/References/Webster-Dictionary/pictures/shire.rtf
./NextLibrary/References/Webster-Dictionary/pictures/seahorse.rtf
./NextLibrary/References/Webster-Dictionary/pictures/scarab.rtf
./NextLibrary/References/Webster-Dictionary/pictures/recorder.rtf
./NextLibrary/References/Webster-Dictionary/pictures/raccoon.rtf
./NextLibrary/References/Webster-Dictionary/pictures/quoin.rtf
./NextLibrary/References/Webster-Dictionary/pictures/quetzal.rtf
./NextLibrary/References/Webster-Dictionary/pictures/quadrant.rtf
./NextLibrary/References/Webster-Dictionary/pictures/pomegranate.rtf
./NextLibrary/References/Webster-Dictionary/pictures/polonaise.rtf
./NextLibrary/References/Webster-Dictionary/pictures/phylactery.rtf
./NextLibrary/References/Webster-Dictionary/pictures/persianlamb.rtf
./NextLibrary/References/Webster-Dictionary/pictures/pekingese.rtf
./NextLibrary/References/Webster-Dictionary/pictures/patchwork.rtf
./NextLibrary/References/Webster-Dictionary/pictures/partridge.rtf
./NextLibrary/References/Webster-Dictionary/pictures/parbuckle.rtf
./NextLibrary/References/Webster-Dictionary/pictures/pantograph.rtf
./NextLibrary/References/Webster-Dictionary/pictures/oxbow.rtf
./NextLibrary/References/Webster-Dictionary/pictures/ovenbird.rtf
./NextLibrary/References/Webster-Dictionary/pictures/otter.rtf
./NextLibrary/References/Webster-Dictionary/pictures/opossum.rtf
./NextLibrary/References/Webster-Dictionary/pictures/onager.rtf
./NextLibrary/References/Webster-Dictionary/pictures/nighthawk.rtf
./NextLibrary/References/Webster-Dictionary/pictures/nautilus.rtf
./NextLibrary/References/Webster-Dictionary/pictures/mute.rtf
./NextLibrary/References/Webster-Dictionary/pictures/mortarboard.rtf
./NextLibrary/References/Webster-Dictionary/pictures/moose.rtf
./NextLibrary/References/Webster-Dictionary/pictures/bible.eps
./NextLibrary/References/Webster-Dictionary/pictures/beaver.rtf
./NextLibrary/References/Webster-Dictionary/pictures/capstan.rtf
./NextLibrary/References/Webster-Dictionary/pictures/civetcat.rtf
./NextLibrary/References/Webster-Dictionary/pictures/davit.rtf
./NextLibrary/References/Webster-Dictionary/pictures/diptych.rtf
./NextLibrary/References/Webster-Dictionary/pictures/discus.rtf
./NextLibrary/References/Webster-Dictionary/pictures/ermine.rtf
./NextLibrary/References/Webster-Dictionary/pictures/exmoor.rtf
./NextLibrary/References/Webster-Dictionary/pictures/facade.rtf
./NextLibrary/References/Webster-Dictionary/pictures/figurehead.rtf
./NextLibrary/References/Webster-Dictionary/pictures/flagon.rtf

./NextLibrary/References/Webster-Dictionary/pictures/fleurdelis.rtf
./NextLibrary/References/Webster-Dictionary/pictures/foolscap.rtf
./NextLibrary/References/Webster-Dictionary/pictures/forehand.rtf
./NextLibrary/References/Webster-Dictionary/pictures/forge.rtf
./NextLibrary/References/Webster-Dictionary/pictures/groin.rtf
./NextLibrary/References/Webster-Dictionary/pictures/hedgehog.rtf
./NextLibrary/References/Webster-Dictionary/pictures/hieroglyphic.rtf
./NextLibrary/References/Webster-Dictionary/pictures/hydrofoil.rtf
./NextLibrary/References/Webster-Dictionary/pictures/imbrication.rtf
./NextLibrary/References/Webster-Dictionary/pictures/intaglio.rtf
./NextLibrary/References/Webster-Dictionary/pictures/intersection.rtf
./NextLibrary/References/Webster-Dictionary/pictures/jodhpur.rtf
./NextLibrary/References/Webster-Dictionary/pictures/karakul.rtf
./NextLibrary/References/Webster-Dictionary/pictures/kayak.rtf
./NextLibrary/References/Webster-Dictionary/pictures/kimono.rtf
./NextLibrary/References/Webster-Dictionary/pictures/kiwi.rtf
./NextLibrary/References/Webster-Dictionary/pictures/leopard.rtf
./NextLibrary/References/Webster-Dictionary/pictures/lichen.rtf
./NextLibrary/References/Webster-Dictionary/pictures/limpet.rtf
./NextLibrary/References/Webster-Dictionary/pictures/loris.rtf
./NextLibrary/References/Webster-Dictionary/pictures/maltese.rtf
./NextLibrary/References/Webster-Dictionary/pictures/geologictime.eps
./NextLibrary/References/Webster-Dictionary/pictures/abscissa.eps
./NextLibrary/References/Webster-Dictionary/pictures/alphabet.eps
./NextLibrary/References/Webster-Dictionary/pictures/element.eps
./NextLibrary/References/Webster-Dictionary/pictures/numbers.eps
./NextLibrary/References/Webster-Dictionary/pictures/proofread.eps
./NextLibrary/References/Webster-Dictionary/pictures/indoeuropeanlanguages.eps
./NextLibrary/References/Webster-Dictionary/pictures/money.eps
./NextLibrary/References/Webster-Dictionary/pictures/month.eps
./NextLibrary/References/Webster-Dictionary/pictures/taylorsseries.eps
./NextLibrary/References/Webster-Dictionary/pictures/weight.eps
./NextLibrary/References/Webster-Dictionary/source
./NextLibrary/References/Webster-Dictionary/tiff
./NextLibrary/References/Webster-Dictionary/tiff/dictionary.tiff
./NextLibrary/References/Webster-Dictionary/tiff/thesaurus.tiff
./NextLibrary/References/Webster-Dictionary/tiff/diamondl.tiff
./NextLibrary/References/Webster-Dictionary/tiff/diamondr.tiff
./NextLibrary/References/Webster-Dictionary/tiff/find.tiff
./NextLibrary/References/Webster-Dictionary/tiff/findH.tiff
./NextLibrary/References/Webster-Dictionary/tiff/thesaurusH.tiff
./NextLibrary/References/Webster-Dictionary/tiff/dictionaryH.tiff
./NextLibrary/References/Webster-Dictionary/tiff/nob.tiff
./NextLibrary/References/Webster-Dictionary/tiff/nobH.tiff
./NextLibrary/References/Webster-Dictionary/tiff/stop.tiff
./NextLibrary/References/Webster-Dictionary/tiff/define.tiff
./NextLibrary/References/Webster-Dictionary/tiff/defineH.tiff
./NextLibrary/References/Webster-Dictionary/tiff/.places
./NextLibrary/References/Webster-Dictionary/.places
./NextLibrary/References/Webster-Thesaurus
./NextLibrary/References/Webster-Thesaurus/index
```

```
./NextLibrary/References/Webster-Thesaurus/source
./NextLibrary/References/Webster-Thesaurus/.places
./NextLibrary/References/README
./NextLibrary/Fonts
./NextLibrary/Fonts/outline
./NextLibrary/Fonts/outline/Courier
./NextLibrary/Fonts/outline/Courier-Bold
./NextLibrary/Fonts/outline/Courier-BoldOblique
./NextLibrary/Fonts/outline/Courier-Oblique
./NextLibrary/Fonts/outline/Helvetica
./NextLibrary/Fonts/outline/Helvetica-Bold
./NextLibrary/Fonts/outline/Helvetica-BoldOblique
./NextLibrary/Fonts/outline/Helvetica-Oblique
./NextLibrary/Fonts/outline/Lexi
./NextLibrary/Fonts/outline/Ohlfs
./NextLibrary/Fonts/outline/Symbol
./NextLibrary/Fonts/outline/Times-Bold
./NextLibrary/Fonts/outline/Times-BoldItalic
./NextLibrary/Fonts/outline/Times-Italic
./NextLibrary/Fonts/outline/Times-Roman
./NextLibrary/Fonts/outline/.places
./NextLibrary/Fonts/bitmap
./NextLibrary/Fonts/bitmap/Courier-Bold.bepf
./NextLibrary/Fonts/bitmap/Courier-BoldOblique.bepf
./NextLibrary/Fonts/bitmap/Courier-Oblique.bepf
./NextLibrary/Fonts/bitmap/Courier.bepf
./NextLibrary/Fonts/bitmap/Helvetica-Bold.bepf
./NextLibrary/Fonts/bitmap/Helvetica-BoldOblique.bepf
./NextLibrary/Fonts/bitmap/Helvetica-Oblique.bepf
./NextLibrary/Fonts/bitmap/Helvetica.bepf
./NextLibrary/Fonts/bitmap/Lexi.bepf
./NextLibrary/Fonts/bitmap/Ohlfs.bepf
./NextLibrary/Fonts/bitmap/Symbol.bepf
./NextLibrary/Fonts/bitmap/Times-Bold.bepf
./NextLibrary/Fonts/bitmap/Times-BoldItalic.bepf
./NextLibrary/Fonts/bitmap/Times-Italic.bepf
./NextLibrary/Fonts/bitmap/Times-Roman.bepf
./NextLibrary/Fonts/bitmap/.places
./NextLibrary/Fonts/afm
./NextLibrary/Fonts/afm/Courier-Bold.afm
./NextLibrary/Fonts/afm/Courier-BoldOblique.afm
./NextLibrary/Fonts/afm/Courier-Oblique.afm
./NextLibrary/Fonts/afm/Courier.afm
./NextLibrary/Fonts/afm/Helvetica-Bold.afm
./NextLibrary/Fonts/afm/Helvetica-BoldOblique.afm
./NextLibrary/Fonts/afm/Helvetica-Oblique.afm
./NextLibrary/Fonts/afm/Helvetica.afm
./NextLibrary/Fonts/afm/Lexi.afm
./NextLibrary/Fonts/afm/Ohlfs.afm
./NextLibrary/Fonts/afm/Symbol.afm
./NextLibrary/Fonts/afm/Times-Bold.afm
```

```
./NextLibrary/Fonts/afm/Times-BoldItalic.afm
./NextLibrary/Fonts/afm/Times-Italic.afm
./NextLibrary/Fonts/afm/Times-Roman.afm
./NextLibrary/Fonts/afm/Screen-Courier-Bold.10.afm
./NextLibrary/Fonts/afm/Screen-Courier-Bold.12.afm
./NextLibrary/Fonts/afm/Screen-Courier-Bold.14.afm
./NextLibrary/Fonts/afm/Screen-Courier-Bold.18.afm
./NextLibrary/Fonts/afm/Screen-Courier-Bold.24.afm
./NextLibrary/Fonts/afm/Screen-Courier-BoldOblique.10.afm
./NextLibrary/Fonts/afm/Screen-Courier-BoldOblique.12.afm
./NextLibrary/Fonts/afm/Screen-Courier-BoldOblique.14.afm
./NextLibrary/Fonts/afm/Screen-Courier-BoldOblique.18.afm
./NextLibrary/Fonts/afm/Screen-Courier-BoldOblique.24.afm
./NextLibrary/Fonts/afm/Screen-Courier-Oblique.10.afm
./NextLibrary/Fonts/afm/Screen-Courier-Oblique.12.afm
./NextLibrary/Fonts/afm/Screen-Courier-Oblique.14.afm
./NextLibrary/Fonts/afm/Screen-Courier-Oblique.18.afm
./NextLibrary/Fonts/afm/Screen-Courier-Oblique.24.afm
./NextLibrary/Fonts/afm/Screen-Courier.10.afm
./NextLibrary/Fonts/afm/Screen-Courier.12.afm
./NextLibrary/Fonts/afm/Screen-Courier.14.afm
./NextLibrary/Fonts/afm/Screen-Courier.18.afm
./NextLibrary/Fonts/afm/Screen-Courier.24.afm
./NextLibrary/Fonts/afm/Screen-Helvetica-Bold.10.afm
./NextLibrary/Fonts/afm/Screen-Helvetica-Bold.12.afm
./NextLibrary/Fonts/afm/Screen-Helvetica-Bold.14.afm
./NextLibrary/Fonts/afm/Screen-Helvetica-Bold.18.afm
./NextLibrary/Fonts/afm/Screen-Helvetica-Bold.24.afm
./NextLibrary/Fonts/afm/Screen-Helvetica-Bold.8.afm
./NextLibrary/Fonts/afm/Screen-Helvetica-BoldOblique.10.afm
./NextLibrary/Fonts/afm/Screen-Helvetica-BoldOblique.12.afm
./NextLibrary/Fonts/afm/Screen-Helvetica-BoldOblique.14.afm
./NextLibrary/Fonts/afm/Screen-Helvetica-BoldOblique.18.afm
./NextLibrary/Fonts/afm/Screen-Helvetica-BoldOblique.24.afm
./NextLibrary/Fonts/afm/Screen-Helvetica-BoldOblique.8.afm
./NextLibrary/Fonts/afm/Screen-Helvetica-Oblique.10.afm
./NextLibrary/Fonts/afm/Screen-Helvetica-Oblique.12.afm
./NextLibrary/Fonts/afm/Screen-Helvetica-Oblique.14.afm
./NextLibrary/Fonts/afm/Screen-Helvetica-Oblique.18.afm
./NextLibrary/Fonts/afm/Screen-Helvetica-Oblique.24.afm
./NextLibrary/Fonts/afm/Screen-Helvetica-Oblique.8.afm
./NextLibrary/Fonts/afm/Screen-Helvetica.10.afm
./NextLibrary/Fonts/afm/Screen-Helvetica.12.afm
./NextLibrary/Fonts/afm/Screen-Helvetica.14.afm
./NextLibrary/Fonts/afm/Screen-Lexi.10.afm
./NextLibrary/Fonts/afm/Screen-Helvetica.18.afm
./NextLibrary/Fonts/afm/Screen-Helvetica.24.afm
./NextLibrary/Fonts/afm/Screen-Helvetica.7.afm
./NextLibrary/Fonts/afm/Screen-Helvetica.8.afm
./NextLibrary/Fonts/afm/Screen-Helvetica.9.afm
./NextLibrary/Fonts/afm/Screen-Lexi.12.afm
```

```
./NextLibrary/Fonts/afm/Screen-Lexi.14.afm
./NextLibrary/Fonts/afm/Screen-Lexi.18.afm
./NextLibrary/Fonts/afm/Screen-Lexi.24.afm
./NextLibrary/Fonts/afm/Screen-Ohlfs.10.afm
./NextLibrary/Fonts/afm/Screen-Ohlfs.12.afm
./NextLibrary/Fonts/afm/Screen-Ohlfs.16.afm
./NextLibrary/Fonts/afm/Screen-Ohlfs.24.afm
./NextLibrary/Fonts/afm/Screen-Ohlfs.9.afm
./NextLibrary/Fonts/afm/Screen-Symbol.10.afm
./NextLibrary/Fonts/afm/Screen-Symbol.12.afm
./NextLibrary/Fonts/afm/Screen-Symbol.14.afm
./NextLibrary/Fonts/afm/Screen-Symbol.18.afm
./NextLibrary/Fonts/afm/Screen-Symbol.24.afm
./NextLibrary/Fonts/afm/Screen-Times-Bold.10.afm
./NextLibrary/Fonts/afm/Screen-Times-Bold.12.afm
./NextLibrary/Fonts/afm/Screen-Times-Bold.14.afm
./NextLibrary/Fonts/afm/Screen-Times-Bold.18.afm
./NextLibrary/Fonts/afm/Screen-Times-Bold.24.afm
./NextLibrary/Fonts/afm/Screen-Times-BoldItalic.10.afm
./NextLibrary/Fonts/afm/Screen-Times-BoldItalic.12.afm
./NextLibrary/Fonts/afm/Screen-Times-BoldItalic.14.afm
./NextLibrary/Fonts/afm/Screen-Times-BoldItalic.18.afm
./NextLibrary/Fonts/afm/Screen-Times-BoldItalic.24.afm
./NextLibrary/Fonts/afm/Screen-Times-Italic.10.afm
./NextLibrary/Fonts/afm/Screen-Times-Italic.12.afm
./NextLibrary/Fonts/afm/Screen-Times-Italic.14.afm
./NextLibrary/Fonts/afm/Screen-Times-Italic.18.afm
./NextLibrary/Fonts/afm/Screen-Times-Italic.24.afm
./NextLibrary/Fonts/afm/Screen-Times-Roman.10.afm
./NextLibrary/Fonts/afm/Screen-Times-Roman.12.afm
./NextLibrary/Fonts/afm/Screen-Times-Roman.14.afm
./NextLibrary/Fonts/afm/Screen-Times-Roman.18.afm
./NextLibrary/Fonts/afm/Screen-Times-Roman.24.afm
./NextLibrary/Fonts/afm/Screen-Times-Roman.7.afm
./NextLibrary/Fonts/afm/Screen-Times-Roman.9.afm
./NextLibrary/Fonts/afm/.places
./NextLibrary/Fonts/.fontdirectory
./NextLibrary/Fonts/.places
./NextLibrary/Images
./NextLibrary/Images/Scene_movies
./NextLibrary/Images/Scene_movies/.list
./NextLibrary/Images/Scene_movies/snake.movie
./NextLibrary/Images/Scene_movies/snake.movie/snake.script.ps
./NextLibrary/Images/Scene_movies/snake.movie/.list
./NextLibrary/Images/Scene_movies/snake.movie/.places
./NextLibrary/Images/Scene_movies/.places
./NextLibrary/Images/Scene_movies/spotlight.movie
./NextLibrary/Images/Scene_movies/spotlight.movie/spotlight.script.ps
./NextLibrary/Images/Scene_movies/spotlight.movie/.places
./NextLibrary/Images/Scene_movies/NeXT.movie
./NextLibrary/Images/Scene_movies/NeXT.movie/.list

./NextLibrary/Images/Scene_movies/NeXT.movie/.places
./NextLibrary/Images/Scene_movies/NeXT.movie/NeXT.script.ps
./NextLibrary/Images/Scene_movies/clouds.movie
./NextLibrary/Images/Scene_movies/clouds.movie/clouds.script.ps
./NextLibrary/Images/Scene_movies/clouds.movie/.list
./NextLibrary/Images/Scene_movies/clouds.movie/transparentnext.ps
./NextLibrary/Images/Scene_movies/clouds.movie/nextsky1.ps
./NextLibrary/Images/Scene_movies/clouds.movie/nextsky2.ps
./NextLibrary/Images/Scene_movies/clouds.movie/.places
./NextLibrary/Images/Scene_movies/eagle.movie
./NextLibrary/Images/Scene_movies/eagle.movie/eagle.script.ps
./NextLibrary/Images/Scene_movies/eagle.movie/.list
./NextLibrary/Images/Scene_movies/eagle.movie/birds.ps
./NextLibrary/Images/Scene_movies/eagle.movie/.places
./NextLibrary/Images/Scene_movies/hostspin.movie
./NextLibrary/Images/Scene_movies/hostspin.movie/hostspin.script.ps
./NextLibrary/Images/Scene_movies/hostspin.movie/.list
./NextLibrary/Images/Scene_movies/hostspin.movie/.places
./NextLibrary/Images/Scene_movies/lines.movie
./NextLibrary/Images/Scene_movies/lines.movie/lines.script.ps
./NextLibrary/Images/Scene_movies/lines.movie/.places
./NextLibrary/Images/Scene_movies/lines.movie/.list
./NextLibrary/Images/Scene_movies/star.movie
./NextLibrary/Images/Scene_movies/star.movie/star.script.ps
./NextLibrary/Images/Scene_movies/star.movie/.places
./NextLibrary/Images/Scene_movies/fish.movie
./NextLibrary/Images/Scene_movies/fish.movie/fish.script.ps
./NextLibrary/Images/Scene_movies/fish.movie/TheFish.eps
./NextLibrary/Images/Scene_movies/fish.movie/TheFish2.eps
./NextLibrary/Images/Scene_movies/fish.movie/TheFish2A.eps
./NextLibrary/Images/Scene_movies/fish.movie/TheFish3.eps
./NextLibrary/Images/Scene_movies/fish.movie/TheFish4.eps
./NextLibrary/Images/Scene_movies/fish.movie/TheFishFront.eps
./NextLibrary/Images/Scene_movies/fish.movie/TheFishRight.eps
./NextLibrary/Images/Scene_movies/fish.movie/TheFishRight2.eps
./NextLibrary/Images/Scene_movies/fish.movie/TheFishRight2A.eps
./NextLibrary/Images/Scene_movies/fish.movie/TheFishRight3.eps
./NextLibrary/Images/Scene_movies/fish.movie/TheFishRight4.eps
./NextLibrary/Images/Scene_movies/fish.movie/LoadBkgrnd
./NextLibrary/Images/Scene_movies/fish.movie/.list
./NextLibrary/Images/Scene_movies/fish.movie/.places
./NextLibrary/Images/Scene_movies/fish.movie/TheFishFrontLeft.eps
./NextLibrary/Images/Scene_movies/fish.movie/TheFishFrontRight.eps
./NextLibrary/Images/Scene_movies/hostfont.movie
./NextLibrary/Images/Scene_movies/hostfont.movie/.list
./NextLibrary/Images/Scene_movies/hostfont.movie/hostfont.script.ps
./NextLibrary/Images/Scene_movies/hostfont.movie/.places
./NextLibrary/Images/Scene_movies/holey.movie
./NextLibrary/Images/Scene_movies/holey.movie/guns.snd
./NextLibrary/Images/Scene_movies/holey.movie/.places
./NextLibrary/Images/Scene_movies/holey.movie/holey.script.ps
```

```
./NextLibrary/Images/Scene_movies/holey.movie/.list
./NextLibrary/Images/Scene_movies/bezier.movie
./NextLibrary/Images/Scene_movies/bezier.movie/bezier.script.ps
./NextLibrary/Images/Scene_movies/bezier.movie/.places
./NextLibrary/Images/Scene_movies/gravity.movie
./NextLibrary/Images/Scene_movies/gravity.movie/gravity.script.ps
./NextLibrary/Images/Scene_movies/gravity.movie/Bonk.snd
./NextLibrary/Images/Scene_movies/gravity.movie/.list
./NextLibrary/Images/Scene_movies/gravity.movie/.places
./NextLibrary/Images/Scene_movies/mosaic.movie
./NextLibrary/Images/Scene_movies/mosaic.movie/mosaic.script.ps
./NextLibrary/Images/Scene_movies/mosaic.movie/.places
./NextLibrary/Images/Scene_movies/NeXTshades.movie
./NextLibrary/Images/Scene_movies/NeXTshades.movie/.places
./NextLibrary/Images/Scene_movies/NeXTshades.movie/NeXTshades.script.ps
./NextLibrary/Images/Scene_movies/NeXTInc.movie
./NextLibrary/Images/Scene_movies/NeXTInc.movie/NeXTInc.script.ps
./NextLibrary/Images/Scene_movies/NeXTInc.movie/NeXTmovie1b.eps
./NextLibrary/Images/Scene_movies/NeXTInc.movie/NeXTmovie2b.eps
./NextLibrary/Images/Scene_movies/NeXTInc.movie/.places
./NextLibrary/Images/Scene_screens
./NextLibrary/Images/Scene_screens/.places
./NextLibrary/Images/Scene_screens/eye.tiff
./NextLibrary/Images/Scene_screens/.list
./NextLibrary/Images/Scene_screens/Marble1.tiff
./NextLibrary/Images/Scene_screens/LightMezzotint.tiff
./NextLibrary/Images/Scene_screens/Marble2.tiff
./NextLibrary/Images/Scene_screens/Marble3.tiff
./NextLibrary/Images/Scene_screens/eyeshadow.tiff
./NextLibrary/Images/Scene_screens/Oak.tiff
./NextLibrary/Images/Scene_screens/NeXT.eps
./NextLibrary/Images/Scene_screens/LightGranite.tiff
./NextLibrary/Images/Scene_screens/DarkGranite.tiff
./NextLibrary/Images/Scene_screens/DarkMezzotint.tiff
./NextLibrary/Images/.places
./NextLibrary/Music
./NextLibrary/Music/Scores
./NextLibrary/Music/Scores/Examp1.score
./NextLibrary/Music/Scores/Examp2.score
./NextLibrary/Music/Scores/Examp3.score
./NextLibrary/Music/Scores/Examp4.score
./NextLibrary/Music/Scores/Examp5.score
./NextLibrary/Music/Scores/Examp6.score
./NextLibrary/Music/Scores/Examp7.score
./NextLibrary/Music/Scores/Emma.score
./NextLibrary/Music/Scores/Gamelan.score
./NextLibrary/Music/Scores/Jungle.score
./NextLibrary/Music/Scores/Twilight.score
./NextLibrary/Music/Scores/Suntan.score
./NextLibrary/Music/Scores/BachFugue.score
./NextLibrary/Music/Scores/BeadGame.score
./NextLibrary/Music/Scores/Throb.score
./NextLibrary/Music/Scores/WTC1.score
./NextLibrary/Music/Scores/.places
./NextLibrary/Music/.places
./odmach
./sdmach
./vmunix
./me
./me/Apps
./me/Apps/README.wn
./me/Apps/.places
./me/.NeXT
./me/.NeXT/.dock
./me/.NeXT/.places
./me/.NeXT/.NeXTdefaults.D
./me/.NeXT/.NeXTdefaults.L
./me/.NeXT/.NeXTtrash
./me/.NeXT/.NeXTtrash/.places
./me/.NeXT/targets
./me/.NeXT/targets/targetFile
./me/.NeXT/targets/Targets1.0
./me/.NeXT/targets/.places
./me/Mailboxes
./me/Mailboxes/.places
./me/Mailboxes/Active.mbox
./me/Mailboxes/Active.mbox/mbox
./me/Mailboxes/Active.mbox/table_of_contents
./me/.cshrc
./me/.mailrc
./me/.logout
./me/.plan
./me/.profile
./me/.login
./me/.places
./me/.list
./LocalLibrary
./LocalLibrary/Images
./LocalLibrary/Images/People
./LocalLibrary/.places
./Mailboxes
./Mailboxes/Active.mbox
./Mailboxes/Active.mbox/mbox
./Mailboxes/Active.mbox/table_of_contents
./Mailboxes/Active.mbox/mbox~
./Mailboxes/Active.mbox/No_subject.attach
./Mailboxes/Active.mbox/No_subject.attach/index.rtf
./Mailboxes/Active.mbox/No_subject.attach/VoiceMail_root0.vox
./Mailboxes/.places
./.dataviz
./.userdict
./clients
./clients/lost+found
./clients/.placesA
```

# Appendix F

# Third-Party Products

*"There's nothing like eating hay when you're faint."..."I didn't say there was nothing better," the King replied, "I said there was nothing like it."*

— **LEWIS CARROLL**  1832–1898

*Greet the unseen with a cheer.*

— **ROBERT BROWNING**  1812–1889

This is an incomplete, frequently erroneous listing of products available for The NeXT Computer. It's incomplete because time marches on. The NeXT Computer is increasingly popular. Hardware and applications are appearing—if not daily or weekly, at least frequently.

It's erroneous because I haven't personally used (or even seen) many of these products. Some were mere prototypes when this listing was created. Others were only wishful thinking. I'll try to note which products were "real" as this list was compiled, but be warned.

Still, if you're interested, write directly to the companies below, or give them a call.

## Abaton

*Scan 300/GS*

The first scanner for NeXT. It's an 8-bit, flatbed scanner capable of 300 dpi resolution, and 256 levels of gray scale. Document to scan may be up to 8.5 by 14 inches. Scanned images are converted to TIFF files. Call for price and availability.

Abaton/Everex Systems, Inc.
Milmont Drive, Fremont, CA 94538
(415) 683-2226

## Absoft Corporation

*FORTRAN 77 Compiler*

This one is both real and shipping. It's an object-oriented version of the popular (at least in academic circles) FORTRAN language. Absoft has been in the FORTRAN compiler business a long time. It shows. Their compiler for NeXT is solid—a good piece of work. It's also fully object-oriented. What's more, the NeXT system lets you "mix and match" objects created in different languages. FORTRAN-made objects get along fine with objects created with NeXT's Objective-C development system.

*Figure F-1*

Includes many sample programs and professional, complete documentation. If you want a FORTRAN compiler, this is highly recommended. $950.

Absoft Corporation
Bond Street, Rochester Hills, MI 48309
(313) 853-0050, (313) 853-0108 fax

## Adamation, Inc.

### Who's Calling

A business-oriented application to keep track of phone calls and client information. It has four parts, according to the press release. A Client Database holds information used by the rest of the program. A Dialer makes calls and records call time, duration, and other comments. A Tickler tickles your memory (by voice) about calls to make. Finally, Reports generates call history, mailing labels, form letters, and other reports. Price to be determined.

Adamation, Inc.
1435 Center Street, Oakland, CA 94607
(415) 452-5252

## Adobe Systems, Inc.

### Adobe Ilustrator

Adobe, the provider of Display PostScript, will offer Adobe Illustrator: a popular drawing program. Versions of Illustrator are also available for Macintosh and IBM computers, but the NeXT version should shine. One reason to expect a killer version of Illustrator/NeXT is that, on other computers, Adobe implements a complete PostScript environment "beneath" Illustrator. So when you use Illustrator on Macintosh, for example, the application runs in its own Display PostScript-like world, forgoing the extensive Quickdraw calls available to Macintosh programs.

This is quite a low-level technical feat. To the user, it means that you can grab a piece of text and freely rotate it by hand—and the text moves as you move the mouse—quite a "gee whiz" feature. That's only one feature in this ultrasophisticated, bezier-curve-based drawing program. Next time you pick up the Sunday paper, turn to the want ads and check out the display advertisements for cars. Odds are, you'll see many detailed illustrations of cars. Odds are, most of the auto illustrations were drawn by hand, using Adobe Illustrator. Multi-Ad Services, the largest U.S. firm offering advertising art to newspapers, has an army of artists using Illustrator. They create most of the product illustrations you see in newspapers; everything from Pepsi cans to cornflakes boxes.

Needless to say, Illustrator is a powerful program, not for the casual user. The more artistic talent you bring to Illustrator, the more you'll get out of it. For less talented users, the program lets you "trace" over scanned images, then clean up your work with a variety of tools.

I hadn't yet seen the NeXT version of Illustrator as this description was written. I had talked with officials at Adobe, where much prideful effort was being expended on the NeXT version of Illustrator. Expect something wonderful.

### Adobe Type Library

Adobe has a font library of over 400 PostScript fonts, all of which should be available for NeXT. This is great, because the cube is shipped with only a few fonts (a Display PostScript computer shipped with only a few PostScript fonts! Shame, shame). Contact Adobe for information about what's available now, and pricing information.

Adobe Systems, Inc.
1585 Charleston Road, Mountain View, CA 94039
(415) 961-4400

## Ariel Corporation

### Ariel Digital Microphone, model DM-N

This is a high-tech, high-resolution microphone. A CD-quality analog-to-digital converter is built-in. The microphone can sample at rates from 5.5 kHz to 88.2 kHz, or use the 44.1-kHz digital-audio standard sampling rate. The numbers are great: dynamic range up to 92 decibels, and total harmonic distortion of less than 0.005%.

The microphone also has left and right jacks for connecting other input devices, including compact disk players, or laboratory or test equipment. It comes with a removable windscreen, 2.5 meters of cable, and a direct input cable. It works with all DSP software that makes use of the DSP port. It's available now. $595.

Ariel Corporation
433 River Road, Highland Park, NJ 08904
(201) 249-2900, (201) 249-2123 fax

## Cayman Systems, Inc.

### GatorBox

This is a gateway used to connect NeXT Ethernet networks and Apple LocalTalk networks. With GatorBox, you can share files between NeXTs and Macintoshes. You can also use Gatorbox to allow a cube to be used as a file server for Apple Localtalk networks. It's an odd idea, but it probably works well. Available now. Call for pricing.

Cayman Systems, Inc.
University Park at MIT
26 Landsdowne Street, Cambridge, MA 02139
(617) 494-1999, (616) 494-9270 fax

## Data Transforms, Inc.

### GEMS (Generalized Equilibrium Modeling System)

An application to model economic systems. Models may include information about primary resource extraction, manufacturing and conversion, market transactions, transportation, transmission, distribution, and consumption of goods and services. This is a port of an application already in use on other computers. Price unknown.

### InDia (Influence Diagram Processor)

An application that represents decision-making in graphic form. Problems may be broken down, it seems, into graphic "diagram nodes" which allow you to see the events and probabilities of...are you following this? Me neither. Sounds neat, though. Call or write for information.

Data Transforms, Inc.
616 Washington Street, Denver, CO 80203
(303) 832-1501

# DataViz, Inc.

## *MacLinkPlus/PC*

This product is now shipping. You may find it invaluable if you need to transfer files between the cube and other computers.

And that's what it does: makes it easy to transfer files. You can use a modem or the supplied cable. One end goes into the NeXT serial port; the other into a Macintosh, IBM PC, or Sun. The supplied software runs on the non-NeXT computer. You can transfer text, eps, TIFF, binary, RTF, or WriteNow/NeXT files.

Also included is software to translate WriteNow/NeXT files into these Macintosh file types:

* MacWrite, Microsoft Word, WriteNow/Macintosh, WordPerfect, or Microsoft Words WP.

You can also translate WriteNow/NeXT files to these IBM file types:

* DCA-RTF, MultiMate, OfficeWriter, text, WordPerfect, WordStart, WPS-Plus, and XYWrite II.

I used MacLinkPlus/PC to transfer over 27 megabytes of NeXT files to Macintosh. This entire book, in other words: WriteNow files, eps files, you name it. It worked great. Recommended. $199.

DataViz, Inc.
35 Corporate Drive, Trumbull, CT 06611
(203) 368-0030, (203) 268-4345 fax

# Dayna Communications, Inc.

## *DaynaFILE*

A rumored floppy disk drive is the subject here. Dayna was making no official announcements as this section was finalized. Let's note that making a floppy drive for the cube may be a deceptively simple task. Cheaper flopticals, on the face of it, seem like a better solution.

Dayna Communications, Inc.
50 South Main Street, Fifth Floor
Salt Lake City, UT 84144
(801) 531-0600

# Emerald City Software, Inc.

## *Displaytalk*

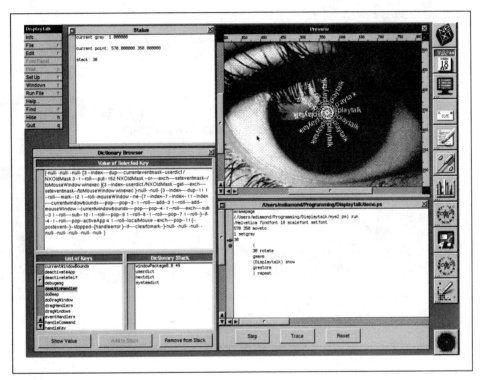

*Figure F-2*

Displaytalk takes the idea of on-screen PostScript "previewing" and turns it into a complete development environment for PostScript programming. The package allows interactive source-level debugging, a multiwindow display, PostScript dictionary browser, and more. If you're writing more than a smidgen of PostScript, this is a mandatory buy. $995.

## *Smart Art*

A truly nifty program to create truly nifty PostScript text.

With Smart Art, you modify text. Boy, can you modify text! Possible effects include:

*Figure F-3*

- faded text;
- text on an arc;
- rotated text;
- perspective text;
- drop shadow text;
- fitted text;
- fountain-filled text; and

about 40 other effects. Smart Art creates EPS files, which can be pasted into documents or saved to disk for use in other programs. Great for use with FrameMaker, Adobe Illustrator, or other NeXT programs. Super for brochures, fliers, and advertisements. $595.

Emerald City Software, Inc.
1040 Menlo Avenue, Suite 102, Menlo Park, CA 94025
(800) 223-0417, (415) 324-8080 (in California), (415) 324-0316 fax

## Extron Electronics

### RGB 66/33 Scan Converter

This is the first add-on hardware board to surface for NeXT. It allows you to send video from the NeXT to "medium resolution" monitors, including large-screen projectors. The board provides a 33-kHz horizontal scan frequency, the key to using lower-res displays. A good add-on for educational or trade-show uses. Should be available now; call for price.

### RGB 111 NeXT Computer Interface

Converts the NeXT video to red, green, blue, and composite sync output. Why? To use any of these monitors to display NeXT video: Contac 7550, Mitsubishi 6605 or 6905, and the Monitronix MX-210. Also provides video to these projectors: Barco Graphics Series, Electrohome Graphics, ESP ESPRIT 1000, and the Hitachi Graphics Projector. $370.

Extron Electronics
13554 Larwin Circle, Santa Fe Springs, CA 90670
(800) 633-9876 (outside California), (213) 802-8804, (213) 802-2741 fax

## Farallon Computing, Inc.

### Ethernet PhoneNET, Sound, and Interpersonal Communications

Farallon made a splash in the Apple market by offering LocalTalk networks using phone cords. Phone cords are cheap. Did it work? You bet. We use PhoneNET at my office; like the best networking products, you don't even know it's there. It just works. Is it real or is it Memorex? That kind of thing.

Farallon hopes to duplicate their success with NeXT products. If they do, you'll be able to use inexpensive "twisted-pair" phone cords to connect cubes, and connect with LocalTalk networks. Keep your fingers crossed. Farallon also markets sound and network communications software for Macintosh. Those applications (or offshoots) may migrate over to NeXT. Call for more information.

Farallon Computing, Inc.
2201 Dwight Way, Berkeley, CA 94704
(415) 849-2331, (415) 841-5770 fax

# Frame Technology Corporation

*FrameMaker 2.0*

Ah, FrameMaker. The jewel of desktop publishing software. FrameMaker is what Aldus PageMaker and Quark Express may be when they grow up. NeXT has anointed FrameMaker as their "desktop publishing solution."

FrameMaker isn't a new, "maybe it's good, maybe it isn't" program. It's a standard on workstations. It's used everyday, on a variety of computers, for everything from designing business cards, to complete layout of complex books. The NeXT version of FrameMaker is only FrameMaker in a new guise. It's a versatile, proven program. If time permitted, and my skills were adequate, I would have loved to have produced this book using FrameMaker. Maybe next time.

If you're familiar with any other desktop publishing software, you'll be right at home in FrameMaker. The program combines the best features of other DTP programs, adds a slew of additional features, and throws in all the features of complete object-oriented drawing programs for good measure. It's all here: word processing, style sheets, hyphenation, spelling, baseline synchronization, text flow around graphics, drawing, index generation, easy inclusion of mathematical equations, and the features just go on and on.

Thankfully, the interface is done well. Commands are well-grouped. Actions are intuitive and consistent. Again, the feeling is similar to other well-crafted DTP programs; there's just "more of everything." The "Intermission" section of this book shows off a bit of FrameMaker's stuff.

Price: $995 (from BusinessLand; educational institutions offer the program for $495).

Frame Technology Corporation
1010 Rincon Circle, San Jose, CA 95134
(408) 433-3311, (408) 433-1928 fax

# Informix Software, Inc.

*Wingz*

This is it: The Spreadsheet for NeXT.

Wingz is a power spreadsheet that's giving Microsoft Excel a run for the money on Macintosh. A version for MS-DOS machines is also in development. The glamour team at Informix, however, gets to work on the NeXT version.

Wingz for NeXT should be similar to Macintosh Wingz: big (32,768 rows and 32,768 columns), fast, and bursting with knockout graphing options. Wingz also boasts a HyperScript language for creating macros or other Wingz-based concoctions. Price and availability not known.

Wingz Brand Marketing
Informix Software, Inc., 16011 College Boulevard
Lenexa, KA 66219
(913) 599-7100, (913) 599-7350 fax

## Kinetics

### Etherport NL

Allows the NeXT to be connected to standard or twisted-pair Ethernet networks. Supports TCP/IP and other network protocols. Comes with 32K of memory and a built-in LattisNet transceiver. Available fourth quarter of 1989. Price not available.

Kinetics, a division of Excelan, Inc.
1340 Trept Blvd, Walnut Creek, CA 94596
(415) 947-0998

## Knowledgeset Corporation

### Knowledge Retrieval System (KRS)

The Knowledge Retrieval System is used to search and retrieve information from extremely large text databases.

The KRS system is pricey, but good. It's the brainchild of Gary Kindall, creator of the CP/M operating system. It's also available for DOS, UNIX, and Macintosh computers. For other computers, this much searching power is overkill—this product has been "ahead" of most hardware for some time. With NeXT, KRS makes perfect sense: You can use it to perform sophisticated searches within megabytes and megabytes of information.

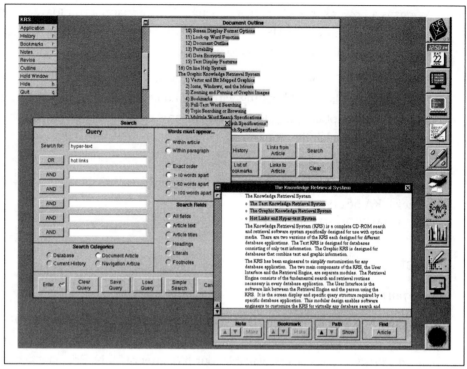

*Figure F-4*

Knowledgeset Corporation
888 Villa Street, Suite 500, Mountain View, CA 94041
(415) 968-9888

## Lotus Development Corporation

Lotus promised something big for Macintosh. Apple touted Lotus during Macintosh's introduction. What finally appeared was Jazz: a flawed program that was trammeled (somewhat unjustly) by the Macintosh community. Jazz was a flop and Microsoft walked away with the Macintosh software market.

This time, Microsoft isn't an initial player. And once again, something big is promised from Lotus. This time, they may deliver. Lotus—and NeXT, in the form of Steve Jobs—are taking pains to deliver a big product, and do it right. What we may see from Lotus is a next-generation spreadsheet (or is that a "NeXT generation spreadsheet"?).

Lotus Development Corporation
55 Cambridge Parkway, Cambridge, MA 02142
(617) 577-8500

# Media Logic, Inc.

*Artisan*

*TopDraw*

Two megafeature, complementary programs.

*Artisan 3.0*

A grayscale image manipulation program with complete touch-up and image processing features. Artisan imports and exports 1-, 2-, or 8-bit TIFF files, and also, optionally, exports EPS files. It supports popular scanners. Features include:

- match shade from within existing shade;
- user-definable brush shapes;
- adjustable "paint flow";
- paint with variable-level opacity;
- invert, blur, sharpen, or otherwise adjust image contrast; and
- user-editable image correction maps.

And more.

*TopDraw*

From slickly done press releases, TopDraw looks to be a megafeature, object-based drawing program with a raft of text processing features, and the ability to edit grayscale images.

If FrameMaker is a sophisticated page-layout program with advanced drawing features (which it is), then TopDraw seems to be a sophisticated drawing program with advanced page-layout features. The press material takes some pains to convince readers that TopDraw "is an excellent companion" to FrameMaker.

That may be. The drawing features do seem to go on and on:

- autotrace of bitmaps;
- rotate, scale, reflect, and skew for objects or groups of objects;
- gradient object fill;

- image cropping;
- adjustable image contrast and brightness;
- "spline editing," including moving, adding, or removing points, and adjusting tangents;
- use of text as a masking boundary;

and more and more and more.

The feature list (above is just a fraction) is massive, but software like this, especially on a new platform such as NeXT's, is difficult to deliver. Media Logic mentions that a demonstration disk (with all features enabled except "Save") is available. That's probably your best starting point, if the price is reasonable.

Artisan and TopDraw are priced identically. For either program:

Single-user license, documentation, and optical: $595.

Single-user license, documentation, no optical: $495.

Additional single-user license, no documentation: $395.

Documentation only: $75.

Media Logic, Inc.
2501 Colorado Avenue, Suite 350, Santa Monica, CA 90404
(213) 453-7744, 453-9565 fax

## Metaresearch, Inc.

### Digital Ears

An all-around wonderful product. Metaresearch is staking out NeXT sound as their territory. And doing a good job of it. Their Digital Ears product combines a CD-quality audio digitizer with all the software you need to capture, then edit sounds. The digitizer is first-rate: small, capable, rugged, and easy-to-use. The software is just fine. These people both know and love this computer, and it shows. If you're a developer or a sound enthusiast, get it. $795.

### Digital Eye

This is a video frame grabber. Use it to capture still frames, or sequences of frames, from video cameras, laserdisk players, the NTSC video sources. Maximum resolution is 640 by 480 pixels, with a maximum 256 shades of gray. Lower resolutions and/or fewer gray shades make for smaller files.

This is a hardware/software combination. The software lets you grab or preview images, save images in EPS or TIFF format, and perform "basic image manipulation." $975.

Metaresearch, Inc.
516 SE Morrison, Suite M-1, Portland, OR 97214
(503) 238-5728, (503) 294-1409 fax

## Microstat Development Corporation

### OMEN III

A sophisticated stock quotation application for stockbrokers and serious investors. Features: stock quotes, limit alarms, charting (with real-time updating, if you wish), statistical reports, real-time tickers, access to Dow Jones News Service, automated order entry and client management, and many, many more features. This looks to be one of those applications you change careers for—just to get your hands on it. Available first quarter of 1990.

Microstat Development Corporation
2150 Western Parkway, Vancouver, BC V6T 1V6
(604) 228-1612

## Motorola, Inc.

### DSP56000 Family Simulator Program (SIM56000)

### DSP96000 Family Simulator Program (SIM96000)

The simulator programs are useful aids during development of DSP programs. Both exactly model all functions of the respective DSP chips. Available now.

Motorola, Inc.
Digital Signal Processors
6501 William Cannon Drive West, Austin, TX 78735-8598
(512) 891-2030

## Neuron Data

### NEXPERT

This is a pricey expert system which first appeared on Macintosh. It consists of an expert system development environment, and a "run-time" system for delivering completed expert systems. The run-time system has been ported to NeXT, so developers can create expert systems on other computers, then "deliver" them on NeXT to users. It's not known if Neuron Data will also port the development environment to NeXT. Call and ask.

> Neuron Data
> 444 High Street, Palo Alto, CA 94301
> (415) 321-4488, 321-3728 fax

## Personal Computer Peripherals Corporation

### JETSTREAM Tape Backup System

Personal Computer Peripherals Corporation first surfaced with a hard disk, MacBottom, for Macintosh. It was a good hard disk. The company has since broadened their product line to include other hard disk drives, color and grayscale monitors, even an "Optical Erasable Removable Drive." The optical drive looks good, but you won't need it. (I wonder what the price is?)

The JetStream tape backup unit is the same unit offered for other computers—though the firm says they'll probably offer it in black for NeXT. It can back up 2.3 gigabytes of information, using widely available, inexpensive 8-mm videotape cartridges. The unit boasts backup speeds of 14.4 megabytes per minute and unattended network backup, when used with PCPC's "NetStreamTM" software. Price unavailable.

> Personal Computer Peripherals Corporation
> Eisenhower Boulevard, Building A4, Tampa, FL 33634
> (813) 884-3092

## T/Maker Company

*ClickArt EPS Business Art/EPS Illustrations*

A disk of 400 EPS images: computers, desk items, people, symbols, sports, corporation icons, borders, bullets, globes, maps, and more. $295, introductory price.

T/Maker Company
1390 Villa Street, Mountain View, CA 94041
(415) 962-0195

## White Pine Software, Inc.

*DEC terminal emulation software*

White Pine is well-known for software to emulate DEC terminals, including the popular DEC VT-100.

But doesn't Terminal, bundled with NeXT, emulate a DEC VT-100? Yes, but White Pine software does it better. Call or write for information.

White Pine Software, Inc.
94 Route 101A, P.O. Box 1108, Amherst, NH 03031
(603) 886-9050

## Copy Protection

Copy protection is universally despised by users. Once common for IBM and Apple applications, it's now rare, thanks to incessant blasts from the Computer Journalism Establishment. For software developers, copy protecting applications results in an invitation to a lynching: their own.

These days, copy protection is mainly confined to game software. The computing populace puts up with this, maybe because of an unspoken feeling that "kids will pirate software if they have the chance."

But copy protection may return from the grave (a moldy hand thrusts through the dirt...) to grace NeXT software applications.

Why? A few reasons. First, the NeXT market is small. Developers need every buck they can get. It's not greed, it's survival.

And NeXT applications might—*might*—be pirated more often.

Why would users pirate NeXT applications more frequently than they'd pirate applications for other computers? Simple. Most cubes will be networked. On a network, other users file systems show up on your display, just like your own files do. It's an invitation to rip-off software. The act of theft takes one little mouse drag. Imagine wandering through a deserted Saks Fifth Avenue...not that you or I would ever pirate software, of course.

For standalone computers, copy protection is usually put in place by software duplicators. It costs extra, it often limits the software's utility, and it's often incompatible with new system releases.

For networked NeXT's, however, implementing copy protection is easy. Every cube has a unique Ethernet address. That address can be read by applications. Once known, applications can check it each time they're run. No tickee, no washee. Developers might also implement some method of "de-installing and re-installing"so users can move applications between cubes, yet only use the software on one cube at a time.

Is this good? I don't mind. If the application isn't otherwise compromised, why not? I'd rather that developers live and prosper. Less piracy might also mean lower prices.

At any rate, don't be surprised to see "Ethernet copy protection schemes"for cubes. And give it some thought before complaining.

# Appendix G

# Further Reading

*A man ought to read just as inclination leads him; for what he reads as a task will do him little good.*

— **SAMUEL JOHNSON** 1709–1784

## NeXT

Webster, Bruce F., *The NeXT Book*. Reading, MA: Addison-Wesley Publishing Company, 1989.

Oh, buy it. It's good, comprehensive, and well-written. A wealth of solid information about The NeXT Computer. Many facts, well organized.

## UNIX

Libes, Don, and Ressler, Sandy, *Life with UNIX: A Guide for Everyone*. Englewood Cliffs, NJ: Prentice Hall, 1989.

If you only buy one UNIX book, buy this. It's fun, useful, fun, fascinating, and fun. UNIX is a universe of people and things. This book touches on everything. Read it and you'll never be cowed by UNIX again. You still may not *understand* UNIX, but you won't be cowed by it. You might even like UNIX. Also includes the best-ever, appropriately irreverent guide to all other UNIX books.

Sobel, Mark G., *A Practical Guide to the UNIX System*. Redwood City, CA: The Benjamin/Cummings Publishing Company, Inc. 1989.

A good, workmanlike effort. Well organized (UNIX books typically are), with many examples.

Kernighan, Brian W., and Pike, Rob, *The UNIX Programming Environment*. Englewood Cliffs, NJ: Prentice Hall, 1984.

The creators of C and UNIX, here showing you how to program UNIX. Obviously the definitive work. Well written, but moves at breakneck speed. Not for beginners or the faint-hearted. Still, who you gonna call?

Kochan, Stephen G., and Wood, Patrick H. *UNIX Shell Programming*. Indianapolis, IN: Howard W. Sams & Company / Hayden Books, 1985.

When I bought *UNIX Shell Programming* last fall, it was in its eighth printing.

The reason for its popularity is clear: *UNIX Shell Programming* is an "easy does it" guide to using the Shell that doesn't presume much, advances at a gentle pace, and offers example after example after example. It was just my speed. I found the book listed above—*The UNIX Programming Environment*—to be too much, too fast. This one was just right. Highly recommended.

The book is also a good example of how to typeset a book using a laser printer, and still have it look good. The key: lots of white space.

Bourne, S.R., *The UNIX System V Environment*. Reading, MA: Addison-Wesley Publishing Company, 1987.

Stephen Bourne is the author of "The Bourne Shell" for UNIX and thus eminently qualified to write about UNIX. His book, while not specific to the version of UNIX used by NeXT, is a clear, detailed explanation of UNIX. A good reference.

Bach, Maurice J., *The Design of the UNIX Operating System*. Englewood Cliffs, NJ: Prentice Hall, 1986.

The title says it all. A respected UNIX book.

*The Nutshell Handbooks*

This is an engaging line of small books about UNIX. They're published by a consulting company specializing in technical documentation and training. I suspect they'll soon specialize in publishing UNIX books.

These are modest productions: small in format, ring-bound, typeset on laser printers. For all that, they're well-done, and filled with detailed information about using UNIX. Not *about* UNIX, about *using* UNIX. Lots of real-life examples, including "what if it doesn't work?" discussions. The current Nutshell Handbooks are:

*Learning the UNIX Operating System* (75 pp.)
*Learning the VI Editor* (131 pp.)
*Termcap and Terminfo* (approx. 170 pp.)
*Programming with Curses* (71 pp.)
*Managing UUCP and Usenet* ( 242 ppp.)
*Using UUCP and Usenet* (185 pp.)
*Managing Projects with Make* (77 pp.)
*DOS Meets UNIX* (134 pp.)
*UNIX in a Nutshell, System V Edition* (270 pp.)
*UNIX in a Nutshell, Berkeley Edition* (284 pp.)
*UNIX Text Processing* (665 pp.)
*X Windows Programming Manual* (2 vol-750 pp.)

For pricing, more information, or to order, call (800) 338-NUTS. In Massachusetts: (617) 527-1392. E-mail: uunet!ora!nuts. Snail-mail: O'Reilly & Associates, Inc., 981 Chestnut Street, Newton, MA 02164.

## Mathematica

Wolfram, Stephen, *Mathematica: A System for Doing Mathematics by Computers.* Reading, MA: Addison-Wesley Publishing Company, 1988.

Buy it and read it before using Mathematica. It's a tremendous book: comprehensive, browsy, interesting. The screen illustrations are taken from Macintosh, but we can overlook that.

If you can't find *Mathematica* at your local bookstore, check at a university bookstore. Mathematica has taken academia by storm; the book is a campus bookstore fixture. For some reason, you'll often find this book shrink-wrapped, despite the fact that it contains not a single naked human. Maybe it's all those revealing graphics.

## Networking

Comer, Douglas, *Internetworking with TCP/IP; Principles, Protocols, and Architecture.* Englewood Cliffs, NJ: Prentice Hall, 1988.

I looked high and low for a good book on networking. This is it. Internet and networking are fascinating, complex subjects. Comer gives them their due, and more. After finishing (or even skimming) this book, you'll know where all this networking stuff came from, how it works, and why. Unless you're interested in designing networks, parts of the book will be more technical than you'd prefer. Still, recommended as a thorough networking overview and, considering the subject matter, a good read.

Hassig, Lee, and Kelly, Susan V., Editors, *Understanding Computers: Communications.* Alexandria, VA: Time-Life Books Inc., 1986.

Time-Life is releasing a series of computer books. This volume covers telephones, networks, modems...the gamut of modern electronic communications. I hesitated to pick this up. After all, it's for a general audience. It wouldn't have anything for me, Mr. Computer Expert.

Wrooong. Like most Time-Life books, this is full of good prose and beautiful, informative illustrations. I learned a lot, and enjoyed every minute of it. In particular, the superb illustrations that detail network protocols and packet switching are great. Graphics truly help convey this complex information. Highly recommended. If this book is indicative of the series, it's a tremendous series.

## Programming | NeXT

Not much yet. Addison-Wesley has announced *Scientific Applications for the NeXT Computer,* by Richard Crandall and Marianne Colgrove, which may be out soon. Crandall contributed some of the sample programs shipped with NeXT. He knows what he's doing. Expect a good book.

## Programming | General

Burge, W. H., *Recursive Programming Techniques.* Reading, MA: Addison-Wesley Publishing Company, 1975.

Good reading for anyone interested in programming. The techniques are applicable to all high-level languages.

Aho, A. V., and Ullman, J. D., *Principles of Compiler Design.* Reading, MA: Addison-Wesley Publishing Company, 1977.

Want to write your own language compiler? This is the standard text. If you're interested in computer languages, this is worth browsing in. Good programmers don't just know their languages; they know their compilers. This shows how it's done.

Knuth, Donald E., *The Art of Computer Programming, Volume 1, Fundamental Algorithms*. Reading, MA: Addison-Wesley Publishing Company, 1968.

————, *The Art of Computer Programming, Volume 2, Sorting and Searching*. Reading, MA: Addison-Wesley Publishing Company, 1975.

————, *The Art of Computer Programming, Volume 3, Seminumerical Algorithms*. Reading, MA: Addison-Wesley Publishing Company, 1981.

Don't even think about reading these unless programming is your profession. If you *do* program for a living, you probably already have all three volumes of "Knuth."

Sedgewick, Robert, *Algorithms*. Reading, MA: Addison-Wesley Publishing Company, 1968.

This one's popularity also shows in its nickname: "Sedgewick," as in "Beats me. Have you looked in Sedgewick?" In short, all the common programming algorithms are here, carefully presented. A working knowledge of a high-level language is assumed.

## Programming | C

There were, at last count, a billion books about C. Enough so that you can pretty much match the C book both to your own knowledge level, and your own idiosyncrasies. Long C books, short C books; they fill shelf after shelf. Here are just a handful:

Cox, Brad J., *Object-Oriented Programming: An Evolutionary Approach*. Reading, MA: Addison-Wesley Publishing Company, 1987.

*The* Objective-C book by the man behind Objective-C. "Read Cox's book: It'll change your life!" sputtered one Objective-C zealot recently on the BIX Information Service.

I wouldn't go that far. (*This* book changed my life; just ask my wife and kids!)

But Cox's book is extremely well-written and must reading for anyone interested in the nuts and bolts of Objective-C. The book begins with a masterful rationale for objective programming, then proceeds, gradually, into the depths of "how it *really* works." A terrific, landmark book. Watch for Cox's next effort, which he says will concentrate "More on the war than on the weapon."

*Objective-C 4.0 User Reference Manual.* Productivity Products International, Inc., 1988.

The complete documentation for Objective-C, from the creators of Objective-C. It's a three-volume set. Cost: $95, plus $5 shipping, to make it an even $100 and worth every penny. To get yours, contact The Stepstone Corporation, 75 Glen Road, Sandy Hook, CT 06482; (203) 426-0699.

Mark Williams Company, *ANSI C: A Lexical Guide.* Englewood Cliffs, NJ: Prentice Hall, 1988.

Good to have if you're starting out with C. It's in dictionary format, and covers the entire C language. Includes a tutorial.

Kernighan, Brian W., and Ritchie, Dennis M., *The C Programming Language. Second Edition.* Englewood Cliffs, NJ: Prentice Hall, 1988.

The C programming classic by the creators of C. Known merely as "K&R," which testifies to its stature. Written with amazing clarity. This, the second edition, has been updated to conform with the "Draft Proposed ANSI C standard" version of C. If these guys say this is how C works, this is how C works, period.

A handy companion volume is "The C Answer Book," which contains answers to the chapter-end exercises. No, you're not cheating, you're learning. As always, the answers are better than the questions. Make sure you get the answer book for the *second* edition.

Steele, Guy L., and Harbison, Samuel P., *C: A Reference Manual. Second Edition.* Englewood Cliffs, NJ: Prentice Hall, 1987.

A complete reference, up to date with the draft ANSI standard version of C. Professional programmers will want a copy in their cubicle and another at bedside.

Parker, Scott, Croy, Gregory S., and Kenyon, Rebecca, eds., *C Quick Reference.* Carmel, IN: Que Corporation.

A little handbook of C. These paperback-sized quick reference guides are justly popular. The Que guide is listed here, but Microsoft also makes a quick reference guide to C, and you should also be able to find small guides to UNIX. The Que guide costs $7.95, a nice break from pricey computer books. Present company excepted. Now, if there were only a quick reference for the NeXT Application Kit...

## Programming I LISP

Steele, G. L. Jr., *COMMON LISP Reference Manual*. Bedford, MA: Digital Press, 1984.

——, *COMMON LISP: The Language*. Bedford, MA: Digital Press, 1984.

The definitive (sorry about bringing up that word again and again) references to the Common LISP language. Professional LISPers need these books. If you're merely LISP curious, pass them by.

Touretzky, David S., *LISP: A Gentle Introduction to Symbolic Computation*. New York, NY: Harper & Row Publishers, 1984.

LISP has been around now for over two decades. Not surprisingly, the language has garnered a raft of books. This one's a classic. It is, indeed, a gentle introduction.

Friedman, Daniel P., and Felleison, Matthias. *The Little LISPer.* Cambridge, MA: The MIT Press.

Another well-known "first book of LISP." This one's presented entirely in two columns. Like this:

| | |
|---|---|
| Is it true that this is a list? | Yes, |
| ((atom turkey) or) | because the two S-expressions |
| | are now enclosed by |
| | parentheses. |

A fun book. If you don't peek at the answers, you'll learn the rudiments of LISP. If you enjoy crossword puzzles, you'll probably enjoy the book.

Hasemer, Tony, *Looking at LISP*. Reading, MA: Addison-Wesley Publishing Company, 1984.

My favorite "first" LISP book. Why? Because it doesn't assume too much about the reader. The author's assumption is only that the reader knows a little BASIC and has a small computer. It's a pleasant book, written in an engaging, somewhat amateurish way. Not LISP puzzle after LISP puzzle, but an attempt to tell you about a language that the author, quite obviously, thinks is really, really neat. By the time you finish, you'll think it's pretty neat, too.

Winston, Patrick Henry, and Berthold, Klaus Paul Horn, *LISP. Second Edition.* Reading, MA: Addison-Wesley Publishing Company, 1984.

Patrick Winston is the Boswell of LISP. This book, billed as an introductory text, is the classic introduction to LISP. It's clear, lucid, and gets deep fast. If LISP will be a "second language" for you, go for it. Put the coffee pot on first. (The second edition is listed here, but the book is faithfully updated. A third edition may be out by now. Check with your bookstore.)

## Hardware I DSP Programming

Motorola, Inc., *MC68030 Enhanced 32-Bit Microprocessor User's Manual.* Englewood Cliffs, NJ: Prentice Hall, 1987.

————, *MC68882 Floating-Point Coprocessor User's Manual.* Englewood Cliffs, NJ: Prentice Hall, 1988.

————, *DSP560 Digital Signal Processor User's Manual.* Englewood Cliffs, NJ: Prentice Hall, 1986.

————, *DSP560/DSP56001 Digital Signal Processor Simulator Reference Manual.* Englewood Cliffs, NJ: Prentice Hall, 1986.

————, *DSP560/DSP56001 Digital Signal Processor Macro Assembler Reference Manual.* Englewood Cliffs, NJ: Prentice Hall, 1986.

The titles say it all. These are hardware manuals for hardware engineers. They're also only the tip of the information iceberg (tip of the motherboard? Corner of the motherboard?). If you wish, Motorola will inundate you with product literature: spec sheets, comparisons between Motorola processors and processors from other companies, papers on networking, papers on multitasking, and more. And more.

If you're really interested in hardware, you might also consider taking a course from Motorola. At last count, Motorola offered nine hardware courses: everything from "Understanding Microprocessor Basics," to "DSP56000/1 Digital Signal Processing." The courses run from one to four days. They're given in Austin,

Chicago, Phoenix, San Jose, Toronto, and Washington, D.C. For course information, call (800)521-6274.

For those unable to attend instructor-led courses, Motorola offers audio and video courses. Audio-cassette-based courses are available for the M68000 family, the DSP56000/1 (*that's* the one to take, if you wish to get started with this incredible chip), and the MC88000. A video course (on 18 video cartridges) is available for the MC68000.

A personal note. In the course of making books like this one, you talk—or at least *try* to talk—with many people, at many companies. I've badgered people at Motorola for years. My experiences with Motorola have always been the same: wonderful. The Motorola employees have always been courteous and helpful. They return calls. They send you whatever you need. They talk freely, and honestly, about their products. They are very helpful.

Take that, Japan.

Although Prentice-Hall publishes the manuals above, you may have more specific needs. For those, try Motorola's toll-free telephone number:

(800)247-2346

Rabiner, Lawrence R., and Gold, Bernard, *Theory and Application of Digital Signal Processing.* Englewood Cliffs, NJ: Prentice Hall, 1975.

Haven't read it. NeXT lists it as a reference, however, and the copyright date, which is dated, leads one to believe that it is a seminal work in the field.

*Dr. BuB's BBS*

If you've got a modem and a thirst for more information about Motorola's DSP, you should give the "Dr. BuB" bulletin board a ring. The BBS is devoted to DSP information and DSP source code. The software library has over 100 files: FFT routines, code for various filters, matrix algebra, floating point routines—a bunch of DSP-related source code. The necessary parameters are 7 data bits, 1 stop bit, and even parity. Type "guest" for user ID. The numbers:

(512) 891-DSP1 (300/1200 baud),
(512) 891-DSP2 (1200 baud), and
(512) 891-DSP3 (2400 baud).

## Sound and Music

Backus, John, *The Acoustical Foundations of Music (2nd Edition)*. Norton 1977.

Chamberlain, Hal, *Musical Applications of Microprocessors*. Hayden Books, 1980.

At one time, the best and only book on the subject. Chamberlain poured his heart into this one and it shows. Unfortunately, it now cries for an update. 1980 is a long time ago. But pick it up and look it over; Chamberlain does a good job of covering basic notions, especially basic sound hardware. There's also a program listing of a fast Fourier transform.

Dodge, Charles, and Jerse, Thomas A., *Computer Music*. Schimer Books, 1985.
*Beginning Synthesizer*
The Keyboard Synthesizer Library:
*Volume I: Synthesizer Basics*
*Volume II: Synthesizer Technique*
*Volume III: Synthesizers and Computers*

If you're starting out with synthesizers, these books are a must. They're published by GPI Publications, a division of Hal Leonard Publishing Corporation, 8112 West Bluemound Road, Milwaukee, WI 53213. GPI publishes Keyboard Magazine, and the books are compilations of articles which appeared in the magazine. They're $8.95 each: a bargain.

It's all here: theory and technique—how it works, and how to do it. Each is stuffed with fascinating information. You'll even find scores of well-known solos. Jan Hammer's "Birds of Fire" solo? It's here. Pick up an issue of Keyboard Magazine to get a feel for what's in the books. Highly recommended: I love 'em.

## PostScript

Adobe Systems, Inc., *PostScript Language Tutorial and Cookbook*. Reading, MA: Addison-Wesley Publishing Company, 1985.

Read this first if you want to learn PostScript. Includes a good tutorial and many sample programs. Like the next two entries, this is required reading for would-be PostScript programmers. It's known as "the blue book." By their covers you shall know them.

Reid, Glenn C., and Adobe Systems, Inc., *PostScript Language Program Design*. Reading, MA: Addison-Wesley Publishing Company, 1988.

Finished with "the blue book"? This is "the green book," a more advanced discussion of PostScript.

Adobe Systems, Inc., *PostScript Language Reference Manual*. Reading, MA: Addison-Wesley Publishing Company, 1985.

Blue...green...this one's "the red book," and also mandatory if you're learning or writing PostScript. As the title says, it's a thorough reference to the PostScript language. Not, you should note, Display PostScript, which builds on the fundamentals of PostScript. The following manuals discuss Display PostScript:

*PostScript Language Color Extensions.*
*An Overview of the Display PostScript System.*
*PostScript Language Extensions for the Display PostScript System.*
*pswrap Reference Manual.*
*Client Library Reference Manual.*

All are available from Adobe Systems, Inc., and are included with the NeXT documentation. If you're currently NeXTless, contact Adobe Systems, Inc., 15875 Charleston Road, Mountain View, CA 94039; (415) 961-4400.

## Other

Greene, Micheal. *Zen and the Art of the Macintosh*. Philadelphia, PA: Running Press Book Publishers, 1986.

Jeez, a Macintosh book! How'd this get here?

Well...just go out and buy a copy. It's inspired artistic Macintosh craziness. Leaf through the book and think, "If you can do this on a Macintosh, think what you could do on a NeXT!"

Krasner, Glen (ed.), *Smalltalk-80: Bits of History, Words of Advice*. Reading, MA: Addison-Wesley Publishing Company, 1987.

Goldberg, Adele, and Robson, David, *Smalltalk-80: The Language and Its Implementation*. Reading, MA: Addison-Wesley Publishing Company, 1985.

No, Smalltalk isn't available yet for NeXT. (Look for it in 1990, maybe.) But reading about Smalltalk is good preparation for programming Objective-C, or any other object-oriented language. The first book listed, "Bits of History...," is a compilation of early users' experience with Smalltalk and is quite interesting.

# Appendix H

# NeXT Hardware Specifications

## Computer

### Dimensions:
1' cube, die-cast magnesium

Holds two full-height 5.25" mass storage devices

### Weight:
29 lbs. to 37 lbs., depending on configuration

### Power:
300 watt, auto-adjusting power supply; adjusts to line frequencies
of 47 Hz to 63 Hz; adjusts to voltages of 90 V to 270 V

Powers four NeXTBuss slots; 25 watts/slot

### Processors:
Motorola 68030 CPU, 25 Mhz

Motorola 6882 Floating Point Unit, 25 MHz

Motorola 56001 Digital Signal Processor, 25 MHz

NeXT-designed Integrated Channel Processor (IPC)

    12 DMA channels
    32 MB/sec bandwidth

NeXT-designed Optical Storage Processor (OSP)

### RAM:
8 to 16 megabytes of RAM memory, expandable in 4 megabyte increments

**Interfaces:**

Two RS-422 compatible serial ports

Printer port

SCSI interface with maximum (burst rate) transfer speed of 4.8 MB/sec

Digital Signal Processor Port

Thin-wire, IEEE 802.3 compatible Ethernet port

Three NeXTBus (enhanced NuBus) card slots

**Environment:**

Ambient temperature from 32 to 104 Fahrenheit (0 to 40 centigrade)

Allowable humidity: 10% to 90%

Maximum altitude: 15,000 feet (4,572 meters)

**Certifications:**

UL listed

CSA certified

Compliant with FCC Part 15 Class A requirements

# MegaPixel Display

**Dimensions:**

16" (w) x 17.3" (h) x 14" (d)

50 lbs.

**Monitor:**

Manufactured by Sony Corporation

17", flat screen display

Resolution: 92 dpi; 1120 x 832 x 2; four gray levels

Refresh rate: 68 Hz non-interlaced

Built-in speaker

Display swivels on horizontal axis

Integrated cast-metal stand with "tractor rollers"

**Interfaces:**

16-bit 44.1 kHz stereo output jacks; gold-plated; RCA standard

8-bit 8 kHz  high-impedance monophonic microphone input jack

Headphone jack ("Walkman" type)

Keyboard jack

## Keyboard

### System controls:
Power; sound up; sound down; brightness up; brightness down

### Keys:
85 keys, including 4 cursor keys, numeric keypad, Command keys (2),

Alternate keys (2), Control key, Esc key

### Mouse
Two-button opto-mechanical mouse

## Mass Storage

### 256 Megabyte (formatted) Optical Drive :
Removeable, read/write/erasable disk; magneto-optical technology

Drive manufactured by Canon

92 ms average seek time

5 ms average seek time in 5 megabyte range

9.1 MB/sec raw transfer rate

2.1 to 6.6 MB/sec raw sustained transfer rate

### Internal 330 Megabyte (formatted) SCSI Hard Disk:
14.8 ms average seek time

45 kB dual-ported FIFO buffer

4.8 MB/sec raw transfer rate

1.4 MB/sec raw sustained transfer rate

### Internal 660 Megabyte (formatted) SCSI Hard Disk:
16.5 ms average seek time

45 kB dual-ported FIFO buffer

4.8 MB/sec raw transfer rate

1.4 MB/sec raw sustained transfer rate

## NeXT Laser Printer

### Dimensions:
with paper trays: 14.3" (w) x 7" (h) x 16.7" (d)

38 pounds

### Power:
115/220 V switching power supply

Standby mode: 110 watts, 115 V

Printing mode: 640 watts, 115 V

### General:
Printer engine manufactured by Canon

Straight paper path

Auto and manual paper feed

Uses standard 20 lb. or similar general-use paper

### Resolution:
300 dpi or 400 dpi, software-selectable

### Speed:
8 pages/minute, average

### Duty cycle:
No monthly page limit

300,000 page life expectancy

### Toner:
Uses Apple LaserWriter-compatible, SX, EP-S toner cartridge

### Paper trays:
150-200 sheet input paper cassette; adjustable for A4, letter-size, or envelopes

Adjustable manual feed adjustable

50-sheet output tray (optional use)

### Environment:
Ambient temperature from 50 to 90 Fahrenheit (10 to 32 centigrade)

Allowable humidity: 10% to 80%

Maximum altitude: 8,000 feet (2,438 meters)

## Certifications:

UL listed

CSA certified

Compliant with FCC Part 15 Class A requirements

Conforms with DCRH radiation performance standard,

21 CFR Chapter 1, Subchapter J

# Index

# P

pagination, 282–283
Panel (Application Kit) class, 299–300
panels, 77, 99–100
    canceling, 82–84
    modal, 84–86
    Print panel, 184–186
    resizing, 87
    standard, 86–88
paper for laser printer, 190–191
Pascal programming, 249
passwords
    changing or installing, 458, 499
    editing files, 521
    encrypting, 460
Pasteboard, 93–94, 283
pathnames, 30–32
pixels. *See* display
plugs, 141–142
PMMU processors, 153–154
pointing devices. *See* mouse
ports, I/O, 163–164
PostScript
    converting files to, 471, 472, 503
    converting graphics to, 364
    creating C code from, 503
    Display PostScript, 253–258
    EPS files, 39–40
    managing file order, 503
    NeXT's choice of, 103
    previewing, 205, 643
    PSWraps, 255
    reading material on, 664–665
    text modification, 643–644
    width tables, 503
power key, 143
power supply, 166–167
Preferences applications, 35
Preview application, 185
print, queueing, 453
Printer application, 188–190

printer definition files, 186–188
printers
    characteristics, 500–502
    color, 418
    NeXT laser. *See* laser printer
    ports, 163
    third-party, 422
PrintInfo (Application Kit) class,
    282–283
printing
    Application Kit PrintInfo class,
        282–283
    libraries, 499
    object files, 496, 499
    Preview application, 185
    with UNIX, 57–58
processors
    68882 FPU, 154–156
    DSP56001, 156–160
    future NeXT, 420–421
    ICP, 161–163
    MC68030, 150–153
    NeXT's specifications, 667
    OSP (Optical Storage Processor), 174
    PMMUs, 153–154
    VSLI, 172, 174
programming
    Application Kit. *See* Application Kit
    BASIC, 250
    books on, 658–663
    C, 248–249, 659–661
    Hypercard, 250
    LISP, 404–407, 660–662
    Mathematica, 369
    NeXT computer, 241–250. *See also*
    UNIX
        advice, 248–250
        books, 658
        encapsulation concept, 242
        environment. *See* Mach
    programming environment
        inheritance concept, 244–247

# About the Author

Doug Clapp is a former newspaper editor who's been associated with personal computers for the past ten years as a writer, speaker, columnist, author, and software designer. President of Foundation Publishing and Douglas Publishing, he lives in Edina, Minnesota with his beautiful wife Patti and two little girls. He can be reached through MCI Mail: dclapp; AppleLink: D2178; BIX: dclapp; Portal: Doug Clapp; MacNet: Doug Clapp; or Usenet: Doug_Clapp@cup.portal.com.